The International Institute for Strategic Studies

THE MILITARY BALANCE 1997/98

Published by **Oxford University Press** for
The International Institute for Strategic Studies
23 Tavistock Street, London WC2E 7NQ

The Military Balance 1997/98

Published by Oxford University Press for
The International Institute for Strategic Studies
23 Tavistock Street, London WC2E 7NQ
http:\\www.isn.ethz.ch\iiss

Director   Dr John Chipman

Assistant Director and Editor   Colonel Terence Taylor

Defence Analysts
Ground Forces   Phillip Mitchell
Aerospace   Wg Cdr Kenneth Petrie RAF
Naval Forces   Lt Cdr John Downing RN
Defence Economist   Digby Waller

Editorial   Rachel Neaman
Editorial Assistant   Natalie Shelotchkova

Design and Production   Mark Taylor

Production Assistant   Anna Clarke
Research Assistants   Michaela Bauer   Eleanore Gallet
Stefan Elbe   Mathew Lefevre
Tom Everett-Heath   Charles Siegel

This publication has been prepared by the Director of the Institute and his staff, who accept full responsibility for its contents. These do not, and indeed cannot, represent a consensus of views among the world-wide membership of the Institute.

First published October 1997

ISBN 0-19-829355-0
ISSN 0459-7222

© The International Institute for Strategic Studies 1997

The Military Balance (ISSN 0459 7222) is published annually in October by Oxford University Press, Great Clarendon Street, Oxford OX2 6DP, UK. The 1997 annual subscription rate is: UK£49; overseas US$79.

Payment is required with all orders and subscriptions are accepted and entered by the volume (one issue). Prices include air-speeded delivery to Australia, Canada, India, Japan, New Zealand and the USA. Delivery elsewhere is by surface mail. Air-mail rates are available on request. Payment may be made by cheque or Eurocheque (payable to Oxford University Press), National Girobank (account 500 1056), credit card (Access, Mastercard, Visa, American Express, Diners' Club), direct debit (please send for details) or UNESCO coupons. Bankers: Barclays Bank plc, PO Box 333, Oxford, UK, code 20-65-18, account 00715654. Claims for non-receipt must be made within four months of dispatch/order (whichever is later).

Please send subscription orders to the Journals Subscription Department, Oxford University Press, Great Clarendon Street, Oxford, OX2 6DP, UK *tel* +44 (0) 1865 267907 *fax* +44 (0) 1865 267485.

In North America *The Military Balance* is distributed by M.A.I.L. America, 2323 Randolph Avenue, New Jersey, NJ 07001, USA. Periodical postage paid at Rahway, NJ, and additional entry points.

US POSTMASTER: Send address corrections to *The Military Balance*, c/o M.A.I.L. America, 2323 Randolph Avenue, New Jersey, NJ 07001, USA.

Printed in Great Britain by Bell & Bain Ltd, Glasgow.

UA
15
.M55
1997-98

Contents

United States

NATO and Non-NATO Europe

Russia

Middle East and North Africa

Central and South Asia

East Asia and Australasia

Caribbean and Latin America

Sub-Saharan Africa

Analyses and Tables

The Military Balance is updated each year to provide an accurate assessment of the military forces and defence expenditures of 169 countries. This current edition contains data as at 1 August 1997.

Developments in Europe, in particular NATO enlargement and Partnership for Peace (PFP), make it appropriate for Europe to be dealt with as a single region in the book. While the United States and Russia have their own sections, all other NATO countries are covered in the Europe section (including Canada). The remaining regions are unchanged from last year's edition. Countries are listed alphabetically within each region.

GENERAL ARRANGEMENT

Part I of *The Military Balance* comprises national entries grouped by region. Regional groupings are preceded by a short introduction describing the military issues facing the region, and significant changes in the weapons and other military equipment holdings of the countries concerned. The regional tables showing international arms transfers and national procurement, introduced for the first time in the 1996/97 edition, are retained. Inclusion of a country or state in *The Military Balance* does not imply legal recognition or indicate support for a particular government.

Part II contains analyses and tables. New elements in this edition include analyses of industrial restructuring in the US and Western Europe and the costs of NATO enlargement. A shortened account of the global arms trade is retained. There are tables on armoured infantry fighting vehicles, armoured personnel carriers and military satellites. Issues related to weapons of mass destruction are combined in one section with arms-control developments. The table on international comparisons of defence expenditure appears as usual, as does the summary of the composition and missions of UN and other peacekeeping forces. A loose wall-map shows data on recent and current armed conflicts.

USING THE MILITARY BALANCE

The Military Balance is a quantitative assessment of the personnel strengths and equipment holdings of the world's armed forces. It is not an assessment of their capabilities. It does not attempt to evaluate the quality of units or equipment, nor the impact of geography, doctrine, military technology, deployment, training, logistic support, morale, leadership, tactical or strategic initiative, terrain, weather, political will or support from alliance partners. *The Military Balance* does not evaluate and compare directly the performance of items of equipment. Those who wish to do so can use the data provided to construct their own force comparisons. *The Military Balance* provides the actual numbers of nuclear and conventional forces and weapons based on the most accurate data available, or, failing that, on the best estimate that can be made with a reasonable degree of confidence. The data presented each year in *The Military Balance* reflect judgements based on information available to the Director and staff of the IISS at the time the book is compiled. Information may differ from previous editions for a variety of reasons, generally as a result of substantive changes in national forces, but in some cases because of IISS reassessment of the evidence supporting past entries. Hence, care has to be taken in constructing time-series comparisons from information given in successive editions, although in the text that introduces each regional section an attempt is made to distinguish between new acquisitions and revised assessments. **In order to interpret correctly the data shown in the country entries it is essential to read the explanatory notes beginning at page 5.**

entry includes all reservists committed to rejoining the armed forces in an emergency, except when national reserve service obligations following conscription last almost a lifetime. *The Military Balance* bases its estimates of effective reservist strengths on the numbers available within five years of completing full-time service, unless there is good evidence that obligations are enforced for longer. Some countries have more than one category of Reserves, often kept at varying degrees of readiness. Where possible, these differences are denoted using the national descriptive title, but always under the heading of 'Reserves' to distinguish them from full-time active forces.

Other Forces

Many countries maintain paramilitary forces whose training, organisation, equipment and control suggest they may be used to support, or in place of, regular military forces. These are listed, and their roles described, after the military forces of each country. Their manpower is not normally included in the Armed Forces totals at the start of each entry. Home Guard units are counted as paramilitary. Where paramilitary groups are not on full-time active duty, '(R)' is added after the title to indicate that they have reserve status. When internal opposition forces are armed and appear to pose a significant threat to a state's security, their details are listed separately after national paramilitary forces.

Equipment

Quantities are shown by function and type and represent what are believed to be total holdings, including active and reserve operational and training units and 'in store' stocks. Inventory totals for missile systems (such as SSM, SAM, ATGW) relate to launchers and not to missiles.

Stocks of equipment held in reserve and not assigned to either active or reserve units are listed as 'in store'. However, aircraft in excess of unit establishment holdings, held to allow for repair and modification or immediate replacement, are not shown 'in store'. This accounts for apparent disparities between unit strengths and aircraft inventory strengths.

Operational Deployments

The Military Balance does not normally list short-term operational deployments, particularly where military operations are in progress. An exception to this rule is made in the case of peace-keeping operations. The contribution or deployment of forces to peacekeeping operations are shown on pp. 274–84. Recent changes and developments are also described in the text of each regional section.

GROUND FORCES

The national designation is normally used for army formations. The term 'regiment' can be misleading. In some cases it is essentially a brigade of all arms; in others, a grouping of battalions of a single arm; and lastly (for example, in UK usage) a battalion-sized unit. The sense intended is indicated in each case. Where there is no standard organisation, the intermediate levels of command are shown as headquarters (HQs), followed by the total numbers of units that could be allocated to them. Where a unit's title overstates its real capability, the title is given in inverted commas, with an estimate of the comparable NATO unit size given in parentheses: 'bde' (coy).

Equipment

The Military Balance uses similar equipment definitions as the Treaty on Conventional Armed Forces in Europe (CFE). Those used are:

Main Battle Tank (MBT) An armoured tracked combat vehicle weighing at least 16.5 metric

ATTRIBUTION AND ACKNOWLEDGEMENTS

The International Institute for Strategic Studies owes no allegiance to any government, group of governments, or any political or other organisation. Its assessments are its own, based on the material available to it from a wide variety of sources. The cooperation of governments has been sought and, in many cases, received. Not all countries have been equally cooperative, and some of the figures in *The Military Balance* are estimates. Care is taken to ensure that these estimates are as accurate and free from bias as possible. The Institute owes a considerable debt to a number of its own Members, consultants and all those who have helped in compiling and checking material. The Director and staff of the Institute assume full responsibility for the facts and judgements contained in this book. Comments and suggestions on the data presented are welcomed. Suggestions on the style and method of presentation are also much appreciated.

Readers may use items of information from *The Military Balance* as required, without applying for permission from the Institute, on condition that the IISS and *The Military Balance* are cited as the source in any published work. However, applications to reproduce major portions of *The Military Balance* must be addressed to: Journals Rights and Permissions, Oxford University Press, Great Clarendon Street, Oxford OX2 6DP, UK, prior to publication.

Explanatory Notes

ABBREVIATIONS AND DEFINITIONS

Abbreviations are used throughout to save space and avoid repetition. The abbreviations may have both singular or plural meanings; for example, 'elm' = 'element' or 'elements'. The qualification 'some' means *up to*, while 'about' means *the total could be higher than given*. In financial data, '$' refers to US dollars unless otherwise stated; billion (bn) signifies 1,000 million (m). Footnotes particular to a country entry or table are indicated by letters, while those that apply throughout the book are marked by symbols (* for training aircraft counted by the IISS as combat-capable, and † where serviceability of equipment is in doubt). A full list of abbreviations is at page 319.

COUNTRY ENTRIES

Information on each country is shown in a standard format, although the varied availability of information results in some differences. Each entry includes economic, demographic and military data. Military data include manpower, length of conscript service, outline organisation, number of formations and units, and an inventory of the major equipment of each service. This is followed, where applicable, by a description of the deployment of each service. Details of national forces stationed abroad and of foreign stationed forces are also given.

GENERAL MILITARY DATA

Manpower

The 'Active' total comprises all servicemen and women on full-time duty (including conscripts and long-term assignments from the Reserves). Under the heading 'Terms of Service', only the length of conscript service is shown; where service is voluntary there is no entry. 'Reserve' describes formations and units not fully manned or operational in peacetime, but that can be mobilised by recalling reservists in an emergency. Unless otherwise indicated, the 'Reserves' tonnes unladen, that may be armed with a 360° traverse gun of at least 75mm calibre. Any new wheeled combat vehicles entering service that meet these criteria will be considered MBTs.

Armoured Combat Vehicles (ACV) A self-propelled vehicle with armoured protection and cross-country capability. ACVs include:

Armoured Personnel Carrier (APC) A lightly armoured combat vehicle designed and equipped to transport an infantry squad, armed with integral/organic weapons of less than 20mm calibre. Variants of APCs converted for other uses (such as weapons platforms, command posts and communications terminals) are included and indicated as such.

Armoured Infantry Fighting Vehicle (AIFV) An armoured combat vehicle designed and equipped to transport an infantry squad, armed with an integral/organic cannon of at least 20mm calibre. Variants of AIFVs are also included and indicated as such.

Heavy Armoured Combat Vehicle (HACV) An armoured combat vehicle weighing more than six metric tonnes unladen, with an integral/organic direct-fire gun of at least 75mm (which does not fall within the definitions of APC, AIFV or MBT). *The Military Balance* does not list HACVs separately, but under their equipment type (light tank, reconnaissance or assault gun), and where appropriate annotates them as HACV.

Artillery Systems with a calibre of 100mm and above, capable of engaging ground targets by delivering primarily indirect fire, namely guns, howitzers, gun/howitzers, multiple-rocket launchers and mortars.

Military Formation Strengths

The manpower strength, equipment holdings and organisation of formations such as brigades and divisions differ widely from country to country. Where possible, the normal composition of formations is given in parentheses. It should be noted that where divisions and brigades are listed, only separate brigades are counted, not those included in divisions.

NAVAL FORCES

Categorisation is based on operational role, weapon fit and displacement. Ship classes are identified by the name of the first ship of that class, except where a class is recognised by another name (such as *Udalay, Petya*). Where the class is based on a foreign design or has been acquired from another country, the original class name is added in parentheses.

Each class of vessel is given an acronym based on the NATO system. All such designators are included in the list of abbreviations at the end of the book.

The term 'ship' refers to vessels with over 1,000 tonnes full-load displacement that are more than 60 metres in overall length; vessels of lesser displacement, but of 16m or more overall length, are termed 'craft'. Vessels of less than 16m overall length are not included.

The term 'commissioning' has different meanings in a number of navies. In *The Military Balance* the term is used to mean that a ship has completed fitting out and initial sea trials, and has a naval crew; operational training may not have been completed, but in all other respects the ship is available for service. 'Decommissioning' means that a ship has been removed from operational duty and the bulk of its naval crew transferred. Removing equipment and stores and dismantling weapons, however, may not have started. Where known, ships in long-term refit are shown as such.

Classifications and Definitions

To aid comparison between fleets, naval entries have been subdivided into the following categories, which do not necessarily conform to national categorisation:

Submarines Those vessels with submarine-launched ballistic missiles are listed separately under 'Strategic Nuclear Forces'. In this issue of *The Military Balance*, a table of submarines on pp. 299–301 shows all classes and numbers of submarines world-wide.

Principal Surface Combatants These include all surface ships with both 1,000 tonnes full-load displacement and a weapons system other than for self-protection. All ships in this category are assumed to have an anti-surface ship capability. They comprise: aircraft carriers (defined below); cruisers (over 8,000 tonnes) and destroyers (less than 8,000 tonnes), both of which normally have an anti-air role and may also have an anti-submarine capability; frigates (less than 8,000 tonnes) which normally have an anti-submarine role. Only ships with a flight deck that extends beyond two-thirds of the vessel's length are classified as aircraft carriers. This distinguishes them from other classes that also carry significant weapon systems and are listed as helicopter cruisers.

Patrol and Coastal Combatants These are ships and craft which have the primary role of protecting a state's sea approaches and coastline. Included are corvettes (600–1,000 tonnes carrying weapons systems other than for self-protection); missile craft (with permanently fitted missile-launcher ramps and control equipment); and torpedo craft (with an anti-surface-ship capability). Ships and craft that fall outside these definitions are classified as 'patrol'.

Mine Warfare This category covers surface vessels configured primarily for mine-laying or mine countermeasures (such as mine-hunters, mine-sweepers or dual-capable vessels). A further classification divides both coastal and patrol combatants and mine-warfare vessels into offshore (over 600 tonnes); coastal (300–600 tonnes); and inshore (less than 300 tonnes).

Amphibious This category includes ships specifically procured and employed to disembark troops and their equipment over unprepared beachheads or directly to support amphibious operations. The term 'Landing Ship' (as opposed to 'Landing Craft') refers to vessels capable of an ocean passage that can deliver their troops and equipment in a fit state to fight. Vessels with an amphibious capability, but which are known not to be assigned to amphibious duties, are not included. Amphibious craft are listed at the end of each entry.

Support and Miscellaneous This category of essentially non-military vessels provides some indication of the sustainability and range of naval forces.

Weapons Systems Weapons are listed in the order in which they contribute to the ship's primary operational role. Significant weapons relating to the ship's secondary role are added after the word 'plus'. Short-range self-defence weapons are not listed. To merit inclusion, a surface-to-air missile system must have an anti-missile range of 10km or more, and guns must be of 100mm bore or greater. Exceptions may be made in the case of some minor combatants with a primary gun armament of a lesser calibre.

Aircraft All armed aircraft, including anti-submarine-warfare and some maritime-reconnaissance aircraft, are included as combat aircraft in naval inventories.

Organisations Naval groupings such as fleets and squadrons are often temporary and change-able; organisation is only shown where it is meaningful.

AIR FORCES

The term 'combat aircraft' refers to aircraft normally equipped to deliver air-to-air or air-to-surface ordnance. The 'combat' totals include aircraft in operational conversion units whose main role is weapons training, and training aircraft of the same type as those in front-line squadrons that are assumed to be available for operations at short notice. (Training aircraft considered to be combat-capable are marked *.) Armed maritime aircraft are not included in combat aircraft totals.

However, naval armed maritime aircraft are included in their respective combat aircraft total. Air force operational groupings are shown where known. Squadron aircraft strengths can vary from country to country.

The number of aircraft categories listed is kept to a minimum. 'Fighter' denotes aircraft with the capability (weapons, avionics, performance) for aerial combat. Multi-role aircraft are shown as fighter ground attack (FGA), fighter, reconnaissance and so on, according to the role in which they are deployed. Different countries often use the same basic aircraft in different roles; the key to determining these roles lies mainly in air-crew training. For bombers, 'long-range' means having an unrefuelled radius of action of over 5,000km, 'medium-range' 1,000–5,000km and 'short-range' less than 1,000km; light bombers are those with a payload of under 10,000kg (no greater than the payload of many FGA).

The CFE Treaty lists three types of helicopters: attack (equipped to employ anti-armour, air-to-ground or air-to-air guided weapons by means of an integrated fire-control and aiming system); combat support (which may be armed with self-defence or area-suppression weapons, but do not have a control and guidance system); and unarmed transport helicopters. *The Military Balance* uses the term 'attack' in the same way as the CFE Treaty, and the term 'assault' to describe armed helicopters used to deliver infantry or other troops to the battlefield. Except in the case of CFE signatories, *The Military Balance* continues to employ the term 'armed helicopters' to cover those equipped to deliver ordnance, including anti-submarine warfare ordnance.

ARMS ORDERS AND DELIVERIES

Tables in the regional texts show confirmed arms orders and deliveries listed by country buyer for the past and current years, together with country supplier and future delivery dates, if known. Every effort has been made to ensure that the information on arms acquisitions and orders is correct. However, some transactions may not be fulfilled or may differ in detail from those reported.

DEFENCE ECONOMICS

Country entries in **Part I** show defence expenditure, selected economic performance indicators and demographic aggregates. **Part II**, *Analyses and Tables*, contains an international comparison of defence expenditure and military manpower which gives expenditure figures for the last two years against the bench-mark year in constant US dollars. The aim is to provide an accurate measure of military expenditure and of the allocation of economic resources to defence. All country entries are subject to year-on-year revision as new information, particularly regarding defence expenditure, becomes available. The information on defence economics in **Parts I** and **II** of *The Military Balance* is necessarily selective. A wider range of economic and defence statistics is available to readers on request.

In **Part I**, individual country entries typically show economic performance over the last two years, and current-year demographic data. Where these data are unavailable, information from the last available year is provided. Defence expenditure is generally shown for the last two years where official outlays are available, or sufficient data for reliable estimates exist. Current-year defence budgets and, where available, defence budgets for the following year are also listed. Foreign Military Assistance (FMA) data cover outlays for the past year, and budgetary estimates for the current and next years. Unless otherwise indicated, the US is the donor country. All financial data in the country entries are shown in both national currency and US dollars at current-year, not constant, prices. US dollar conversions are generally, but not invariably, calculated from the exchange rates listed in the entry. In a few cases, notably Russia and China, purchasing-power-parity (PPP) rates are used in preference to official or market-exchange rates.

Definitions of terms

Definitions of defence expenditure are important if interpretation errors are to be avoided. Both the UN and NATO have developed standardised definitions, but in many cases countries prefer to use their own definitions (which are not in the public domain). For consistency in the estimating process, the IISS applies the NATO definition of military spending to all its defence-expenditure estimates.

NATO defines military expenditure as the cash outlays of central or federal government to meet the costs of national armed forces. The term 'armed forces' includes strategic, land, naval, air, command, administration and support forces. It also includes paramilitary forces such as the *gendarmerie*, customs service and border guard if these are trained in military tactics, equipped as a military force and operate under military authority in the event of war. NATO defence expenditures are reported in four categories: Operating Costs; Procurement and Construction; Research and Development (R&D); and Other Expenditure. Operating costs include salaries and pensions for military and civilian personnel; the cost of maintaining and training units, service organisations, headquarters and support elements; and the cost of servicing and repairing military equipment and infrastructure. Procurement and construction expenditure covers national equipment and infrastructure spending, as well as common infrastructure programmes. It also includes financial contributions to multinational military organisations, host-nation support in cash and in kind, and payments made to other countries under bilateral agreements. Foreign Military Assistance counts as expenditure by the donor, and not recipient, government. R&D is defence expenditure up to the point at which new equipment can be put in service, regardless of whether new equipment is actually procured. The fact that NATO definitions of military expenditure are generally more inclusive than those applied by national governments and the standardised UN format means that NATO-calculated expenditure figures may be higher than national and UN equivalents. Since the IISS uses NATO definitions in estimating non-transparent cases, it follows that IISS estimates may differ from official figures.

The issue of transparency in reporting military expenditures is a fundamental one. Only a minority of the governments of UN member-states report defence expenditures to their electorates, the UN, the International Monetary Fund (IMF) and other multilateral organisations. In the case of governments with a proven record of transparency, official figures generally conform to a standardised definition of defence expenditure, and consistency problems are not usually a major issue. Where these conditions of transparency and consistency are met, the IISS cites official defence budgets and outlays as reported by national governments, NATO, the UN, the Organisation for Security and Cooperation in Europe (OSCE) and the IMF. On the other hand, some governments do not report defence expenditures until several years have elapsed, while others appear to understate the figures they report. Where these reporting conditions exist, *The Military Balance* gives IISS estimates of military expenditures for the country concerned, together with official defence budgets, in order to provide a measure of the discrepancy between official and IISS-estimated real defence outlays. In these cases *The Military Balance* does not cite official defence expenditures (actual outlays), as these rarely differ significantly from official budgetary data. The IISS defence-expenditure estimates are based on information from several sources, and are marked 'ε'. The most frequent instances of budgetary falsification typically involve equipment procurement, R&D, defence-industrial investment, covert weapons programmes, pensions for retired military and civilian personnel, paramilitary forces, and non-budgetary sources of revenue for the military arising from ownership of industrial, property and land assets.

In general, no similar transparency problems arise with regard to economic statistics cited in the country entries. Some exceptions are found among the former communist economies in transition, and also countries where civil war is taking place or where hostilities have recently ended. The principal sources for economic statistics are the IMF, the Organisation for Economic Cooperation and Development (OECD), the World Bank and three regional banks (the Inter-American, Asian and African Development Banks).

The Gross Domestic Product (GDP) figures are nominal (current) values at market prices, but GDP per capita figures are nominal values at PPP prices. GDP growth is real not nominal growth, and inflation is the year-on-year change in consumer prices. Two different measures of debt are used to distinguish between OECD and non-OECD countries: for OECD countries, debt is gross public debt (or, more exactly, general government gross financial liabilities) expressed as a proportion of GDP. For all other countries, debt is gross foreign debt denominated in current US dollars. Dollar exchange rates relate to the last two years plus the current year. Values for the past two years are annual averages while current values are the latest monthly value.

Calculating exchange rates

Typically, but not invariably, the exchange rates shown in the country entries are also used to calculate GDP and defence-expenditure dollar conversions. Where they are not used, it is because exchange-rate dollar conversions can misrepresent both GDP and defence expenditure. These cases are clearly annotated. They may arise under the following conditions: when the official exchange rate is overvalued (as with some Latin American and African countries); whenever relatively large currency appreciations or depreciations occur over the short to medium term; and whenever a substantial medium-to-long-term discrepancy between the exchange rate and the dollar PPP exists. In the case of exchange-rate fluctuations, dollar values are converted using lagged exchange rates (generally by no more than six months). The GDP estimates of the Inter-American Development Bank, usually lower than those derived from official exchange rates, are used for Latin American countries. For former communist countries, PPP rather than market exchange rates are sometimes used for dollar conversions of both GDP and defence expenditures, and are marked as such.

The arguments for using PPP are strongest for Russia and China. Both the UN and IMF have issued caveats concerning the reliability of official economic statistics on transitional economies, particularly those of Russia and the former Soviet republics. Non-reporting, lags in the publication of current statistics and frequent revisions of recent data (not always accompanied by timely revision of previously published figures in the same series) pose transparency and consistency problems. A problem arises in the cases of certain transitional economies with productive capabilities similar to those of developed economies, but where cost and price structures are often much lower than world levels. PPP dollar values are used in preference to market exchange rates in cases where using such exchange rates may result in excessively low dollar-conversion values for GDP and defence expenditure.

Demographic data

Population aggregates are based on the most recent official census data or, in their absence, demographic statistics taken from *World Population Projections* published annually by the World Bank. Data on ethnic and religious minorities are also provided under country entries where a related security issue exists.

MILITARY CAPABILITY

The United States is the only country in the world with the weapons, mobility, logistics, intelligence and communications capabilities to conduct effective, large-scale military operations with a global reach. This scale of military capability has been maintained despite force reductions: both defence spending (in real terms) and personnel have been cut by about one-third since 1990. However, further significant reductions are not envisaged. Projections in the 1998 budget (published on 6 February 1997), as adjusted by the recommendations in the May 1997 Quadrennial Defense Review (QDR), indicate that the re-elected Clinton administration plans to maintain spending at current levels, allowing for inflation. Introducing the QDR report on 20 May 1997, Secretary of Defense William Cohen stated that a balance was being struck between exploiting advanced technologies to enhance capabilities, and maintaining a sufficient number of active forces and logistic support to be, in the words of the 1998 budget statement, 'capable of prevailing in two nearly simultaneous regional conflicts'.

The QDR's strategy for force development to meet this fundamental requirement has three elements:

- preventing or reducing conflicts and threats and deterring coercion and aggression on a day-to-day basis in key regions of the world;
- continuing to develop the ability to respond rapidly to a spectrum of crises, from concurrent small-scale operations to winning two major regional conflicts; and
- developing and implementing advanced technologies to defend against future threats and deter prospective rivals from entering into a conflict with the US.

The main changes in force capabilities as a result of the 1998 budget plans, assuming acceptance of the QDR recommendations, are:

- Army active personnel will be reduced by 15,000 through streamlining headquarters and support facilities. The Army will still retain ten active divisions. The plan to enhance information-technology capabilities (known as the Force XXI modernisation plan) will be accelerated.
- The Army's reserve component will be reduced by some 45,000, and several reserve combat units will be reassigned to combat-service support roles. This restructuring will partly compensate for a shortfall in the active-duty force.
- Navy surface ships will be reduced from 128 to 116, and attack submarines from 73 to 50. The procurement plan for the F/A-18 E/F aircraft will be cut back on the assumption that the Joint Strike Fighter (JSF) will enter production for the Navy in 2008. These reductions, as well as restructured combat support and infrastructure, will enable the Navy to cut active personnel by 18,000 and reserves by 4,100. Despite these reductions, the Navy plans to retain 12 carrier battle groups (11 active and one reserve) and 12 amphibious groups. The reduced number of vessels will be offset by the introduction of more capable systems.
- The Air Force will move an air wing from the active force to the reserves. Other reductions will be made in the national air-defence force structure and by contracting out some support functions. The QDR proposes to reduce the number of F-22 aircraft to be procured. The F-22, unlike the F-15 C/D which it replaces, will be able to conduct air-to-ground tasks as well as air defence. The first B-2 bomber wing became operational in April 1997. Implementation of the QDR proposals will reduce active-duty personnel by 27,000.
- While the Marine Corps is not immune from proposed reductions, it is likely to remain at

about the same strength, with three Marine Expeditionary Forces. The introduction of the MV-22 tilt-rotor aircraft (*Osprey*) will be accelerated, although the number to be procured will be reduced. Some modest reductions in personnel will be achieved through adjustments to support elements.

Table I **US military force developments**

	1990	1998	Target
Active Forces			
Army Divisions	18	10	10
Navy Aircraft Carriers	15	11	11
Navy Air Wings	13	10	10
Navy Surface Combatants and Attack Submarines	287	192	166
Marine Divisions and Air Wings	3	3	3
Air Force Tactical Wings	24	12	12
Reserve Forces			
National Guard Divisions	10	8	8
Navy Air Wings	2	1	1
Navy Aircraft Carriers (training)	1	1	1
Marine Divisions and Air Wings	1	1	1
Air Force Tactical Wings	12	8	8
Strategic Nuclear Forces			
ICBMs/Warheads	1,000/2,450	550/2,000	500/500[1]
SSBNs	31	18	18
SLBMs/Warheads	568/4,864	432/3,456	336[1]/<1,750[1]
Bombers	324	87[2]	92[2]
Military Personnel			
Active Forces	2,069,000	1,431,000	1,360,000
National Guard and Reserve Forces	1,128,000	892,000	835,000

Notes [1] On entry into force of the Strategic Arms Reduction Treaty (START) II

[2] Does not include 95 B-1 bombers assigned for conventional missions

The planned force structure outlined above would enable the US to participate in a major regional conflict, while also being engaged in one or more lesser peacekeeping operations, such as the NATO-led Stabilisation Force (SFOR) in Bosnia and Herzegovina. Whether it could conduct two major regional conflicts simultaneously, or, in the words of the 1998 budget statement, nearly simultaneously, is questionable; much would depend on the quantity and quality of allied support. Nevertheless, the budgetary objective of maintaining such a capability enables the US to sustain a powerful, broad spectrum of forces with the command, control, surveillance and intelligence systems essential for the US to remain the world's dominant military power.

DEFENCE SPENDING

Fiscal Year 1997

The administration's defence-budget request for 1997 – released on 5 February 1996 – amounted to $254 billion, about 7% less in real terms than the revised 1996 budget. Following its presentation to Congress on 4 March, the Republican majority made clear its intention to increase the proposed spend (as in the previous year). As a result, the 1997 Budget Authority (BA) was raised to $262bn, about 4% less than in 1996.[1] Most of the additional funding was allocated to Operations and Maintenance (O&M – $4bn), Procurement ($3bn) and Research and Development (R&D – $2bn).

Fiscal Year 1998

The second Clinton administration's $265bn Fiscal Year (FY) 1998 defence-budget request released on 6 February 1997 represented a real decline of 1% over the revised 1997 authorisation. Congress has raised the request by nearly $4bn to $269bn.

Table 2 US National Defense Budget Authority, 1985, 1990, 1996–2002

(Constant 1998 US$bn)			Actual		Req.			Planned		Real fall (%)	
Fiscal Year	*1985*	*1990*	*1996*	*1997*	*1998*	*1999*	*2000*	*2001*	*2002*	*1985–97*	*1985–02*
Military Personnel	100.0	100.2	73.7	71.8	69.5	68.1	67.5	67.3	67.1	28	33
O&M	114.3	109.3	98.8	95.7	93.7	89.9	88.7	88.5	84.9	16	26
Procurement	136.7	96.7	44.2	45.1	42.6	49.7	54.6	56.9	62.6	67	54
R&D, Test and Evaluation	45.0	43.9	36.5	37.4	35.9	34.3	32.0	30.9	31.5	17	30
Military Construction	7.9	6.1	7.2	6.0	4.7	4.2	4.1	3.9	3.1	24	61
Family Housing	4.1	3.8	4.4	4.2	3.7	3.8	3.8	3.7	3.6	+3	12
Other	6.7	-1.0	2.6	-3.7	0.6	0.8	0.6	0.6	0.4	155	94
Total – DoD	**414.7**	**359.0**	**267.4**	**256.5**	**250.7**	**250.8**	**251.3**	**251.8**	**253.0**	**38**	**39**
DoE – defense-related	10.6	11.9	11.2	11.6	13.6	11.6	10.7	10.1	9.6	+10	9
Other defense-related	0.7	0.8	1.0	1.0	1.0	1.0	1.0	1.0	1.0	+40	+32
Total – National Defense	**426.0**	**371.7**	**279.6**	**269.1**	**265.3**	**263.4**	**263.0**	**262.9**	**263.8**	**37**	**38**

DoD = Department of Defense DoE = Department of Energy Req. = Request

Notes [1] Data for FY1990–92 exclude *Operations Desert Shield* and *Desert Storm* costs and receipts

[2] FY1997 figures assume Congressional approval of proposed supplemental appropriations and rescissions

IFOR and SFOR

By September 1996, the official estimate for the incremental cost to the US of the 12-month NATO-led Implementation Force (IFOR) operation in Bosnia had increased from $1.9bn to $3.3bn. The 1996 budget request released in February 1995 – well before the General Framework Agreement for Peace in Bosnia and Herzegovina (the Dayton Accord) and IFOR had materialised – included $700 million for contingency operations, augmented later in the year by a supplemental budget request for $820m. The 1997 O&M appropriation provided $1.3bn to cover military operations in Bosnia, as well as South-west Asia and Iraq-related contingencies (see below).[2] In November 1996, the Clinton administration committed US forces to the follow-on SFOR in Bosnia, at an estimated cost of almost $1.9bn, necessitating a further supplement to the 1997 budget. The 1998 request includes $1.5bn in the Overseas Contingency Operations Transfer Account to cover remaining SFOR costs, yielding a total cost estimate for the 12-month operation of nearly $3.4bn. The six-month extension of US participation in SFOR to 30 June 1998 will raise the incremental cost of the 18-month operation to $5bn.

Other Contingency Costs

The DoD continues to prevent the unbudgeted costs of contingency operations from absorbing funds required to ensure readiness, modernisation and other priorities. Bosnia apart, other recent contingencies strengthened the US military presence in the Taiwan Strait in March 1996, when

Chinese exercises threatened the Taiwanese election, and in the Gulf region following Iraqi provocations in September 1996. The latter required a $124m supplement to the 1997 budget, while for 1998 the Military Service/Defense Agency accounts include $700m for continuing operations in the Gulf region.

Ballistic Missile Defence

The US Ballistic Missile Defense (BMD) programme forms part of a broader counter-proliferation strategy to reduce, deter and defend against the threat of weapons of mass destruction (WMD) and the ballistic missiles that deliver them. The 1998 BMD budget request is $3.5bn (down from the $4bn authorised in 1997). For FY1999–2003, an additional $18bn spending is planned. The highest priority remains Theater Missile Defense (TMD), which takes most of the funding. Major programmes include: the *Patriot* PAC-3; Navy Area TMD; the Medium Extended Air Defense System (MEADS) in cooperation with France, Germany and Italy (although France's commitment is uncertain); Navy theatre-wide TMD; Theater High Altitude Area Defense (THAAD); and the Airborne Laser. Developing a limited National Missile Defense (NMD) is the second priority, and the NMD request for 1998 is $505m ($2.3bn for 1998–2003). The administration intends to develop NMD for three further years before deciding whether to deploy it over the following three years, while Republicans in Congress want a firm commitment to deploy NMD in 2003.

The Cooperative Threat Reduction (Nunn–Lugar) Programme

Congress established the Nunn–Lugar programme in 1991 to deal with concerns about the security and safety of Russian nuclear weapons. Since 1992, the DoD budget has allocated $300–400m a year to the CTR programme. Initially, outlays lagged behind authorisations by a wide margin, but by September 1996 nearly $600m of an authorised $1.5bn had been spent. The programme focuses on four objectives:
- to destroy WMD;
- to transport, store, disable and safeguard WMD before their destruction;
- to establish verifiable safeguards against WMD proliferation, their components and weapons-usable materials; and
- to prevent the diversion of scientific expertise that could contribute to WMD programmes in other countries.

Table 3 Allocation of funds in the Cooperative Threat Reduction (CTR) programme, 1992–1996 (as of September 1996)

By recipient country (US$m)	Budget	Expenditure	By function	Budget	Expenditure
Russia	754	328	Destruction and Dismantlement	737	269
Ukraine	395	171	Chain of Custody[1]	432	143
Kazakstan	173	35	Demilitarisation	254	147
Belarus	119	44	Other	109	48
Total	**1,441**	**578**	**Total**	**1,532**	**607**

Note [1] Security of weapons during transit and handling
Source Congressional Research Service, Washington DC

The Quadrennial Defense Review

Since the Bottom Up Review in 1993 (the last QDR), defence spending has declined by around 15%. In contrast, the 1997 QDR projects stable annual defence spending of about $250bn in constant 1997 dollars, notwithstanding the now-bipartisan US commitment to a balanced federal budget. Readiness remains the priority; modernisation takes second place. The sharp decline in procurement since 1990 will be slowed, and, while the QDR notes the present commitment to an annual $60bn procurement spend, it takes into account the potential for unplanned expenditure contingencies which might reduce procurement by as much as $10–12bn a year, particularly in the latter stages of the current six-year plan. To offset the impact of such contingencies, the QDR recommends reducing some larger procurement programmes, including the F-18 (from 1,000 to 548, up to a maximum of 748), the F-22 (from 438 to 339) and the V-22 (from 425 to 360). The QDR recommends a higher priority for NMD, involving an additional $2bn, largely at the expense of the technically risky THAAD programme. Savings are expected from, among others, two further rounds of Base Realignment and Closure (BRAC), and reduced costs of support services through greater outsourcing of their procurement.

Table 4 US National Defense Budget Function and other selected budgets, 1989–2000

(US$bn)	National Defense Budget Function		Department of Defense		Atomic Energy Defense Activities	International Security Assistance	Veterans Administration	Total Federal Government Expenditure	Total Federal Budget Deficit
FY	(BA)	(outlay)	(BA)	(outlay)	(outlay)	(outlay)	(outlay)	(outlay)	(outlay)
1989	299.6	303.6	290.8	294.9	8.1	1.5	30.0	1,143.7	152.5
1990	301.2	297.9	291.0	288.3	9.0	8.7	29.1	1,253.2	221.2
1991	296.2	296.7	283.5	285.8	10.0	9.8	31.3	1,324.4	269.4
1992	287.7	286.1	274.8	274.7	10.6	7.5	34.1	1,381.7	290.4
1993	281.1	283.9	267.2	271.4	11.0	7.6	35.7	1,409.4	255.0
1994	263.3	278.9	251.4	265.8	11.9	6.6	37.6	1,461.7	203.1
1995	266.3	271.0	255.7	258.4	11.8	5.3	37.9	1,515.7	163.9
1996	266.0	265.2	254.4	252.7	11.6	4.6	37.0	1,560.2	107.3
1997	262.3	267.1	250.0	254.2	11.9	5.1	39.7	1,631.0	125.6
1998[R]	265.3	259.4	250.7	247.5	10.9	5.4	41.0	1,687.5	120.6
1999[P]	269.2	261.4	256.3	249.3	11.1	5.7	41.9	1,760.7	117.4
2000[P]	275.0	267.2	262.8	255.2	11.0	5.7	43.9	1,814.4	87.1

FY = Fiscal Year (1 October–30 September) [R] = Request [P] = Projection

Note The National Defense Budget Function subsumes funding for the DoD, the DoE Atomic Energy Defense Activities and some smaller support agencies (including Federal Emergency Management and Selective Service System). It does not include funding for International Security Assistance (under International Affairs), the Veterans Administration, the US Coast Guard (Department of Transport), nor for the National Aeronautics and Space Administration (NASA). Funding for civil projects administered by the DoD is excluded from the figures cited here.

[1] Early in each calendar year, the US government presents its defence budget to Congress for the next fiscal year which begins on 1 October. It also presents its Future Years' Defense Program, which covers the next fiscal year plus the following five. Until approved by Congress, the Budget is called the Budget Request; after approval, it becomes the Budget Authority.

[2] Definitions of US budget terms: *Authorisation* establishes or maintains a government programme or agency by defining its scope. Authorising legislation is normally a prerequisite for appropriations and may set specific limits on the amount that may be appropriated. An authorisation, however, does not make money available. *Budget Authority* is the legal authority for an agency to enter into obligations for the provision of goods or services. It may be available for one or more years. *Appropriation* is one form of Budget Authority provided by Congress for funding an agency, department or programme for a given amount of time and for specific purposes. Funds will not necessarily all be spent in the year in which they are initially provided. *Obligation* is an order placed, contract awarded, service agreement undertaken or other commitment made by federal agencies during a given period which will require outlays during the same or some future period. *Outlays* are money spent by a federal agency from funds provided by Congress. Outlays in a given fiscal year are a result of obligations that in turn follow the provision of Budget Authority.

Table 5 **Major US weapon systems on order, FY1998–2003**

Equipment	Type	Units	Comment
Strategic Forces			
BMD			FY1998 exp $3.5bn, FYDP projection $21.5bn
sat	*Milstar*		Coms sat with FYDP exp $3.3bn
sat	NAVSTAR	3	GPS sat with FY1998 cost $363m
Air Force			
bbr	B-1B		Upgrade; FYDP exp $1.7bn
bbr	B-2		21 previously ordered; FY1998 exp $331m on procurement and R&D
FGA	F-15E	3	FY1998 exp $308m
FGA	F-16		Upgrade; FY1998 exp $100m
FGA	F-22	70	FYDP exp $20.4bn; initial production 1999; planned purchase 438; QDR plans 339
FGA	JSF		FYDP exp $10.1bn; No joined US and UK programme April 1997; QDR plans 2,852
JSTARS	E-8	1	FY1998 exp $456m; planned purchase 20
tpt	C-130J	1	FY1998 exp $54m
tpt	C-17	9	FY1998 exp $2.3bn; planned purchase 120
trg	JPATS	18	FY1998 exp $129m; total planned purchase 711; primary trainer
Army			
AIFV	M-2		Upgrade; FYDP exp $2.1bn; $201m for mod of 18 FY1998
cbt hel	AH-64D	400	Upgrade; FYDP exp $3.7bn; $525m FY1998 for 44 upgrades
cbt hel	RAH-66		R&D; FYDP exp $3.7bn
MBT	M1	552	Upgrade; FYDP exp $3,842m; $655m FY1998 for 120 upgrades
recce hel	OH-58D		Upgrade; FY1998 exp $39m
SPA	*Crusader*		R&D; FY1998 exp $322m
tac hel	UH-60	18	FY1998 exp $208m for 18
UAV		91	FYDP exp $1.8bn
Marines			
FGA	AV-8B	44	FYDP exp $1.2bn
tac hel	V-22	91	FYDP exp $8.3bn; planned purchase 425 reduced by QDR to 360
Navy			
AGOR	T-AGS-60	1	Oceanographic research vessel
AKR	T-AKR	12	Fast sealift vessel; another 3 already delivered
CVN	CVN-68	1	Upgrade; USS *Nimitz* to undergo overhaul costing FY1998 $1.7bn
DDG	DDG-51	3	FY1998 exp $2.9bn for 3 units; planned purchase 12 by FY2001
FF	arsenal ship		R&D; concept development to receive $150m FY1998
LHD	LHD-5	7	4 operational, 6th launched; 5 more being built, 7 by 2000
ro-ro	T-AKR-300	8	First for delivery Jan 1998, the rest by Jun 2000
SSN	NSSN	4	FYDP exp $10.7bn
SSN	SSN-23		FY1998 exp $227m
FGA	F-14		Upgrade; mod costing FY1998 $302m
FGA	F/A-18 C/D		FY1998 exp $50m
FGA	F/A-18 E/F	248	FYDP exp $20.5bn; purchase 1,000 reduced by QDR to 785
trg	T-45	12	FY1998 exp $250m; 12 a year since 1992

United States

	1995	1996	1997	1998
GDP	$7.2tr	$7.6tr		
per capita	$26,600	$27,600		
Growth	2.0%	2.4%		
Inflation	2.8%	2.9%		
Publ debt	64.3%	64.2%		
Def bdgt				
BA		$266.0bn	$262.3bn	
Outlay		$265.2bn	$267.1bn	
Request				
BA				$265.3bn
Outlay				$259.4bn
Population			268,126,000	
Age	*13–17*	*18–22*	*23–32*	
Men	9,328,000	9,234,000	19,966,000	
Women	8,879,000	8,794,000	19,244,000	

Total Armed Forces

ACTIVE 1,447,600

(198,500 women, excl Coast Guard)

RESERVES 1,711,700

(total incl Stand-by and Retired Reserve)

READY RESERVE 1,433,000

Selected Reserve and Individual Ready Reserve to augment active units and provide reserve formations and units

NATIONAL GUARD 476,200

Army (ARNG) 367,000 **Air Force** (ANG) 109,200

RESERVE 956,800

Army 519,800 **Navy** 262,400 **Marines** 101,300 **Air Force** 73,300

STAND-BY RESERVE 27,500

Trained individuals for mob **Army** 900 **Navy** 12,000 **Marines** 200 **Air Force** 14,400

RETIRED RESERVE 251,200

Trained individuals to augment spt and trg facilities (retired in the past 5 years, are under 60 and not disabled) **Army** 152,000 **Navy** 19,800 **Marines** 25,000 **Air Force** 54,400

US Strategic Command (US STRATCOM)

HQ: Offutt AFB, NE (manpower incl in Navy and Air Force totals)

NAVY 432 SLBM in 18 SSBN

(Plus 48 *Poseidon*-C3 launchers in 1 non-op SSBN, 2 op ex-SSBN re-designated SSN, and 16 *Trident*-C4 launchers in 1 non-op SSBN, all START-accountable)

SSBN 18 *Ohio*

10 (SSBN-734) with 24 UGM-133A *Trident* D-5 (240 msl)

8 (SSBN-726) with 24 UGM-93A *Trident* C-4 (192 msl)

AIR FORCE

ICBM (Air Force Space Command (AFSPC)) 580
2 strategic msl wg, 2 gp (1 test wg with 13 test silo launchers)
530 *Minuteman* III (LGM-30G)
50 *Peacekeeper* (MX; LGM-118A) in mod *Minuteman* silos

AC (Air Combat Command (ACC)): 174 hy bbr (346 START-accountable)
13 bbr sqn (6 B-1B, 2 B-2A, 5 B-52)
6 sqn (2 ANG (not yet op)) with 95 B-1B
5 sqn (1 AFR) with 66 B-52H (with AGM-86B ALCM)
2 sqn with 13 B-2A (plus 2 at production site)

FLIGHT TEST CENTRE 9
1 B-52, 2 B-1, 6 B-2A (not START-accountable)

Strategic Recce/Intelligence Collection (Satellites)

(see satellite table pp. 303–6)

IMAGERY Improved *Crystal* (advanced **KH-11**) visible and infra-red imagery (perhaps 3 op)
Lacrosse (formerly *Indigo*) radar-imaging satellite

ELECTRONIC OCEAN RECCE SATELLITE (EORSAT) to detect ships by infra-red and radar

NAVIGATIONAL SATELLITE TIMING AND RANGING (NAVSTAR) 24 satellites, components of Global Positioning System (GPS)

ELINT/SIGINT 2 *Orion* (formerly *Magnum*), 2 *Trumpet* (successor to *Jumpseat*)

NUCLEAR DETONATION DETECTION SYSTEM detects and evaluates nuclear detonations; sensors to be deployed in NAVSTAR satellites

Strategic Defences

US Space Command (HQ: Peterson AFB, CO)

North American Aerospace Defense Command (NORAD), a combined US–Canadian org (HQ: Peterson AFB, CO)

US Strategic Command (HQ: Offutt AFB, NE)

EARLY WARNING

DEFENSE SUPPORT PROGRAM (DSP) infra-red surveillance and warning system. Approved constellation: 3 op satellites and 1 op on-orbit spare

BALLISTIC-MISSILE EARLY-WARNING SYSTEM (BMEWS) 3 stations: Clear (AK), Thule (Greenland), Fylingdales Moor (UK). Primary mission to track ICBM and SLBM; also used to track satellites

SPACETRACK USAF radars at Incirlik (Turkey),

Eglin (FL), Cavalier AFS (ND), Clear, Thule,
Fylingdales Moor, Beale AFB (CA), Cape Cod
(MA); optical tracking systems in Socorro (NM),
Maui (HI), Diego Garcia (Indian Ocean)

**USN SPACE SURVEILLANCE SYSTEM
(NAVSPASUR)** 3 transmitting, 6 receiving-site field
stations in south-east US

**PERIMETER ACQUISITION RADAR ATTACK
CHARACTERISATION SYSTEM (PARCS)** 1
north-facing phased-array system at Cavalier AFS
(ND); 2,800km range

PAVE PAWS phased-array radars in Massachusetts,
GA; 5,500km range

**MISCELLANEOUS DETECTION AND TRACK-
ING RADARS US Army** Kwajalein Atoll (Pacific)
USAF Ascension Island (Atlantic), Antigua
(Caribbean), Kaena Point (HI), MIT Lincoln
Laboratory (MA)

**GROUND-BASED ELECTRO-OPTICAL DEEP
SPACE SURVEILLANCE SYSTEM (GEODSS)**
Socorro, Maui, Diego Garcia

AIR DEFENCE

RADARS

**OVER-THE-HORIZON-BACKSCATTER RADAR
(OTH-B)** 1 in Maine (mothballed), 1 in Mountain
Home AFB (mothballed); range 500nm (mini-
mum) to 3,000nm

NORTH WARNING SYSTEM to replace DEW line
15 automated long-range (200nm) radar stations
40 short-range (110–150km) stations

DEW LINE system deactivated

AC ANG 90
6 sqn: 3 with 45 F-15A/B, 3 with 45 F-16A/B
ac also on call from Navy, Marine Corps and Air
Force

AAM *Sidewinder, Sparrow*, AMRAAM

Army 495,000

(72,000 women)
3 Army HQ, 4 Corps HQ (1 AB)
2 armd div (3 bde HQ, 5 tk, 4 mech inf, 3 SP arty bn; 1
MLRS bty, 1 AD bn; 1 avn bde)
2 mech div (3 bde HQ, 5 tk, 4 mech inf, 3 SP arty bn; 1
MLRS bty, 1 ADA bn; 1 avn bde)
1 mech div (3 bde HQ, 4 tk, 5 mech inf, 3 SP arty bn; 1
MLRS bty, 1 ADA bn; 1 avn bde)
1 mech div (3 bde HQ, 4 tk, 3 mech inf, 2 lt inf, 3 SP
arty bn; 1 ADA bn; 1 avn bde)
2 lt inf div (3 bde HQ, 9 inf, 3 arty, 1 AD bn; 1 avn bde)
1 air aslt div (3 bde HQ, 9 air aslt, 3 arty bn; avn bde (7
hel bn: 3 ATK, 2 aslt, 1 comd, 1 med tpt))
1 AB div (3 bde HQ, 9 AB, 1 lt tk, 3 arty, 1 AD, 1 cbt
avn bn)
5 avn bde (1 army, 3 corps, 1 trg)
3 armd cav regt (1 hy, 1 lt, 1 trg)
6 arty bde (3 with 1 SP arty, 2 MLRS bn; 1 with 3 arty, 1

MLRS bn; 1 with 3 MLRS bn; 1 with 1 MLRS bn)
3 indep inf bn, 1 AB Task Force
9 *Patriot* SAM bn (5 with 6 bty, 2 with 4 bty, 2 with 3
bty)
2 *Avenger* SAM bn

READY RESERVE

ARMY NATIONAL GUARD (ARNG) 367,100
(31,500 women): capable after mob of manning 8 div
(1 armd, 4 mech, 2 inf, 1 lt inf) • 18 indep bde, incl 15
enhanced (2 armd, 5 mech, 5 inf, 2 lt inf, 1 armd
cav), 1 armd, 1 lt inf, 1 inf scout (3 bn) • 16 fd arty
bde HQ • Indep bn: 3 inf, 36 arty, 18 avn, 9 AD (1
Patriot, 8 *Avenger*), 37 engr

ARMY RESERVE (AR) 519,800 (105,400 women): 7
trg div, 5 exercise div, 13 AR/Regional Spt Cmd
(Of these, 215,000 Standing Reservists receive
regular trg and have mob assignment; the remainder receive no trg, but as former active-duty soldiers
could be recalled in an emergency)

EQUIPMENT

MBT some 7,836: 192 M-60A3, 7,644 M-1 *Abrams*
incl M-1A1, M-1A2
LT TK 131 M-551 *Sheridan*
RECCE 113 *Fuchs*
AIFV 6,720 M-2/-3 *Bradley*
APC 18,200 M-113 incl variants
TOTAL ARTY 7,428
  TOWED 1,926: **105mm**: 940 M-102, 423 M-119;
  155mm: 563 M-198
  SP 2,818: **155mm**: 2,568 M-109A1/A2/A6;
  203mm: 250 M-110A1/A2
  MRL 227mm: 734 MLRS (all ATACMS-capable)
  (plus 123 reserve/trg)
  MOR 1,950: **107mm**: 1,355 M-30 (incl SP); **120mm**:
  595 M-120/121
ATGW 8,457 TOW (1,237 *Hummer*, 500 M-901, 6,720
M-2/M-3 *Bradley*), 24,400 *Dragon*, 500 *Javelin*
RL 84mm: AT-4
SAM FIM-92A *Stinger*, 660 *Avenger* (veh-mounted
Stinger), 474 *Patriot* (plus 104 reserve/trg)
SURV Ground 44 AN/TPQ-36 (arty), 16 AN/TPQ-
37 (arty), 62 AN/TRQ-32 (COMINT), 37 AN/
TSQ-138 (COMINT), AN/TLQ-17A (EW) **Air-
borne** 4 *Guardrail* (RC-12D/H/K, RU-21H ac), 6
EO-5ARL (DHC-7), 35 OV/RV-1D
AMPH 54 ships:
  6 *Frank Besson* LST: capacity 32 tk
  34 LCU-2000, 14 LCU-1600
  Plus craft: some 107 LCM
UAV 7 *Hunter* (5 in store)
AC some 264: 31 **C-12C**, 104 **C-12D/-F**, 43 **C-23A/B**,
10 **C-26**, 2 **C-182**, 2 **O-2**, 55 **RC-12D/G/H/K**, 3 **T-34**,
4 **U-21**, 6 **UV-18A**, 4 **UV-20A**
HEL some 5,002 (1,460 armed): 483 **AH-1S**, 724 **AH-
64A**, 59 **AH-6/MH-6**, 867 **UH-1** (being replaced),
1,391 **UH/MH-60A**, 66 **EH-60A (ECM)**, 456 **CH/**

MH-47, 510 OH-58A/C, 311 OH-58D (incl 194 armed), 135 TH-67 *Creek*

Navy (USN) 395,500

(53,000 women)

5 Fleets: **2nd** Atlantic, **3rd** Pacific, **5th** (Indian Ocean, Persian Gulf, Red Sea, **6th** Mediterranean, **7th** W. Pacific; plus Military Sealift Command, Naval Reserve Force (NRF)

SUBMARINES 95

STRATEGIC SUBMARINES 18 (see p. 18)

TACTICAL SUBMARINES 75 (incl about 8 in refit)

  SSGN 32
  1 *Seawolf* (SSN-21) with up to 45 *Tomahawk* SLCM plus 660mm TT; about 50 tube-launched missiles and torpedoes
  23 imp *Los Angeles* (SSN-751) with 12 *Tomahawk* SLCM (VLS), 533mm TT (Mk 48 HWT, *Harpoon*, *Tomahawk*)
  8 mod *Los Angeles* (SSN-719) with 12 *Tomahawk* SLCM (VLS); plus 533mm TT (Mk 48 HWT, *Harpoon*, *Tomahawk*)
  SSN 43
  24 *Los Angeles* (SSN-688) with Mk 48 HWT, plus *Harpoon*, *Tomahawk* SLCM
  18 *Sturgeon* (SSN-637) with Mk 48 HWT; plus *Harpoon*, 21 with *Tomahawk* SLCM (incl 10 capable of special ops)
  1 *Narwhal* (SSN-671) with Mk 48 HWT, *Harpoon*, *Tomahawk*

OTHER ROLES 2 ex-SSBN (SSBN 642 and 645) (special ops, included in the START-accountable launcher figures)

PRINCIPAL SURFACE COMBATANTS 143

AIRCRAFT CARRIERS 12 (incl 1 in long refit/refuel)

  CVN 7 *Nimitz* (CVN-68) (96/102,000t)
  CV 5
  3 *Kitty Hawk* (CV-63) (81,000t)
  1 *J. F. Kennedy* (CV-67) (NRF but op)
  1 *Forrestal* (CV-59) (79,250/81,100t)
  AIR WING 12 (11 active, 1 reserve); average Air Wing comprises 9 sqn
    3 with 12 F/A-18A/C, 1 with 14 F-14, 1 with 8 S-3B and 2 ES-3, 1 with 6 SH-60, 1 with 4 EA-6B, 1 with 4 E-2C, 1 spt with C-2

CRUISERS 30

  CGN 3
  1 *Virginia* (CGN-38) with 2 x 2 SM-2 MR SAM/ ASROC SUGW; plus 2 x 4 *Tomahawk* SLCM, 2 x 4 *Harpoon*, SH-2F hel (Mk 46 LWT), 2 x 3 ASTT, 2 127mm guns
  2 *California* (CGN-36) with 2 SM-2 MR; plus 2 x 4 *Harpoon*, 1 x 8 ASROC, 2 x 3 ASTT, 2 127mm guns
  CG 27 *Ticonderoga* (CG-47 *Aegis*)
  5 *Baseline* 1 (CG-47–51) with 2 x 2 SM-2 MR/

ASROC; plus 2 x 4 *Harpoon*, 2 x 1 127mm guns, 2 x 3 ASTT, 2 SH-2F or SH-60B hel
  22 *Baseline* 2/3 (CG-52) with 2 VLS Mk 41 (61 tubes each) for combination of SM-2 ER, and *Tomahawk*; other weapons as *Baseline* 1

DESTROYERS 57 (incl some 6 in refit)

  DDG 26
  22 *Arleigh Burke* (DDG-51 *Aegis*) with 2 VLS Mk 41 (32 tubes fwd, 64 tubes aft) for combination of *Tomahawk*, SM-2 ER and ASROC; plus 2 x 4 *Harpoon*, 1 127mm gun, 2 x 3 ASTT, 1 SH-60B hel
  4 *Kidd* (DDG-993) with 2 x 2 SM-2 MR/ASROC; plus 2 x 3 ASTT, 2 SH-2F hel, 2 x 4 *Harpoon*, 2 127mm guns
  DD 31 *Spruance* (DD-963) (ASW)
  7 with 1 x 8 ASROC, 2 x 3 ASTT, 1 SH-2F hel; plus 2 x 4 *Harpoon*, 1 with 2 RAM, 2 127mm guns, 2 x 4 *Tomahawk*
  24 with 1 VLS Mk 41 (*Tomahawk*), 2 x 3 ASTT, 1 SH-60B hel; plus 2 127mm guns, 2 x 4 *Harpoon*

FRIGATES 44 (incl some 5 in refit)

  FFG 44 *Oliver Hazard Perry* (FFG-7) (10 in NRF) all with 2 x 3 ASTT; 24 with 2 SH-60B hel; 27 with 2 SH-2F hel; all plus 1 SM-1 MR/*Harpoon*

PATROL AND COASTAL COMBATANTS 20

(mainly responsibility of Coast Guard)

PATROL, COASTAL 13 *Cyclone* PFC with SEAL team

PATROL, INSHORE 7<

MINE WARFARE 25

MINELAYERS none dedicated, but mines can be laid from attack submarines, aircraft and surface ships.

MCM 25
  1 *Inchon* MCMCS
  10 *Osprey* (MHC-51) MHC
  14 *Avenger* (MCM-1) MCO

AMPHIBIOUS 42

COMD 2 *Blue Ridge*, capacity 700 tps

LHA 9
  4 *Wasp*, capacity 1,892 tps, 60 tk; with 6 AV-8B ac, 12 CH-46E, 4 CH-53E, 4 UH-1N, 4 AH-1W hel; plus 3 LCAC, 2 x RAM
  5 *Tarawa*, capacity 1,713 tps, 100 tk, 4 LCU or 1 LCAC, 6 AV-8B ac, 12 CH-46E, 4 CH-53E, 4 UH-1N, 4 AH-1T/W hel, 2 x RAM

LPH 2 *Iwo Jima*, capacity 1,489 tps, 12 CH-46E, 4 CH-53E, 4 UH-1N hel, 4 AH-1T/W

LPD 11 *Austin*, capacity 788 tps, 4 tk

LSD 16
  8 *Whidbey Island* with 4 LCAC: capacity 450 tps, 40 tk, 1 with 2 x RAM
  3 *Harpers Ferry* with 4 LCAC, capacity 500 tps 40tk
  5 *Anchorage* with 3 LCAC, capacity 302 tps, 38 tk

LST 2 *Newport*, capacity 347 tps, 10 tk

CRAFT 210

90 LCAC, capacity 1 MBT, about 37 LCU-1610,

capacity 3 MBT, 8 LCVP, 75 LCM, numerous LCU

SUPPORT AND MISCELLANEOUS 93
UNDER WAY SPT 40
AO 17
5 *Cimarron*, 12 *Henry Kaiser* (MSC)
AOE 7
3 *Supply*, 4 *Sacramento*
AE 8 *Kilauea* (MSC)
T-AFS 8
5 *Mars* (MSC), 3 *Sirius* (MSC)
MAINT AND LOG 21
3 AS, 7 AT (MSC), 7 TAO-T (MSC), 2 T-AH (MSC), 2 T-AVB
SPECIAL PURPOSES 8
2 LCC, 6 AGS (4 MSC)
SURVEY AND RESEARCH 24
10 AGOS (towed array) (MSC), 5 AGOR, 9 AGS

MILITARY SEALIFT
Military Sealift Command (MSC) operates 123 ships, incl 53 Naval Fleet Auxiliary Force ships deployed in direct fleet spt and special mission ships for survey, range and research activities incl in Spt and Misc. Other assets are:

MSC Active Force 52

Operating Vessels 18
8 dry cargo (3 ro-ro, 1 *Combo*, 2 freighters, 2 other)
10 tkr

Afloat Prepositioning Force 34
13 maritime prepositioning ships (MPS) (in 3 sqn each to spt an MEB)
21 prepositioned ships (7 ro-ro, 5 lash, 1 tac, 1 flo-flo, 1 flt, AH, 3 tkr, 3 container)
Based in Diego Garcia, Guam and the Mediterranean

MSC Strategic Sealift Force 10
1 sqn of 8 fast sealift ships (30 kt ro-ro at 4 days' readiness), 2 hosp ships

Additional Military Sealift

Ready Reserve Force 82
32 breakbulk, 29 ro-ro, 4 lash, 3 'Seebee', 4 tkr, 2 tps, 8 tac (at 4–20 days' readiness, maintained by Department of Transport)

National Defence Reserve Fleet (NDRF) 62
30 dry cargo, 9 tkr, 4 tps, 4 container, 1 crane, 3 ro-ro, 2 hy lift, 7 research, 2 Maritime Academy

Naval Reserve Surface Forces 20
1 CV (*J. F. Kennedy*) fully op with assigned air wg, 10 FFG, 4 MCM, 2 MHC, 2 LST, 1 mine-control ship (*Inchon*) generally crewed by 70% active and 30% reserve

Augment Forces
28 MIUW units and 12 cargo handling bn

NAVAL INACTIVE FLEET about 122
includes about 25 'mothballed' USN ships, 2 CV, about 25 dry cargo ships, 10 tkr and some 60 *Victory* Second World War cargo ships (60–90 days' reactivation, but many ships are of doubtful serviceability). 89 awaiting scrap/sale

COMMERCIAL SEALIFT about 303
US-flag and effective US-controlled (EUSC) ships potentially available to augment military sealift

NAVAL AVIATION 58,650
(10,500 women), incl 12 carrier air wg (11 active, 1 reserve) **Flying hours** F-14: 240; F-18: 264; A-6: 240
Average air wg comprises 9 sqn
3 with 12 F/A-18A/C, 1 with 14 F-14, 1 with 8 S-3B and 2 ES-3, 1 with 6 SH-60, 1 with 4 EA-6B, 1 with 4 E-2C, 1 spt with C-2

AIRCRAFT
FTR 12 sqn
5 with F-14A, 4 with F-14B, 3 with F-14D
FGA/ATTACK 24 sqn with F/A-18C/D
3 with A-6E
ELINT 4 sqn
2 with EP-3, 2 with ES-3A
ECM 13 sqn with EA-6B
MR 12 land-based sqn
1 with P-3CII, 11 with P-3CIII
ASW 10 sqn with S-3B
AEW 10 sqn with E-2C
COMD 2 sqn with E-6A (TACAMO)
OTHER 4 sqn
2 with C-2A, 2 with C-130T
TRG 11 sqn
2 'Aggressor' with F/A-18
9 trg with T-2C, T-34C, T-44, T-45A

HELICOPTERS
ASW 20 sqn
10 with SH-60B (LAMPS Mk III)
10 with SH-60F/HH-60H
MCM 2 sqn with MH-53E
MISC 6 sqn
5 with CH-46, 1 with MH-53E
TRG 2 sqn with TH-57B/C

NAVY RESERVE 27,350
(3,285 women) 1,598 cbt ac; 501 armed hel
FTR ATTACK 2 sqn with F-18
FTR 1 sqn with F-14
AEW 2 sqn with E-2C
ECM 1 sqn with EA-6B
MPA 9 sqn with P-3B/C
FLEET LOG SPT 1 wg
8 sqn with C-9B/DC-9, 4 sqn with C-130T
HEL 1 wg
3 ASW sqn with SH-2G and SH-3H
2 HCS sqn with HH-60H

AIRCRAFT

(Naval Inventory includes Marine Corps ac and hel)
298* **F-14** (168 **-A** (ftr, incl 16 NR) plus 21 in store, 80 (ftr) **-B**, 50 (ftr) **-D**) • 762* **F/A-18** (209 **-A** (FGA, incl 35 NR, 89 MC (51 MCR)), 33 **-B** (FGA, incl 2 NR (5 MC)), 389 **-C** (FGA, incl 87 MC), 130-**D** (FGA, incl 93 MC), 1 **-F**) • 34* **F-5E/F** (trg, incl 12 MCR) • 59* **TA-4J** (trg) plus 24 in store • 129 **A-6** (18* **-E** (FGA), 111 **EA-6B** (ECM, incl 4 NR, 28 MC) plus 125 in store) • 174* **AV-8B** (FGA, incl 154 MC) plus 18 in store • 17* **TAV-8B** (trg, incl 14 MC) plus 1 in store • 81 **E-2** (80 -**C** (AEW, incl 11 NR) plus 4 in store, 1 **TE-2C** (trg) plus 4 in store) • 280 **P-3** (3 **-B**, 236* **-C** (MR, incl 70, NR), 12 **EP-3** (ELINT), 13 **NP-3D** (trials), 11 **U/VP-3A** (utl/VIP), 5 **TP-3A** (trg) plus 51 P-3 in store) • 133 **S-3** plus 21 in store (117 **-B** (ASW), 16 **ES-3A** (ECM)) • 105 **C-130** (20 **-T** (tpt NR), 80 **-KC-130F/R/T** (incl 79 MC (28 MCR)), 1 **-TC-130G/Q** (tpt/trg), 4 **LC-130** (Antarctic)) • 4 **CT-39G** (misc) • 43 **C-2A** (tpt) (19 **C-9B** (tpt, 17 NR, 2 MC), 10 **DC-9** (tpt), 7 **C-20**, 2 **-D** (VIP/NR), 5 **-G** (tpt/4 NR, 1 MC)) • 76 **UC-12** (utl) (56 **-B** (incl 11 MC, 3 MCR), 10 **-F** (incl 4 MC), 10 **-M**) • 1 **NU-1B** (utl) • 2 **U-6A** (utl) • 109 **T-2** (trg) plus 13 in store • 1 **T-39D** (trg) • 55 **T-44** (trg) • 66 **T-45** (trg) • 290 **T-34C** (incl 3 MC) plus 29 in store • 11 **T-38A/B** (trg) • 2 **TC-18F** (trg)

HELICOPTERS

106 **UH-1N** (utl, incl 103 MC (20 MCR)) • 27 **HH-1H** (utl, incl 7 MC) • 148 **CH-53E** (tpt, incl 144 MC (5 MCR)) • 44 **MH-53** (tpt, incl 12 NR, 5 MC) • 246 **SH-60**: 169 **-B** (ASW), 77 **-F** (ASW) • 39 **HH-60H** (cbt spt, incl 16 NR) • 14 **SH-2G** (ASW, 14 NR) plus 3 in store • 8 **VH-60** (ASW/SAR MC) • 53 **UH-3H** (ASW/SAR) • 27 **CH-46D** (tpt, trg) • 233 **CH-46E** (tpt, incl 231 MC (26 MCR)) • 46 **UH/HH-46D** (utl) • 120 **TH-57** (45 **-B** (trg), 75 **-C** (trg) (plus B-2, C-12 in store)) • 16 **VH-3A/B** (VIP) • 180 **AH-1W** (atk, incl 159 MC (29 MCR)) • 47 **CH-53D** (tpt, incl 37 MC) plus 25 in store • 7 **RH-53D** (tpt MCR) plus 4 in store

MISSILES

AAM AIM-120 AMRAAM, AIM-7 *Sparrow*, AIM-54A/C *Phoenix*, AIM-9 *Sidewinder*
ASM AGM-45 *Shrike*, AGM-88A HARM; AGM-84 *Harpoon*, AGM-119 *Penguin* Mk-3

Marine Corps 174,900

(8,500 women)

GROUND

3 div
1 with 3 inf regt (10bn), 1 tk, 2 lt armd recce (LAV-25), 1 aslt amph, 1 cbt engr bn, 1 arty regt (4 bn)
1 with 3 inf regt (8 bn), 1 tk, 1 lt armd recce (LAV-25), 1 aslt amph, 1 cbt engr bn, 1 arty regt (4 bn)
1 with 2 inf regt (6 bn), 1 cbt aslt bn (1 AAV, 1 LAR coy), 1 arty regt (2 bn)
3 Force Service Spt Gp
1 bn Marine Corps Security Force (Atlantic and Pacific)
Marine Security Guard bn (1 HQ, 7 region coy)

RESERVES (MCR)

1 div (3 inf (9 bn), 1 arty regt (5 bn); 2 tk, 1 lt armd inf (LAV-25), 1 aslt amph, 1 recce, 1 cbt engr bn)
1 Force Service Spt Gp

EQUIPMENT

MBT 403 M-1A1 *Abrams*
LAV 401 LAV-25 (**25mm gun**), 189 LAV (variants, excl MOR and ATGW)
AAV 1,258 AAV-7A1 (all roles)
TOWED ARTY 105mm: 248 M-101A1; **155mm**: 599 M-198
MOR 81mm: 613 (incl 50 LAV-M)
ATGW 1,147 TOW, 1,978 *Dragon*, 95 LAV-TOW
RL 83mm: 1,842 SMAW; **84mm**: 1,300 AT-4
SURV 22 AN/TPQ-36 (arty)

AVIATION 34,362

(1,270 women)
3 active air wg and 1 MCR air wg
Flying hours cbt aircrew: 264
AIR WING no standard org, but a notional wg comprises
AC 130 fixed-wing: 48 **F/A-18A/C/D**, 60 **AV-8B**, 10 **EA-6B**, 12 **KC-130**
HEL 167: 12 **CH-53D**, 32 **CH-53E**, 36 **AH-1W**, 27 **UH-1N**, 60 **CH-46E**
1 MC C^2 system, wg support gp

AIRCRAFT

FTR/ATTACK 14 sqn with 168 F/A-18A/C/D
FGA 7 sqn with 140 AV-8B
ECM 4 sqn with 20 EA-6B
TKR 3 sqn with KC-130F/R
TRG 4 sqn
　1 with 14 AV-8B, 12 TAV-8B
　1 with 40 F/A-18A/B/C/D, 3 T-34C
　1 with 12 F-5E, 1 F-5F
　1 with 8 KC-130F

HELICOPTERS

ARMED 6 lt attack/utl with 108 AH-1W and 54 UH-1N
TPT 15 **med** sqn with 180 CH-46E, 4 sqn with 32 CH-53D; 6 **hy** sqn with 96 CH-53E
TRG 4 sqn
　1 with 20 AH-1W, 10 UH-1N, 4 HH-1N
　1 with 20 CH-46
　1 with 6 CH-53D
　1 with 20 CH-53E, 5 MH-53E
SAM 3+ bn
　2 (1 MCR) with phase III I HAWK
　2+ (5 bty + 1 MCR) with *Stinger* and *Avenger*
UAV 2 sqn with *Pioneer*

RESERVES 4,820

(200 women) (MCR); 1 air wg

AIRCRAFT

FTR/ATTACK 4 sqn with 48 F-18A

1 *Aggressor* sqn with 13 F5-E/F

TKR 2 tkr/tpt sqn with 24 KC-130T

HELICOPTERS

ARMED 2 attack/utl sqn with 36 AH-1W, 18 UH-1N

TPT 4 sqn

2 **med** with 24 CH-46E, 2 **hy** with 16 RH-53A

SAM 1 bn (3 bty) with I HAWK, 1 bn (2 bty) with *Stinger* and *Avenger*

EQUIPMENT (incl MCR): 454 cbt ac; 159 armed hel

Totals included in the Navy inventory

AIRCRAFT

274 **F-18A/-B/-C/-D** (FGA incl 51 MCR) • 154 **AV-8B**, 14* **TAV-8B** (trg) • 28 **EA-6B** (ECM) • 12* **F-5E/F** (trg, MCR) • 79 **KC-130F/R/T** (tkr, incl 28 MCR) • 2 **C-9B** (tpt) • 1 **C-20G** (MCR) (tpt) • 3 **CT-39G** (MCR) • 18 **UC-12B/F** (utl, incl 3 MCR) • 3 **T-34C** (trg)

HELICOPTERS

159 **AH-1W** (GA, incl 29 MCR) • 103 **UH-1N** (utl, incl 20 MCR) • 7 **HH-1H** (utl) • 231 **CH-46E** (tpt) • 9 **UH/HH-46D** (utl) • 144 **CH-53-E** (tpt, incl 5 MCR) • 5 **MH-53E**, 37 **CH-53D** (tpt, incl 26 MCR) • 16 **RH-53D** (MCR) plus 2 in store • 8 **VH-60** (VIP tpt) • 11 **VH-3A/D** (VIP tpt)

MISSILES

SAM 60 phase III I HAWK launcher, 1,929 *Stinger*, 235 *Avenger*

AAM *Sparrow, Sidewinder*

ASM *Maverick*

Coast Guard 34,700

(includes 3,200 women)

By law a branch of the Armed Forces; in peacetime operates under, and is funded by, the Department of Transport

Bdgt Authority

1993	$3.6bn	1996	$3.7bn
1994	$3.7bn	1997	$3.8bn
1995	$3.7bn	1998	request $4.0bn

PATROL VESSELS 157

OFFSHORE 71

12 *Hamilton* high-endurance with HH-60J LAMPS HU-65A *Dolphin* hel, all with 76mm gun

13 *Bear* med-endurance with 76mm gun, HH-65A hel

16 *Reliance* med-endurance with 25mm gun, hel deck

2 *Vindicator* (USN *Stalwart*) med-endurance cutter

4 other med-endurance cutters

24 buoy tenders

INSHORE 86

49 *Farallon*, 37 *Point Hope*<

SPT AND OTHER 12

2 icebreakers, 9 icebreaking tugs, 1 trg

AVIATION

AC 18 HU-25 (plus 23 in store), 26 HC-130H (plus 4 in store), 2 RU-38A, 5 HH-60J (plus 7 in store), 80 HH-65A (plus 15 in store), 1 VC-4A, 1 C-20B

RESERVES 14,400

Air Force 382,200

(65,000 women) **Flying hours** ftr 240, bbr 236

Air Combat Comd (ACC) 5 air force (incl 1 ICBM), 23 ac wg **Air Mobility Comd** (AMC) 2 air force, 13 ac wg

TACTICAL 52 ftr sqn

incl active duty sqn ACC, USAFE and PACAF (sqn may be 12 to 24 ac)

14 with F-15, 6 with F-15E, 23 with F-16C/D (incl 3 AD), 7 with A-10/OA-10, 2 with F-117

SUPPORT

RECCE 3 sqn with U-2R and RC-135

AEW 1 Airborne Warning and Control wg, 6 sqn (incl 1 trg) with E-3

EW 3 sqn

2 with EC-130, 1 with EF-111

FAC 7 tac air control sqn, mixed A-10A/OA-10A

TRG 36 sqn

1 *Aggressor* with F-16

35 trg with **ac** F-15, F-16, A-10/OA-10, T-37, T-38, AT-38, T-1A, -3A, C-5, -130, -141 **hel** HH-60, U/TH-1

TPT 28 sqn

17 strategic: 5 with C-5 (1 trg), 9 with C-141 (2 trg), 3 with C-17

11 tac airlift with C-130

Units with C-135, VC-137, C-9, C-12, C-20, C-21

TKR 23 sqn

19 with KC-135 (1 trg), 4 with KC-10A

SAR 8 sqn (incl STRATCOM msl spt), HH-60, HC-130N/P

MEDICAL 3 medical evacuation sqn with C-9A

WEATHER RECCE WC-135

TRIALS weapons trg units with **ac** A-10, F-4, F-15, F-16, F-111, T-38, C-141 **hel** UH-1

UAV 2 sqn with *Predators*

RESERVES

AIR NATIONAL GUARD (ANG) 109,180

(17,250 women)

BBR 2 sqn with B-1B

FTR 6 AD sqn with F-15, F-16

FGA 43 sqn

6 with A-10/ OA-10

31 with F-16 (incl 3 AD)

6 with F-15A/B (incl 3 AD)

TPT 27 sqn
  24 tac (1 trg) with C-130E/H
  3 strategic: 1 with C-5, 2 with C-141B

TKR 23 sqn with KC-135E/R (11 with KC-135E, 12 with KC-135R)

SPECIAL OPS 1 sqn (AFSOC) with EC-130E

SAR 3 sqn with **ac** HC-130 **hel** HH-60

TRG 7 sqn

AIR FORCE RESERVE (AFR) 73,310

(14,880 women), 35 wg

BBR 1 sqn with B-52H

FGA 7 sqn
  4 with F-16C/D, 3 with A-10/OA-10 (incl 1 trg)

TPT 19 sqn
  7 strategic: 2 with C-5A, 5 with C-141B
  11 tac with 8 C-130H, 3 C-130E
  1 weather recce with WC-130E/H

TKR 7 sqn with KC-135E/R (5 KC-135R, 2 KC-135E)

SAR 3 sqn (ACC) with **ac** HC-130N/P **hel** HH-60

ASSOCIATE 20 sqn (personnel only)
  4 for C-5, 8 for C-141, 1 aero-medical for C-9, 2 C-17A, 4 for KC-10, 1 for KC-135

AIRCRAFT

LONG-RANGE STRIKE/ATTACK 175 cbt ac
  67 strike **B-52H** (with AGM-86 ALCM, 1 test) • 95 **B-1B** (2 test) •13 **B-2A** (5 test)

RECCE 31 U-2R/S • 4 TU-2 R/S • 19 RC-135 • SR-71 (6 in store)

COMD 32 E-3B/C • 4 E-4B • 16 EC-135

TAC 2,644 cbt ac (incl ANG, AFR plus 1098 in store); no armed hel
  14 (FGA) F-4E (plus 364 -C, -D, -E, -G models in store) • 707 F-15 (505 -A/B/C/D (ftr incl 95 ANG, 119 OCU, test), 202 -E (FGA) (plus 140 F-15A/B in store)) • 1,503 F-16 (136 -A (incl 133 ANG), 59 -B (incl 41 ANG), 1,113 -C (incl 402 ANG, 68 AFR), 195 -D (incl 46 ANG, 8 AFR) (plus 410 F-16A/B in store)) • 37 EF-111A (ECM) • 53 F-117 (42 (FGA), 10* (trg), plus 1 test) • 233 A-10A (FGA, incl 78 ANG, 27 AFR), plus 184 in store • 134* OA-10A (FAC incl 18 ANG, 24 AFR) • 4 EC-18B/D (Advanced Range Instrumentation) • 3 E-8C (JSTARS) • 2 E-9A • 2 WC-135B (weather recce) • 4 OC-135 ('Open Skies' Treaty) • 21* AC-130H/U (special ops, USAF) • 33 HC-130N/P • 27 EC-130E/H (special ops incl 8 SOF) • 66 MC-130E/H/P (special ops) • 13 WC-130H/W (weather recce, 10 AFR) • 14 EC-135

TPT 126 C-5 (74 -A (strategic tpt, incl 14 ANG, 32 AFR), 50 -B, 2 -C) • 33 C-17A (1 test) • 188 C-141B (incl 18 ANG, 45 AFR) • 513 C-130B/D/E/H/J (tac tpt, incl 215 ANG, 112 AFR), plus 71 in store • 7 C-135A/B/C/E • 6 C-137B/C (VIP tpt) • 23 C-9A/C • 36 C-12C/-D/-J (liaison) • 12 C-20 (2 -A, 5 -B, 3 -C, 2 -H) • 79 C-21A • 3 C-22B (ANG) • 3 C-23A • 2 VC-25A • 28 C-26A/B (ANG) • 10 C-27A (tpt)

TKR 548 KC-135 (224 ANG, 76 AFR) • 59 KC-10A tkr/tpt

TRG 183 T-1A • 112 T-3A • 419 T-37B • 418 T-38 • 12 T-43A • 1 TC-135S • 1 TC-135W • 2 UV-18B • 73 AT-38B • 2 TC-18E • 2 CT-43A

HELICOPTERS

40 MH-53-J *Pave Low* (special ops) • 13 MH-60G (incl 10 SOC) • 8 HH-1H • 87 HH-60G (incl 21 AFR, 17 ANG) • 62 UH-1N, 6 TH-53A

MISSILES

AAM AIM-9P/L/M *Sidewinder*, AIM-7E/F/M *Sparrow*, AIM 120, A/B AMRAAM

ASM AGM-86B/C ALCM, AGM-65A/B/D/G *Maverick*, AGM-88A/B HARM, AGM-84A *Harpoon*, AGM-86C ALCM, AGM-142A/B/C/D

CIVIL RESERVE AIR FLEET (CRAF) 683

commercial ac (numbers fluctuate)

LONG-RANGE 501
  passenger 271 (A-310, B-747, B-757, B-767, DC-10, L-1011, MD-11)
  cargo 230 (B-747, DC-8, DC-10, L-1011, MD-11)

SHORT-RANGE 95
  passenger 81 (A-300, B-727, B-737, MD-80/83)
  cargo 14 (L-100, B-727, DC-9)

DOMESTIC AND AERO-MEDICAL 34 (B-767)

Special Operations Forces

Units only listed

ARMY (15,500)

5 SF gp (each 3 bn) • 1 Ranger inf regt (3 bn) • 1 special ops avn regt (3 bn) • 1 Psychological Ops gp (5 bn) • 1 Civil Affairs bn (5 coy) • 1 sigs, 1 spt bn

RESERVES (2,800 ARNG, 7,800 AR)
  2 ARNG SF gp (3 bn) • 12 AR Civil Affairs HQ (3 comd, 9 bde) • 2 AR Psychological Ops gp • 36 AR Civil Affairs 'bn' (coy)

NAVY (4,000)

1 Naval Special Warfare Comd • 1 Naval Special Warfare Centre • 3 Naval Special Warfare gp • 6 Naval Special Warfare units • 6 SEAL teams • 2 SEAL delivery veh teams • 2 Special Boat sqn • 6 DDS

RESERVES (1,400)
  1 Naval Special Warfare Comd • 6 Naval Special Warfare gp det • 3 Naval Special Warfare unit det • 6 SEAL team det • 2 Special Boat unit • 2 Special Boat sqn • 1 SEAL delivery veh det • 1 CINCSOC det

AIR FORCE (9,335 – AFRES 1,383, ANG 1,025)

1 air force HQ, 1 wg, 13 sqn
  4 with MC-130, 2 with AC-130, 3 with HC-130, 3 with MH-53 hel, 1 with MH-60 hel

RESERVES (1,383)
1 wg, 2 sqn (AFSOC) with 8 MC-130E, 5 MC-130P, 2 C-130E
ANG (1,025)
1 wg, 1 sqn with 6 EC-130E, 4 C-130E

Deployment

Commanders' NATO appointments also shown (e.g., COMEUCOM is also SACEUR)

EUROPEAN COMMAND (EUCOM)

some 121,600, incl Mediterranean 6th Fleet: HQ Stuttgart-Vaihingen (Commander is SACEUR)
ARMY HQ US Army Europe (USAREUR), Heidelberg
NAVY HQ US Navy Europe (USNAVEUR), London (Commander is also CINCAFSOUTH)
AIR FORCE HQ US Air Force Europe (USAFE), Ramstein (Commander is COMAIRCENT)

GERMANY

ARMY 60,500
V Corps with 1 armd(-), 1 mech inf div(-), 1 arty, 1 AD (1 *Patriot* (6 bty), 1 *Avenger* bn), 1 engr, 1 avn bde
Prepositioned eqpt (POMCUS) for 4 armd/mech bde, approx 57% stored in Ge
    EQPT (incl POMCUS in Ge, Be and Nl)
    some 1,108 MBT, 885 AIFV, 959 APC, 583 arty/MRL/mor, 104 ATK hel
AIR FORCE 15,165, 72 cbt ac
1 air force HQ: USAFE
1 ftr wg: 4 sqn (2 with 36 F-16C/D, 1 with 18 F-15C/D, 1 with 12 A-10 and 6 OA-10)
1 airlift wg: incl 16 C-130E and 4 C-9A, 9C-21, 2C-20, 1CT-43

BELGIUM

ARMY 740; approx 22% of POMCUS
NAVY 100
AIR FORCE 520

GREECE

ARMY 18
NAVY 250; base facilities at Soudha Bay, Makri (Crete)
AIR FORCE 167; air base gp. Facilities at Iraklion (Crete)

ITALY

ARMY 2,500; HQ: Vicenza. 1 inf bn gp, 1 arty bty
    EQPT for Theater Reserve Unit/Army Readiness Package South (TRU/ARPS), incl 122 MBT, 133 AIFV, 81 APC, 64 arty/MLRS/mor
NAVY 4,600; HQ: Gaeta; bases at Naples, La Maddalena, 1 MR sqn with 9 P-3C at Sigonella
AIR FORCE 4,200; 1 AF HQ (16th Air Force), 1 ftr wg, 2 sqn with 36 F-16C/D
    SFOR Air Element 6 F-16, 1 AC-130, 3 EC-130, 1 MC-130, 4 KC-135, 4 C-12, 6 EA-6B, 2 MH-53J

LUXEMBOURG

ARMY approx 21% of POMCUS

MEDITERRANEAN

NAVY some 14,000 (incl 2,500 Marines). 6th Fleet (HQ Gaeta, Italy): typically 4 SSN, 1 CVBG (1 CV, 5 surface combatants, 1 fast spt ship), 1 T-AO. MPS-1 (4 ships with equipment for 1 MEB). MEU (SOC) embarked aboard Amphibious Ready Group ships

NETHERLANDS

ARMY 490; approx 7% of POMCUS
AIR FORCE 295

NORWAY

prepositioning for 1 MEB (24 arty, no aviation assets)
ARMY 23
AIR FORCE 60

PORTUGAL

(for Azores, see Atlantic Command)
NAVY 65
AIR FORCE 973

SPAIN

NAVY 2,200; base at Rota
AIR FORCE 233

TURKEY

ARMY 314
NAVY 20, spt facilities at Izmir and Ankara
AIR FORCE 2,695; facilities at Incirlik. 1 wg (ac on det only), numbers vary (incl F-15, F-16, EA-6B, KC-135, E-3B/C, C-12, HC-130, HH-60)
Installations for SIGINT, space tracking and seismic monitoring

UNITED KINGDOM

ARMY 376
NAVY 1,550; HQ: London, admin and spt facilities, 1 SEAL det
AIR FORCE 9,570
1 air force HQ (3rd Air Force): 1 ftr wg, 66 cbt ac, 2 sqn with 48 F-15E, 1 sqn with 18 F-15C/D
1 special ops gp with 3 sqn: 1 with 5 MH-53J, 1 with 4 HC-130, 1 with 4 MC-130H
1 air refuelling wg with 9 KC-135

PACIFIC COMMAND (USPACOM)

HQ: Hawaii

ALASKA

ARMY 6,735; 1 lt inf bde
AIR FORCE 9,472; 1 air force HQ (11th Air Force) 1 ftr wg with 2 sqn (1 with 18 F-16, 1 with 6 A-10, 6 OA-10), 1 wg with 2 sqn with 36 F-15C/D, with 18 F-15E, 1 sqn with 10 C-130H, 2 E-3B, 3 C-12, 1 air tkr wg with 8 KC-135R

HAWAII

ARMY 15,800; HQ: US Army Pacific (USARPAC)

1 lt inf div (2 lt inf bde)

AIR FORCE 4,605; HQ: Pacific Air Forces (PACAF)
1 wg with 2 C-135B/C, 1 wg (ANG) with 15 F-15A/B, 4 C-130H and 8 KC-135R

NAVY 19,500; HQ: US Pacific Fleet
Homeport for some 7 SS, 16 PSC and 10 spt and misc ships

MARINES 6,100; HQ: Marine Forces Pacific; 1 MEB

SINGAPORE

NAVY about 100; log facilities
AIR FORCE 40 det spt sqn

JAPAN

ARMY 1,530; 1 corps HQ, base and spt units
AIR FORCE 14,400; 1 air force HQ (5th Air Force):
90 cbt ac
1 ftr wg, 2 sqn with 36 F-16 • 1 wg, 3 sqn with 54 F-15C/D • 1 sqn with 15 KC-135 • 1 SAR sqn with 8 HH-60 • 1 sqn with 2 E-3 AWACS • 1 Airlift Wg with 16 C-130 E/H, 4 C-21, 3 C-9 • 1 special ops gp with 4 MC-130P and 4 MC-130E

NAVY 6,700; bases: Yokosuka (HQ 7th Fleet)
homeport for 1 CV, 8 surface combatants Sasebo homeport for 4 amph ships, 2 MCM

MARINES 14,300; 1 MEF

SOUTH KOREA

ARMY 27,260; 1 Army HQ (UN command), 1 inf div (2 bde, (6 bn)), 2 SP arty, 1 MLRS, 1 AD bn
AIR FORCE 8,660; 1 air force HQ (7th Air Force): 2 ftr wg, 90 cbt ac; 3 sqn with 72 F-16, 1 sqn with 6 A-10, 12 OA-10, 1 special ops sqn, 5 MH-53J

GUAM

AIR FORCE 2,090; 1 air force HQ (13th Air Force)
NAVY 4,600; MPS-3 (4 ships with eqpt for 1 MEB)
Naval air station, comms and spt facilities

AUSTRALIA

NAVY some 35; comms facility at NW Cape, SEWS/SIGINT station at Pine Gap, and SEWS station at Nurrungar

DIEGO GARCIA

NAVY 900; MPS-2 (5 ships with eqpt for 1 MEB)
Naval air station, spt facilities

US WEST COAST

MARINES 1 MEF

AT SEA

PACIFIC FLEET (HQ: Pearl Harbor) **Main base**
Pearl Harbor **Other bases** Bangor, Everett, Bremerton (WA), San Diego (CA)
Submarines 7 Ohio SSBN, 5 SSGN, 27 SSN
Surface Combatants 6 CV/CVN, 29 CG/CGN, 2 DDG, 15 DD, 12 FFG
Amph 1 comd, 3 LHA, 3 LPH, 7 LPD, 6 LSD, 2 LST
Surface Combatants divided between two fleets
3rd Fleet (HQ: San Diego) covers Eastern and Central Pacific, Aleutian Islands, Bering Sea;

typically 4 CVBG, 4 URG, amph gp

7th Fleet (HQ: Yokosuka) covers Western Pacific, Japan, Philippines, ANZUS responsibilities, Indian Ocean; typically 1 CVBG, 1 URG, amph ready gp (1 MEU embarked)

CENTRAL COMMAND (USCENTCOM)

commands all deployed forces in its region; HQ: MacDill AFB, FL

ARMY 2,070
AT SEA
5th Fleet, HQ Manama. Average US Naval Forces deployed in Indian Ocean, Persian Gulf, Red Sea: 1 CVBG (1 CV/CVN, 2 CG/CGN, 2 DD/DDG, 1-2 AO/AOE/AE, 2 SSN) (forces provided from Atlantic and Pacific)

KUWAIT

ARMY 250; prepositioned eqpt for 1 armd bde (2 tk, 1 mech bn, 1 arty bn)
NAVY 1,000
AIR FORCE 9 (force structure varies)

QATAR

ARMY 50; prepositioned eqpt for 1 armd bde (forming)
AIR FORCE 2

SAUDI ARABIA

ARMY 274; 1 Patriot SAM, 1 sigs unit plus some 1,250 on short-term (6 months) duty
AIR FORCE ε170 plus some 2,900 on temporary duty. Units on rotational detachment, ac numbers vary (incl F-15, F-16, F-117, C-130, KC-135, U-2, E-3)

SOUTHERN COMMAND (USSOUTHCOM)

HQ: Quarry Heights, Panama (to relocate to Miami 1 Oct 1997)

PANAMA

ARMY 3,370; HQ: US Army South, Fort Clayton, Panama; 1 inf, 1 avn bn
NAVY 700; HQ: US Naval Forces Southern Command, Fort Amador, Panama; special boat unit, fleet spt
MARINES 200
AIR FORCE 1,960; 1 wg (1 C-21, 9 C-27, 1 CT-43)

HONDURAS

ARMY 6
AIR FORCE 50

ATLANTIC COMMAND (USACOM)

HQ: Norfolk, VA (CINC has op control of all CONUS-based army and air forces)

US EAST COAST

MARINES 1 MEF

BERMUDA

NAVY 800

CUBA

NAVY 1,000 (Guantánamo)
MARINES 640 (Guantánamo)

ICELAND

NAVY 1,800; 1 MR sqn with 6 P-3, 1 UP-3
MARINES 80
AIR FORCE 630; 4 F-15C/D, 1 KC-135, 1 HC-130, 4 HH-60G

PORTUGAL (AZORES)

NAVY 10; limited facilities at Lajes
AIR FORCE 950; periodic SAR detachments to spt space shuttle ops

UNITED KINGDOM

NAVY 150; comms and int facilities, Edzell, Thurso

AT SEA

ATLANTIC FLEET (HQ: Norfolk, VA) **Other main bases** Groton (CT), King's Bay (GA), Mayport (FL)
Submarines 7 *Ohio*, 3 other SSBN, 16 SSGN, 35 SSN
Surface Combatants 6 CV/CVN, 23 CG/CGN, 5 DDG, 16 DD, 23 FFG. Amph: 1 LCC, 2 LHA, 4 LPH, 6 LPD, 5 LSD, 6 LST, 1 LKA
Surface Forces divided into 2 fleets:
2nd Fleet (HQ: Norfolk) covers Atlantic; typically 4–5 CVBG, amph gp, 4 URG
6th Fleet (HQ: Gaeta, Italy) under op comd of EUCOM

Continental United States (CONUS)

major units/formations only listed

ARMY (USACOM)

200,500 provides general reserve of cbt-ready ground forces for other comd
Active 1 Army HQ, 3 Corps HQ (1 AB), 1 armd, 2 mech, 1 lt inf, 1 AB, 1 air aslt div; 6 arty bde; 3 armd cav regt, 6 AD bn (1 *Avenger*, 5 *Patriot*)
Reserve (ARNG): 3 armd, 1 mech, 3 inf, 1 lt inf div;18 indep bde

US STRATEGIC COMMAND (USSTRATCOM)

HQ: Offutt AFB, NE
See entry on p. 18

AIR COMBAT COMMAND (ACC)

HQ: Langley AFB, VA. Provides strategic AD units and cbt-ready Air Force units for rapid deployment

SPACE COMMAND (AFSPACECOM)

HQ: Peterson AFB, CO. Provides ballistic-missile warning, space control, satellite operations around the world, and maintains ICBM force

US SPECIAL OPERATIONS COMMAND (USSOCOM)

HQ: MacDill AFB, FL. Comd all active, reserve and National Guard special ops forces of all services based in CONUS. See p. 24

US TRANSPORTATION COMMAND (USTRANSCOM)

HQ: Scott AFB, IL. Provides all common-user airlift, sealift and land transport to deploy and maintain US forces on a global basis

AIR MOBILITY COMMAND (AMC)

HQ: Scott AFB, IL. Provides strategic, tac and special op airlift, aero-medical evacuation, SAR and weather recce

Forces Abroad

UN AND PEACEKEEPING

BOSNIA (SFOR): 8,427; 1 inf bde plus spt tps; (UNMIBH): 228 civ pol. **CROATIA** (SFOR): 701; (UNTAES): 3 plus 36 civ pol. **EGYPT** (MFO): 917; 1 inf bn. **FYROM** (UNPREDEP): 502; 1 inf bn, incl 3 UH-60 hel. **GEORGIA** (UNOMIG): 4 Obs. **HAITI** (UNTMIH): 47 civ pol. **HUNGARY** (SFOR): 4,900. **IRAQ/KUWAIT** (UNIKOM): 15 Obs. **ITALY** (SFOR Air Element) **Air Force** 2,000: 6 F-16, 3 EC-130, 1 MC-130, 4 KC-135, 2 MH-53J, 4 C-12 **Marines** 6 EA-6B **Navy** 1 FF, P-3C **ac**. **MIDDLE EAST**(UNTSO): 2 Obs. **WESTERN SAHARA** (MINURSO): 15 Obs. **SAUDI ARABIA** (*Southern Watch*) **Air Force** units on rotation, numbers vary (incl F-15, F-16, F-117, C-130, KC-135, E-3). **TURKEY** (*Provide Comfort*) **Army** 145 **Air Force** 1,400; 1 tac, 1 Air Base gp (ac on det only), numbers vary but include F-16, F-15, EA-6B, KC-135, E3B/C, C-12, HC-130

Paramilitary

CIVIL AIR PATROL (CAP) 51,000

(17,500 cadets); HQ, 8 geographical regions, 52 wg, 1,700 units, 530 CAP ac, plus 4,450 private ac

MILITARY DEVELOPMENTS

Regional Trends

The NATO summit, held on 8 and 9 July in Madrid, took the decision to enlarge NATO to include the Czech Republic, Hungary and Poland. NATO also strengthened its links with non-members by establishing the Euro-Atlantic Partnership Council (EAPC) and a reinforced Partnership for Peace (PFP) programme. The signing of a Founding Act and a Charter between NATO, Russia and Ukraine completed a heavy round of diplomacy.

The NATO-led Stabilisation Force (SFOR) in Bosnia remains the most important military deployment in 1997. In August 1997, the force strength was about 36,000 troops, nearly half the size of its predecessor, the Implementation Force (IFOR), when it first deployed in December 1995. SFOR's mandate is now due to run until June 1998. Crisis in Albania led to the deployment from April to August 1997 of a small coalition force – *Operation Alba* – around 7,000 personnel at its height, drawn from seven NATO members, plus contingents from Austria, Romania and Slovenia. In other parts of Europe, military forces remain engaged, either as peacekeepers or combatants, in Azerbaijan (Nagorno Karabakh), Cyprus and Georgia (Abkhazia). The military continues to be called upon to support the civilian police in counter-terrorist operations, for example, the British forces in Northern Ireland. Military forces also supported the police in dealing with organised crime in southern Italy in June 1997. The traditional role of military aid in civil emergencies was much exercised in Europe, particularly in eastern Germany, during major floods in summer 1997 in Central Europe. Cooperation between NATO Allies and PFP partners on military support for civil emergency planning is becoming more extensive. By 31 July 1997, 14 NATO and PFP partners had sent aid for flood relief to Poland in the form of finance, equipment and specialist teams under the NATO Civil Emergency Planning system.

European defence budgets still show a slight decline and there are steadily fewer European military forces available for deployment on active operations, as sea, land and air forces continue to be cut. However, the process of ending conscription may, over time, enhance the readiness and operational capability of those remaining. Re-equipment programmes are beginning to reflect the changed roles for European forces which now need to be lighter and more mobile. However, the largest single European military programme in financial terms is the *Eurofighter* which, while a role remains for advanced combat aircraft, is more a product of the Cold War. Budgetary constraints make it difficult for European forces, even those of the UK and France, best equipped and trained for rapid deployments, to conduct combined-arms operations in a variety of conflict situations. The same constraints inhibit their ability to exploit new technologies to improve capabilities which may partially compensate for the force reductions.

NATO Enlargement

The NATO enlargement process has only just begun. Following the decisions taken at Madrid in July 1997, the next steps involve accession preparations with the Czech Republic, Hungary and Poland, leading to the signature by all NATO allies of Accession Protocols which will be subject to national ratification procedures in each member-state. Once the ratification procedures are complete, prospective new members will be invited, in accordance with their own national procedures, to deposit their instrument of accession with the US government, the depositary state for the North Atlantic Treaty. Only then do those invited become members of the Alliance. NATO hopes that the new members will be accepted by the time of its 50th anniversary in 1999. In

NATO and Non-NATO Europe

Logistic Support HQ

Zagreb

HUNGARY

CROATIA

UK Divisional HQ MND (SW)

Nordic Brigade HQ

US Divisional HQ MND (N)

SERBIA

Russian Brigade HQ

Coralici

Bihac

Bos Gradiska

Orasje

Brcko

Banja Luka

Doboj

Ugljevik

SW✕✕N

Kljuc

Maglaj

Tuzla

Mrkonjic Grad

Dubrave

Zvornik

BOSNIA AND HERZEGOVINA

Sipovo

Vlasenica

Zenica

Srebrenica

Turkish Brigade HQ

Kiseljak

N✕✕SE

Zepa

Gornji Vakuf

Sarajevo

Visegrad

SW✕✕SE

Gorazde

CROATIA

Foca

F R Y

Medugorje

Mostar

Main SFOR HQ

Spanish Brigade HQ

Blieca

French/ German Brigade HQ (at Rajlovac)

MONTENEGRO

French Divisional HQ MND (SE)

Trebinje

Italian Brigade HQ (at Zetra)

Adriatic Sea

- - - - - - Dayton Agreement line
☐ Bosnian Croat–Muslim Federation
▨ Republika Srpska
– – military sector boundary
N Sector North
SW Sector South-west
SE Sector South-east
— international boundary
■ capital city

All data as at 1 August 1997

0   100km

0   50 miles

accordance with Article 10 of the North Atlantic Treaty, the Alliance remains open to further accessions.

Euro-Atlantic Partnership Council

The EAPC was created at a NATO Foreign Ministers' meeting in May 1997 to provide a framework for both an expanded political dimension to PFP, and for closer practical military cooperation. It brings together the 16 NATO allies and 28 other European countries, and replaces the former North Atlantic Cooperation Council (NACC). At a ministerial-level meeting in autumn 1997, a new 'Work Plan' will be drawn up to implement the EAPC's 'Basic Document'. Initially, the Work Plan is likely to follow a similar pattern to that of NACC and will include the following topics: consultations on specific political and security-related matters, such as crisis management; arms-control issues; nuclear, biological and chemical (NBC) defence and proliferation; international terrorism; defence-policy planning and budgets; and the security impact of economic developments. There is also scope for: consultations and cooperation on issues such as civil emergency and disaster preparedness; armaments cooperation under the NATO Conference of National Armaments Directors (CNAD); nuclear safety; defence-related environmental issues; civil–military coordination of air-traffic management and control; scientific cooperation; and issues related to peace-support operations.

The Enhanced Partnership for Peace Programme

Originally set up in January 1994, PFP allows the Alliance's Cooperation Partners to take part in security cooperation programmes with NATO, including military exercises and civil-emergency operations. Following the May 1997 NATO Foreign Ministers' meeting, Cooperation Partners will have a greater say in planning and directing future programmes. The objectives of PFP enhancement are to:

- strengthen the political consultation element in PFP;
- develop a more operational role for PFP; and
- provide for greater involvement of Partners in PFP decision-making and planning.

To meet each of these objectives, a series of enhancements has been agreed which aims to build on the existing programme. They include:

- increased involvement of Partners in the political guidance and oversight of future NATO-led operations in which they participate;
- the development of a new political–military framework for PFP operations; and
- establishing a Political/Military Steering Committee in which all members may participate.

In order to make PFP more operational, in a military sense, a number of steps have been taken. The most significant are:

- Expanding the scope of NATO/PFP exercises to practise the full range of the Alliance's new missions, including peace-support operations.
- Partner involvement in planning and conducting PFP activities, including NATO/PFP exercises and other operations, by establishing PFP staff elements at different NATO headquarters. Partner countries can now assume international roles in these headquarters and can carry out international functions at the Partnership Coordination Cell (PCC) in Brussels.
- Participation of PFP staff elements in Combined Joint Task Force (CJTF) exercise planning, concept and doctrine development, and operations.
- Arrangements for national liaison representatives from Partner countries to be stationed at NATO headquarters as full diplomatic missions formerly accredited to NATO under the terms of the Brussels Agreement.
- Expanding the Planning and Review Process (PARP) modelled on the NATO defence

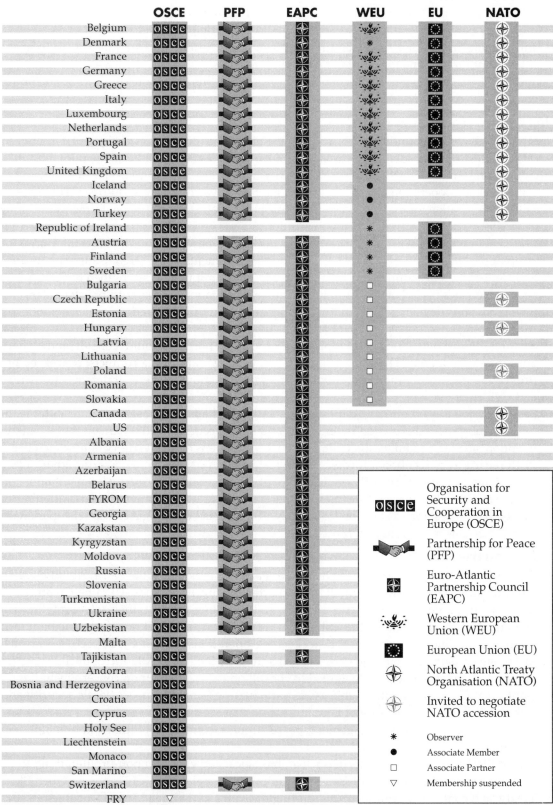

	OSCE	PFP	EAPC	WEU	EU	NATO
Belgium	OSCE	PFP	EAPC	member	EU	NATO
Denmark	OSCE	PFP	EAPC	observer ✳	EU	NATO
France	OSCE	PFP	EAPC	member	EU	NATO
Germany	OSCE	PFP	EAPC	member	EU	NATO
Greece	OSCE	PFP	EAPC	member	EU	NATO
Italy	OSCE	PFP	EAPC	member	EU	NATO
Luxembourg	OSCE	PFP	EAPC	member	EU	NATO
Netherlands	OSCE	PFP	EAPC	member	EU	NATO
Portugal	OSCE	PFP	EAPC	member	EU	NATO
Spain	OSCE	PFP	EAPC	member	EU	NATO
United Kingdom	OSCE	PFP	EAPC	member	EU	NATO
Iceland	OSCE	PFP	EAPC	●		NATO
Norway	OSCE	PFP	EAPC	●		NATO
Turkey	OSCE	PFP	EAPC	●		NATO
Republic of Ireland	OSCE			✳	EU	
Austria	OSCE	PFP	EAPC	✳	EU	
Finland	OSCE	PFP	EAPC	✳	EU	
Sweden	OSCE	PFP	EAPC	✳	EU	
Bulgaria	OSCE	PFP	EAPC	□		
Czech Republic	OSCE	PFP	EAPC	□		invited
Estonia	OSCE	PFP	EAPC	□		
Hungary	OSCE	PFP	EAPC	□		invited
Latvia	OSCE	PFP	EAPC	□		
Lithuania	OSCE	PFP	EAPC	□		
Poland	OSCE	PFP	EAPC	□		invited
Romania	OSCE	PFP	EAPC	□		
Slovakia	OSCE	PFP	EAPC	□		
Canada	OSCE	PFP	EAPC			NATO
US	OSCE	PFP	EAPC			NATO
Albania	OSCE	PFP	EAPC			
Armenia	OSCE	PFP	EAPC			
Azerbaijan	OSCE	PFP	EAPC			
Belarus	OSCE	PFP	EAPC			
FYROM	OSCE	PFP	EAPC			
Georgia	OSCE	PFP	EAPC			
Kazakstan	OSCE	PFP	EAPC			
Kyrgyzstan	OSCE	PFP	EAPC			
Moldova	OSCE	PFP	EAPC			
Russia	OSCE	PFP	EAPC			
Slovenia	OSCE	PFP	EAPC			
Turkmenistan	OSCE	PFP	EAPC			
Ukraine	OSCE	PFP	EAPC			
Uzbekistan	OSCE	PFP	EAPC			
Malta	OSCE					
Tajikistan	OSCE	PFP	EAPC			
Andorra	OSCE					
Bosnia and Herzegovina	OSCE					
Croatia	OSCE					
Cyprus	OSCE					
Holy See	OSCE					
Liechtenstein	OSCE					
Monaco	OSCE					
San Marino	OSCE					
Switzerland	OSCE	PFP	EAPC			
FRY	▽					

Legend

OSCE	Organisation for Security and Cooperation (OSCE)
(handshake)	Partnership for Peace (PFP)
(star)	Euro-Atlantic Partnership Council (EAPC)
(flower)	Western European Union (WEU)
(circle of stars)	European Union (EU)
(compass)	North Atlantic Treaty Organisation (NATO)
(compass, light)	Invited to negotiate NATO accession
✳	Observer
●	Associate Member
□	Associate Partner
▽	Membership suspended

planning system. This measure will be combined with increased opportunities to develop more transparency in military matters among PARP participants.

- Introducing modalities for extending the scope and orientation of the NATO Security Investment Programme to include Partnership projects.
- Increased scope for regional cooperation activities in the context of PFP, including consultations on both regional security matters and on practical cooperation.

NATO–Russia Founding Act

On 27 May 1997, the Founding Act on Mutual Relations, Cooperation and Security between NATO and the Russian Federation was signed in Paris. The Act set up a Permanent Joint Council (PJC) of representatives of the 16 allies and Russia. It will provide a special mechanism for consultation and cooperation on security-policy matters between NATO and Russia. The Act was part of the preparation for the Madrid summit, in a bid to make the enlargement process easier for Russia to bear. The Act is divided into four sections:

- Section I sets out the principles on which the Act is based. These include the norms of international behaviour in the UN Charter and the documents of the Organisation for Security and Cooperation in Europe (OSCE), and includes a commitment to strengthen the OSCE.
- Section II creates the PJC, which is to hold regular consultations on security-policy matters and where possible, develop joint initiatives which may result in joint action in such activities as peacekeeping operations under UN or OSCE auspices.
- Section III sets out a range of topics on which the parties should consult and, where appropriate, cooperate. The subjects include: preventing and settling conflicts; peacekeeping; preventing the proliferation of weapons of mass destruction; converting defence industries; and civil-emergency preparedness.
- Section IV focuses on military deployments and is perhaps the most important in terms of military substance. This section reiterates NATO's 10 December 1996 statement that it had 'no intention, no plan and no reason to deploy nuclear weapons on the territory of new members'. With regard to conventional forces, NATO restates its 14 March 1997 assertion that in 'the current and foreseeable security environment' it would assure its security by maintaining an adequate capability for reinforcement rather than by 'additional permanent stationing of substantial combat forces'. Section IV of the NATO–Russia Founding Act also sets up military liaison missions in Brussels and Moscow.

NATO–Ukraine Charter

At the Madrid summit, a Charter on a Distinctive Partnership between the North Atlantic Treaty Organisation and Ukraine was signed. This Charter sets up the NATO–Ukraine Commission which is to meet not less than twice a year. The parties commit themselves to the full development of the EAPC and the enhanced PFP. This includes Ukrainian participation in operations, including UN and OSCE peacekeeping operations, and, if CJTFs are used in such cases, Ukrainian participation at an early stage if agreed by the North Atlantic Council (NAC) for specific operations. The parties also agreed to consult on issues of common concern including:

- political and security-related subjects, in particular developing Euro-Atlantic security and stability, including the security of Ukraine;
- conflict-prevention, crisis-management, peace-support, conflict-resolution and humanitarian operations;
- the political and defence aspects of nuclear, biological and chemical non-proliferation;
- disarmament and arms-control issues, including those related to CFE and the Open Skies Treaty, and confidence- and security-building measures in the 1994 Vienna Document;

- arms exports and related technology transfers; and
- combating drug-trafficking and terrorism.

A whole range of other areas of cooperation are mentioned in the Charter, including military training, aerospace research, civil-emergency planning and defence conversion. A Ukrainian military liaison mission will be established as part of a Ukrainian mission to NATO in Brussels.

Conventional Armed Forces in Europe Treaty

In Section IV of their Founding Act, NATO and Russia committed themselves to work promptly to adapt the Conventional Armed Forces in Europe (CFE) Treaty 'in order to further reduce the levels of Treaty Limited Equipment [TLE]' and 'reflect the changed security environment' since the Treaty entered into force. Since 1990, over 58,000 pieces of TLE have been destroyed under the terms of the Treaty. After the Founding Act was signed, negotiations intensified in Vienna and an accord was reached on 24 July between NATO, Russia and the other 13 members of the CFE Treaty, on an outline agreement. Negotiations based on this outline agreement began again in Vienna in September 1997 with the aim of drawing up a revised Treaty text by the end of 1998. The main points of the outline agreement are:

- the bloc-to-bloc basis of the Treaty will be abolished and the limitations will apply to national equipment holdings except for some regional allowances;
- national equipment quotas will be reduced;
- flank limitations which constrain deployment in the Caucasus region and on the borders of Norway and the Baltic States will be maintained;
- the Treaty will continue to allow stationing and temporary deployments, enabling new NATO member-states to participate on equal terms in the Alliance, while regional limitations will continue to rule out any destabilising build up of forces;
- all members remain commited to the scope and detail of the Treaty's transparency provisions and to considering additional transparency measures; and
- the option of other European states joining the Treaty will remain open.

NATO countries have said they will cut their quotas for stored equipment by 80% in the revised Treaty. Some countries have already announced their national cuts unilaterally. The UK, for example, has announced a 5% cut. The overall cuts in NATO countries' quotas will result in reductions of more than 3,000 tanks, and similar numbers of armoured combat vehicles and artillery. This is roughly the equivalent of the equipment held by ten armoured divisions. As many NATO members' current holdings are well below their existing quotas, very little additional equipment, if any, will have to be destroyed.

DEFENCE SPENDING

NATO Europe

In 1996, NATO European member-states spent just over $187 billion on defence, slightly down on 1995 levels, and accounted for around 40% of NATO's spending overall, compared to a US share of some 58%. The European share of this spending has also been around 40% since Spain joined the Alliance in 1981. The three countries invited to negotiate NATO membership in June 1997 – the Czech Republic, Hungary, and Poland – together spent an estimated $4.7bn on defence in 1996. Should these countries accede, they will boost the European share of NATO defence expenditure by around 1%, at current spending levels. After virtually static outlays in 1996, NATO European defence spending looks set to fall by about 9% in real terms in 1997. For several

Table 6 Defence R&D and procurement spending, NATO and Non-NATO Western Europe, 1994–1997

(constant 1996 US$m)	Defence budget				R&D				Procurement			
	1994	1995	1996	1997	1994	1995	1996	1997	1994	1995	1996	1997
Belgium	3,198	3,460	3,118	2,743	2	2	2	1	292	287	213	221
Denmark	2,869	3,182	3,034	2,706	0	0	0	0	0	397	376	336
France	36,254	41,351	37,064	32,434	6,041	6,888	5,456	4,586	8,856	10,670	11,293	9,108
Germany	30,765	33,896	32,055	26,500	1,613	1,940	1,811	1,771	3,548	3,885	3,627	3,367
Greece	3,225	3,400	3,522	3,609	0	0	83	91	0	0	665	667
Italy	16,853	16,269	20,244	17,962	589	567	740	740	1,615	1,608	1,983	2,069
Luxembourg	115	125	121	108	0	0	0	0	53	58	6	6
Netherlands	7,703	8,591	8,076	6,923	63	78	119	102	0	1,310	1,545	1,323
Norway	3,384	3,819	3,740	3,416	153	167	171	155	820	808	822	731
Portugal	1,568	1,830	1,718	1,698	0	0	4	4	112	137	258	352
Spain	6,244	7,090	6,867	5,897	258	293	276	240	748	977	1,217	1,004
Turkey	5,593	5,880	5,066	4,546	6	7	6	6	2,042	2,341	2,067	1,881
United Kingdom	35,803	34,973	33,477	35,904	3,615	3,616	3,439	3,542	10,517	10,910	10,705	12,006
Total NATO Europe	153,573	163,865	158,101	144,447	12,341	13,557	12,107	11,236	28,603	33,389	34,777	33,071
Austria	1,935	2,148	1,959	1,641	0	0	0	0	415	442	364	297
Finland	2,042	2,180	1,934	1,778	8	11	9	8	730	775	727	649
Ireland	648	708	741	755	0	0	0	0	26	27	24	27
Sweden	5,485	6,158	6,122	4,842	88	76	116	88	2,191	2,433	1,902	1,751
Switzerland	4,401	5,013	4,439	3,652	91	99	95	76	1,755	2,123	1,801	1,614
Total Non-NATO EU	14,511	16,207	15,195	12,667	187	186	219	172	5,117	5,799	4,817	4,338
Total NATO and EU	168,084	180,071	173,296	157,114	12,528	13,743	12,326	11,408	33,720	39,188	39,594	37,409
Canada	8,950	8,481	7,741	6,964	189	83	91	73	2,280	1,754	2,120	1,839
US	272,388	268,843	266,018	256,788	35,931	35,827	34,970	35,820	45,796	45,277	42,420	43,208
Total US and Ca	281,339	277,323	273,759	263,751	36,120	35,910	35,061	35,893	48,076	47,031	44,540	45,046

Notes [1] Table cites budgetary data which may differ from out-turn data shown in country entries

[2] Austria includes R&D under procurement

[3] UK procurement includes expenditure on spare parts for equipment repair and maintenance

[4] Expenditure on spare parts for equipment repair and maintenance excluded from procurement except in UK case

Alliance countries which are also EU member-states, the effort to qualify for Economic and Monetary Union (EMU) is providing an additional incentive for spending cuts.

NATO European Defence Procurement Organisations

Collectively, European NATO countries spent some $35bn on procurement and $12bn on research and development (R&D) in 1996 – a total of $47bn or 26% of total defence spending under NATO definitions. By comparison, the US spent $77bn or 28% of total defence spending. The most significant difference between NATO Europe and the US is expenditure on R&D; Europe collectively spent just $12bn in 1996 while the US spent $35bn. The search for ways to deal with the imbalance has long occupied policy-makers in NATO, the Western European Union (WEU) and, increasingly, the European Commission, although the last has no direct competence for defence procurement. Moreover, escalating costs for weapons acquisition continues to be a dominant feature of Alliance equipment programmes. While there was no agreement on a more independent defence role for the WEU at the 1996–97 EU Inter-Governmental Conference, three European procurement organisations were created in 1996. In April 1997, following a NAC mandate to review NATO's procurement procedures, the CNAD set in motion a 12-month study on the future of Alliance armaments cooperation. Since the Independent European Programme Group (IEPG) became the Western European Armaments Group (WEAG) in 1992, the rationale for a European armaments agency has been vigorously championed by France, supported by Germany. Frustrated by the lack of WEAG consensus, France and Germany decided to create a joint procurement agency in 1993 which was launched in early 1996. In November 1996, the UK and Italy joined France and Germany and the new organisation was named the Joint Armaments Cooperation Organisation (JACO) or OCCAR in French (*Organisme Conjoint de Coopération en Matière d'Armament*). Joining JACO is conditional on participation in collaborative development and production programmes with at least one of the founder member-states. Shortly after JACO's formation, and also in November 1996, the ten WEU members announced the creation of the Western European Armaments Organisation (WEAO), which includes Denmark, Norway and Turkey. The WEAO focuses on defence research (for which it has a contracting function), rather than on development and production. For countries currently unwilling or unable to participate in the present generation of major collaborative programmes, and therefore excluded from JACO, the WEAO presents an opportunity to join in the research for the next generation of weapons and military equipment. Thus, while neither JACO nor the WEAO qualify as an inclusive European armaments agency, some progress towards that objective was made in 1996.

European Procurement Programmes

So far, defence budget cuts have not resulted in the cancellation of any major weapons programme. Instead, governments have tried to save money by reducing the size of orders and by delaying the schedules of development and production programmes. The EF-2000 *Eurofighter*, as Europe's largest collaborative programme, has been the focus of intense political scrutiny. During 1997, the UK confirmed its requirement for 232 aircraft (with an option for a further 65) and, having already put its share of production investment funding in place, attempted to persuade its partners to follow suit. In July 1997, the German government finally approved production investment funding to buy 180 aircraft. This decision is certain to be challenged in the German Bundestag later in the year. While Italy (121 aircraft) and Spain (87 aircraft) are also *Eurofighter* partners, Anglo-German agreement on requirements at existing levels may be enough to secure the programme's continuation. Other large and long-running collaborative programmes whose production status is assured include: the Anglo-Italian EH-101 maritime and utility helicopter, for which the Italian government finally approved an order for 16 in July 1997 (as opposed to the original requirement for 38) to complement the current UK order for 66; the Franco-German *Tiger* attack helicopter, for which the two governments have confirmed a joint requirement for 427 (production funding was approved in June 1997 and first deliveries are expected in 2003–25); the four-nation NH-90 maritime and utility helicopter is also about to enter production after prolonged uncertainty (which may re-surface), and orders from France, Germany, Italy and the Netherlands currently total 647 (down from 720).

Collaborative shipbuilding has also escaped cancellation so far, although programmes increasingly take on a national appearance: the UK is driving the *Horizon* frigate programme with uncertain French and Italian commitment, while the Trilateral Frigate Cooperation programme of Germany, Netherlands and Spain has forfeited much of its commonality in the face of differing national operational requirements. Severe funding difficulties confront two important programmes – surveillance satellites and strategic lift – most identified with developing an independent European operational capability. Germany's unwillingness (as the major partner in the development of the *Horus* radar-imaging satellite) to fund the development of two *Hélios* 2 infra-red optical satellites leaves the financial burden on France, although Spain offered to take a 3% share in June 1997. There is no development funding for the Future Large Aircraft (FLA) after France and Germany decided in early 1996 to place the onus of development funding on the private sector while confirming the possibility of a European collaborative project and appointed Airbus Industries as a prime contractor. Apart from Germany (with a potential requirement for 75) and France (50), the 1993 European Staff Target was also signed by Italy (44), Spain (36), Turkey (26), Belgium (12) and Portugal (9). The UK (with a reported requirement for 25), which purchased 25 C-130J *Hercules* aircraft from the US in 1994, has left its options open on the FLA. In July 1997, the UK government announced that it would join its European partners in requesting proposals from Airbus Industries to supply the FLA in a competition which may also involve the US company Boeing.

Table 7 UN Register of Conventional Arms imports, NATO, 1996

(as at 30 July 1997)	MBT	ACV	Artillery	Combat aircraft	Attack helicopters	Warships	Missiles
US and Canada							
Canada	—	—	20	—	—	—	74
US	1	1	12	—	—	—	63
Total	1	1	32	0	0	0	137
NATO Europe							
Denmark	—	10	—	—	—	—	—
France	—	—	—	—	—	—	8
Germany	—	6	—	—	—	—	—
Greece	—	—	—	—	—	1	10
Italy	—	—	—	3	—	—	200
Netherlands	—	—	—	1	—	—	—
Norway	—	67	—	—	—	—	98
Portugal	1	10	—	—	—	—	—
Spain	—	—	18	11	—	—	19
Turkey	—	25	—	12	—	—	35
UK	—	—	—	—	—	—	111
Total	1	118	18	27	0	1	481

ARMS TRANSFERS

NATO Europe is one of the three largest defence markets. The others are the Middle East and East Asia. While the major producers (France, Germany, Italy and the UK) meet most of their requirements from domestic sources or through European collaboration, Germany, Italy and the UK are also large importers (both of complete systems and sub-systems), while the remaining NATO member-states mostly depend on imported equipment. The US is the dominant non-European supplier to NATO Europe, with annual deliveries valued at $3–7bn over the last decade. Among major recent US transactions, deliveries of 25 C-130J *Hercules* from the US to the UK have slipped a year, and first delivery is expected in November 1997. Deliveries of 17 CH-47 *Chinook* D-models to the UK and 30 AH-64 *Apache* attack helicopters are expected in 1998, while the 67 licence-produced and re-engined *Apaches* ordered by the UK in 1995 are expected to start delivery in 2000.

Non-NATO Europe

In 1996, military spending in non-NATO European countries declined by around 10% compared to 1995, according to *The Military Balance* estimates. Against this trend, emphatic spending increases took place in the Baltic and Transcaucasus regions, Cyprus and Poland. As in Russia, real spending levels in Ukraine remain uncertain, although official data suggest that outlays grew in 1996. Defence budgets for the year suggest a further fall of about 8% in 1997. Cyprus is the one country committed to a substantial spending increase in 1997 as a result of major weapons procurement, including the Russian S-300 surface-to-air missile (SAM) air-defence system. Bulgaria's economic difficulties for 1996–97 are squeezing defence outlays, despite a large nominal increase in 1997.

Non-NATO European Union member-states collectively account for around half of non-NATO European defence spending. The weakening of the European Monetary System (EMS) currencies against the dollar in 1997 has driven the dollar value of 1997 defence budgets down. It particularly affects countries such as Finland, Sweden and Switzerland which have commitments to purchase major weapons systems and sub-systems from the US.

Table 8 **Defence spending by function, Czech Republic, Hungary and Poland, 1995–1997**

(1996 US$m)	Czech Republic			Hungary			Poland			Total		
	1995	1996	1997	1995	1996	1997	1995	1996	1997	1995	1996	1997
Personnel	368	470	384	324	287	256	1,786	2,158	1,815	2,478	2,915	2,455
O&M	452	345	232	226	216	210	226	588	458	228	1,019	671
Procurement	151	139	83	48	31	11	327	449	596	526	619	690
R&D	38	27	24	0	1	1	43	22	0	81	50	24
Infrastructure and other	38	45	87	27	49	45	29	40	252	93	134	384
Total	1,047	1,026	810	625	584	524	2,772	3,127	2,891	4,443	4,737	4,224

The Czech Republic, Hungary and Poland collectively spent $4–5bn on defence in 1995–96, around 15% of non-NATO Europe outlays. In July 1997, these countries (together with Cyprus, Estonia and Slovenia) were named as the preferred candidates for EU membership, and negotiations are expected to start in 1998. Meeting the criteria for both NATO and EU membership will require a prudent balancing of security and economic commitments. Joining

NATO will certainly involve additional costs for the prospective new member-states (although these might be offset by cuts elsewhere in the defence budget or subsumed under modernisation costs which would have in any case taken place). According to reports, the Polish government estimates the incremental costs of joining NATO at an annual $100–200 million over 10–15 years, or around 3–6% of the defence budget at current levels. Estimates by the Hungarian government are reported as an annual $50m (about 10% of the defence budget). If the three countries also join the EU, they are all likely to benefit directly from net financial transfers arising from EU membership, as well as from improved economic prospects.

ARMS SALES

The three most expensive procurements in the region concern combat aircraft. Some 40 of 140 JAS-39 *Gripen* on order from the Swedish Air Force were delivered by mid-1997. Ten F/A-18 aircraft of 34 on order (32 of which are to be assembled in Switzerland) were delivered to the Swiss Air Force by mid-1997, while 18 F/A-18s have been delivered to the Finnish Air Force (out of an order for 64, 57 of which are to be assembled in Finland). Slovakia was to have been the first former Warsaw Pact country to make a major acquisition from NATO suppliers, ordering 19 helicopters from the Franco-German group Eurocopter, although the status of this transaction is now uncertain following Slovakia's exclusion from the first stage of NATO enlargement. In June 1997, the Czech government approved an order for 72 L-159 light combat aircraft for its Air Force. These aircraft are to be manufactured by the Czech firm Aero Vodochody in which the US company Boeing took a minority share-holding of around one-third in May 1997.

Table 9 **UN Register of Conventional Arms imports, Non-NATO Europe, 1996**

(as at 30 July 1997)	MBT	ACV	Artillery	Combat aircraft	Attack helicopters	Warships	Missiles
Bosnia-Herzegovina	45	80	—	—	—	—	—
Bulgaria	100	100	—	—	—	—	—
Cyprus	42	51	—	—	—	—	—
Finland	—	2	—	9	—	—	3
Hungary	—	119	—	—	—	—	—
Poland	—	—	—	4	18	—	—
Romania	—	—	—	2	—	—	—
Slovakia	—	—	—	8	—	—	—
Slovenia	—	—	66	4	—	1	—
Sweden	1	164	—	—	—	—	—
Switzerland	—	—	—	16	—	—	—
Total	**188**	**516**	**66**	**43**	**18**	**1**	**3**

In 1997, controversies developed over arms acquisitions by Cyprus and Armenia, with Russia the supplier in both cases. In January 1997, the Cypriot government announced that it had signed an agreement to purchase the S-300 SAM air-defence system from Russia. This followed the purchase of 41 T-80 main battle tanks (MBTs) and 43 BMP-3 armoured infantry fighting vehicles (AIFVs) from Russia for delivery in 1996–97. Reports began to circulate in February 1997 of large-scale transfers of major weapons systems from Russia to Armenia in 1993–96, including *Scud* launchers and missiles, T-72 MBTs and BMP-2 AIFVs. Members of the Russian Duma were concerned that there was no record of any payments by Armenia for these weapons. The Russian government denied knowledge of the alleged transactions, but conceded that they may have taken place without the government's formal involvement. External observers noted that, if *Scud* missile transfers had taken place after 1995 (the year Russia joined the Missile Technology Control Regime – MTCR), Russia would be in breach of its commitments. The controversy also raised the question of whether Russia and Armenia were in breach of their CFE Treaty obligations. There have been counter-allegations from Armenia relating to transfers of combat aircraft, MBTs and other weapons and equipment from Ukraine to Azerbaijan over the same period.

Table 10 **Arms orders and deliveries, NATO Europe and Canada, 1995–1997**

Equipment	Type	Unit	Supplier	Order Date	Delivery Date	Comment
Belgium						
APC	*Pandur*	54	A	1997	1998	Deliveries to 1999
arty	105mm	14	Fr	1996	1996	Deliveries 1997
MSC	KMV-type	4	Domestic	1994	2000	
Canada						
trg	*Hawk* 100	25	UK	1997		For NATO trg programme in Ca
trg	*Super Tucano*	27	Br	1997		For NATO trg programme in Ca
AD arty	GDF-005	20	CH	1996		Upgrade
AAW	SM 2	21	US		1996	
arty	C3 105mm	12	Fr	1994	1996	Towed howitzer
arty	LG1 Mk II	8	Nl	1994	1996	
APC	*Piranha* III	240	Domestic	1997	1998	Deliveries to 1999
FFG	*Halifax*	12	Domestic	1983	1996	
MCMV	*Kingston*	12	Domestic	1991	1996	Deliveries to 1999
Denmark						
tpt	*Gulfstream* IV	1	US	1997	1997	
FGA	F-16		Domestic	1996	2002	Upgrade
SAM	MIM-23 *Hawk*	25	No		1996	
LAV	*Mowag Eagle*	10	CH	1993	1995	
PCI	*Stanflex* 300	14	Domestic	1985	1996	
PCI	MHV-800	6	Domestic	1996	1997	
France						
AEW	E2-D	3	US	1994	1997	First 2 delivered 1997, last by 1999
FGA	*Mirage* 2000-D	41	Domestic		1997	Deliveries to 2002
FGA	*Mirage* 2000-5	37	Domestic		1997	Upgrade; deliveries to 2002
FGA	*Rafale*	320	Domestic	1984	2000	86 for Navy
ALCM	*Scalp* EG	420	Collab.	1997		Joint UK–Fr
tkr	KC-135	7	US	1995	1995	EDA
tpt	FLA	52	Collab.	1995	2002	With Ge, It, Sp, UK
tpt	CN 235	7	Sp	1996		
hel	NH-90	160	Collab.	1987	2003	With Ge, It, Nl
sat	*Horus*		Collab.		2005	Development with Ge
sat	*Hélios* 1A	1	Collab.		1996	With Ge, It, Sp; *Hélios* 1B launch 1997
sat	*Hélios* 2	1	Collab.		2001	Development with Ge
MBT	*Leclerc*	320	Domestic	1986	1994	33 deliveries a year to 2002
APC	VAB recce NBC	40	Domestic	1988	1997	1 of 40 delivered by Apr 1997
LAV	MRAV		Collab.			With UK, Ge and Nl
hel	*Tiger*	215	Collab.	1984	2003	With Ge; initial 160
PCI	*Stellis*	4	Domestic		1997	
CVN	*Charles de Gaulle*	1	Domestic	1987	1999	To commission 1999
FF	*La Fayette*-class	6	Domestic	1988	1996	Deliveries to 2003
FF	*Horizon*	2	Collab.	1994	2005	With UK and It
LSD	*Foudre*-class	1	Domestic	1994	1998	Sea trials 1997, to commission 1998

Equipment	Type	Unit	Supplier	Order Date	Delivery Date	Comment
LSD		2	Domestic	1997	2004	2 to be ordered; design not chosen
MPC	*Falcon* 50	4	Domestic	1997		Conversion of second-hand jets
MHC	*Tripartite*-class	1	Domestic	1992	1996	
MHC	*Tripartite*-class	3	Be	1997	1997	Be Navy surplus
OPV		3	Domestic	1992	1996	
SAM	FSAF		Collab.		2006	With It for carrier use
SAM	PAAMS		Collab.		2003	With UK, It for *Horizon*
SLBM	M-45		Domestic			For *Le Triomphant* SSBN class
SSBN	*Le Triomphant*	3	Domestic	1986	1996	2nd to deliver 1998, 3rd 2001
Germany						
sat	*Horus*	1	Collab.		2005	With Fr
sat	*Hélios* 1A		Collab.		1996	With Ge, It, Sp; *Hélios* 1B launch 1997
sat	*Hélios* 2		Collab.		2001	With Fr
FGA	*Eurofighter* 2000	180	Collab.	1985	2001	With UK, It, Sp
BMD	MEADS		Collab.			With US, It
tpt	FLA		Collab.	1995	2002	With Ge, It, Sp, UK; status uncertain
hel	*Tiger*	212	Collab.	1984	2001	With Fr; initial batch 80
hel	NH-90	272	Collab.	1987	2003	With Fr, It, Nl
hel	EC 135	15	Ge	1997		For trg
MBT	*Leopard* II	225	Domestic	1995		Upgrade
arty	PzH 2000		Domestic	1996	1998	To replace M109 and FH70
AD guns	*Gepard*	147	Domestic	1996	1998	Upgrade
APC	OT-810	8	Slvk		1995	
LAV	GTK		Collab.			With UK, Fr, Nl
AMCV	*Keiler*	24	Domestic		1997	2 delivered 1997; option for 48 more
UAV	*Taifun*		Domestic			Development
FFG	Type 124	3	Collab.	1996	2002	With Nl; deliveries to 2006
FFG	Type 123	4	Domestic	1988	1994	Deliveries completed 1996
FAC	Type 143A/B	20	Domestic	1997	1999	Upgrade
corvette	Type 130	15	Domestic	1995	2004	Design to complete end 1997
SSK	Type 212	4	Domestic	1987	2003	Development
hel	*Super Lynx*	7	UK	1996	1999	
Greece						
FGA	A-7	8	US	1990	1995	82 delivered since 1991
FGA	F-16C/D	40	US	1993	1997	5 delivered by Jun 1997
FGA	F-4	40	Il	1997		Upgrade
MPA	P-3 *Orion*	20	US	1991	1995	EDA
tpt	C-130	8	US	1992	1995	EDA
APC	M-113A	100	Ge	1993	1995	Cascading
MRL	MLRS	10	US	1992	1995	
MRL	ATACM	40	US			
hel	AH-64	20	US		1995	
FF	*Kortenaer*-class	4	Nl	1992	1995	Deliveries to 1997
FFG	*Hydra*-class	4	Domestic	1989	1996	2 delivered by 1996, 2 more by 1999
LST	*Jason*-class	5	Domestic	1987	1996	2 delivered by 1996, 3 more by 1999
PCC	FPBGs-148	2	Ge		1995	
ASSM	*Penguin*	10	No		1996	
Italy						
FGA	*Tornado* F-3	24	UK	1993	1996	Final deliveries 1997
FGA	AMX	136	Collab.	1985		With Br; deliveries by end 1997
FGA	*Eurofighter* 2000	121	Collab.	1985		With UK, Ge, Sp; option for 9 more
FGA	F-104	45	Domestic	1996		Upgrade; option to upgrade 108 more
tpt	FLA		Collab.	1995	2002	With Fr, Ge, Sp, UK; status uncertain
tpt	C-130J	18	US	1997	1999	
trg	MB-339CD	15	Domestic	1995	1996	2 delivered Jan 1997, 10 1997, 3 1998

Equipment	Type	Unit	Supplier	Order Date	Delivery Date	Comment
BMD	MEADS		Collab.			With US, Ge
hel	NH-90	214	Collab.	1987	2003	With Fr, Ge, Nl
ASM	AGM-88B	200	US	1996		HARM
sat	*Hélios* 1A		Collab.		1996	With Ge, It, Sp; *Hélios* 1B launch 1997
APC	*Puma*	250	Domestic	1996	1997	Deliveries to 2002
MBT	*Ariete*	200	Domestic	1988	1995	Deliveries to 2001
CV	*Project* NUM	1	Domestic			
FFG	*Artigliere*-class	4	Domestic	1992	1994	Deliveries completed Mar 1996
FF	*Horizon*	6	Collab.	1994	2003	Development with UK, Fr
PC	*Esploratore*-class	4	Domestic	1993	1997	Deliveries to 1998
MHC	*Gaeta*-class	2	Domestic	1992	1996	
SAM	FSAF		Collab.		2006	With Fr, UK, It for *Horizon*
SSK	Type 212A	2	Ge	1997	2004	Built in It under licence
FGA	*Harrier* II	16	US		1994	Deliveries to 1997
hel	EH101	16	Collab.	1979	1998	With UK; approved Jun 1997
PCI	*Zara* 2-class	1	Domestic	1996	1998	
MPA	ATR 42MP	1	It		1997	
Netherlands						
FGA	F-16	136	US			Upgrade
hel	AS-532	17	Fr		1996	9 delivered 1996, 8 1997
hel	CH-47D	13	US		1995	7 remanufactured ex-Ca CH-7D
hel	AH-64A	12	US	1995	1996	For RNAF until AH-64Ds in 1998
hel	AH-64D	30	US	1995	1998	
tpt	F-50	4	Domestic		1996	2 delivered by Dec 1996
msl		40	US		1995	
AD guns	*Gepard*	60	Ge	1996	1998	Upgrade
LAV	MRAV		Collab.			Development with Fr, Ge, UK
APC	XA-188	90	SF		1998	
VLA	LSV	180	Fr	1997	1998	Manufactued under licence in Nl
arty	FH-70	15	Ge		1995	Towed howitzer
MBT	*Leopard* 2A5	180	Ge		1996	Upgrade, first deliveries 1996
OPV		3	Domestic	1997	1998	Deliveries from Jun 1998
AO	A 836	1	Collab.	1988	1995	Fast combat support ship with Sp
FF	*Karel Doorman*	8	Domestic	1985	1991	Last delivered Sept 1995
FF	*De Zeven Provincien*	4	Collab.	1995	2001	Development with Ge, Sp
LCU		4	Domestic	1996	1997	Option for 5th
LPD	L 800	1	Domestic	1994	1997	Hangar space for 4 hel
torpedo	Mk-48	10	US	1995	1995	EDA
hel	NH-90	20	Collab.	1987	2003	With Fr, Ge, It
Norway						
AAM	AMRAAM	500	US	1995	1996	98 delivered 1996
AIFV	CV9030N	104	Swe	1994	1996	Deliveries to 2000
APC	*Sisu* XA-185	31	SF		1995	
ATGW	M-901	126	US	1995	1995	EDA
MRL	227mm	12	US	1995		
ASSM			Domestic	1997	2003	Development to replace *Penguin*
ASSM	RBS-17		Swe	1996		
FAC	*Skjold*-class	8	Domestic	1996	1998	Deliveries to 2004
LCA	*Stridsbat*	16	Swe		1997	Deliveries to 1998
MSC	*Alta*-class	5	Domestic	1989	1996	Deliveries to Oct 1997
PFC	*Hauk Erle* P999	14		1997		Upgrade
Portugal						
arty	L119 105mm	21	UK	1997	1997	
MBT	M-60	13	US	1993	1995	EDA; 1 delivered 1996

Equipment	Type	Unit	Supplier	Order Date	Delivery Date	Comment
APC	M-577	10	US	1995	1996	
mor	107mm	30	US	1994	1995	EDA
AGOS	*Stalwart*	1	US		1997	SURTASS towed array sonar removed
Spain						
FGA	*Mirage* F-1	3	Fr		1995	
FGA	*Eurofighter* 2000	87	Collab.	1994	2001	With Ge, It, UK
FGA	F/A-18A	43	US	1994	1995	Deliveries to 1998
FGA	EF-4C	6	US		1995	
FGA	AV-8B	5	US		1996	
hel	AS-532	15	Fr	1996	1998	Deliveries to 2003
hel	CH-47D	3	US	1997	1999	Upgrade
recce	Cessna 560	2	US		1997	
tpt	FLA		Collab.	1995	2002	With Fr, Ge, It, UK
tpt	C-295		Domestic		2000	Derivative of CN-235
tpt	C-130	12	Domestic	1995	1999	Upgrade
msl	LAU 116A	12	US		1996	Launcher
sat	*Hélios* 1A		Collab.		1996	With Ge, It, Sp; *Hélios* 1B launch 1997
AIFV	*Pizarro*	144	Collab.	1996	1997	Licensed manufacture Sp with A
MBT	*Leopard* 2A4	108	Ge		1997	Deliveries completed
arty	L-119	23	UK	1994	1996	Deliveries to 1997
AO	*Patino*	1	Domestic		1995	Combat supply vessel
FFG	F-100	4	Domestic	1996	2002	With Nl, Ge, Sp
LPD	*Galicia*-class	2	Domestic	1994	1998	
MHC	*Segura*-class	4	Domestic	1989	1998	Deliveries to 2000
OPV	*Alboran*-class	1	Domestic	1991	1996	
Turkey						
FGA	F-16	184	US	1984	1995	Licensed production; deliveries to 1999
FGA	F-5	70	Fr	1996		Upgrade; 34 for export
FGA	F-4	54	Il	1996	1997	Upgrade; delivery to 2002
MPA	CN-235	9	Sp	1997		Licensed production Tu
AAM	AIM-7 *Sparrow*	126	US	1994	1995	EDA
ASM	*Popeye* I	50	Il	1996	1999	
SAM	*Rapier*	515	US	1994	1995	EDA; includes 14 launchers
tkr	KC-135	12	US	1994	1994	EDA; last 2 delivered 1995
hel	AS-532	50	Fr	1994	1995	Deliveries to 2002
APC	BTR-80	70	RF	1994	1995	
MRL	ATACM	72	US		1998	
SAM	*Rapier*		UK	1996	1998	Upgrade
hel	Mi-17	19	RF	1994	1996	16 delivered Apr 1996
SSK	*Preveze*-class	4	Domestic	1987	1994	2 delivered end 1995, 2 by 1999
AO		1	Domestic		1995	
FF	*Perry*-class	3	US	1995	1996	Delivery suspended
FFG	MEKO 200 TFF	4	Ge	1990	1995	2 delivered 1996, 2 by 2000
ASSM	*Harpoon*	22	US		1995	
hel	SH-60	4	US	1997	1999	Deliveries to 2001
United Kingdom						
ASM	*Brimstone*		UK	1996		
ALCM	*Storm Shadow*		UK	1996		
FGA	*Tornado* GR4 IDS	142	Domestic		1998	Upgrade; deliveries to 2002
FGA	*Eurofighter*	232	Collab.	1984	2001	With Ge, It, Sp; option for 65 more
FGA	JSF		Collab.	1995		Development with US
FGA	*Tornado* F-3	100	Domestic	1996	1998	Upgrade
hel	CH-47D/E	17	US	1995	1998	
hel	EH101	66	Collab.	1979	1998	With It; 44 for RN, 22 for RAF
hel	AS-550	47	Fr	1996	1997	For trg

Equipment	Type	Unit	Supplier	Order Date	Delivery Date	Comment
MPA	*Nimrod* 2000	21	UK	1996	2001	Upgrade
SAM	*Rapier*	618	US		1995	EDA
tpt	FLA		Collab.	1995	2002	With Fr, Ge, It, Sp
tpt	C-130J	25	US	1994	1998	Option for 5 more
trg	*Harrier* T10	13	Domestic		1994	13 delivered by May 1996
lt tk	CVRT	21	Be		1995	For re-export
LAV	MRAV		Collab.			With Fr, Ge, Nl
arty	AS90	179	Domestic	1989	1993	Deliveries of last 12 1996
MBT	*Challenger* 2	386	Domestic	1993	1996	36 delivered by May 1996
hel	AH-64D	67	US	1995	2000	Licensed manufacture in UK
AAM	AMRAAM	210	US		1995	150 delivered by Jul 1996
AO	Fast Fleet tkr	2	Domestic	1997		
FFG	*Horizon*	12	Collab.	1994	2003	Development with Fr, It
FFG	Type-23	6	Domestic	1996		12 in service
LPD		2	Domestic	1996	2000	
LPH	*Ocean*	1	Domestic	1993	1998	First sea trials 1996
MHC	*Sandown*	7	Domestic		1998	Delivery Jan 1998
PCI		2	Domestic			
ro-ro		1	J		1996	Chartered from J
SAM	PAAMS		Collab.		2003	With UK, It
SLCM	*Tomahawk*	65	US	1995	1998	SSN launched Block 3 variant
SSBN	*Vanguard*-class	4	Domestic	1982	1993	Deliveries to March 1999
SSN	*Astute*-class	3	Domestic	1997	2004	
FGA	*Sea Harrier*	35	Domestic		1994	Update; 28 delivered by May 1996
hel	*Sea King*	6	Domestic		1996	

Table II Arms orders and deliveries, Non-NATO Europe, 1995–1997

Equipment	Type	Unit	Supplier	Order Date	Delivery Date	Comment
Albania						
PFC		5	US	1996	1997	Ex-US 42 and 65 foot patrol boats
Austria						
AIFV	ASCOD	112	Collab.	1990	1999	With Sp for Sp Army
APC	*Pandur*	337	Domestic	1997	1995	68 for UN operations
arty	M-109	54	UK	1994	1995	
ATGW	*Jaguar* 1	90	Ge	1997	1998	Surplus; 3 for evaluation 1995
MBT	*Leopard* 2A4	114	Nl	1996	1998	Surplus
Bosnia-Herzegovina						
APC	M-113	80	US	1995	1996	EDA
arty	105mm	36	UAE	1995	1996	
arty	130mm	12	Et			
arty	M114 155mm	116	US	1996	1997	EDA
arty	122mm	12	Et			
MBT	OF-40	50	UAE	1996	1997	Plus 41 armoured transporters
MBT	M-60	45	US	1995	1996	EDA
hel	UH-1H	15	US	1995	1996	EDA; located in Ge, for trg
Bulgaria						
ftr	MiG-29SM	14	RF	1997		Bg delaying order
trg	Yak-18T	6	RF	1996	1996	
AIFV	BMP-1/2	100	RF	1995	1996	Debt repayment
MBT	T-72	100	RF	1995	1996	Debt repayment; 25 delivered Jul 1996
Croatia						
hel	Bell-206B-3	3	US	1996	1997	Number not given
trg	PC-9	20	CH	1996	1997	
MBT	M-84		Domestic		1995	In production

Equipment	Type	Unit	Supplier	Order Date	Delivery Date	Comment
APC	LOV		Domestic	1992	1995	Several variants in production
LCT		1	Domestic		1995	Second of type delivered 1995
Cyprus						
AIFV	BMP-3	43	RF	1995	1995	18 delivered 1995, 25 1996
APC	*Leonidas*	26	Gr		1996	
MBT	T-80U	41	RF	1996	1996	Deliveries to 1997
MBT	AMX-30	52	Gr		1996	B-2 upgrades, deliveries to 1997
SAM	SA-10		RF	1997	1998	
SSM	MM-40 *Exocet*	24	Fr	1994	1995	
PCI		1	Il		1997	Reportedly torpedo boat
Czech Republic						
FGA	L-159	72	Domestic	1997	1999	Production due 1997
hel	W-3	11	Pl	1995	1995	Exchange for 10 Cz MiG-29
MBT	T-72		Domestic	1997		Upgrade
Estonia						
hel	Mi-8	4	Ge		1995	Ex-East Ge, FMA
PCI		1	Domestic		1996	
Finland						
FGA	F/A-18C/D	64	US	1992	1995	57 for assembly in SF to 2000
SAM	SA-11	6	RF	1995	1996	Debt repayment
APC	XA-185		Domestic	1982		Deliveries to 1995
APC	RA-140	10	Domestic	1997		For mine clearing
LAV	CAV 100	2	UK		1996	For IFOR/SFOR duties
arty	155mm		Domestic			Development completed,
SAM	*Crotale*		Fr		1995	Deliveries completed 1996
FAC	*Rauma* 2000	1	Domestic	1997	1997	
PFM	*Helsinki*-class	4	Domestic		1995	
MPA	DO-228	2	Ge		1995	For Frontier Guard
PFC		1	Domestic		1995	For Frontier Guard
Georgia						
PCI	*Zhuk*	1	Ukr	1997	1997	
FAC	*Koncar*	1	Domestic		1995	
SS	Mod *Una*	1	Domestic		1996	Mini-sub; stretched version of *Una*
Hungary						
hel	Mi-24	20	Ge	1994	1995	
trg	L-39	20	Cz	1993	1995	Ex-East Ge, Ge FMA
SAM	*Mistral*		Fr	1997		
APC	BTR-80	540	RF	1995	1996	Deliveries to 1997
MBT	T-72	100	Bel	1995	1996	Ex-Bel
MBT	T-72	31	Bel	1995	1996	
Ireland						
OPV		1				Request for proposals
recce	*Defender* 4000	1	UK		1997	Surveillance ac
Latvia						
arty	120mm	26	Cz		1995	Ex-Cz, FMA
arty	100mm	26	Cz		1995	
PCI	*Storm*	1	No		1995	
PFC	*Osa*-class	1	Ge		1995	Ex-East Ge
Lithuania						
hel	Mi-2	5	Pl		1996	Ex-Pl, FMA
arty	120mm	18	Cz		1995	
Malta						
hel	*Alouette* 3	2	Nl		1997	Surplus, to join 3 operated by M
Moldova						
APC	TAB-71	80	R		1995	

Equipment	Type	Unit	Supplier	Order Date	Delivery Date	Comment
Poland						
FGA	MiG-29	10	Cz		1995	Ex-Cz, exchange; 4 delivered 1996
FGA	I-22	6	Domestic	1996	1998	Plus upgrades for 11
tpt	PZL M-20	2	Domestic			Licensed variant of US *Piper Seneca* II
trg	M-96	17	Pl	1996	1997	Delivery by end 1997
trg	M-93K *Iryda*	12	Domestic	1995	1996	Upgrade
FGA	*Mirage* 5	1	Be		1995	
MBT	T-72	2	Ukr		1995	
hel	Mi-24	18	Ge		1996	Ex-East Ge
MHC	*Golpo*	1	Domestic			Launched early 1994
hel	*Kania*	2	Domestic			For Border Guard
Romania						
FGA	MiG-23UB	2	RF		1996	
FGA	MiG-21	110	Domestic	1995	1997	Upgrade with Il
cbt hel	AH-1RO	90	US	1997		Licensed production; uncertain
hel	SA-330 *Puma*	24	Domestic	1997	1998	Upgrade with Fr, Il
tpt	C-130B	4	US	1995	1996	Ex-US
Slovakia						
FGA	MiG-29	8	RF	1995	1996	Debt repayment
msl	R27RI	14	Ukr		1995	
arty	155mm SP	8	Domestic		1997	
MBT	M-2 *Moderna*		Domestic	1994		T-72 upgrade
Slovenia						
arty	120mm	56	Il		1996	
arty	155mm	10	Il		1996	
PCI	*Super Dvora*	1	Il		1996	
Sweden						
FGA	JAS-39	204	Domestic	1980	1995	40 delivered mid-1997
AAM	AMRAAM	110	US	1995	1998	Option for 700 more
SAM	RBS 23		Domestic	1995	2000	Medium-range SAM system
AEW	Saab-340	6	Domestic	1992	1997	4 of 6 to be delivered 1997
MBT	*Leopard* II	289	Ge	1995	1996	Incl 120 second-hand
AIFV	CV-90	600	Domestic	1984	1993	Deliveries to 2003
AIFV	BMP-1	350	Ge	1995	1997	Following refurbishment
APC	MT-LB	550	Ge	1994	1995	Deliveries to 1997
LCA	155mm SPA		Domestic			SP variant of FH-77 with Fr
hel	AS-532	12	Fr	1995	1997	Deliveries to 2002
corvette	YS-2000	4	Domestic	1995	1997	Deliveries to 2003
MCM	YSB	4	Domestic		1997	Deliveries to 1998
SS	Sub-2000		Domestic	1997		Development
SSK	*Gotland*-class	3	Domestic		1998	
supply ship		16	Domestic		1997	7th of 16 delivered Mar 1997
Switzerland						
FGA	F/A-18C/D	34	US	1993	1997	32 assembled in CH; deliveries to 1999
arty	M-109	456	US	1995	1997	Domestic upgrade
LAV	*Recce Eagle*	329	Domestic	1993	1995	Deliveries to 2001
UAV	*Ranger*	28	Domestic	1995	1998	4 *Ranger* 95 systems
Ukraine						
bbr	Tu-22	20	RF	1995	1996	Transfer in situ in Ukr
FGA	SU-27	4	RF	1996		Transfer in situ in Ukr
FGA	MiG-29	8	RF	1996		Transfer in situ in Ukr
tpt	AN-24/26		RF	1996		Transfer in situ in Ukr
hel	Mi-8		RF	1996		Transfer in situ in Ukr
Yugoslavia						
MCM	S-25 *Nestin*	1	Domestic			Launched Jun 1996

NATO

Belgium

	1995	1996	1997	1998
GDP	fr7.9tr	fr8.1tr		
	($245bn)	($262bn)		
per capita	$21,200	$21,900		
Growth	1.9%	1.4%		
Inflation	1.4%	2.1%		
Publ debt	134%	130%		
Def exp	fr131.2bn	fr132.4bn		
	($4.4bn)	($4.3bn)		
Def bdgt			fr98.9bn	fr102.1bn
			($2.8bn)	($2.9bn)
$1 = franc	29.5	31.0	35.3	
Population		10,093,000		
Age	*13–17*	*18–22*	*23–32*	
Men	310,000	323,000	734,000	
Women	296,000	311,000	712,000	

Total Armed Forces

ACTIVE 44,450

(incl 1,250 Medical Service, 2,760 women)

RESERVES 144,200 (to be 62,000)

Army 97,000 **Navy** 5,700 **Air Force** 22,000 **Medical Service** 19,500

Army 28,500

(incl 1,600 women)
1 op comd HQ
1 mech inf div with 3 mech inf bde (each 1 tk, 2 mech inf, 1 SP arty bn) (2 bde at 70%, 1 bde at 50% cbt str), 1 AD arty bn, 2 recce coy (Eurocorps); 1 recce bn (MNDC)
1 cbt spt div (11 mil schools forming, 1 arty, 1 engr bn – augment mech inf div, plus 1 inf, 1 tk bn for bde at 50% cbt str)
1 para-cdo bde (3 para-cdo, 1 ATK/recce bn, 1 arty, 1 AD bty, 1 engr coy)
1 lt avn gp (2 ATK, 1 obs bn)

RESERVES

Territorial Defence 11 lt inf bn (1 per province, 1 gd, 1 reserve)

EQUIPMENT

MBT 326: 132 *Leopard* 1A5, 194 *Leopard* 1A1 (8 trg, 78 for sale, remainder for mod or destruction)
RECCE 141 *Scimitar* (29 in store)
AIFV 236 YPR-765 (14 in store) (plus 278 'look-alikes')
APC 434 M-113 (incl 'look-alikes') (110 in store)

TOTAL ARTY 255
TOWED 25: **105mm**: 11 M-101, 14 LG Mk II (being delivered)
SP 138: **105mm**: 19 M-108 (trg, 5 in store); **155mm**: 108 M-109A2 (12 in store), plus 1-A3 (trials); **203mm**: 10 M-110A2 (for sale)
MOR **107mm**: 90 M-30; **120mm**: 2 (for sale), plus **81mm**: 220
ATGW 498: 420 *Milan* (incl 218 YPR-765 (24 in store), 56 M-113 (4 in store)), 22 *Striker* (in store)
AD GUNS **35mm**: 54 *Gepard* SP (all for sale)
SAM 118 *Mistral*
AC 10 BN-2A *Islander*
HELICOPTERS 78
ASLT 28 A-109BA (6 in store)
OBS 18 A-109A (2 in store)
SPT 32 SA-318 (3 in store)
UAV 22 *Epervier*

Navy 2,700

(incl 260 women)
BASES Ostend, Zeebrugge. Be and Nl Navies under joint op comd based at Den Helder (Nl)
FRIGATES 3
3 *Wielingen* with 2 dual role (Fr L-5 HWT), 1 x 6 ASW mor; plus 4 MM-38 *Exocet* SSM, 1 100mm gun and 1 x 8 *Sea Sparrow* SAM
MINE COUNTERMEASURES 11
4 *Van Haverbeke* (US *Aggressive* MSO) (incl 1 used for trials)
7 *Aster* (tripartite) MHC
SUPPORT AND MISCELLANEOUS 4
2 log spt/comd with hel deck, 1 research/survey, 1 sail trg **hel** 3 SA-316B
ADDITIONAL IN STORE 1 FF for sale

Air Force 12,000

(incl 900 women) **Flying hours** 165
FGA 3 sqn with F-16A/B
FTR 3 sqn with F-16A/B
TPT 2 sqn
1 with 11 C-130H, 1 with 2 Boeing 727QC, 3 HS-748, 5 *Merlin* IIIA, 2 *Falcon* 20, 1 *Falcon* 900
TRG 4 sqn
2 with *Alpha Jet*, 1 with SF-260, 1 with CM-170
SAR 1 sqn with *Sea King* Mk 48

EQUIPMENT

132 cbt ac (plus 59 in store), no armed hel
AC 132 **F-16** (112 -A, 20 -B (plus 32 in store) • 11 **C-130** (tpt) • 2 **Boeing 727QC** (tpt) • 3 **HS-748** (tpt) • 2 *Falcon* **20** (VIP) • 1 *Falcon* **900B** • 5 **SW 111** *Merlin* (VIP, photo, cal) • 11 **CM-170** (trg, liaison) • 34 **SF-260** (trg) • 31 *Alpha Jet* (trg)
HEL 5 (SAR) *Sea King*
IN STORE 27 *Mirage* 5 (12 -BA, 12 -BR, 3 -BD)

MISSILES
  AAM AIM-9 *Sidewinder*
  SAM 24 *Mistral*

Forces Abroad

GERMANY 2,000; 1 mech inf bde (1 inf, 1 arty bn, 1 recce coy)
UN AND PEACEKEEPING
BOSNIA (SFOR): 123. **CROATIA** (SFOR): 12.
(UNTAES): 827; 1 inf bn plus 4 Obs; (UNMOP): 1 Obs.
FYROM (UNPREDEP): 1 Obs. **INDIA/PAKISTAN**
(UNMOGIP): 2 Obs. **ITALY** (SFOR): 70; 3 F-16A.
MIDDLE EAST (UNTSO): 6 Obs

Foreign Forces

NATO HQ NATO Brussels; HQ SHAPE Mons
WEU Military Planning Cell
US 1,365 **Army** 740 **Navy** 100 **Air Force** 525

Canada

	1995	1996	1997	1998
GDP	C$776bn	C$798bn		
	($569bn)	($585bn)		
per capita	$21,400	$22,100		
Growth	2.3%	1.5%		
Inflation	2.2%	1.5%		
Publ debt	100.5%	100.3%		
Def exp	C$12.5bn	C$11.7bn		
	($9.1bn)	($8.6bn)		
Def bdgt			C$9.9bn	C$9.4bn
			($7.1bn)	($6.7bn)
US$1 = C$	1.37	1.36	1.39	
Population		28,683,000		
Age	*13–17*	*18–22*	*23–32*	
Men	974,000	968,000	2,154,000	
Women	931,000	934,000	2,107,000	

Canadian Armed Forces are unified and org in functional comds. Land Force Comd has op control of TAG. Maritime Comd has op control of maritime air. This entry is set out in traditional single-service manner

Total Armed Forces

ACTIVE 61,600

(6,500 women); of the total str some 15,700 are not identified by service

RESERVES

Primary 28,700 **Army** (Militia) (incl comms) 21,700

Navy 4,600 **Air Force** 2,100 **Primary Reserve List** 300
Supplementary **Ready Reserve** 14,700

Army (Land Forces) 21,900

(ε1,600 women)
1 Task Force HQ • 3 mech inf bde gp, each with 1 armd regt, 3 inf bn (1 lt), 1 arty, 1 engr regt, 1 AD bty • 1 indep AD regt • 1 indep engr spt regt

RESERVES

Militia 20,100 (excl comms); 18 armd, 19 arty, 51 inf, 12 engr, 20 log bn level units, 14 med coy
Canadian Rangers 3,250; 127 patrols
EQUIPMENT
  MBT 114 *Leopard* C-1
  RECCE 5 *Lynx* (in store), 195 *Cougar*, 170 *Coyote*
  APC 1,858: 1,329 M-113 A2 (1,247 to be upgraded,
    82 in store), 61 M-577, 269 *Grizzly*, 199 *Bison*
  TOWED ARTY 196: **105mm**: 185 C1/C3 (M-101), 11
    LG1 Mk II
  SP ARTY 155mm: 76 M-109A4
  MOR 81mm: 167
  ATGW 150 TOW (incl 72 TUA M-113 SP), 425 *Eryx*
  RL 66mm: M-72
  RCL 84mm: 1,040 *Carl Gustav*; **106mm**: 111
  AD GUNS 35mm: 34 GDF-005 with *Skyguard*;
    40mm: 57 L40/60 (in store)
  SAM 34 ADATS, 96 *Javelin, Starburst*

Navy (Maritime Command) 9,400

(incl 650 women)
SUBMARINES 3
  3 *Ojibwa* (UK *Oberon*) SS with Mk 48 HWT
    (equipped for, but not with, *Harpoon* USGW)
PRINCIPAL SURFACE COMBATANTS 20
DESTROYERS 4
  DDG 4 *Iroquois* (incl 1 in conversion refit) with 1
    Mk-41 VLS for 29 SM-2 MR, 2 CH-124 *Sea King*
    ASW hel (Mk 46 LWT), 2 x 3 ASTT, plus 1 76mm
    gun
FRIGATES 16
  FFH 14
  12 *Halifax* with 1 CH-124A *Sea King* ASW hel (Mk 46
    LWT), 2 x 2 ASTT; plus 2 x 4 *Harpoon* and 2 x 8 *Sea
    Sparrow* SAM
  2 *Annapolis* with 1 *Sea King* hel, 2 x 3 ASTT, 1 x 3
    ASW mot; plus 2 76mm gun
  FF 2 improved *Restigouche* with 1 x 8 ASROC, 2 x 3
    ASTT, 1 x 3 ASW mor, plus 2 76mm gun
PATROL AND COASTAL COMBATANTS 16
  4 *Kingston* MCDV, 6 *Fundy* PCC (trg), 5 *Porte St Jean*
    PCC, 1 PCI (reserve trg)
MINE COUNTERMEASURES 2
  2 *Anticosti* MSO (converted offshore spt vessels)

SUPPORT AND MISCELLANEOUS 8

2 *Protecteur* AO with 3 *Sea King*, 1 *Provider* AO with 2 *Sea King*, 1 AOT, 2 AGOR, 1 diving spt, 1 *Riverton* spt

DEPLOYMENT AND BASES

ATLANTIC Halifax (National and Marlant HQ;Commander Marlant is also COMCANLANT): 3 SS, 2 DDG, 7 FFH, 2 FF, 1 AO, 1 AGOR; 2 MR plus 1 MR (trg) sqn with CP-140 and 3 CP-140A, 1 ASW and 1 ASW (trg) hel sqn with 26 CH-125 hel
PACIFIC Esquimalt (HQ): 2 DDG, 5 FFH, 1 FF, 6 PCC, 2 AO, 1 AGOR; 1 MR sqn with 4 CP-140 and 1 ASW hel sqn with 6 CH-124 hel

RESERVES

4,000 in 24 div: patrol craft, coastal def, MCM, Naval Control of Shipping, augmentation of regular units

Air Force 14,600

(women 825) **Flying hours** 210

FIGHTER GROUP

FTR 5 sqn (1 trg) with CF-18
EW 2 sqn with CECC-144 (CL-601), CT-133, CH-146
EARLY WARNING Canadian NORAD Regional HQ at North Bay; 47 North Warning radar sites: 11 long-range, 36 short-range; Regional Op Control Centre (ROCC) (2 Sector Op Control Centres (SOCC)). 4 Coastal Radars and 2 Transportable Radars. Canadian Component – NATO Airborne Early Warning (NAEW)

MARITIME AIR GROUP

MR 4 sqn (1 trg) with CP-140 *Aurora*
ASW 3 hel sqn (1 trg) with CH-124, *Sea King*

TACTICAL AIR GROUP (TAG)

HEL 3 sqn with CH-135 (1 trg), 2 reserve sqn with CH-146, 1 test sqn with CH-135 and CH-146

AIR TRANSPORT GROUP

TPT 6 sqn
4 (1 trg) with CC-130E/H *Hercules*, KCC-130 (tkr)
1 with CC-150 (*Airbus* A-310)
1 with CC-109, CC-144
COMBAT SUPPORT CH-146, CT-133
SAR 4 tpt/SAR sqn with ac CC-115, CC-130, CC-138 **hel** CH-113/-113A
TRG (reports direct to HQ Air Comd)
2 flying schools with **ac** CT-114 **hel** CH-139
1 Air Navigation Trg sqn with CC-142 (DHC-8)
1 demonstration sqn with CT-114

EQUIPMENT

140 (incl 18 MR) cbt **ac** (104 in store), 30 armed **hel**
AC 122 CF-18 (83 **-A**, 39 **-B**) • 18 CP-140 (MR) • 3 **CP-140A** (environmental patrol) • 30 **CC-130E/H** (tpt) • 5 **KCC-130** (tkr) • 5 **CC-150** • 7 **CC-109** (tpt) • 16 **CC/E-144** (6 EW trg, 3 coastal patrol, 7 VIP/tpt) • 7 **CC-138** (SAR/tpt) • 6 **CC-115** (SAR/ tpt) • 45 **CT-133** (EW trg/tpt plus 9 in store) • 108 **CT-114** (trg) • 6 **CT-142** (2 tpt, 4 trg)
HEL 30 **CH-124** (ASW, afloat) • 14 **CH-135** • 13 **CH-113** (SAR/tpt) • 45 **CH-146**
IN STORE ac 64 CF-116 (CF-5), 40 CF-18

Forces Abroad

UN AND PEACEKEEPING

BOSNIA (SFOR): 982; 1 inf coy gp, 1 armd recce, 1 engr sqn; CC-130 relief missions; (UNMIBH): 1 plus 15 civ pol. **CROATIA** (SFOR): 8. (UNMOP): 1 Obs. **CYPRUS** (UNFICYP): 2. **EGYPT** (MFO): 28. **FYROM** (UNPREDEP): 1 Obs. **HAITI** (UNTMIH): 754 (incl 84 Air Force), hel 7 CH-146 plus 62 civ pol. **IRAQ/ KUWAIT** (UNIKOM): 4 Obs. **MIDDLE EAST** (UNTSO): 12 Obs. **SYRIA/ISRAEL** (UNDOF): 189; log unit

Paramilitary 11,100

Canadian Coast Guard has merged with **Department of Fisheries and Oceans.** Both are civilian-manned
CANADIAN COAST GUARD (CCG) 4,900
some 82 vessels incl 1 survey ship, 1 trg vessel, 17 icebreakers plus various NAVAID and SAR vessels; plus **hel** 1 S-61, 5 Bell 206L, 16 BO-104
DEPARTMENT OF FISHERIES AND OCEANS (DFO) 6,200
some 67 vessels incl 23 survey and research, 44 patrol

Denmark

	1995	1996	1997	1998
GDP	kr968bn	kr1,010bn		
	($173bn)	($174bn)		
per capita	$20,900	$21,800		
Growth	2.6%	2.4%		
Inflation	2.0%	2.2%		
Publ debt	76.9%	74.8%		
Def exp	kr17.5bn	kr17.6bn		
	($3.1bn)	($3.0bn)		
Def bdgt			kr18.0bn	kr17.5bn
			($3.1bn)	($3.0bn)
$1 = kroner	5.6	5.8	6.5	
Population		5,235,000		
Age	*13–17*	*18–22*	*23–32*	
Men	149,000	169,000	395,000	
Women	144,000	163,000	381,000	

Total Armed Forces

ACTIVE 32,900

(7,810 conscripts, 960 women)

Terms of service: 4–12 months (up to 24 months in certain ranks)

RESERVES 70,450

Army 51,800 **Navy** 5,850 **Air Force** 12,800
Home Guard (*Hjemmevaernet*) (volunteers to age 50)
Army 52,300 **Navy** 4,200 **Air Force** 7,800

Army 19,000

(6,900 conscripts, 460 women)
1 op comd, 1 land comd (east) • 1 mech inf div (3 mech inf bde (1 reserve) each 2 mech, inf, 1 tk, 1 arty bn), 1 recce, 1 tk (reserve), 1 AD, 1 engr bn (reserve), div arty (reserve)) • 1 rapid-reaction bde with 1 mech inf, 1 tk, 1 SP arty bn • 1 regt cbt gp, 1 mot inf, 1 recce, 1 indep engr bn • Army avn (1 attack hel coy, 1 recce hel det) • 1 SF unit

RESERVES

7 mil region (regt cbt gp or 1–2 inf bn), 2 regt cbt gp HQ, 1 mech inf, 4 mot inf, 2 inf • 1 arty comd, 6 arty, 1 AD, 1 engr bn

EQUIPMENT

MBT 353: 230 *Leopard* 1A5 (58 in store), 70 *Centurion*, 53 M-41DK-1
AIFV 50 M-113A2 (with **25mm** gun)
APC 594 M-113 (incl look-alikes)
TOTAL ARTY 503
    TOWED 105mm: 134 M-101; **155mm:** 24 M-59, 97 M-114/39; **203mm:** 12 M-115
    SP 155mm: 76 M-109
    MOR 120mm: 160 Brandt; plus **81mm:** 313 (incl 55 SP)
ATGW 140 TOW (incl 56 SP)
RCL 1,151: **84mm:** 1,131 *Carl Gustav;* **106mm:** 20 M-40
SAM *Stinger*
SURV *Green Archer*
ATTACK HEL 12 AS-550C2
SPT HEL 13 Hughes 500M/OH-6

Navy 6,000

(incl 480 conscripts, 200 women)
BASES Korsør, Frederikshavn
SUBMARINES 5
    3 *Tumleren* (mod No *Kobben*) SSC with Swe FFV Type 61 HWT
    2 *Narhvalen,* SSC with FFV Type 61 HWT
FRIGATES 3
    3 *Niels Juel* with 2 x 4 *Harpoon* SSM and 1 x 8 *Sea Sparrow* SAM, 1 76mm gun
PATROL AND COASTAL COMBATANTS 65
MISSILE CRAFT 10 *Willemoes* PFM with 2 x 4 *Harpoon*, 2 or 4 533mm TT, 1 76mm gun

PATROL CRAFT 55
    OFFSHORE 5
    1 *Beskytteren,* 4 *Thetis* PCO all with 1 *Lynx* hel
    COASTAL 17
    14 *Flyvefisken* (Stanflex 300) PFC, 3 *Agdlek* PCC
    INSHORE 33
    9 *Barsø,* 12 *Aldebaran,* 6 *Bopa,* 6 *Baunen*
MINE WARFARE 9
(All units of *Flyvefisken* class can also lay up to 60 mines)
MINELAYERS 6
    4 *Falster* (400 mines), 2 *Lindormen* (50 mines)
MINE COUNTERMEASURES 3
    1 *Alssund* (US MSC-128) MSC
    2 *Flyvefisken* (SF300) MHC
SUPPORT AND MISCELLANEOUS 8
    2 AOT (small), 4 icebreakers (civilian-manned), 1 tpt, 1 Royal Yacht
HEL 8 *Lynx* (up to 4 embarked)

COASTAL DEFENCE

1 coastal fortress; **150mm** guns, coastal radar
2 mobile coastal missile batteries: 2 x 8 *Harpoon*
RESERVES (Home Guard)
37 inshore patrol craft

Air Force 7,900

(430 conscripts, 300 women) **Flying hours** 180
TACTICAL AIR COMD
FGA/FTR 4 sqn with F-16A/B
TPT 1 sqn with C-130H, *Gulfstream* III
SAR 1 sqn with S-61A hel
TRG 1 flying school with SAAB T-17
AIR DEFENCE GROUP
2 SAM bn: 8 bty with 36 I HAWK, 32 **40mm**/L70
CONTROL/REPORTING GROUP
5 radar stations, one in the Faroe Islands
EQUIPMENT
64 cbt ac, no armed hel
AC 64 **F-16A/B** (FGA/ftr) (52 **-A**, 12 **-B**) • 3 **C-130H** (tpt) • 3 *Gulfstream* III (tpt) • 28 **SAAB T-17**
HEL 8 **S-61** (SAR)
MISSILES
ASM AGM-12 *Bullpup*
AAM AIM-9 *Sidewinder*
SAM 36 I HAWK

Forces Abroad

UN AND PEACEKEEPING
ALBANIA (*Operation Alba*): ε60, to withdraw Aug 1997. **BOSNIA** (SFOR): 658; 1 inf bn gp incl 1 tk sqn (10 *Leopard* MBT); aircrew with NATO E-3A operations; Air Force personnel in tac air-control

parties (TACP); (UNMIBH): 1 plus 37 civ pol. **CROATIA** (SFOR): 4. (UNTAES): 8 civ pol; (UNMOP): 1 Obs. **FYROM** (UNPREDEP): 47 plus 1 Obs. **GEORGIA** (UNOMIG): 4 Obs. **INDIA/PAKISTAN** (UNMOGIP): 5 Obs. **IRAQ/KUWAIT** (UNIKOM): 6 Obs. **MIDDLE EAST** (UNTSO): 9 Obs. **TAJIKISTAN** (UNMOT): 2 Obs

Foreign Forces

NATO HQ Allied Forces Baltic Approaches (BALTAP) **US** 1,360 **Army** 740 **Navy** 100 **Air Force** 520

France

	1995	1996	1997	1998
GDP	fr7.7tr	fr7.9tr		
	($1.5tr)	($1.5tr)		
per capita	$20,500	$21,100		
Growth	2.1%	1.5%		
Inflation	1.7%	2.1%		
Publ debt	60.7%	63.0%		
Def exp	fr238.4bn	fr241.4bn		
	($47.8bn)	($47.2bn)		
Def bdgt			fr190.9bn	fr185.0bn
			($37.1bn)	($33.1bn)
$1 = franc	4.99	5.12	5.76	
Population		58,645,000		
Age	*13–17*	*18–22*	*23–32*	
Men	1,953,000	2,025,000	4,365,000	
Women	1,865,000	1,935,000	4,215,000	

Total Armed Forces

ACTIVE 380,820

(17,350 women, 156,950 conscripts; incl 5,200 **Central Staff**, 8,600 (2,300 conscripts) *Service de santé*, 400 *Service des essences* not listed)
Terms of service: 10 months (can be voluntarily extended to 12–24 months)

RESERVES 292,500

Army 195,500 **Navy** 27,000 **Air Force** 70,000 *Potential* 1,096,500 **Army** 782,000 **Navy** 135,000 **Air Force** 179,500

Strategic Nuclear Forces (10,400)

(**Army** some 1,700 **Navy** 5,000 **Air Force** 3,100 *Gendarmerie* 600)
NAVY 64 SLBM in 4 SSBN
  SSBN 4
  3 mod *Le Redoutable* with 16 M-4/TN-75 or -71; plus SM-39 *Exocet* USGW and 4 533mm HWT
  1 *Le Triomphant* with 16 M45/TN-71 SLBM; plus SM-

39 *Exocet* and 4 533mm HWT
AIR FORCE
  IRBM 18 SSBS S-3D/TN-61 msl in 2 sqn
  BBR 2 sqn with 15 *Mirage* IVP (*Air-Sol, Moyenne-Portée* (*ASMP*) nuclear ASM), plus 3 in store
  TRG 1 *Mystère-Falcon* 20P, 1 *Alpha Jet*
  TKR 2 sqn with 11 C-135FR

'PRE-STRATEGIC' NUCLEAR FORCES

NAVY 36 *Super Etendard* strike **ac** (ASMP); plus 16 in store
AIR FORCE 3 sqn with 60 *Mirage* 2000 N(ASMP)
  TRG 3 *Mystère-Falcon* 20 SNA

Army 219,900

(9,000 women, 111,000 conscripts) regt normally bn size
1 Int and EW bde
1 corps with 2 armd, 1 mtn inf div (48,200)
Summary of div cbt units
  5 armd regt • 6 arty regt • 4 mech inf regt • 3 recce sqn • 4 mot inf regt • 2 ATK sqn • 3 mtn inf regt
Corps units: 1 armd recce, 1 mot inf, 1 arty bde (1 MLRS, 2 *Roland* SAM (each of 4 bty), 1 HAWK SAM regt • 1 air mobile bde with 2 cbt hel regt (**hel** 26 SA-330, 48 SA-342 HOT ATK, 20 SA-341 gunships) • 1 engr bde (4 regt)
1 armd div (in Eurocorps): 2 armd, 1 mech inf, 2 arty regt
1 Fr/Ge bde (2,100): Fr units incl 1 lt armd, 1 mot inf regt; 1 recce sqn
Rapid Action Force (FAR) (41,500)
  1 para div: 6 para inf, 1 armd cavalry, 1 arty, 1 engr regt • 1 lt armd marine div: 2 APC inf, 2 lt armd, 1 arty, 1 engr regt • 1 lt armd div: 2 armd cavalry, 2 APC inf, 1 arty, 1 engr regt • 1 air-mobile div: 1 inf, 3 cbt hel, 1 spt hel regt (234 **hel** 62 SA-330, 90 SA-342/HOT, 20 AS-532, 62 SA-341 (20 gun, 42 recce/liaison))
Corps units: 1 arty bde (1 MLRS, 1 *Roland* SAM, 1 HAWK SAM regt) • 1 engr regt
Territorial def forces incl spt of UN missions: 7 regt

FOREIGN LEGION (8,500)

1 armd, 1 para, 6 inf, 1 engr regt (incl in units listed above)

MARINES (31,000)

(incl 13,000 conscripts, mainly overseas enlisted)
1 div (see FAR), 4 regt in France (see div cbt units above), 11 regt overseas

SPECIAL OPERATIONS FORCES

(see also above) 1 Marine para regt, 1 para regt, 2 hel units (EW, special ops)

RESERVES

Indiv reinforcements for 1 corps (incl Eurocorps) and

FAR (75,000)
Territorial def forces: 44 regt
EQUIPMENT
MBT 768: 658 AMX-30B2 (plus 388 in store), 110 *Leclerc*
RECCE 337 AMX-10RC, 192 ERC-90F4 *Sagaie*, 155 AML-60/-90, 899 VBL M-11
AIFV 713 AMX-10P/PC
APC 3,820 VAB (incl variants)
TOTAL ARTY 1,081
  TOWED 155mm: 133 BF-50, 105 TR-F-1
  SP 155mm: 264 AU-F-1
  MRL 380mm: 59 MLRS
  MOR 520: **120mm**: 361 RT-F1, 159 M-51
ATGW 354 *Eryx*, 1,390 *Milan*, HOT (incl 135 VAB SP)
RL 21,180: **89mm**: 10,380; **112mm**: 10,800 APILAS
AD GUNS 20mm: 782 53T2
SAM 570: 69 HAWK, 156 *Roland* I/II, 345 *Mistral*
SURV STENTOR (veh), RASIT-B/-E (veh, arty), RATAC (veh, arty)
AC 2 Cessna *Caravan* II , 5 PC-6
HELICOPTERS 508
  ATTACK 342: 157 SA-341F, 155 SA-342M, 30 SA-342AATCP
  RECCE 2 AS-532 *Horizon*
  SPT 164: 24 AS-532, 10 AS-555, 130 SA-330
UAV CL-89 (AN/USD-501), CL-289 (AN/USD-502), MART Mk II, *Crecerelle* (replacing MART)

Navy 63,300

(incl 7,600 Naval Air, 2,900 Marines, 2,400 women, 17,250 conscripts)
COMMANDS Atlantic (CECLANT) HQ Brest **North Sea/Channel** (COMAR CHERBOURG) HQ Cherbourg **Mediterranean** (CECMED) HQ Toulon **Indian Ocean** (ALINDIEN) HQ afloat **Pacific Ocean** (ALPACI) HQ Papeete
BASES France Cherbourg, Brest (HQ), Lorient, Toulon (HQ) **Overseas** Papeete (HQ) (Tahiti), La Réunion, Noumea (New Caledonia), Fort de France (Martinique), Cayenne (French Guinea)
SUBMARINES 14
STRATEGIC SUBMARINES 4 SSBN (see p. 50)
TACTICAL SUBMARINES 10
  SSN 6 *Rubis* ASW/ASUW with F-17 HWT, L-5 LWT and SM-39 *Exocet* USGW
  SS 4
  3 *Agosta* with F-17 HWT and L-5 LWT; plus *Exocet* USGW
  1 *Daphné*, with E-15 HWT and L-5 LWT (plus 5 in store)
PRINCIPAL SURFACE COMBATANTS 42
CARRIERS 2 *Clémenceau* CVS (33,300t), capacity 40 ac (typically 2 flt with 16 *Super Etendard*, 1 with 6 *Alizé*;

1 det with 2 *Etendard* IVP, 8 *Crusader* F8/P, 2 *Super Frelon*, 2 *Dauphin* hel)
CRUISERS 1 *Jeanne d'Arc* CCH (trg/ASW) with 6 MM-38 *Exocet* SSM, 2 x 2 100mm guns, capacity 8 SA-319B hel
DDG 4
2 *Cassard* with 1 x 1 *Standard* SM-1 MR; plus 8 MM-40 *Exocet*, 1 100mm gun, 2 ASTT, 1 *Lynx* hel (ASW/OTHT)
2 *Suffren* with 1 x 2 *Masurca* SAM; plus 1 *Malafon* SUGW, 4 ASTT, 4 MM-38 *Exocet*, 2 100mm guns
FRIGATES 35
6 *Floréal* with 2 MM-38 *Exocet*, 1 AS-365 hel and 1 100mm gun
7 *Georges Leygues* with 2 *Lynx* hel (Mk 46 LWT), 2 ASTT; plus 5 with 8 MM-40, 2 with 4 MM-38 *Exocet*, all with 1 100mm gun
3 *Tourville* with 2 *Lynx* hel, 1 *Malafon* SUGW, 2 ASTT; plus 6 MM-38 *Exocet*, 2 100mm guns
16 *D'Estienne d'Orves* with 4 ASTT, 1 x 6 ASW mor; plus 6 with 2 MM-38, 6 with 4 MM-40 *Exocet*, all with 1 100mm gun
3 *La Fayette* with 8 MM-40 Exocet, CN-2 SAM, 1 100mm gun, 1 *Panther* hel
PATROL AND COASTAL COMBATANTS 36
PATROL, OFFSHORE 1 *Albatross* PCO (Public Service Force)
PATROL, COASTAL 23
  10 *L'Audacieuse*, 8 *Léopard* PCC (trg), 3 *Flamant* PCC, 1 *Sterne* PCC, 1 *Grebe* PCC (Public Service Force)
PATROL, INSHORE 12
  2 *Athos* PCI, 4 *Patra* PCI, 1 *La Combattante* PCI, 5 PCI< (manned by *Gendarmerie Maritime*)
MINE WARFARE 25
MINELAYERS nil, but submarines and *Thetis* (trials ship) have capability
MINE COUNTERMEASURES 25
  13 *Eridan* MHC, 5 *Circé* MHC, 4 *Vulcain* MCM diver spt, 3 *Antares* (route survey/trg)
AMPHIBIOUS 9
1 *Foudre* LPD, capacity 450 tps, 30 tk, 4 *Super Puma* hel, 2 CDIC LCT or 10 LCM
2 *Ouragan* LPD: capacity 350 tps, 25 tk, 2 *Super Frelon* hel
1 *Bougainville* LSD: capacity 500 tps, 6 tk, 2 AS-332 hel (assigned to spt DIRCEN nuclear test centre South Pacific)
5 *Champlain* LSM: capacity 140 tps, tk
Plus craft: 6 LCT, 24 LCM
SUPPORT AND MISCELLANEOUS 38
UNDER WAY SUPPORT 5 *Durance* AO with 1 SA-319 hel
MAINTENANCE AND LOGISTIC 20
  1 AOT, 1 *Jules Verne* AR with 2 SA-319 hel, 3 *Rhin* depot/spt, 1 *Rance* med and trg spt, all with hel; 8 tpt, 6 ocean tugs (3 civil charter)

SPECIAL PURPOSES 7
5 trial ships, 2 *Glycine* trg
SURVEY/RESEARCH 6
5 AGHS, 1 AGOR

DEPLOYMENT
CECLAND (HQ, Brest): 5 SSBN, 6 SS, 6 ASW FF, 10 FF, 1 CCH, 1 FFA, 1 AO, 3 ML, 12 MHC, 1 AGOS, 1 clearance diving ship, 1 AG, 3 AGS, 1 AGOR, 2 PB
COMAR CHERBOURG (HQ, Cherbourg): 1 clearance diving ship plus craft
CECMED (HQ, Toulon): 6 SSN, 1 SS, 2 CV, 4 DDG, 8 FF, 5 ASW FF, 2 MCMV, 3 amph, 3 AO, 1 LSM, 2 LCT, 1 AH, 1 AGOR, 2 clearance diving ships, 3 MHC

NAVAL AIR (7,600)
(incl 700 women, 410 conscripts)
Flying hours *Etendard* and *Crusader*: 190
NUCLEAR STRIKE 2 flt with *Super Etendard* (ASMP nuc ASM)
FTR 1 flt with F-8E (FN) *Crusader*
ASW 2 flt with *Alizé*
MR 4 flt
1 with *Atlantic*, 3 with *Atlantic*-2
OCU *Alizé*
TRG 5 units with N-262 *Frégate*, EMB-121 *Xingu*, MS-760 *Paris*, *Falcon* 10MER, *Rallye* 880, CAP 10
MISC 4 comms/liaison units (1 VIP) with *Falcon* 10 MER, N-262, EMB 121, *Xingu*
1 trial unit with *Atlantique* 2, MS-760 *Paris*
2 lt ac units with 12 *Rallye* 880, 6 CAP-10
ASW 2 sqn with *Lynx*
COMMANDOS 2 aslt sqn with SA-321
TRG SA-316
MISC 2 comms/SAR units with SE-313B, SA-316B, SA-319B, 1 trials unit with SA-319, *Lynx*, SA-321

EQUIPMENT
69 cbt ac (plus 29 in store); 25 armed hel (plus 9 in store)
AC 32* *Super Etendard* plus 21 in store (53 to be mod for ASMP) • 11* *Crusader* plus 4 in store • 15 *Alizé* (AEW) plus 8 in store • 6* *Atlantic* (MR) plus 1 in store • 20* *Atlantique* 2 (MR) plus 3 in store • 24 *Nord 262* (9 MR trg, 15 misc) • 18 *Xingu* (8 trg, 10 misc) • 14 *Rallye 880* (4 trg, 10 misc) • 8 **CAP-10** (misc) • 6 **MS-760** (trg) • 5 *Falcon* **10MER** (3 trg, 2 misc)
HEL 25 *Lynx* (ASW) plus 9 in store • 12 **SA-321** (SAR, trg) plus 4 in store • 10 **SA-313** (2 trg, 8 misc) • 3 **AS-565SA** (SAR, trg) plus 2 in store

MISSILES
ASM *Exocet* AM-39
AAM R-550 *Magic* 2, AIM-9 *Sidewinder*

MARINES (2,900)
COMMANDO UNITS (400) 4 aslt gp
1 attack swimmer unit

FUSILIERS-MARIN (2,500) 14 naval-base protection gp
PUBLIC SERVICE FORCE naval personnel, performing general coast guard, fishery, SAR, anti-pollution and traffic surv duties: 1 *Albatross*, 1 *Sterne*, 1 *Grebe*, 1 *Flamant* PCC; **ac** 4 N-262 **hel** 4 SA-365 (ships incl in naval patrol and coastal totals). Comd exercised through *Maritime Préfectures* (Premar): *Manche* (Cherbourg), *Atlantique* (Brest), *Méditerranée* (Toulon)

Air Force 83,420

(5,950 women, 26,400 conscripts, incl strategic and pre-strategic forces) **Flying hours** 170

AIR SIGNALS AND GROUND ENVIRONMENT COMMAND
CONTROL automatic *STRIDA* II, 10 radar stations, 1 sqn with 4 E3F
SAM 10 sqn (1 trg) with 24 *Crotale* bty (48 fire, 30 radar units), 36 *Mistral*
AA GUNS 12 sections with 170 AA gun bty (**20mm**)

AIR COMBAT COMMAND
FTR 5 sqn with *Mirage* 2000C/B
FGA 7 sqn
3 with *Mirage* 2000D, 2 with *Jaguar* A, 2 with *Mirage* F1-CT
RECCE 2 sqn with *Mirage* F-1CR
TRG 3 OCU sqn
1 with *Jaguar* A/E, 1 with F1-C/B, 1 with *Mirage* 2000/BC
EW 1 sqn with C-160 ELINT/ESM

AIR MOBILITY COMMAND (CFAP)
TPT 13 sqn
1 hy with DC-8F, A310-300
5 tac with C-160/-160NG, C-130H
7 lt tpt/trg/SAR/misc with C-160, DHC-6, CN235, *Falcon* 20, *Falcon* 50, *Falcon* 900, TBM-700, N-262, AS-555
EW 1 sqn with DC-8 ELINT
HEL 6 sqn with AS-332, SA-330, AS-555, AS-355, SA-319
TRG 1 OCU with C-160, N-262, 1 OCU with SA-319, AS-555, SA-330

AIR TRAINING COMMAND
TRG *Alpha Jet*, EMB-121, TB-30, EMB-312, CAP-10/-20/-231, CR-100, N262

EQUIPMENT
505 cbt ac, no armed hel
AC 345 *Mirage* (10 **F-1B** (OCU), 10 **F-1C** (OCU plus 6 in Djibouti), 40 **F-1CR** (recce),• 40 **F-1CT** (FGA), 5 **MIVP** (recce), 120 -**M-2000B/C** (95 -C (ftr), 25 -B (OCU)), 60 -**M-2000N** (strike, FGA), 60 -**M-2000D** (FGA) • 50 *Jaguar* (30 -**A**, 20* -**E** (strike, FGA)) • 110* *Alpha Jet* (trg, 6 test plus 39 in store) • 4 **E-3F** (AEW) • 2 **A** 310-300 (tpt) • 3 **DC-8F** (tpt) • 14 **C-130** (5 -**H** (tpt), 9 -**H-30** (tpt)) • 11 **C-135FR** (tkr) •

60 **C-160** (40 **-AG**, 20 **-NG** (tpt of which 14 tkr)) • 8 **CN-235M** (tpt) • 22 **N-262** (14 lt tpt, 3 OCU, 5 trg, plus 2 in store) • 17 *Falcon* (11 **-20** (4 tpt, 7 misc plus 3 in store), 4 **-50** (VIP), 2 **-900** (VIP)) • 12 **TBM-700** (tpt) • 24 **MS-760** (misc) • 11 **CM-170** (*Fouga*) (misc) • 10 **DHC-6** (tpt) • 25 **EMB-121** (trg) • 97 **TB-30** (trg plus 50 in store) • 4 **CAP-10/ 20/231** (trg) • 49 **EMB-312** (trg) • 2 **CR-100** (trg)

HEL 14 **SA-319** (12 tpt, 2 OCU) (*Alouette* III) • 28 **SA-330** (25 tpt, SAR, 3 OCU) (*Puma*) • 7 **AS-332** (tpt/VIP) (*Super Puma*) • 3 **AS-532** (tpt) (*Cougar*) • 6 **AS-355** (*Ecureuil*) • 39 **AS-555** (30 tpt, 9 OCU) (*Fennec*)

MISSILES

ASM AS-30/-30L
AAM *Super* 530F/D, R-550 *Magic* 1/II

Forces Abroad

GERMANY 11,700; Eurocorps with 1 armd div *Gendarmerie* 260

ANTILLES (HQ Fort de France) 5,000; 3 marine inf regt (incl 2 SMA), 1 marine inf bn, 1 air tpt unit **ac** 2 C-160 **hel** 2 SA-330, 1 SA-319

FRENCH GUIANA (HQ Cayenne) 3,600; 2 marine inf (incl 1 SMA), 1 Foreign Legion regt, 6 ships (incl 1 FF and 2 amph) **ac** 1 *Atlantic*, 1 air tpt unit **hel** 4 SA-330, 3 AS-555 *Gendarmerie* 1,400

INDIAN OCEAN (Mayotte, La Réunion) 4,000; 2 Marine inf (incl 1 SMA) regt, 1 spt bn, 1 Foreign Legion coy, 1 air tpt unit **ac** 2 C-160 **hel** 2 AS 555; *Gendarmerie* 700 **Navy** Indian Ocean Squadron, Comd ALINDIEN (HQ afloat): 1,400; 3 FF, 2 patrol combatants, 2 amph, 3 spt (1 comd), reinforcement 1 FF, 1 *Atlantic* ac

NEW CALEDONIA (HQ Nouméa) 3,900; 1 Marine inf regt; some 12 AML recce, 5 **120mm** mor; 1 air tpt unit, det **ac** 2 C-160 **hel** 2 AS-555, 6 SA-330 **Navy** 1 FF, 2 patrol combatants, 1 survey, 1 amp, 1 spt **ac** 2 *Guardian* MR *Gendarmerie* 1,100

POLYNESIA (HQ Papeete) 3,800 (incl *Centre d'Expérimentation du Pacifique*); 1 Marine inf regt, 1 Foreign Legion bn, 1 air tpt unit, 2 CN-235, 3 AS-332 *Gendarmerie* 350 **Navy** 2 FF, 3 patrol combatants, 1 amph, 1 survey, 5 spt **ac** 3 *Guardian* MR

CAR 1,500 **Garrison** 1 bn gp incl 1 motor coy; spt coy with O-1E lt ac, **120mm** mor, *Milan* ATGW **From France** 1 AML armd car sqn and 1 tp (13 AML), 2 inf coy, 1 arty bty (**105mm**), 1 avn det (4 SA-330 **hel**); air elm with **ac** 3 F-1CT, 2 F-1CR, 2 C-160

CHAD 800; 2 inf coy, 1 AML sqn (-) **ac** 2 C-160

CÔTE D'IVOIRE 500; 1 marine inf bn (18 AML-60/- 90) **hel** 1 AS-555

DJIBOUTI 3,200; 1 marine inf(-), 1 Foreign Legion regt(-); 26 ERC-90 recce, 6 **155mm** arty, 16 AA arty; 3 amph craft, 1 sqn with **ac** 6 *Mirage* F-1C (plus 4 in store), 1 C-160 **hel** 3 SA-319

GABON 600; 1 marine inf bn (4 AML-60) **ac** 1 C-160

hel 1 AS-555

SENEGAL 1,300; 1 marine inf bn (14 AML-60/-90) **ac** 1 *Atlantic* MR, 1 C-160 tpt **hel** 1 SA-319

UN AND PEACEKEEPING

ALBANIA (*Operation Alba*): ε1,000, to withdraw Aug 1997. **ANGOLA** (UNOMA): 22 incl 7 Obs. **BOSNIA** (SFOR): 3,594: 2 mech inf bde, 1 N-262, 1 *Falcon* 20; (UNMIBH): 120 civ pol. **CROATIA** (SFOR): 52. **EGYPT** (MFO): 17; incl 1 DHC-6. **GEORGIA** (UNOMIG): 5 Obs. **HAITI** (UNTMIH): 46 civ pol. **IRAQ/KUWAIT** (UNIKOM): 1 Obs. **ITALY** (SFOR Air Component): 10 *Mirage* 2000C/D, 1 C-135, 1 E-3F, 11 *Jaguar*, 3 SA-330 (*Puma*), 1 N-262. **LEBANON** (UNIFIL): 247; elm 1 log bn; *Gendarmerie* (11). **MIDDLE EAST** (UNTSO): 4 Obs. **SAUDI ARABIA** (*Southern Watch*): 170; 5 *Mirage* 2000C, 3 F-1CR, 1 C-135, 1 N-262. **WESTERN SAHARA** (MINURSO): 25 Obs (*Gendarmerie*)

Paramilitary 92,300

GENDARMERIE 92,300

(2,900 women, 13,000 conscripts, 1,200 civilians); incl **Territorial** 58,900 **Mobile** 17,000 **Schools** 5,500 **Overseas** 3,100 **Maritime, Air** (personnel drawn from other Dept.) **Republican Guard, Air tpt, Arsenals** 4,800 **Administration** 3,000 **Reserves** 139,000

EQPT 121 AML, 28 VBC-90 armd cars; 33 AMX-VTT, 155 VBRG-170 APC; 278 **81mm** mor; 5 PCIs (listed under Navy), plus 11 other patrol craft and 4 tugs, **hel** 3 SA-316, 9 SA-319, 30 AS-350

Germany

	1995	1996	1997	1998
GDP	DM3.5tr	DM3.5tr		
	($2.2tr)	($2.2tr)		
per capita	$20,400	$21,100		
Growth	1.9%	1.3%		
Inflation	1.9%	1.5%		
Publ debt	62.2%	64.9%		
Def exp	DM59.0bn	DM59.1bn		
	($41.2bn)	($39.2bn)		
Def bdgt			DM46.3bn	DM46.7bn
			($27.1bn)	($27.3bn)
$1 = DM	1.43	1.5	1.71	
Population		81,104,000		
Age	*13–17*	*18–22*	*23–32*	
Men	2,281,000	2,294,000	6,156,000	
Women	2,160,000	2,200,000	5,907,000	

Total Armed Forces

ACTIVE some 347,100

(152,560 conscripts; incl 2,500 active Reserve trg posts, all services)
Terms of service: 10 months; 12–23 months voluntary

RESERVES 315,000

(men to age 45, officers/NCO to 60) **Army** 258,000
Navy 10,200 **Air Force** 46,800

Army 239,950

(124,700 conscripts)
ARMY FORCES COMMAND
1 air-mobile force comd (div HQ) with 2 AB (1 Crisis Reaction Force (CRF)) • 1 cdo SF bde •1 army avn bde with 6 regt •1 SIGINT/ELINT bde •1 spt bde
ARMY SUPPORT COMMAND
3 log, 1 medical bde
CORPS COMMANDS
I Ge/Nl Corps 2 MDC/armd div
II Corps 2 MDC/armd div; 1 MDC/mtn div
IV Corps 3 MDC/armd inf div
Corps Units 2 spt bde and Ge elm of Ge/Nl Corps, 1 air mech bde (CRF), 1 ATGW hel regt
Military District Commands (MDC)/Divisions
8 MDC/div comd and control 9 armd inf and the Ge elm of the Ge/Fr bde, 2 mech (not active), 1 inf, 1 mtn bde. Bde differ in their basic org, peacetime str, eqpt and mob capability; 4 (2 mech, 1 inf and Ge/Fr bde) are allocated to the CRF, the remainder to the Main Defence Forces (MDF). The MDC also comd and control 41 Military Region Commands (MRC). One armd div earmarked for Eurocorps, another for Allied Rapid Reaction Corps (ARRC). 8 recce bn, 8 arty regt, 8 engr bde and 7 AD regt available for cbt spt
EQUIPMENT
MBT 3,248: 1,460 *Leopard* 1A1/A3/A4/A5, 1,788 *Leopard* 2 (225 to be upgraded to A5)
RECCE 523: 409 SPz-2 *Luchs*, 114 TPz-1 *Fuchs* (NBC)
AIFV 2,089 *Marder* A2/A3, 343 *Wiesel* (210 TOW, 133 **20mm** gun), 1 BMP-2
APC 924 TPz-1 *Fuchs* (incl 87 EW plus variants), 2,760 M-113 (incl variants, 320 arty obs)
TOTAL ARTY 2,058
TOWED 359: **105mm**: 19 Geb H, 144 M-101; **155mm**: 196 FH-70
SP 155mm: 559 M-109A3G
MRL 234: **110mm**: 80 LARS; **227mm**: 154 MLRS
MOR 906: **120mm**: 391 Brandt, 515 Tampella
ATGW 2,435: 1,975 *Milan*, 98 TOW, 226 RJPz-(HOT) *Jaguar* 1, 136 RJPz-(TOW) *Jaguar* 2
ATK GUNS 90mm: 2 JPz-4-5 SP
AD GUNS 1,724: 20mm: 1,345 Rh 202 towed; **35mm**: 379 *Gepard* SP
SAM 143 *Roland* SP, *Stinger*
SURV 28 *Green Archer* (mor), 110 RASIT (veh, arty), 77 RATAC (veh, arty)

HELICOPTERS 626
ATTACK 204 PAH-1 (BO-105 with HOT)
SPT 422: 176 UH-1D, 108 CH-53G, 96 BO-105M, 42 *Alouette*
UAV CL-289 (AN/USD-502)
MARINE (River Engineers) 24 LCM, 24 PCI (river)

Navy 27,760

(incl 4,500 Naval Air, 5,460 conscripts and 420 women)
FLEET COMMAND Type comds Frigate, Patrol Boat, MCMV, Submarine, Support Flotillas, Naval Air **Spt comds** Naval Comms, Electronics
BASES Glücksburg (Maritime HQ), Wilhelmshaven, Kiel, Olpenitz, Eckernförde, Warnemünde. Bases with limited spt facilities **Baltic** Flensburg, Neustadt **North Sea** Emden
SUBMARINES 16
14 Type 206/206A SSC with *Seeaal* DM2 533mm HWT (12 conversions to T-206A complete, plus 2 in store)
2 Type 205 SSC with DM3 HWT
PRINCIPAL SURFACE COMBATANTS 15
DESTROYERS 3
DDG 3 *Lütjens* (mod US *Adams*) with 1 x 1 SM-1 MR SAM/*Harpoon* SSM launcher, 2 127mm guns; plus 1 x 8 ASROC (Mk 46 LWT), 2 x 3 ASTT
FRIGATES 12
FF 8 *Bremen* with 2 *Lynx* hel (ASW/OTHT), 2 x 2 ASTT; plus 2 x 4 *Harpoon*
FFG 4 *Brandenburg* with 4 MM-38 *Exocet*, 1 VLS Mk-41 SAM, 2 RAM, 21 Mk-49 SAM, 1 76mm gun, 4 324mm TT, 2 *Lynx* hel
PATROL AND COASTAL COMBATANTS 34
MISSILE CRAFT 34
10 *Albatross* (Type 143) PFM with 2 x 2 *Exocet*, and 2 533mm TT
10 *Gepard* (T-143A) PFM with 2 x 2 *Exocet*
14 *Tiger* (Type 148) PFM with 2 x 2 *Exocet*
MINE COUNTERMEASURES 40
10 *Hameln* (T-343) comb ML/MCC
6 *Lindau Troika* MSC control and guidance, each with 3 unmanned sweep craft
8 converted *Lindau* (T-331) MHC
10 *Frankenthal* (T-332) MHC
5 *Frauenlob* MSI
1 MCM diver spt ship
AMPHIBIOUS craft only
some 13 LCU/LCM
SUPPORT AND MISCELLANEOUS 42
UNDER WAY SUPPORT 2 *Spessart* AO
MAINTENANCE AND LOGISTIC 26
6 *Elbe* spt, 4 small (2,000t) AOT, 4 *Lüneburg* log spt, 2 AE, 8 tugs, 2 icebreakers (civil)
SPECIAL PURPOSE 10
3 AGI, 2 trials, 3 multi-purpose (T-748), 2 trg

RESEARCH AND SURVEY 4

1 AGOR, 3 AGHS (civil-manned for Ministry of Transport)

NAVAL AIR (4,500)

Flying hours *Tornado*: 160

3 wg, 7 sqn

1 wg with *Tornado*, 2 sqn FGA/recce, 1 sqn trg

1 wg with ASW/SIGINT/SAR/pollution control/ tpt, 1 sqn with *Atlantic* (MPA/SIGINT), 1 sqn with *Atlantic* (pollution control/tpt) and Do-228, 1 sqn with *Lynx* (ASW)

1 SAR/tpt wg with 1 sqn *Sea King* Mk 41 hel

EQUIPMENT

53 cbt ac, 17 armed hel

AC 53 *Tornado* • **18** *Atlantic* (14 MR, 4 ELINT) • 2 **Do-228** (pollution control) • 2 **Do-228** (tpt)

HEL 17 *Sea Lynx* **Mk 88** (ASW) • 22 *Sea King* **Mk 41** (SAR/tpt)

MISSILES

ASM *Kormoran*, *Sea Skua*, HARM

AAM AIM-9 *Sidewinder*

Air Force 76,900

(22,400 conscripts, 230 women) **Flying hours** 150

AIR FORCE COMMAND

2 TAC cmds, 4 air div

FGA 4 wg with 8 sqn *Tornado*

FTR 4 wg (with F-4F (7 sqn); MiG-29 1 sqn)

RECCE 1 wg with 2 sqn *Tornado*

ECR 1 wg with 2 sqn *Tornado*

SAM 6 mixed wg (each 1 gp *Patriot* (6 sqn) plus 1 gp HAWK (4 sqn plus 2 reserve sqn)); 14 sqn *Roland*

RADAR 2 tac Air Control regts, 7 sites; 10 remote radar posts

TRANSPORT COMMAND (GAFTC)

TPT 3 wg, 4 sqn with *Transall* C-160, incl 1 (OCU) with C-160, 4 sqn (incl 1 OCU) with Bell UH-1D, 1 special air mission wg with Boeing 707-320C, Tu-154, Airbus A-310, VFW-614, CL-601, L-410S (VIP), Mi-8S (VIP)

TRAINING

FGA OCU 1 det (Cottesmore, UK) with 19 *Tornado*

FTR OCU (Holloman AFB, NM) with 24 F-4E (17 F-4E leased from USAF)

NATO joint jet pilot trg (Sheppard AFB, TX) with 35 T-37B, 40 T-38A; primary trg sqn with Beech *Bonanza* (Goodyear AFB, AZ)

EQUIPMENT

455 cbt ac (36 trg (overseas)) (plus 105 in store); no attack hel

AC 154 **F-4** (147 **-F** (FGA, ftr), 7 **-E** (OCU, in US)) • 278 *Tornado* (196 FGA, 35* ECR, 28* OCU, 19* in tri-national trg sqn (in UK)) • 23 **MiG-29** (19 (ftr), 4* **-UB** (trg)) • *Alpha Jet* (105 in store) • 84

Transall **C-160** (tpt, trg) • 2 **Boeing 707** (VIP) • 5 **A-310** (VIP, tpt) • 2 **Tu-154** • 7 **CL-601** (VIP) • 4 **L-410-S** (VIP) • 35 **T-37B** • 40 **T-38A** • 3 **VFW-614** (VIP)

HEL 103 **UH-1D** (99 SAR, tpt, liaison; 4 VIP) • 6 **Mi-8S** (VIP)

MISSILES

ASM AGM-65 *Maverick*, AGM-88 HARM

AAM AIM-9 *Sidewinder*, AA-8 *Aphid*, AA-10 *Alamo*, AA-11 *Archer*

SAM 72 HAWK launchers, 84 *Roland* launchers, 36 *Patriot* launchers

Forces Abroad

NAVY 1 DD/FF with STANAVFORLANT, 1 DD/FF with STANAVFORMED, 1 MCMV with STANAVFORCHAN, 3 MPA in ELMAS/Sardinia

US 650 flying trg at Goodyear, Sheppard, Holloman AFBs, NAS Pensacola, Fort Rucker AFBs with 35 T-37, 40 T-38, 7 F-4E; 11 *Tornado*, missile trg at El Paso

UK 70 OCU at RAF Cottesmore with 19 *Tornado*

UN AND PEACEKEEPING

BOSNIA (SFOR): 2,516. (UNMIBH): 165 civ pol. **CROATIA** (SFOR): 87. **GEORGIA** (UNOMIG): 10 Obs. **IRAQ** (UNSCOM): 35; **ac** 1 C-160 **hel** 2 CH-53. **IRAQ/KUWAIT** (UNIKOM): 26. **ITALY** (SFOR Air Component): 14 *Tornado* (8 ECR, 6 recce) 7 C-160

Foreign Forces

NATO HQ Allied Land Forces Central Europe (LANDCENT), HQ Allied Rapid Reaction Corps (ARRC), HQ Allied Air Forces Central Europe (AIRCENT), HQ Allied Land Forces Jutland and Schleswig-Holstein (LANDJUT), HQ Multi-National Division (Central) (MND(C)), HQ Allied Command Europe Mobile Force (AMF), Airborne Early Warning Force: 18 E-3A *Sentry*

BELGIUM 2,000; 1 mech inf bde(-)

FRANCE 11,700; 1 armd div (Eurocorps)

ITALY Air Force 92 NAEW Force

NETHERLANDS 3,000; 1 lt bde

UK 27,920 **Army** 23,600; 1 corps HQ (multinational), 1 armd div, 2 armd recce, 4 fd arty, 2 AD regt **Air Force** 4,320; 2 air bases, 4 sqn with **ac** 54 *Tornado* GR1, 2 sqn with 36 *Harrier* RAF regt, 1 *Rapier* SAM sqn, 2 fd sqn

US 75,665 **Army** 60,500; 1 army HQ, 1 corps HQ; 1 armd(-), 1 mech inf div (-) **Air Force** 15,165, HQ USAFE, (HQ 17th Air Force), 1 tac ftr wg with 4 sqn FGA/ftr, 1 cbt spt wg, 1 air-control wg, 1 tac airlift wg; 1 air base wg, 54 F-16C/D, 12 A-10, 6 OA-10, 16 C-130E, 9 C-9A, 9 C-21, 2 C-20, 1 CT-43

Greece

	1995	1996	1997	1998
GDP	dr26.5tr	dr29.6tr		
	($114bn)	($123bn)		
per capita	$11,400	$11,900		
Growth	2.0%	2.6%		
Inflation	8.9%	8.2%		
Publ debt	111.8%	111.9%		
Def exp	dr1.2tr	dr1.4tr		
	($5.1bn)	($5.9bn)		
Def bdgt			dr996bn	
			($3.7bn)	
FMA (US)	$269m	$225m	$123m	$123m
$1 = drachma	232	241	270	
Population[a]		10,550,000 (Muslim 1%)		
Age	*13–17*	*18–22*	*23–32*	
Men	359,000	384,000	826,000	
Women	336,000	364,000	785,000	

[a] ε400,000 Albanian legal and illegal immigrants and temporary workers live in Greece in 1997

Total Armed Forces

ACTIVE 162,300

(119,200 conscripts, 5,100 women)
Terms of service: **Army** up to 19 months **Navy** up to 21 months **Air Force** up to 21 months

RESERVES some 291,000

(to age 50) **Army** some 235,000 (Field Army 200,000, Territorial Army/National Guard 35,000) **Navy** about 24,000 **Air Force** about 32,000

Army 116,000

(95,000 conscripts, 2,700 women)

FIELD ARMY

3 Mil Regions • 1 Army, 5 corps HQ • 4 div HQ (1 armd, 3 mech) • 7 inf div (3 inf, 1 arty regt, 1 armd bn) • 5 indep armd bde (each 2 armd, 1 mech inf, 1 SP arty bn) • 7 indep mech bde (2 mech, 1 armd, 1 SP arty bn) • 2 inf bde • 1 amph bn • 4 recce bn • 3 army avn bn (incl 1 ATK) • 15 fd arty bn • 1 indep avn coy • 10 AD arty bn • 2 SAM bn with I HAWK
Units are manned at 3 different levels
Cat A 85% fully ready **Cat B** 60% ready in 24 hours
Cat C 20% ready in 48 hours

TERRITORIAL DEFENCE

Higher Mil Comd of Interior and Islands HQ
4 Mil Comd HQ (incl Athens) • 1 inf div • 4 AD arty bn • 2 inf regt • 1 army avn bn • 1 para regt • 8 fd arty bn

RESERVES 34,000

National Guard internal security role

EQUIPMENT

MBT 1,735: 714 M-48 (15 A3, 303 A5, 396 A5 MOLF), 669 M-60 (357 A1, 312 A3), 352 *Leopard* (105 -1CR, 170 -1V, 77 -1A5)
RECCE 48 M-8
AIFV 501 BMP-1
APC 308 *Leonidas* Mk1/Mk2, 1,669 M-113A1/A2
TOTAL ARTY 1,878
  TOWED 730: **105mm**: 18 M-56, 445 M-101; **155mm**: 267 M-114
  SP 399: **105mm**: 73 M-52A1; **155mm**: 133 M-109A1/A2, **175mm**: 12 M-107; **203mm**: 181 M-110A2
  MRL 122mm: 116 RM-70; **227mm**: 9 MLRS (+9 being delivered)
  MOR 107mm: 624 M-30 (incl 191 SP); plus **81mm**: 2,900
ATGW 290 *Milan*, 336 TOW (incl 212 M-901), 250 AT-4 *Spigot*
RL 64mm: RPG-18; **66mm**: M-72
RCL 90mm: 1,346 EM-67; **106mm**: 1,313 M-40A1
AD GUNS 20mm: 101 Rh-202 twin; **23mm**: 506 ZU-23-2; **40mm**: 227 M-1, 95 M-42A twin SP
SAM 500 *Stinger*, 42 I HAWK, 12 SA-8B
SURV AN/TPQ-36 (arty, mor)
AC 1 U-9E, 1 C-12A, 43 U-17A
HELICOPTERS
  ATTACK 20 AH-64
  SPT 9 CH-47D (1 in store), 73 UH-1H, 34 AB-205A, 1 AB-212, 14 AB-206, 14 Bell 47G, 15 Hughes 300C

Navy 19,500

(9,800 conscripts, 1,300 women)
BASES Salamis, Patras, Soudha Bay
SUBMARINES 8
  4 *Glavkos* (Ge T-209/1100) with 533mm TT (2 with *Harpoon* USGW)
  4 *Poseidon* (Ge T-209/1200) with 533mm TT
PRINCIPAL SURFACE COMBATANTS 15
DESTROYERS 4 *Kimon* (US *Adams*) (US lease) with 1 SM-1; plus 1 x 8 ASROC, 2 x 3 ASTT, 2 127mm guns, 6 *Harpoon* SSM
FRIGATES 11
  2 *Hydra* (Ge MEKO 200) with 2 x 3 ASTT; plus 2 x 4 *Harpoon* SSM and 1 127mm gun (1 SH-60 hel, 1 DC)
  6 *Elli* (Nl *Kortenaer*) with 2 AB-212 hel, 2 x 2 ASTT; plus 2 x 4 *Harpoon*
  3 *Makedonia* (ex-US *Knox*) (US lease) with 1 x 8 ASROC, 4 ASTT; plus *Harpoon* (from ASROC launcher), 1 127mm gun
PATROL AND COASTAL COMBATANTS 41
CORVETTES 5 *Niki* (ex-Ge *Thetis*) (ASW) with 1 x 4

ASW RL, 4 533mm TT

MISSILE CRAFT 19

13 *Laskos* (Fr *La Combattante* II, III, IIIB) PFM, 8 with 4 MM-38 *Exocet*, 5 with 6 *Penguin* SSM, all with 2 533mm TT

4 *Votis* (Fr *La Combattante* IIA) PFM 2 with 4 MM-38 *Exocet*, 2 with *Harpoon*

2 *Stamou* with 4 SS-12 SSM

TORPEDO CRAFT 8

4 *Hesperos* (Ge *Jaguar*) PFT with 4 533mm TT

4 *Andromeda* (No *Nasty*) PFT with 4 533mm TT

PATROL CRAFT 9

COASTAL 4

2 *Armatolos* (Dk *Osprey*) PCC, 2 *Pirpolitis* PCC

INSHORE 5

2 *Tolmi*, 3 PCI

MINE WARFARE 16

MINELAYERS 2 *Aktion* (US LSM-1) (100–130 mines)

MINE COUNTERMEASURES 14

9 *Alkyon* (US MSC-294) MSC

5 *Atalanti* (US *Adjutant*) MSC, plus 4 MSR

AMPHIBIOUS 10

2 *Chios* LST with hel deck: capacity 300 tps, 4 LCVP plus veh

1 *Nafkratoussa* (US *Cabildo*) LSD: capacity 200 tps, 18 tk, 1 hel

2 *Inouse* (US *County*) LST: capacity 400 tps, 18 tk

3 *Ikaria* (US LST-510): capacity 200 tps, 16 tk

2 *Roussen* (US LSM-1) LSM, capacity 50 tps, 4 tk

Plus about 57 craft: 2 LCT, 6 LCU, 11 LCM, some 31 LCVP, 7 LCA

SUPPORT AND MISCELLANEOUS 14

2 AOT, 4 AOT (small), 1 *Axios* (ex-Ge *Lüneburg*) log spt, 1 AE, 5 AGHS, 1 trg

NAVAL AIR (250)

6 cbt ac, 15 armed hel

AC 6P-3B (MR)

HEL 2 sqn with 8 AB-212 (ASW), 2 AB-212 (EW), 2 SA-319 (ASW), 5 S-70B (ASW)

Air Force 26,800

(14,400 conscripts, 1,100 women)

TACTICAL AIR FORCE

8 cbt wg, 1 tpt wg

FGA 7 sqn

2 with A-7H, 1 with F-16, 3 with A-7E, 1 with F-4E

FTR 10 sqn

2 with *Mirage* F-1CG, 2 with F-5A/B, 1 with NF-5A/B, RF-5A, 1 with F-16 C/D, 2 with *Mirage* 2000 EG/BG, 2 with F-4E

RECCE 1 sqn with RF-4E

TPT 3 sqn with C-130H/B, YS-11, C-47, Do-28, *Gulfstream*

LIAISON 4 T-33A

HEL 2 sqn with AB-205A, Bell 47G, AB-212

AD 1 bn with *Nike Hercules* SAM (36 launchers), 12 bty with *Skyguard*/*Sparrow* SAM, twin **35mm** guns

AIR TRAINING COMMAND

TRG 4 sqn

1 with T-41A, 1 with T-37B/C, 2 with T-2E

EQUIPMENT

342 cbt ac, no armed hel

AC 93 **A-7** (43 **-H** (FGA), 4 **TA-7H** (FGA), 40 **A-7E** (plus 15 in store), 6 **A-7C**) • 84 **F-5** (60 **-A/B**, 7 **-B**, 10 **NF-5A**, 1 **NF-5B**, 6 **RF-5A**) • 66 **F-4E/RF-4E** • 37 **F-16** (30 **-C** (FGA/ftr), 7 **-D**) • 26 *Mirage* **F-1 CG** (ftr) • 36 *Mirage* **2000** (32 **-EG**, 4* **BG** (trg)) • 4 **C-47** (tpt) • 11 **C-130H** (tpt) • 3 **C-130B** (tpt) • 10 **CL-215** (tpt, fire-fighting) • 4 **Do-28** (lt tpt) • 1 *Gulfstream* I (VIP tpt) • 35* **T-2** (trg) • 28 **T-33A** (liaison) • 33 **T-37B/C** (trg) • 19 **T-41D** (trg) • 3 **YS-11-200** (tpt)

HEL 11 **AB-205A** (SAR) • 1 **AB-206** • 4 **AB-212** (VIP, tpt) • 5 **Bell 47G** (liaison)

MISSILES

ASM AGM-65 *Maverick*

AAM AIM-7 *Sparrow,* AIM-9 *Sidewinder* L/P, R-550 *Magic* 2, AIM 120 AMRAAM, *Super* 530D

SAM 36 *Nike Hercules,* 40 *Sparrow*

Forces Abroad

CYPRUS 1,250; incl 1 mech bde (forming) and officers/NCO seconded to Greek-Cypriot forces

UN AND PEACEKEEPING

ADRIATIC (*Sharp Guard* if re-implemented): 2 MSC. **ALBANIA** (*Operation Alba*): ε600, to withdraw Aug 1997. **BOSNIA** (SFOR): 217. **CROATIA** (SFOR): 1. **GEORGIA** (UNOMIG): 4 Obs. **IRAQ/KUWAIT** (UNIKOM): 5 Obs. **ITALY** (SFOR Air Component): 2 C-130

Paramilitary 4,000

COAST GUARD AND CUSTOMS 4,000

some 100 patrol craft, ac 2 Cessna *Cutlass,* 2 TB-20 *Trinidad*

Foreign Forces

US 435 **Army** 18 **Navy** 250; facilities at Soudha Bay **Air Force** 167; air base gp; facilities at Iraklion

Iceland

	1995	1996	1997	1998
GDP	K452bn	K487bn		
	($7.0bn)	($7.3bn)		
per capita	$19,700	$21,100		

contd	1995	1996	1997	1998
Growth	1.2%	5.7%		
Inflation	1.6%	2.3%		
Publ debt	58.8%	57.6%		
Sy exp[a]	K3.1bn	K3.1bn		
	($48m)	($46m)		
Sy bdgt[a]			K3.3bn	
			($46m)	
$1 = kronur	64.7	66.5	71.0	

[a] Iceland has no Armed Forces. Sy bdgt is part of public order and safety bdgt

Population		275,000		
Age	*13–17*	*18–22*	*23–32*	
Men	11,000	11,000	22,000	
Women	10,000	10,000	20,000	

Total Armed Forces

ACTIVE Nil

Paramilitary 120

COAST GUARD 120
BASE Reykjavik
  PATROL CRAFT 4
  2 *Aegir* PCO with hel, 1 *Odinn* PCO with hel deck, 1 PCI<
  AVN 1 F-27 **ac** 1 SA-360 **hel**

Foreign Forces

NATO Island Commander Iceland (ISCOMICE, responsible to CINCEASTLANT)
US 2,520 **Navy** 1,800; MR: 1 sqn with 6 P-3C, 1 UP-3 **Marines** 91 **Air Force** 629; 4 F-15C/D, 1 HC-130, 1 KC-135, 4 HH-60G
NETHERLANDS 30 **Navy** 1 P-3C

Italy

	1995	1996	1997	1998
GDP	L1,769tr	L1,834tr		
	($1.1tr)	($1.1tr)		
per capita	$19,500	$20,000		
Growth	2.9%	0.7%		
Inflation	5.2%	3.9%		
Publ debt	122.0%	121.7%		
Def exp	L31.6tr	L36.7tr		
	($19.4bn)	($23.8bn)		
Def bdgt			L31.1tr	
			($18.3bn)	
$1 = lira	1,629	1,543	1,693	

Population		57,900,000		
Age	*13–17*	*18–22*	*23–32*	
Men	1,660,000	1,962,000	4,633,000	
Women	1,578,000	1,875,000	4,492,000	

Total Armed Forces

ACTIVE 325,150

(163,800 conscripts; incl 29,250 Central Staff and centrally controlled formations/units)
Terms of service: all services 10 months

RESERVES 484,000 (immediate mobilisation)
Army 800,000 (obligation to age 45) (immediate mob 420,000) **Navy** 36,000 (to age 39 for men, variable for officers to 73) **Air Force** 28,000 (to age 25 or 45 (specialists))

Army 188,300

(127,550 conscripts)

FIELD ARMY
(Regt are normally of bn size)
3 Corps HQ (1 mtn)
  1 with 2 mech bde, 1 armd cav, 1 arty, 1 avn regt
  1 with 1 armd, 1 armd cav bde, 1 amph, 2 arty, 1 avn regt
  1 with 3 mtn bde, 1 hy arty, 1 avn regt
1 AD comd: 3 HAWK SAM, 3 AAA regt
1 avn gp (1 sqn AB-412, 2 sqn CH-47, 1 flt Do-228)

TERRITORIAL DEFENCE
7 Mil Regions • 5 indep mech, 1 AB bde (incl 1 SF bn, 1 avn sqn) • Rapid Intervention Force (FIR) formed from 1 mech, 1 AB bde (see above), plus 1 Marine bn (see Navy), 1 hel unit (Army), 1 air tpt unit (Air Force) • 4 armd cav regt • 1 inf regt • 4 engr regt • 5 avn units

RESERVES
on mob: 1 armd, 1 mech, 1 mtn bde

EQUIPMENT
  MBT 1,325: 920 *Leopard* (incl 120 -1A5), 400 *Centauro* B-1, 5 *Ariete*
  APC 1,002 M-113, 1,794 VCC1/-2, 57 Fiat 6614, 14 LVTP-7
  TOTAL ARTY 1,939
    TOWED 857: **105mm**: 272 Model 56 pack (233 in store); **155mm**: 164 FH-70, 421 M-114 (in store)
    SP 286: **155mm**: 260 M-109G/-L; **203mm**: 26 M-110A2
    MRL 227mm: 22 MLRS
    MOR 120mm: 774 (389 in store); plus **81mm**: 1,205 (381 in store)
  ATGW 432 TOW 2A/2B (incl 270 SP), 1,000 *Milan*
  RL 1,000 *Panzerfaust* 3

RCL 80mm: 720 *Folgore*
AD GUNS 25mm: 219 SIDAM SP; 40mm: 234
SAM 66 HAWK, 128 *Stinger*, 24 *Skyguard/Aspide*
AC 30 SM-1019, 3 Do-228
HELICOPTERS
  ATTACK 45 A-129
  ASLT 27 A-109, 62 AB-206
SPT 87 AB-205A, 40 AB-206 (obs), 14 AB-212, 23 AB-412, 38 CH-47C
UAV CL-89 (AN/USD-501), *Mirach* 20/-150

Navy 44,000

(incl 1,600 Naval Air, 1,000 Marines and 17,250 conscripts)
COMMANDS 1 Fleet Commander CINCNAV (also NATO COMEDCENT) Area Commands Upper Tyrrhenian, Adriatic, Lower Tyrrhenian, Ionian and Strait of Otranto, Sicily, Sardinia
BASES La Spezia (HQ), Taranto (HQ), Ancona (HQ), Brindisi, Augusta, Messina (HQ), La Maddalena (HQ), Cagliari, Naples (HQ), Venice (HQ)
SUBMARINES 8
  4 *Pelosi* (imp *Sauro*) with Type 184 HWT
  4 *Sauro* with Type 184 HWT (includes 2 non-op, undergoing mod)
PRINCIPAL SURFACE COMBATANTS 32
CARRIERS 1 *G. Garibaldi* CVV with 16 SH-3 *Sea King* hel, 3 AV-8B (plus 2 trg) V/STOL ac, 4 *Teseo* SSM, 2 x 3 ASTT
CRUISERS 1 *Vittorio Veneto* CGH with 1 x 2 SM-1 ER SAM, 6 AB-212 ASW hel (Mk 46 LWT); plus 4 *Teseo* SSM, 2 x 3 ASTT
DESTROYERS 4
  2 *Luigi Durand de la Penne* (ex-*Animoso*) DDGH with 1 SM-1 MR SAM, 2 x 4 *Teseo* SSM, plus 2 AB-312 hel, 1 127mm gun, 2 x 3 ASTT
  2 *Audace* DDGH, with 1 SM-1 MR SAM, 4 *Teseo* SSM, plus 2 AB-212 hel, 1 127mm gun, 2 x 3 ASTT
FRIGATES 26
  8 *Maestrale* FFH with 2 AB-212 hel, 2 533mm DP TT; plus 4 *Teseo* SSM, 1 127mm gun
  4 *Lupo* FFH with 1 AB-212 hel, 2 x 3 ASTT; plus 8 *Teseo* SSM, 1 127mm gun
  4 *Artigliere* FFG (ex-*Lupo* for Iraq) with 8 *Tesco* SSM, 8 *Aspide* SAM, 1 127mm gun, 1 AB-212 hel
  2 *Alpino* FFH with 1 AB-212 hel, 2 x 3 ASTT, 1 ASW mor
  8 *Minerva* FF with 2 x 3 ASTT
PATROL AND COASTAL COMBATANTS 14
MISSILE CRAFT 5 *Sparviero* PHM with 2 *Teseo* SSM
PATROL, OFFSHORE 6
  4 *Cassiopea* with 1 AB-212 hel
  2 *Storione* (US *Aggressive*) ex-MSO
PATROL, COASTAL 3 *Bambu* (ex-MSC) PCC
MINE COUNTERMEASURES 12

4 *Lerici* MHC
8 *Gaeta* MSC
AMPHIBIOUS 3
  3 *San Giorgio* LPD: capacity 350 tps, 30 trucks, 2 SH-3D or CH-47 hel, 7 craft
  Plus some 33 craft: about 3 LCU, 10 LCM and 20 LCVP
SUPPORT AND MISCELLANEOUS 42
  2 *Stromboli* AO, 8 tugs, 9 coastal tugs, 6 water tkr, 4 trials, 2 trg, 3 AGOR, 6 tpt, 2 salvage
SPECIAL FORCES (Special Forces Command – COMSUBIN)
3 gp; 1 underwater ops; 1 school; 1 research
MARINES (San Marco gp) (1,000)
1 bn gp, 1 trg gp, 1 log gp
  EQUIPMENT
    30 VCC-1, 10 LVTP-7 APC, 16 81mm mor, 8 106mm RCL, 6 *Milan* ATGW
NAVAL AIR (1,600)
18 cbt ac, 74 armed hel
FGA 1 sqn with 16 AV-8B plus and 2*TAV-8B plus
ASW 5 hel sqn with 30 SH-3D, 53 AB-212
AAM AIM-9L *Sidewinder*
ASM *Marte* Mk 2, AS-12

Air Force 63,600

(19,000 conscripts)
FGA 8 sqn
  4 with *Tornado*, 4 with AMX
FTR 7 sqn
  5 with F-104 ASA, 2 with *Tornado* F-3
RECCE 2 sqn with AMX
MR 2 sqn with *Atlantic* (OPCON to Navy)
EW 1 ECM/recce sqn with G-222VS, PD-808
CAL 1 navigation-aid calibration sqn with G-222RM, PD-808
TPT 2 with G-222, 1 with C-130H
TKR/TPT 1 sqn with B707-320
LIAISON 3 sqn with ac *Gulfstream* III, *Falcon* 50, DC-9, P-166, P-180 hel SH-3D
TRG 1 OCU with TF-104G; 1 det (Cottesmore, UK) with *Tornado*; 4 sqn with ac AMX T, MB-339A, SF-260M, 1 sqn with MB-339 (Aerobatic Team), 1 sqn with MB-339CD (ftr lead-in trg) hel 1 sqn with NH-500
SAR 1 sqn and 3 det with HH-3F
  6 det with AB-212
AD 6 SAM sqn with *Nike Hercules*, 14 SAM sqn with *Spada*
EQUIPMENT
  286 cbt ac (plus 110 in store), no armed hel
  AC 77 *Tornado* (53 FGA (4* in tri-national sqn), 24 F-3 (plus 36 FGA in store)) • 65 F-104 ASA (plus 40

in store) • 7 **TF104G** (plus 12 in store) • 99 **AMX** (81 (FGA), 18* **-T** (trg)) • 77 **MB-339** (13* tac, 64 trg Acrobatic Team) (plus 17 in store) • 12* **MB-339CD** • 13* *Atlantic* (MR) (plus 5 in store) • 4 **Boeing-707-320** (tkr/tpt) • 7 **C-130H** (tpt) • 36 **G-222** (31 tpt, 4 cal), 1 **-GE** (ECM) • 2 **DC9-32** (VIP) • 2 *Gulfstream* III (VIP) • 3 *Falcon* 50 (VIP) • 7 **P-166** (2 **-M**, 5 **-DL3** (liaison and trg)) • 5 **P-180** (liaison) • 6 **PD-808** (ECM, cal, VIP tpt) • 29 **SF-260M** (trg) • 29 **SIAI-208** (liaison)

HEL 19 **HH-3F** (SAR) • 1 **SH-3D** (liaison) • 26 **AB-212** (SAR) • 51 **NH-500D** (trg)

MISSILES

ASM AGM-88 HARM, *Kormoran*
AAM AIM-7E *Sparrow*, AIM-9B/L *Sidewinder*, *Aspide*
SAM *Nike Hercules*, *Aspide*

Forces Abroad

GERMANY 92 **Air Force**, NAEW Force
MALTA 16 **Air Force** with 2 AB-212
UK 21 **Air Force** tri-national *Tornado* sqn with 4 ac
US 33 **Air Force** flying trg

UN AND PEACEKEEPING

ALBANIA (*Operation Alba*): 2,972, to withdraw Aug 1997. **BOSNIA** (SFOR): 1,812; 1 mech inf bde gp; (UNMIBH): 23 civ pol. **CROATIA** (SFOR): 13. **EGYPT** (MFO): 81; 3 PCC. **INDIA/PAKISTAN** (UNMOGIP): 7 Obs. **ITALY** (SFOR Air Component): 8 *Tornado*, 6 AMX, 1 B-707 (tkr). **IRAQ** (UNSCOM): 1 Obs. **IRAQ/KUWAIT** (UNIKOM): 5 Obs. **LEBANON** (UNIFIL): 46; hel unit. **MIDDLE EAST** (UNTSO): 8 Obs. **WESTERN SAHARA** (MINURSO): 5 Obs

Paramilitary 255,700

CARABINIERI (Ministry of Defence) 113,200

Territorial 5 bde, 18 regt, 94 gp **Trg** 1 bde **Mobile def** 1 div, 2 bde, 1 cav regt, 1 special ops gp, 13 mobile bn, 1 AB bn, avn and naval units
    EQPT 40 Fiat 6616 armd cars; 40 VCC2, 91 M-113 APC **hel** 24 A-109, 4 AB-205, 39 AB-206, 24 AB-412

PUBLIC SECURITY GUARD (Ministry of Interior) 79,000

11 mobile units; 40 Fiat 6614 APC **ac** 5 P-68 **hel** 12 A-109, 20 AB-206, 9 AB-212

FINANCE GUARDS (Treasury Department) 63,500

14 Zones, 20 Legions, 128 gps **ac** 5 P-166-DL3 **hel** 15 A-109, 65 Breda-Nardi NH-500M/MC/MD; 3 PCI; plus about 300 boats

HARBOUR CONTROL (*Capitanerie di Porto*)

(subordinated to Navy in emergencies): some 12 PCI, 130+ boats and 4 AB-412 (SAR)

Foreign Forces

NATO HQ Allied Forces Southern Europe (AFSOUTH), HQ 5 Allied Tactical Air Force (5 ATAF)
US 11,300 **Army** 2,500; 1 inf bn gp **Navy** 4,600 **Air Force** 4,200; 2 ftr sqn with 36 F-16C/D
SFOR AIR COMPONENT: Be (3 F-16A), **Fr** (10 *Mirage* 2000C/D, 11 *Jaguar*, 1 E-3F, 1 C-135, 3 SA-330 (*Puma*), 1 N-262), **Ge** (14 *Tornado* ECR/recce, 2 C-160), **Gr** (1 C-130), **It** (8 *Tornado*, 6 AMX, 1 B-707 (tkr)), **NATO** (4 E-3A), **Nl** (7 F-16, 1 C-130, 1 F-60, 1 KDC-10 (tkr)), **No** (1 C-130), **Sp** (8 F/A -18, 2 KC-130 (tkr), 1 CASA 212 (spt ac)), **Tu** (8 F-16C), **UK** (14 *Jaguar*, 1 K-1 *Tristar* (tkr), 2 E-3D *Sentry*, 1 C-130), **US** 6 F-16C (USAF), 3 EC-130 (USAF), 1 AC-130 (USAF), 6 EA-6B (USMC), 4 KC-135 (USAF), 7 P-3 (USN), 2 MH-53J (SAR), 1 MC-130 P (SAR), 4 C-12

Luxembourg

	1995	1996	1997	1998
GDP	fr570bn	fr593bn		
	($18.0bn)	($19.3bn)		
per capita	$23,000	$24,200		
Growth	3.2%	3.9%		
Inflation	2.0%	1.4%		
Publ debt	6.3%	6.5%		
Def exp	fr4.2bn	fr4.2bn		
	($142m)	($135m)		
Def bdgt			fr3.9bn	fr3.9bn
			($111m)	($111m)
$1 = franc	31.0	35.3	35.0	
Population	412,000 (ε122,000 foreign citizens)			
Age	13–17	18–22	23–32	
Men	12,000	12,000	30,000	
Women	12,000	12,200	30,000	

Total Armed Forces

ACTIVE 800

Army 800

1 lt inf bn (recce coy to Eurocorps/BE div)
EQUIPMENT
    APC 5 *Commando*
    MOR 81mm: 6
    ATGW TOW some 6 SP
    RL LAW

Air Force

(none, but for legal purposes NATO's E-3A AEW ac have Lu registration)

1 sqn with 17 E-3A *Sentry* (NATO standard), 2 Boeing 707 (trg) (4 E-3A in SFOR Air Element)

Forces Abroad

UN AND PEACEKEEPING
BOSNIA (SFOR): 22

Paramilitary 560

GENDARMERIE 560

Netherlands

	1995	1996	1997	1998
GDP	gld635bn	gld662bn		
	($352bn)	($393bn)		
per capita	$19,600	$20,600		
Growth	2.4%	3.5%		
Inflation	2.0%	2.1%		
Publ debt	79.5%	78.5%		
Def exp	gld12.9bn	gld13.6bn		
	($8.0bn)	($8.1bn)		
Def bdgt			gld13.6bn	gld13.6bn
			($7.1bn)	($7.2bn)
$1 = guilder	1.61	1.68	1.92	
Population		15,585,000		
Age	*13–17*	*18–22*	*23–32*	
Men	446,000	487,000	1,225,000	
Women	427,000	465,000	1,161,000	

Total Armed Forces

ACTIVE 57,180
(incl 3,600 Royal Military Constabulary, 800 Inter-Service Organisation; 2,600 women)

RESERVES 75,000
(men to age 35, NCO to 40, officers to 45) **Army** 60,000 **Navy** some 5,000 **Air Force** 10,000 (immediate recall)

Army 27,000

1 Corps HQ (Ge/Nl), 1 mech div HQ • 3 mech inf bde (2 cadre) • 1 lt bde • 1 air-mobile bde (3 inf bn) • 1 fd arty, 1 AD gp • 1 engr gp
Summary of cbt arm units
    7 tk bn • 7 armd inf bn • 3 air-mobile bn • 3 recce bn • 7 arty bn • 1 AD bn • 2 MLRS bty

RESERVES
(cadre bde and corps tps completed by call-up of reservists)
National Command (incl Territorial Comd): 3 inf, 1 SF,

2 engr bn spt units, could be mob for territorial defence
Home Guard 3 sectors; lt inf weapons
EQUIPMENT
  MBT 600: 270 *Leopard* 1A4 (in store; for sale), 330 *Leopard* 2 (180 to be A5)
  AIFV 383 YPR-765, 65 M-113C/-R all with **25mm**
  APC 269 YPR-765 (plus 491 look-a-likes)
  TOTAL ARTY 439
    TOWED 125: **105mm**: 1 M-101 (in store); **155mm**: 27 M-114/23, 82 M-114/39, 15 FH-70 (trg)
    SP 159: **155mm**: 129 M-109A3; **203mm**: 30 M-110 (in store; for sale)
    MRL 227mm: 22 MLRS
    MOR 81mm: 40; **120mm**: 133
  ATGW 753 (incl 135 in store): 427 *Dragon*, 326 (incl 90 YPR-765) TOW
  RL 84mm: *Carl Gustav,* AT-4
  RCL 106mm: 185 M-40 (in store)
  AD GUNS 35mm: 77 *Gepard* SP (60 to be up-graded); **40mm**: 60 L/70 towed
  SAM 312 *Stinger*
  SURV AN/TPQ-36 (arty, mor)
  MARINE 1 tk tpt, 3 coastal, 3 river patrol boats

Navy 13,800

(incl 950 Naval Air, 2,800 Marines, 1,200 women)
BASES Netherlands Den Helder (HQ). Nl and Be Navies under joint op comd based Den Helder **Overseas** Willemstad (Curaçao)
SUBMARINES 4
  4 *Walrus* with Mk 48 HWT; plus provision for *Harpoon* USGW
PRINCIPAL SURFACE COMBATANTS 16
DESTROYERS 4
  DDG (Nl desig = FFG) 4
  2 *Tromp* with 1 SM-1 MR SAM; plus 2 x 4 *Harpoon* SSM, 1 x 2 120mm guns, 1 *Lynx* hel (ASW/OTHT), 2 x 3 ASTT (Mk 46 LWT)
  2 *Van Heemskerck* with 1 SM-1 MR SAM; plus 2 x 4 *Harpoon*, 2 x 2 ASTT
FRIGATES 12
  8 *Karel Doorman* FF with 2 x 4 *Harpoon* SSM, plus 2 x 2 ASTT; 1 *Lynx* (ASW/OTHT) hel
  4 *Kortenaer* FF with 2 *Lynx* (ASW/OTHT) hel, 2 x 2 ASTT; plus 2 x 4 *Harpoon*
MINE WARFARE 17
MINELAYERS none, but *Mercuur*, listed under spt and misc, has capability
MINE COUNTERMEASURES 17
  15 *Alkmaar* (tripartite) MHC
  2 *Dokkum* MSC
AMPHIBIOUS 1
  1 *Rotterdam* LPD: capacity 4 LCU or 6 LCA, 600 troops

SUPPORT AND MISCELLANEOUS 11

1 *Amsterdam* AOR (4 *Lynx* or 3 NH-90 or 2 EH-101 hel), 1 *Mercuur* torpedo tender, 2 trg, 4 *Cerberus* div spt, 1 *Zuideruis* AOR (2 *Lynx* hel), 1 *Pelikaan* spt

NAVAL AIR (950)

MR 1 sqn with F-27M (see Air Force)
MR/ASW 2 sqn with P-3C
ASW/SAR 2 sqn with *Lynx* hel
EQPT 13 cbt ac, 22 armed hel
AC 13 P-3C (MR)
HEL 22 *Lynx* (ASW, SAR)

MARINES (2,800)

3 Marine bn (1 cadre); 1 spt bn

RESERVES

1 Marine bn

EQUIPMENT

TOWED ARTY 105mm: 16 lt
MOR 81mm: 18; **120mm**: 28 (2 in store)
ATGW *Dragon*
RL AT-4
SAM *Stinger*

Air Force 11,980

(720 women) **Flying hours** 180
FTR/FGA 6 sqn with F-16A/B (1 sqn is tac trg, evaluation and standardisation sqn)
FTR/RECCE 1 sqn with F-16A
MR 2 F-27M (assigned to Navy)
TPT 1 sqn with F-50, F-60, C-130H-30, DC-10-30
TRG 1 sqn with PC-7
HEL SA-316, BO-105, CH-47D, AH-64D, AS-532U2
SAR 1 sqn with SA-316
AD 8 bty with HAWK SAM (4 in Ge), 4 bty with *Patriot* SAM (in Ge)

EQUIPMENT

171 cbt ac (plus 11 in store), 12 armed hel
AC 171 **F-16A/B** (plus 11 in store) • 2 F-27M (MR) • 2 **F-50** • 4 **F-60** • 2 **C-130H-30** • 2 **DC-10-30** (tkr/tpt) • 1 *Gulfstream* III • 10 **PC-7** (trg)
HEL 3 **AB-412 SP** (SAR) • 9 **SA-316** • 27 **BO-105** • 12 **AH-64D** • 7 **CH-47D** • 15 **AS-532U2**

MISSILES

AAM AIM-9/L/N *Sidewinder*
SAM 48 HAWK, 5 *Patriot*, 100 *Stinger*
AD GUNS 25 VL 4/41 *Flycatcher* radar, 75 L/70 **40mm** systems

Forces Abroad

GERMANY 3,000; 1 lt bde (1 armd inf, 1 tk bn), plus spt elms
ICELAND 30 **Navy** 1 P-3C

NETHERLANDS ANTILLES Netherlands, Aruba and the Netherlands Antilles operate a Coast Guard Force to combat org crime and drug smuggling. Comd by Netherlands Commander Caribbean. HQ Curaçao, bases Aruba and St Maarten **Navy** 20 (to expand); 1 frigate, 1 amph cbt det, 2 P-3C **Air Force** 25; 2 F-27MPA

UN AND PEACEKEEPING

ADRIATIC (*Sharp Guard* if re-implemented): 1 FFG.
ANGOLA (UNOMA): 16 incl 14 Obs, plus 10 civ pol.
BOSNIA (SFOR): 988; 1 mech inf bn gp; (UNMIBH): 50 civ pol. **CROATIA** (SFOR): 71. (UNTAES): 6. **ITALY**: 155 (SFOR Air Component) 7 F-16, 1 C-130, 1 F-60, 1 KDC-10. **MIDDLE EAST** (UNTSO): 16 Obs

Paramilitary 3,600

ROYAL MILITARY CONSTABULARY (*Koninklijke Marechaussee*) 3,600

(500 conscripts); 3 'div' comprising 10 districts with 72 'bde'

Foreign Forces

NATO HQ Allied Forces Central Europe
US 785 **Army** 490 **Air Force** 295

Norway

	1995	1996	1997	1998
GDP	kr926bn	kr1,011bn		
	($132bn)	($157bn)		
per capita	$21,300	$22,700		
Growth	3.3%	4.9%		
Inflation	2.5%	1.2%		
Publ debt	42.8%	40.1%		
Def exp	kr22.2bn	kr24.3bn		
	($3.5bn)	($3.8bn)		
Def bdgt			kr24.3bn	
			($3.5bn)	
$1 = kroner	6.43	6.45	6.97	
Population		4,392,000		
Age	*13–17*	*18–22*	*23–32*	
Men	138,000	149,000	340,000	
Women	130,000	140,000	319,000	

Total Armed Forces

ACTIVE 33,600

(incl recalled reservists, 400 Joint Services org, 500 Home Guard permanent staff, and 19,700 conscripts)
Terms of service: **Army**, **Navy**, **Air Force**, 12 months, plus 4–5 refresher trg periods

RESERVES

234,000 mobilisable in 24–72 hours; obligation to 44
(conscripts remain with fd army units to age 35,
officers to age 55, regulars to age 60)
Army 101,000 **Navy** 25,000 **Air Force** 25,000 **Home
Guard** some 83,000 on mob

Army 15,800

(incl 11,000 conscripts)
2 Comd, 4 district comd, 14 'regimental' comd
North Norway 1 inf bn, border gd, cadre and trg units
for 1 div (1 armd, 2 inf bde) and 1 indep mech inf bde
South Norway 2 inf bn (incl Royal Guard), indep units
plus cadre units for 1 mech inf and 1 armd bde

RESERVES

20 inf, 1 arty bn; 10 inf coy, engr coy, sigs units

LAND HOME GUARD 77,000

18 districts each divided into 2–6 sub-districts and
some 465 sub-units (pl)

EQUIPMENT

MBT 170 *Leopard* (111 -1A5NO, 59 -1A1NO)
AIFV 53 NM-135 (M-113/**20mm**), 4 CV 9030N
APC 194 M-113 (incl variants), 18 XA-186 *Sisu*
TOTAL ARTY 252
 TOWED 120: **105mm**: 72 M-101; **155mm**: 48 M-
 114
 SP **155mm**: 126 M-109A3GN SP
 MRL **227mm**: 6 MLRS
MOR **81mm**: 454 (40 SP incl 28 M-106A1, 12 M-
125A2)
ATGW 320 TOW-1/-2 incl 126 NM-142 (M-901)
RCL **84mm**: 2,517 *Carl Gustav*
AD GUNS **20mm**: 252 Rh-202 (192 in store)
SAM 300 RBS-70 (120 in store)
SURV *Cymberline* (mor)

Navy 9,000

(incl 1,000 Coastal Defence, 700 Coast Guard and 4,900
conscripts)
OPERATIONAL COMMANDS COMNAVSONOR
and COMNAVNON with 7 regional Naval districts
BASES Horten, Haakonsvern (Bergen), Olavsvern
(Tromsø)

SUBMARINES 12

6 *Ula* SS with 8 533mm TT
6 *Kobben* SSC with 8 533mm TT

FRIGATES 4

4 *Oslo* with 2 x 3 ASTT, 1 x 6 *Terne* ASW RL; plus 4
Penguin 1 SSM, *Sea Sparrow*

PATROL AND COASTAL COMBATANTS 24

MISSILE CRAFT 24

14 *Hauk* PFM with 6 *Penguin* 1, 2 (Swe TP-613)
HWT, 8 *Storm* PFM with 6 *Penguin* 1

MINE WARFARE 14

MINELAYERS 3

2 *Vidar*, coastal (300–400 mines), 1 *Tyr* (amph craft
also fitted for minelaying)

MINE COUNTERMEASURES 11

4 *Oskøy* MHC, 5 *Alta* MSC, 2 diver spt

AMPHIBIOUS craft only

5 LCT, 4 S90N LCA

SUPPORT AND MISCELLANEOUS 7

1 *Horten* sub/patrol craft depot ship, 1 *Mariata*
AGOR (civ manned), 1 *Valkyrien Torpedo* recovery,
1 *Sverdrup* II, 1 Royal Yacht, 2 *Hessa* trg

ADDITIONAL IN STORE 1 *Sauda* MSC

NAVAL HOME GUARD 5,000

on mob assigned to 10 sub-districts incl 33 areas
Some 400 fishing craft

COASTAL DEFENCE

FORTRESS 17 **75mm**: 6; **120mm**: 3; **127mm**: 6;
150mm: 2 guns; 6 cable mine and 4 torpedo bty

COAST GUARD (700)

PATROL AND COASTAL CRAFT 20

PATROL, OFFSHORE 13

3 *Nordkapp* with 1 *Lynx* hel (SAR/recce), fitted for 6
Penguin Mk 2 SSM, 1 *Nornen*, 7 chartered (partly
civ manned), 2 *Chartered* (Coast Guard spec)

PATROL INSHSORE 7 PCI

AVN ac 2 P-3N *Orion* **hel** 6 *Lynx* Mk 86 (Air Force-
manned)

Air Force 7,900

(3,800 conscripts) **Flying hours** 180
OPERATIONAL COMMANDS 2 joint with
COMAIRSONOR and COMAIRNON
FGA 4 sqn with F-16A/B
FTR 1 trg sqn with F-5A/B
MR 1 sqn with 6 P-3D/N *Orion* (2 assigned to Coast
Guard)
TPT 3 sqn
 1 with C-130, 1 with DHC-6, 1 with *Falcon* 20C
 (CAL, ECM)
TRG MFI-15
SAR 1 sqn with *Sea King* Mk 43B
TAC HEL 2 sqn with Bell-412SP
SAM 6 bty NASAMS, 6 bty RB-70
AAA 10 bty L70 (with Fire-Control System 2000) org
into 5 gps

EQUIPMENT

79 cbt ac (incl 4 MR), no armed hel
AC 15 **F-5A/B** (ftr/trg) • 58 **F-16A/B** • 6* **P-3** (4 -**D**
(MR), 2 -**N** (Coast Guard)) • 6 **C-130H** (tpt) • 3
Falcon **20C** (EW/tpt Cal) • 3 **DHC-6** (tpt) • 15
MFI-15 (trg)

HEL 18 **Bell 412 SP** (tpt) • 12 *Sea King* **Mk 43B** (SAR) • 6 *Lynx* **Mk 86** (Coast Guard)

MISSILES

ASM CRV-7, *Penguin* Mk-3
AAM AIM-9L/N *Sidewinder*, AIM 120 AMRAAM

AA HOME GUARD

(on mob under comd of Air Force): 2,500; 2 bn (9 bty) AA **20mm** NM45

Forces Abroad

UN AND PEACEKEEPING

ANGOLA (UNOMA): 4 Obs. **BOSNIA** (SFOR): 579; log bn, incl hel unit with 4 Bell-412SP, fd hospital; (UNMIBH): 1 plus 10 civ pol. **CROATIA** (SFOR): 14. (UNTAES): 6 Obs, plus 34 civ pol; (UNMOP): 1 Obs. **EGYPT** (MFO): 4 Staff Officers. **FYROM** (UNPREDEP): 43 (elm Nordic bn) plus 2 Obs. **LEBANON** (UNIFIL): 616; 1 inf bn, 1 service coy, plus HQ personnel. **MIDDLE EAST** (UNTSO): 11 Obs. **WESTERN SAHARA** (MINURSO): 1 civ pol

Foreign Forces

US prepositioned eqpt for 1 MEB **Army** 23 **Air Force** 60
NATO HQ Allied Forces North Europe (HQ North)

Portugal

	1995	1996	1997	1998
GDP	esc15.1tr	esc15.8tr		
	($87bn)	($97bn)		
per capita	$12,500	$13,100		
Growth	1.9%	3.0%		
Inflation	4.0%	3.2%		
Publ debt	68.4%	67.6%		
Def exp	esc403bn	esc449bn		
	($2.7bn)	($2.9bn)		
Def bdgt			esc298bn	
			($1.7bn)	
FMA (US)	$0.5m	$0.5m	$0.8m	0.8m
$1 = escudo	151	154	172	
Population		9,871,000		
Age	*13–17*	*18–22*	*23–32*	
Men	357,000	394,000	817,000	
Women	338,000	378,000	800,000	

Total Armed Forces

ACTIVE 59,300

(12,700 conscripts; incl 4,300 Central Staff, 400 in centrally controlled formations/units)

Terms of service: **Army** 4–8 months **Navy** and **Air Force** 4–18 months

RESERVES 210,900

(all services) (obligation to age 35) **Army** 210,000 **Navy** 900

Army 32,100

(11,800 conscripts)
5 Territorial Comd (1 mil governance, 2 mil, zone, 2 mil region) • 1 mech inf bde (2 mech, 1 tk, 1 fd arty bn) • 3 inf bde, 1 AB bde • 1 lt intervention bde • 3 composite regt (3 inf bn, 2 coast arty, 2 AA bty) • 2 armd cav regt • 8 inf regt • 2 fd, 1 AD, 1 coast arty regt • 2 engr regt • 1 MP regt • 1 special ops centre

EQUIPMENT

MBT 186: 86 M-48A5, 100 M-60 (8 -A2, 92 -A3)
RECCE 15 V-150 *Chaimite*, 18 VBL M-11
APC 249 M-113, 26 M-557, 81 V-200 *Chaimite*
TOTAL ARTY 284
   TOWED 118: **105mm**: 54 M-101, 24 M-56; **155mm**: 40 M-114A1
   SP **155mm**: 6 M-109A2
   MOR 160: **107mm**: 42 M-30 (incl 14 SP); **120mm**:118 Tampella; **81mm**: incl 21 SP
   COASTAL 27: **150mm**: 15; **152mm**: 6; **234mm**: 6
RCL **84mm**: 162 *Carl Gustav*; **89mm**: 53; **90mm**: 46; **106mm**: 128 M-40
ATGW 51 TOW (incl 18 M-113, 4 M-901), 93 *Milan* (incl 6 VBL M-11)
AD GUNS 105, incl **20mm**: Rh202; **40mm**: L/60
SAM 15 *Stinger*, 5 *Chaparral*

DEPLOYMENT

AZORES AND MADEIRA 2,000; 3 composite regt (3 inf bn, 2 coast arty, 2 AA bty)

Navy 14,800

(incl 1,700 Marines and 900 conscripts plus 116 recalled reserves)
COMMANDS Naval Area Comd 1 **Subordinate Comds** Azores, Madeira, North Continental, Centre Continental, South Continental
BASES Lisbon (Alfeite), Portimão (HQ Continental Comd), Ponta Delgada (HQ Azores), Funchal (HQ Madeira)

SUBMARINES 3

3 *Albacora* (Fr *Daphné*) SS with 12 550mm TT

FRIGATES 10

3 *Vasco Da Gama* (MEKO 200) with 2 x 3 ASTT (US Mk 46), plus 2 x 4 Harpoon SSM, 1 x 8 *Sea Sparrow* SAM, 1 100mm gun (with 2 *Super Lynx* hel in some)
3 *Commandante João Belo* (Fr *Cdt Rivière*) with 2 x 3 ASTT, 2 x 100mm gun

4 *Baptista de Andrade* with 2 x 3 ASTT; plus 1 100mm gun

PATROL AND COASTAL COMBATANTS 29
PATROL, OFFSHORE 6 *João Coutinho* PCO, hel deck
PATROL, COASTAL 10 *Cacine* PCC
PATROL, INSHORE 12
5 *Argos*, 6< PCI, 1 *Dom Aleixo* PCI
RIVERINE 1 *Rio Minho*<
AMPHIBIOUS craft only
3 LCU, about 7 LCM
SUPPORT AND MISCELLANEOUS 14
1 *Berrio* (UK *Green Rover*) AO, 8 AGHS, 1 *D. Carlos 1* (ex-US *Stalwart*) AGOS, 2 trg, 1 ocean trg, 1 div spt
AIR 5 *Lynx*-Mk 95

MARINES (1,700)
3 bn (2 lt inf, 1 police), spt units
EQUIPMENT
MOR 120mm: 36

Air Force 7,700

Flying hours F-16: 180; A-7P: 160
1 op air com (COFA)
FGA 3 sqn
1 with A-7P, 1 with F-16A/B, 1 with *Alpha Jet*
SURVEY 1 sqn with C-212
MR 1 sqn with P-3P
TPT 4 sqn
1 with C-130, 1 with C-212, 1 with *Falcon* 20 and *Falcon* 50, 1 with SA-330 hel
SAR 2 sqn
1 with SA-330 hel, 1 with SA-330 hel and C-212
LIAISON 1 sqn with Reims-Cessna FTB-337G
TRG 2 sqn
1 with *Socata* TB-30 *Epsilon*, 1 with *Alpha Jet*
EQUIPMENT
96 cbt ac, no attack hel
AC 40 *Alpha Jet* (FGA trg) (plus 10 in store) • 31 **A-7** (25 **-7P** (FGA), 6* **TA-7P** (trg)) • 20 **F-16A/B** (17 -A, 3 -B) • 5* **P-3P** (MR) (plus 1 in store) • 6 **C-130H** (tpt plus SAR) • 24 **C-212** (20 -A (12 tpt/SAR, 1 Nav trg, 2 ECM trg, 5 fisheries protection), 4 **-B** (survey)) • 12 **Cessna 337** (liaison) • 1 *Falcon* 20 (tpt, cal) • 3 *Falcon* 50 (tpt) • 16 *Epsilon* (trg)
HEL 10 **SA-330** (SAR/tpt) • 18 **SA-316** (trg, utl)

Forces Abroad

UN AND PEACEKEEPING
ANGOLA (UNOMA): 296 plus 6 Obs, 39 civ pol.
BOSNIA (SFOR): 319; 1 inf bn. (UNMIBH): 60 civ pol.
CROATIA (UNMOP): 1 Obs. **FYROM** (UNPREDEP): 1 Obs. **WESTERN SAHARA** (MINURSO): 5 Obs

Paramilitary 40,900

NATIONAL REPUBLICAN GUARD 20,900
Commando Mk III APC **hel** 7 SA-315
PUBLIC SECURITY POLICE 20,000

Foreign Forces

NATO HQ IBERLANT area at Lisbon (Oeiras)
US 1,050 **Navy** 75 **Air Force** 975 (incl Azores)

Spain

	1995	1996	1997	1998
GDP	pts69.8tr	pts73.7tr		
	($560bn)	($582bn)		
per capita	$14,500	$15,100		
Growth	2.8%	2.2%		
Inflation	4.6%	3.6%		
Publ debt	69.6%	71.6%		
Def exp	pts1.1tr	pts1.1tr		
	($8.7bn)	($8.6bn)		
Def bdgt			pts870bn	
			($6.0bn)	
FMA (US)	$0.05m	$0.05m		
$1 = peseta	125	127	144	
Population		39,181,000		
Age	*13–17*	*18–22*	*23–32*	
Men	1,370,000	1,581,000	3,336,000	
Women	1,289,000	1,495,000	3,195,000	

Total Armed Forces

ACTIVE 197,500
(108,000 conscripts (to be reduced), some 200 women)
Terms of service: 9 months

RESERVES 431,900
Army 420,000 **Navy** 3,900 **Air Force** 8,000

Army 128,500

(81,500 conscripts)
8 Regional Op Comd incl 2 overseas: 1 mech div (1 armd, 2 mech bde) • 2 armd cav bde (1 cadre) • 1 mtn bde • 3 lt inf bde (cadre) • 1 air-portable bde • 1 AB bde • Spanish Legion: 1 bde (3 lt inf, 1 arty, 1 engr bn, 1 ATK coy), 2 regt (each with 1 mech, 1 mot bn, 1 ATK coy) • 3 island garrison: Ceuta and Melilla, Balearic, Canary • 1 arty bde; 1 AD regt • 1 engr bde • 1 Army Avn bde (1 attack, 1 tpt hel bn, 4 utl units) • 1 AD comd: 5 AD regt incl 1 HAWK SAM, 1 composite *Aspide*/**35mm**, 1 *Roland* bn • 1 Coastal Arty Comd (2 coast arty regt) • 3 special ops bn • Rapid Action Force

(FAR) formed from 1 Spanish Legion, 1 AB and 1 airportable bde (see above)

EQUIPMENT

MBT 776: 210 AMX-30 (150 EM2, 60 ER1), 164 M-48A5E, 294 M-60 (50 -A1, 244 -A3TTS), 108 *Leopard* 2 A4 (Ge tempy transfer)

RECCE 340 BMR-VEC (100 **90mm**, 208 **25mm**, 32 **20mm** gun)

AIFV some *Pizarro*

APC 1,995: 1,313 M-113 (incl variants), 682 BMR-600

TOTAL ARTY 1,252 (excluding coastal)

  TOWED 565: **105mm**: 283 M-26, 170 M-56 pack, 28 L 118; **155mm**: 84 M-114

  SP 208: **105mm**: 48 M-108; **155mm**: 96 M-109A1; **203mm**: 64 M-110A2

  COASTAL ARTY 53: **6in**: 44; **305mm**: 6; **381mm**: 3

  MRL 140mm: 14 *Teruel*

  MOR 120mm: 465 (incl 192 SP); plus **81mm**: 1,314 (incl 187 SP)

ATGW 442 *Milan*, 28 HOT, 200 TOW

RCL 106mm: 638

AD GUNS 20mm: 329 GAI-BO1; **35mm**: 92 GDF-002 twin; **40mm**: 183 L/70

SAM 24 I HAWK, 18 *Roland*, 13 *Skyguard/Aspide*, 108 *Mistral*

HELICOPTERS 175 (28 attack)

  53 HU-10B, 70 HA/HR-15 (31 with **20mm** guns, 28 with HOT, 9 trg), 6 HU-18, 11 HR-12B, 18 HT-21, 17 HT-17 (incl 9-D models)

SURV 2 AN/TPQ-36 (arty, mor)

DEPLOYMENT

CEUTA AND MELILLA 10,000; 2 armd cav, 2 Spanish Legion, 2 mot inf, 2 engr, 2 arty regt; 2 lt AD bn, 1 coast arty gp

BALEARIC ISLANDS 2,500; 1 mot inf regt: 3 mot inf bn; 1 mixed arty regt: 1 fd arty, 1 AD; 1 engr bn

CANARY ISLANDS 6,500; 3 mot inf regt: 2 mot inf bn; 1 mot inf bn, 2 mixed arty regt: 1 fd arty, 1 AD bn; 2 engr bn

Navy 39,000

(incl 1,000 Naval Air, 7,200 Marines and 13,500 conscripts) plus 8,000 civilians

FLEET COMMANDS 5

NAVAL ZONES Cantabrian, Strait (of Gibraltar), Mediterranean, Canary (Islands)

BASES El Ferrol (La Coruña) (Cantabrian HQ), San Fernando (Cadiz) (Strait HQ), Rota (Cadiz) (Fleet HQ), Cartagena (Murcia) (Mediterranean HQ), Las Palmas (Canary Islands HQ), Palma de Mallorca and Mahón (Menorca)

SUBMARINES 8

4 *Galerna* (Fr *Agosta*) with F-17 and L-5 HWT
4 *Delfín* (Fr *Daphné*) with F-17 and L-5 HWT

PRINCIPAL SURFACE COMBATANTS 18

CARRIERS 1 (CVV) *Príncipe de Asturias* (16,200t); air gp: typically 6 to 10 AV-8S/EAV-8B FGA, 4 to 6 SH-3D ASW hel, 2 SH-3D AEW hel, 2 utl hel

FRIGATES 17

  FFG 11 (AAW/ASW)

  6 *Santa Maria* (US *Perry*) with 1 x 1 SM-1 MR SAM/ *Harpoon* SSM launcher, 2 SH-60B hel, 2 x 3 ASTT; plus 1 76mm gun, 1–2 S-70L hel

  5 *Baleares* with 1 x 1 SM-1 MR SAM, 1 x 8 ASROC, 4 324mm and 2 484mm ASTT; plus 2 x 4 *Harpoon*, 1 127mm gun

  FF 6 *Descubierta* with 2 x 3 ASTT, 1 x 2 ASW RL; plus 2 x 2 *Harpoon* SSM

PATROL AND COASTAL COMBATANTS 32

PATROL, OFFSHORE 6

  4 *Serviola*, 2 *Chilreu*

PATROL, COASTAL 10 *Anaga* PCC

PATROL, INSHORE 16

  6 *Barceló* PFI, 10 PCI<

MINE COUNTERMEASURES 12

4 *Guadalete* (US *Aggressive*) MSO
8 *Júcar* (US *Adjutant*) MSC

AMPHIBIOUS 4

2 *Castilla* (US *Paul Revere*) amph tpt, capacity: 1,600 tps; plus some 15 amph craft
2 *Hernán Cortés* (US *Newport*) LST, capacity: 400 troops, 500t vehicles, 3 LCVPs, 1 LCPL
Plus 13 craft: 3 LCT, 2 LCU, 8 LCM

SUPPORT AND MISCELLANEOUS 34

1 AOR, 2 AO, 5 ocean tugs, 3 diver spt, 2 tpt/spt, 3 water carriers, 6 AGHS, 1 AGOR, 1 sub salvage, 1 AK, 5 trg craft, 4 sail trg

NAVAL AIR (1,000)

(290 conscripts)

Flying hours 160

FGA 1 sqn with 10 AV-8B/8 AV-8B+

LIAISON 1 sqn with 3 *Citation* II

HELICOPTERS 4 sqn

  ASW 2 sqn

    1 with SH-3D/G *Sea King* (mod to SH-3H standard)

    1 with SH-60B (LAMPS-III fit)

  COMD/TPT 1 sqn with AB-212

  TRG 1 sqn with Hughes 500

AEW 1 flt with SH-3D (*Searchwater* radar)

EQUIPMENT

18 cbt ac, 25 armed hel

AC 10 **EAV-8B**, 8 **EAV-8B** plus (trg) • 3 *Citation* II (liaison)

HEL 10 **AB-212** (ASW/SAR) • 12 **SH-3D** (9 -H ASW, 3 -D AEW) • 10 **Hughes 500** (trg) • 6 **SH-60B** (ASW)

MARINES (7,200)

(3,500 conscripts)

1 marine bde (3,500); 2 inf, 1 spt bn; 3 arty bty

5 marine garrison gp

EQUIPMENT

MBT 16 M-60A3
AFV 17 *Scorpion* lt tk, 19 LVTP-7 AAV, 28 BLR APC
TOWED ARTY 105mm: 12 M-56 pack
SP ARTY 155mm: 6 M-109A
ATGW 12 TOW, 18 *Dragon*
RL 90mm: C-90C
RCL 106mm: 54
SAM 12 *Mistral*

Air Force 30,000

(13,000 conscripts)
Flying hours EF-18: 155; F-5: 219; *Mirage* F-1: 150
CENTRAL AIR COMMAND (MACEN) 4 wg
FTR 2 sqn with EF-18 (F-18 *Hornet*)
RECCE 1 sqn with RF-4C
TPT 7 sqn
  2 with C-212, 2 with CN-235, 1 with *Falcon* (20, 50, 900), 1 with Boeing 707 (tkr/tpt), 1 with AS-332 (tpt)
SPT 5 sqn
  1 with CL-215, 1 with C-212 (EW) and *Falcon* 20, 1 with C-212, AS-332 (SAR), 1 with C-212 and Cessna *Citation*, 1 with Boeing 707
TRG 4 sqn
  1 with C-212, 1 with Beech (*Baron*), 1 with C-101, 1 with Beech (*Bonanza*)
EASTERN AIR COMMAND (MALEV) 2 wg
FTR 4 sqn
  2 with EF-18 (F-18 *Hornet*), 1 with EF-18 (/trg/FTR), 1 with *Mirage* F1
TPT 2 sqn
  1 with C-130H, 1 tkr/tpt with KC-130H
SPT 1 sqn with **ac** C-212 (SAR) **hel** AS-330
STRAIT AIR COMMAND (MAEST) 4 wg
FTR 3 sqn
  2 with *Mirage* F-1 CE/BE
  1 with EF/A-18
FGA 2 sqn with F-5B
MR 1 sqn with P-3A/B
TRG 6 sqn
  2 hel with, *Hughes* 300C, S-76C, 1 with C-212, 1 with E-26 (*Tamiz*), 1 with C-101, 1 with C-212
CANARY ISLANDS AIR COMMAND (MACAN) 1 wg
FGA 1 sqn with *Mirage* F-1EE
TPT 1 sqn with C-212
SAR 1 sqn with **ac** F-27 **hel** AS-332 (SAR)
LOGISTIC SUPPORT COMMAND (MALOG)
1 trials sqn with C-101, C-212 and F-5A
EQUIPMENT

199 cbt ac, no armed hel
AC 87 **EF/A-18 A/B** (ftr, OCU) • 29 **F-5B** (FGA) • 62 *Mirage* **F-1CF/-BE/-EE** • 14* **RF-4C** (recce) 7* **P-3** (2 **-A** (MR), 5 **-B** (MR)) • 3 **Boeing 707** (tkr/tpt) •

12 **C-130**: 7 **-H** (tpt), 5 **KC-130H** (tkr) • 76 **C-212** (31 tpt, 9 SAR, 6 recce, 26 trg, 2 EW, 2 trials) • 2 **Cessna** *Citation* (recce) • 78 **C-101** (trg) • 15 **CL-215** (spt) • 5 *Falcon* **20** (3 VIP tpt, 2 EW) • 1 *Falcon* **50** (VIP tpt) • 2 *Falcon* **900** (VIP tpt) • 3 **F-27** (SAR) • 37 **E-26** (trg) • 20 **CN-235** (18 tpt, 2 VIP tpt) • 5 **E-20** (*Baron*) trg • 23 **E-24** (*Bonanza*) trg
HEL 5 **SA-330** (SAR) • 16 **AS-332** (10 SAR, 6 tpt) • 15 **Hughes 300C** (trg) • 8 **S-76C** (trg)
MISSILES

AAM AIM-7 *Sparrow*, AIM-9 *Sidewinder*
ASM *Maverick*, *Harpoon*, HARM

Forces Abroad

UN AND PEACEKEEPING

ADRIATIC (*Sharp Guard* if re-implemented): 1 FFG.
ALBANIA (*Operation Alba*): 333, to withdraw Aug 1997; 1 inf bn. **BOSNIA** (SFOR): 1,554; 1 inf bn gp, 12 Obs, 2 TACP; (UNMIBH): 56 civ pol. **CROATIA** (SFOR): 1. **ITALY** (SFOR Air Component) 280; 8 F/A-18, 2 KC-130 (tkr), 1 CASA-212 (spt ac)

Paramilitary 75,750

GUARDIA CIVIL 75,000

(2,200 conscripts); 9 regions, 19 inf *tercios* (regt) with 56 rural bn, 6 traffic security gp, 6 rural special ops gp, 1 special sy bn; 22 BLR APC, 18 Bo-105, 5 BK-117 hel
GUARDIA CIVIL DEL MAR 750
about 27 PCI

Foreign Forces

US 2,430 **Navy** 2,200 **Air Force** 230

Turkey				
	1995	**1996**	**1997**	**1998**
GDP	L7,926tr	L14,777tr		
	($173bn)	($182bn)		
per capita	$4,500	$4,800		
Growth	7.0%	7.2%		
Inflation	88.1%	77.5%		
Debt	$73.6bn	$78.5bn		
Def exp	L303tr	L570tr		
	($6.6bn)	($7.0bn)		
Def bdgt			L610tr	L1,223tr
			($4.6bn)	($6.8bn)
FMA (US)	$413m	$321m	$177m	$177m
$1 = lira	45,845	81,405	137,257	
Population	63,222,000 (Kurds 20%)			
Age	*13–17*	*18–22*	*23–32*	
Men	3,270,000	3,262,000	5,665,000	
Women	3,132,000	3,067,000	5,401,000	

NATO *and* Non-NATO Europe

Total Armed Forces

ACTIVE ε639,000

(ε528,000 conscripts) *Terms of service:* 18 months

RESERVES 378,700

(all to age 41) **Army** 258,700 **Navy** 55,000 **Air Force** 65,000

Army ε525,000

(ε462,000 conscripts)
4 army HQ: 9 corps HQ • 1 mech div (1 mech, 1 armd bde) • 1 mech div HQ • 1 inf div • 14 armd bde (each 2 armd, 2 mech inf, 2 arty bn) • 17 mech bde (each 2 armd, 2 mech inf, 1 arty bn) • 9 inf bde (each 4 inf, 1 arty bn) • 4 cdo bde (each 4 cdo bn) • 1 inf regt • 1 Presidential Guard regt • 5 border def regt • 26 border def bn

RESERVES

4 coastal def regt • 23 coastal def bn

EQUIPMENT

MBT 4,205: 2,876 M-48 A5T1/T2, 932 M-60 (658 - A3, 274-A1), 397 *Leopard* (170-1A1, 227-1A3)
RECCE some *Akrep*
AIFV 98 AIFV
APC 738 AAPC, 2,813 M-113/-A1/-A2
TOTAL ARTY 4,274
  TOWED 1,552: **105mm**: M-101A1; **150mm**: 62 Skoda (in store); **155mm**: 517 M-114A1\A2, 171 M-59 (in store); **203mm**: 162 M-115
  SP 820: **105mm**: 362 M-52A1, 26 M-108T; **155mm**: 4 M-44A1, 164 M-44T1; **175mm**: 36 M-107; **203mm**: 9 M-55, 219 M-110A2
  MRL 60: **107mm**: 48; **227mm**: 12 MLRS
  MOR 1,842: **107mm**: 1,264 M-30 (some SP); **120mm**: 578 (some 170 SP); plus **81mm**: 3,792 incl SP
ATGW 943: 186 *Cobra*, 365 TOW SP, 392 *Milan*
RL M-72
RCL **57mm**: 923 M-18; **75mm**: 617; **106mm**: 2,329 M-40A1
AD GUNS 1,664: **20mm**: 439 GAI-DO1; **35mm**: 120 GDF-001/-003; **40mm**: 803 L60/70, 40 T-1, 262 M-42A1
SAM 108 *Stinger*, 789 *Redeye* (being withdrawn)
SURV AN/TPQ-36 (arty, mor)
AC 168: 3 Cessna 421, 34 *Citabria*, 4 B-200, 4 T-42A, 98 U-17B, 25 T-41D
ATTACK HEL 38 AH-1W/P
SPT HEL 241: 9 S-70A, 19 AS-532UL, 12 AB-204B, 64 AB-205A, 10 AB-206, 2 AB-212, 28 H-300C, 3 OH-58B, 94 UH-1H
UAV CL-89 (AN/USD-501), *Gnat* 750

Navy 51,000

(incl 3,100 Marines and 34,500 conscripts)
BASES Ankara (Navy HQ and COMEDNOREAST), Gölcük (HQ Fleet), Istanbul (HQ Northern area and Bosphorus), Izmir (HQ Southern area and Aegean), Eregli (HQ Black Sea), Iskenderun, Aksaz Bay, Mersin (HQ Mediterranean)

SUBMARINES 15

  6 *Atilay* (Ge Type 209/1200) with SST-4 HWT
  5 *Canakkale/Burakreis†* (plus 2 non-op) (US *Guppy*) with Mk 37 HWT
  2 *Hizirreis* (US *Tang*) with Mk 37 HWT
  2 *Preveze* (Ge Type 209/1400)

PRINCIPAL SURFACE COMBATANTS 21

DESTROYERS 5

  3 *Yücetepe* (US *Gearing*) (ASW/ASUW) with 2 x 3 ASTT (Mk 46 LWT); 1 with 1 x 8 ASROC, 2 with *Harpoon* SSM, all with 2 x 2 127mm guns
  2 *Alcitepe* (US *Carpenter*) with 1 x 8 ASROC, 2 x 3 ASTT, 1 x 2 127mm guns

FRIGATES 16

  4 *Yavuz* (Ge MEKO 200) with 1 AB-212 hel (ASW/OTHT), 2 x 3 ASTT; plus 2 x 4 *Harpoon* SSM, 1 127mm gun
  2 *Berk* with 2 x 3 ASTT, 2 Mk 11 *Hedgehog*
  8 *Muavenet* (US *Knox*-class) with 1 x 8 ASROC, 4 ASTT; plus *Harpoon* (from ASROC launcher), 1 127mm gun
  2 *Barbaros* (MOD Ge MEKO 200) with 2 x 4 *Harpoon* SSM, 8 x *Sea Sparrow* SSM, 1 127mm gun, 6 324mm TT, 1 AB-212 hel

PATROL AND COASTAL COMBATANTS 50

MISSILE CRAFT 18

  8 *Dogan* (Ge Lürssen-57) PFM with 2 x 4 *Harpoon* SSM
  8 *Kartal* (Ge *Jaguar*) PFM with 4 *Penguin* 2 SSM, 2 533mm TT
  2 *Yildiz* with 2 x 4 *Harpoon* SSM, 1 76mm gun

PATROL CRAFT 32

  COASTAL 11
  1 *Girne* PFC, 6 *Sultanhisar* PCC, 4 *Trabzon* PCC (1 used as AGI)
  INSHORE 21
  1 *Bora* (US *Asheville*) PFI, 12 AB-25 PCI, 4 AB-21, 4 PGM-71

MINE WARFARE 24

MINELAYERS 3

  1 *Nusret* (400 mines), 1 *Mersin* (US LSM) coastal (400 mines), 1 *Mehmetcik* (plus 3 ML tenders)
  (*Bayraktar*, *Sarucabey* and *Çakabey* LST have minelaying capability)

MINE COUNTERMEASURES 21

  11 *Selcuk* (US *Adjutant*) MSC
  6 *Karamürsel* (Ge *Vegesack*) MSC
  4 *Foça* (US *Cape*) MSI (plus 8 MCM tenders)

AMPHIBIOUS 8

1 *Osman Gazi*: capacity 980 tps, 17 tk, 4 LCVP
2 *Ertugal* (US *Terrebonne Parish*): capacity 400 tps, 18 tk
2 *Bayraktar* (US LST-512): capacity 200 tps, 16 tk
2 *Sarucabey*: capacity 600 tps, 11 tk
1 *Çakabey*: capacity 400 tps, 9 tk
Plus about 59 craft: 35 LCT, 2 LCU, 22 LCM

SUPPORT AND MISCELLANEOUS 24

1 *Akar* AO, 5 spt tkr, 2 Ge *Rhein* plus 3 other depot ships, 3 salvage/rescue, 2 survey, 3 tpt, 5 tugs, 2 repair, 1 div spt

NAVAL AVIATION

13 armed hel
ASW 3 AB-204AS, 13* AB-212 ASW
TRG 7 TB-20

MARINES (3,100)

1 regt, HQ, 3 bn, 1 arty bn (18 guns), spt units

Air Force 63,000

(31,500 conscripts) 2 tac air forces, 1 tpt comd, 1 air trg comd, 1 air log comd **Flying hours** 180
FGA 11 sqn
1 OCU with F-5A/B, 4 (1 OCU) with F-4E, 6 (1 OCU) with F-16C/D
FTR 7 sqn
2 with F-5A/B, 2 with F-4E, 3 with F-16C/D
RECCE 2 sqn with RF-4E
TPT 5 sqn
1 with C-130B/E, 1 with C-160D, 2 with CN-235, 1 VIP tpt unit with *Gulfstream*, *Citation* and CN 235
TKR 2 KC-135R
LIAISON 10 base flts with **ac** T-33 **hel** UH-1H
TRG 3 sqn
1 with T-41, 1 with SF-260D, 1 with T-38 trg schools with **ac** CN-235 **hel** UH-1H
SAM 4 sqn with 92 *Nike Hercules*, 2 sqn with 86 *Rapier*
EQUIPMENT
501 cbt ac, no attack hel
AC 175 **F-16C/D** (149 -**C**, 26 -**D**)• 107 **F-5** (63 **A/B**, 44 **NF-5A/B** (FGA)) • 181 **F-4E** (95 FGA, 47 ftr, 39 **RF-4E** (recce)) • 13 **C-130** (tpt) • 2 **KC-135R** • 19 **C-160D** (tpt) • 2 *Citation* (VIP) • 44 **CN-235** (tpt) • 39 **SF-260D** (trg) • 34 **T-33** (trg) • 60 **T-37** trg • 70 **T-38** (trg) • 28 **T-41** (trg)
HEL 21 **UH-1H** (tpt, liaison, base flt, trg schools)
MISSILES
AAM AIM-7E *Sparrow*, AIM 9 S *Sidewinder*, AIM-120 AMRAAM
ASM AGM-65 *Maverick*, AGM-88 HARM

Forces Abroad

CYPRUS 25–30,000; 1 corps; 265 M-48A5 MBT; 200 M-

113, 50 AAPC APC; 90 **105mm**, 36 **155mm**, 8 **203mm** towed; 30 **155mm** SP; 30 **120mm**, 102 **107mm**, 175 **81mm** mor; 84 **40mm** AA guns; **ac** 5 **hel** 3–4
UN AND PEACEKEEPING
ALBANIA (*Operation Alba*): ε700, to withdraw Aug 1997. **BOSNIA** (SFOR): 1,488; 1 inf bn gp; (UNMIBH): 27 civ pol. **CROATIA** (SFOR): 34. (UNPF): 2. **GEORGIA** (UNOMIG): 5 Obs. **ITALY** (SFOR Air Component): 170; 8 F-16 C. **FYROM** (UNPREDEP): 1 civ pol

Paramilitary 182,200

GENDARMERIE/NATIONAL GUARD (Ministry of Interior, Ministry of Defence in war) 180,000
50,000 reserve; some *Akrep* recce, 535 BTR-60/-80, 25 *Condor* APC **ac** 0-1E **hel** 19 Mi-17, 36 S-70A, 10 AB-206A
COAST GUARD 2,200
(1,400 conscripts); 48 PCI, 16 PCI<, plus boats, 2 tpt

Opposition

KURDISTAN WORKERS PARTY (PKK) ε5,000
plus 50,000 spt militia

Foreign Forces

NATO HQ Allied Land Forces South Eastern Europe (LANDSOUTHEAST), HQ 6 Allied Tactical Air Force (6 ATAF)
OPERATION NORTHERN WATCH
UK Air Force 230; 6 *Tornado*, 1 VC-10 (tkr)
US 3,034 **Army** 314 **Navy** 20 **Air Force** 2,700; 1 wg (**ac** on det only), numbers vary (incl F-16, F-15C, KC-135, E-3B/C, C-12, HC-130, HH-60)
ISRAEL Periodic det of F-16 at Akinci
US Installations for seismic monitoring

United Kingdom

	1995	1996	1997	1998
GDP	£700bn	£737bn		
	($1.1tr)	($1.2tr)		
per capita	$18,800	$19,600		
Growth	2.5%	2.1%		
Inflation	3.4%	2.5%		
Publ debt	60.0%	61.3%		
Def exp	£21.2bn	£21.4bn		
	($33.4bn)	($33.5bn)		
Def bdgt			£21.1bn	£22.3bn
			($35.5bn)	($37.1bn)
$1 = pound	0.63	0.64	0.60	

Population	58,526,000		

(*Northern Ireland* 1,600,000; Protestant 56%, Roman Catholic 41%)

Age	*13–17*	*18–22*	*23–32*
Men	1,840,000	1,861,000	4,391,000
Women	1,753,000	1,773,000	4,223,000

Total Armed Forces

ACTIVE 213,800

(incl 14,950 women, some 4,000 locally enlisted)

RESERVES

Army 246,900 (Regular 189,300) **Territorial Army** (TA) 57,600 **Navy/Marines** 27,200 (Regular 23,600, Volunteers and Auxiliary Forces 3,600) **Air Force** 46,700 (Regular 45,300, Volunteers and Auxiliary Forces 1,400)

Strategic Forces (1,900)

SLBM 48 msl in 3 SSBN
  SSBN 3
  3 *Vanguard* SSBN with 16 *Trident* (D5); will not deploy with more than 96 warheads (some *Trident* D5 missiles loaded with single warheads for sub-strategic role)
EARLY WARNING
Ballistic-Missile Early-Warning System (BMEWS) station at Fylingdales

Army 112,200

(incl 6,800 women and 4,100 enlisted outisde the UK, of whom 3,500 are Gurkhas)
regt normally bn size
1 Land Comd HQ • 3 Mil Districts, 3 (regenerative) div HQ (former mil districts), 1 UK Spt Comd (Germany) (UKSC(G)) • Joint Rapid Deployment Force HQ • 1 armd div with 3 armd bde, 3 arty, 4 engr, 1 avn, 1 AD regt • 1 mech div with 2 mech (*Warrior/Saxon*), 1 AB bde, 3 arty, 2 engr, 1 avn, 1 AD regt • ARRC Corps tps: 3 armd recce, 3 MLRS, 2 AD, 1 engr regt (EOD) • 1 air-mobile bde • 14 inf bde HQ (3 control ops in N. Ireland, remainder mixed regular and TA for trg/administrative purposes only)
Summary of combat arm units
  8 armd regt • 3 armd recce regt • 4 mech inf bn (*Saxon*) • 8 armd inf bn (*Warrior*) • 25 inf bn (incl 2 air mobile, 2 Gurkha) • 3 AB bn (2 only in para role) • 1 SF (SAS) regt • 12 arty regt (3 MLRS, 5 SP, 3 fd (1 cdo, 1 AB, 1 air-mobile), 1 trg) • 4 AD regt (2 *Rapier*, 2 *Javelin*) • 10 engr regt • 5 avn regt (2 ATK, 2 air mobile, 1 general)

HOME SERVICE FORCES

N. Ireland 4,700: 6 inf bn (2,700 full-time)

Gibraltar 350: 1 regt (150 full-time)

RESERVES

Territorial Army 1 armd recce, 4 lt recce, 1 NBC def, 1 armd delivery regt, 31 inf bn, 2 AB (not in role), 2 SF (SAS), 3 arty (2 fd, 1 obs), 3 AD, 9 engr, 1 avn regt

EQUIPMENT

MBT 541: 36 *Challenger* 2, 426 *Challenger*, 79 *Chieftain* (in store)
LT TK 6 *Scorpion* in store
RECCE 315 *Scimitar*, 127 *Sabre*, 11 *Fuchs*
AIFV 555 *Warrior* (plus 227 'look-alikes'), 11 AFV 432 *Rarden*
APC 892 AFV 432 (plus 808 'look-alikes'), 526 FV 103 *Spartan*, 657 *Saxon* (incl 'look-alikes'), 3 *Saracen* (in store)
TOTAL ARTY 461 (incl 2 in store)
  TOWED 217: **105mm**: 162 L-118, 7 L-119; **140mm**: 1 5.5in; **155mm**: 47 FH-70
  SP 181: 2 **105mm** *Abbot* in store; **155mm**: 179 AS-90
  MRL 227mm: 63 MLRS
MOR 81mm: 543 (incl 110 SP)
ATGW 793 *Milan*, 58 *Swingfire* (FV 102 *Striker* SP), TOW
RL 94mm: LAW-80
RCL 84mm: 302 *Carl Gustav* (in store)
SAM 56 *Starstreak* (SP), some 298 *Javelin* and *Starburst* (incl 72 FV-103 *Spartan*), 30 *Rapier* (some 24 SP)
SURV 42 *Cymbeline* (mor)
AC 7 BN-2
ATTACK HEL 270: 154 SA-341, 116 *Lynx* AH-1/-7/-9
UAV CL-89 (AN/USD-501)
LANDING CRAFT 2 LCL, 6 RCL, 4 LCVP, 4 workboats

Navy (RN) 44,900

(incl 6,750 Fleet Air Arm, 6,700 Royal Marines Command, 3,200 women)

ROYAL FLEET AUXILIARY (RFA)

(2,050 civilians) mans major spt vessels

ROYAL MARITIME AUXILIARY SERVICE (RMAS)

(290 civilians) provides harbour/coastal services
BASES UK Northwood (HQ Fleet, CINCEASTLANT), Devonport (HQ), Faslane, Portsmouth **Overseas** Gibraltar

SUBMARINES 15

STRATEGIC SUBMARINES 3 SSBN
TACTICAL SUBMARINES 12
  SSN 12
  7 *Trafalgar*
  5 *Swiftsure* with *Spearfish* or Mk 24 HWT and *Harpoon* USGW

PRINCIPAL SURFACE COMBATANTS 38

CARRIERS 3 *Invincible* CVS each with **ac** 8 *Sea Harrier*

V/STOL **hel** 12 *Sea King,* up to 9 ASW, 3 AEW; plus
1 x 2 *Sea Dart* SAM (includes 1 *Invincible* at extended
readiness)

DDG 12 *Birmingham* with 1 x 2 *Sea Dart* SAM; plus 1
Lynx hel, 2 x 3 ASTT, 1 114mm gun (2 in refit)

FRIGATES 23

4 *Cornwall* (Type 22 Batch 3) with 1 *Sea King* or 2
Lynx hel (*Sting Ray* LWT), 2 x 3 ASTT; plus 2 x 4
Harpoon SSM, 1 114mm gun

6 *Broadsword* Type 22 Batch 2 with 2 *Lynx* hel (2 with
1 *Sea King*), 2 x 3 ASTT; plus 4 MM-38 *Exocet* SSM

13 *Norfolk* (Type 23) with 1 *Lynx* hel, 2 x 2 ASTT, plus
2 x 4 *Harpoon* SSM, 1 114mm gun

PATROL AND COASTAL COMBATANTS 26

PATROL, OFFSHORE 12

2 *Castle*, 6 *Island*, 4 *River* PCO

PATROL, INSHORE 14

12 *Archer* (incl 4 trg), 2 *Ranger* PCI

MINE WARFARE 18

MINELAYER no dedicated minelayer, but all
submarines have limited minelaying capability

MINE COUNTERMEASURES 18

13 *Hunt* MCO, 5 *Sandown* MHC

AMPHIBIOUS 7

2 *Fearless* LPD (incl 1 in extended readiness) with 4
LCU, 4 LCVP; capacity 400 tps, 15 tk, 3 hel

5 *Sir Bedivere* LSL; capacity 340 tps, 16 tk, 1 hel (RFA
manned)

Plus 33 craft: 12 LCU, 21 LCVP

(see Army for additional amph lift capability)

SUPPORT AND MISCELLANEOUS 21

UNDER WAY SUPPORT 9

2 *Fort Victoria* AOR, 2 *Olwen*, 3 *Rover* AO, 2 *Fort
Grange* AF

MAINTENANCE AND LOGISTIC 4 AOT

SPECIAL PURPOSE 2

1 *Endurance*, 1 avn trg ship

SURVEY 6

2 *Bulldog*, 1 *Roebuck*, 1 *Herald*, 1 *Gleaner*, 1 *Hecla*

FLEET AIR ARM (6,750)

(300 women)

A typical CVS air group consists of 8 *Harrier*, 9 *Sea King*
(ASW), 3 *Sea King* (AEW)

Flying hours *Sea Harrier*: 180

FTR/ATK 3 ac sqn with *Sea Harrier* F/A2 plus 1 trg sqn
with *Harrier* T-4/-8

ASW 5 hel sqn with *Sea King* Mk-5/6

ASW/ATK 2 sqn with *Lynx* HAS-3 HMA8 (in indep flt)

AEW 1 hel sqn with *Sea King* AEW-2

COMMANDO SPT 3 hel sqn with *Sea King* HC-4

SAR 1 hel sqn with *Sea King* MK-5

TRG 1 sqn with *Jetstream*

FLEET SPT *Hawk*, *Mystère-Falcon* 20 (civil
registration), 1 Cessna *Conquest* (civil registration), 1
Beech *Baron* (civil registration) (op under contract)

TPT *Jetstream*

EQUIPMENT

33 cbt ac (plus 16 in store), 114 armed hel (plus 27 in
store)

AC 28 *Sea Harrier* FRS-2 (plus 14 in store) • 5* **T-4/
T-8** (trg) plus 2 in store • 15 *Hawk* (spt) • 11
Jetstream • 9 T-2 (trg) • 2 T-3 (spt) (plus 4 in store)

HEL 97 *Sea King* (54 HAS-5/6 (plus 11 in store), 33
HC-4 (plus 3 in store), 10 AEW-2) • 45 *Lynx* HAS-
3 (plus 13 in store) • 15 *Lynx* HAS-8 (plus 3 in
store)

MISSILES

ASM *Sea Skua*, *Sea Eagle*

AAM AIM-9 *Sidewinder*, AIM-120C AMRAAM

ROYAL MARINES COMMAND (6,700, incl RN and
Army)

1 cdo bde: 3 cdo; 1 cdo arty regt (Army) incl 1 bty (TA);
1 cdo log regt (joint service); 1 cdo AD bty (Army), 2
cdo engr (1 Army, 1 TA), 1 aslt sqn; 3 hel sqn ((RN) 1 lt,
2 spt) • 1 bde patrol • 1 AD tp • 2 aslt sqn • 1 gp
(*Commachio*) • Special Boat Service (SF) HQ: 5 sqn

EQUIPMENT

MOR 81mm

ATGW *Milan*

SAM *Javelin*, *Blowpipe*

HEL 9 SA-341 (*Gazelle*); plus 3 in store, 6 *Lynx* AH-7

AMPH 24 RRC, 1 LCVP, 4 LACV

Air Force (RAF) 56,700

(incl 4,950 women) **Flying hours** Tornado F-3: 183;
Tornado GR1: 210; *Harrier*: 206; *Jaguar*: 197

FGA/BBR 6 (nuclear-capable) sqn

4 with *Tornado* GR-1, 2 with *Tornado* GR-1B (maritime attack)

FGA 5 sqn

3 with *Harrier* GR-7, 2 with *Jaguar* GR-1A/B

FTR 6 sqn with *Tornado* F-3 plus 1 flt in the Falklands

RECCE 4 sqn

2 with *Tornado* GR-1A, 1 with *Canberra* PR-9, 1 with
Jaguar GR-1A/B

MR 3 sqn with *Nimrod* MR-2

AEW 2 sqn with E-3D *Sentry*

ELINT 1 ELINT with *Nimrod* R-1

TPT/TKR 3 sqn

2 with VC-10 K-2/-3/-4, 1 with *Tristar* K-1/KC-1/-2
(tkr/tpt), plus 1 flt in the Falklands

TPT 4 sqn with *Hercules* C-1/-3

LIAISON 1 comms VIP sqn with **ac** HS-125, BAe 146
hel *Wessex*, AS-355 (*Twin Squirrel*)

TARGET FACILITY/CAL 1 sqn with *Hawk* T-1/T-1A

OCU 8: *Tornado* GR-1 (with 1 wpn conversion unit),
Tornado F-3, *Jaguar* GR-1A/T2A, *Harrier* GR-7/-T10,
Hercules, *Nimrod* MR-2, SA-330/CH-47

TRG *Hawk* T-1/-1A/-1W, *Jetstream* T-1, *Bulldog* T-1,
HS-125 *Dominie* T-1, *Tucano* T-1, SA-341 (*Gazelle*),

Firefly
TAC HEL 8 sqn
  1 with CH-47 (*Chinook*), SA-341 (*Gazelle* HT3), 1 with
  CH-47 (*Chinook*) and SA-330 (*Puma*), 3 with
  Wessex HC-2, 2 with SA-330 (*Puma*), 1 with CH-47
  and *Sea King* HAR3
SAR 2 hel sqn with *Sea King* HAR-3
TRG *Sea King*, Tri-Service Defence Helicopter School
with AS-350 (*Single Squirrel*) and Bell 412

EQUIPMENT
  452 cbt ac, incl 25 MR (plus 105 in store), no armed
  hel
  AC 249 *Tornado* (90 **GR-1**, 26 **GR-1A**, 26 **GR-1B**, 107
  F-3 (plus 43 *Tornado* in store))• 54 *Jaguar* (44 **GR-
  1A/-B**, 10 **T-2A/B** (plus 27 in store) • 70 *Harrier*
  (59 **GR-7**, 11 **T-10** (plus 22 **GR-7** in store)) • 98
  Hawk **T-1/1-A-W** (54* (T1-A) tac weapons unit
  Sidewinder-capable) (plus 21 in store) • 9 *Canberra*
  (2 **T-4**, 2 **PR-7**, 5 **PR-9**) • 28 *Nimrod* (3 **R-1** (ECM),
  25* **MR-2** (MR) • 7 *Sentry* (**E-3D**) (AEW) • 9
  Tristar (2 **K-1** (tkr/tpt), 4 **KC-1** (tkr/cgo), 3 **C-2A**
  (tpt)) • 26 *VC-10* (12 **C-1/C-1K** (strategic tpt to be
  mod to tkr/tpt), 5 **K-2** (tkr), 4 **K-3** (tkr), 5 **K-4**) •
  55 *Hercules* **C-1/C-3** • 18 **BAe-125** (10 **T-1** (trg), 8
  CC-2/-3 (liaison)) • 2 *Islander* **CC-MK2** • 3 **BAe-
  146** (VIP tpt) • 73 *Tucano* (trg) (plus 44 in store) •
  11 *Jetstream* (trg) • 114 *Bulldog* (trg) • 18 *Firefly*
  HEL 17 *Wessex* • 34 **CH-47** • 39 **SA-330** • 25 *Sea
  King* • 38 **AS-350** (*Single Squirrel*) • 2 **AS-355**
  (*Twin Squirrel*) • 9 **Bell 412**

MISSILES
  ASM *Martel*, AGM-84D-1 *Harpoon*, *Sea Eagle*
  AAM ASRAAM, AIM-9G *Sidewinder*, *Sky Flash*
  ARM ALARM

ROYAL AIR FORCE REGIMENT
5 fd sqn (with 5 *Scorpion* lt tk, 11 *Saxon*, 12 *Spartan* and
81mm mor), 6 SAM sqn with 36 *Rapier* fire units
RESERVES (Royal Auxiliary Air Force): 5 fd def sqn, 1
  sqn Air Movements, 1 sqn Aero-medical
  6 flt, one each covering Intelligence, Photographic
  Interpretation, Security, Public Relations, Helicopter
  Support, Meteorological Services

Deployment

ARMY
LAND COMMAND
Assigned to ACE Rapid Reaction Corps **Germany** 1
armd div plus Corps cbt spt tps **UK** 1 mech inf div, 1
air mobile bde; additional TA units incl 8 inf bn, 2 SAS,
3 AD regt **Allied Command Europe Mobile Force**
(*Land*) (AMF(L)): UK contribution 1 inf BG (incl 1 inf
bn, 1 arty bty, 1 sigs sqn)
HQ NORTHERN IRELAND
(some 10,600, plus 4,700 Home Service); 3 inf bde HQ,
up to 12 major units in inf role (6 resident, up to 6

roulement inf bn), 1 engr, 1 avn egt, 6 Home Service inf
bn. Remainder of Army regular and TA units for
Home Defence and the defence of Dependent
Territories, the Cyprus Sovereign Base Areas and
Brunei

NAVY
FLEET (CinC is also CINCEASTLANT and
COMNAVNORTHWEST): almost all regular RN
forces are declared to NATO, split between SACLANT
and SACEUR
MARINES 1 cdo bde (declared to SACLANT)

AIR FORCE
STRIKE COMMAND responsible for all RAF front-
line forces. Day-to-day control delegated to 3 Groups
No. 1 (Strike, Attack) **No. 11/18** (Air Defence/
Maritime) **No. 38** (Transport/AAR)
PERSONNEL AND TRAINING COMMAND
responsible for personnel management and ground/
flying trg; incl Training Group Defence Agency and
Personnel Management Agency
LOGISTIC COMMAND responsible for log spt for
RAF units world-wide; Joint Service spt for RN and
Army units for rationalised eqpt

Forces Abroad

ANTARCTICA 1 ice patrol ship (in seasonal summer)
ASCENSION ISLAND RAF some 150
BRUNEI Army some 900; 1 Gurkha inf bn, 1 hel flt (3
  hel)
CANADA Army trg and liaison unit **RAF** 250; routine
  training deployment of **ac** *Tornado* GR1, *Harrier*,
  Jaguar
CYPRUS 3,700 **Army** 2,500; 2 inf bn, 1 engr spt sqn, 1
  hel flt **RAF** 1,200; 1 hel sqn (5 *Wessex* HC-2), plus **ac**
  on det
FALKLAND ISLANDS Army 1 inf coy gp, 1 engr sqn
  (fd, plant) **RN** 1 DD/FF, 1 OPV, 1 spt, 1 AR **RAF**
  (750 incl Ascension Island), 4 *Tornado* F-3, 2 *Hercules*
  C-1, 1 VC-10 K-2 (tkr), 2 *Sea King* HAR-3, 2 CH-47
  hel, 1 sqn RAF regt (*Rapier* SAM)
GERMANY 27,920 **Army** 23,600; 1 corps HQ
  (multinational), 1 armd div, 1 armd recce, 3 fd arty, 1
  AD regt **RAF** 4,320; 4 sqn with 54 *Tornado*, 2 sqn
  with 36 *Harrier*, RAF regt; 1 *Rapier* SAM sqn, 2 fd sqn
GIBRALTAR 440 **Army** 70; Gibraltar regt (350) **RN/
  Marines** 270; 2 PCI; Marine det, 2 twin *Exocet*
  launchers (coastal defence), base unit **RAF** some
  100; periodic ac det
INDIAN OCEAN (*Armilla Patrol*): 2 DD/FF, 1 spt
  Diego Garcia 1 Marine/naval party
NEPAL Army ε500 (Gurkha trg org)
WEST INDIES 1 DD/FF, 1 spt
MILITARY ADVISERS 455 in 30 countries
UN AND PEACEKEEPING
BAHRAIN (*Southern Watch*): RAF 40. **BOSNIA**

(SFOR): 3,610; 1 Augmented Brigade HQ (multinational) with 2 recce sqn, 1 armd regt(-), 1 armd inf bn, 1 tk sqn, 3 arty bty (2 hy, 1 lt), 1 engr regt **hel** 4 *Sea King* H-C4 (RN), 9 *Lynx* AH-7 (Army), 4 *Gazelle* (Army) 4 CH-47 *Chinook* (RAF); (UNMIBH): 30 civ pol. (UNTAES): 1. **CROATIA** (SFOR): 1,793 incl log and spt tpts. **CYPRUS** (UNFICYP): 390; 1 bn in inf role, 1 hel flt, engr spt (incl spt for UNIFIL). **GEORGIA** (UNOMIG): 8 Obs. **IRAQ/KUWAIT** (UNIKOM): 11 Obs. **ITALY** (SFOR Air Component): 350; 14 *Jaguar* GR-1B, 1 K-1 *Tristar* (tkr), 2 E-3D *Sentry*; 1 C-130 (tpr, tpt). **SAUDI ARABIA** (*Southern Watch*): 400; 6 *Tornado* GR-IA, 1 VC-10 (tkr). **TURKEY** (*Northern Watch*): RAF: 330; 6 *Tornado*, GRI, 1 VC-10 tkr

Foreign Forces

US 11,646 **Army** 376 **Navy** 1,700 **Air Force** 9,570; 1 Air Force HQ (3rd Air Force) 1 ftr wg, 66 cbt ac, 2 sqn with 48 F-15E, 1 sqn with 18 F-15C/D. 1 Special Ops Gp, 3 sqn: 1 with 5 MH-53J, 1 with 4 HC-130, 1 with 4 MC-130H, 1 air refuelling wg with 9 KC-135
GERMANY/ITALY tri-national *Tornado* trg sqn
NATO HQ Allied Forces North-west Europe (AFNORTHWEST), HQ Allied Naval Forces North-west Europe (NAVNORTHWEST), HQ Allied Air Forces North-west Europe (AIR NORTH WEST), HQ Eastern Atlantic Area (EASTLANT)

Non-NATO Europe

Albania

	1995	1996	1997	1998
GDP	leke225bn	leke266bn		
	($1.4bn)	($1.5bn)		
per capita	$3,300	$3,600		
Growth	8.6%	8.2%		
Inflation	8.0%	12.0%		
Debt	$709m	$824m		
Def exp	εleke8.2bn	εleke10.5bn		
	($89m)	($100m)		
Def bdgt			εleke8.3bn	
			($55m)	
FMA[a] (US)	$0.6m	$0.4m	$0.6m	$0.6m
$1 = leke	93	105	152	
[a] Operation Alba 1997 ε$150m				
Population		3,638,000		

(Muslim 70%, Greek Orthodox 20%, Roman Catholic 10%; Greek ε3–8%)

Age	13–17	18–22	23–32
Men	182,000	173,000	322,000
Women	167,000	158,000	299,000

Total Armed Forces

The Albanian armed forces have yet to be re-constituted following the civil unrest in early 1997. Personnel str and eqpt details are those reported prior to the unrest and should be treated with caution.

EQUIPMENT
MBT 138 T-34 (in store), 721 T-59
LT TK 35 Type-62
RECCE 15 BRDM-1
APC 103 PRC Type-531
TOWED ARTY 122mm: 425 M-1931/37, M-30, 208 PRC Type-60; **130mm**: 100 PRC Type-59-1; **152mm**: 90 PRC Type-66
MRL 107mm: 270 PRC Type-63
MOR 82mm: 259; **120mm**: 550 M-120; **160mm**: 100 M-43
RCL 82mm: T-21
ATK GUNS 45mm: M-1942; **57mm**: M-1943; **85mm**: 61 D-44 PRC Type-56; **100mm**: 50 Type-86
AD GUNS 23mm: 12 ZU-23-2/ZPU-1; **37mm**: 100 M-1939; **57mm**: 82 S-60; **85mm**: 30 KS-12; **100mm**: 56 KS-19

Navy 2,500

(incl ε250 conscripts)
BASES Durrës, Sarandë, Shëngjin Vlorë
SUBMARINES I
  1 Sov *Whiskey* with 533mm TT †
PATROL AND COASTAL COMBATANTS† 3I
TORPEDO CRAFT 24 PRC *Huchuan* PHT with 2 533mm TT
PATROL CRAFT 7
  2 Sov *Kronshdat* PCO, 3 PRC *Shanghai* II, 2 Sov Po-2 PFI
MINE COUNTERMEASURES† 3
  1 Sov T-43 (in reserve), 2 Sov T-301 MSI (2 in reserve)
SUPPORT I4
  2 Sov *Khobi* harbour tkr, 2 Sov *Shalanda* AK, 1 *Sekstan*, 1 *Poluchat*, 1 *Nyryat*, 1 *Toplivo*, 2 *Tugur*, 4 *Arcor* 25

Air Force 6,000

(1,500 conscripts); 98 cbt ac†, no armed hel
Flying hours 10–15
FGA 1 air regt with 10 J-2 (MiG-15), 14 J-6 (MiG-17), 23 J-6 (MiG-19)
FTR 2 air regt
  1 with 20 J-6 (MiG-19), 10 J-7 (MiG-21)
  1 with 21 J-6 (MiG-19)
TPT 1 sqn with 10 C-5 (An-2), 3 Il-14M, 6 Li-2 (C-47)
HEL 1 regt with 20 Z-5 (Mi-4)
TRG 8 CJ-5, 15 MiG-15UTI, 6 Yak-11
SAM† some 4 SA-2 sites, 22 launchers

Forces Abroad

UN AND PEACEKEEPING
BOSNIA (SFOR): 36. GEORGIA (UNOMIG): 1 Obs

Paramilitary

INTERNAL SECURITY FORCE
PEOPLE'S MILITIA
BORDER POLICE (Ministry of Public Order)

Foreign Forces

OPERATION ALBA some 6,000
A, Da, Fr, Gr, It, Sp, R (to withdraw by Aug 1997)

Armenia

	1995	1996	1997	1998
GDP	d543bn	d660bn		
	($1.3bn)	($1.4bn)		
per capita	$2,400	$2,500		
Growth	6.9%	5.9%		
Inflation	176%	20%		
Debt	$374m	$469m		
Def exp	εd32bn	εd37bn		
	($79m)	($89m)		
Def bdgt		εd47bn		
		($92m)		
FMA (US)		$0.3m	$0.3m	
$1 = dram	406	415	510	
Population		3,782,000		
(Azeri 3%, Kurd 2%, Russian 2%)				
Age	*13–17*	*18–22*	*23–32*	
Men	181,000	164,000	282,000	
Women	176,000	160,000	275,000	

Total Armed Forces some 60,000

incl 1,400 MoD and comd staff
Terms of service: conscription, 18 months

RESERVES
some mob reported, possibly 300,000 with mil service within 15 years

Army some 58,600

(incl 4,000 Air Component; conscripts)
1 Army HQ • 3 MR bde; 10 indep MRR • 1 SF regt • 1 arty bde; 1 SP arty regt • 1 ATK regt • 1 SAM bde, 1 SAM, 1 AA regt • 1 ground attack sqn • 1 indep hel sqn, 1 avn trg centre
EQUIPMENT (CFE declared totals as at 1 Jan 1997)

MBT 102 T-72
AIFV 168 BMP-1/-2, 10 BMD-1
APC some 50 BTR-60/-70/-80
TOTAL ARTY 225
  TOWED 121: **122mm**: 59 D-30; **152mm**: 2 D-1, 34 D-20, 26 2A36
  SP 38: **122mm**: 10 2S1; **152mm**: 28 2S3
  MRL 122mm: 47 BM-21
  MOR 120mm: 19 M-120
ATK GUNS 105: **85mm**: D-44; **100mm**: T-12
ATGW 18 AT-3 *Sagger*, 27 AT-6 *Spiral*
SAM 25 SA-2/-3, 54 SA-4, 20 SA-8, SA-13
SURV GS-13 (veh), *Long Trough* ((SNAR-1) arty), *Pork Trough* ((SNAR-2/-6) arty), *Small Fred/Small Yawn* (arty), *Big Fred* ((SNAR-10) veh/arty)
AIR COMPONENT (4,000 incl AD):
  FGA 6 cbt ac, 7 armd hel
    5* Su-25, 1* MiG-25 1 hel sqn with 7 Mi-24 (attack), 2 Mi-9, 8 Mi-8, 5 Mi-24K/P
  AIR TRG CENTRE 7 Mi-2 hel, 24 ac (An-2, Yak-52, Yak-55, Yak-18T)

Paramilitary 1,000

MINISTRY OF INTERIOR ε1,000
4 bn: 34 BMP-1, 30 BTR-60/-70/-152

Foreign Forces

RUSSIA 4,300 **Army** 1 mil base (bde+) with 74 MBT, 158 ACV, 84 arty/MRL/mor **Air Defence** 1 sqn MiG-23

Austria

	1995	1996	1997	1998
GDP	OS2.4tr	OS2.4tr		
	($206bn)	($228bn)		
per capita	$20,000	$21,000		
Growth	1.8%	3.0%		
Inflation	2.3%	2.3%		
Publ Debt	69.3%	69.8%		
Def exp	OS21.5bn	OS21.7bn		
	($2.1bn)	($2.1bn)		
Def bdgt			OS20.9bn	OS21.4bn
			($1.7bn)	($1.7bn)
$1 = OS	10.1	10.6	12.5	
OS = Austrian schilling				
Population		8,044,000		
Age	*13–17*	*18–22*	*23–32*	
Men	239,000	253,000	639,000	
Women	228,000	242,000	616,000	

Total Armed Forces

(Air Service forms part of the Army)

ACTIVE some 45,500

(incl 28,400 active and short term; 16,600 conscripts; some 66,000 reservists a year undergo refresher trg, a proportion at a time)
Terms of service: 7 months recruit trg, 30 days reservist refresher trg during 10 years (or 8 months trg, no refresher); 60–90 days additional for officers, NCO and specialists

RESERVES

100,700 ready (72 hrs) reserves; 990,000 with reserve trg, but no commitment. Officers, NCO and specialists to age 65, remainder to age 50

Army some 45,500

(16,600 conscripts)
3 Corps
  2 each with 1 engr bn, 1 recce, 1 arty regt, 3 Provincial mil comd, 9 inf regt (total)
  1 with 3 mech inf bde (1 tk, 1 mech inf, 1 SP arty bn), 1 engr, 1 recce bn, 1 arty regt, 2 Provincial mil comd, 2 inf regt
1 Provincial mil comd with 1 inf regt, 1 inf bn
EQUIPMENT
  MBT 169 M-60A3, 5 *Leopard*
  APC 465 Saurer 4K4E/F, ε68 *Pandur* (being delivered)
  TOWED ARTY 105mm: 108 IFH (M-2A1)
  SP ARTY 155mm: 124 M-109/-A2 (plus 54 -A5Ö being delivered)
  FORTRESS ARTY 155mm: 24 SFK M-2 (deactivated)
  MRL 128mm: 18 M-51 (in store)
  MOR 81mm: 498; **120mm**: 242 M-43
  ATGW 226 RBS-56 *Bill*
  RCL 2,196 incl **74mm**: *Miniman*; **84mm**: *Carl Gustav*; **106mm**: 445 M-40A1 (in store)
  ANTI-TANK GUNS
    SP 105mm: 284 *Kuerassier* JPz SK (50 in store)
    TOWED 85mm: 205 M-52/-55 (in store)
    STATIC 105mm: some 227 L7A1 (*Centurion* tk)
  AD GUNS 20mm: 426

MARINE WING
  (under School of Military Engineering)
  2 river patrol craft<; 10 unarmed boats

Air Force (4,250)

(3,400 conscripts); 53 cbt ac, no armed hel
Flying hours 130
1 air div HQ, 3 air regt, 3 AD regt, 1 air surv regt
FTR/FGA 1 wg with 24 SAAB J-35Oe
HELICOPTERS
  LIAISON 11 OH-58B, 11 AB-206A
  TPT 23 AB-212; 8 AB-204 (9 in store)
  SAR 24 SA-319 *Alouette* III

TPT 2 *Skyvan* 3M
LIAISON 14 O-1 (L-19A/E), 12 PC-6B
TRG 16 PC-7, 29* SAAB 105Oe
AD 76 *Mistral*; 132 **20mm** AA guns: 74 Twin **35mm** AA towed guns with *Skyguard* radars; air surv *Goldhaube* with *Selenia* MRS-403 3D radars

Forces Abroad

UN AND PEACEKEEPING
ALBANIA (*Operation Alba*): ε100, to withdraw by Aug 1997. **BOSNIA** (SFOR): 225. (UNMBIH): 23 civ pol. **CROATIA** (UNTAES): 11 civ pol. (SFOR): 5. **CYPRUS** (UNFICYP): 314; 1 inf bn. **GEORGIA** (UNOMIG): 4 Obs. **IRAQ/KUWAIT** (UNIKOM): 34 plus 5 Obs. **MIDDLE EAST** (UNTSO): 12 Obs. **SYRIA** (UNDOF): 464; 1 inf bn. **TAJIKISTAN** (UNMOT): 3 Obs. **WESTERN SAHARA** (MINURSO): 4 Obs, plus 2 civ pol

Azerbaijan

	1995	1996	1997	1998
GDP	m9.7tr	m10.5tr		
	($2.2bn)	($2.3bn)		
per capita	$1,400	$1,400		
Growth	-8.3%	1.2%		
Inflation	412%	20%		
Debt	$321m	$572m		
Def exp	εm480bn	εm560bn		
	($107m)	($133m)		
Def bdgt			εm477bn	
			($120m)	
FMA (US)		$0.25m	$0.25m	
$ = manat	4,500	4,200	3,968	
Population		7,718,000		
(Daghestani 3%, Armenian 2%, Russian 2%,)				
Age	*13–17*	*18–22*	*23–32*	
Men	386,000	341,000	607,000	
Women	363,000	326,000	651,000	

Total Armed Forces

ACTIVE 66,700
Terms of service: 17 months, but can be extended for ground forces

RESERVES
some mob 560,000 with mil service within 15 years

Army 53,300

1 MRD • 18 MR bde (incl 2 trg) • 2 arty bde, 1 ATK regt
EQUIPMENT (CFE declared totals as at 1 Jan 1997)

MBT 270: 147 T-72, 123 T-55
AIFV 287: 114 BMP-1, 96 BMP-2, 3 BMP-3, 41 BMD,
   33 BRM-1
APC 270: 25 BTR-60, 28 BTR-70, 11 BTR-80, 10 BTR-
   D, 196 MT-LB
TOTAL ARTY 301
   TOWED 151: **122mm**: 95 D-30; **152mm**: 32 D-20,
   24 2A36
   SP 122mm: 14 2S1
   COMBINED GUN/MOR 120mm: 28 2S9
   MRL 122mm: 56 BM-21
   MOR 120mm: 52 PM-38
SAM 60+ SA-4/-8/-13
SURV GS-13 (veh); *Long Trough* ((SNAR-1) arty),
   Pork Trough (SNAR-2/-6) arty), *Small Fred/Small
   Yawn* (veh, arty), *Big Fred* ((SNAR-10) veh, arty)

Navy 2,200

As a member of the CIS, Azerbaijan's naval forces
operate under CIS (Russian) control
BASE Baku
PRINCIPAL SURFACE COMBATANTS 2
FRIGATES 2 *Petya* II with 4 76mm gun, 5 406mm TT
PATROL AND COASTAL COMBATANTS 18
MISSILE CRAFT 3 *Osa* II PFM with 4 SS-N-2B *Styx*
   SSM
PATROL, INSHORE 15
   10 *Stenka* PFI, 1 *Zhuk* PCI, 3 SO-1 PCI, 1 *Svetlyak* PCI
MINE COUNTERMEASURES 15
   5 *Sonya* MSC, 4 *Yevgenya* MSI, 2 *Yurka* MCC, 3 *Vanya*
   MCC, 1 T-43 MSC
AMPHIBIOUS 4
   4 *Polnochny* LSM capacity 180 tps
SUPPORT AND MISCELLANEOUS 2
   1 *Vadim Popov* (research), 1 *Balerian Uryvayev*
   (research)

Air Force 11,200

36 cbt ac, 15 attack hel
FGA regt with 4* Su-17, 5* Su-24, 2* Su-25, 4* MiG-21,
   18 L-29, 12 L-39
FTR sqn with 16 MiG-25, 3 MiG-25UB
RECCE sqn with 2 MiG-25
TPT 5 ac (An-2, An-12, Yak-40)
HEL 1 regt with 7 Mi-2, 13 Mi-8, 15* Mi-24 (20 **ac** incl
   17 MiG-25, MiG-21, Su-24 in store)
SAM 100 SA-2/-3/-5

Paramilitary ε40,000

MILITIA (Ministry of Internal Affairs) 20,000+

POPULAR FRONT (Karabakh People's Defence)
ε20,000

Opposition

ARMED FORCES OF NAGORNO-KARABAKH
ε20–25,000
(incl ε8,000 personnel from Armenia)
   EQPT (reported) incl 120+ T-72, T-55 MBT; 200 ACV
   incl BTR-70/-80, BMP-1/-2; 200 arty incl D-44, D-
   30, 2S1, 2S3, BM-21, KS-19

Belarus

	1995	1996	1997	1998
GDP	r118.5tr	r179.8tr		
	($10.3bn)	($11.6bn)		
per capita	$5,200	$5,400		
Growth	-10.2%	2.0%		
Inflation	709%	53%		
Debt	$1.6bn	$2.0bn		
Def exp	εr5.7tr	εr7.6tr		
	($496m)	($490m)		
Def bdgt			εr2.7tr	
			($117m)	
FMA[a] (US)	$0.1m	$0.8m	$0.8m	$0.3m
$1 = rubel	11,500	15,500	43,350	

[a] Excl US Cooperative Threat Reduction programme: 1992–
96 $119m budget, of which $44m spent by Sept 1996.
Programme continues in 1997–98

Population	10,421,000		
(Russian 13%, Polish 4%, Ukrainian 3%)			
Age	13–17	18–22	23–32
Men	400,000	380,000	696,000
Women	387,000	372,000	699,000

Total Armed Forces

ACTIVE ε81,800

incl about 1,200 MoD staff, 3,400 women and ε4,700 in
centrally controlled units; 40,000 conscripts
Terms of service: 18 months

RESERVES some 289,500

with mil service within last 5 years

Army 50,500

MoD tps: 2 MRD (1 trg), 1 ABD, 1 indep AB bde, 1 arty
   div, 2 arty, 2 MRL regt
1 rear defence div (reserve inf units only)
1 SSM, 1 ATK, 1 *Spetsnaz*, 2 SAM bde
3 Corps
   1 with 3 mech, 1 SSM, 1 SAM bde, 1 arty, 1 MRL regt
   1 with 1 mech, 1 SSM, 1 SAM bde, 1 arty, 1 MRL regt
   1 with no manned cbt units
EQUIPMENT
   MBT 1,778: T-55, T-62, T-72

LT TK 8 PT-76
AIFV 1,956: 388 BMP-1, 1,265 BMP-2, 161 BRM, 142
BMD-1
APC 1,020: 188 BTR-60, 451 BTR-70, 195 BTR-80, 115
BTR-D, 71 MT-LB
TOTAL ARTY 1,519 incl
  TOWED 382: **122mm**: 190 D-30; **152mm**: 6 M-1943
  (D-1), 136 2A65, 50 2A36
  SP 586: **122mm**: 239 2S1; **152mm**: 166 2S3, 120 2S5;
  152mm: 13 2S19; **203mm**: 48 2S7
  COMBINED GUN/MOR 120mm: 54 2S9
  MRL 419: **122mm**: 275 BM-21, 11 9P138; **130mm**: 1
  BM-13; **220mm**: 84 9P140; **300mm**: 48 9A52
  MOR 120mm: 78 2S12
ATGW 480: AT-4 *Spigot*, AT-5 *Spandrel* (some SP),
AT-6 *Spiral* (some SP), AT-7 *Saxhorn*
SSM 60 *Scud*, 36 FROG/SS-21
SAM 350 SA-8/-11/-12/-13
SURV GS-13 (arty), *Long Trough* ((SNAR-1) arty),
Pork Trough ((SNAR-2/-6) arty), *Small Fred/Small
Yawn* (veh, arty), *Big Fred* ((SNAR-10) veh, arty)

Air Force 22,000

(incl 10,000 Air Defence); 1 air army, 230 cbt ac, 74
attack hel **Flying hours** 40
FGA 30 Su-24, 99 Su-25
FTR 67 MiG-29, 22 Su-27
RECCE 12* Su-24
HELICOPTERS
  ATTACK 74 Mi-24
  EW 25 Mi-8
  CBT SPT 4 Mi-24K, 6 Mi-24P, 100 Mi-8
TPT ac 29 Il-76, 6 An-12, 7 An-24, 1 An-26, 1 Tu-134 **hel**
26 Mi-2, 14 Mi-26
AWAITING ELIMINATION 4 MiG-23, 16 Su-17

AIR DEFENCE (10,000)
SAM 175 SA-3/-5/-10

Paramilitary 8,000

BORDER GUARDS (Ministry of Interior) 8,000

Bosnia-Herzegovina

	1995	1996	1997	1998
GDP		ε$4bn		
per capita		ε$4,000		
Growth		ε25%		
Debt		ε$2bn		
Def exp	ε$600m	ε$250m		
Def bdgt[a]			ε$250m	
FMA[bc] (US)		$0.3m	$0.5m	$0.6m
$ = dinar		65	150	

[a] Excl Bosnian Serb def bdgt of ε$62m

[b] Eqpt and trg valued at ε$450m from US, Sau, Kwt, UAE,
Et and Tu in 1996–97
[c] UNPROFOR **1995** $1.5bn; UNMIBH **1996** $163m **1997**
$170m; IFOR **1996** ε$5bn; SFOR **1997** ε$4bn

Population	ε4,000,000		
(Serb 40%, Muslim 38%, Croat 22%)			
Age	*13–17*	*18–22*	*23–32*
Men	190,000	177,000	350,000
Women	180,000	167,000	331,000

The data outlined below represent the situation prior to the
signing of a comprehensive peace agreement on 14 December
1995. BiH and HVO forces are to merge and form the armed
forces of a Muslim–Croat Federation with a probable structure
of 4 Corps, 15 bde (incl 1 rapid-reaction) and an arty div. It is
reported that this force will be equipped with 273 MBT (45),
227 ACV (80), 1,000 arty (60), 14 attack hel. Figures in ( )
denote eqpt delivered in country, but under US control.

Total Armed Forces

ACTIVE some 40,000

RESERVES some 100,000

Army (BiH) some 40,000

1 'Army' HQ • 5 'Corps' HQ • 2 div HQ • 40+ inf/
armd/mot inf bde • 1 SF 'bde' • 1 recce bde • 19 arty/
ATK/AD regt
EQUIPMENT
  MBT 80 incl T-34, T-55
  APC 70
  TOTAL ARTY (incl hy mor) 2,500
    ARTY incl **122mm**, **130mm**, **203mm**
    MRL incl **262mm**: M-87 *Orkan*
    MOR 82mm; **120mm**
  ATGW 100 AT-3 *Sagger*, *Red Arrow* (TF-8) reported
  AD GUNS 20mm, **30mm**
  SAM SA-7/-14
  HEL 10 Mi-8/-17, 15 UH-1H
  AC 3 UTVA-75

Other Forces

CROAT (Croatian Defence Council (HVO)) 16,000
4 MD • 4 guard, 1 arty bde, 1 inf regt, 1 armd, 1 MP
bn, 1 Home Def regt
  RESERVES 24 Home Def, 1 inf, 1 arty regt, 7 Home
  Def, 2 arty, 1 AD, 1 SF bn

  EQUIPMENT
  MBT ε50, incl T-34, T-55, M-84/T-72M, M-47
  AFV ε30 M-60, M-80
  TOTAL ARTY some 1,250 incl
    TOWED incl **76mm**: M-48; **105mm**: M-56; **122mm**:

D-30; **130mm**: M-46
MRL **122mm**: BM-21; **128mm**: M-63, M-77
MOR **82mm**
ATGW AT-3 *Sagger*, AT-4 *Fagot*, AT-6 (reported)
RL ε100 *Armbrust*, M-79, RPG-7/-22
RCL **84mm**: 30 *Carl Gustav*
AD GUNS **20mm**: M-55, Bov-3; **30mm**: M-53;
57mm: S-60
SAM SA-7/-9/-14/-16
HEL Mi-8, Mi-24, MD-500

SERB (Army of the Serbian Republic of Bosnia and Herzegovina–SRB (BH)) 30,000+
3 'Corps' HQ • 40+ inf/armd/mot inf bde • 1 SF 'bde'
• 11 arty/ATK/AD regt

EQUIPMENT
MBT 570 incl T-34, T-55, M-84, T-72
APC 360
TOTAL ARTY some 4,000 incl
TOWED **122mm**: D-30, M-1938 (M-30); **130mm**:
M-46; **152mm**: D-20
SP **122mm**: 2S1
MRL **128mm**: M-63; **262mm**: M-87 *Orkan*
MOR **120mm**
SSM FROG-7
AD GUNS 975: incl **20mm**, **23mm** incl ZSU 23-4;
30mm: M53/59SP; **57mm**: ZSU-57-2; **90mm**
SAM SA-2, some SA-6/-7B/-9/-13
AC some 20 *Galeb*, *Jastreb*, G-4 *Super Galeb* and *Orao*,
UTVA, *Kraguj*, Cessna
HEL 12 Mi-8, 12 SA-341 *Gazela*

Foreign Forces

NATO (SFOR): some 33,000: Be, Ca, Da, Fr, Ge, Gr, It, Lu, Nl, No, Por, Sp, Tu, UK, US **Non-NATO** Alb, Aus, A, Cz, Ea, Et, SF, HKJ, Hu, Lat, L, Mal, Mor, NZ, Pl, R, RSA, RF, Swe, Ukr
UN (UNMIBH): 1,902 civ pol from 38 countries

Bulgaria

	1995	1996	1997	1998
GDP	L871bn	L1,981bn		
	($13.0bn)	($10.4bn)		
per capita	$4,600	$4,300		
Growth	2.6%	-10%		
Inflation	62%	123%		
Debt	$10.9bn	$10.2bn		
Def exp	L28.0bn	L65.0bn		
	($417m)	($342m)		
Def bdgt			L570bn	
			($324m)	
FMA (US)	$0.4m	$5.0m	$0.8m	$0.9m
$1 = leva	67	190	1,758	

Population	8,339,000		
(Turk 9%, Macedonian 3%, Romany 3%)			
Age	*13–17*	*18–22*	*23–32*
Men	300,000	313,000	581,000
Women	285,000	297,000	559,000

Total Armed Forces

ACTIVE ε101,500
(incl ε49,300 conscripts, about 22,300 centrally controlled, 3,400 MoD staff, but excl some 10,000 construction tps)
Terms of service: 18 months

RESERVES 303,000
Army 250,500 **Navy** (to age 55, officers 60 or 65) 7,500
Air Force (to age 60) 45,000

Army 50,400

(ε33,300 conscripts)
3 Mil Districts/Army HQ
1 with 1 tk bde • 1 with 1 MRD, 1 Regional Training Centre (RTC), 1 tk, 1 mech bde • 1 with 2 MRD, 2 RTC, 2 tk bde
Army tps: 4 *Scud*, 1 SS-23, 1 SAM bde, 3 arty, 3 ATK, 3 AD arty, 1 SAM regt
1 AB bde

EQUIPMENT
MBT ε1,475: ε1,042 T-55, 433 T-72
ASLT GUN 68 SU-100
RECCE 58 BRDM-1/-2
AIFV 100 BMP-1, 114 BMP-23, BMP-30
APC 1,894: 781 BTR-60, 1,113 MT-LB (plus 1,270 'look-alikes')
TOTAL ARTY 1,750 (CFE total as at 1 Jan 97)
TOWED **100mm**: M-1944 (BS-3); **122mm**: M-30, M-1931/37 (A-19); **130mm**: M-46; **152mm**: M-1937 (ML-20), D-20
SP **122mm**: 2S1
MRL **122mm**: BM-21
MOR 444: **120mm**: M-38, 2B11, B-24, *Tundzha* SP
SSM launchers: 28 FROG-7, 36 *Scud*, 8 SS-23
ATGW 200 AT-3 *Sagger*
ATK GUNS **85mm**: 150 D-44; **100mm**: 200 T-12
AD GUNS 400: **23mm**: ZU-23, ZSU-23-4 SP; **57mm**: S-60; **85mm**: KS-12; **100mm**: KS-19
SAM 20 SA-3, 27 SA-4, 20 SA-6
SURV GS-13 (veh), *Long Trough* ((SNAR-1) arty), *Pork Trough* ((SNAR-2/-6) arty), *Small Fred/Small Yawn* (veh, arty), *Big Fred* ((SNAR-10) veh, arty)

Navy ε6,100

(ε2,000 conscripts)
BASES Coastal Varna (HQ), Atya **Danube** Vidin (HQ), Balchik, Sozopol. Zones of operational control at Varna and Burgas

SUBMARINES 2

2 *Pobeda* (Sov *Romeo*)-class with 533mm TT†

FRIGATES 1

1 *Smeli* (Sov *Koni*) with 1 x 2 SA-N-4 SAM, 2 x 12 ASW RL; plus 2 x 2 76mm guns

PATROL AND COASTAL COMBATANTS 23

CORVETTES 7

4 *Poti* ASW with 2 ASW RL, 4 ASTT

1 *Tarantul* II ASUW with 2 x 2 SS-N-2C *Styx*, 2 x 4 SA-N-5 *Grail* SAM; plus 1 76mm gun

2 *Pauk* I with 1 SA-N-5 SAM, 2 x 5 ASW RL; plus 4 406mm TT

MISSILE CRAFT 6 *Osa* I/II PFM with 4 SS-N-2A/B *Styx* SSM

PATROL, INSHORE about 10 *Zhuk* PFI

MINE WARFARE 29

MINELAYERS 10 *Vydra*

MINE COUNTERMEASURES 19

4 *Sonya* MSC, 15 MSI (4 *Vanya*, 4 *Yevgenya*, 5 *Olya*, 2 PO-2)

AMPHIBIOUS 2

2 Sov *Polnocny* LSM, capacity 150 tps, 6 tk Plus 7 LCU and 16 in reserve

SUPPORT AND MISCELLANEOUS 7

2 AOT, 2 AGHS, 1 AGI, 1 trg, 1 AT

NAVAL AVIATION

9 armed hel
HEL 1 ASW sqn with 6 Mi-14, 3 Ka-25
COASTAL ARTY 2 regt, 20 bty
GUNS 100mm: ε150; **130mm:** 4 SM-4-1
SSM SS-C-1B *Sepal*, SSC-3 *Styx*

NAVAL GUARD

3 coy

Air Force 19,300

(14,000 conscripts); 217 cbt ac, 44 attack hel, 1 Tactical Aviation corps, 1 AD corps **Flying hours** 30–40
FGA 3 regt
1 with 39 Su-25
2 with 41 MiG-21, 1 regt with 32 MiG-23
FTR 4 regt with some 40 MiG-23, 23 MiG-21, 21 MiG-29
RECCE 1 regt with 21 Su-22
TPT 1 regt with 2 Tu-134, 3 An-24, 4 An-26, 5 L-410, 3 Yak-40 (VIP)
SURVEY 1 An-30
HEL 2 regt with 14 Mi-2, 7 Mi-8, 25 Mi-17, 44 Mi-24 (attack)
TRG 3 trg regt with 6 Yak-18, 73 L-29, 35 L-39
MISSILES
ASM AS-7 *Kerry*
AAM AA-2 *Atoll*, AA-7 *Apex*, AA-8 *Aphid*
SAM SA-2/-3/-5/-10 (20 sites, some 110 launchers)

Forces Abroad

UN AND PEACEKEEPING
ANGOLA (UNOMA): 10 Obs plus 16 civ pol.
BOSNIA (UNMBIH): 16 civ pol. **TAJIKISTAN** (UNMOT): 2 Obs.

Paramilitary 34,000

BORDER GUARDS (Ministry of Interior) 12,000
12 regt; some 50 craft incl about 12 Sov PO2 PCI<
SECURITY POLICE 4,000
RAILWAY AND CONSTRUCTION TROOPS 18,000

Croatia

	1995	1996	1997	1998
GDP	k90bn	k102bn		
	($18.1bn)	($18.8bn)		
per capita	$5,300	$5,700		
Growth	1.7%	4.5%		
Inflation	2.0%	3.5%		
Debt	$3.9bn	$4.9bn		
Def exp	k9.3bn	k7.0bn		
	($1.8bn)	($1.3bn)		
Def bdgt			k7.8bn	
			($1.2bn)	
FMA[a] (US)	$0.1m	$0.2m	$0.4m	$0.4m
$1 = kuna	5.23	5.43	6.29	

[a] UNPROFOR **1995** $1.5bn; UNTAES **1996** $292m **1997** $266m; UNMOP (UNMIBH) **1996** $163m **1997** $170m

Population	ε4,700,000		
(Serb 3%, Muslim 1%, Slovene 1%)			
Age	*13–17*	*18–22*	*23–32*
Men	168,000	168,000	333,000
Women	158,000	159,000	321,000

Total Armed Forces

ACTIVE 58,000
(incl ε33,500 conscripts)
Terms of service: 10 months

RESERVES 220,000
Army 150,000 **Home Defence** 70,000

Army 50,000

(incl ε33,500 conscripts)
6 Mil Districts • 7 Guard bde (each 3 mech, 1 tk, 1 arty bn) • 10 inf 'bde' (each 2-5 inf bn, 1 tk, 1 arty unit) • 1 mech bde • 7 mixed arty 'div' • 1 MRL bde • 3 ATK bde • 4 AD bde • 3 SF bde • 1 engr bde • 27 Home Def regt

RESERVES

17 inf 'bde' (incl 1 trg), 10 Home Def regt

EQUIPMENT

MBT 285: T-34, T-55, M-47, M-84/T-72M

LT TK 5 PT-76

RECCE 5 BRDM-2

AIFV ε100 M-80

APC BTR-50, 19 M-60PB plus 22 'look-alikes', ε150 BIV (reported)

TOTAL ARTY some 2,500 incl

TOWED 400+ **76mm:** ZIS-3; **85mm; 105mm:** M-56, M-2A1; **122mm:** M-1938, D-30; **130mm:** M-46; **152mm:** D-20, M-84; **203mm:** some **SP 122mm:** 2S1

MRL 220: **122mm:** BM-21; **128mm:** M-63; **262mm:** M-87 *Orkan* reported

MOR 325 incl: **82mm; 120mm:** M-74/-75, UBM-52; **240mm:** reported

ATGW AT-3 *Sagger*, AT-4 *Spigot*, AT-7 *Saxhorn*, *Milan* reported

ATK GUNS 100mm: 200 T-12

RL 73mm: RPG-7/-22. **90mm:** M-79

AD GUNS 600+: **14.5mm:** ZPU-2/-4; **20mm:** BOV-1 SP, M-55; **30mm:** M-53/59, BOV-3SP

Navy 3,000

BASES Split, Pula, Sibenik, Ploce, Dubrovnik **Minor facilities** Lastovo, Vis

SUBMARINES 1

1 Velebit (Mod *Una*) SSI for SF ops (4 SDV or 4 mines)

PATROL AND COASTAL COMBATANTS 8

CORVETTES 1 *Kralj Petar* with 4 or 8 Saab RBS-15 SSM

MISSILE CRAFT 2

1 *Rade Koncar* PFM with 2 RBS-15 SSM

1 *Dubrovnik* (Sov *Osa* I) with 4 SS-N-2A *Styx* SSM

TORPEDO CRAFT 1 *Vukovar* (Sov *Shershen*) with 4 533mm TT

PATROL, INSHORE 4 *Mirna*

MINE WARFARE 3

MINELAYERS 2 *Cetina* (*Silba*-class, LCT hull), 94 mines

MINECOUNTERMEASURES 1

1 *Dubrovnik* (Converted Sov *Osa* 1) MCI

AMPHIBIOUS craft only

1 DTM LCT/ML, 1 DSM-501 LCT/ML, 3 LCU, 4 LCVP

SUPPORT AND MISCELLANEOUS 5

1 *Spasilac* salvage, 1 Sov *Moma* survey, 1 AE, 2 tugs

MARINES

2 indep inf coy

COASTAL DEFENCE

some 10 coast arty bty, 2 RBS-15 SSM bty (reported)

Air Force 5,000

30 cbt ac, 15 armed hel

FGA/FTR 20 MiG-21

TPT 4 An-2, 2 An-26, 2 An-32, 5 UTVA, 2 Do-28

HEL 20 Mi-8/17, 15* Mi-24, 2 MD-500, 1 UH-1, 3 Bell-206B

TRG 10* PC-9

SAM SA-6, SA-7, SA-9, SA-10 (non-op), SA-13, SA-14/-16

Paramilitary 40,000

POLICE 40,000 armed

Foreign Forces

UN (UNTAES): 5,059; 6 inf bn, incl 100 Obs and 438 civ pol from 31 countries. (UNPF): 45 tps from HKJ. (UNMOP): 27 Obs from 24 countries; (SFOR): 3,175 tps from 22 countries

Cyprus

	1995	1996	1997	1998
GDP	C£3.9bn ($7.9bn)	C£4.0bn ($8.3bn)		
per capita	$10,900	$11,300		
Growth	5.0%	2.4%		
Inflation	2.6%	3.0%		
Debt	$1.9bn	$2.1bn		
Def exp	C£166m ($368m)	C£200m ($429m)		
Def bdgt			C£259m ($500m)	
$1 = pound	0.45	0.47	0.52	

UNFICYP **1995** $43m **1996** $44m **1997** $46m

Population	850,000 (Turkish 24%)		
Age	*13–17*	*18–22*	*23–32*
Men	31,000	28,000	56,000
Women	29,000	26,000	53,000

Total Armed Forces

ACTIVE 10,000

(8,700 conscripts; 445 women)

Terms of service: conscription, 26 months, then reserve to age 50 (officers 65)

RESERVES 88,000

45,000 first-line (age 20–34), 43,000 second-line (age 35–50)

National Guard 10,000

(8,700 conscripts) (all units classified non-active under
Vienna Document)
1 Corps HQ • 2 lt inf div HQ • 2 lt inf bde HQ • 1
armd bde (3 bn) • 1 SF bn • 1 ATK bn • 1 cdo regt (3
bn) • 7 arty bn • 1 coastal def SSM bty with MM-40
Exocet

EQUIPMENT

MBT 102 AMX-30 (incl 52 -B2), 41 T-80U (being
delivered)
RECCE 124 EE-9 *Cascavel*, 15 EE-3 *Jararaca*
AIFV 27 VAB-VCI, 43 BMP-3
APC 268 *Leonidas*, 118 VAB (incl variants), 16 AMX-
VCI
TOWED ARTY 75mm: 4 M-116A1 pack; **88mm**: 24
25-pdr (in store); **100mm**: 10 M-1944; **105mm**: 72
M-56; **155mm**: 12 TR F1
SP ARTY 155mm: 12 F3
MRL 128mm: 12 FRY M-63 (YMRL-32)
MOR 386+: **81mm**: 180 E-44, 70+ M1/M29 (in
store); **107mm**: 20 M-30/M-2; **120mm**: 116 RT61
SSM 3 MM-40 *Exocet*
ATGW 45 *Milan* (15 on EE-3 *Jararaca*), 72 HOT (18
on VAB), AT-10 (on BMP-3)
RL 66mm: M-72 LAW; **73mm**: ε450 RPG-7; **112mm**:
ε900 *Apilas*
RCL 90mm: 40 EM-67; **106mm**: 144 M-40A1
AD GUNS 20mm: 36 M-55; **35mm**: 24 GDF-005
with *Skyguard*; **40mm**: 20 M-1 (in store)
SAM 60 *Mistral* (some SP), 12 *Aspide*

MARITIME WING

1 *Salamis* PFI (plus 11 boats)
AC 1 BN-2 *Islander*, 2 PC-9
HEL 3 Bell 206C, 4 SA-342 *Gazelle* (with HOT), 2 Mi-2
(in store)

Paramilitary some 570

ARMED POLICE some 250

1 mech rapid-reaction unit, 2 VAB/VTT APC, 1 BN-2A
Maritime Defender ac, 2 Bell 412 hel

MARITIME POLICE 320

2 *Evagoras* and 1 *Kinon* PFI (plus boats)

Foreign Forces

GREECE 1 mech bde incl 950 (ELDYK) (Army); 2
mech inf bn, plus ε300 officers/NCO seconded to
Greek-Cypriot National Guard
UK (in Sovereign Base Areas) 3,800 **Army** 2 inf bn, 1
armd recce sqn **Air Force** 1,200; 1 hel sqn, plus ac on
det
UN (UNFICYP): some 1,180; 3 inf bn (Arg, A, UK),
plus 35 civ pol from 4 countries

'Turkish Republic of Northern Cyprus'

Data presented here represent the *de facto* situation on the
island. This in no way implies international recognition as a
sovereign state

	1995	1996	1997	1998
GNP		ε$837m		
Def exp				
(Tu)	ε$510–540m			
Population		ε200,000		

Total Armed Forces

ACTIVE some 4,000

Terms of service: conscription, 24 months, then reserve
to age 50

RESERVES 26,000

11,000 **first-line** 10,000 **second-line** 5,000 **third-line**

Army some 4,000

7 inf bn
MARITIME WING
3 patrol boats

Foreign Forces

TURKEY 25–30,000; 1 corps, 265 M-48A5 MBT; 200 M-
113, 50 AAPC APC; 90 **105mm**, 36 **155mm**, 8 **203mm**
towed arty; 30 **155mm** SP arty; 102 **107mm**, 30 **120mm**,
175 **81mm** mor; ε45 *Milan*, 38 TOW ATGW; some
35mm, 84 **40mm** AA guns; *Stinger* SAM; 5 **ac** 3–4 **hel**

Czech Republic

	1995	1996	1997	1998
GDP	Kc1.3tr	Kc1.4tr		
	($39bn)	($42bn)		
per capita	$9,600	$10,200		
Growth	4.8%	4.4%		
Inflation	9.2%	8.8%		
Debt	$16.6bn	$17.9bn		
Def exp	Kc28.4bn	Kc26.8bn		
	($1.1bn)	($988.0m)		
Def bdgt			Kc27.8bn	
			($826m)	
FMA (US)	$0.5m	$9.7m	$0.8m	$1.3m
$1 = koruna	26.5	27.2	33.6	
Population		10,350,000		
(Slovak 3%, Polish 0.6%, German 0.5%)				
Age	13–17	18–22	23–32	
Men	387,000	422,000	748,000	
Women	370,000	405,000	720,000	

Total Armed Forces

ACTIVE 61,700

(incl ε37,000 conscripts, about 17,700 MoD, centrally controlled formations and HQ units)
Terms of service: 12 months

Army 27,000

(ε15,400 conscripts)
General Staff 1 rapid-reaction bde (2 mech, 1 AB, 1 recce, 1 arty bn), 1 SF bde
MoD tps: 5 civil defence regt
2 Corps HQ
7 mech bde (each with 4 mech/trg, 1 recce, 1 arty, 1 ATK, 1 AD bn). Manning state assessed as 2 bde above 50%, 2 bde at 50%, 3 bde at 10%
Corps tps:
2 arty bde • 2 recce bde, 1 AD regt; 2 AD bn • 2 engr bde, 2 op bn

RESERVES
14–15 territorial def bde
EQUIPMENT
MBT 952: 411 T-54/-55, 541 T-72M (250 to be upgraded)
RECCE some 182 BRDM, OT-65
AIFV 945: 129 BPZV, 615 BMP-1, 186 BMP-2, 15 BRM-1K
APC 422 OT-90 plus 711 'look-alikes'
TOTAL ARTY 767
TOWED 122mm: 154 D-30
SP 370: **122mm:** 97 2S1; **152mm:** 273 *Dana* (M-77)
MRL 122mm: 150 RM-70
MOR 93: **120mm:** 85 M-1982, 8 MSP-85
SSM FROG-7, SS-21, *Scud*
ATGW 721 AT-3 *Sagger* (incl 621 on BMP-1, 100 on BRDM-2), 21 AT-5 *Spandrel*
AD GUNS 30mm: M-53/-59; **57mm:** S-60
SAM SA-7, ε140 SA-9/-13
SURV GS-13 (veh), *Long Trough* ((SNAR-1) arty), *Pork Trough* ((SNAR-2/-6) arty), *Small Fred/Small Yawn* (veh, arty), *Big Fred* ((SNAR-10) veh arty)

Air Force 17,000

(incl AD and 3,800 conscripts); 129 cbt ac, 36 attack hel
Flying hours 50
FGA/RECCE 2 sqn
1 with 32 Su-22, 1 with 25 Su-25
FTR 2 sqn
1 with 21 MiG-23, 1 with 37 MiG-21
TPT 2 sqn
1 with 12 L-410, 4 An-24, 1 Tu-134, 1 Tu-154 **hel** 2 Mi-2, 6 Mi-8, 1 Mi-9, 6 Mi-17
1 with 1 Il-14, 1 An-30, 1 An-12, 4 An-26
HEL 2 sqn (aslt/tpt/attack) with 21 Mi-2, 6 Mi-8, 17 Mi-17, 36* Mi-24, 11 PZL W-3
TEST CENTRE 7* Mig-21, 2 L-29, 2 L-39, 1 Mi-17, 1 Mi-2
TRG 1 regt with **ac** *7 MiG-21 U/MF, 18 L-29, 19 L-39 **hel** 8 Mi-2, 3 Mi-8
AAM AA-2 *Atoll*, AA-7 *Apex*, AA-8 *Aphid*
SAM 2 AD div (7 AD units), SA-2, SA-3, SA-5, SA-6, SA-10

Forces Abroad

UN AND PEACEKEEPING
BOSNIA (SFOR): 636; 1 mech inf bn. **CROATIA** (UNTAES): 43 incl 4 Obs; (UNMOP): 1 Obs. (SFOR): 7. **FYROM** (UNPREDEP): 1 Obs. **GEORGIA** (UNOMIG): 4 Obs. **LIBERIA** (UNOMIL): 5 Obs

Paramilitary 5,600

BORDER GUARDS 4,000
(1,000 conscripts)
INTERNAL SECURITY FORCES 1,600
(1,500 conscripts)

Estonia

	1995	1996	1997	1998
GDP	kn41.5bn	kn53.1bn		
	($3.6bn)	($4.4bn)		
per capita	$6,500	$7,000		
Growth	2.9%	3.3%		
Inflation	28.8%	14.8%		
Debt	$309m	$441m		
Def exp	εkn1.2bn	εkn1.3bn		
	($101m)	($108m)		
Def bdgt			kn736m	kn805m
			($52m)	($57m)
FMA (US)	$1.2m	$1.9m	$0.5m	$0.7m
$1 = kroon	11.5	12.0	14.2	
Population		1,472,000		
(Russian 30%, Ukrainian 3%, Belarussian 2%)				
Age	*13–17*	*18–22*	*23–32*	
Men	58,000	55,000	105,000	
Women	56,000	54,000	101,000	

Total Armed Forces

ACTIVE 3,510
(incl 1,630 conscripts)
Terms of service: 12 months

RESERVES some 14,000
Militia

Army 3,350

(incl 250 Air Wing; 1,500 conscripts)
3 inf bn (2 more to form) • 3 inf coy • 1 guard • 1
peacekeeping coy

RESERVES

Militia 6,000 (2,000 armed), 17 *Kaitseliit* (Defence
League) units

EQUIPMENT

    RECCE 7 BRDM-2
    APC 32 BTR-60/-70/-80
    MOR 81mm: 41; **120mm**: 16
    ATGW 5 *Mapats*
    RL 82mm: 200 B-300
    RCL 106mm: 30 M-40A1
    AIR WING (250): 1 AD bn
    AD GUNS 23mm: 100 ZU-23-2
    HEL 2 Mi-2

Navy 160

(incl 95 conscripts)
Latvia, Estonia and Lithuania are setting up a joint Baltic
Naval unit (BALTRON) to be operational by May 1998. Ger-
many will play a leading role in the formation of this unit.
BASE Paldiski

PATROL CRAFT 3

    PATROL, INSHORE 3
    2 *Grif* (RF *Zhuk*) PCI, 1 *Ahti* (*Da Maagen*) PCI

MINE COUNTERMEASURES 2

    2 *Sulev* (Ge *Kondor*-1) MSO

SUPPORT AND MISCELLANEOUS 2

    1 *Mardus* AK, 1 *Laine* (Ru *Mayak*) AK

Forces Abroad

UN AND PEACEKEEPING

BOSNIA (SFOR): 44. (UNMIBH): 18 civ pol.
CROATIA (SFOR): 2. **MIDDLE EAST** (UNTSO): 2
Obs

Paramilitary 2,800

BORDER GUARD (Ministry of Interior) 2,800

(970 conscripts); 1 regt, 3 rescue coy; maritime elm of
Border Guard also fulfils task of Coast Guard
    BASES Tallinn, Miinisdam
    PATROL CRAFT 8
    1 *Torm* PCC, 1 *Kõu* (SF *Silma*) PCO, 3 *Koskelo* (SF
    Telkkä) PCI, 1 *Tiiv* (RF *Serna*) LCU capacity 100 tps,
    1 *Maru* (SF *Viima*) PCI, 1 *Pikker* (RF new build) PCI
    SPT AND MISC 1 *Linda* (SF *Kemio*) PCI (trg)
    AVN 2 L-410 UVP-1 *Turbolet*, 5 Mi-8

Finland

	1995	1996	1997	1998
GDP	m546bn	m570bn		
	($105bn)	($110bn)		
per capita	$17,200	$18,100		
Growth	4.2%	3.3%		
Inflation	0.9%	0.6%		
Publ debt	61.8%	61.4%		
Def exp	m10.4bn	m10.1bn		
	($2.4bn)	($2.2bn)		
Def bdgt			m9.5bn	m10.5bn
			($1.8bn)	($2.0bn)
$1 = markka	4.37	4.59	5.24	
Population		5,136,000		
Age	*13–17*	*18–22*	*23–32*	
Men	169,000	165,000	353,000	
Women	159,000	157,000	337,000	

Total Armed Forces

ACTIVE 31,000

(23,700 conscripts, some 300 women)
Terms of service: 8–11 months (11 months for officers, NCO
and soldiers with special duties). Some 29,000 a year do
conscript service

RESERVES some 500,000

Total str on mob some 500,000 (all services), with 300,000
in general forces (bde etc) and 200,000 in local forces.
Some 35,000 reservists a year do refresher trg: total
obligation 40 days (75 for NCO, 100 for officers) between
conscript service and age 50 (NCO and officers to age 60)

Army 27,000

(21,000 conscripts)
(all bdes reserve, some with peacetime trg role)
3 Mil Comd
    1 with 5 mil provinces, 2 armd (1 trg), 3 *Jaeger* (trg), 9
    inf, 1 coastal bde (trg)
    1 with 2 mil provinces, 3 *Jaeger* (trg) bde
    1 with 5 mil provinces, 4 *Jaeger* (trg), 5 inf bde
Other units
    4 AD regt, 4 engr bn

RESERVES

some 200 local bn and coy

EQUIPMENT

    MBT 70 T-55M, 126 T-72
    AIFV 163 BMP-1, 110 BMP-2 (incl 'look-alikes')
    APC 120 BTR-60, 450 XA-180/185 *Sisu*, 220 MT-LB
    (incl 'look-alikes')
    TOWED ARTY 105mm: 54 H 61-37; **122mm**: 486 H
    63 (D-30); **130mm**: 36 K 54, **152mm**: 324 incl: H 55
    (D-20), H 88-40, H 88-37 (ML-20), H 38 (M-10);

155mm: 108 M-74 (K-83)
SP ARTY 122mm: 72 PsH 74 (2S1); **152mm**: 18 *Telak* 91 (2S5)
COASTAL ARTY 100mm: D-10T (tank turrets); **130mm**: 195 K-54 (static)
COASTAL SSM 5 RBS-15
MRL 122mm: 24 Rak H 76 (BM-21), 36 Rak H 89 (RM-70)
MOR 81mm: 800; **120mm**: 789: KRH 40, KRH 92
ATGW 100: incl 24 M-82 (AT-4 *Spigot*), 12 M-83 (BGM-71D TOW 2), M-82M (AT-5 *Spandrel)*
RL 112mm: APILAS
RCL 66mm: 66 KES-75, 66 KES-88; **95mm**: 100 SM-58-61
AD GUNS 23mm: 400 ZU-23; **30mm; 35mm**: GDF-005, *Marksman* GDF-005 SP; **57mm**: 12 S-60 towed, 12 ZSU-57-2 SP
SAM SAM-78 (SA-7), SAM-79 (SA-3), SAM-86M (SA-18), SAM-86 (SA-16), 20 SAM-90 (*Crotale* NG), 18 SAM-96 (SA-11)
SURV *Cymbeline* (mor)
HEL 2 Hughes 500D, 7 Mi-8

Navy 2,100

(1,200 conscripts)
BASES Upinniemi (Helsinki), Turku
4 functional sqn (msl, patrol, two mine warfare). Approx 50% of units kept fully manned; others in short-notice storage, rotated regularly
PATROL AND COASTAL COMBATANTS 14
CORVETTES 2 *Turunmaa* with 1 120mm gun, 2 x 5 ASW RL
MISSILE CRAFT 8
4 *Helsinki* PFM with 4 x 2 MTO-85 (Swe RBS-15SF) SSM
4 *Rauma* PFM with 2 x 2 and 2 x 1 MTO-85 (Sw RBS-15SF) SSM
PATROL CRAFT, INSHORE 4
2 *Rihtniemi* with 2 ASW RL
2 *Ruissalo* with 2 ASW RL
MINE WARFARE 23
MINELAYERS 10
2 *Hämeenmaa*, 150–200 mines, plus 1 x 6 Matra *Mistral* SAM
1 *Pohjanmaa*, 100–150 mines; plus 1 120mm gun and 2 x 5 ASW RL
3 *Pansio* aux minelayer, 50 mines
4 *Tuima* (ex-PFM), 20 mines
MINE COUNTERMEASURES 13
6 *Kuha* MSI, 7 *Kiiski* MSI
AMPHIBIOUS craft only
3 *Kampela* LCU tpt, 3 *Kala* LCU
SUPPORT AND MISCELLANEOUS 37
1 *Kustaanmiekka* command ship, 5 *Valas* tpt, 6 *Hauki* tpt, 4 *Hila* tpt, 2 *Lohi* tpt, 1 *Aranda* AGOR (Ministry

of Trade control), 9 *Prisma* AGS, 9 icebreakers (Board of Navigation control)

Air Force 1,900

(1,500 conscripts); 98 cbt ac, no armed hel, 3 AD areas: 3 ftr wg **Flying hours** 150
FTR 3 wg
1 with 14 MiG-21bis, 10 *Hawk* Mk 51 and 51A
2 with 27 J-35, 20 *Hawk* Mk 51 and 51A
OCU 4* MiG-21U/UM, 5* SAAB SK-35C, 11 F/A-18C, 7 F/A-18D
RECCE some *Hawk* Mk 51 and MiG-21T (incl in ftr sqn)
SURVEY 3 *Learjet* 35A (survey, ECM trg, target-towing)
TPT 1 **ac** sqn with 3 F-27
TRG 24 *Hawk** Mk 51, 28 L-70 *Vinka*
LIAISON 13 Piper (7 *Cherokee Arrow*, 6 *Chieftain*), 9 L-90 *Redigo*
AAM AA-2 *Atoll*, AA-8 *Aphid*, AIM-9 *Sidewinder*, RB-27, RB-28 (*Falcon*)

Forces Abroad

UN AND PEACEKEEPING

BOSNIA (SFOR): 339; 1 mech bn; (UNMIBH): 18 civ pol. **CROATIA** (UNTAES): 4 Obs plus 16 civ pol; (UNPF): 69; (UNMOP): 1 Obs. **CYPRUS** (UNFICYP): 1. **FYROM** (UNPREDEP): 365; 1 inf bn, 1 Obs plus 5 civ pol. **INDIA/PAKISTAN** (UNMOGIP): 5 Obs. **IRAQ/KUWAIT** (UNIKOM): 5 Obs. **LEBANON** (UNIFIL): 490; 1 inf bn. **MIDDLE EAST** (UNTSO): 16 Obs

Paramilitary 3,400

FRONTIER GUARD (Ministry of Interior) 3,400
(on mob 23,000); 4 frontier, 3 Coast Guard districts, 1 air comd; 5 offshore, 2 coastal, 4 inshore patrol craft (plus boats and ACVs); air patrol sqn with **hel** 3 AS-332, 4 AB-206L, 4 AB-412 **ac** 2 Do-228 (Maritime Surv)

Georgia

	1995	1996	1997	1998
GDP	lari 3.7bn	lari 4.1bn		
	($3.0bn)	($3.3bn)		
per capita	$3,400	$3,800		
Growth	2.4%	10.0%		
Inflation	163.0%	40.0%		
Debt	$1.2m	$1.3bn		
Def exp	εlari 130m	lari 140m		
	($106m)	($112m)		

contd	1995	1996	1997	1998
Def bdgt[a]			lari 79m	lari 82m
			($60m)	($55m)
FMA[b] (US)	$0.1m	$0.3m	$0.3m	$0.4m
$1 = lari	1.23	1.25	1.31	

[a] Abkhazia def bdgt 1997 ε$5m
[b] UNOMIG 1995 $18m 1996 $16m 1997 $18m

Population		5,380,000		

(Armenian 8%, Azeri 6%, Russian 4%, Ossetian 3%, Abkhaz 2%)

Age	13–17	18–22	23–32
Men	214,000	205,000	379,000
Women	207,000	197,000	362,000

Total Armed Forces 33,200

(incl 15,600 MoD and centrally controlled units)
Terms of service: conscription, 2 years

RESERVES up to 250,000

with mil service in last 15 years

Army 12,600

up to 24,000 planned
2 Corps HQ • Some 6 bde (incl 5 mech inf, 1 gd mech, plus trg centre) • 1 arty bde (3 bn) • 1 peacekeeping bn
EQUIPMENT
  MBT 48 T-55, 31 T-72
  AIFV/APC 67 BMP-1, 12 BMP-2, 7 BRM-1K, 6 BTR-70/-80
  TOTAL ARTY 92 incl
    TOWED 85mm: D-44; **100mm**: KS-19 (ground role); **122mm**: 45 D-30; **152mm**: 3 2A36, 10 2A65
    SP 152mm: 1 2S3; **203mm**: 1 2S7
    MRL 122mm: 18 BM-21
    MOR 120mm: 14 M-120

Navy 2,000

BASES Tbilisi (HQ), Poti
PATROL AND COASTAL COMBATANTS 16
FRIGATES 2 *Grisha* I/V with 2 SA-N-4 SAM, 4 533mm TT
TORPEDO CRAFT 1 *Turya* PFT with 4 533mm TT
PATROL CRAFT 13
  9 *Stenka* PFC with 4 406mm TT, 1 76mm gun
  3 *Muravey* PHT with 2 406mm TT, 1 *Zhuk* PCI

Air Force 3,000

(incl Air Defence); some 7 Su-25 **ac**, 1 Mi-2, 4 Mi-8, 3 Mi-24 **hel**

AIR DEFENCE
SAM 75 SA-2/-3/-5

Opposition

ABKHAZIA ε5,000
50+ T-72, T-55 MBT, 80+ AIFV/APC, 80+ arty
SOUTH OSSETIA ε2,000
5–10 MBT, 30 AIFV/APC, 25 arty incl BM-21

Foreign Forces

RUSSIA 8,500 **Army** 3 mil bases (each = bde+) 140 T-72 MBT, 360 ACV, 155 arty incl **122mm** D-30, 2S1; **152mm** 2S3; **122mm** BM-21 MRL; **120mm** mor plus 118 ACV and some arty deployed in Abkhazia **Air Force** 1 composite regt, some 35 tpt **ac** and **hel** incl An-12, An-26 and Mi-8
PEACEKEEPING: 2,100; 1 AB regt, 2 MR, 1 inf bn (Russia)
UN (UNOMIG): some 117 Obs from 23 countries

Hungary

	1995	1996	1997	1998
GDP	f5.5tr	f6.8tr		
	($43bn)	($45bn)		
per capita	$6,400	$6,500		
Growth	1.5%	0.8%		
Inflation	28.0%	23.5%		
Debt	$31.2bn	$30.2bn		
Def exp	f77.1bn	f79.0bn		
	($613m)	($517m)		
Def bdgt			f97.0bn	f122.5bn
			($511m)	($613m)
FMA (US)	$0.8m	$4.2m	$1.0m	$1.5m
$1 = forint	126	153	190	

Population		10,159,000		

(Romany 4%, German 3%, Serb 2%, Romanian 1%, Slovak 1%)

Age	13–17	18–22	23–32
Men	368,000	394,000	685,000
Women	346,000	368,000	642,000

Total Armed Forces

ACTIVE 49,100
(ε30,200 conscripts)
Terms of service: 12 months (to be 9 months from Nov 1997)

RESERVES ε186,400
Army ε175,000 **Air Force** 11,400 (to age 50)

Land Forces 31,600

(ε19,000 conscripts; incl 10,400 centrally controlled tps)
Land Forces HQ • 1 Mil District/Corps HQ

2 mech div
  1 with 2 mech inf, 1 arty, 1 ATK bde, 1 engr regt, 1
    recce bn
  1 with 1 mech inf bde, 1 ATK, 1 engr regt, 1 recce
Corps tps
  2 mech inf bde (1 indep) • 2 trg bde • 1 MRL regt •
  1 engr regt • 2 recce bn • 1 MP regt • 1 river bde
MoD tps (Budapest): 1 MP regt

RESERVES
2 mech
EQUIPMENT
  MBT 797: 597 T-55 (177 in store), 200 T-72M1
  RECCE 161 FUG D-442
  AIFV 502 BMP-1, BRM-1K
  APC 798: 229 BTR-80, 539 PSZH D-944 (83 in store),
    30 MT-LB (plus some 400 'look-alike' types)
  TOTAL ARTY 840
    TOWED -532: 122mm: 230 M-1938 (M-30) (18 in
    store); **152mm**: 302 D-20 (108 in store)
    SP -122mm: 151 2S1
    MRL 122mm: 56 BM-21
    MOR 120mm: 101 M-120 (26 in store)
  ATGW 353: 117 AT-3 *Sagger*, 30 AT-4 *Spigot* (incl
    BRDM-2 SP), 206 AT-5 *Spandrel*
  ATK GUNS 85mm: 162 D-44 (62 in store); **100mm**:
    106 MT-12 (10 in store)
  AD GUNS 57mm: 189 S-60 (43 in store)
  SAM 244 SA-7, 60 SA-14
  SURV GS-13 (veh), *Long Trough* ((SNAR-1) arty),
    Pork Trough ((SNAR-2/-6) veh, arty), *Small Fred/
    Small Yawn* (veh, arty), *Big Fred* ((SNAR-10) veh,
    arty)

Army Maritime Wing (400)

BASE Budapest

RIVER CRAFT ε51

6 *Nestin* MSI (riverine), some 45 An-2 mine warfare/
patrol boats (plus 6 in reserve)

Air Force 17,500

(11,200 conscripts)
AIR DEFENCE COMMAND
80 cbt ac, 59 attack hel
Flying hours 50
FTR 2 regt with 52 MiG-21bis/MF/UM, 28 MiG-29
ATTACK HEL 59 Mi-24
SPT HEL 30 Mi-2, 50 Mi-8/-17
TPT 2 An-24, 9 An-26
TRG 19 L-39, 12 Yak-52
AAM AA-2 *Atoll*
SAM some 14 sites, 1 bde, 3 regt with 82 SA-2/-3/-5,
  18 SA-4, 40 SA-6, 45 SA-9, 4 SA-13

Forces Abroad

UN AND PEACEKEEPING
ANGOLA (UNOMA): 10 Obs plus 7 civ pol. **BOSNIA**
(SFOR): 2. **CROATIA** (SFOR): 271; 1 engr bn;
(UNMIBH): 31 civ pol. **CYPRUS** (UNFICYP): 39.
EGYPT (MFO): 41 mil pol. **GEORGIA** (UNIKOM): 5
Obs. **IRAQ/KUWAIT** (UNIKOM): 5 Obs. **WESTERN
SAHARA** (MINURSO): 2 civ pol.

Paramilitary 14,100

BORDER GUARDS (Ministry of Interior) 12,000 (to
reduce)
11 districts/regts plus 1 Budapest district (incl 25
  rapid-reaction coy; 100 PSZH, 26 BTR-80 APC)
INTERNAL SECURITY FORCES (Police) 2,100

Ireland

	1995	1996	1997	1998
GDP	I£38.6bn	I£42.0bn		
	($62bn)	($67bn)		
per capita	$15,200	$16,600		
Growth	10.3%	7.3%		
Inflation	2.5%	1.7%		
Publ debt	84.9%	76.5%		
Def exp	I£429m	I£463m		
	($688m)	($741m)		
Def bdgt			I£493m	
			($771m)	
$1 = pound	0.62	0.63	0.64	
Population		3,647,000		
Age	*13–17*	*18–22*	*23–32*	
Men	162,000	170,000	313,000	
Women	154,000	161,000	298,000	

Total Armed Forces

ACTIVE 12,700
(incl 200 women)
Terms of service: voluntary, 3-year terms to age 60,
officers 56–65

RESERVES 15,640
(obligation to age 60, officers 57–65) **Army** first-line
540, second-line 14,750 **Navy** 350

Army 10,500

4 Territorial Comds
1 inf force (2 inf bn)
4 inf bde
  2 with 2 inf bn

1 with 3 inf bn, all with 1 fd arty regt, 1 cav recce
   sqn, 1 engr coy
1 with 2 inf bn, 1 armd recce sqn, 1 fd arty bty
Army tps: 1 lt tk sqn, 1 AD regt, 1 Ranger coy
Total units: 11 inf bn • 1 UNIFIL bn *ad hoc* with elm
from other bn, 1 lt tk sqn, 4 recce sqn (1 armd), 3 fd
arty regt (each of 2 bty) • 1 indep bty, 1 AD regt (1
regular, 3 reserve bty), 4 fd engr coy, 1 Ranger coy)

RESERVES

4 Army Gp (garrisons), 18 inf bn, 6 fd arty regt, 3 cav
sqn, 3 engr sqn, 3 AD bty

EQUIPMENT

LT TK 14 *Scorpion*
RECCE 15 AML-90, 32 AML-60
APC 47 Panhard VTT/M3, 5 *Timoney*, 2 A-180 *Sisu*
TOWED ARTY 88mm: 48 25-pdr; **105mm**: 12 L-118
MOR 81mm: 400; **120mm**: 67
ATGW 21 *Milan*
RCL 84mm: 444 *Carl Gustav*; **90mm**: 96 PV-1110
AD GUNS 40mm: 24 L/60, 2 L/70
SAM 7 RBS-70

Navy 1,100

BASE Cork
PATROL AND COASTAL COMBATANTS 7
   PATROL, COASTAL 7
   1 *Eithne* with 1 *Dauphin* hel, 3 *Emer*, 1 *Deirdre*, 2 *Orla*
   (UK *Peacock*)

Air Force 1,100

13 cbt ac, 15 armed hel; 3 wg (1 trg)
CCT 2 sqn
   1 with 7 SF-260WE,
   1 with 6 CM-170-2 *Super Magister*
MR 2 CN-235MP
TPT 1 *Super King Air* 200, 1 *Gulfstream* IV
LIAISON 1 sqn with 6 Cessna Reims FR-172H, 1 FR-172K
HEL 4 sqn
   1 Army spt with 8 SA-316B (*Alouette* III)
   1 Navy spt with 2 SA-365FI (*Dauphin*)
   1 SAR with 3 SA-365FI (*Dauphin*)
   1 trg with 2 SA-342L (*Gazelle*)

Forces Abroad

UN AND PEACEKEEPING

BOSNIA (UNMIBH): 36 civ pol. **CROATIA** (UNTAES):
4 Obs plus 10 civ pol; (UNMOP): 1 Obs. **CYPRUS**
(UNFICYP): 31 plus 15 civ pol. **FYROM** (UNPREDEP):
2 Obs. **IRAQ/KUWAIT** (UNIKOM): 6 Obs. **LEBANON**
(UNIFIL): 613; 1 bn; 4 AML-90 armd cars, 10 *Sisu* APC,
4 **120mm** mor. **MIDDLE EAST** (UNTSO): 11 Obs.
WESTERN SAHARA (MINURSO): 8 Obs

Latvia

	1995	1996	1997	1998
GDP	L2.4bn	L2.8bn		
	($3.7bn)	($3.8bn)		
per capita	$4,700	$4,800		
Growth	-1.6%	2.8%		
Inflation	25.0%	13.1%		
Debt	$462m	$501m		
Def exp	εL64m	εL73m		
	($121m)	($133m)		
Def bdgt			L27.0m	
			($47m)	
FMA (US)	$1.2m	$1.9m	$0.5m	$0.7m
(Swe)			$1.5m	
$1 = lats	0.53	0.55	0.57	
Population		2,587,000		

(Russian 34%, Belarussian 5%, Ukrainian 3%, Polish
2%)

Age	*13–17*	*18–22*	*23–32*	
Men	97,000	90,000	171,000	
Women	93,000	87,000	166,000	

Total Armed Forces

ACTIVE 4,500

(incl 2,200 conscripts, 1,900 National Guard)
Terms of service: 12 months

RESERVES 16,600
National Guard

Army 3,400

(incl 1,685 conscripts)
1 inf bn • 1 recce bn • 1 engr bn • 1 peacekeeping coy
• 1 SF team

RESERVES

National Guard 5 bde each of 5–7 bn

EQUIPMENT

RECCE 2 BRDM-2
APC 13 *Pskbil* M/42
TOWED ARTY 100mm: 24 K-53
MOR 82mm: 4; **120mm**: 24
AD GUNS 12.7mm

Navy 980

(incl 520 conscripts, 220 Coastal Defence)
Latvia, Estonia and Lithuania are setting up a joint Baltic
Naval unit (BALTRON) to be operational by May 1998. Ger-
many will play a leading role in the formation of this unit.
BASES Liepaja, Riga
PATROL CRAFT 13

1 *Osa* PFM (unarmed), 1 *Storm* PCC (unarmed), 1
Selga PCI, 2 *Ribnadzor* PC, 5 KBV 236 PC<, 3 PCH
(plus 1 tug, 1 diving vessel)
MINE COUNTERMEASURES 2 *Kondor* II MCO

SUPPORT AND MISCELLANEOUS 2

1 *Nyrat* AT , 1 *Goliat* AT

COASTAL DEFENCE (220)

1 coastal def bn

Air Force 120

AC 2 An-2, 1 An-26, 1 L-410
HEL 5 Mi-2, 2 Mi-8

Forces Abroad

UN AND PEACEKEEPING

BOSNIA (SFOR): 40

Paramilitary 3,600

BORDER GUARD (Ministry of Internal Affairs) 3,500

1 bde (7 bn)

COAST GUARD 100

5 PCI<, 3 converted fishing boats, 3 PCH

Lithuania

	1995	1996	1997	1998
GDP	L24bn	L31bn		
	($2.8bn)	($2.9bn)		
per capita	$4,600	$4,800		
Growth	3.0%	3.6%		
Inflation	39.7%	13.1%		
Debt	$802m	$871m		
Def exp	εL460m	εL500m		
	($115m)	($125m)		
Def bdgt			L317m	
			($79m)	
FMA (US)	$1.0m	$1.9m	$0.5m	$0.7m
$1 = litas	4.0	4.0	4.0	
Population		3,709,000		
(Russian 9%, Polish 8%, Belarussian 2%)				
Age	*13–17*	*18–22*	*23–32*	
Men	141,000	133,000	266,000	
Women	136,000	130,000	258,000	

Total Armed Forces

ACTIVE ε5,250

(2,000 conscripts)
Terms of service: 12 months

RESERVES 11,000

Army 4,200

(incl 2,000 conscripts)
1 motor rifle bde (6 bn) • 1 Ranger, 1 Guard bn • 1
peacekeeping coy
EQUIPMENT
   RECCE 10 BRDM-2
   APC 14BTR-60, 10 *Pskbil* M/42
   MOR 120mm: 18 M-43
   RCL 84mm: *Carl Gustav*

RESERVES 11,000
Voluntary National Defence Service 8 district units,
18 territorial def bn, 127 territorial def coy

Navy ε500

Latvia, Estonia and Lithuania are setting up a joint Baltic
Naval unit (BALTRON) to be operational by May 1998. Ger-
many will play a leading role in the formation of this unit.
BASE Klaipeda
FRIGATES 2
   2 Sov *Grisha* III, with 2 x 12 ASW RL, 4 533mm TT
PATROL AND COASTAL COMBATANTS 3
   2 Sov *Turya* PHT (no TT), 1 KBV 236 (ex-Swe) PCI
SUPPORT AND MISCELLANEOUS 2
   1 *Kondor* (ex-Ge) AG, 1 *Valerian Uryvayev* AG

Air Force 550

no cbt ac
AC 4 L-39, 2 L-410, 4 AN-26, 1 AN-24
HEL 3 Mi-8, 5 Mi-2

Forces Abroad

UN AND PEACEKEEPING
BOSNIA (SFOR): 140. **CROATIA** (UNTAES): 8 civ pol

Paramilitary 4,800

BORDER GUARD 4,800

4 bn

Macedonia, Former Yugoslav Republic of

	1995	1996	1997	1998
GDP	d60bn	d64bn		
	($1.3bn)	($1.3bn)		
per capita	$3,400	$3,500		
Growth	-1.5%	1.1%		

contd	1995	1996	1997	1998
Inflation	8.6%	-0.7%		
Debt	$1.2bn	$1.2bn		
Def exp	d4.4bn	d4.8bn		
	($116m)	($120m)		
Def bdgt			d6.6bn	
			($121m)	
FMA[a] (US)	$0.1m	$0.3m	ε$0.3m	$0.4m
$1 = dinar	38.0	40.0	54.0	

[a] UNPREDEP **1995** $38m **1996** $50m **1997** $45m

Population		2,266,000		

(Albanian 22%, Turkish 4%, Romany 3%, Serb 2%)

Age	*13–17*	*18–22*	*23–32*	
Men	95,000	90,000	179,000	
Women	86,000	82,000	162,000	

Total Armed Forces

ACTIVE 15,400

Terms of service: 9 months (8,000 conscripts)

RESERVES 100,000 planned

Army 15,400 (to be 20,000)

3 Corps HQ (cadre) each of 3 bde (planned)
1 border gd bde
EQUIPMENT
   MBT 4 T-34
   AFV 10 BRDM-2, M-80
   TOWED ARTY 76mm: 55 M-48
   MRL 128mm: 60 M-71 (single barrel), 15 M-63
   MOR 1,200 incl **60mm**, **82mm** and 130 **120mm**
   ATGW AT-3 *Sagger*
   RCL 57mm: 2,400; **82mm**
   ATK GUNS 76mm: M-1942
   MARINE WING (400)
   9 river patrol craft

Air Force

ac 4 *Zlin* (trg), 10 lt tpt **hel** 4 Mi-17
AD GUNS 100: **20mm**; **40mm**
SAM 200 SA-7

Paramilitary 7,500

POLICE 7,500
(some 4,500 armed)

Foreign Forces

UN (UNPREDEP): some 1,105; 2 inf bn (US, SF), incl
35 Obs and 22 civ pol from 25 countries

Malta

	1995	1996	1997	1998
GDP	ML1.0bn	εML1.1bn		
	($3.0bn)	($3.1bn)		
per capita	$7,500	$7,800		
Growth	6.2%	ε3.5%		
Inflation	4.0%	ε2.6%		
Debt	$955m	$951m		
Def exp	ML11.4m	ML11.8m		
	($32m)	($33m)		
Def bdgt			ML12m	
			($33m)	
FMA (US)	$0.06m	$0.03m	$0.10m	$0.10m
$1 = lira	0.35	0.36	0.36	

Population		372,000		

Age	*13–17*	*18–22*	*23–32*	
Men	14,000	14,000	26,000	
Women	14,000	13,000	25,000	

Total Armed Forces

ACTIVE 1,950

Armed Forces of Malta 1,950

Comd HQ, spt tps
No. 1 Regt (inf bn): 3 rifle, 1 spt coy
No. 2 Regt (composite regt)
   1 air wg (76) with **ac** 4 0-1 *Bird Dog*, 1 BN-2 *Islander* **hel**
      3 SA-316B, 2 NH-369M Hughes, 1 AB-206A, 4 AB-
      47G2
   1 maritime sqn (220) with 2 ex-GDR *Kondor* 1 PCC,
      2 PCI<, 1 LCVP plus boats
   1 AD bty; **14.5mm**: 50 ZPU-4; **40mm**: 40 Bofors
No. 3 Regt (Depot Regt): 1 engr sqn, 1 workshop, 1
   ordnance, 1 airport coy

Foreign Forces

ITALY 16 **Air Force** 2 AB-212 **hel**

Moldova

	1995	1996	1997	1998
GDP	L8.0bn	L10.3bn		
	($1.2bn)	($1.1bn)		
per capita	$3,700	$3,500		
Growth	-3.0%	-8.0%		
Inflation	30.0%	23.5%		
Debt	$691m	$703m		
Def exp	L203m	L215m		
	($45m)	($47m)		

NATO *and* Non-NATO Europe

contd	1995	1996	1997	1998
Def bdgt			L70m	
			($15m)	
FMA (US)	$0.1m	$0.6m	$0.3m	$0.4m
$1 = leu	4.5	4.6	4.6	
Population			4,319,000	

(Moldovan/Romanian 65%, Ukrainian 14%, Russian 13%, Gaguaz 4%, Bulgarian 2%, Jewish <2%)

Age	13–17	18–22	23–32
Men	194,000	174,000	289,000
Women	187,000	169,000	299,000

Total Armed Forces

ACTIVE 11,030

(incl ε5,200 conscripts)
Terms of service: up to 18 months

RESERVES some 66,000

with mil service within last 5 years

Army some 9,300

(ε5,200 conscripts)
3 MR bde • 1 arty bde • 1 recce/assault, 1 gd, 1 SF, 1 engr bn

EQUIPMENT
AIFV 54 BMD
APC 11 BTR-80, 11 BTR-D, 2 BTR-60PB, 131 TAB-71, plus 126 'look-alikes'
TOWED ARTY 122mm: 18 M-30; **152mm**: 32 D-20, 21 2A36
COMBINED GUN/MOR 120mm: 9 2S9
MRL 220mm: 15 9P140 *Uragan*
MOR 82mm: 54; **120mm**: 60 M-120
ATGW 70 AT-4 *Spigot*, 19 AT-5 *Spandral*, 27 AT-6 *Spiral*
RCL 73mm: SPG-9
ATK GUNS 100mm: 26 MT-12
AD GUNS 23mm: 30 ZU-23; **57mm**: 12 S-60
SURV GS-13 (arty), 1 L219/200 PARK-1 (arty), *Long Trough* ((SNAR-1) arty), *Pork Trough* ((SNAR-2/-6) veh, arty), *Small Fred/Small Yawn* (veh, arty), *Big Fred* ((SNAR-10) veh, arty)

Air Force 1,730

(incl AD)
FTR 1 regt with 27 MiG-29
TPT 1 mixed sqn **ac** An-24, 2 An-72, 1 Tu-134, 1 IL-18 **hel** 8 Mi-8
SAM 1 bde with 25 SA-3/-5

Paramilitary 3,400

INTERNAL TROOPS (Ministry of Interior) 2,500

OPON (riot police) (Ministry of Interior) 900

Opposition

DNIESTR 5,000

incl Republican Guard (Dniestr bn), Delta bn, ε1,000 Cossacks

Foreign Forces

RUSSIA 4,900 reducing to 2,500 by end 1997; 1 op gp, incl 1 indep MR bde
PEACEKEEPING: 1 inf bn **Russia** 3 inf bn **Moldova** 3 bn **Dniestr**

Poland

	1995	1996	1997	1998
GDP	z293bn	z360bn		
	($100bn)	($109bn)		
per capita	$6,000	$6,400		
Growth	6.5%	6.0%		
Inflation	26.8%	20.1%		
Debt	$42.3bn	$42.2bn		
Def exp	z6.7bn	z8.3bn		
	($2.8bn)	($3.1bn)		
Def bdgt			z9.8bn	z10.2bn
			($3.0bn)	($3.1bn)
FMA (US)	$1.7m	$17.5m	$1.0m	$1.5m
$1 = zloty	2.43	2.70	3.33	
Population		38,673,000		

(Belarussian 1%, German 1%, Ukrainian 1%)

Age	13–17	18–22	23–32
Men	1,665,000	1,567,000	2,680,000
Women	1,581,000	1,491,000	2,565,000

Total Armed Forces

ACTIVE 241,750

(incl 141,600 conscripts) *Terms of service:* all services 18 months

RESERVES

Army 343,000 **Navy** 14,000 (to age 50) **Air Force** 49,000 (to age 60)

Army 168,650

(incl 101,670 conscripts, 1,760 centrally controlled staffs, 23,200 trg, 14,130 log units)
4 Mil Districts/Army HQ
Pomerania 3 mech div (incl 1 coast def), 1 arty, 1 engr, 1 territorial def bde, 1 SSM, 1 cbt hel, 2 AA arty, 1 SA-6 regt
Silesia 3 mech, 1 armd cav div, 1 mtn, 2 arty, 2 engr, 1

AD arty bde, 2 SSM regt
Warsaw 3 mech div, 1 arty, 1 engr, 1 territorial def bde,
1 cbt hel regt
Krakow 1 air cavalry div HQ, 1 armd, 1mech, 1 air
aslt, 1 mtn, 1 territorial def bde, 1 mech, 2 engr, 1
recce regt
Div tps: 10 SA-6/-8 regt
General Staff tps: 1 special ops, 1 gd regt
EQUIPMENT
   MBT 1,729: 862 T-55, 809 T-72, 58 PT-91
   RECCE 510 BRDM-2
   AIFV 1,405: 1,367 BMP-1, 38 BRM-1
   APC 37 OT-64 plus some 693 'look-alike' types
   TOTAL ARTY 1,581
      TOWED 440: **122mm**: 280 M-1938 (M-30); **152mm**:
      160 M-1938 (ML-20)
      SP 652: **122mm**: 533 2S1; **152mm**: 111 *Dana* (M-77);
      203mm: 8 2S7
      MRL 258: **122mm**: 228 BM-21, 30 RM-70
      MOR 231: **120mm**: 215 M-120, 16 2B11/2S12
   SSM launchers: 35 FROG, SS-C-2B
   ATGW 403: 263 AT-3 *Sagger*, 115 AT-4 *Spigot*, 18 AT-5
   Spandrel, 7 AT-6 *Spiral*
   ATK GUNS 85mm: 711 D-44
   AD GUNS 1,116: **23mm**: ZU-23-2, ZSU-23-4 SP;
   57mm: S-60
   SAM 1,290: SA-6/-7/-8/-9/-13
   HELICOPTERS
      ATTACK 16 PZL-W3, 35 Mi-24, 37 Mi-2URP
      SPT 26 Mi-2URN
      TPT 35 Mi-8, 3 Mi-17, 36 Mi-2
   SURV GS-13 (arty), 1 L219/200 PARK-1 (arty), *Long
   Trough* ((SNAR-1) arty), *Pork Trough* ((SNAR-2/-6)
   veh, arty), *Small Fred/Small Yawn* (veh, arty), *Big
   Fred* ((SNAR-10) veh, arty)

Navy 17,000

(incl 2,460 Naval Aviation, 9,500 conscripts)
BASES Gdynia, Hel, Swinoujscie; Kolobrzeg, Gdansk
(Coast Guard)
SUBMARINES 3
   1 *Orzel* SS (RF *Kilo*) with 533mm TT
   2 *Wilk* (RF *Foxtrot*) with 533mm TT
PRINCIPAL SURFACE COMBATANTS 2
DESTROYERS 1 *Warszawa* DDG (Sov mod *Kashin*)
   with 2 x 2 SA-N-1 *Goa* SAM, 4 SS-N-2C *Styx* SSM, 5
   533mm TT, 2 ASW RL
FRIGATES 1 *Kaszub* with 2 ASW RL, 4 533mm TT,
   76mm gun
PATROL AND COASTAL COMBATANTS 33
CORVETTES 4 *Gornik* (Sov *Tarantul* I) with 2 x 2 SS-N-
   2C *Styx* SSM, 76mm gun
MISSILE CRAFT 7 Sov *Osa* I PFM with 4 SS-N-2A
   SSM
PATROL CRAFT 22
   COASTAL 3 *Sassnitz*

INSHORE 19
   8 *Obluze* PCI, 11 *Pilica* PCI<
MINE WARFARE 24
MINELAYERS none, but SS, *Krogulec* MSC and *Lublin*
   LSM have capability
MINE COUNTERMEASURES 24
   5 *Krogulec* MSC, 13 *Goplo* (*Notec*) MSI, 4 *Mamry*
   (*Notec*) MHI, 2 *Leniwka* MSI
AMPHIBIOUS 5
   5 *Lublin* LSM, capacity 135 tps, 9 tk
   Plus craft: 3 *Deba* LCU (none employed in amph
   role)
SUPPORT AND MISCELLANEOUS 12
   1 comd ship, 2 AGI, 3 AGHS, 2 ARS, 4 spt tkr

NAVAL AVIATION (2,460)
28 cbt ac, 10 armed hel
Flying hours (MiG-21) 60
3 regt
   1 with 28 MiG-21 BIS/U
   1 with **ac** 17 TS-11, 4 An-2, 3 An-28 **hel** 6 PZL-W3
   1 with 6 Mi-2R, 10* Mi-14 PL, 2 Mi-14 PS

Air Force 56,100

(incl AD tps, 30,430 conscripts); 356 cbt ac, 17 attack
hel **Flying hours** 60
FTR 3 AD Corps
   7 regt with 178 MiG-21/U, 31 MiG-23, 22 MiG-29/U
FGA 4 regt with 10 Su-20, 99 Su-22
RECCE 16 MiG-21R/U
TPT 2 regt with 32 An-2, 10 An-26, 5 An-28, 13 Yak-40,
   2 Tu-154
HEL 17* PZL-W3, 109 Mi-2, 5 Mi-8, 7 PZL-W3
TRG 184 TS-11 *Iskra*, 11 PZL I-22 *Iryda*, 25 PZL-130 *Orlik*
IN STORE 13 MiG-17, 1 MiG-21
AAM AA-2 *Atoll*, AA-8 *Aphid*
ASM AS-7 *Kerry*
SAM 5 bde; 1 indep regt with about 200 SA-2/-3/-4/-5

Forces Abroad

UN AND PEACEKEEPING
ANGOLA (UNOMA): 7 Obs. **BOSNIA** (SFOR): 396; 1
AB bn; (UNMIBH): 40 civ pol. **CROATIA** (UNTAES):
58 incl 5 Obs plus 8 civ pol; (UNMOP): 1 Obs. **GEOR-
GIA** (UNOMIG): 4 Obs. **IRAQ/KUWAIT** (UNIKOM): 5
Obs. **LEBANON** (UNIFIL): 632; 1 inf bn, mil hospital.
FYROM (UNPREDEP): 2 Obs. **ROK** (Neutral Nations
Supervisory Commission – NNSC): staff. **SYRIA**
(UNDOF): 355; 1 inf bn. **TAJIKISTAN** (UNMOT): 1
Obs. **WESTERN SAHARA** (MINURSO): 3 Obs

Paramilitary 23,400

BORDER GUARDS (Ministry of Interior) 16,000
14 Provincial Comd: 14 units

MARITIME BORDER GUARD
about 28 patrol craft: 2 PCC, 9 PCI and 17 PC1<
PREVENTION UNITS OF POLICE (OPP) 7,400
(1,400 conscripts)

Romania

	1995	1996	1997	1998
GDP	lei 72.3tr	lei 101.9tr		
	($30bn)	($33bn)		
per capita	$4,500	$4,800		
Growth	6.9%	4.3%		
Inflation	32.2%	45.0%		
Debt	$6.7bn	$8.8bn		
Def exp	lei 1.8tr	lei 2.3tr		
	($872m)	($745m)		
Def bdgt			lei 5.5tr	
			($770m)	
FMA (US)	$0.5m	$10.0m	$0.8m	$0.9m
$1 = lei	2,033	3,085	7,120	
Population		22,769,000 (Hungarian 9%)		
Age	*13–17*	*18–22*	*23–32*	
Men	901,000	935,000	1,784,000	
Women	868,000	900,000	1,724,000	

Total Armed Forces

ACTIVE 226,950
(incl 127,200 conscripts, 2,900 MoD staff and 29,600
centrally controlled units)
Terms of service: **Army**, **Air Force** 12 months, **Navy** 18
months

RESERVES 427,000
Army 400,000 **Navy** 6,000 **Air Force** 21,000

Army 129,350

(90,000 conscripts, 8,000 Naval Infantry)
3 Army HQ, 8 Corps HQ (incl HQ for naval inf) each
    with 2–3 mech 1 tk, 1 mtn, 1 arty, 1 ATK, 1 mixed
    AAA bde
Army tps: 1 tk, 1 mech, 1 mtn, 1 arty, 1 ATK, 3 AAA
    bde, 1 mech, 1 arty, 4 AAA, 4 SAM, 3 engr regt
MoD tps: 3 AB (Air Force), 1 gd bde, 2 recce bn
Land Force tps: 2 Scud, 1 arty, 1 engr bde; 2 engr regt
Determining the manning state of units is difficult. The
following is based on the latest available information: one-
third at 100%, one-third at 50–70%, one-third at 10–20%
EQUIPMENT
  MBT 1,255: 822 T-55, 30 T-72, 315 TR-85, 88 TR-580
  ASLT GUN 66 SU-100
  RECCE 129: 121 BRDM-2, 8 TAB-80
  AIFV 178 MLI-84
  APC 1,704: 168 TAB-77, 398 TABC-79, 1,050 TAB-71,

  88 MLVM, plus 976 'look-alikes'
  TOTAL ARTY 1,359
    TOWED 790: **100mm**: 8 Skoda (various models);
    105mm: 72 Schneider; **122mm**: 212 M-1938 (M-
    30) (A-19); **130mm**: 90 Gun 82; **150mm**: 12 Skoda
    (Model 1934); **152mm**: 108 Gun-how 85, 288
    Model 81
    SP 48: **122mm**: 6 2S1, 42 Model 89
    MRL 122mm: 189 APR-40
    MOR 332: **120mm**: M-38, Model 1982
  SSM launchers: 12 *Scud* (in store), 9 FROG
  ATGW 520: AT-1 *Snapper*, AT-3 *Sagger* (incl BRDM-2)
  ATK GUNS 57mm: M-1943; **85mm**: D-44; **100mm**:
    871: Gun 77, Gun 75
  AD GUNS 1,118: **30mm; 37mm; 57mm; 85mm;
    100mm**
  SAM 62 SA-6/-7
  SURV GS-13 (arty), 1 L219/200 PARK-1 (arty), *Long
    Trough* ((SNAR-1) arty), *Pork Trough* ((SNAR-2/-6)
    veh, arty), *Small Fred/Small Yawn* ((veh, arty), *Big
    Fred* ((SNAR-10) veh, arty)

Navy 17,500

(9,500 conscripts and 800 Coastal Defence) 1 maritime
div, 1 patrol boat bde, 1 river bde, 1 maritime/river
bde
BASES Coastal Mangalia, Constanta **Danube** Braila,
Giurgiu, Tulcea, Galati
SUBMARINES 1
  1 Sov Kilo SS with 533mm TT
PRINCIPAL SURFACE COMBATANTS 7
DESTROYERS 1 *Muntena* DDG with 4 x 2 SS-N-2C
  Styx SSM, plus SA-N-5 *Grail* SAM, 2 IAR-316 hel, 2 x
  3 533mm TT, RBU 6000
FRIGATES 6
  4 *Tetal* 1 with 2 ASW RL, 4 ASTT
  2 *Tetal* II with 2 ASW RL, 4 ASTT, plus 1 SA-316 hel
PATROL AND COASTAL COMBATANTS 100
CORVETTES 3 *Zborul* (Sov *Tarantul* I) with 2 x 2 SS-N-
  2C *Styx*, 1 76mm gun
MISSILE CRAFT 6 Sov *Osa* I PFM with 4 SS-N-2A
  Styx
TORPEDO CRAFT 36
  12 *Epitrop* PFT with 4 533mm TT
  24 PRC *Huchuan* PHT with 2 533mm TT
PATROL CRAFT 55
  OFFSHORE 4 *Democratia* (GDR M-40) PCO
  INSHORE 29
  25 PRC *Shanghai* PFI, 4 PRC *Huchuan*
  RIVERINE 22
  some 4 *Brutar* with 1 100mm gun, 1 122mm RL
  18<
MINE WARFARE 43
MINELAYERS 2 *Cosar*, capacity 100 mines
MINE COUNTERMEASURES 41
  4 *Musca* MSC, 12 T-301 MSI (plus some 9 non-op), 25

VD141 MSI<

SUPPORT AND MISCELLANEOUS 10

2 *Constanta* log spt with 1 *Alouette* hel, 3 spt tkr, 2
AGOR, 1 trg, 2 tugs

HELICOPTERS 7

3 1AR-316, 4 Mi-14 PL

NAVAL INFANTRY (8,000)

1 Corps HQ (Army – subordinated to Navy HQ)
2 mech, 1 mot inf, 1 arty bde, 1 AD arty regt, 1 ATK, 1
recce bn • 1 indep inf bn

EQUIPMENT

MBT 120 TR-580
ASLT GUN 12 SU-76
APC 123: 90 TAB-71, 33 TABC-79 plus 79 'look-
alikes'
TOTAL ARTY 120
TOWED 72: **122mm**: 36 M-1938 (M-30); **152mm**:
36 Model 81
MRL 122mm: 12 APR-40
MOR 36: **120mm**: 24 Model 1982, 12 M-38

COASTAL DEFENCE (800)

HQ Constanta 4 sectors
4 coastal arty bty with 32 **130mm**
10 AA arty bty
3 with 18 **30mm**, 5 with 30 **37mm**, 2 with 12 **57mm**

Air Force 47,600

(incl 5,300 AB, 27,700 conscripts); 315 cbt ac, 16 attack
hel **Flying hours** 40
Air Force comd: 2 Corps, 1 AD msl bde, 2 AD arty bde,
3 para bde
FGA 2 regt with 75 IAR-93, 13 IAR-99
FTR 6 regt with 150 MiG-21, 38 MiG-23, 15 MiG-29
RECCE 2 sqn
1 with 12* Il-28 (recce/ECM), 1 with 12* MiG-21
TPT 1 regt with **ac** 9 An-24, 14 An-26, 2 Il-18, 2 Boeing
707, 2 Rombac 1-11 4 C-130B **hel** 5 IAR-330, 5 Mi-8, 2
Mi-17, 4 SA-365, 10 IAR-316
SURVEY 3 An-30
HELICOPTERS
ATTACK 16 IAR 316A
CBT SPT 73 IAR-330, 78 IAR-316, 19 Mi-8
TRG ac 45 L-29, 31 L-39, 36 IAR-823, 23 Yak-52, 17 An-
2
AAM AA-2 *Atoll*, AA-3 *Anab*, AA-7 *Apex*
ASM AS-7 *Kerry*
AD 1 div
20 SAM sites with 120 SA-2

Forces Abroad

UN AND PEACEKEEPING

ALBANIA (*Operation Alba*): ε390 to withdraw by Aug
1997. **ANGOLA** (UNOMA): 150. **BOSNIA** (SFOR):

204; 1 engr bn. **CROATIA** (SFOR): 4. **KUWAIT**
(UNIKOM): 5 Obs

Paramilitary 79,100

BORDER GUARDS (Ministry of Interior) 22,300

(incl conscripts) 6 bde, 7 naval gp
33 TAB-71 APC, 18 SU-100 aslt gun, 12 M-1931/37
(A19) **122mm** how, 18 M-38 **120mm** mor, 20 PRC
Shanghai II PFI (included in navy))

GENDARMERIE (Ministry of Interior) 10,000

8 bde; some APC

SECURITY GUARDS (Ministry of Interior) 46,800

Slovakia

	1995	1996	1997	1998
GDP	Ks515bn	Ks581bn		
	($15.4bn)	($16.8bn)		
per capita	$6,000	$6,600		
Growth	6.8%	7.0%		
Inflation	9.9%	5.8%		
Debt	$5.8bn	$6.0bn		
Def exp	Ks13.2bn	Ks13.4bn		
	($446m)	($438m)		
Def bdgt			Ks14.3bn	
			($424m)	
FMA (US)	$0.3m	$4.2m	$0.6m	$0.6m
$ = koruna	29.7	30.7	33.8	
Population		5,370,000		
(Hungarian 11%, Romany ε5%, Czech 1%)				
Age	13–17	18–22	23–32	
Men	232,000	230,000	405,000	
Women	229,000	223,000	395,000	

Total Armed Forces

ACTIVE 41,200

(incl ε30,000 conscripts, 2,000 centrally controlled
staffs, 3,400 log and spt)
Terms of service: 12 months

RESERVES ε20,000 on mob
National Guard Force

Army 23,800

(incl 15,000 conscripts)
2 Corps HQ
2 tk bde (each 3 tk, 1 mech, 1 recce, 1 arty bn)
4 mech inf bde (each 3 mech inf, 1 tk, 1 recce, 1 arty bn)

RESERVES
National Guard Force 6 bde plus 32 indep coy

EQUIPMENT

MBT 478 (103 in store): 272 T-72M, 206 T-55
RECCE 219: 129 BRDM, 90 OT-65
AIFV 383 BMP-1, 93 BMP-2, BPZV, BRM-1K
APC 207 OT-90
TOTAL ARTY 383 (69 in store)
   TOWED 122mm: 76 D-30
   SP 184: **122mm** 49 2S1; **152mm**: 135 *Dana* (M-77)
   MRL 122mm: 87 RM-70
   MOR 120mm: 36 M-1982
SSM 9 FROG-7, SS-21, SS-23, *Scud*
ATGW ε480 (incl BMP-1 mounted): AT-3 *Sagger*, AT-5 *Spandrel*
ATK GUNS 100mm: 52 M-53
AD GUNS ε200: **30mm**: M-53/-59, *Strop* SP; **57mm**: S-60
SAM SA-7, ε48 SA-9/-13
SURV GS-13 (veh), *Long Trough* (SNAR-1), *Pork Trough* ((SNAR-2/-6) arty), *Small Fred/Small Yawn* (veh, arty), *Big Fred* (SNAR-10) veh, arty)

Air Force 12,000

114 cbt ac, 19 attack hel **Flying hours** 50
FGA 20 Su-22, 13 Su-25
FTR 52 MiG-21, 24 MiG-29
RECCE 5* MiG-21 RF
TPT 1 An-12, 2 An-24, 2 An-26, 1 Tu-154, 4 L410M
TRG 14 L-29, 24 L-39
ATTACK HEL 19 Mi-24
ASLT TPT 3 Mi-2, 3 Mi-8, 12 Mi-17
AAM AA-2 *Atoll*, AA-7 *Apex*, AA-8 *Aphid*, AA-10 *Alamo*, AA-11 *Archer*
AD SA-2, SA-3, SA-6, SA-10

Forces Abroad

UN AND PEACEKEEPING

ANGOLA (UNOMA): 5 Obs. **CROATIA** (UNTAES): 560; 1 engr bn

Paramilitary 3,950

BORDER GUARDS 600

INTERNAL SECURITY FORCES 250

CIVIL DEFENCE TROOPS 3,100

Slovenia

	1995	1996	1997	1998
GDP	t2.2tr	t2.7tr		
	($15bn)	($16bn)		
per capita	$6,700	$7,100		
Growth	4.8%	3.5%		
Inflation	12.6%	9.7%		

contd	1995	1996	1997	1998
Debt	$3.5bn	$4.0bn		
Def exp	t32.9bn	εt38.0bn		
	($277m)	($281m)		
Def bdgt			t35.0bn	
			($214m)	
FMA (US)	$0.2m	$0.7m	$0.4m	$0.6m
$1 = tolar	119	135	163	
Population		2,012,000		
(Croat 3%, Serb 2%, Muslim 1%)				
Age	13–17	18–22	23–32	
Men	73,000	75,000	149,000	
Women	68,000	71,000	147,000	

Total Armed Forces

ACTIVE 9,550

(5,500 conscripts) *Terms of service:* 7 months

RESERVES 53,000

Army (incl 300 maritime)

Army 9,550

(5,500 conscripts)
7 Mil Regions, 27 Mil Districts • 7 inf bde (each 1 active, 3 reserve inf bn) • 1 SF 'bde' • 1 SAM 'bde' (bn) • 2 indep mech bn • 1 avn 'bde'

RESERVES

2 indep mech, 1 arty, 1 coast def, 1 ATK bn

EQUIPMENT

MBT 50 M-84, 53 T-55, 6 T-34
RECCE 16 BRDM-2
AIFV 62 M-80
TOWED ARTY 105mm: 8 M-2; **155mm**: 10
SP ARTY 122mm: 8 2S1
MRL 128mm: 56 M-71 (single tube), 4 M-63
MOR 120mm: 120 M-52
ATGW AT-3 *Sagger* (incl 12 BOV-1SP)

MARITIME ELEMENT (100)

(effectively police) (plus 300 reserve)
BASE Koper
2 PCI<

AIR ELEMENT (120)

AC 3 PC-9, 3 *Zlin*-242, 1 LET L-410, 3 UTVA-75
HEL 1 AB-109, 2 B-206, 7 B-412
SAM 9 SA-9
AD GUNS 20mm: 9 SP; **30mm**: 9 SP; **57mm**: 21 SP

Paramilitary 4,500

POLICE 4,500

armed (plus 5,000 reserve) **hel** 2 AB-206 *Jet Ranger*, 1 AB-109A, 1 AB-212, 1 AB-412

Sweden

	1995	1996	1997	1998
GDP	Skr1.6tr	Skr1.6tr		
	($206bn)	($213bn)		
per capita	$19,300	$19,800		
Growth	3.0%	1.1%		
Inflation	2.5%	0.0%		
Publ Debt	80.3%	79.8%		
Def exp	Skr43.1bn	Skr40.7bn		
	($6.0bn)	($6.1bn)		
Def bdgt			Skr38.3bn	Skr35.9bn
			($4.9bn)	($4.6bn)
$1 = kronor	7.13	6.71	7.75	
Population		8,850,000		
Age	*13–17*	*18–22*	*23–32*	
Men	262,000	274,000	619,000	
Women	247,000	260,000	587,000	

Total Armed Forces

ACTIVE 53,350

(38,750 conscripts and active reservists)
Terms of service: **Army**, **Navy** 7–15 months **Air Force** 8–12 months

RESERVES[a] 570,000

(obligation to age 47) **Army** (incl Local Defence and Home Guard) 450,000 **Navy** 50,000 **Air Force** 70,000

[a] 48,000 reservists carried out refresher trg in 1995–96; length of trg depends on rank (officers up to 31 days, NCO and specialists, 24 days, others 17 days). Commitment is five exercises during reserve service period, plus mob call-outs.

Army 35,100

(26,400 conscripts and active reservists)
3 joint (tri-service) comd each with: Army div and def districts, Naval Comd (2 in Central Joint Comd)
Air Comd, logistics regt
No active units (as defined by Vienna Document)
6 div with total of 2 armd, 4 mech, 6 inf, 4 arctic bde, 7 arty regt HQ, 17 arty bn
22 def districts (4 mech, 18 inf)
EQUIPMENT
MBT 153 *Centurion*, 240 Strv-103B, 80 Strv-121 (*Leopard* 2), 66 Strv-122 (*Leopard* 2 (S))
LT TK 206 Ikv-91
AIFV 490 Pbv-302 plus 203 'look-alikes', 100+ Strf-9040
APC 415 Pbv 401A (MT-LB), 126 *Pskbil* M/42
TOWED ARTY 105mm: 508 Type-40; 155mm: 252 FH-77A/B, 170 Type F
SP ARTY 155mm: 26 BK-1A
MOR 81mm: 200; 120mm: 605

ATGW 57 TOW (Pvrbv 551 SP), RB-55, RB-56 *Bill*
RL 84mm: AT-4
RCL 84mm: *Carl Gustav*; 90mm: PV-1110
AD GUNS 40mm: 600
SAM RBS-70 (incl Lvrbv SP), RB-77 (I HAWK), RBS-90
SURV *Green Archer* (mor)
HEL 21 Hkp-9A ATK, 16 Hkp-3 tpt, 12 Hkp-4, 25 Hkp-5B trg, 28 Hkp-6A utl, 5 Hkp-11

Navy 9,500

(incl 1,100 Coastal Defence, 320 Naval Air, 4,200 conscripts and 2,500 reserve officers)
BASES Muskö, Karlskrona, Härnösand, Göteborg (spt only)
SUBMARINES 10
2 *Gotland* with 4 533mm TT, TP-613 and TP-431/451 (AIP powered)
4 *Västergötland* with 6 533mm TT, TP-613 and TP-431/451
1 mod *Näcken* (AIP) with TP-613 and TP-421
2 *Näcken* with 6 533mm TT, TP-613 and TP-421
1 *Spiggen* II (ASW target) submarine
PATROL AND COASTAL COMBATANTS 31
MISSILE CRAFT 28 PFM
4 *Göteborg* with 4 x 2 RBS-15 SSM; plus 4 400mm TT, 4 ASW mor
2 *Stockholm* with 4 x 2 RBS-15 SSM (or up to 4 additional 533 TT); plus 2 533mm, 4 400mm TT, 4 ASW mor
4 *Hugin* with 6 RB-12 *Penguin* SSM
8 *Kaparen* with 6 RB-12 *Penguin* SSM
10 *Norrköping* with 4 x 2 RBS-15 SSM or up to 6 533mm TT
PATROL CRAFT 3 PCI
MINE WARFARE 29
MINELAYERS 2
1 *Carlskrona* (200 mines) trg, 1 *Visborg* (200 mines)
(Mines can be laid by all submarine classes)
MINE COUNTERMEASURES 27
3 *Styrsö* MSO, 1 *Utö* MCMV spt, 1 *Skedsrik* MCM/diver support, 7 *Landsort* MHC, 15 MSI
SUPPORT AND MISCELLANEOUS 29
1 AGI, 1 sub rescue/salvage ship, 3 survey, 7 icebreakers, 16 tugs, 1 SES PCI (trials)

COASTAL DEFENCE (1,100)
2 coastal arty bde: 5 naval bde, 6 amph, 3 mobile arty (120mm), 12 specialist protection (incl inf, static arty (75mm, 105mm, 120mm), SSM and mor units)
EQUIPMENT
APC 47 *Piranha* (being delivered)
GUNS 40mm, incl L/70 AA; 75mm, 105mm, 120mm incl CD-80 *Karin* (mobile); 120mm *Ersta* (static)

MOR **81mm, 120mm**: 70
SSM RBS-17 *Hellfire*, 6 RBS-15KA
MINELAYERS 7 inshore, 10 inshore<
PATROL CRAFT 17 PCI
AMPH 10 LCM, 65 LCU, about 77 LCA

NAVAL AIR (320)

1 cbt ac, no armed hel
ASW 1 C-212 ac
HEL 14 Hkp4C (KV-107)(ASW), 10 Hkp6 (Bell-206) (utl)

Air Force 8,750

(incl 4,000 conscripts and 1,650 active reservists); 387
cbt ac, no armed hel **Flying hours** 110–140
3 Air Comd
FGA/RECCE 4 sqn with 58 SAAB AJS-37; plus *32
   SAAB SH/SF-37 (recce), 1 (OCU) with 14 SAAB SK-
   37, 37 JAS-39 (*Gripen*)
FTR 9 sqn
   1 with 50 SAAB J-35, 10 SAAB SK-35C
   8 with 133 SAAB JA-37
ECM 2 *Caravelle*, 2 *Gulfstream* IV
TPT 1 sqn with 8 C-130E/H, 3 *King Air* 200, 1 *Metro*
   III, 13 SK-60D/E, 1 SAAB 340B, 1 *Gulfstream* IV
   (VIP)
TRG 105 Sk-60 (includes 53* Sk-60B/C with lt attack/
   recce role) 71 SK-61
SAR 12 Hkp10 (*Super Puma*), 6 Hkp3 (Bell 204)
AAM RB-24 (AIM-9B/3 *Sidewinder*), RB-27 (*Improved
   Falcon*), RB-28 (*Falcon*), RB-71 (*Skyflash*), RB-74 AIM
   9L (*Sidewinder*), AIM 120 (AMRAAM)
ASM RB-04E, RB-05A, RB-15F, RB-75 (*Maverick*)
AD semi-automatic control and surv system, *Stric*,
   coordinates all AD components

Forces Abroad

UN AND PEACEKEEPING

ANGOLA (UNOMA): 19 Obs plus 18 civ pol.
BOSNIA (SFOR): 487; 1 mech inf bn; (UNMIBH): 50
civ pol. CROATIA (UNTAES): 5 Obs plus 16 civ pol;
(UNMOP): 1 Obs; (SFOR): 1. FYROM (UNPREDEP):
41 plus 1 Obs. GEORGIA (UNOMIG): 5 Obs. INDIA/
PAKISTAN (UNMOGIP): 9 Obs. IRAQ/KUWAIT
(UNIKOM): 5 Obs. MIDDLE EAST (UNTSO): 16 Obs.
ROK (NNSC): 6 staff

Paramilitary 600

COAST GUARD 600

   1 *Gotland* PCO and 1 KBV-171 PCC (fishery protection), some 65 PCI
   AIR ARM 3 C-212 MR, 1 Cessna 337G

CIVIL DEFENCE shelters for 6,300,000

All between ages 16–25 liable for civil defence duty

VOLUNTARY AUXILIARY ORGANISATIONS some
35,000

Switzerland

	1995	1996	1997	1998
GDP	fr362bn	fr360bn		
	($306bn)	($291bn)		
per capita	$25,900	$26,200		
Growth	0.7%	-0.7%		
Inflation	1.8%	0.9%		
Publ Debt	47.1%	48.7%		
Def exp	fr5.9bn	fr5.7bn		
	($5.0bn)	($4.6bn)		
Def bdgt			fr5.4bn	
			($3.7bn)	
$1 = franc	1.2	1.2	1.5	
Population		7,080,000		
Age	*13–17*	*18–22*	*23–32*	
Men	207,000	210,000	554,000	
Women	195,000	204,000	560,000	

Total Armed Forces

ACTIVE about 3,300 (357,460 on mobilisation)

plus recruits (2 intakes in 1996 (1 of 8,160, 1 of 14,800) each
for 15 weeks only)
Terms of service: 15 weeks compulsory recruit trg at age
19–20, followed by 10 refresher trg courses of 3 weeks
over a 22-year period between ages 20–42. Some 240,900
attended trg in 1996

RESERVES 390,000

Army 357,460 (to be mobilised)

Armed Forces Comd (All units non-active/Reserve
status)
Comd tps: 2 armd bde, 2 inf, 1 arty, 1 airport, 2 engr regt
3 fd Army Corps, each 2 fd div (3 inf, 1 arty regt), 1
   armd bde, 1 arty, 1 engr, 1 cyclist, 1 fortress regt, 1
   territorial div (4/6 regt)
1 mtn Army corps with 3 mtn div (2 mtn inf, 1 arty
   regt), 3 fortress bde (each 1 mtn inf regt), 2 mtn inf, 2
   fortress, 1 engr regt, 1 territorial div (6 regt), 2
   territorial bde (1 regt)
EQUIPMENT
   MBT 769 (incl 27 in store): 186 Pz-68, 186 Pz-68/88,
      370 Pz-87 (*Leopard* 2)
   AIFV 513 (incl 6 in store): 192 M-63/73, 315 M-63/
      89 (all M-113 with **20mm**)
   APC 836 M-63/73 (M-113) incl variants, 62 *Piranha*
   TOTAL ARTY 796 (incl 22 in store)
      TOWED **105mm**: 216 Model-46
      SP **155mm**: 558 PzHb 66/74/-74/-79/-88
      (M-109U)
   MOR **81mm**: 1,200 M-33, M-72; **120mm**: 577 (incl 44
      in store): 402 M-87, 132 M-64 (M-113)
   ATGW 2,850 *Dragon*, 303 TOW-2 SP (MOWAG)

Piranha
RL 13,540 incl: **60mm**: *Panzerfaust*; **83mm**: M-80
AD GUNS 20mm: 630
SAM 56 B/L-84 (*Rapier*), some *Stinger*
UAV *Scout*
HEL 60 *Alouette* III

MARINES

10 *Aquarius* patrol boats

Air Force 32,600 (to be mobilised)

(incl AD units, mil airfield guard units); 161 cbt ac, no
armed hel
1 Air Force bde, 1 AAA bde, 1 Air-Base bde and 1
Comd-and-Control bde
Flying hours: 150–200; reserves 50–70
FTR 10 sqn
7 with 89 *Tiger* II/F-5E, 12 *Tiger* II/F-5F
2 with 29 *Mirage* IIIS, 4 -III DS
1 with 10 F/A-18 C/D
RECCE 3 sqn with 17* *Mirage* IIIRS 2
TPT 1 sqn with 17 PC-6, 1 *Learjet* 36, 2 Do-27, 1 *Falcon*-
50
HEL 3 sqn with 15 AS-332 M-1 (*Super Puma*), 12 SA-
316 (*Alouette* III)
TRG 19 *Hawk* Mk 66, 38 PC-7, 12 PC-9 (tgt towing)
ASM AGM-65A/B *Maverick*
AAM AIM-9 *Sidewinder*, AIM-26 *Falcon*

AIR DEFENCE

1 SAM regt with 2 bn (each with 3 bty, *Bloodhound*)
1 AD bde: 1 SAM regt (3 bn, each with 2 or 3 bty:
Rapier); 7 AD regt (each with 2 or 3 bn of 3 bty;
35mm guns, *Skyguard* fire control radar)

Forces Abroad

UN AND PEACEKEEPING

BOSNIA (UNMIBH): 6 civ pol. **CROATIA** (UNTAES):
3 Obs; (UNMOP): 1 Obs. **FYROM** (UNPREDEP): 1
Obs plus 4 civ pol. **GEORGIA** (UNOMIG): 5 Obs.
KOREA (NNSC): 6 Staff. **MIDDLE EAST** (UNTSO): 7
Obs. **TAJIKISTAN** (UNMOT): 6 Obs

Paramilitary

CIVIL DEFENCE 350,000 (not part of Armed Forces)
300,000 trained

Ukraine

	1995	1996	1997	1998
GDP	h48.4bn	h80.5bn		
	($46bn)	($44bn)		
per capita	$4,300	$4,200		

contd	1995	1996	1997	1998
Growth	-11.4%	-10.0%		
Inflation	377%	ε80.3%		
Debt	$8.4bn	$9.3bn		
Def exp	εh1.5bn	εh2.4bn		
	($1.0bn)	($1.3bn)		
Def bdgt			εh1.4bn	
			($810m)	
FMA[a] (US)	$0.8m	$3.5m	$1.0m	$1.2m
$1 = hryvna	1.47	1.83	1.77	

[a] Excl US Cooperative Threat Reduction programme: 1992–
96 $395m, of which $171m spent by Sept 1996. Programme
continues in 1997–98

Population		50,853,000	
(Russian 22%, Polish ε4%, Jewish 1%)			
Age	*13–17*	*18–22*	*23–32*
Men	1,887,000	1,843,000	3,519,000
Women	1,824,000	1,803,000	3,494,000

Total Armed Forces

ACTIVE ε387,400

(excl Strategic Nuclear Forces and Black Sea Fleet; incl
83,600 in central staffs, plus 1,900 in units not covered
below)
Terms of service: **Army, Air Force** 18 months **Navy** 2
years

RESERVES some 1,000,000

mil service within 5 years

Strategic Nuclear Forces

(to be eliminated under START)
ICBM 115 (none with warheads)
69 SS-19 *Stiletto* (RS-18); at two sites
46 SS-24 *Scalpel* (RS-22); silo-based, one site co-
located with SS-19
BBR 44
20 Tu-95H16
5 Tu-95H6 (with AS-15 ALCM)
19 Tu-160 (with AS-15 ALCM)
plus 2 Tu-95A/B in store (under Ukr comd)

Ground Forces 161,500

MoD tps: 1 TD (trg), 1 arty bde (trg), 1 *Spetsnaz*, 1 arty,
1 SSM, 1 ATK, 2 engr bde, 1 attack, 1 tpt hel regt
CARPATHIAN MD
Comd tps 1 arty div (2 arty, 1 MRL, 1 ATK regt), 1
SSM, 1 avn bde, 1 engr regt
3 Corps 1 with 2 MRD (1 res), 1 mech, 1 SSM, 1 arty, 1
SAM, 1 engr bde, 1 MRL, 1 ATK, 1 attack hel regt
1 with 2 mech div, 2 mech, 1 SSM, 1 arty, 2 SAM bde,
1 ATK (res), 1 MRL (res), 1 attack hel regt
1 with 1 TD, 1 SAM, 1 ATK, 1 attack hel regt

ODESSA MD

Comd tps 1 mech div (trg), 1 mech bde, 1 arty div, 1
Spetsnaz, 1 SSM, 1 SAM, 1 avn bde

4 Corps 1 with 2 mech bde, 1 arty, 1 SAM bde, 1 ATK,
1 MRL regt (res) • 1 with 1 TD (trg), 1 mech div, 1
SSM bde, 1 MRL, 1 ATK (res), 1 attack hel regt • 1
with 2 mech div, 1 SSM, 1 SAM bde, 1 arty, 1 MRL, 1
avn bde •1 with 1 mech div, 1 MRL regt

EQUIPMENT

MBT 4,063 (940 in store): 154 T-55, 1 T-62, 2,282 T-64,
1,304 T-72, 322 T-80

RECCE some 1,500

AIFV 3,080: 1,016 BMP-1, 457 BRM-1K, 1,464 BMP-
2, 4 BMP-3, 61 BMD-1, 78 BMD-2

APC 1,762: 204 BTR-60, 1,059 BTR-70, 457 BTR-80,
42 BTR-D; plus 2,000 MT-LB, 4,700 'look-alikes'

TOTAL ARTY 3,764 (561 in store)

TOWED 1,146: **122mm**: 436 D-30, 3 M-30; **152mm**:
224 D-20, 8 ML-20, 186 2A65, 289 2A36

SP 1,308: **122mm**: 643 2S1; **152mm**: 501 2S3, 24
2S5, 40 2S19; **203mm**: 100 2S7

COMBINED GUN/MOR 120mm: 70 2S9, 2 2B16

MRL 634: **122mm**: 373 BM-21, 24 9P138; **132mm**: 4
BM-13; **220mm**: 139 9P140; **300mm**: 94 9A52

MOR 604: **120mm**: 347 2S12, 255 PM-38; **160mm**:
2 M-160

SSM 132 *Scud*, 140 FROG/SS-21

ATGW AT-4 *Spigot*, AT-5 *Spandrel*, AT-6 *Spiral*

SAM SA-4/-6/-8/-11/-12A/-15

ATTACK HEL 270 Mi-24

SPT HEL 14 Mi-2, 33 Mi-6, 136 Mi-8, 40 Mi-24 P-K,
16 Mi-26

SURV SNAR-10 (*Big Fred*), *Small Fred* (arty)

Navy† ε16,000

On 31 May 1997, Russian President Yeltsin and Ukrainian
President Kuchma signed an inter-governmental agreement
on the status and terms of the Black Sea Fleet's deployment
on the territory of Ukraine and parametres for the Fleet's
division. The Russian Fleet will lease bases in Sevastopol for
the next 20 years. It will be based at Sevastopol and
Karantinnaya Bays and jointly with Ukrainian warships at
Streletskaya Bay. The overall serviceability of the Fleet is very
low. The following order of battle is interim; more units will
be transferred from Russia.

BASES Sevastopol, Donuzlav, Odessa, Kerch,
Balaklava, Nikolaev

SUBMARINES 3

3 prob *Foxtrot*

PRINCIPAL SURFACE COMBATANTS 4

1 *Krivak* 2 with 4 SS-N-14 SSM, 2 100mm gun, 8
533mm TT

2 *Krivak* 3 with 2 SA-N-4 SAM, 1 100mm gun, 8
533mm TT, 1 KA-27 hel

1 *Petya* III with 4 76mm gun, 3 533mm TT

PATROL AND COASTAL COMBATANTS 9

3 *Grisha* PCP (type n.k.)

1 *Pauk* PFT with 4 SA-N-5 SAM, 1 76mm gun, 4
406mm TT

4 *Matka* PHM with 2 SS-N-2C SSM, 1 76mm gun

1 *Mukha* PHT with 8 406mm TT, 1 76mm gun

MINE COUNTERMEASURES 3

2 *Yurka* MSO, 1 *Yevgenya* MHC

AMPHIBIOUS 7

4 *Pomornik* ACV with 2 SA-N-5 capacity 30 tps and
crew

1 *Ropucha* LST with 4 SA-N-5 SAM, 2 x 2 57mm gun,
92 mines; capacity 190 tps or 24 veh

1 *Alligator* LST with 2/3 SA-N-5 SAM capacity 300
tps and 20 tk

1 *Polnocny* LSM capacity 180 tps and 6 tk

SUPPORT AND MISCELLANEOUS 9

1 Mod *Kamkatka* research, 2 *Vytegrales* AK, 1 *Lama*
msl spt, 1 Mod *Moma* AGI, 1 *Primore* AGI, 1
Kashtan buoytender, 1 *Passat* AGOS, 1 *Elbrus* ASR

NAVAL AVIATION (7,000)

32 MiG-29, 69 Su-17, 44 Su-25, 39 Tu-22M

NAVAL INFANTRY (Marines – 1,250)

2 inf bn

Air Force 124,400

(incl Air Defence) some 790 cbt ac, plus 380 in store
(MiG-21, MiG-23, MiG-25, MiG-27, MiG-29, Su-24,
Yak-28), 24 attack hel

2 air corps, 1 PVO army

BBR 1 div HQ, 2 regt with 28 Tu-22M

FGA/BBR 2 div HQ, 5 regt (1 trg) with 166 Su-24

FGA 1 regt with 34 Su-25

FTR 2 div, 6 PVO regt with 140 MiG-23, 73 MiG-25,
145 MiG-29, 66 Su-27

RECCE 4 regt (1 trg) with 17* Tu-22, 41* Su-17, 41* Su-
24, 13* MiG-25

ECM 1 sqn with 29 Mi-8

TPT 174 Il-76, 100 others incl An-12

TRG 7 regt with 23* Tu-22M, 3* Tu-16, 430 L-39

ATTACK HEL 24 Mi-24

SPT HEL 16 Mi-6, 144 Mi-8, 8 Mi-26

SAM 825: SA-2/-3/-5/-10/-12A

Forces Abroad

UN AND PEACEKEEPING

ANGOLA (UNOMA): 4 Obs. **BOSNIA** (SFOR): 371;
(UNMIBH): 39 civ pol. **CROATIA** (UNTAES): 260; 1
inf bn, incl 4 Obs and 19 civ pol; (UNMOP): 1 Obs.
FYROM (UNPREDEP): 1 Obs plus 4 civ pol.

Paramilitary ε36,000

MVS (Ministry of Internal Affairs) ε6,000

internal security tps
NATIONAL GUARD 30,000
1 'div', 5 'bde' (incl 1 AB) reported
BORDER GUARD (incl Coast Guard) str n.k.
some minor vessels

Yugoslavia, Federal Republic of (Serbia–Montenegro)

	1995	1996	1997	1998
GDP	sd38bn	sd58bn		
	($16bn)	($17bn)		
per capita	$4,100	$4,300		
Growth	6.0%	5.5%		
Inflation	120%	58.7%		
Debt	$10.5bn	$10.0bn		
Def exp	εsd8.4bn	εsd7.5bn		
	($3.1bn)	($1.5bn)		
Def bdgt			sd6.5bn	
			($1.1bn)	
$1 = super dinar	2.70	5.10	5.71	
Population		ε11,350,000		

Serbia ε10,500,000 (Serb 66%, Albanian 17%,
Hungarian 4%, Muslim 2%)
Montenegro ε850,000(Montenegrin 62%, Muslim
15%, Serb 9%, Albanian 7%)
(ε2,032,000 Serbs were living in the other Yugoslav
republics before the civil war)

Age	*13–17*	*18–22*	*23–32*
Men	422,000	426,000	835,000
Women	398,000	403,000	793,000

Total Armed Forces

ACTIVE some 114,200
(43,000 conscripts)
Terms of service: 12–15 months

RESERVES some 400,000

Army (JA) some 90,000

(37,000 conscripts)
3 Army, 7 Corps (incl 1 capital def) • 3 div HQ • 6 tk
bde • 1 gd bde (-), 1 SF bde • 4 mech bde • 1 AB bde •
8 mot inf bde (incl 1 protection) • 5 mixed arty bde • 7
AD bde • 1 SAM bde

RESERVES
27 mot inf, 42 inf, 6 mixed arty bde
EQUIPMENT
    MBT 785 T-55, 239 M-84 (T-74; mod T-72), 181 T-34,
    65 T-72
    LT TK PT-76

RECCE 88 BRDM-2
AIFV 568 M-80
APC 169 M-60P, 68 BOV VP M-86
TOWED 105mm: 265 M-56, 15 M-18, 54 M2A1;
    122mm: 90 M-38, 310 D-30; **130mm**: 276 M-46;
    152mm: 25 D-20, 52 M-84; **155mm**: 139 M-1, 6 M-
    65
SP 122mm: 83 2S1
MRL 107mm; 122mm: BM-21; **128mm**: 103 M-63, 64
    M-77, **262mm**: M-87 *Orkan*
MOR 82mm: 1,665; **120mm**: 6 M-38/-39, 123 M-52,
    320 M-74, 854 M-75
SSM 4 FROG
ATGW 135 AT-3 *Sagger* incl SP (BOV-1, BRDM-1/2),
    AT-4 *Fagot*
RCL 57mm: 1,550; **82mm**: 1,000 M-60PB SP; **105mm**:
    650 M-65
ATK GUNS 750: **76mm**: 24 M-42, 94 M-48; **90mm**:
    M-36B2 (incl SP), M-3; **100mm**: 138 T-12, MT-12
AD GUNS 1,850: **20mm**: M-55/-75, BOV-3 SP triple;
    30mm: M-53, M-53/-59, BOV-30 SP; **57mm**: ZSU-
    57-2 SP
SAM 60 SA-6, SA-7/-9/-13/-14/-16

Navy ε7,500

(incl 3,000 conscripts and 900 Marines)
BASES Kumbor, Tivat, Bar, Novi Sad (River Comd)
(Most former Yugoslav bases are now in Croatian
hands)
SUBMARINES 4
    2 *Sava* SS with 533mm TT (1 in refit)
    2 *Heroj* SS with 533mm TT (1 in refit)
    (Plus 5 *Una* SSI for SF ops, 3 non-op)
FRIGATES 4
    2 *Kotor* with 4 SS-N-2C *Styx* SSM, 1 x 2 SA-N-4
    SAM, 2 x 12 ASW RL, 2 x 3 ASTT
    2 *Split* (Sov *Koni*) with 4 SS-N-2C, 1 x 2 SA-N-4 SAM,
    Styx SSM, 2 x 12 ASW RL
PATROL AND COASTAL COMBATANTS 34
MISSILE CRAFT 10
    5 *Rade Koncar* PFM with 2 SS-N-2B *Styx* (some †)
    5 *Mitar Acev* (Sov *Osa* I) PFM with 4 SS-N-2A
PATROL CRAFT 24
    PATROL, INSHORE 6 *Mirna*
    PATROL, RIVERINE about 18 < (some in reserve)
MINE WARFARE 16
MINELAYERS 1 *Sibla*-class, 94 mines
    D-3 and D-501 LCTs can also lay 100 mines
MINE COUNTERMEASURES 15
    2 *Vukov Klanac* MHC, 2 UK *Ham* MSI, 7 *Nestin* MSI, 4
    Type M-301 MSR
AMPHIBIOUS 20
    1 *Silba* LCT/ML: capacity 6 tk or 300 tps, 1 x 4 SA-
    N-5 SAM, 94 SAG-1 mines
    1 DSM 501 LCT/ML capacity 3 mbt or 200 tps
    8 Type 22 LCU

6 Type 21 LCU
4 Type 11 LCVP

SUPPORT AND MISCELLANEOUS 9

1 PO-91 *Lubin* tpt, 1 water carrier, 4 tugs, 2 AK, 1 degassing

MARINES (900)

2 mot inf 'bde' (2 regt each of 2 bn) • 1 lt inf bde (reserve) • 1 coast arty bde • 1 MP bn

Air Force 16,700

(3,000 conscripts); 241 cbt ac, 56 armed hel
2 Corps (1 AD)
FGA 4 sqn with 30 *Orao* 2, 50 *Galeb*, 10 *Super Galeb* G-4
FTR 5 sqn with 48 MiG-21F/PF/M/bis, 17 MiG-21U, 15 MiG-29
RECCE 2 sqn with some 20* *Orao*, 18* MiG-21R

ARMED HEL 48 *Gazelle*
ASW 1 hel sqn with 3* Mi-14, 3* Ka-25, 2* Ka-28
TPT 15 An-26, 4 CL-215 (SAR, fire-fighting), 2 *Falcon* 50 (VIP), 6 Yak-40
LIAISON ac 32 UTVA-66 **hel** 14 *Partizan*
TRG ac 17* *Super Galeb*, 16* *Orao*, 25 UTVA **hel** 16 *Gazelle*
AAM AA-2 *Atoll*, AA-8 *Aphid*, AA-10 *Alamo*, AA-11 *Archer*
ASM AGM-65 *Maverick*, AS-7 *Kerry*
AD 8 SAM bn, 8 sites with 24 SA-2, 16 SA-3 15 regt AD arty

Paramilitary

MINISTRY OF INTERIOR TROOPS str n.k.
internal security; eqpt incl 150 AFV, 170 mor

MILITARY DEVELOPMENTS

The major threat to the Russian armed forces in 1997 was not military, but financial. A dire lack of funding was compounded by delays and genuine difficulties in implementing urgently needed structural reforms. Although the military receives nearly 20% of the total federal budget, the money is not being managed properly to continue the reform programme; rather, it is being used, at least in mid-1997, to maintain as far as possible the inefficient status quo. The appointment of General Igor Sergeyev on 21 May 1997 as Minister of Defence, in place of General Igor Rodionov, raised expectations that the reform programme would be accelerated. However, crisis management, rather than managed restructuring, still seems the order of the day.

The decrees announced by President Boris Yeltsin on 16 July 1997 appeared to acknowledge reality, not herald a rigorous programme of action. Yeltsin announced cuts in the authorised numbers of armed forces personnel of 0.5–1.2 million; the latter figure represents the current force strength according to *The Military Balance* estimates. There may well be some further savings as the structure supporting the unfilled posts is removed by cuts and mergers in accordance with the presidential decrees. In particular, a large number of senior officers' posts should disappear. For example, the Strategic Rocket Forces, Space Commands and anti-aircraft missile units are to be merged, and the Air Defence Force is to be absorbed into the Air Force. Apart from airborne and special forces, the command of Army field formations will be devolved to military districts, and the centralised command structure will be sharply reduced. If effected, these cuts will bring the force level nearer to one which can be maintained by conscription and with contract soldiers.

In his 16 July decree, the President re-affirmed his commitment to ending conscription by 2005, although his pre-election decree of 16 May 1996 stated that this would be achieved by 2000. The later date will still be difficult to meet. In 1997, some estimates indicate that only about one-third of those liable for conscription are reporting for duty; half go to the main branches of the armed forces, the other half to the Interior and Border Troops.

Since the war in Chechnya ended in August 1996, the regular armed forces have seen little military action apart from in Tajikistan. Even there, the June 1997 General Agreement of National Reconciliation and Peace Establishment halted fighting for a while. However, Russian Border Troops are fully occupied with frontier controls along the Tajik border with Afghanistan. Russian Army and Border Troops in Tajikistan total some 20,000 personnel, although the Commander of the Russian Federal Border Troops, General Andrei Nikolaev, said in July 1997 that Moscow is considering reductions, but they would not take place for several months. In July 1997, there were still nearly 2,000 Russian troops in the Abkhazia region of Georgia; little progress had been made in negotiations to replace them with a UN peacekeeping force. In other parts of the Trans-caucasus, the Russian Army is supporting Border Troops in dealing with terrorist activities arising from the territorial dispute between North Ossetia and Ingushetia.

Another method of dealing with border security, this time in relation to China, was the Agreement on Confidence-Building in the Military Field in Border Areas signed in Shanghai in April 1996. This agreement was followed by another on conventional force reductions signed in Moscow on 24 April 1997. The principal parties to this second agreement are Russia and China, but the three Central Asian states sharing borders with China – Kazakstan, Kyrgyzstan and Tajikistan – are also signatories. The agreement – to remain valid, but renewable, until 31 December 2020 – covers 7,000 kilometres of borders between China and the other states. It requires each party to have no more than 130,400 military personnel in an area 100km-wide on their side of the border. Details of the timetable for the reductions, data exchanges and how the implementation is to be supervised have yet to be finalised. Given Russia's current deployments, it is hard to see what reductions, if any, are necessary on its part. The agreement does not apply to strategic forces or long-range aviation. The timing of this agreement, and its predecessor in 1996, had more to do with political manoeuvring in negotiating the NATO–Russia Founding Act of 29 May 1997 prior to the NATO summit in Madrid in July 1997 (when the first stage of NATO enlargement was announced) than partnership with China.

The most significant naval development in 1997 was a final agreement between Russia and Ukraine over the division of the Black Sea Fleet. On 31 May 1997 in Kiev, Presidents Yeltsin and Leonid Kuchma signed an inter-governmental agreement on the status and terms of the Fleet's deployment in Ukrainian territory, the parametres for its division and mutual payments. Russia will lease bases in the north and south bays of Sevastopol for the next 20 years. Russian warships will be based in Sevastopol and Karantinnaya Bays and Ukrainian warships in Streletskaya Bay and others to the west. In addition, units of the Russian Naval Infantry will be stationed at Kamiyshovaya Bay. By June 1997, Russia had transferred 35 submarines, surface warships and support vessels to Ukraine; more are expected to follow. Among the branches of the Russian armed forces, despite severe lack of funding, the Navy probably maintains the highest degree of combat readiness. The numbers of ballistic-missile submarines (SSBN) available for patrol have fallen; only one boat is maintained on station in each of the Northern and Pacific Fleet areas. However, all four fleets continue to exercise modestly, although their activities have been greatly curtailed. The submarine branch continues to be highly valued and receives a substantial percentage of the naval budget allocation for construction and operations.

The Air Force is critically short of spares; less than half its aircraft are serviceable. Although the number of active airfields has been reduced by half over the past decade, nearly half of those remaining desperately require repair and modernisation. Shortage of money, lack of fuel and poor aircraft serviceability also seriously limit flying training. Flying standards are now considered to be below basic safety levels, let alone combat efficiency. Those pilots that obtain some flying time, usually only more experienced air crew, will average between 10 and 40 hours per year, compared to the NATO combat air crew average of 180–240 hours per year.

FUTURE DEVELOPMENTS

There are three outstanding priorities for Russian military reform. First, the armed forces command structure must be reorganised as soon as possible and clear lines of responsibility drawn between the armed forces and the various types of Interior Troops. Also, personnel numbers, in particular in senior officer posts, must be reduced. Second, resources need to be allocated to improve the training and equipment of a lighter, all-professional force for roles relevant to Russia's current security requirements. Third, these changes can only work if a new system of financial controls is introduced to make best use of the budgetary resources available and eliminate corruption and waste. On 22 May 1997, the President formed two commissions to oversee military reform headed by civilian members of the government, Prime Minister Viktor Chernomyrdin and First Deputy Prime Minister Anatoli Chubais.

DEFENCE SPENDING

During 1996–97, defence has continued to receive relatively favourable budgetary allocations, accounting for around one-fifth of government spending. However, the federal government has been collecting only a fraction of its tax revenue, resulting in actual defence outlays being around one-fifth less than budgeted. Other spending departments have had to cope with the same shortfall. The Defence Ministry, because of its political clout, receives more than most ministries.

Defence Budgets 1996–1998

Despite the Chechnya *débâcle*, the armed forces' political influence secured large increases in defence spending in both 1996 and 1997. A similar situation arose in 1994. As then, the prospective boost to defence spending did not materialise after the sequestration of around one-fifth of the defence budget. Following the December 1995 parliamentary elections, when the communists became the largest single party in the Duma, and with a presidential election due in June 1996, the Russian military had cause for optimism. This optimism was justified, as, in budgetary terms, the armed forces had their best year (1994 apart) since the Soviet Union collapsed in 1991. The Budget Law was published on 10 January 1996 – nearly three months earlier than in 1995 – and the armed forces were allocated some R80.2 trillion. At the then prevailing inflation forecast, this represented a decline from the revised 1995 budget of R59.4tr, but a real increase over the actual 1995 outlay. In the event, inflation was higher than expected, despite falling steeply from 197% in 1995 to 48% in 1996, according to International Monetary Fund (IMF) figures. Meanwhile, 1996 outlays have been reported as R64tr, signifying that actual government outlays in the defence budget fell by some 10% in 1996 compared to 1995.

Table 12 **Official Russian defence budgets and outlays, 1992–1998**			
(current roubles bn)	**Defence budget**	**% Federal budget**	**Defence outlay**
1992	384	*16.0*	855.3
1993 (revised)	3,116 (8,327)	*16.6 (n.a.)*	n.a. (7,210)
1994	40,626	*20.9*	28,028
1995 (revised)	48,577 (59,379)	*19.6 (21.3)*	n.a (47,800)
1996	80,185	*18.4*	63,900
1997 (revised)	104,300 (83,000)	*19.7 (19.7)*	n.a. (n.a.)
1998	94,000	*n.a.*	n.a.

When the 1997 budget process began in autumn 1996, the military was quick to renew its case for more money from the government. The strong showing of Communist Party leader Gennadi Zhuganov and the nationalist former General Alexander Lebed in the June presidential election had raised expectations. The initial target was an unrealistic R260tr, including R40tr for unpaid debts from previous years. This figure was subsequently reduced to R160.3tr, but still far from the Finance Ministry target of R90tr. Eventually, the Finance Ministry figure was adjusted upwards as the defence-budget bill progressed through the Duma and Federation Council. Most of the increase went to equipment procurement and Research and Development (R&D) accounts; their combined share of the budget rose from 24% to 31% in 1996. Salaries and pensions continue to take priority over Operations and Maintenance (O&M). The peacekeeping budget in 1997, for example, amounts to just R512bn ($100m at the market exchange rate) to cover the deployment of Russian forces in the Dniestr region of Moldova, and the South Ossetia and Abkhazia regions in Georgia and Tajikistan. The incremental cost of Russia's contribution to the NATO-led Implementation Force (IFOR) in Bosnia was $23m in 1996, funded in foreign currency by the Ministry of Finance. A new account was created for payments and housing benefits to discharged servicemen. The defence budget of R104.3tr was finally approved under the Federal Budget Law of 25 February 1997. Under the prevailing inflation forecasts, the defence budget represented a rise of around one-third in real terms over the 1996 out-turn – one of the reasons why Yeltsin was reluctant to sign what was overall an unrealistic federal budget into law.

Table 13 **Official Russian defence budgets by function, 1993–1997**											
(current roubles bn)	1993	%	1994	%	1995	%	1995 (revised)	%	1996	%	1997	%
Personnel, O&M	1,556	50.0	22,105	54.4	21,982	45.3	31,880	53.7	41,120	51.3	48,364	46.4
Procurement	570	18.3	8,442	20.8	10,275	21.2	10,275	17.3	13,213	16.5	20,963	20.1
R&D	225	7.2	2,433	6.0	4,936	10.2	4,936	8.3	6,475	8.1	11,574	11.1
Infrastructure	514	16.5	4,778	11.8	6,138	12.6	6,138	10.3	7,637	9.5	5,017	4.8
Pensions	171	5.5	1,994	4.9	4,015	8.3	4,867	8.2	9,899	12.3	13,858	13.3
Nuclear, other	80	2.6	874	2.2	1,231	2.5	1,283	2.2	1,842	2.3	2,095	2.0
Military reform	–	–	–	–	–	–	–	–	–	–	2,429	2.3
Total	3,116	100	40,626	100	48,577	100	59,379	100	80,185	100	104,300	100

Note The 1993 defence budget of R3.1tr (May 1993) was later adjusted to R8.3tr. The 1995 budget was adjusted to R59.4tr in December 1995. The government reduced the 1997 defence budget to R83.0tr in May 1997.

The Federal Budget Law, however, proved short lived. In March 1997, a government reshuffle aimed primarily at strengthening economic management took place. The IMF had already signalled its disapproval of the government's inadequate tax collection by suspending the Extended Fund Facility (EFF) monthly disbursements to Russia, due in the first quarter of 1997 (subsequently released at the end of May). Also in May, the government's financial crisis forced a revised federal budget of 20% less than the original, with defence spending expected to take a pro-rata share of the cuts. The government proposed a new defence budget of R83tr. Since the military had already warned the government that the 1997 R104tr defence budget would be exhausted after nine months, the government faces a difficult time in the later part of this year. Following the appointment of Defence Minister Sergeyev, the government set a target of R94tr for the 1998 defence budget – a 5% real increase on 1997 at prevailing inflation projections.

The question of funding military reform remains unresolved. Soon after taking office in May 1997, Sergeyev outlined his priorities and the sources from which he believed funding should come: increased O&M allocations, with an emphasis on improving training, funded by the defence budget; improving redundancy and pensions to retiring personnel, funded under a federal budget article outside the defence budget; and extra-budgetary funding from the sale of military property, businesses and surplus arms and equipment.

PROCUREMENT, THE DEFENCE INDUSTRY AND ARMS SALES

The range of Russia's weapons programmes remains wide icompared to any country except the United States. Similarly, although production levels have fallen drastically since the Cold War, Russian defence-industrial output remains high in comparison with other major industrialised countries, even though it exports a relatively larger proportion. The revenue from exports has helped several R&D programmes currently under way across the spectrum of conventional and strategic weapons programmes, as well aso modernisation programmes (in some cases, involving joint ventures with foreign enterprises, including French, German and Israeli companies).

Table 14 Estimated production of major weapon systems, 1990–1996

	1990[1]	1991[1]	1992	1993	1994	1995	1996
Main battle tanks	1,600	850	500	200	40	30	5
Infantry fighting vehicles	3,400	3,000	700	300	380	400	250
SP artillery	500	300	200	100	85	15	20
Bombers	40	30	20	10	2	2	1
Fighters/FGA	430	250	150	100	50	20	25
Transport aircraft[2]	70	60	60	60	35	30	15
Helicopters[2]	450	350	175	150	100	95	75
Submarines	12	6	6	4	4	3	2
Major surface ships	2	3	1	1	0	1	1
ICBMs/SLBMs	115	100	55	35	25	10	10
SRBMs[3]	0	0	80	105	55	45	35

Notes [1] USSR

[2] Includes civilian production

[3] Production relocated from Kazakstan to Russia in 1992

Source UK Ministry of Defence, London

Government policy towards the defence industry has been to promote conversion, concentration and privatisation. The decline in Russian arms procurement since the Cold War ended did not produce any immediate rationalisation in the defence industry. Initially, great hopes were placed on the plan to convert defence firms into enterprises producing mainly civilian goods, while remaining within the defence-industrial complex. The government's procurement policy has attempted to reduce the number of defence firms by awarding contracts to a select number of preferred contractors (thereby initiating the current process of industrial concentration), and, more recently, by introducing competitive tendering. However, the privatisation programme, due to start in 1993, appears to have stalled. The intention at the time was to reduce the number of state-controlled defence firms from some 2,000 to below 500. In April 1997, the government abolished the Ministry of Defence Industries and incorporated it into the Ministry of Economics. While this change has produced considerable short-term confusion, it remains to be seen how this reorganisation will affect the defence industry's bargaining power within government in the long term.

There is still a large degree of over-capacity and duplication among the larger defence firms in Russia. This is starting to create the merger and acquisition activity prevalent in US and West European defence industries. To date, the largest defence conglomerate to emerge is VPK MAPO (Moscow Aircraft Production Association) – established in January 1996 and grouping together the firms involved in manufacturing MiG combat aircraft. VPK MAPO is a Financial-Industrial Group (FIG, similar to the Airbus structure known as *Groupement d'Intérêt Economique*), as opposed to an equity-driven set of mergers and acquisitions. Later, in October 1996, Sukhoi AVPK, the most successful Russian military aircraft company, in terms of both Russian government contracts and exports, teamed up with the Beriev design bureau and three production plants. Sukhoi also proposed a new structure combining itself with two other aircraft firms, Tupolev and Yakolev, together with the helicopter manufacturer, Mil. The creation of the Ilyushin Transnational Financial Industrial Group followed in February 1997 (a major part of the group is located in Tashkent, Uzbekistan).

Table 15 Comparison of Russian arms trade, procurement and foreign trade, 1992–1997

	Arms trade (US$bn)	Arms trade (Rbn)	Domestic procurement incl R&D (Rbn)	Arms trade as % of domestic procurement	Arms trade as % of merchandise exports
1992	2.5	450	228	197.4	5.9
1993	3.1	3,075	2,130	144.4	7.0
1994	2.7	5,916	10,875	54.4	4.1
1995	3.3	15,045	15,211	98.9	4.2
1996	3.5	17,924	19,688	91.0	3.9
1997ε	4.0	23,020	32,537	70.8	4.0
Total	**19.1**	**65,429**	**80,669**	–	–

Russia's arms trade represents an increasingly important source of foreign currency. At present, the defence sector is a principal manufacturing-industry exporter. The arms trade is also a significant extra-budgetary source of income for company R&D activity – generating relatively large revenues in comparison with official outlays on procurement and R&D.

Table 16 Military-related expenditure outside the defence budget, 1995–1997

(roubles bn)	1995	1996	1997
Arms control	2,549	3,324	3,110
Space Agency	1,402	3,000	n.a.
of which Baikonur lease	161	720	625
Internal Troops	1,536	3,252	3,878
Border Troops	2,401	3,988	5,888
State Security	2,458	5,142	6,632
Subsidies to military regions	1,043	1,932	n.a.
Defence conversion	2,315	3,862	1,711
Debts to industry	3,553	2,200	n.a.
Science (R&D)[1]	2,614	6,509	7,629
Civil defence, mobilisation	304	388	1,388
Emergencies	2,438	5,798	7,690
Service housing	2,462	n.a.	n.a.
Sub-total	*25,237*	*39,036*	*38,551*
Defence budget	48,577	80,185	104,300
Total military budget	**73,814**	**119,221**	**142,851**
Federal budget	248,344	435,750	529,600
% Military spending/Federal budget	*29.7*	*27.4*	*27.0*

Note [1] Figure assumes 50% of the budget is for military-related R&D

INDEPENDENT ESTIMATES OF RUSSIAN MILITARY SPENDING

The Russian defence budget continues to exclude substantial funding for paramilitary forces, arms control, participation in UN operations, and various subsidies to military regions and industries. As the Russian Federation law 'On Defence' of 31 May 1996 makes clear, both the Border Troops and Internal Troops among the paramilitary agencies are involved in defence, although they are funded under the Law Enforcement and State Security budget. About half of the budget's science allocation may still be spent on military-related research (one reason why R&D appears low when measured against the range of current Russian programmes). When military-related spending is added to the defence budget, these outlays may raise the proportion of the military component of the federal budget to over one-quarter.

Various independent estimates of Russia's military spending are shown in the table below. Discrepancies arise for two reasons: first, because definitions of military outlays vary so that different treatment is afforded to paramilitary spending and various regional and industrial subsidies; and, second, because estimates of rouble purchasing-power parity (PPP) with the US dollar vary considerably. Estimates in *The Military Balance* show that Russian defence expenditure – under NATO definitions and using PPP values rather than formal exchange rates – currently amounts to around 7% of gross domestic product (GDP) – 2–3 times more than present levels in developed countries. This estimate excludes revenue and expenditure accruing to the armed forces of the several 'power ministries' through association with the black economy, officially estimated in 1997 at R750tr, or 45% of GDP.

Russia

Table 17 Independent estimates of Russian military expenditure, 1992–1997

	IMF (% of GDP)	NATO (% of GDP)	ACDA (1995$bn)	ACDA (% of GDP)	IISS (1995$bn)	IISS (% of GDP)
1992	4.7	>10	171	20	140	12
1993	4.4	>10	131	17	109	9
1994	4.6	>10	95	14	97	9
1995	2.9	7–10	76	11	82	8
1996	3.6	7–8	n.a.	n.a.	70	7
1997	3.3	n.a.	n.a.	n.a.	70	7

Russia

	1995	1996	1997	1998
GDP[a]	εr1,888tr	εr2,256tr		
	($1.1tr)	($1.1tr)		
per capita	$6,600	$6,500		
Growth	ε-4.0%	ε-2.8%		
Inflation	ε197.0%	ε47.5%		
Debt	$120bn	$129bn		
Def exp[a]	ε$82bn	ε$71bn		
Def bdgt[a]			r83tr	r94tr
			($31bn)	($32bn)
FMA[b] (US)	$0.4m	$2.3m	$0.8m	$0.9m
(Ge) 1991–97		$5.0bn		
$1 = rouble	4,559	5,121	5,750	

[a] PPP est

[b] Under the US Cooperative Threat Reduction programme, $754m has been authorised for FY1992–96 to support START implementation and demilitarisation in Russia. By September 1996, $328m had been spent. The 1998 budget request is $382m (1997 $328m) of which Russia's share is 50–60%

Population	148,000,000

(Ukrainian 5%, Tatar 4%, Belarussian 1%, Moldovan 1%, other 10%)

Age	13–17	18–22	23–32
Men	5,768,000	5,417,000	10,307,000
Women	5,560,000	5,258,000	10,013,000

Total Armed Forces

ACTIVE ε1,240,000

(perhaps 381,000 conscripts, 153,000 women; incl about 200,000 MoD staff, centrally controlled units for EW, trg, rear services, not incl elsewhere)
Terms of service: 18–24 months. Women with medical and other special skills may volunteer

RESERVES some 20,000,000

some 2,400,000 with service within last 5 years; Reserve obligation to age 50

Strategic Nuclear Forces ε149,000

(incl 49,000 assigned from Air Force, Air Defence and Navy)

NAVY (ε13,000)

452 msl in 29 operational SSBN
SSBN 29 (all based in Russian ports)
   4 *Typhoon* with 20 SS-N-20 *Sturgeon* (80 msl)
   7 *Delta* IV with 16 SS-N-23 *Skiff* (112 msl)
   10 *Delta* III with 16 SS-N-18 *Stingray* (160 msl)
   1 *Delta* II with 16 SS-N-8 *Sawfly* (16 msl)
   7 *Delta* I with 12 SS-N-8 *Sawfly* (84 msl)
(The following non-op SSBNs remain START-accountable)
   1 *Yankee* 1 with 16 SS-N-6

   3 *Delta* II with a total of 48 SS-N-8
   7 *Delta* I with a total of 84 SS-N-8)

STRATEGIC ROCKET FORCES (ε100,000)

(incl 50,000 conscripts)
5 rocket armies, org in div, regt, bn and bty, launcher gp normally with 10 silos (6 for SS-18) and one control centre; 12 SS-24 rail each 3 launchers
ICBM 877
   186 SS-18 *Satan* (RS-20) at 4 fields; mostly mod 4/5, 10 MIRV; in **Russia**
   239 SS-19 *Stiletto* (RS-18) at 4 fields; mostly mod 3, 6 MIRV; 170 in **Russia**, 69 in **Ukraine** (without warheads)
   92 SS-24 *Scalpel* (RS-22) 10 MIRV; 10 silo, 36 rail in **Russia**, 46 silo in **Ukraine** (without warheads)
   360 SS-25 *Sickle* (RS-12M) mobile, single-warhead msl; 10 bases with some 40 units in **Russia**

STRATEGIC AVIATION (ε3,000)

Long-Range Forces (Moscow)
BBR 66, plus 5 trg, 14 test ac (plus 44 in Ukraine)
   28 Tu-95H6 (with AS-15 ALCM) (plus 5 in Ukraine)
   32 Tu-95H16 (with AS-15 ALCM) (plus 20 in Ukraine)
   6 Tu-160 (with AS-15 ALCM) (plus 19 in Ukraine)
TEST AC 8 Tu-95, 6 Tu-160
TRG AC 5 Tu-95G

STRATEGIC DEFENCE (21,000)

ABM 100: 36 SH-11 (mod *Galosh*), 64 SH-08 *Gazelle*
   WARNING SYSTEMS (see satellite table pp. 303–6)
   ICBM/SLBM launch-detection capability, others include photo recce and ELINT
   RADARS
   OVER-THE-HORIZON-BACKSCATTER (OTH-B)
   2 near Kiev and Komsomolsk (Ukraine), covering US and polar areas
   1 near Nikolayevsk-na-Amure, covering China (these sites are non-op)
   LONG-RANGE EARLY-WARNING ABM-ASSOCIATED
   6 long-range phased-array systems **Operational** Olenegorsk (Kola), Lyaki (Azerbaijan), Pechora (Urals) **Under test** Sary-Shagan (Kazakstan) **Under construction** Baranovichi (Belarus), Mishelevka (Irkutsk)
   11 *Hen House*-series; range 6,000km, 6 locations covering approaches from the west and south-west, north-east and south-east and (partially) south. Engagement, guidance, battle management: 1 *Pill Box* phased-array at Pushkino (Moscow)

Army ε420,000

reported to reduce to 200,000 (ε144,000 conscripts, ε170,000 on contract)
8 Mil Districts (MD)

8 Army HQ, 9 Corps HQ

12 TD (incl 3 trg) (3 tk, 1 motor rifle, 1 arty, 1 SAM regt; 1 armd recce bn; spt units)

27 MRD (incl 4 trg) (3 motor rifle, 1 arty, 1 SAM regt; 1 indep tk, 1 ATK, 1 armd recce bn; spt units)

5 ABD (each 3 para, 1 arty regt; 1 AA bn) (plus 1 trg div)

4 MG/arty div

4 arty div incl 1 trg; no standard org: perhaps 4 bde (12 bn): 152mm SP, 152mm towed and MRL: plus ATK bde

Some 47 arty bde/regt; no standard org, perhaps 4 bn: 2 each of 24 152mm towed guns, 2 each of 24 152mm SP guns, some only MRL

4 hy arty bde (each with 4 bn of 12 203mm 2S7 SP guns)

7 AB bde (each 4 inf bn; arty, SAM, ATK; spt tps)

2 indep tk bde

17 indep (1 under airborne comd) MR bde (more forming)

8 (1 airborne) SF (*Spetsnaz*) bde

23 SSM bde (incl 3 trg)

19 ATK bde/regt

28 SAM bde/regt

20 attack hel regt

8 aslt tpt hel regt

6 hel trg regt

Other Front and Army tps

engr, pontoon-bridge, pipe-line, signals, EW, CW def, tpt, supply bde/regt/bn

EQUIPMENT

Figures in () were reported to CFE on 1 Jan 1997 and include those held by Naval Infantry and Coastal Defence units

MBT about 15,500 (5,541), incl: T-54/-55 (66), T-62 (97), T-64A/-B (186), T-72L/-M (1,980) and T-80/-M 9 (3,210), T-90 (2), plus some 11,000 in store east of Urals (incl Kazakstan, Uzbekistan)

LT TK 200 PT-76 (5)

RECCE some 2,000 BRDM-2

TOTAL AIFV/APC ε26,300 (10,193)

AIFV (6,886): BMP-1 (1,699), BMP-2 (3,364), BMP-3 (26), some 1,600 BMD-1/-2/-3 (AB) (1,222), BRM (575)

APC (3,307): BTR-60P/-70/-80 (2,193), BTR-D (465); MT-LB (649), plus 'look-alikes'

TOTAL ARTY ε15,700 (6,011), plus some 13,000, mainly obsolete types, in store east of the Urals

TOWED (1,904) incl: **122mm**: D-30 (837); **152mm**: D-20 (213), *Giatsint-B* 2A36 (524), *MSTA-B* 2A65 (330); **203mm**: B-4M

SP (2,622) incl: **122mm**: *Gvozdika* 2S1 (643); **152mm**: *Acatsia* 2S3 (1,087), *Giatsint-S* 2S5 (449), *MSTA-S* 2S19 (411); **203mm**: *Pion* 2S7 (32)

COMBINED GUN/MOR (333): **120mm**: *Nona-S* 2S9 SP (329), *Nona-K* 2B16 (2), 2 S23 (2)

MRL (895) incl: **122mm**: BM-21 (356), BM-13 (6), 9P138 (13); **220mm**: 800 (415) 9P140 *Uragan*; **300mm**: 105 (105) *Smerch* 9A52

MOR (252) incl: **120mm**: 2S12 (171), PM-38 (61); **160mm**: M-160 (1); **240mm**: *Tulpan* 2S4 SP (19)

SSM (nuclear-capable) ε200 SS-21 *Scarab* (*Tochka*), ε116 *Scud*-B/-C mod (R-17) (FROG (*Luna*) units mostly disbanded)

ATGW AT-2 *Swatter*, AT-3 *Sagger*, AT-4 *Spigot*, AT-5 *Spandrel*, AT-6 *Spiral*, AT-7 *Saxhorn*, AT-9, AT-10

RL 64mm: RPG-18; **73mm**: RPG-7/-16/-22/-26; **105mm**: RPG-27/-29

RCL 73mm: SPG-9; **82mm**: B-10

ATK GUNS 57mm: ASU-57 SP; **76mm; 85mm**: D-44/SD-44, ASU-85 SP; **100mm**: T-12/-12A/M-55 towed

AD GUNS 23mm: ZU-23, ZSU-23-4 SP; **37mm; 57mm**: S-60, ZSU-57-2 SP; **85mm**: M-1939; **100mm**: KS-19; **130mm**: KS-30

SAM

500 SA-4 A/B *Ganef* (twin) (Army/Front weapon)

400 SA-6 *Gainful* (triple) (div weapon)

400 SA-8 *Gecko* (2 triple) (div weapon)

200 SA-9 *Gaskin* (2 twin) (regt weapon)

250 SA-11 *Gadfly* (quad) (replacing SA-4/-6)

100 SA-12A/B (*Gladiator/Giant*)

350 SA-13 *Gopher* (2 twin) (replacing SA-9)

100 SA-15 (replacing SA-6/SA-8)

SA-19 (2S6 SP) (8 SAM, plus twin **30mm** gun)

SA-7, SA-14 being replaced by SA-16, SA-18 (man-portable)

HELICOPTERS some 2,565

ATTACK 1,050 Mi-24 (812), 15 Ka-50 *Hokum*

TPT some 1,300 Mi-6, Mi-8 (some armed), Mi-26 (hy)

GENERAL PURPOSE 200 incl Mi-2, Mi-8 (comms)

DEPLOYMENT

The manning state of Russian units is difficult to determine. The following assessment is based on the latest available information. Above 75% – none reported; above 50% – possibly 6 TD, 16 MRD, 5 ABD, 2 arty and 2 MG/arty div. The remainder are assessed as 20–50%. All bde are maintained at or above 50%. TLE in each MD includes active and trg units and in store

RUSSIAN MILITARY DISTRICTS

KALININGRAD MD

GROUND 19,000: 1 Army HQ, 2 MRD, 2 tk, 3 arty, 1 SSM, 1 SAM bde/regt, 1 ATK, 1 attack hel regt, 850 MBT, 925 ACV, 426 arty/MRL/mor, 12 Scud, 50 attack hel

AD 1 regt: 28 Su-27 (Baltic Fleet)

SAM 50

LENINGRAD MD (HQ St Petersburg)

GROUND 63,400: 1 Army HQ, 1 Corps HQ; 5 MRD (1 trg), 1 ABD; plus 3 indep MR bde, 7 arty bde/regt, 4 SSM, 1 AB, 1 *Spetsnaz*, 4 SAM bde, 3 ATK, 2 attack hel, 1 aslt tpt hel regt, 870 MBT, 740 ACV, 1,000 arty/MRL/mor, 12 Scud, 36 SS-21, 60 attack hel

AIR 1 hy bbr regt (20 Tu-22M), 1 tac air army: 1 bbr

div (80 Su-24), 1 recce regt (25 MiG-25, 10 Su-24), 1 ftr div (35 Su-27, 60 MiG-29), 1 hel ECM sqn (20 Mi-8)

AD 7 regt: 100 MiG-31, 90 Su-27

SAM 525

MOSCOW MD (HQ Moscow)

GROUND 87,000: 2 Army HQ, 1 Corps HQ, 5 TD (1 trg), 2 MRD, 2 ABD, plus 1 arty div (5 bde), 8 arty bde/regt, 4 ATK, 4 SSM, 4 indep MR, 1 *Spetsnaz*, 5 SAM bde, 6 attack hel, 1 aslt tpt hel regt, 1,950 MBT, 3,700 ACV, 2,650 arty/MRL/mor, 24 *Scud*, 18 SS-21, 240 attack hel

AIR 1 hy bbr regt (20 Tu-22M), 1 tac air army: 1 bbr div (90 Su-24), 1 ftr div (120 MiG-29), 1 FGA regt (50 Su-25), 1 recce regt (30 Su-24/MiG-25), 2 hel ECM sqn with 40 Mi-8

   TRG 1 Long Range Aviation trg centre, 2 Tactical Aviation trg centre, trg regts of Air Force Aviation Schools; storage bases

   AD 6 regt: 30 MiG-23, 75 MiG-31, 65 Su-27, 1 trg centre

   SAM 850

VOLGA MD (HQ Kuybyshev (Samarra))

GROUND 44,800: 1 Army HQ, 2 TD, 2 MRD (1 trg), 1 ABD plus 1 AB, 2 arty bde/regt, 2 SSM, 2 SAM bde, 1 ATK, 2 attack hel, 2 aslt tpt hel, 6 hel trg regt, 1,100 MBT, 1,840 ACV, 750 arty/MRL/mor, 18 SS-21, 230 attack hel

AIR trg regts of tac aviation; trg centres and Air Force aviation schools, storage bases

   AD 1 PVO Corps, 2 regt: 30 MiG-23, 25 MiG-31

NORTH CAUCASUS MD (HQ Rostov)

GROUND 70,500: 1 Army HQ, 2 Corps HQ, 2 MRD, 1 ABD, 2 AB, 4 MR bde, 1 *Spetsnaz*, 5 arty bde, 3 SSM, 5 SAM bde, 3 ATK, 2 attack hel, 1 aslt tpt hel regt, 380 MBT, 1,270 ACV, 630 arty/MRL/mor, 12 *Scud*, 60 attack hel

AIR 1 tac Air Army: 1 bbr div (90 Su-24), 1 FGA div (100 Su-25), 1 ftr div (100 MiG-29), 1 recce regt (35 Su-24), 1 hel ECM sqn with 20 Mi-8, trg regt of tac aviation and Air Force aviation schools

   AD 1 PVO Corps, 3 regt: 25 MiG-31, 60 Su-27; 1 aviation school, 4 regt: 165 MiG-23, 200 L-39

   SAM 125

URAL MD (HQ Yekaterinburg)

GROUND 2 TD (1 trg), 1 MRD, 4 arty bde/regt, 2 ATK bde/regt, 1 SAM bde, 1,100 MBT, 1,500 ACV, 900 arty/MRL/mor

AIR Air Force aviation schools

   AD Covering Ural, Siberian, Transbaykal and Far Eastern MDs: 40 MiG-23, 200 MiG-31, 65 Su-27

   SAM 600

SIBERIAN MD (HQ Novosibirsk)

GROUND 1 Corps HQ, 1 MRD, 1 AB (trg), 1 arty div, 1 AB, 3 MR bde, 4 arty bde/regt, 2 SSM, 2 SAM, 1 *Spetsnaz* bde, 1 ATK, 1 attack hel regt, 1,468 MBT, 3,400 ACV, 2,200 arty/MRL/mor, 24 *Scud*, 40 attack hel

AIR Air Force aviation schools

   AD See Ural MD

TRANSBAYKAL MD (HQ Chita)

GROUND 2 Corps HQ, 3 TD (1 trg), 1 MRD, plus 2 MG/arty div, 1 arty div, 2 MR bde, 5 arty bde/regt, 3 SSM, 1 AB, 1 *Spetsnaz*, 2 ATK, 3 SAM bde, 2 attack hel, 1 aslt tpt hel regt, 3,000 MBT, 4,000 ACV, 3,500 arty/MRL/mor, 12 *Scud*, 18-SS-21, 80 attack hel

AIR Covering Transbaykal and Far Eastern MDs: 2 LRA DIV, 2 tac air armies

   BBR 85 Tu-22M

   FGA 315 Su-24/25

   FTR 100 Su-27/MiG-29

   RECCE 100 Su-24

   AD See Ural MD

FAR EASTERN MD (HQ Khabarovsk)

GROUND 2 Army, 2 Corps HQ, 10 MRD (2 trg), plus 2 MG/arty div, 1 arty div, 9 arty bde/regt, 1 MR, 1 AB, 4 SSM, 5 SAM, 1 *Spetsnaz*, 2 ATK bde, 3 attack hel, 2 aslt tpt hel regt, 5,600 MBT, 7,000 ACV, 5,800 arty/MRL/mor, 48 *Scud*, 190 attack hel

AIR See Transbaykal MD

   AD See Ural MD

FORCES IN OTHER FORMER SOVIET REPUBLICS

Declared str of forces deployed in Armenia and Georgia as at 1 Jan 1997 was 13,100. These forces are now subordinate to the North Caucasus MD. Total probably excludes locally enlisted personnel

ARMENIA

   GROUND (4,300): 1 mil base (bde), 74 MBT, 158 ACV, 84 arty/MRL/mors

   AD 1 sqn MiG-23

GEORGIA

   GROUND (8,500): 3 mil bases (each = bde+), 140 T-72 MBT, 360 ACV, 155 arty incl **122mm** D-30, 2S1 SP; **152mm** 2S3; **122mm** BM-21 MRL; **120mm** mor. Plus 118 ACV and some arty deployed in Abkhazia

   AD 60 SA-6

   AIR 1 composite regt with some 35 **ac** An-12, An-26 **hel** Mi-8

MOLDOVA (Dniestr)

   GROUND (4,900 reducing to 2,500 by end 1997): 1 indep MR bde, 120 MBT, 166 ACV, 129 arty/MRL/mor

TAJIKISTAN

   GROUND (e6,000): 1 MRD, 190 MBT, 303 ACV, 180 arty/MRL/mor; plus e25,000 Frontier Forces (Tajik conscripts, Russian-controlled)

Navy ε220,000

(ε142,000 conscripts, ε13,000 Strategic Forces, ε35,000 Naval Aviation, ε19,000 Coastal Defence Forces/Naval Infantry)

SUBMARINES 128

STRATEGIC 29 (see p. 108)

TACTICAL 87

  SSGN 18

  12 *Oscar* with 24 SS-N-19 *Shipwreck* USGW (VLS); plus T-65 HWT

  1 *Charlie* II with 8 SS-N-7 *Starbright* USGW; plus T-53 HWT

  1 *Echo* II with 8 SS-N-12 *Sandbox* SSM; plus T-53 HWT

  3 *Yankee* 'Notch' with 20+ SS-N-21 *Sampson* SLCM

  1 *Yankee* (trials) with ε12 SS-NX-24 SLCM

  SSN 43

  13 *Akula* with T-65 HWT; plus SS-N-21

  4 *Sierra* with T-65 HWT; plus SS-N-21

  26 *Victor* III with T-65 HWT; plus SS-N-15

  SS 26

  17 *Kilo*, 5 *Tango*, 4 *Foxtrot* (all with T-53 HWT)

OTHER ROLES 12

  SSN 7

  3 *Uniform*, 1 *Alfa*, 1 *Echo* II experimental/trials, 2 *Yankee*

  SS 5

  1 *Beluga*, 1 *Bravo* wpn targets, 1 *X-Ray* trials, 2 *Losos* SF

IN STORE probably some *Foxtrot*, *Tango* and *Kilo*

PRINCIPAL SURFACE COMBATANTS 60

CARRIERS 1 *Kuznetsov* CVV (67,500t) capacity 20 fixed wing ac (Su-33) and 15–17 ASW hel with 12 SS-N-19 *Shipwreck* SSM, 4 x 6 SA-N-9 SAM, 8 CADS-1, 2 RBU-12 (not fully op)

CRUISERS 22

  CGN 4 *Kirov* (AAW/ASUW) with 12 x 8 SA-N-6 *Grumble*, 20 SS-N-19 *Shipwreck* SSM, 3 Ka-25/-27 hel for OTHT/AEW/ASW; plus 1 with 1 x 2 130mm guns, 1 with 1 x 2 SS-N-14 *Silex* SUGW (LWT or nuc payload), 10 533mm TT

  CG 18

  3 *Slava* (AAW/ASUW) with 8 x 8 SA-N-6 *Grumble*, 8 x 2 SS-N-12 *Sandbox* SSM, 1 Ka-25/-27 hel (AEW/ASW); plus 8 533mm TT, 1 x 2 130mm guns

  11 *Udaloy* (ASW) with 2 x 4 SS-N-14 *Silex* SUGW, 2 x 12 ASW RL, 8 533mm TT, 2 Ka-27 hel; plus 2 100mm guns

  1 *Udaloy* II with 8 x 4 SS-N-22 *Sunburn*, 8 SA-N-9, 2 Cads-N-1, 8 SA-N-11, 10 533mm TT, 2 Ka-27 hel plus 2 100mm guns

  3 *Kara* (ASW) with 2 x 4 SS-N-14 *Silex* SUGW, 10 533mm TT, 1 Ka-25 hel; plus 2 x 2 SA-N-3 *Goblet* (1 (*Azov*) with 3 x 8 SA-N-6, only 1 SA-N-3 and other differences)

DDG 19

  16 *Sovremennyy* with 2 x 4 SS-N-22 *Sunburn* SSM, 2 x 1 SA-N-7 *Gadfly* SAM, 2 x 2 130mm guns, 1 Ka-25 (B) hel (OTHT); plus 4 533mm TT

  1 *Kynda* (ASUW) with 2 x 4 SS-N-3B; plus 1 x 2 SA-N-1 *Goa* SAM, 6 533mm TT

  1 mod *Kashin* with 4 SS-N-2C *Styx* SSM, 2 x 2 SA-N-1 SAM; plus 5 533mm TT (non-op)

  1 *Kashin* with 2 x 12 ASW RL, 5 533mm TT; plus 2 x 2 SA-N-1 SAM

FRIGATES 18

  5 *Krivak* II with 1 x 4 SS-N-14 *Silex* SUGW, 8 533mm TT, 2 x 12 ASW RL; plus 2 100mm guns

  12 *Krivak* I (weapons as *Krivak* II, but with 2 twin 76mm guns)

  1 *Neustrashimyy* with 2 x 12 ASW RL

PATROL AND COASTAL COMBATANTS 182

CORVETTES 72

  59 *Grisha* I, -III, -IV, -V, with 2 x 12 ASW RL, 4 533mm TT

  12 *Parchim* II (ASW) with 2 x 12 ASW RL, 4 406mm ASTT

  1 *Petya* with ASW RL, 5 or 10 406mm ASTT

MISSILE CRAFT 80

  about 42 *Tarantul* (ASUW), 3 -I, 17 -II, both with 2 x 2 SS-N-2C *Styx*; 29 -III with 2 x 2 SS-N-22 *Sunburn*

  25 *Nanuchka* (ASUW) -I, -III and -IV with 2 x 3 SS-N-9 *Siren*

  2 *Dergash* ACV with 8 x SS-N-22 SSM, 1 SAN-4 SAM, 1 76mm gun

  3 *Osa* PFM with 4 SS-N-2C (non-op)

  8 *Matka* PHM with 2 x 1 SS-N-2C

TORPEDO CRAFT 15 *Turya* PHT with 4 533mm TT

PATROL CRAFT 15

  OFFSHORE 3 T-43

  COASTAL 12

  1 *Vtka* PCI

  8 *Pauk* PFC (ASW) with 2 ASW RL, 4 ASTT

  1 *Babochka* PHT (ASW) with 8 ASTT

  2 *Mukha* PHT (ASW) with 8 ASTT

MINE WARFARE about 155

MINELAYERS 2 *Alesha*, capacity 300 mines (non-op) (most submarines and many surface combatants are equipped for minelaying)

MINE COUNTERMEASURES about 153

  OFFSHORE 25

  2 *Gorya* MCO

  23 *Natya* I and -II MSO

  COASTAL about 80

  10 *Yurka* MSC

  About 70 *Sonya* MSC

  INSHORE about 48

  8 *Vanya*

  40 MSI<

AMPHIBIOUS about 55

  LPD 2 *Ivan Rogov* with 4–5 Ka-27 hel, capacity 520 tps, 20 tk

  LST 30

  22 *Ropucha*, capacity 225 tps, 9 tk

  8 *Alligator*, capacity 300 tps, 20 tk

  LSM about 23 *Polnocny* (3 types), capacity 180 tps, 6 tk (some adapted for mine warfare, but retain amph primary role)

Russia

Plus about 40 craft: about 6 *Ondatra* LCM; about 34 LCAC and SES (incl 6 *Pomornik*, 6 *Aist*, 6 *Tsaplya*, 12 *Lebed*, 1 *Utenok*, 2 *Orlan* WIG and 1 *Utka* WIG (wing-in-ground-experimental))

Plus about 80 smaller craft

SUPPORT AND MISCELLANEOUS about 507

UNDER WAY SUPPORT 25
1 *Berezina*, 6 *Chilikin*, 18 other AO

MAINTENANCE AND LOGISTIC about 219
some 15 AS, 38 AR, 20 AOT, 15 msl spt/resupply, 90 tugs, 12 special liquid carriers, 12 water carriers, 17 AK

SPECIAL PURPOSES about 63
some 26 AGI (some armed), 2 msl range instrumentation, 7 trg, about 24 icebreakers (civil-manned), 4 AH

SURVEY/RESEARCH about 200
some 40 naval, 39 civil AGOR; 80 naval, 35 civil AGHS; 6 space-associated ships (civil-manned)

MERCHANT FLEET (aux/augmentation)
about 2,800 ocean-going vessels (17 in Arctic service) incl 125 ramp-fitted and ro-ro, some with rails for rolling stock, 3 roll-on/float-off, 14 barge carriers, 48 passenger liners, 500 coastal and river ships, plus miscellaneous craft

NAVAL AVIATION (ε35,000)
some 329 cbt ac; 387 armed hel

HQ Naval Air Force

FLEET AIR FORCES 4
each org in air div, each with 2–3 regt of HQ elm and 2 sqn of 9–10 ac each; recce, ASW, tpt/utl org in indep regt or sqn

BBR some 71
5 regt with some 71 Tu-22M (AS-4 ASM)

FGA 75 Su-24, 9 Su-25, 30 Su-27

ASW ac 9 Tu-142, 35 Il-38, 54 Be-12 **hel** 70 Mi-14, 53 Ka-25, 119 Ka-27

MR/EW ac incl 14 Tu-95, 8 Tu-22, 24 Su-24, 7 An-12, 2 Il-20 **hel** 20 Ka-25

MCM 25 Mi-14 hel

CBT ASLT 25 Ka-29 hel

TPT ac 120 An-12, An-24, An-26 **hel** 70 Mi-6/-8

ASM AS-4 *Kitchen*, AS-7 *Kerry*, AS-10 *Karen*, AS-11 *Kilter*, AS-12 *Kegler*, AS-13 *Kingbolt*, AS-14 *Kedge*

COASTAL DEFENCE (ε19,000)
(incl Naval Infantry, Coastal Defence Troops)

NAVAL INFANTRY (Marines) (ε14,000)
1 inf div (8,000: 3 inf, 1 tk, 1 arty regt) (Pacific Fleet)

3 indep bde (4 inf, 1 tk, 1 arty, 1 MRL, 1 ATK bn)

3 fleet SF bde: 2–3 underwater, 1 para bn, spt elm

EQUIPMENT
MBT 280: T-55, T-64, T-72, T-80

LT TK 120 PT-76

RECCE 60 BRDM-2/*Sagger* ATGW

APC some 1,500: BTR-60/-70/-80, 250 MT-LB

TOTAL ARTY 389
SP 122mm: 96 2S1; **152mm**: 18 2S3

MRL 122mm: 96 9P138

COMBINED GUN/MOR 120mm: 168 2S9 SP, 11 2S23 SP

ATGW 72 AT-3/-5

AD GUNS 23mm: 60 ZSU-23-4 SP

SAM 250 SA-7, 20 SA-8, 50 SA-9/-13

COASTAL DEFENCE TROOPS (5,000)
(all units reserve status)

1 coastal defence div

1 coastal defence bde

1 arty regt

2 SAM regt

EQUIPMENT
MBT 350 T-64

AIFV 450 BMP

APC 280 BTR-60/-70/-80, 400 MT-LB

TOTAL ARTY 364 (152)
TOWED 280: **122mm**: 140 D-30; **152mm**: 40 D-20, 50 2A65, 50 2A36

SP 152mm: 48 2S5

MRL 122mm: 36 BM-21

NAVAL DEPLOYMENT

NORTHERN FLEET (Arctic and Atlantic)
(HQ Severomorsk)

BASES Kola Inlet, Motovskiy Gulf, Gremikha, Polyarnyy, Litsa Gulf, Ura Guba, Severodvinsk

SUBMARINES 73
strategic 18 SSBN **tactical** 49 (12 SSGN, 29 SSN, 8 SS) **other roles** 6

PRINCIPAL SURFACE COMBATANTS 43
1 CV, 11 cruisers, 9 destroyers, 5 frigates, 17 corvettes

OTHER SURFACE SHIPS about 18 patrol and coastal combatants, 30 MCM, 24 amph, some 154 spt and misc

NAVAL AVIATION
108 cbt ac; 85 armed hel

BBR 37 Tu-22M

FTR/FGA 30 Su-24/-25, 30 Su-27

ASW ac 11 Il-38, 5 Be-12 **hel** (afloat) 5 Ka-25, 55 Ka-27

MR/EW ac 2 An-12, 30 Tu-95 **hel** 5 Ka-25

MCM 8* Mi-14 hel

CBT ASLT HEL 12 Ka-29

COMMS 5 Tu-142

NAVAL INFANTRY
1 bde (96 MBT, 122 ACV, 95 arty)

COASTAL DEFENCE
1 Coastal Defence (360 MT-LB, 134 arty), 1 SAM regt

BALTIC FLEET (HQ Kaliningrad)
BASES Kronshtadt, Baltiysk

SUBMARINES 6
tactical 4 **other roles** 2

PRINCIPAL SURFACE COMBATANTS 25

2 destroyers, 6 frigates, 17 corvettes

OTHER SURFACE SHIPS about 32 patrol and coastal combatants, 37 MCM, 12 amph, some 111 spt and misc

NAVAL AVIATION

93 cbt ac, 25 armed hel

FGA 5 regt: 55 Su-24, 28 Su-27

ASW ac 10 Be-12 **hel** 3* Ka-25, 22* Ka-27

MR/EW ac 2 An-12, 5 Su-24 **hel** 5 Ka-25

MCM 6 Mi-14 BT hel

CBT ASLT HEL 4 Ka-29

NAVAL INFANTRY

1 bde (25 MBT, 34 arty/MRL) (Kaliningrad)

COASTAL DEFENCE

2 arty regt (133 arty)

1 SSM regt: some 8 SS-C-1b *Sepal*

BLACK SEA FLEET ε48,000 (HQ Sevastopol)

(incl Naval Aviation, Naval Infantry). On 31 May 1997, Russian President Boris Yeltsin and Ukrainian President Leonid Kuchma signed an intergovernmental agreement on the status and terms of the Black Sea Fleet's deployment on the territory of Ukraine, and parametres for the Fleet's division. The Russian Fleet will lease bases in Sevastopol for the next 20 years, and will be based at Sevastopol and Karantinnaya Bays, and jointly with Ukrainian warships at Streletskaya Bay. The Fleet's overall serviceability is low
BASES Sevastopol, Temryuk, Novorossiysk
SUBMARINES 11

tactical 8 **other roles** 3

PRINCIPAL SURFACE COMBATANTS 25

4 cruisers, 2 destroyers, 3 frigates, 16 corvettes

OTHER SURFACE SHIPS about 25 patrol and coastal combatants, 26 MCM, 7 amph, some 88 spt and misc

NAVAL AVIATION

17 cbt ac; 30 armed hel

BBR some 7 Tu-22M

ASW ac 10* Be-12 **hel** 35 Mi-14, 25* Ka-25, 5* Ka-27

MR/EW ac 4 An-12 **hel** 3 Ka-25

MCM 5 Mi-14 BT hel

NAVAL INFANTRY (2,000)

1 bde (50 MBT, 218 APC, 45 arty (2S1, 2S9))

CASPIAN SEA FLOTILLA

BASE Astrakhan (Russia)

The Caspian Sea Flotilla has been divided among Azerbaijan (about 25%), and Russia, Kazakstan and Turkmenistan, which are operating a joint flotilla under Russian command currently based at Astrakhan
PRINCIPAL SURFACE COMBATANTS 1 corvette
OTHER SURFACE SHIPS 14 patrol and coastal combatants, 12 MCM, some 8 amph, about 20 spt

PACIFIC FLEET (HQ Vladivostok)

BASES Vladivostok, Petropavlovsk, Kamchatskiy, Magadan, Sovetskaya Gavan
SUBMARINES 39

strategic 11 SSBN **tactical** 26 (6 SSGN, 14 SSN, 6 SS)
other roles 2 SS
PRINCIPAL SURFACE COMBATANTS 39

7 cruisers, 6 destroyers, 4 frigates, 22 corvettes

OTHER SURFACE SHIPS about 35 patrol and coastal combatants, 60 MCM, 12 amph, some 154 spt and misc

NAVAL AVIATION (Pacific Fleet Air Force)

(HQ Vladivostok) 96 cbt ac, 80 cbt hel

BBR 1 regt with 9 Tu-22M

FGA 1 regt with 15 Su-24

ASW ac 27 Tu-142, 20 Il-38, 25 Be-12 **hel** afloat 25 Ka-25, 30 Ka-27; ashore 25 Mi-14

MR/EW ac some 8 An-12, Tu-95

MCM hel 6 Mi-14 BT

CBT ASLT HEL 10 Ka-29

COMMS 7 Tu-142

NAVAL INFANTRY

1 div HQ, 3 inf, 1 tk and 1 arty regt

COASTAL DEFENCE

1 Coastal Defence div

Air Force ε130,000

some 1,855 cbt ac, 2 comd, 5 tac air armies, trg org. Force strengths vary, mostly org with div of 3 regt of 3 sqn (total 90–120 ac), indep regt (30–40 ac). Regt roles incl AD, interdiction, recce, tac air spt

LONG-RANGE AVIATION COMMAND (DA)

3 div

BB about 125 Tu-22M-3, plus 30 decommissioned Tu-22M-2 in store and 92 Tu-22 (incl 30 recce) awaiting destruction

TKR 20 Il-78

TRG 10 Tu-22M-2/3, 60 Tu-134

TACTICAL AVIATION

5 tac air armies

Flying hours 40

BBR/FGA some 725: incl 475 Su-24, 250 Su-25

FTR some 415: incl 315 MiG-29, 100 Su-27

RECCE some 200: incl 40 MiG-25, 160 Su-24

ECM 60 Mi-8

TRG 1 centre for op conversion: 180 **ac** incl 80 MiG-29, 80 Su-24, 20 Su-25

1 centre for instructor trg: 65 **ac** incl 10 MiG-25, 20 MiG-29, 15 Su-24, 10 Su-25, 10 Su-27

AAM AA-8 *Aphid*, AA-10 *Alamo*, AA-11 *Archer*

ASM AS-7 *Kerry*, AS-10 *Karen*, AS-11 *Kilter*, AS-12 *Kegler*, AS-13 *Kingbolt*, AS-14 *Kedge*, AS-16 *Kickback*, AS-17 *Krypton*, AS-18 *Kazoo*

MILITARY TRANSPORT AVIATION COMMAND (VTA)

3 div, each 3 regt, each 30 ac; some indep regt
EQUIPMENT
some 350 **ac**, incl Il-76M/MD *Candid* B, An-12, An-

Russia

22, An-124
Additional long- and medium-range tpt **ac** in comd other than VTA some 250: Tu-134, Tu-154, An-12, An-72, Il-18, Il-62
CIVILIAN FLEET 1,500 medium- and long-range passenger ac, incl some 350 An-12 and Il-76

AIR FORCE AVIATION TRAINING SCHOOLS

TRG 5 schools (incl 1 for foreign students) subordinate to Air Force HQ: 1,225 **ac** incl 900 L-39, 250 L-410/Tu-134, 75 MiG-29/Su-22/Su-25/Su-27
DECOMMISSIONED AIRCRAFT IN STORE some 1,000 **ac** incl MiG-23, MiG-27, Su-17, Su-22

Air Defence Troops (VPVO) 170,000

3 AD armies: 4 indep AD corps: air regt and indep sqn; SAM bde/regt, 965 cbt ac
AIRCRAFT (Aviation of Air Defence – APVO)
  FTR some 800, incl, 100 MiG-23, 425 MiG-31, 275 Su-27 (plus some 20 cbt capable MiG-23 trg variants in regts)
  TRG 1 trg school, 4 regt: 165 MiG-23, 200 L-39
  DECOMMISSIONED AIRCRAFT IN STORE 300 **ac** inc MiG-23, MiG-25
AEW AND CONTROL 20 Il-76
MISSILES
  AAM AA-8 *Aphid*, AA-9 *Amos*, AA-10 *Alamo*, AA-11 *Archer*
  SAM some 2,150 launchers in some 225 sites
    50 SA-2 *Guideline* (being replaced by SA-10)
    200 SA-5 *Gammon* (being replaced by SA-10)
    some 1,900 SA-10 *Grumble*
COMBAT AIRCRAFT (CFE totals as at 1 Jan 1997 for all air forces less maritime)
  ac 2,891: 192 **Su-17** • 58 **Su-22** • 413 **Su-24** • 195 **Su-25** • 298 **Su-27** • 20 **MiG-21** • 555 **MiG-23** • 143 **MiG-25** • 176 **MiG-27** • 461 **MiG-29** • 229 **MiG-31** • 92 **Tu-22** • 59 **Tu-22M**
  hel 824: 747 **Mi-24** • 34 **Mi-24(K)** • 43 **Mi-24(R)**

Forces Abroad

(other than in the former Soviet republics)
AFRICA 100
CUBA some 800 SIGINT and ε10 mil advisers
GEORGIA/ABKHAZIA ε1,600; 1 AB regt, 2 MR bn
GEORGIA/SOUTH OSSETIA ε500; 1 MR bn
MOLDOVA/TRANSDNIESTR 500; 1 MR bn**SYRIA** 50
VIETNAM 700; naval facility and SIGINT station. Used by RF aircraft and surface ships on reduced basis

Peacekeeping

BOSNIA (SFOR): 1,387; 2 AB bn

UNITED NATIONS

ANGOLA (UNOMA): 130 incl 7 Obs. **BOSNIA** (UNMIBH): 1 plus 37 civ pol. **CROATIA** (UNTAES): 853 incl 6 Obs plus 3 civ pol; (UNMOP): 1 Obs. **FYROM** (UNPREDEP): 2 Obs plus 2 civ pol. **GEORGIA**: (UNOMIG) 3 Obs. **IRAQ/KUWAIT** (UNIKOM): 11 Obs. **MIDDLE EAST** (UNTSO): 4 Obs. **WESTERN SAHARA** (MINURSO): 25 Obs

Paramilitary ε583,000 active

FRONTIER FORCES 220,000

directly subordinate to the President; 7 frontier districts, Arctic, Kaliningrad, Moscow units
  EQUIPMENT
    1,700 ACV (incl BMP, BTR), 90 arty (incl 2S1, 2S9, 2S12)
    ac some 70 Il-76, Tu-134, An-72, An-24, An-26, Yak-40, 16 SM-92 **hel** some 200+ Mi-8, Mi-24, Mi-26, Ku-27
  PATROL AND COASTAL COMBATANTS about 237
    PATROL, OFFSHORE 23
    7 *Krivak*-III with 1 Ka-27 hel, 1 100mm gun, 12 *Grisha*-II, 4 *Grisha*-III
    PATROL, COASTAL 35
    20 *Pauk*, 15 *Svetlyak*
    PATROL, INSHORE 95
    65 *Stenka*, 10 *Muravey*, 20 *Zhuk*
    RIVERINE MONITORS about 84
    10 *Yaz*, 7 *Piyavka*, 7 *Vosh*, 60 *Shmel*
    SUPPORT AND MISCELLANEOUS about 26
    8 *Ivan Susanin* armed icebreakers, 18 *Sorum* armed ocean tugs

FORCES FOR THE PROTECTION OF THE RUSSIAN FEDERATION 25,000

org incl elm of Ground Forces (1 mech inf bde, 1 AB regt, 1 Presidential Guard)

FEDERAL SECURITY SERVICE ε9,000 armed incl Alfa, Beta and Zenit cdo units

MINISTERSTVO VNUTRENNIKH DEL (MVD) ε329,000

internal security tps; some 20 div incl 3 indep special purpose div (ODON – 2 to 5 op regt), 29 bde incl 5 indep special designation bde (OBRON – 3 mech, 1 mor bn); 65 regt/bn incl special motorised units guards and escorts
  EQUIPMENT
    incl 1,700 ACV (incl BMP-1/-2, BTR-80), 20 D-30

MILITARY DEVELOPMENTS

Regional Trends

The Middle East and North Africa remains the largest arms market in the world, with deliveries of major conventional weapon systems at a high level in 1996 and 1997, as a result of orders made three or four years earlier. The Middle East peace process continues to suffer setbacks, principally because of the actions of extremist elements on both sides. While UN Security Council Resolution (UNSCR) 986 authorised the 'oil-for-food' arrangements for **Iraq** to begin with the first delivery of oil in December 1996, Iraq has yet to satisfy the conditions of cease-fire Resolution 687 if the Security Council is to lift the full sanctions regime. **Iran** conducted major military exercises in April 1997 while electing a more moderate cleric, Mohammad Khatami, as President. In **Algeria**, now with a multi-party parliament, the *Groupe Islamique Armée* (GIA) continued its campaign of atrocities, principally against unarmed civilians.

The Middle East

1997 began badly for the Middle East peace process when, on 1 January, an Israeli soldier opened fire on a crowded Arab market in Hebron wounding seven Palestinians. This attempt to destabilise the hand-over of Hebron did not succeed. By 17 January, the Israeli Defence Forces (IDF) had handed over 80% of Hebron to the Palestinian Authority (PA) after 30 years of occupation. Despite Palestinian protests over breaking ground for a new Jewish settlement on the edge of Arab East Jerusalem in March 1997, by July there were some glimmers of hope that talks between **Israel** and the PA might begin again. These hopes were dashed on 30 July when two suicide bomb attacks in a market place in Jerusalem killed 14 and wounded 170. This was the first bombing since 21 March when three Israeli women were killed in Tel Aviv. In the south **Lebanon** 'security zone', the IDF faced fewer *Hizbollah* rocket attacks into northern Israel in 1997 than the previous year. When these attacks occurred the IDF response was as vigorous as ever. The Israeli–Turkish military cooperation programmes continued throughout the government of the Islamic-led coalition in Ankara. The Israeli Navy carried out joint naval exercises with its Greek counterpart in July 1997.

The Gulf

Iraq was still found wanting in its declarations on its weapon-of-mass-destruction (WMD) programmes, in particular regarding biological weapons. The authorities continue to put obstacles in the way of UN inspectors and access to facilities is sometimes denied. While oil began to flow under UNSCR 986 in December 1996, there were delays in distributing the food to all parts of Iraq – in particular to the north – as required by the Security Council. Supported by the Republican Guard and his security service, Saddam Hussein remains firmly in control. The Turkish armed forces carried out a major offensive against Kurdistan Workers' Party (PKK) guerrillas in northern Iraq mainly from May to July 1997. At one stage, in May, up to 50,000 Turkish troops were deployed in northern Iraq on the operation.

In Iran, the moderate cleric Mohammad Khatami assumed the presidency on 3 August 1997 following his landslide election victory on 23 May. He made a number of important new appointments on taking office, but the impact of these developments on regional security policy is yet to become clear. The Iranian armed forces held a number of major exercises from April to July 1997 involving land, sea and air forces. The largest exercise, held in April and known as *Tariq ol-Qods* (Road to Jerusalem), reportedly involved up to 200,000 personnel across four of the country's provinces and along the Gulf coast. This was the largest exercise deployment for a number of years. While Iran's land forces do not pose a threat beyond its borders, the naval force – with a sea mine-laying capability and more than 20 fast patrol boats fitted with missiles (including the Chinese-built C-802) – could disrupt shipping in the Gulf. Iran's operational submarine capability, with the three Russian-built *Kilo*-class vessels, remains very limited. Its naval capability is no match for the US 5th Fleet, which continues to exercise regularly in the region and helps to enforce the sanctions regime against Iraq.

North Africa

In Algeria, President Liamine Zeroual's government successfully held multi-party elections on 5 June 1997 which resulted in a parliament representing 11 different political parties. The government's main ally, the National Democratic Union (RND), took 156 of the 380 seats. Religious parties are banned. The security forces faced a mounting campaign of violence conducted by the GIA in the run-up to the election in which many civilians lost their lives, particularly in the rural areas. In the internationally supervised election the turnout was reported to be a respectable 65%. The violence continued prior to the country's regional elections in August 1997. With regard to the Western Sahara, In 1997 , former US Secretary of State James Baker was appointed the UN Secretary-General's Special Representative in **Western Sahara** to try to achieve a final settlement between the Moroccan government and the former guerrilla movement the *Frente Popular para la Liberacion de Saguia el-Hamma y de Rio de Oro* (POLISARIO). The general framework of a UN-sponsored peace plan has been agreed, and the possibility of renewed conflict is remote. Nevertheless, a final political settlement remains elusive.

DEFENCE SPENDING

Regional defence outlays in 1996 were slightly up in real terms over 1995, according to *The Military Balance* estimates. Saudi Arabia and Israel account for over half of regional spending – one-third and one-fifth respectively. 1997 budget trends suggest a further real increase in defence spending reflecting the stalled Middle East peace process and several large equipment orders dating back to 1993 (involving Israel, **Kuwait** and **Saudi Arabia** in particular) translating into volume deliveries. Uncertainties remain over the actual outlays of Iran and Iraq, while real defence spending in **Egypt**, **Libya** and **Syria** is also difficult to assess.

Israel

Israel's 1997 defence budget was raised by NS300 million ($90m) to NS22 billion ($7bn excluding $3bn of US Foreign Military Assistance – FMA) in January 1997 in the light of higher-than-expected inflation and currency depreciation. The military reportedly asked for an additional $910m to offset its loss of purchasing power over the past year. The US is proposing to cut some $50m in its annual aid packages to both Israel ($3.0m) and Egypt ($2.1bn), with funds going to other countries (mainly **Jordan**) which support the Middle East peace process. At present, $1.8bn of US military aid to Israel goes directly towards purchasing equipment and military research and development (R&D), while most of the Economic Aid tranche ($1.2bn) is used to repay military loans. The Israeli government includes US FMA worth an annual $3bn in its defence budget figure. Previous editions of *The Military Balance* have subtracted US FMA and cited the lower figure of the actual defence budget funded from Israeli government revenues. The International Monetary Fund (IMF) figures also reflect this lower value. This year, *The Military Balance* has revised upwards estimates of Israeli expenditure on the basis of new evidence of military-related expenditure outside the defence budget. According to this revised assessment, Israeli defence expenditure (as released in the official budget, but excluding US FMA) amounts to some 10% of gross domestic product (GDP). Military-related accounts outside the defence budget include the Intelligence Services (funded under the General Reserve), funds for emergency construction and inventory build-up (also under the General Reserve), and protecting civil government ministries, and effectively increases the military share of GDP to some 12%. In addition, Israel's defence industry exports military equipment and services worth up to $1bn or more annually.

The Gulf States

The Gulf states account for about half of regional defence outlays. Real defence expenditures continue to exceed budgetary allocations as governments take advantage of improved oil prices to finance expensive weapon acquisitions in the aftermath of the 1991 Gulf War. Although the Saudi Arabian government has not disclosed its defence budgets for 1996 and 1997, *The Military Balance* estimates that Saudi Arabia spent over $17bn on defence in 1996 and 1997 outlays are expected to be of the same order. Although defence and security allocations are not specifically identified in the government budget, government spending overall is set to increase by 21% in 1997. The Kingdom imported arms and services worth $8–9bn (around half the actual defence outlays) in 1995 and 1996, and these levels will be sustained in 1997. Riyadh has reportedly pledged to repay some $3.5m in accumulated US Foreign Military Sales debt. Accounting for the Al-Yamamah oil-for-arms barter transaction between Saudi Arabia and the UK, worth a reported $3–4bn annually, appears to lie outside the defence budget. Kuwait and the **United Arab Emirates** (UAE) also continue to spend heavily on defence, although reporting lags of up to two years make current spending trends difficult to verify. **Oman**, which makes timely reports on defence budgets and outlays, budgeted R699m ($1.8bn) for defence in 1996 and spent R737m ($1.9bn).

Table 18 **IMF estimates of Iran's military expenditure**							
(US$bn)	1991 outlay	1992 outlay	1993 outlay	1994 outlay	1995 budget	1995 outlay	1996 budget
Total government expenditure	31.6	32.7	28.2	22.4	26.5	30.0	34.9
of which							
National defence	2.9	2.4	1.4	1.4	1.4	1.4	2.0
Other military expenditure	3.9	2.1	0.3	1.1	1.6	1.2	1.3
Total military expenditure	6.8	4.5	1.7	2.5	3.0	2.6	3.3
% military expenditure/GDP	21.4	13.7	6.1	11.3	11.1	8.5	9.4

Note　US$ conversions are IISS estimates of real exchange rates

Iran

Iran's defence budget rises by a nominal 40% from R5.9tr ($3.4bn) in 1996 to R8.23tr ($4.7bn) in 1997. In real terms, the spending difference between the two years should be less, given high rates of annual inflation and the variance between official and market exchange rates. A recent audit of Iranian government spending by the IMF found that military spending was higher than that suggested by the National Defence allocation. Actual military expenditures are likely to be higher still, since the defence budget is believed to exclude funding for the defence industry and some military imports. The Iranian government has made no secret of its plans to build up Iran's defence-industrial capability in order to reduce dependence on external arms suppliers, but has always denied the existence of programmes involving WMD. IMF figures also suggest that military spending levels fluctuated during the 1990s as a consequence of additional outlays after the Gulf War, followed by a steep decline in 1993 as Iran's external balance deteriorated under the dual influence of uncontrolled credit expansion and falling oil prices.

Algeria

The cost of fighting terrorism in Algeria has risen over the last two years, and defence spending in 1996 increased to $1.8bn. Whereas the 1997 defence budget is D94bn ($1.6bn), overall spending on security including internal law enforcement accounts for over 17% of government spending, or some $2.7bn in 1996 and 1997.

ARMS SALES

In 1996, regional arms sales of some $15bn accounted for 40% of the global arms trade. The 1993 surge in orders is now translating into several large-scale transfers in the region. Saudi Arabia is taking delivery of 72 F-15 combat aircraft from the US (1995–2001); 48 *Tornado* strike aircraft and 20 *Hawk* advanced trainers from the UK (both 1996–98); and the first of three *La Fayette* frigates from France in 1998. Israel is to take delivery of 25 F-15s from late 1997 and the first of three *Dolphin*-class submarines from Germany. Kuwait's lengthy acquisition of the *Patriot* air-defence system continues. *Warrior* armoured infantry fighting vehicle (AIFV) deliveries from the UK continued at a rate of ten per month in 1996 and are due to be completed in 1997. The UAE's acquisition of 390 *Leclerc* main battle tanks (MBTs) (plus 46 armoured response vehicles – ARVs) is approaching the half-way point with 150 delivered by mid-1997. An order for a further 10 AH-64 *Apaches* was placed in the US in 1997. Egypt continues to take delivery of Turkish-assembled F-16 combat aircraft and locally assembled M-1 *Abrams* MBTs.

Table 19 UN Register of Conventional Arms imports, Middle East and North Africa, 1996

(as at 11 August 1997)	MBT	ACV	Artillery	Combat aircraft	Attack helicopters	Warships	Missiles
Algeria	—	6	—	—	—	—	—
Bahrain	—	125	—	—	—	1	—
Egypt	60	662	—	—	—	—	16
Iran	2	2	—	5	—	5	103
Israel	—	1	6	—	14	—	15
Jordan	60	—	—	—	—	—	—
Kuwait	174	143	18	—	—	—	—
Lebanon	—	108	—	—	—	—	—
Oman	6	51	—	—	1	—	—
Qatar	—	—	—	—	—	—	1
Saudi Arabia	124	340	—	17	—	—	48
Tunisia	—	—	26	6	—	—	—
UAE	58	25	—	—	10	—	168
Total	**484**	**1463**	**50**	**28**	**25**	**6**	**351**

Iran remains the major regional source for concern with regard to ballistic- and cruise-missile proliferation and associated WMD programmes. Russia is reported to have supplied Iran with SS-4 missile-related equipment and possibly civil nuclear-power technology in late 1996. Iran is also believed to have acquired technology from North Korea for the *Scud*-derivative *Nodong* surface-to-surface missile (SSM) and to be involved in a cooperative programme with Pyongyang to improve the *Nodong*. Iran continues to develop the C-801 cruise missile.

During 1996, Egypt and Syria obtained spare parts for *Scud* missile inventories from Russia and North Korea, according to an unclassified Central Intelligence Agency (CIA) report to the US Congress.

Israel's Theater Missile Defense (TMD) joint venture with the US on the *Arrow* programme is progressing well, with two successful intercepts reported to date (at an estimated cost of $1.2bn largely funded by the US). Initial deployment is planned for 1998. In addition to this programme, substantial US support is being given to *Nautilus*, a development programme for a missile system to defend against multiple rocket-launcher attacks of the type used by *Hizbollah* with *Katushya* rockets against northern Israel over the past several years.

Table 20 Orders and deliveries, Middle East and North Africa, 1995–1997

Equipment	Type	Unit	Supplier	Order Date	Delivery Date	Comment
Algeria						
AIFV	BVP-2	48	Slvk	1994	1995	Deliveries completed 1996
APC	OT-64	150	Slvk		1995	
APC	*Fahd*	200	Et	1992	1992	Deliveries completed 1995
hel	AS-350B	9	Fr	1994	1995	
corvette		3	Ag	1983	1988	Delivered 1988, 1995; third delayed
Bahrain						
FGA	F-16		US	1997		Unconfirmed; 10 -C/Ds or 20 -A/Bs
hel	AH-1	12	US	1994	1995	EDA
MBT	M-60A3	60	US	1995	1996	Ex-ROK, on lease
SAM	Improved *Hawk*	8	US	1996	1997	EDA
FFG	*Perry*-class	1	US	1995	1997	
Egypt						
cbt hel	AH-64	36	US	1990	1994	Deliveries to 1999
FGA	F-16C/D	67	US	1991	1994	Deliveries to 1999
hel	UH-60L	2	US	1995	1998	
AIFV	YPR-765	611	Nl	1995	1996	
APC	M-113	498	US	1994	1995	EDA
arty	SP 122	24	US		1998	122mm; AA upgrade
ATGW	M-901	130	US	1995	1996	Deliveries continue
MBT	M1A1	635	US	1988	1993	Deliveries to 1999
FFG	*Perry*-class	3	US	1994	1997	3 delivered 1997
FF	*Knox*-class	2	US	1994	1995	EDA
SS	*Romeo*-class	4	US		1995	*Harpoon* upgrade by US, Dec 1995
hel	SH-2F	10	US	1994	1996	EDA
Iran						
tpt	Y-7	14	PRC	1996	1998	Deliveries 1998–2006
tpt	An-74T-200	2	Ukr		1997	Total order n.k.
trg	TB-21	12	Fr	1996		6 TB-21, 6 TB-200
MBT	*Zulfiqar*		Domestic		1994	Production
MBT	T-72M1	70	Pl	1993	1994	Deliveries completed 1995
MBT	T-72	2	RF	1989	1996	120 delivered 1993–94
AIFV	BMP-1	2	RF	1989	1996	40 *Boragh* under licence to 1997
MRL	FADJR-3		Domestic			240mm; development completed
corvette		1	Domestic			Reported under construction 1996
mine	MC-52		PRC	1992		Delivery unconfirmed
PFM	*Hudong*-class	10	PRC	1992	1994	5 delivered 1994, 5 Mar 1996
SS	*Kilo*-class	3	RF	1989	1996	
SSM	*Nodong*		Collab.			Development with DPRK

Equipment	Type	Unit	Supplier	Order Date	Delivery Date	Comment
SSM	SS-1/9P117M		DPRK	1991	1994	Deliveries continuing
SSM	C-802	18	PRC	1992	1995	For *Hudong*-class PFM
Israel						
SAM	*Nautilus*		Collab.	1995		Development with US
TMD	*Arrow*		Collab.			Development with US
FGA	F-16A/B	50	US		1995	
FGA	F-15I	25	US	1993	1997	
AAM	AIM-9S	300	US	1990	1993	Deliveries completed 1995
hel	AH-1	14	US	1995	1995	EDA
tkr	Boeing 707	1	US		1997	Multi-role tpt/tkr
hel	UH-60	14	US		1997	
MBT	*Merkava* IV		Domestic	1996		Development
MRL	MLRS (M203)	42	US	1994	1995	6 delivered 1995, continuing to 1998
hel	AS-565SA	5	Fr	1994	1997	5 delivered 1997; requirement 20 ASW
corvette	*Saar* 5	3	US	1989	1995	
SSK	*Dolphin*	3	Ge	1994	1997	Sea trials late 1996 Ge
Jordan						
FGA	F-16A/B	16	US	1995	1997	Surplus; 12 -A, 4 -B; deliveries to 1998
hel	UH-60L	4	US	1995	1995	2 delivered 1995, 2 by 1998
hel	UH-1H	18	US	1995	1996	
tpt	C-130	2	US	1995	1996	1 C-130H, 1 C-130B
MBT	M-60A3	50	US	1995	1996	
Kuwait						
hel	UH-60L	16	US	1996		Armed attack variant; halted by US
SAM	*Patriot*	5	US	1992		5 batteries, 210 missiles
AIFV	BMP-2	46	RF	1993	1995	4 delivered 1993, 5 1994; rest 1995–96
AIFV	*Warrior*	254	UK	1993	1995	66 delivered 1995, 116 1996
AIFV	BMP-3	126	RF	1994	1995	76 delivered by Apr 1997
LAV	*Pandur*	70	A	1996		Options for 200 total
APC	S-600	22	Aus	1997	1998	
MBT	M1A2	218	US	1992	1994	130 delivered 1996; deliveries continue
PFC	*Combattante*-4	8	Fr	1995	1999	
PFM	P-37 BRL	8	Fr	1995	1997	Deliveries 1997–99
Lebanon						
hel	UH-1	32	US		1995	EDA
APC	M113	225	US		1995	EDA
Mauritania						
PCI	*Amgram*-class	1	Fr		1996	Coast Guard vessel
Morocco						
FGA	A-37	14	US	1995	1995	EDA
arty	M198 155mm	26	US	1996		EDA
ATGW	M-901	80	US	1995	1995	EDA
OPV	OPV 64	5	Fr		1995	1 delivered Dec 1995, rest 1997
Oman						
LAV	*Piranha*	80	UK	1993	1994	First delivery 1994, 50 1996, rest 1997
arty	155mm	25	RSA	1995	1996	
MBT	*Challenger* II	19	UK	1993	1995	Includes 1 ARV
MBT	M60A3	50	US	1995	1996	EDA; 30 delivered 1995
corvette	VT-83	2	UK	1992	1996	Second commissioned Apr 1997
Qatar						
FGA	*Mirage* 2000-5	12	Fr	1995	1997	
trg	*Hawk* 100	15	UK	1996		Option for three more
LAV	*Piranha*	36	UK	1996	1997	Deliveries 1997–98
MBT	AMX-30	10	Fr		1997	FMA
SAM	*Starburst*		UK	1996		

Equipment	Type	Unit	Supplier	Order Date	Delivery Date	Comment
SSM	*Exocet* MM 40	8	Fr	1996		To equip *Barzan*-class PFCs
PFC	*Barzan*-class	4	UK	1992	1995	Deliveries 1995–97
PFC		2	UK	1996	2000	
Saudi Arabia						
hel	AS-532 Mk 2	12	Fr	1996		Armed with AM-39 Mk2 *Exocet*
FGA	F-15S	72	US	1992	1995	Deliveries to 2001
FGA	*Tornado* IDS	48	UK	1993	1996	Deliveries to 1998
trg	PC-9	20	CH	1993	1996	Assembled under licence in UK
trg	*Hawk* 65	20	UK	1993	1996	Deliveries to 1997
AIFV	M-2 *Bradley*	306	US	1990	1993	Deliveries completed 1995
MBT	M1A1	315	US	1990	1993	Final deliveries 1995
arty	G-6 155mm	30	RSA	1997		Unconfirmed
SAM	*Aster* 15	3	Fr	1997		3 launchers with 60 missiles
FFG	*La Fayette*-class	3	Fr	1994	1998	First delivered 1998, second 2002
FF	*Medina*-class	4	Fr		1997	Overhaul of 4 ASW; final delivery 1999
MHC	*Sandown*-class	3	UK	1988	1993	Final due late 1997
Tunisia						
trg	L-59	6	Cz	1995	1996	
tpt	C-130B	5	US	1993	1995	EDA
arty	M-30	26	A	1996	1997	
United Arab Emirates						
cbt hel	AH-64A	10	US	1997		
hel	AS-565	6	Fr	1995	1998	Armed with AS-15TT missiles
hel	*Gazelle*	5	Fr	1997		Surplus; 5 ordered, option for 5 more
tpt	CN-235	7	Indo	1997		
trg	G-115 TA	12	Ge	1996	1997	12 delivered 1997, option for 12 more
trg	*Hawk*	26	UK	1989	1992	Deliveries completed 1996
AIFV	BMP-3	330	RF	1992	1996	Deliveries completed 1996
APC	AAPC	136	Tu	1997	1998	
MBT	*Leclerc*	436	Fr	1993	1994	Includes 46 ARVs; deliveries continue
FF	*Kortenaer*-class	2	Nl	1996	1997	Surplus; second delivery 1998
Yemen						
FGA	Su-22	4	Ukr		1995	
FAC	*Baklan*-class	6	Fr	1996	1996	First 5 delivered 1996, last early 1997
PFC	*Huangfen*	3	PRC	1991	1995	

Algeria

	1995	1996	1997	1998
GDP	D2.0tr	D2.5tr		
	($43bn)	($45bn)		
per capita	$6,200	$6,300		
Growth	3.7%	4.0%		
Inflation	21.8%	15.1%		
Debt	$32.6bn	$36.3bn		
Def exp	D68bn	D99bn		
	($1.4bn)	($1.8bn)		
Def bdgt			D94.0bn	
			($1.6bn)	
FMA (US)	$0.07m	$0.08m	$0.08m	$0.08m
$1 = dinar	47.7	54.5	57.0	

Population		28,865,000		
Age		13–17	18–22	23–32
Men		1,860,000	1,646,000	2,598,000
Women		1,732,000	1,542,000	2,437,000

Total Armed Forces

ACTIVE ε124,000

(ε75,000 conscripts)

Terms of service: **Army** 18 months (6 months basic, 12 months civil projects)

RESERVES

Army some 150,000, to age 50

Army 107,000

(ε75,000 conscripts)
6 Mil Regions; re-org into div structure on hold
2 armd div (each 3 tk, 1 mech regt) • 2 mech div (each
3 mech, 1 tk regt) • 1 AB div • 1 indep armd bde • 4–5
indep mot/mech inf bde • 7 arty, 5 AD bn

EQUIPMENT

MBT 890: 275 T-54/-55, 330 T-62, 285 T-72
RECCE 75 BRDM-2
AIFV 690 BMP-1, 225 BMP-2
APC 530 BTR-50/-60, 150 OT-64, some BTR-80
   (reported)
TOWED ARTY 122mm: 28 D-74, 100 M-1931/37, 60
   M-30 (M-1938), 198 D-30; **130mm**: 10 M-46;
   152mm: 20 ML-20 (M-1937)
SP ARTY 185: **122mm**: 150 2S1; **152mm**: 35 2S3
MRL 122mm: 48 BM-21; **140mm**: 48 BM-14-16;
   240mm: 30 BM-24
MOR 82mm: 150 M-37; **120mm**: 120 M-1943;
   160mm: 60 M-1943
ATGW AT-2 *Swatter*, AT-3 *Sagger*
RCL 82mm: 120 B-10; **107mm**: 58 B-11
ATK GUNS 57mm: 156 ZIS-2; **85mm**: 80 D-44;
   100mm: 12 T-12, 50 SU-100 SP
AD GUNS 14.5mm: 80 ZPU-2/-4; **20mm**: 100;
   23mm: 100 ZU-23 towed, 210 ZSU-23-4 SP;
   37mm: 150 M-1939; **57mm**: 75 S-60; **85mm**: 20 KS-
   12; **100mm**: 150 KS-19; **130mm**: 10 KS-30
SAM SA-7/-8/-9

Navy ε7,000

(incl ε500 Coast Guard)
BASES Mers el Kebir, Algiers, Annaba, Jijel
SUBMARINES 2
   2 Sov *Kilo* with 533mm TT
FRIGATES 3
   3 *Mourad Rais* (Sov *Koni*) with 2 x 12 ASW RL
PATROL AND COASTAL COMBATANTS 22
CORVETTES 3 *Rais Hamidou* (Sov *Nanuchka* II) with 4
   SS-N-2C *Styx* SSM, 2 C-58
MISSILE CRAFT 11 *Osa* with 4 SS-N-2 SSM
PATROL CRAFT 8
   COASTAL 2 *Djebel Chinoise*
   INSHORE 6 *El Yadekh* PCI
MINE COUNTERMEASURES 11
   11 Sov T-43 MSC
AMPHIBIOUS 3
   2 *Kalaat beni Hammad* LST: capacity 240 tps, 10 tk, hel
   deck
   1 *Polnocny* LSM: capacity 180 tps, 6 tk
SUPPORT AND MISCELLANEOUS 3
   1 *El Idrissi* AGHS, 1 div spt, 1 *Poluchat* torpedo
   recovery vessel

COAST GUARD (ε500)

Some 7 PRC *Chui-E* PCC, about 6 *El Yadekh* PCI, 16
   PCI<, 1 spt, plus boats

Air Force 10,000

181 cbt ac, 65 armed hel **Flying hours** ε160
FGA 3 sqn
   1 with 10 Su-24
   2 with 40 MiG-23BN
FTR 5 sqn
   1 with 10 MiG-25
   1 with 30 MiG-23B/E
   3 with 70 MiG-21MF/bis
RECCE 1 sqn with 4* MiG-25R, 1 sqn with 6* MiG-21
MR 2 sqn with 15 *Super King Air* B-200T
TPT 2 sqn with 10 C-130H, 6 C-130H-30, 5 Il-76
VIP 2 *Falcon* 900, 3 *Gulfstream* III, 2 F-27
HELICOPTERS
   ATTACK 35 Mi-24, 1 with 30 Mi-8/-17
   TPT 2 Mi-4, 5 Mi-6, 46 Mi-8/17, 10 AS 355
TRG 3* MiG-21U, 5* MiG-23U, 3* MiG-25U, 6 T-34C,
   30 L-39, plus 30 ZLIN-142
AAM AA-2, AA-6
AD GUNS 3 bde+: **85mm**, **100mm**, **130mm**
SAM 3 regt with SA-3, SA-6, SA-8

Forces Abroad

UN AND PEACEKEEPING
HAITI (UNTMIH): 14 civ pol

Paramilitary ε146,200

GENDARMERIE (Ministry of Defence) 25,000
6 regions; 44 Panhard AML-60/M-3, 200 *Fahd* APC,
   BRDM-2 recce **hel** Mi-2
NATIONAL SECURITY FORCES (Directorate of
National Security) 20,000
small arms
REPUBLICAN GUARD 1,200
AML-60, M-3 recce
**COMMUNAL GUARDS / LEGITIMATE DEFENCE
GROUPS** ε100,000
Local militia

Opposition

ARMÉE ISLAMIQUE DU SALUT (AIS) perhaps 2,000+
armed wing of the *Front Islamique du Salut* (FIS)
GROUPE ISLAMIQUE ARMÉE (GIA) small groups each
ε50–100
ARMED FRONT FOR ISLAMIC JIHAD (FIDA)
ISLAMIC LEAGUE FOR THE CALL AND JIHAD
(LIDO)

Bahrain

	1995	1996	1997	1998
GDP	D1.9bn	D1.9bn		
	($5.1bn)	($5.1bn)		
per capita	$8,200	$8,300		
Growth	1.0%	1.6%		
Inflation	2.7%	-0.2%		
Debt	$7.3bn	$8.3bn		
Def exp	D103m	D107m		
	($273m)	($285m)		
Def bdgt			D109m	
			($290m)	
FMA (US)	$0.1m	$0.1m	$0.1m	$0.2m
$1 = dinar	0.38	0.38	0.38	
Population		599,400		

(Nationals 68%, Asian 13%, other Arab 10%, Iranian 8%, European 1%)

Age	13–17	18–22	23–32
Men	29,000	23,000	41,000
Women	28,000	22,000	39,000

Total Armed Forces

ACTIVE 11,000

Army 8,500

1 armd bde (-) (2 tk, 1 recce bn) • 1 inf bde (2 mech, 1 mot inf bn) • 1 arty 'bde' (1 hy, 2 med, 1 lt, 1 MRL bty) • 1 SF, 1 *Amiri* gd bn • 1 AD bn (2 SAM, 1 AD gun bty)

EQUIPMENT
MBT 106 M-60A3
RECCE 22 AML-90, 8 *Saladin*, 8 *Ferret*, 8 Shorland
AIFV 25 YPR-765 (with **25mm**)
APC some 10 AT-105 *Saxon*, 110 Panhard M-3, 220 M-113A2
TOWED ARTY 105mm: 8 lt; **155mm**: 28 M-198
SP ARTY 203mm: 13 M-110
MRL 227mm: 9 MLRS
MOR 81mm: 9; **120mm**: 9
ATGW 15 TOW
RCL 106mm: 30 M-40A1; **120mm**: 6 MOBAT
AD GUNS 35mm: 12 Oerlikon; **40mm**: 12 L/70
SAM 40+ RBS-70, 15 *Stinger*, 7 *Crotale*, 8 I HAWK (being delivered)

Navy 1,000

BASE Mina Sulman
PRINCIPAL SURFACE COMBATANTS 1
FRIGATES 1 *Sabah* (US OH *Perry*) with 4 *Harpoon* SSM, 1 *Standard* SAM, 1 76mm gun
PATROL AND COASTAL COMBATANTS 12

CORVETTES 2 *Al Manama* (Ge Lürssen 62m) with 2 x 2 MM-40 *Exocet* SSM, hel deck
MISSILE CRAFT 4 *Ahmad el Fateh* (Ge Lürssen 45m) with 2 x 2 MM-40 *Exocet*
PATROL CRAFT 6
  INSHORE 6
  2 *Al Riffa* (Ge Lürssen 38m) PFI
  2 PFI<
  2 *Swift* FPB-20
SUPPORT AND MISCELLANEOUS 5
4 *Ajeera* LCU-type spt
1 *Tiger* ACV, **hel** 2 B-105 (SAR)

Air Force 1,500

24 cbt ac, 24 armed hel
FGA 1 sqn with 8 F-5E, 4 F-5F
FTR 1 sqn with 8 F-16C, 4 F-16D
TPT 2 *Gulfstream* (1 -II, 1 -III; VIP), 1 Boeing 727
HEL 1 sqn with 12 AB-212 (10 armed), 12 AH-1E (atk), 5 Bo-105, 1 UH-60L (VIP), 1 S-70A (VIP)
MISSILES
  ASM AS-12, AGM-65 *Maverick*
  AAM AIM-9P *Sidewinder*, AIM-7F *Sparrow*

Paramilitary ε9,850

POLICE (Ministry of Interior) 9,000
2 Hughes 500, 2 Bell 412, 1 Bell 205 hel
NATIONAL GUARD str ε600
3 bn to form; 1 PCI, some 20 PCI<, 2 spt/landing craft, 1 hovercraft
COAST GUARD (Ministry of Interior) ε250
1 PCI, some 20 PCI<, 2 spt/landing craft, 1 hovercraft

Foreign Forces

US Air Force periodic detachments of ftr and support ac **Navy** (HQ CENTCOM and 5th Fleet) 230
UK RAF 40 (*Southern Watch*)

Egypt

	1995	1996	1997	1998
GDP	E£205bn	E£257bn		
	($56bn)	($60bn)		
per capita	$3,800	$4,000		
Growth	4.4%	4.9%		
Inflation	15.7%	5.4%		
Debt	$34.1bn	$33.6bn		
Def exp	εE£8.5bn	εE£9.1bn		
	($2.5bn)	($2.7bn)		
Def bdgt			E£8.7bn	
			($2.6bn)	
FMA[a] (US)	$2.1bn	$2.1bn	$2.1bn	$2.1bn

contd	1995	1996	1997	1998
$1 = pound	3.39	3.39	3.39	

ª UNTSO **1995** $28m **1996** $27m

Population		63,000,000		
Age	*13–17*	*18–22*	*23–32*
Men	3,412,000	2,931,000	4,817,000
Women	3,218,000	2,758,000	4,514,000

Total Armed Forces

ACTIVE 450,000

(some 320,000 conscripts)
Terms of service: 3 years (selective)

RESERVES 254,000

Army 150,000 **Navy** 14,000 **Air Force** 20,000 **AD** 70,000

Army 320,000

(perhaps 250,000+ conscripts)
4 Mil Districts, 2 Army HQ • 4 armd div (each with 2 armd, 1 mech, 1 arty bde) • 8 mech inf div (each with 2 mech, 1 armd, 1 arty bde) • 1 Republican Guard armd bde • 4 indep armd bde • 1 air-mobile bde • 2 indep inf bde • 1 para bde • 4 indep mech bde • 6 cdo gp • 15 indep arty bde • 2 SSM bde (1 with FROG-7, 1 with *Scud*-B)

EQUIPMENTª

MBT 840 T-54/-55, 260 *Ramses* II (mod T-54/55), 500 T-62, 1,700 M-60 (400 M-60A1, 1,300 M-60A3), 400 M1A1 *Abrams*

RECCE 300 BRDM-2, 112 *Commando Scout*

AIFV 220 BMP-1 (in store), 260 BMR-600P, 310 YPR-765 (with **25mm**)

APC 650 *Walid*, 165 *Fahd*/-30, 1,075 BTR-50/OT-62 (most in store), 1,944 M-113A2 (incl variants), 70 YPR-765

TOWED ARTY 122mm: 36 M-31/37, 359 M-1938, 156 D-30M; **130mm**: 420 M-46

SP ARTY 122mm: 76 SP 122 (delivery reported), **155mm**: 200 M-109A2

MRL 122mm: 96 BM-11, 200 BM-21/*as-Saqr*-10/-18/-36

MOR 82mm: 500 (some 50 SP); **107mm**: 100+ M-30 SP; **120mm**: 1,800 M-38; **160mm**: 60 M-160

SSM 12 FROG-7, *Saqr*-80 (trials), 9 *Scud*-B

ATGW 1,400 AT-3 *Sagger* (incl BRDM-2); 220 *Milan*; 200 *Swingfire*; 840 TOW (incl I-TOW, TOW-2A (with 52 on M-901, 210 on YPR-765 SP))

RCL 107mm: B-11

AD GUNS 14.5mm: 475 ZPU-2/-4; **23mm**: 550 ZU-23-2, 117 ZSU-23-4 SP, 45 *Sinai*; **37mm**: 150 M-1939; **57mm**: 300 S-60, 40 ZSU-57-2 SP

SAM 2,000 SA-7/'*Ayn as-Saqr*, 20 SA-9, 26 M-54 SP *Chaparral*

SURV AN/TPQ-37 (arty/mor), RASIT (veh, arty), *Cymbeline* (mor)

UAV R4E-50 *Skyeye*

ª Most Sov eqpt now in store, incl MBT and some cbt ac

Navy ε20,000

(incl ε2,000 Coast Guards and ε10,000 conscripts)
BASES Mediterranean Alexandria (HQ), Port Said, Mersa Matruh, Safaqa, Port Tewfig **Red Sea** Hurghada (HQ)

SUBMARINES 8
   4 Sov *Romeo* with 533mm TT (poss non-op)
   4 PRC Romeo with sub-*Harpoon* and 533mm TT

PRINCIPAL SURFACE COMBATANTS 9

DESTROYERS 1 *El Fateh* (UK 'Z') (trg) with 4 114mm guns, 5 533mm TT

FRIGATES 8
   2 *Mubarak* (ex-US *Perry*) with 4 *Harpoon* SSM, 36 *Standard* SAM, 1 76mm gun, 2 hel
   2 *El Suez* (Sp *Descubierta*) with 2 x 3 ASTT, 1 x 2 ASW RL; plus 2 x 4 *Harpoon* SSM
   2 *Al Zaffir* (PRC *Jianghu* I) with 2 ASW RL; plus 2 CSS-N-2 (*HY* 2) SSM
   2 *Damyat* (US *Knox*) with 8 *Harpoon*, 127mm gun, 4 324mm TT

PATROL AND COASTAL COMBATANTS 43

MISSILE CRAFT 25
   6 *Ramadan* with 4 *Otomat* SSM
   5 Sov *Osa* I with 4 SS-N-2A *Styx* SSM (plus 1 non-op)
   6 *6th October* with 2 *Otomat* SSM
   2 Sov *Komar* with 2 SSN-2A *Styx* (plus 2 non-op)
   6 PRC *Hegu* (*Komar*-type) with 2 SSN-2A *Styx* SSM

PATROL CRAFT 18
   8 PRC *Hainan* PFC with 4 ASW RL
   6 Sov *Shershen* PFI; 2 with 4 533mm TT and BM-21 (8-tube) 122mm MRL; 4 with SA-N-5 and 1 BM-24 (12-tube) 240mm MRL
   4 PRC *Shanghai* II PFI

MINE COUNTERMEASURES 11
   4 *Aswan* (Sov *Yurka*) MSC (plus 1 non-op)
   4 *Assiout* (Sov T-43 class) MSC (plus 2 non-op)
   3 *Swiftship* MHI

AMPHIBIOUS 12
   3 Sov *Polnocny* LSM, capacity 100 tps, 5 tk
   9 *Vydra* LCU, capacity 200 tps

SUPPORT AND MISCELLANEOUS 20
   7 AOT (small), 5 trg, 6 tugs, 1 diving spt, 1 *Tariq* (ex-UK FF) trg

NAVAL AVIATION
24 armed Air Force **hel** 5 *Sea King* Mk 47 (ASW, anti-ship), 9 SA-342 (anti-ship), 10 SH-2G

COASTAL DEFENCE (Army tps, Navy control)
GUNS 130mm: SM-4-1
SSM *Otomat*

Air Force 30,000

(10,000 conscripts); 572 cbt ac, 125 armed hel
FGA 7 sqn
  2 with 42 *Alpha Jet*, 2 with 44 PRC J-6, 2 with 29 F-4E,
  1 with 20 *Mirage* 5E2
FTR 21 sqn
  2 with 25 F-16A, 6 with 74 MiG-21, 6 with 115 F-16C,
  3 with 53 *Mirage* 5D/E, 3 with 53 PRC J-7, 1 with
  18 *Mirage* 2000C
RECCE 2 sqn with 6* *Mirage* 5SDR, 14* MiG-21
EW ac 2 C-130H (ELINT), 4 Beech 1900 (ELINT) **hel** 4
  Commando 2E (ECM)
AEW 5 E-2C
ASW 9* SA-342L, 5* *Sea King* 47, 10* SH-2G (with
  Navy)
MR 2 Beech 1900C surv **ac**
TPT 19 C-130H, 5 DHC-5D, 1 *Super King Air*, 3
  Gulfstream III, 1 *Gulfstream* IV, 3 *Falcon* 20
HELICOPTERS
  ATTACK 4 sqn with 65 SA-342K (44 with HOT, 25
  with 20mm gun), 36 AH-64A
  TAC TPT hy 14 CH-47C **med** 40 Mi-8, 25 *Commando*
  (3 VIP), 2 S-70 (VIP) **lt** 12 Mi-4, 17 UH-12E (trg), 2
  UH-60A, 3 AS-61
TRG incl 4 DHC-5, 54 EMB-312, 10* F-16B, 15* F-16D,
  36 *Gumhuria*, 16* JJ-6, 40 L-29, 48 L-39, 30* L-59E,
  MiG-21U, 5* *Mirage* 5SDD, 3* *Mirage* 2000B
UAV 29 Teledyne-Ryan 324 *Scarab*
MISSILES
  ASM AGM-65 *Maverick*, *Exocet* AM-39, AS-12, AS-
  30, AS-30L HOT
  ARM *Armat*
  AAM AA-2 *Atoll*, AIM-7E/F/M *Sparrow*, AIM-9F/
  L/P *Sidewinder*, R-530, R-550 *Magic*

Air Defence Command 80,000

(50,000 conscripts)
4 div: regional bde, 100 AD arty bn, 40 SA-2, 53 SA-3,
  14 SA-6 bn, 12 bty I HAWK, 12 bty *Chaparral*, 14 bty
  Crotale
EQUIPMENT
  AD GUNS some 2,000: **20mm, 23mm, 37mm,
  57mm, 85mm, 100mm**
  SAM some 282 SA-2, 212 SA-3, 56 SA-6, 78 I
  HAWK, 36 *Crotale*
  AD SYSTEMS some 18 *Amoun* (*Skyguard*/RIM-7F
  Sparrow, some 36 twin **35mm** guns, some 36 quad
  SAM); *Sinai*-23 short-range AD (Dassault 6SD-20S
  radar, **23mm** guns, '*Ayn as-Saqr* SAM)

Forces Abroad

Advisers in Oman, Saudi Arabia, Zaire
UN AND PEACEKEEPING
ANGOLA (UNOMA): 11 incl 10 Obs plus 14 civ pol.
BOSNIA (SFOR): 270. (UNMIBH): 34 civ pol.
CROATIA (UNTAES): 4 Obs plus 16 civ pol;
(UNMOP): 1 Obs. FYROM (UNPREDEP): 1 Obs.
GEORGIA (UNOMIG): 5 Obs. LIBERIA (UNOMIL):
14 Obs. WESTERN SAHARA (MINURSO):19 Obs

Paramilitary 230,000 active

CENTRAL SECURITY FORCES (Ministry of Interior)
150,000
  110 *Hotspur Hussar*, *Walid* APC
NATIONAL GUARD 60,000
8 bde (each of 3 bn; cadre status); lt wpns only
BORDER GUARD FORCES 20,000
19 Border Guard Regt; lt wpns only
COAST GUARD ε2,000 (incl in Naval entry)
  PATROL, INSHORE 39
  18 *Timsah* PCI, 10 *Swiftships*, 5 *Nisr*†, 6 *Crestitalia*
  PFI<, plus some 60 boats

Foreign Forces

PEACEKEEPING (MFO Sinai): some 1,896 from **Aus,
Ca, Co, Fji, Fr, Hu, It, NZ, No, Ury, US**

Iran

	1995	1996	1997	1998
GDP[a]	r184tr	r283tr		
	($62.5bn)	($67.3bn)		
per capita	$4,900	$5,100		
Growth	4.0%	5.2%		
Inflation	50.0%	28.9%		
Debt	$21.9bn	$21.4bn		
Def exp[a]	r4.3tr	r5.9tr		
	($2.5bn)	($3.4bn)		
Def bdgt			r8.2tr	
			($4.7bn)	
$1 = rial[b]	1,748	1,751	1,754	

[a] Excl defence industry funding
[b] Market rate **1997** $1 = r4,200–4,500

Population	68,735,000		
(Persian 51%, Azeri 24%, Gilaki/Mazandarani 8%, Kurdish 7%, Sunni Muslim 4%, Arab 3%)			
Age	*13–17*	*18–22*	*23–32*
Men	4,141,000	3,426,000	5,206,000
Women	3,987,000	3,275,000	4,939,000

Total Armed Forces

ACTIVE ε518,000

(perhaps 250,000 plus conscripts)
Terms of service: 24 months

RESERVES
Army 350,000, ex-service volunteers

Army ε350,000

(perhaps 250,000 conscripts)
4 Army HQ • 4 armd div (each 3 armd, 1 mech bde, 4–5 arty bn) • 6 inf div (each 4 inf bde, 4-5 arty bn) • 1 AB bde • 2 SF div (3 bde) • some indep armd, inf, cdo bde • 5 arty gps

EQUIPMENT†
MBT some 1,390, incl: 110 T-54/-55, some 100 T-62, 200 T-72, 250 *Chieftain* Mk 3/5, 150 M-47/-48, 160 M-60A1, 220 PRC Type-59, 200 PRC Type-69
LT TK 80 *Scorpion*
RECCE 35 EE-9 *Cascavel*
AIFV 300 BMP-1, 100 BMP-2
APC 550: BTR-50/-60, M-113
TOWED 1,995: **105mm**: 130 M-101A1; **122mm**: 550 D-30, 100 PRC Type-54; **130mm**: 1,000 M-46/Type-59; **152mm**: 30 D-20; **155mm**: 15 WAC-21, 70 M-114; 80 GHN-45; **203mm**: 20 M-115
SP 289: **122mm**: 60 2S1; **155mm**: 160 M-109; **170mm**: 9 M-1978; **175mm**: 30 M-107; **203mm**: 30 M-110
MRL 659+: **107mm**: 500 PRC Type-63; **122mm**: 50 *Hadid/Arash/Noor*, 100 BM-21, 5 BM-11; **240mm**: 9 M-1985; **320mm**: *Oghab*; **333mm**: *Shahin* 1/-2; **355mm**: *Nazeat*
MOR 6,500 incl: **60mm; 81mm; 82mm; 107mm**: 4.2in M-30; **120mm**
SSM ε10 *Scud*-B/-C (210 msl), ε25 CSS-8 (200 msl), *Fajr*
ATGW TOW, AT-3 *Sagger* (some SP)
RL **73mm**: RPG-7
RCL **75mm**: M-20; **82mm**: B-10; **106mm**: M-40; **107mm**: B-11
AD GUNS 1,700: **14.5mm**: ZPU-2/-4; **23mm**: ZU-23 towed, ZSU-23-4 SP; **35mm; 37mm**: M-1939, PRC Type-55; **57mm**: ZSU-57-2 SP
SAM SA-7
AC incl 50 Cessna (150, 180, 185, 310), 19 F-27, 8 *Falcon* 20
HEL 100 AH-1J **attack**; 40 CH-47C **hy tpt**; 130 Bell 214A, 35 AB-214C; 40 AB-205A; 90 AB-206; 12 AB-212; 30 Bell 204; 5 Hughes 300C; 9 RH-53D; 10 SH-53D; 10 SA-319; 45 UH-1H

Revolutionary Guard Corps (*Pasdaran Inqilab*) some 120,000

GROUND FORCES some 100,000
grouped into perhaps 13 inf, 2 armd div and 15–20 indep bde, incl inf, armd, para, SF, arty (incl SSM), engr, AD and border defence units, serve indep or with Army; limited numbers of tk, APC and arty; controls *Basij* (see Paramilitary) when mob

NAVAL FORCES some 20,000
BASES Al Farsiyah, Halul (oil platform), Sirri, Abu Musa, Larak
some 40 Swe Boghammar Marin boats armed with ATGW, RCL, machine guns; 5 *Hudong* with C-802 SSM; controls coast-defence elm incl arty and CSSC-3 (*HY* 2) *Seersucker* SSM bty. Under joint command with Navy
MARINES I bde

Navy 18,000

(incl 2,000 Naval Air and Marines)
BASES Bandar Abbas (HQ), Bushehr, Kharg, Bandar-e-Anzelli, Bandar-e-Khomeini, Chah Bahar
SUBMARINES 3
3 Sov *Kilo* SS with 6 533mm TT (possibly wake homing) (unit 3 probably not fully op) (plus some 2 SS1s)
PRINCIPAL SURFACE COMBATANTS 4
DESTROYERS 1 *Babr* (US *Sumner*) with 4 x 1 SM-1 SAM (boxed), 2 x 2 127mm guns; plus 2 x 3 ASTT
FRIGATES 3 *Alvand* (UK Vosper Mk 5) with 1 x 5 *Sea Killer* II, 1 x 3 AS mor, 1 114mm gun
PATROL AND COASTAL COMBATANTS 48
CORVETTES 2 *Bayandor* (US PF-103)
MISSILE CRAFT 20
10 *Kaman* (Fr *Combattante* II) PFM, 4 fitted for 4 *Harpoon* SSM, and 6 for C-801/C-802 SSM
10 *Houdong* PFM with 4 C-802 SSM
PATROL, INSHORE 26
3 *Kaivan*, 3 *Parvin* PCI, 1 ex-Irq *Bogomol* PFI, some 10 other PFI<, plus some 9 hovercraft< (not all op), many small craft
MINE COUNTERMEASURES 7
3 *Shahrokh* MSC (in Caspian Sea as trg ship)
2 *Riazi* (US *Cape*) MSI
2 *Iran Ajr* LST (used for mine-laying)
AMPHIBIOUS 8
4 *Hengam* LST, capacity 225 tps, 9 tk, 1 hel
3 *Iran Hormuz* 24 (ROK) LST, capacity 140 tps, 8 tk
1 *Polnochny* (ex Irq) LSM
Plus craft: 3 LCT
SUPPORT AND MISCELLANEOUS 25
1 *Kharg* AOE with 2 hel, 2 *Bandar Abbas* AOR with 1 hel, 1 repair, 4 water tkr, 2 *Delvar* and 13 *Hendijan* spt vessels, 1 AT, 1 *Shahrokh* msc trg

NAVAL AIR (2,000)
9 armed hel
ASW 1 hel sqn with ε3 SH-3D, 6 AB-212 ASW
MCM 1 hel sqn with 2 RH-53D
TPT 1 sqn with 4 *Commander*, 4 F-27, 1 *Falcon* 20 ac AB-205, AB-206 **hel**

MARINES 2 bde

Air Force 30,000

(incl 12,000 Air Defence); some 297 cbt ac (probably less than 50% of US ac types serviceable); no armed hel
FGA 9 sqn
   4 with some 60 F-4D/E, 4 with some 60 F-5E/F, 1 with 30 Su-24 (including former Irq ac)
FTR 7 sqn
   4 with 60 F-14, 1 with 24 F-7, 2 with 30 MiG-29 (incl former Irq ac)
MR 5 P-3F, 1 RC-130
RECCE 1 sqn (det) with some 8* RF-4E
TKR/TPT 1 sqn with 4 Boeing 707, 1 Boeing 747
TPT 5 sqn with 9 Boeing 747F, 11 Boeing 707, 1 Boeing 727, 18 C-130E/H, 3 *Commander* 690, 15 F-27, 4 *Falcon* 20 1 *Jetstar*, 10 PC-6B
HEL 2 AB-206A, 39 Bell 214C, 5 CH-47
TRG incl 26 Beech F-33A/C, 10 EMB-312, 45 PC-7, 7 T-33, 5* MiG-29B, 5* FT-7, 20* F-5B, 8 TB-21, 4 TB-200
MISSILES
   ASM AGM-65A *Maverick*, AS-10, AS-11, AS-14, C-801
   AAM AIM-7 *Sparrow*, AIM-9 *Sidewinder*, AIM-54 *Phoenix*, probably AA-8, AA-10, AA-11 for MiG-29, PL-7
   SAM 12 bn with 150 I HAWK, 5 sqn with 30 *Rapier*, 15 *Tigercat*, 45 HQ-2J (PRC version of SA-2), SA-5, FM-80 (PRC version of *Crotale*)

Forces Abroad

LEBANON ε150 Revolutionary Guard
SUDAN mil advisers

Paramilitary 150,000 active

BASIJ ('Popular Mobilisation Army') (R) ε200,000 peacetime volunteers, mostly youths; str up to 1,000,000 during periods of offensive ops. Small arms only; not currently embodied for mil ops
LAW-ENFORCEMENT FORCES 150,000
incl border-guard elm **ac** Cessna 185/310 lt **hel** AB-205/-206; about 90 patrol inshore, 40 harbour craft

Opposition

KURDISH COMMUNIST PARTY OF IRAN (KOMALA) str n.k.

KURDISH DEMOCRATIC PARTY OF IRAN (KDP–Iran) ε8,000

NATIONAL LIBERATION ARMY (NLA) some 15,000
Iraq-based; org in bde, armed with captured eqpt.
   Perhaps 160+ T-54/-55 tanks, BMP-1 AIFV, D-30 **122mm** arty, BM-21 **122mm** MRL, Mi-8 **hel**

Iraq

	1995	1996	1997	1998
GDP	ε$15bn	ε$15bn		
Growth	ε2%	ε2%		
Inflation	ε50%	ε30%		
Debt	ε$22.2bn	$22.6bn		
Def exp	ε$1.3bn	ε$1.3bn		
$1 = dinar[a]	0.31	0.31	0.31	

[a] Market rate **1997** $1 = d1,000–1,250

Population		22,442,000		

(Arab 75–80% (of which Shi'a Muslim 55%, Sunni Muslim 45%), Kurdish 20–25%)

Age	13–17	18–22	23–32
Men	1,375,000	1,150,000	1,695,000
Women	1,314,000	1,103,000	1,637,000

Total Armed Forces

ACTIVE ε387,500
Terms of service: 18–24 months

RESERVES ε650,000

Army ε350,000

(incl ε100,000 recalled Reserves)
7 corps HQ • 6 armd/mech div[a] • 12 inf div[a] • 6 Republican Guard Force div • 4 Special Republican Guard bde • 10 cdo bde • 2 SF bde
EQUIPMENT[b]
   MBT perhaps 2,700, incl 1,000 T-54/-55/M-77, PRC Type-59/-69, 200 T-62, 700 T-72 (total incl *Chieftain* Mk 3/5, M-60 and M-47, mostly inop)
   RECCE BRDM-2, AML-60/-90, EE-9 *Cascavel*, EE-3 *Jararaca*
   AIFV perhaps 900 BMP-1/-2
   APC perhaps 2,000, incl BTR-50/-60/-152, OT-62/-64, MTLB, YW-531, M-113A1/A2, Panhard M-3, EE-11 *Urutu*
   TOWED ARTY perhaps 1,800, incl **105mm**: incl M-56 pack; **122mm**: D-74, D-30, M-1938; **130mm**: incl M-46, Type 59-1; **155mm**: some G-5, GHN-45, M-114
   SP ARTY 150, incl **122mm**: 2S1; **152mm**: 2S3; **155mm**: M-109A1/A2, AUF-1 (GCT)
   MRL perhaps 150, incl **107mm**; **122mm**: BM-21; **127mm**: ASTROS II; **132mm**: BM-13/-16, **262mm**: *Ababeel*
   MOR 81mm; 120mm; 160mm: M-1943; **240mm**
   SSM up to 6 *Scud* launchers (ε27 msl) reported
   ATGW AT-3 *Sagger* (incl BRDM-2), AT-4 *Spigot* reported, SS-11, *Milan*, HOT (incl 100 VC-TH)
   RCL 73mm: SPG-9; **82mm**: B-10; **107mm**
   ATK GUNS 85mm; **100mm** towed

HELICOPTERS ε500 (120 armed)
   ATTACK ε120 Bo-105 with AS-11/HOT, Mi-24, SA-316 with AS-12, SA-321 (some with *Exocet*), SA-342
   TPT ε350 **hy** Mi-6 **med** AS-61, Bell 214 ST, Mi-4, Mi-8/-17, SA-330 **lt** AB-212, BK-117 (SAR), Hughes 300C, Hughes 500D, Hughes 530F
   AD GUNS ε6,000: **23mm**: ZSU-23-4 SP; **37mm**: M-1939 and twin; **57mm**: incl ZSU-57-2 SP; **85mm**; **100mm; 130mm**
   SAM SA-2/-3/-6/-7/-8/-9/-13/-14/-16, *Roland*
   SURV RASIT (veh, arty), *Cymbeline* (mor)

[a] All divisions less Republican Guard at a reported 50% cbt effectiveness
[b] 50% of all eqpt lacks spares

Navy ε2,500

BASES Basra (limited facilities), Az Zubayr, Umm Qasr (currently closed for navy, commercials only)
FRIGATES 2
   2 *Mussa Ben Nussair* with 2 *Otomat* SSM, 1 *Aspide* SAM, 1 76mm gun, 1 AB 212 hel
PATROL AND COASTAL COMBATANTS 6
MISSILE CRAFT 1 Sov *Osa* I with 4 SS-N-2A *Styx*
PATROL, INSHORE 5
   1 Sov *Bogomol* PFI<, 3 PFI<, 1 PCI< plus 80 boats
MINE COUNTERMEASURES 4
   2 Sov *Yevgenya*, 2 *Nestin* MSI<
SUPPORT AND MISCELLANEOUS 3
   1 *Damen* AGS, 1 *Aka* (Yug *Spasilac*-class) AR, 1 yacht with hel deck
   (Plus 1 *Agnadeen* (It *Stromboli*) AOR laid-up in Alexandria, 3 *Al Zahraa* ro-ro AK with hel deck, capacity 16 tk, 250 tps, inactive in foreign ports)

Air Force ε35,000

(incl 17,000 AD personnel)
Serviceability of fixed-wg **ac** about 55%, serviceability of **hel** poor **Flying hours** 60
BBR ε6, incl H-6D, Tu-22
FGA ε130, incl MiG-23BN, *Mirage* F1EQ5, Su-7, Su-20, Su-25
FTR ε180 incl F-7, MiG-21, MiG-23, MiG-25, *Mirage* F-1EQ, MiG-29
RECCE incl MiG-25
TKR incl 2 Il-76
TPT incl An-2, An-12, An-24, An-26, Il-76
TRG incl AS-202, EMB-312, some 50 L-29, some 50 L-39, *Mirage* F-1BQ, 25 PC-7, 30 PC-9
MISSILES
   ASM AM-39, AS-4, AS-5, AS-11, AS-9, AS-12, AS-30L, C-601
   AAM AA-2/-6/-7/-8/-10, R-530, R-550

Paramilitary ε45–55,400

SECURITY TROOPS ε35–45,000 reported
BORDER GUARDS 10,400
lt wpns and mor only

Opposition

KURDISH DEMOCRATIC PARTY (KDP) ε15,000
(plus 25,000 tribesmen); small arms, some Iranian lt arty, MRL, mor, SAM-7
PATRIOTIC UNION OF KURDISTAN (PUK) ε10,000
(plus 22,000 tribesmen); 450 mor (**60mm, 82mm, 120mm**); **106mm** RCL; some 200 **14.5mm** AA guns; SA-7 SAM
SOCIALIST PARTY OF KURDISTAN ε500
SUPREME ASSEMBLY OF THE ISLAMIC REVOLUTION (SAIRI)
ε4,000; ε1 'bde'; Iran-based; Iraqi dissidents, ex-prisoners of war

Foreign Forces

UN (UNIKOM): some 936 tps and 238 mil obs from 33 countries

Israel

	1995	1996	1997	1998
GDP	NS261bn	NS304bn		
	($76bn)	($79bn)		
per capita	$16,400	$17,400		
Growth	7.2%	4.4%		
Inflation	10.1%	11.3%		
Debt	$45.0bn	$47.5bn		
Def exp	NS28bn	NS31bn		
	($9.3bn)	($9.6bn)		
Def bdgt			NS22.0bn	
			($6.6bn)	
FMA[a] (US)	$3bn	$3bn	$3bn	$3bn
$1 = new sheqalim				
	3.01	3.19	3.39	

[a] UNDOF **1995** $32m **1996** $32m

Population[b]	5,813,000		
(Jewish 81%, Arab 15%, Christian 3%, Druze 2%, Circassian ε3,000)			
Age	*13–17*	*18–22*	*23–32*
Men	272,000	266,000	496,000
Women	258,000	257,000	487,000

[b] Incl ε140,000 Jewish settlers in Gaza and the West Bank, ε200,000 in East Jerusalem, and ε13,000 in Golan

Total Armed Forces

ACTIVE ε175,000

(ε138,500 conscripts)

Terms of service: **officers** 48 months **men** 36 months **women** 21 months (Jews and Druze only; Christians, Circassians and Muslims may volunteer). Annual trg as cbt reservists to age 42 (some specialists to age 54) for men, 24 (or marriage) for women

RESERVES 430,000

Army 365,000 **Navy** 10,000 **Air Force** 55,000. Reserve service can be followed by voluntary service in Civil Guard or Civil Defence

Strategic Forces

Israel is widely believed to have a nuclear capability with up to 100 warheads. Delivery means could include **ac** *Jericho* 1 SSM (range up to 500km), *Jericho* 2 (tested 1987–89, range ε1,500km)

Army 134,000

(114,700 conscripts, male and female); some 598,000 on mob

3 territorial, 1 home front comd • 3 corps HQ • 3 armd div (2 armd, 1 arty bde, plus 1 armd, 1 mech inf bde on mob) • 2 div HQ (op control of anti-*intifada* units) • 3 regional inf div HQ (border def) • 4 mech inf bde (incl 1 para trained) • 3 arty bn with 203mm M-110 SP

RESERVES

9 armd div (2 or 3 armd, 1 affiliated mech inf, 1 arty bde) • 1 air-mobile/mech inf div (3 bde manned by para trained reservists) • 10 regional inf bde (each with own border sector) • 4 arty bde

EQUIPMENT

MBT 4,300: 1,080 *Centurion*, 500 M-48A5, 400 M-60, 600 M-60A1, 200 M-60A3, 150 *Magach* 7, 300 Ti-67 (T-54/-55), 70 T-62, 1,000 *Merkava* I/II/III

RECCE about 400, incl RAMTA RBY, BRDM-2, ε8 *Fuchs*

APC 5,900 M-113A1/A2, ε80 *Nagmashot* (*Centurion*), some *Achzarit*, *Puma*, BTR-50P, 3,500 M-2/-3 half-track

TOWED ARTY 400: **105mm**: 60 M-101; **122mm**: 100 D-30; **130mm**: 100 M-46; **155mm**: 40 Soltam M-68/-71, 50 M-839P/-845P, 50 M-114A1

SP ARTY 1,150: **105mm**: 34 M-7; **155mm**: 200 L-33, 120 M-50, 530 M-109A1/A2; **175mm**: 230 M-107; **203mm**: 36 M-110

MRL 100+: **122mm**: 40 BM-21; **160mm**: LAR-160; **227mm**: 9 MLRS; **240mm**: 30 BM-24; **290mm**: MAR-290.

MOR: 2,740: **81mm**: 1,600; **120mm**: 900; **160mm**: 240 (some SP) plus about 5,000 smaller calibre (**60mm**)

SSM 20 *Lance* (in store), some *Jericho* 1/2
ATGW 200 TOW (incl *Ramta* (M-113) SP), 780 *Dragon*, AT-3 *Sagger*, 25 *Mapats*
RL 82mm: B-300
RCL 84mm: *Carl Gustav*; **106mm**: 250 M-40A1
AD GUNS 20mm: 850: incl TCM-20, M-167 *Vulcan*, 35 M-163 *Vulcan*/M-48 *Chaparral* gun/msl systems; **23mm**: 100 ZU-23 and 60 ZSU-23-4 SP; **37mm**: M-39; **40mm**: L-70
SAM *Stinger*, 900 *Redeye*, 45 *Chaparral*
SURV EL/M-2140 (veh), AN/TPQ-37 (arty), AN/PPS-15 (arty)

Navy ε9,000

(2,000–3,000 conscripts), 10,000–12,000 on mob
BASES Haifa, Ashdod, Eilat
SUBMARINES 3

1 *Dolphin* (Ge prob Type 212 variant)
2 *Gal* (UK Vickers) SSC with Mk 37 HWT, *Harpoon* USGW (plus 1 in maintenance)

PATROL AND COASTAL COMBATANTS 53

CORVETTES 3 *Eilat* (*Sa'ar* 5) with 8 *Harpoon*, 8 *Gabriel* II SSM, 2 *Barak* VLS SAM (2 32 mls), 6 324mm ASTT plus 1 SA-366G hel
MISSILE CRAFT 21 PFM

2 *Aliya* with 4 *Harpoon*, 4 *Gabriel* SSM, 1 SA-366G *Dauphin* hel (OTHT)
3 *Romat* with 8 *Harpoon*, 8 *Gabriel*
4 *Hetz* (*Sa'ar* 4.5) with 4 *Harpoon*, 6 *Gabriel* and *Barak* VLS (plus 1 trials)
6 *Reshef* (*Sa'ar* 4) with 2–4 *Harpoon*, 4–6 *Gabriel*
6 *Mivtach* with 2–4 *Harpoon*, 3–5 *Gabriel*

PATROL, INSHORE 29

14 *Super Dvora/Dabur* PFI<, some with 2 324mm TT, 15 *Dabur* PFI with 2 324mm TT

AMPHIBIOUS 1

1 *Bat Sheva* LST type tpt
Plus craft: 3 *Ashdod* LCT, 1 US type LCM

NAVAL COMMAND 300 mainly underwater trained

Air Force 32,000

(21,800 conscripts, mainly in AD), 37,000 on mob; 448 cbt ac (plus perhaps 250 stored), 130 armed hel
Flying hours regulars: 190; reserves: 75
FGA/FTR 16 sqn

5 with 50 F-4E-2000, 25 F-4E
3 with 62 F-15 (36 -A, 2 -B, 18 -C, 6 -D)
7 with 205 F-16 (67 -A, 8 -B, 76 -C, 54 -D)
1 with 20 *Kfir* C7 (plus 120 C2/C7 in store)

FGA 4 sqn with 50 A-4N, plus 130 in store
RECCE 14* RF-4E, 6* *Kfir* RC-2, 2* F-15D
AEW 2 Boeing 707 with *Phalcon* system
EW 6 Boeing 707 (ELINT/ECM), 6 RC-12D, 3 IAI-200, 15 Do-28, 6 *King Air* 2000

MR 3 IAI-1124 *Seascan*
TKR 3 Boeing-707, 5 KC-130H
TPT 1 wg incl 4 Boeing 707, 12 C-47, 24 C-130H, 7 IAI-201
LIAISON 2 *Islander*, 20 Cessna U-206, 8 *Queen Air* 80
TRG 80 CM-170 *Tzukit*, 10 *Kfir* TC2/7, 30 *Super Cub*, 10* TA-4H, 4* TA-4J, 4 *Queen Air* 80
HELICOPTERS
    ATTACK 14 AH-1, 39 AH-1F, 35 Hughes 500MD, 42 AH-64A
    SAR 1 HH-65A, 4 AS-565
    TPT 40 CH-53D, 10 UH-60; 54 Bell 212, 39 Bell 206
UAV *Scout, Pioneer, Searcher, Firebee, Samson, Delilah, Hunter Silver Arrow*
MISSILES
    ASM AGM-45 *Shrike*, AGM-62A *Walleye*, AGM-65 *Maverick*, AGM-78D *Standard*, *Gabriel* III (mod), *Hellfire*, TOW, *Popeye*
    AAM AIM-7 *Sparrow*, AIM-9 *Sidewinder*, R-530, *Shafrir, Python* III, IV
    SAM 17 bty with MIM-23 I HAWK, 3 bty *Patriot*, 8 bty *Chapparal*

Paramilitary ε6,050

BORDER POLICE 6,000
    some *Walid* 1, 600 BTR-152 APC
COAST GUARD ε50
    1 US PBR, 3 other patrol craft

Forces Abroad

TURKEY periodic det of Air Force F-16 ac to Akinci air base

Jordan

	1995	1996	1997	1998
GDP	D4.7bn	D5.1bn		
	($6.6bn)	($7.0bn)		
per capita	$4,300	$4,500		
Growth	6.5%	5.0%		
Inflation	2.3%	6.5%		
Debt	$7.9bn	$7.0bn		
Def exp	D314m	D282m		
	($448m)	($398m)		
Def bdgt			D300m	
			($423m)	
FMAᵃ (US)	$49m	$271m	$32m	$47m
$1 = dinar	0.70	0.71	0.71	
ᵃ Excl US military debt waiver **1997** $15m **1998** $12m				
Population	4,713,000 (Palestinian ε50–60%)			
Age	*13–17*	*18–22*	*23–32*	
Men	258,000	238,000	425,000	
Women	250,000	230,000	404,000	

Total Armed Forces

ACTIVE ε104,050

RESERVES 35,000 (all services)
Army 30,000 (obligation to age 40)

Army 90,000

2 armd div (each 2 tk, 1 mech inf, 1 arty, 1 AD bde)
2 mech inf div (each 2 mech inf, 1 tk, 1 arty, 1 AD bde)
1 indep Royal Guard bde
1 SF bde (2 SF, 2 AB, 1 arty bn)
1 fd arty bde (4 bn)
Southern Mil Area (3 inf bn)
EQUIPMENT
    MBT some 1,141: 300 M-47/-48A5 (in store), 278 M-60A1/A3, 270 *Khalid/Chieftain*, 293 *Tariq* (*Centurion*)
    LT TKS 19 *Scorpion*
    RECCE 170 *Ferret*
    AIFV some 35 BMP-2
    APC 1,100 M-113
    TOWED ARTY 115: **105mm**: 50 M-102; **155mm**: 30 M-114 towed, 10 M-59/M-1; **203mm**: 25 M-115 towed (in store)
    SP ARTY 370: **105mm**: 30 M-52; **155mm**: 20 M-44, 220 M-109A1/A2; **203mm**: 100 M-110
    MOR 81mm: 450 (incl 130 SP); **107mm**: 50 M-30; **120mm**: 300 Brandt
    ATGW 330 TOW (incl 70 SP), 310 *Dragon*
    RL 94mm: 2,500 LAW-80; **112mm**: 2,300 APILAS
    RCL 106mm: 330 M-40A1
    AD GUNS 360: **20mm**: 100 M-163 *Vulcan* SP; **23mm**: 44 ZSU-23-4 SP; **40mm**: 216 M-42 SP
    SAM SA-7B2, 50 SA-8, 50 SA-13, 300 SA-14, 240 SA-16, 250 *Redeye*
    SURV AN-TPQ-36/-37 (arty, mor)

Navy ε650

BASE Aqaba
PATROL AND COASTAL COMBATANTS 5
PATROL CRAFT, INSHORE 5
    3 *Al Hussein* (Vosper 30m) PFI
    2 Ge *Bremse* PCI< (ex-GDR)
    Plus 3 *Al Hashim* (Rotork) PCI< and other armed boats (Dead Sea)

Air Force 13,400

(incl 3,400 AD); 97 cbt ac, 24 armed hel
Flying hours 180
FGA 3 sqn with 65 F-5E/F
FTR 2 sqn with 30 *Mirage* F-1 (14 -CJ, 16 -E)
TPT 1 sqn with 8 C-130 (3 -B, 5 -H), 4 C-212A

VIP 1 sqn with **ac** 2 *Gulfstream* III, IL-1011 **hel** 3 S-70, SA-319

HELICOPTERS 4 sqn
   ATTACK 3 with 24 AH-1S (with TOW ASM)
   TPT 1 with 9 AS-332M, 3 Bo-105, 8 Hughes 500D, 18 UH-1H, 18 UH-60L

TRG 16 *Bulldog*, 15 C-101, 12 PA-28-161, 6 PA-34-200, 2* *Mirage* F-1B

AD 2 bde: 14 bty with 80 I HAWK

MISSILES
   ASM TOW
   AAM AIM-9 *Sidewinder*, R-530, R-550 *Magic*

Forces Abroad

UN AND PEACEKEEPING
ANGOLA (UNOMA): 19 incl 17 Obs, 21 civ pol.
BOSNIA (SFOR): 10; (UNMIBH): 136 civ pol; (UNPF): 45. **CROATIA** (UNTAES): 876 incl 6 Obs plus 40 civ pol; (UNMOP): 1 Obs. **FYROM** (UNPREDEP): 2 Obs plus 2 civ pol. **GEORGIA** (UNOMIG): 7 Obs.
TAJIKISTAN (UNMOT): 2 Obs

Paramilitary ε10,000 active

PUBLIC SECURITY DIRECTORATE (Ministry of Interior) ε10,000
(incl Police Public Sy bde); some *Scorpion* lt tk, 25 EE-11 *Urutu*, 30 *Saracen* APC

CIVIL MILITIA 'PEOPLE'S ARMY' (R) ε20,000
(to be 5,000) **men** 16–65 **women** 16–45

Kuwait

	1995	1996	1997	1998
GDP	D8.0bn	D8.3bn		
	($26.7bn)	($27.8bn)		
per capita	$16,000	$16,200		
Growth	8.2%	1.6%		
Inflation	2.7%	3.4%		
Debt	$5.9bn	$6.0bn		
Def exp[a]	D1.0bn	εD1.2bn		
	($3.5bn)	($3.6bn)		
Def bdgt			εD1.1bn	
			($3.7bn)	
$1 = dinar	0.30	0.30	0.30	

[a] UNIKOM **1995** $66m **1996** $62m

Population		1,656,000		

(Nationals 39%, other Arab 35%, South Asian 9%, Iranian 4%)

Age	13–17	18–22	23–32
Men	109,000	88,000	143,000
Women	81,000	67,000	103,000

Total Armed Forces

ACTIVE 15,300
(some conscripts)
Terms of service: voluntary, conscripts 2 years

RESERVES 23,700
obligation to age 40; 1 month annual trg

Land Force 11,000

(incl 1,600 foreign personnel)
2 armd bde • 1 force arty bde • 1 mech inf bde • 1 force engr bde • 1 recce (mech) bde

ARMY
1 reserve bde • 1 Amiri gd bde • 1 cdo bn

EQUIPMENT
   MBT 150 M-84 (ε50% in store), 174 M-1A2 (being delivered), 17 *Chieftain* (in store)
   AIFV 46 BMP-2, 55 BMP-3, 182 *Desert Warrior*
   APC 60 M-113, 40 M-577, 40 *Fahd* (in store)
   SP ARTY 155mm: 23 M-109A2, 18 GCT (in store), 18 F-3
   MRL 300mm: 27 *Smerch* 9A52
   MOR 81mm: 44; **107mm**: 6 M-30
   ATGW 118 TOW/TOW II (incl 8 M-901 ITV; 66 HMMWV)

Navy ε1,800

(incl 400 Coast Guard)
BASE Ras al Qalaya

PATROL AND COASTAL COMBATANTS 7
MISSILE CRAFT 2
   1 *Istiqlal* (Ge Lürssen FPB-57) PFM with 2 x 2 MM-40 *Exocet* SSM
   1 *Al Sanbouk* (Ge Lürssen TNC-45) with 2 x 2 MM-40 *Exocet*
PATROL INSHORE 5
   4 OPV 310 PCI, 1 P-37BRL PCI, plus boats

SUPPORT AND MISCELLANEOUS 3
   1 LCM, 2 spt

Air Force ε2,500

76 cbt ac, 20 armed hel
Flying hours 210
FTR/FGA 40 F/A-18 (-C 32, -D 8)
FTR 8 *Mirage* F1-CK/BK
CCT 1 sqn with 12 *Hawk* 64, 16 Shorts *Tucano*
TPT ac 3 L-100-30, 1 DC-9 **hel** 4 AS-332 (tpt/SAR/attack), 8 SA-330
TRG/ATK hel 16 SA-342 (with HOT)

AIR DEFENCE
4 *Hawk* Phase III bty with 24 launchers

6 bty *Amoun* (each bty, 1 *Skyguard* radar, 2 *Aspide*
launchers, 2 twin **35mm** Oerlikon), 48 *Starburst*

Paramilitary 5,000 active

NATIONAL GUARD 5,000

3 gd, 1 armd car, 1 SF, 1 mil police bn

COAST GUARD

4 *Inttisar* (Aust 31.5m) PFI, 3 LCU
Plus some 30 armed boats

Foreign Forces

UN (UNIKOM): some 902 tps and 197 Obs from 32
countries
US Army 250; prepositioned eqpt for 1 armd bde (2 tk,
1 mech, 1 arty bn **Air Force** Force structure varies with
aircraft detachments **Navy** 1,000

Lebanon

	1995	1996	1997	1998
GDP	εLP18.0tr	εLP20.6tr		
	($10.0bn)	($11.0bn)		
per capita	$4,200	$4,400		
Growth	ε6%	ε7%		
Inflation	ε11.0%	ε9.5%		
Debt	$3.0bn	$3.8bn		
Def exp	LP795bn	LP760bn		
	($490m)	($484m)		
Def bdgt			LP805bn	
			($521m)	
FMAᵃ (US)	$4.4m	$4.8m	$0.6m	$0.6m
$1 = pound	1,621	1,571	1,547	
ᵃ UNIFIL **1995** $135m **1996** $135m				
Population		4,141,000		

(Christian 30%, Druze 6%, Armenian 4%) excl
ε300,000 Syrian nationals and ε500,000 Palestinian
refugees

Age	*13–17*	*18–22*	*23–32*
Men	204,000	197,000	373,000
Women	208,000	202,000	390,000

Total Armed Forces

ACTIVE some 55,100

Terms of Service: 1 year

Army 53,300

11 inf bde (-) • 1 Presidential Guard bde • 1 cdo/
Ranger, 3 SF regt • 2 arty regt • 1 air aslt regt
EQUIPMENT
    MBT some 110 M-48A1/A5, 205 T-54/-55

LT TK 35 AMX-13
RECCE 40 *Saladin*, 5 *Ferret*, 80 AML-90, 30 *Staghound*
APC 725 M-113A1/A2, 20 *Saracen*, 30 VAB-VCI, 30
    VAB-VTT, 75 AMX-VCI, 15 Panhard M3/VTT
TOWED ARTY 105mm: 15 M-101A1, 10 M-102;
    122mm: 33 M-1938, 10 D-30; **130mm**: 25 M-46;
    155mm: 60, incl some Model 50, 15 M-114A1, 35
    M-198
MRL 122mm: 5 BM-11, 25 BM-21
MOR 81mm: 150; **120mm**: 130
ATGW ENTAC, *Milan*, 20 BGM-71A TOW
RL 85mm: RPG-7; **89mm**: M-65
RCL 106mm: M-40A1
AD GUNS 20mm; 23mm: ZU-23; **40mm**: 10 M-
    42A1

Navy 1,000

BASES Juniye, Beirut, Tripoli
PATROL AND COASTAL COMBATANTS 14
PATROL CRAFT, INSHORE 14
    7 PCI<, 5 UK *Attacker* PCI<, 2 UK *Tracker* PCI<, plus
    27 armed boats
AMPHIBIOUS craft only
    2 *Sour* (Fr *Edic*) LCT (33 tps)

Air Force some 800

3† cbt ac; 4† armed hel
EQUIPMENT
FTR 3 *Hunter*† (F-70/FGA-70A)
HELICOPTERS
    ATTACK 4 SA-342 with AS-11/-12 ASM
    TPT 16 UH-1H, 5† AB-212, 3 SA-330; 4 SA-319
TRG 3 *Bulldog*, 3 CM-170
TPT 1 *Dove*, 1 *Turbo-Commander* 690A

Paramilitary ε13,000 active

INTERNAL SECURITY FORCE (Ministry of Interior)
ε13,000
(incl Regional and Beirut *Gendarmerie* coy plus Judicial
Police); 30 *Chaimite* APC
CUSTOMS
    2 *Tracker* PCI<, 5 *Aztec* PCI<

Opposition

MILITIAS
most militias, except *Hizbollah* and the SLA, have been
substantially disbanded and hy wpns handed over to
the National Army
HIZBOLLAH ('Party of God'; Shi'a, fundamentalist,
    pro-Iranian): ε3–500 (-) active; about 3,000 in spt
    EQPT arty, MRL, RL, RCL, ATGW (AT-3 *Sagger*, AT-

4 *Spigot*), AA guns, SAM

SOUTH LEBANESE ARMY (SLA) 2–3,000 active (was mainly Christian but increasingly Shi'a, some Druze, trained, equipped and supported by Israel, occupies the 'Security Zone' between Israeli border and area controlled by UNIFIL)

EQUIPMENT
MBT 30 T-54/-55
APC M-113, BTR-50
TOWED ARTY **122mm**: D-30; **130mm**: M-46; **155mm**: M-1950
MOR some **160mm**

Foreign Forces

UN (UNIFIL): some 4,488; 6 inf bn 1 each from **Fji**, **SF**, **Gha**, **Irl**, **N**, **No**, plus spt units from **Ea**, **Fr**, **It**, **No**, **Pl**
IRAN ε150 Revolutionary Guard
SYRIA 30,000 **Beirut** elm 1 mech inf bde, 5 SF regt **Metn** elm 1 mech inf bde **Bekaa** 1 mech inf div HQ, elm 2 mech inf, elm 1 armd bde **Tripoli** 1 SF regt **Batrum** 1 SF Regt **Kpar Fallus** elm 3 SF regt

Libya

	1995	1996	1997	1998
GDP	ε$25bn	ε$26bn		
per capita	$5,300	$5,400		
Growth	ε-2.0%	ε2.0%		
Inflation	ε10.0%	ε7.0%		
Debt	$3.6bn	$3.7bn		
Def exp[a]	εD495m	εD474m		
	($1.4bn)	($1.3bn)		
Def bdgt			εD480.0m	
			($1.3bn)	
$1 = dinar[a]	0.35	0.37	0.38	
[a] Market rate **1997** $1 = D3.5–4.0				
Population		5,806,000		
Age	*13–17*	*18–22*	*23–32*	
Men	337,000	282,000	423,000	
Women	325,000	271,000	402,000	

Total Armed Forces

ACTIVE ε65,000

Terms of service: selective conscription, 1–2 years

RESERVES some 40,000
People's Militia

Army ε35,000

(ε25,000 conscripts)
7 Mil Districts • 5 elite bde (regime sy force) • 10 tk bn • 22 arty bn • 21 inf bn • 8 AD arty bn • 8 mech inf bn

• 15 para/cdo bn • 5 SSM bde

EQUIPMENT
MBT 560 T-54/-55, 280 T-62, 145 T-72 (plus some 1,040 T-54/-55, 70 T-62, 115 T-72 in store†)
RECCE 250 BRDM-2, 380 EE-9 *Cascavel*
AIFV 1,000 BMP-1
APC 750 BTR-50/-60, 100 OT-62/-64, 40 M-113, 100 EE-11 *Urutu*
TOWED ARTY some 720: **105mm**: some 60 M-101; **122mm**: 270 D-30, 60 D-74; **130mm**: 330 M-46.
SP ARTY: 450: **122mm**: 130 2S1; **152mm**: 60 2S3, 80 DANA; **155mm**: 160 *Palmaria*, 20 M-109
MRL 107mm: Type 63; **122mm**: 350 BM-21/RM-70, 300 BM-11
MOR 82mm; **120mm**: M-43; **160mm**: M-160
SSM launchers: 40 FROG-7, 80 *Scud*-B
ATGW 3,000: *Milan*, AT-3 *Sagger* (incl BRDM SP), AT-4 *Spigot*
RCL 106mm: 220 M-40A1
AD GUNS 600: **23mm**: ZU-23, ZSU-23-4 SP; **30mm**: M-53/59 SP
SAM SA-7/-9/-13, 24 quad *Crotale*
SURV RASIT (veh, arty)

Navy 8,000

(incl Coast Guard)
BASES Tripoli, Benghazi, Derna, Tobruk, Sidi Bilal, Al Khums

SUBMARINES 4
4 *Al Badr* † (Sov *Foxtrot*) with 533mm and 406mm TT (3 non-op)

FRIGATES 3
2 *Al Hani* (Sov *Koni*) with 4 ASTT, 2 ASW RL; plus 4 SS-N-2C SSM
1 *Dat Assawari*† (UK Vosper Mk 7) with 2 x 3 ASTT; plus 4 *Otomat* SSM, 1 114mm gun

PATROL AND COASTAL COMBATANTS 36
CORVETTES 4
1 *Assad al Bihar*† (It *Assad*) with 4 *Otomat* SSM; plus 2 x 3 ASTT (A244S LWT) (plus 3 more non-op)
3 *Ean al Gazala* (Sov *Nanuchka* II) with 2 x 2 SS-N-2C *Styx* SSM
MISSILE CRAFT 24
9 *Sharaba* (Fr *Combattante* II) with 4 *Otomat* SSM
12 *Al Katum* (Sov *Osa* II) with 4 SS-N-2C SSM
3 *Susa* with 8 SS-12M SSM
PATROL, INSHORE 8
4 *Garian*, 3 *Benina*, 1 Sov *Poluchat* (diving spt)

MINE COUNTERMEASURES 8
8 *Ras al Gelais* (Sov *Natya* MSO)
(*El Temsah* and about 5 other ro-ro tpt have mine-laying capability)

AMPHIBIOUS 5
2 *Ibn Ouf* LST, capacity 240 tps, 11 tk, 1 SA-316B hel

3 Sov *Polnocny* LSM, capacity 180 tps, 6 tk
Plus craft: 3 LCT

SUPPORT AND MISCELLANEOUS 10

1 *Zeltin* log spt/dock, 1 *Tobruk* trg, 1 salvage, 1
diving spt, 1 *El Temsah* and about 5 other ro-ro tpt

COASTAL DEFENCE

1 SSC-3 *Styx* bty

NAVAL AVIATION

32 armed hel
HEL 2 sqn
1 with 25 Mi-14 PL (ASW), 1 with 7 SA-321 (Air
Force assets)

Air Force 22,000

(incl Air Defence Command); 420 cbt ac, 52 armed hel
(many ac in store, number n.k.) **Flying hours** 85
BBR 1 sqn with 6 Tu-22
FGA 12 sqn with 40 MiG-23BN, 15 MiG-23U, 30
Mirage 5D/DE, 14 *Mirage* 5DD, 14 *Mirage* F-1AD, 6
Su-24, 45 Su-20/-22, 1 sqn with 30 J-1 *Jastreb*
FTR 9 sqn with 50 MiG-21, 75 MiG-23, 60 MiG-25, 3 -
25U, 15 *Mirage* F-1ED, 6 -BD
RECCE 2 sqn with 4 *Mirage* 5DR, 7 MiG-25R
TPT 9 sqn with 15 An-26, 12 Lockheed (7 C-130H, 2 L-
100-20, 3 L-100-30), 16 G-222, 20 Il-76, 15 L-410
ATTACK HEL 40 Mi-25, 12 Mi-35
TPT HEL hy 18 CH-47C **med** 34 Mi-8/17 **lt** 30 Mi-2, 11
SA-316, 5 AB-206
TRG ac 80 *Galeb* G-2 **hel** 20 Mi-2 **other ac** incl 1 Tu-22,
150 L-39ZO, 20 SF-260WL

MISSILES

ASM AT-2 *Swatter* ATGW (hel-borne), AS-7, AS-9,
AS-11
AAM AA-2 *Atoll*, AA-6 *Acrid*, AA-7 *Apex*, AA-8
Aphid, R-530, R-550 *Magic*

AIR DEFENCE COMMAND

Senezh AD comd and control system
4 bde with SA-5A: each 2 bn of 6 launchers, some 4 AD
arty gun bn; radar coy
5 Regions: 5–6 bde each 18 SA-2; 2–3 bde each 12 twin
SA-3; ε3 bde each 20–24 SA-6/-8

Paramilitary

CUSTOMS/COAST GUARD (Naval control)
a few patrol craft incl in naval totals, plus armed boats

Mauritania

	1995	1996	1997	1998
GDP	OM140bn	OM150bn		
	($1.1bn)	($1.1bn)		

contd	1995	1996	1997	1998
per capita	$1,700	$1,700		
Growth	6.1%	4.7%		
Inflation	6.1%	3.0%		
Debt	$2.5bn	$2.4bn		
Def exp	OM3.8bn	OM4.4bn		
	($29m)	($32m)		
Def bdgt			εOM4.8bn	
			($33.0m)	
FMA (Fr)	$1.0m	$1.0m	$1.1m	
$1 = OM*	130	137	145	

* Mauritanian ouguiya

Population		2,397,000		
Age	*13–17*	*18–22*	*23–32*	
Men	132,000	112,000	173,000	
Women	127,000	107,000	170,000	

Total Armed Forces

ACTIVE ε15,650

Terms of service: conscription (2 years) authorised

Army 15,000

6 Mil Regions • 7 mot inf bn • 3 arty bn • 8 inf bn • 4
AD arty bty • 1 para/cdo bn • 1 Presidential sy bn • 2
Camel Corps bn • 1 engr coy • 1 armd recce sqn
EQUIPMENT
MBT 35 T-54/-55
RECCE 60 AML (20 -60, 40 -90), 40 *Saladin*, 5 *Saracen*
TOWED ARTY 105mm: 35 M-101A1/HM-2;
122mm: 20 D-30, 20 D-74
MOR 81mm: 70; **120mm:** 30
ATGW *Milan*
RCL 75mm: M-20; **106mm:** M-40A1
AD GUNS 23mm: 20 ZU-23-2; **37mm:** 15 M-1939;
57mm: S-60; **100mm:** 12 KS-19
SAM SA-7

Navy ε500

BASES Nouadhibou, Nouakchott
PATROL CRAFT 11
OFFSHORE 2
1 *Aboubekr Ben Amer* (Fr OPV 54) OPV
1 *N'Madi* (UK *Jura*) PCO (fishery protection)
INSHORE 9
3 *El Vaiz* (Sp *Barcelo*) PFI†
1 *El Nasr* (Fr *Patra*) PCI
1 *Z'Bar* (Ge *Neustadt*) PFI
4 *Mandovi* PCI

Air Force 150

7 cbt ac, no armed hel
CCT 5 BN-2 *Defender*, 2 FTB-337 *Milirole*

MR 2 *Cheyenne* II
TPT 2 Cessna F-337, 1 DHC-5D, 1 *Gulfstream* II

Paramilitary ε5,000 active

GENDARMERIE (Ministry of Interior) ε3,000
6 regional coy
NATIONAL GUARD (Ministry of Interior) 2,000
plus 1,000 auxiliaries
CUSTOMS
1 *Dah Ould Bah* (Fr *Amgram* 14)

Morocco

	1995	1996	1997	1998
GDP	D277bn	D321bn		
	($32.4bn)	($36.8bn)		
per capita	$3,200	$3,600		
Growth	-7.6%	11.8%		
Inflation	6.1%	6.1%		
Debt	$22.1bn	$21.0bn		
Def exp	D12.5bn	D13.7bn		
	($1.5bn)	($1.6bn)		
Def bdgt			εD14.7bn	
			($1.6bn)	
FMA[a] (US)	$1.2m	$0.8m	$0.8m	$0.9m
$1 = dirham	8.54	8.72	9.45	

[a] MINURSO **1995** $41m **1996** $59m

Population		28,776,000		
Age	*13–17*	*18–22*	*23–32*	
Men	1,660,000	1,497,000	2,452,000	
Women	1,603,000	1,445,000	2,397,000	

Total Armed Forces

ACTIVE 196,300
(ε100,000 conscripts)
Terms of service: conscription 18 months authorised; most enlisted personnel are volunteers

RESERVES
Army 150,000; obligation to age 50

Army 175,000

(ε100,000 conscripts)
2 Comd (Northern Zone, Southern Zone) • 3 mech inf bde • 1 lt sy bde • 2 para bde • 8 mech inf regt •
Indep units
12 arty bn • 3 mot (camel corps) bn • 1 AD gp • 2 cav bn • 10 armd bn • 1 mtn bn • 37 inf bn • 7 engr bn • 4 cdo units • 2 AB bn

ROYAL GUARD 1,500

1 bn, 1 cav sqn
EQUIPMENT
MBT 224 M-48A5, 300 M-60 (60 -A1, 240 -A3)
LT TK 100 SK-105 *Kuerassier*
RECCE 16 EBR-75, 80 AMX-10RC, 190 AML-90, 38 AML-60-7, 20 M-113
AIFV 60 *Ratel* (30 -20, 30 -90), 45 VAB-VCI, 10 AMX-10P
APC 420 M-113, 320 VAB-VTT, some 45 OT-62/-64 may be op
TOWED ARTY 105mm: 35 lt (L-118), 20 M-101, 36 M-1950; **130mm**: 18 M-46; **155mm**: 20 M-114, 35 FH-70, 26 M-198
SP ARTY 105mm: 5 Mk 61; **155mm**: 98 F-3, 44 M-109, 20 M-44
MRL 122mm: 39 BM-21
MOR 81mm: 1,100; **120mm**: 600 (incl 20 VAB SP)
ATGW 440 *Dragon*, 80 *Milan*, 150 TOW (incl 42 SP), 50 AT-3 *Sagger*
RL 89mm: 150 3.5in M-20
RCL 106mm: 350 M-40A1
ATK GUNS 90mm: 28 M-56; **100mm**: 8 SU-100 SP
AD GUNS 14.5mm: 200 ZPU-2, 20 ZPU-4; **20mm**: 40 M-167, 60 M-163 *Vulcan* SP; **23mm**: 90 ZU-23-2; **100mm**: 15 KS-19 towed
SAM 37 M-54 SP *Chaparral*, 70 SA-7
SURV RASIT (veh, arty)
UAV R4E-50 *Skyeye*

Navy 7,800

(incl 1,500 Marines)
BASES Casablanca, Agadir, Al Hoceima, Dakhla, Tangier
FRIGATES 1
1 *Lt Col. Errhamani* (Sp *Descubierta*) with 2 x 3 ASTT (Mk 46 LWT), 1 x 2 375mm AS mor (fitted for 4 MM-38 *Exocet* SSM)
PATROL AND COASTAL COMBATANTS 26
CORVETTES 2 *Assad* with 3 x 2 *Otomat* SSM; plus 2 x 3 ASTT (A244S LWT) (reported purchased, but not yet delivered)
MISSILE CRAFT 4 *Cdt El Khattabi* (Sp *Lazaga* 58m) PFM with 4 MM-38 *Exocet* SSM
PATROL CRAFT 20
COASTAL 14
2 *Okba* (Fr PR-72) PFC
6 *LV Rabhi* (Sp 58m B-200D) PCC
4 *El Hahiq* (Dk *Osprey* 55) PCC (incl 2 with customs)
2 *Rais Bargach*
INSHORE 6 *El Wacil* (Fr P-32) PFI< (incl 4 with customs)
AMPHIBIOUS 4
3 *Ben Aicha* (Fr *Champlain* BATRAL) LSM, capacity 140 tps, 7 tk
1 *Sidi Mohammed Ben Abdallah* (US Newport) LST, capacity 400 troops

Plus craft: 1 *Edic*-type LCU

SUPPORT AND MISCELLANEOUS 4

2 log spt, 1 tpt, 1 AGOR (US lease)

MARINES (1,500)

1 naval inf bn

Air Force 13,500

89 cbt ac, 24 armed hel

Flying hours F-5 and *Mirage*: over 100

FGA 10 F-5A, 3 F-5B, 16 F-5E, 4 F-5F, 14 *Mirage* F-1EH

FTR 1 sqn with 15 *Mirage* F-1CH

RECCE 2 C-130H (with side-looking radar), 4* OV-10

EW 2 C-130 (ELINT), 1 *Falcon* 20 (ELINT)

TKR 1 Boeing 707, 2 KC-130H (tpt/tkr)

TPT 11 C-130H, 7 CN-235, 3 Do-28, 3 *Falcon 20*, 1 *Falcon 50* (VIP), 2 *Gulfstream* II (VIP), 5 *King Air 100*, 3 *King Air 200*

HELICOPTERS

ATTACK 24 SA-342 (12 with HOT, 12 with cannon)

TPT hy 7 CH-47 **med** 27 SA-330, 27 AB-205A **lt** 20 AB-206, 3 AB-212, 4 SA-319

TRG 10 AS-202, 2 CAP-10, 4 CAP-230, 12 T-34C, 23* *Alpha Jet*

LIAISON 2 *King Air 200*, 2 UH-60 *Blackhawk*

AAM AIM-9B/D/J *Sidewinder*, R-530, R-550 *Magic*

ASM AGM-65B *Maverick* (for F-5E), HOT

Forces Abroad

UN AND PEACEKEEPING

BOSNIA (SFOR): ε650; 1 mot inf bn

Paramilitary 42,000 active

GENDARMERIE ROYALE 12,000

1 bde, 4 mobile gp, 1 para sqn, air sqn, coast guard unit

EQPT 18 boats **ac** 2 *Rallye* **hel** 3 SA-315, 3 SA-316, 2 SA-318, 6 *Gazelle*, 6 SA-330, 2 SA-360

FORCE AUXILIAIRE 30,000

incl 5,000 Mobile Intervention Corps

CUSTOMS/COAST GUARD

2 PCC, 4 PFI (incl in Navy), plus boats

Opposition

POLISARIO ε3–6,000

Mil wing of Sahrawi People's Liberation Army, org in bn

EQPT 100 T-55, T-62 tk; 50+ BMP-1, 20–30 EE-9 *Cascavel* MICV; 25 D-30/M-30 **122mm** how; 15 BM-21 **122mm** MRL; 20 **120mm**, mor; AT-3 *Sagger* ATGW; 50 ZSU-23-2, ZSU-23-4 **23mm** SP AA guns; SA-6/-7/-8/-9 SAM (Captured Moroccan

eqpt incl AML-90, *Eland* armd recce, *Ratel* 20, Panhard APC, Steyr SK-105 *Kuerassier* lt tks)

Foreign Forces

UN (MINURSO) some 27 tps, 200 mil obs and 9 civ pol in Western Sahara from 28 countries

Oman

	1995	1996	1997	1998
GDP	R4.6bn	R4.7bn		
	($11.8bn)	($12.3bn)		
per capita	$8,600	$8,800		
Growth	4.6%	3.8%		
Inflation	-1.3%	2.0%		
Debt	$3.1bn	$2.7bn		
Def exp	R776m	R737m		
	($2.0bn)	($1.9bn)		
Def bdgt[a]			R698.0m	
			($1.8bn)	
FMA[b] (US)	$0.1m	$0.1m	$0.2m	$0.2m
$1 = rial	0.38	0.38	0.38	

[a] Five-year plan 1996–2000 allocates R3.3bn ($8.6bn) for defence

[b] Excl ε$100m over 1990–99 from US Access Agreement renewed in 1990

Population		2,047,000 (expatriates 27%)	
Age	*13–17*	*18–22*	*23–32*
Men	116,000	92,000	138,000
Women	112,000	90,000	126,000

Total Armed Forces

ACTIVE 43,500

(incl Royal Household tps, and some 3,700 foreign personnel)

Army 25,000

(regt are bn size)

1 armd, 2 inf bde HQ • 2 armd regt (3 tk sqn) • 1 armd recce regt (3 sqn) • 4 arty (2 fd, 1 med (2 bty), 1 AD (2 bty)) regt • 8 inf regt (incl 2 Baluch) • 1 inf recce regt (3 recce coy), 2 indep recce coy • 1 fd engr regt (3 sqn) • 1 AB regt • Musandam Security Force (indep rifle coy)

EQUIPMENT

MBT 6 M-60A1, 73 M-60A3 (20 to be delivered), 24 *Qayid al-Ardh* (*Chieftain* Mk 7/-15) (in store), 18 *Challenger* 2

LT TK 37 *Scorpion*

APC 6 *Spartan*, 13 *Sultan*, 4 *Stormer*, 50 *Piranha* (being delivered)

TOWED ARTY 91: **105mm**: 42 ROF lt; **122mm**: 25

D-30; **130mm**: 12 M-46, 12 Type 59-1
SP ARTY 155mm: 18 G-6
MOR 81mm: 69; **107mm**: 20 4.2in M-30
ATGW 18 TOW, 50 *Milan* (incl 2 VCAC)
AD GUNS 23mm: 4 ZU-23-2; **40mm**: 12 Bofors L/
60
SAM *Blowpipe*, 28 *Javelin*, 34 SA-7

Navy 4,200

BASES Seeb (HQ), Wudam (main base), Raysut,
Ghanam Island, Alwi
CORVETTES 2
2 *Qahir Al Amwaj* with 8 MM-40 *Exocet* SSM, *Crotale*
SAM, 1 76mm gun
PATROL AND COASTAL COMBATANTS 13
MISSILE CRAFT 4
4 *Dhofar*, 1 with 2 x 3 MM-40, 3 with 2 x 4 MM-40
Exocet SSM
PATROL CRAFT 9
3 *Al Bushra* (Fr P-400) with 1 76m gun, 2 406mm TT
2 *Al Wafi* (Brooke-Marine 37m) PCI
4 *Seeb* (Vosper 25m) PCI<
AMPHIBIOUS 2
1 *Nasr el Bahr* LST†, capacity 240 tps, 7 tk, hel deck
1 *Al Munassir* LST, capacity 200 tps, 8 tk, hel deck
(non-op, harbour trg)
Plus craft: 3 LCM, 1 LCU
SUPPORT AND MISCELLANEOUS 2
1 *Al Sultana*, 1 *Al Mabrukah* trg with hel deck (also
used in offshore patrol role)

Air Force 4,100

47 cbt ac, no armed hel
FGA 2 sqn with 17 *Jaguar* S(O) Mk 1, 2 T-2
FGA/RECCE 12 *Hawk* 203
CCT 1 sqn with 12* BAC-167 Mk 82, 4* *Hawk* 103
TPT 3 sqn
1 with 3 BAC-111
2 with 15 *Skyvan* 3M (7 radar-equipped, for MR), 3
C-130H
HEL 2 med tpt sqn with 20 AB-205, 3 AB-206, 3 AB-
212, 5 AB-214
TRG 4 AS-202-18, 7 MFI-17B *Mushshak*
AD 2 sqn with 28 *Rapier* SAM, *Martello* radar
AAM AIM-9P *Sidewinder*

Royal Household 6,500

(incl HQ staff) 2 SF regt (1,000)
Royal Guard bde (5,000) 9 VBC-90 lt tk, 14 VAB-VCI
APC, 9 VAB-VDAA, *Javelin* SAM
Royal Yacht Squadron (based Muscat) (150) 1 Royal
Yacht, 3,800t with hel deck, 1 *Fulk Al Salamah* tps and
veh tpt with up to 2 AS-332C *Puma* hel, 1 *Zinat Al*

Bihaar Dhow
Royal Flight (250) **ac** 2 Boeing-747 SP, 1 DC-8-73CF, 2
Gulfstream IV **hel** 3 AS-330, 2 AS-332C, 1 AS-332L

Paramilitary 4,400 active

TRIBAL HOME GUARD (*Firqat*) 4,000
org in teams of ε100
POLICE COAST GUARD 400
15 AT-105 APC, some 18 inshore patrol craft
POLICE AIR WING
ac 1 Do-228, 2 CN 235M, 1 BN-2T Islander **hel** 3 Bell
205A, 6 Bell 214ST

Palestinian Autonomous Areas Of Gaza And Jericho

	1995	1996	1997	1998
GDP	ε$3.2bn	ε$3.3bn		
per capita	$1,500	$1,500		
Growth	ε3.5%	ε0.7%		
Inflation	ε11.0%	ε11.0%		
Debt	ε$800m	ε$800m		
Sy bdgt	ε$170m	ε$248m	ε$250m	
FMA(US)	$80m	$75m	$75m	$75m
Population				

West Bank incl East Jerusalem and Gaza ε2,350,000
(Israeli 7%) *Gaza* ε968,000 (Israeli ε5,000) *West Bank*
excl East Jerusalem ε1,382,000 (Israeli ε11%) *Jericho*
Israeli ε18,000 *East Jerusalem* Israeli ε215,000

Gaza	13–17	18–22	23–32	
Men	48,000	40,000	62,000	
Women	47,000	39,000	61,000	
West Bank				
Men	69,000	62,000	106,000	
Women	66,000	59,000	98,000	

Total Armed Forces

ACTIVE Nil

Paramilitary ε35,000

PUBLIC SECURITY 6,000 Gaza, 8,000 West Bank

CIVIL POLICE 4,000 Gaza, 6,000 West Bank

PREVENTIVE SECURITY 1,200 Gaza, 1,800 West Bank
GENERAL INTELLIGENCE 3,000

MILITARY INTELLIGENCE 500

PRESIDENTIAL SECURITY 3,000

Others include **Coastal Police, Civil Defence, Air**

Force, Customs and Excise Police Force, University Security Service

EQPT incl small arms, 45 APC **ac** 1 Lockheed *Jet Star* **hel** 2 Mi-8, 2 Mi-17

PALESTINIAN GROUPS

All significant Palestinian factions are listed irrespective of where they are based. est number of active 'fighters' are given; these could perhaps be doubled to give an all-told figure. In 1991, the Lebanon Armed Forces (LAF), backed by Syria, entered refugee camps in southern Lebanon to disarm many Palestinian groups of their heavier weapons, such as tk, arty and APCs. The LAF conducted further disarming operations against *Fatah* Revolutionary Council (FRC) refugee camps in spring 1994

PLO (Palestine Liberation Organisation) **Leader** Yasser Arafat

FATAH Political wing of the PLO

PNLA (Palestine National Liberation Army) ε8,000 Effectively mil wing of the PLO **Based** Ag, Et, RL, LAR, HKJ, Irq, Sdn, Ye. Units closely monitored by host nations' armed forces.

PLF (Palestine Liberation Front) **Leader** Al Abas; ε300–400 **Based** Irq **Tal al Yaqub faction** ε100–150 **Based** Syr

DFLP (Democratic Front for the Liberation of Palestine) **Leader** Hawatmah; ε500–600 **Based** Syr, RL, elsewhere **Abd Rabbu faction** ε150–20 **Based** HKJ

PFLP (Popular Front for the Liberation of Palestine) **Leader** Habash; ε800 **Based** Syr, RL, Occupied Territories

PSF (Popular Struggle Front) **Leader** Samir Ghansha; ε600–700 **Based** Syr

ARAB LIBERATION FRONT ε500 **Based** RL, Irq

GROUPS OPPOSED TO THE PLO

FATAH **DISSIDENTS** (Abu Musa gp) ε1,000 **Based** Syr, RL

FRC (*Fatah* Revolutionary Council, Abu Nidal Group) ε300 **Based** RL, Syr, Irq, elsewhere

PFLP (GC) (Popular Front for the Liberation of Palestine (General Command)) **Leader** Jibril; ε600

PFLP (SC) (Popular Front for the Liberation of Palestine – Special Command) ε50–100 **Based** RL, Irq, Syr

SAIQA Leader al-Khadi; ε1,000 **Based** Syr

HAMAS ε300 **Based** Occupied Territories

PIJ (Palestine Islamic Jihad) ε350 all factions **Based** Occupied Territories

PALESTINE LIBERATION FRONT Abd al-Fatah Ghanim faction **Based** Syr

PLA (Palestine Liberation Army) ε4,500 Based Syr

Qatar

	1995	1996	1997	1998
GDP	R25.9bn	R26.9bn		
	($7.1bn)	($7.4bn)		
per capita	$15,300	$15,800		
Growth	-1.2%	9.9%		
Inflation	1.5%	3.0%		
Debt	$4.5bn	$7.3bn		
Def exp[a]	εR2.5bn	εR2.8bn		
	($700m)	($755m)		
Def bdgt			εR4.1bn	
			($1.1bn)	
$1 = rial	3.64	3.64	3.64	

[a] Revised from previous years

Population		567,000		

(*nationals* 25% *expatriates* 75%, of which Indian 18%, Iranian 10%, Pakistani 18%)

Age	*13–17*	*18–22*	*23–32*
Men	23,000	19,000	37,000
Women	25,000	20,000	30,000

Total Armed Forces

ACTIVE ε11,800

Army 8,500

1 Royal Guard regt • 1 SF 'bn' (coy) • 1 tk bn • 1 fd arty regt • 4 mech inf bn • 1 mor bn

EQUIPMENT

MBT 34 AMX-30

RECCE 16 VBL, 12 AMX-10RC, 8 V-150

AIFV 40 AMX-10P

APC 160 VAB, 12 AMX-VCI

TOWED ARTY 155mm: 12 G5

SP ARTY 155mm: 28 F-3

MRL 4 ASTROS II

MOR 81mm: 24 L16 (some SP); **120mm**: 15 Brandt

ATGW 100 *Milan*, HOT (incl 24 VAB SP)

RCL 84mm: *Carl Gustav*

Navy ε1,800

(incl Marine Police)

BASE Doha

PATROL AND COASTAL COMBATANTS 7

MISSILE CRAFT 3 *Damsah* (Fr *Combattante* III) with 2 x 4 MM-40 *Exocet* SSM

PATROL, INSHORE 4 *Barzan* (UK *Vita*) PCI with 8 *Exocet* SSM, 6 *Mistral* SAM, 1 76mm gun

Plus some 47 small craft operated by Marine Police

AMPHIBIOUS craft only

1 LCU

COASTAL DEFENCE

4 x 3 *quad* MM-40 *Exocet* bty

Air Force 1,500

11 cbt ac, 20 armed hel

FGA/FTR 1 sqn with 6 *Alpha* jets and 4 *Mirage* F-1 EDA, 1 *Mirage* F1-DDA (first deliveries of 12 *Mirage* 2000-5 commences late 1997)

TPT 1 sqn with 2 Boeing 707, 1 Boeing 727, 2 *Falcon* 900, 1 *Airbus* A340

ATTACK HEL 12 SA-342L (with HOT), 8 *Commando* Mk 3 (*Exocet*)

TPT 4 *Commando* (3 Mk 2A tpt, 1 Mk 2C VIP)

LIAISON 2 SA-341G

MISSILES

  ASM *Exocet* AM-39, *HOT*

  AAM *Magic* R-55, MICA

  SAM 9 *Roland* 2, *Mistral, Stinger, SA-7 Grail*

Foreign Forces

US Army 50; prepositioned eqpt for 1 armd bde (forming)

Saudi Arabia

	1995	1996	1997	1998
GDP	R469bn	R510bn		
	($125bn)	($136bn)		
per capita	$9,900	$10,200		
Growth	0.5%	4.5%		
Inflation	4.9%	1.2%		
Debt	$20.7bn	$21.8bn		
Def exp	R64.4bn	R65.0bn		
	($17.2bn)	($17.4bn)		
Def bdgt			εR67.0bn	
			($17.9bn)	
$1 = rial	3.75	3.75	3.75	
Population		16,948,000		

(*nationals* 73%, of which Bedouin up to 10%, Shi'a 6% *expatriates* 27%, of which Asians 21%, Arabs 8%, Africans 2% and Europeans <1%)

Age	*13–17*	*18–22*	*23–32*
Men	1,216,000	998,000	1,506,000
Women	1,088,000	885,000	1,257,000

Total Armed Forces

ACTIVE ε105,500

(plus 57,000 active National Guard)

Army 70,000

3 armd bde (each 3 tk, 1 mech, 1 fd arty, 1 recce, 1 AD, 1 ATK bn) • 5 mech bde (each 3 mech, 1 tk, 1 fd arty, 1 AD, 1 spt bn) • 1 AB bde (2 AB bn, 3 SF coy) • 1 Royal Guard regt (3 bn) • 8 arty bn • 1 army avn comd

EQUIPMENT

  MBT 315 M-1A2 *Abrams* (ε200 in store), 290 AMX-30 (50% in store), 450 M60A3

  RECCE 235 AML-60/-90

  AIFV 570+ AMX-10P, 400 M-2 *Bradley*

  APC 1,700 M-113 (incl variants), 150 Panhard M-3

  TOWED ARTY 105mm: 100 M-101/-102; **155mm:** 50 FH-70 (in store), 90 M-198, M-114; **203mm:** 8 M-115 (in store)

  SP ARTY 155mm: 110 M-109A1B/A2, 90 GCT

  MRL 60 ASTROS II

  MOR 400, incl: **107mm:** 4.2in M-30; **120mm:** 110 Brandt

  SSM some 10 PRC CSS-2 (40 msl)

  ATGW TOW-2 (incl 200 VCC-1 SP), M-47 *Dragon*, HOT (incl 90 AMX-10P SP)

  RCL 84mm: 300 *Carl Gustav*; **90mm:** M-67; **106mm:** M-40A1

  HEL 12 AH-64, 12 S-70A-1, 10 UH-60 (tpt, 4 medevac), 6 SA-365N (medevac), 15 Bell 406CS

  SAM *Crotale, Stinger*, 500 *Redeye* **SURV** AN/TPQ-36/-37 (arty, mor)

Navy ε13,500

(incl 3,000 Marines)

BASES Riyadh (HQ Naval Forces) **Western Fleet** Jiddah (HQ), Yanbu **Eastern Fleet** Al-Jubayl (HQ), Ad-Dammam, Ras al Mishab, Ras al Ghar, Jubail

FRIGATES 8

  4 *Madina* (Fr F-2000) with 4 533mm, 2 406mm ASTT, 1 AS-365N hel (AS 15 ASM); plus 8 *Otomat* 2 SSM, 1 100mm gun (1 in refit)

  4 *Badr* (US Tacoma) (ASUW) with 2 x 4 *Harpoon* SSM, 2 x 3 ASTT (Mk 46 LWT)

PATROL AND COASTAL COMBATANTS 29

MISSILE CRAFT 9 *Al Siddiq* (US 58m) PFM with 2 x 2 *Harpoon*

TORPEDO CRAFT 3 *Dammam* (Ge *Jaguar*) with 4 533mm TT (trg, incl 1 in reserve)

PATROL CRAFT 17 US Halter Marine PCI< (some with Coast Guard) plus 40 craft

MINE COUNTERMEASURES 6

  2 *Al Jawf* (UK *Sandown* MCC)

  4 *Addriyah* (US MSC-322) MCC

AMPHIBIOUS craft only

  4 LCU, 4 LCM

SUPPORT AND MISCELLANEOUS 7

  2 *Boraida* (mod Fr *Durance*) AO with 1 or 2 hel, 3 ocean tugs, 1 salvage tug, 1 Royal Yacht with hel deck

NAVAL AVIATION

23 armed hel
HEL 21 AS-365N (4 SAR, 17 with AS-15TT ASM), 12 AS 332B/F (6 tpt, 6 with AM-39 *Exocet*)

MARINES (3,000)

1 inf regt (2 bn) with 140 BMR-600P

Air Force 18,000

336 cbt ac, 12 armed hel
FGA 5 sqn
　3 with 56 F-5E, 14 F-5F, 2 with 58 *Tornado* IDS
FTR 6 sqn
　4 with 70 F-15C, 25 F-15D, 20 F-15S
　2 with 24 *Tornado* ADV
RECCE 1 sqn with 10* RF-5E (10 *Tornado* in FGA sqn)
AEW 1 sqn with 5 E-3A
TKR 8 KE-3A (tkr/tpt), 7 KC-130H
OCU 2 sqn with 14* F-5B, 7* F-5F
TPT 3 sqn with 41 C-130 (7 -E, 34 -H), 8 L-100-30HS (hospital ac)
HEL 2 sqn with 22 AB-205, 25 AB-206B, 27 AB-212, 12* AH-64A, 12 AS-332 B/F
TRG 30* *Hawk* Mk 65, 8* *Hawk* Mk 65A, 50 PC-9, 1 *Jetstream* 31, 4 Cessna 172
ROYAL FLT ac 1 Boeing-747SP, 1 Boeing-737-200, 4 BAe 125-800, 2 C-140, 4 CN-235, 2 *Gulfstream* III, 2 *Learjet* 35, 6 VC-130H, 1 Cessna 310 **hel** 3 AS-61, AB-212, 1 -S70
MISSILES
　ASM AGM-65 *Maverick*, AS-15, AS-30, *Sea Eagle*, *Shrike* AGM-45
　ARM ALARM
　AAM AIM-9J/L/P *Sidewinder*, AIM-7F *Sparrow*, *Skyflash*

Air Defence Forces 4,000

33 SAM bty
　16 with 128 I HAWK
　17 with 68 *Shahine* fire units and AMX-30SA 30mm SP AA guns
73 *Shahine/Crotale* fire units as static defence
EQUIPMENT
　AD GUNS 20mm: 92 M-163 *Vulcan*; **30mm**: 50 AMX-30SA; **35mm**: 128; **40mm**: 150 L/70 (in store)
　SAM 141 *Shahine*, 128 MIM-23B I HAWK, 40 *Crotale*

National Guard 77,000

(57,000 active, 20,000 tribal levies)
3 mech inf bde, each 4 all arms bn
5 inf bde
1 ceremonial cav sqn
EQUIPMENT

LAV 450 LAV-25
APC 290 V-150 *Commando* (plus 810 in store), 440 *Piranha*
TOWED ARTY 105mm: 40 M-102; **155mm**: 30 M-198
MOR 81mm
RCL 106mm: M-40A1
ATGW TOW

Paramilitary 15,500+ active

FRONTIER FORCE 10,500
COAST GUARD 4,500
　EQPT 4 *Al Jouf* PFI, about 30 PCI<, 16 hovercraft, 1 trg, 1 Royal Yacht (5,000t) with 1 Bell 206B hel, about 350 armed boats
GENERAL CIVIL DEFENCE ADMINISTRATION UNITS
10 KV-107 **hel**
SPECIAL SECURITY FORCE 500
UR-416 APC

Foreign Forces

PENINSULAR SHIELD FORCE ε7,000
1 inf bde (elm from all GCC states)
FRANCE 130; 6 *Mirage* 2000C, 1 C 135FR, 1 N-262
US ε5,000 **Army** 274; 1 *Patriot* SAM, 1 sigs unit plus some 1,250 on short-term duty (6 months) **Air Force** ε1,500 plus some 2,900 on tempy duty; units on rotational det, numbers vary (incl: F-15, F-16, F-117, C-130, KC-135, U-2, E-3)
UK ε200; 6 *Tornado* GR-1A, 2 VC-10 (tkr)

Syria

	1995	1996	1997	1998
GDP	S£552bn	S£626bn		
	($30.8bn)	($32.7bn)		
per capita	$6,400	$6,500		
Growth	3.6%	4.0%		
Inflation	8.0%	8.3%		
Debt	$21.3bn	$21.6bn		
Def exp[a]	εS£40.0bn	εS£36.4bn		
	($1.7bn)	($1.6bn)		
Def bdgt			εS£59.1bn	
			($1.7bn)	
$1 = pound[a]	11.2	11.2	11.2	

[a] Market rate 1997 $1 = S£45–50

Population		15,344,000		
Age	*13–17*	*18–22*	*23–32*	
Men	939,000	763,000	1,142,000	
Women	904,000	738,000	1,099,000	

Total Armed Forces

ACTIVE ε320,000

Terms of service: conscription, 30 months

RESERVES (to age 45) 500,000
Army 400,000 active **Navy** 8,000 **Air Force** 92,000

Army ε215,000

(incl conscripts)
3 corps HQ • 6 armd div (each 3 armd, 1 mech bde, 1
arty regt) • 3 mech div (-) (each 2 armd, 2 mech bde, 1
arty regt) • 1 Republican Guard div (3 armd, 1 mech
bde, 1 arty regt) • 1 SF div (3 SF regt) • 3 indep inf bde
• 1 Border Guard bde • 2 indep arty bde • 2 indep
ATK bde • 8 indep SF regt • 1 indep tk regt • 3 SSM
bde (each of 3 bn): 1 with FROG, 1 with *Scud*, 1 with
SS-21 • 1 coastal def SSM bde with SS-C-1B *Sepal* and
SS-C-3 *Styx*

RESERVES

1 armd div HQ (cadre), 30 inf, arty regt

EQUIPMENT

    MBT 4,600: 2,100 T-54/-55, 1,000 T-62M/K, 1,500 T-
    72/-72M (incl some 1,200 in static positions and in
    store)
    RECCE 700 BRDM-2
    AIFV 2,250 BMP-1, 60 BMP-2
    APC 1,500 BTR-40/-50/-60/-152
    TOWED ARTY some 1,630, incl: **122mm**: 100 M-
    1931/-37 (in store), 150 M-1938, 500 D-30; **130mm**:
    800 M-46; **152mm**: 20 D-20, 50 M-1937; **180mm**: 10
    S23
    SP ARTY 122mm: 400 2S1; **152mm**: 50 2S3
    MRL 107mm: 200 Type-63; **122mm**: 280 BM-21
    MOR 82mm: 200; **120mm**: 350 M-1943; **160mm**: 100
    M-160; **240mm**: ε8 M-240
    SSM launchers: 18 FROG-7, some 18 SS-21, 26 *Scud*-
    B/-C; SS-C-1B *Sepal*, SS-C-3 coastal
    ATGW 3,000 AT-3 *Sagger* (incl 2,500 SP), 150 AT-4
    Spigot, 40 AT-5 *Spandrel* and 200 *Milan*
    AD GUNS 2,060: **23mm**: 650 ZU-23-2 towed, 400
    ZSU-23-4 SP; **37mm**: 300 M-1939; **57mm**: 675 S-60,
    10 ZSU-57-2 SP; **100mm**: 25 KS-19
    SAM 4,000 SA-7, 20 SA-9, 35 SA-13

Navy ε5,000

(plus 4,000 reserves)
BASES Latakia, Tartus, Minet el-Baida
SUBMARINES 3
    3 Sov *Romeo* with 533mm TT (all non-op)
FRIGATES 4
    2 *Abu Dhabi* (Nl *Kortenaer*) with 8 *Harpoon* SSM, 8 *Sea
    Sparrow* SAM, 1 76mm gun (trg in Nl, unit 1
    delivery 1997)

    2 Sov *Petya* II with 4 ASW RL, 5 533mm TT
PATROL AND COASTAL COMBATANTS 27
MISSILE CRAFT 16
    14 Sov *Osa* I and II PFM with 4 SS-N-2 *Styx* SSM
    2 Sov *Komar<* with 2 SS-N-2 *Styx* SSM (non-op)
PATROL CRAFT 11
    8 Sov *Zhuk* PFI<
    1 Sov *Natya* (ex-MSO)
    About 2 *Hamelin* PFI< (ex-PLF)
MINE COUNTERMEASURES 7
    1 Sov T-43, 1 *Sonya* MSC, 5 *Yevgenya* MSI
AMPHIBIOUS 3
    3 *Polnocny* LSM, capacity 100 tps, 5 tk
SUPPORT AND MISCELLANEOUS 3
    1 spt, 1 trg, 1 div spt

NAVAL AVIATION
24 armed hel
ASW 20 Mi-14, 4 Ka-28 (Air Force manpower)

Air Force 40,000

589 cbt ac; 72 armed hel (some may be in store)
FGA 9 sqn
    5 with 90 Su-22, 2 with 44 MiG-23 BN, 2 with 20 Su-
    24
FTR 17 sqn
    8 with 170 MiG-21, 5 with 90 MiG-23, 2 with 30
    MiG-25, 2 with 20 MiG-29
RECCE 6 MiG-25R, 8 MiG-21H/J
EW 10 Mi-8 *Hip* J/K
TPT 4 An-24, civil-registered **ac** incl 5 An-26, 2 *Falcon*
    20, 4 Il-76, 7 Yak-40, 1 *Falcon* 900, 6 Tu-134 **hel** 10 Mi-
    2, 100 Mi-8/-17
ATTACK HEL 49 Mi-25, 23 SA-342L
TRG incl 80* L-39, 20 MBB-223, 20* MiG-21U, 6* MiG-
    23UM, 5* MiG-25U, 6 *Mashshak*
MISSILES
    ASM AT-2 *Swatter*, AS-7 *Kerry*, AS-12, HOT
    AAM AA-2 *Atoll*, AA-6 *Acrid*, AA-7 *Apex*, AA-8
    Aphid, AA-10 *Alamo*

Air Defence Command ε60,000

25 AD bde (some 130 SAM bty)
Some 450 SA-2/-3, 200 SA-6 and AD arty
2 SAM regt (each 2 bn of 2 bty) with some 48 SA-5, 60
SA-8

Forces Abroad

LEBANON 30,000; 1 mech div HQ, elm 1 armd, 4
mech inf bde, elm 10 SF, 2 arty regt

Paramilitary 8,000+

GENDARMERIE (Ministry of Interior) 8,000

WORKERS' MILITIA (PEOPLE'S ARMY) (*Ba'ath* Party)

Foreign Forces

UN (UNDOF): 1,053; contingents from **A** 464 **Ca** 189 **J** 45 **Pl** 355
RUSSIA ε50 advisers, mainly AD

Tunisia

	1995	1996	1997	1998
GDP	D17.0bn	D19.0bn		
	($18.0bn)	($19.6bn)		
per capita	$5,200	$5,500		
Growth	2.4%	6.9%		
Inflation	6.3%	3.7%		
Debt	$9.9bn	$10.5bn		
Def exp	D349m	D388m		
	($369m)	($399m)		
Def bdgt			εD454m	
			($418m)	
FMA (US)	$5.1m	$0.7m	$0.8m	$0.9m
$1 = dinar	0.95	0.97	1.09	
Population		9,421,000		
Age	*13–17*	*18–22*	*23–32*	
Men	509,000	469,000	814,000	
Women	488,000	451,000	790,000	

Total Armed Forces

ACTIVE ε35,000

(23,400 conscripts)
Terms of service: 12 months selective

Army 27,000

(22,000 conscripts)
3 mech bde (each with 1 armd, 2 mech inf, 1 arty, 1 AD regt) • 1 Sahara bde • 1 SF bde • 1 engr regt
EQUIPMENT
  MBT 84: 54 M-60A3, 30 M-60A1
  LT TK 55 SK-105 *Kuerassier*
  RECCE 24 *Saladin*, 35 AML-90
  APC 268: 140 M-113A1/-A2, 18 EE-11 *Urutu*, 110 Fiat F-6614
  TOWED ARTY 117: **105mm**: 48 M-101A1/A2; **155mm**: 12 M-114A1, 57 M-198
  MOR 81mm: 95; **107mm**: 66 4.2in
  ATGW 65 TOW (incl some SP), 500 *Milan*
  RL 89mm: 300 LRAC-89, 300 3.5in M-20
  RCL 57mm: 140 M-18; **106mm**: 70 M-40A1
  AD GUNS 20mm: 100 M-55; **37mm**: 15 Type-55/-65
  SAM 48 RBS-70, 25 M-48 *Chaparral*
  SURV RASIT (veh, arty)

Navy ε4,500

(ε700 conscripts)
BASES Bizerte, Sfax, Kelibia
PATROL AND COASTAL COMBATANTS 20
MISSILE CRAFT 6
  3 *La Galite* (Fr *Combattante* III) PFM with 8 MM-40 *Exocet* SSM
  3 *Bizerte* (Fr P-48) with 8 SS-12 SSM
PATROL, INSHORE 14
  2 *Gafsah* (PRC *Shanghai*) PFI (plus 3 non-op), 2 *Tazarka* (UK Vosper 31m) PCI, some 10 PCI<
SUPPORT AND MISCELLANEOUS 1
  1 *Salambo* (US *Conrad*) survey/trg

Air Force 3,500

(700 conscripts); 44 cbt ac, 7 armed hel
FGA 15 F-5E/F
CCT 3 MB-326K, 2 MB-326L
TPT 5 C-130B, 2 C-130H, 1 *Falcon* 20, 3 LET-410
LIAISON 2 S-208M
TRG 18 SF-260 (6 -C, 12* -W), 5 MB-326B, 12* L-59
ARMED HEL 5 SA-341 (attack) 2 HH-3 (ASW)
TPT HEL 1 wg with 15 AB-205, 6 AS-350B, 1 AS-365, 6 SA-313, 3 SA-316, 2 UH-1H, 2 UH-1N
AAM AIM-9J *Sidewinder*

Forces Abroad

UN AND PEACEKEEPING
BOSNIA (UNMIBH): 3 civ pol. **CROATIA** (UNTAES): 23 civ pol.

Paramilitary 12,000

NATIONAL GUARD (Ministry of Interior) 12,000
incl Coastal Patrol with 4 (ex-GDR) *Kondor* I-class PCC, 5 (ex-GDR) *Bremse*-class PCI<, 4 *Gabes* PCI<, plus some 10 other PCI< **ac** 5 P-6B **hel** 8 SA-318/SA-319

United Arab Emirates

	1995	1996	1997	1998
GDP	Dh144bn	Dh157bn		
	($38.5bn)	($40.0bn)		
per capita	$21,000	$21,400		
Growth	1.0%	2.0%		
Inflation	5.0%	7.0%		
Debt	$11.5bn	$11.7bn		
Def exp	εDh7.2bn	εDh7.6bn		
	($2.0bn)	($2.1bn)		
Def bdgt			εDh8.0bn	
			($2.2bn)	
$1 = dirham	3.67	3.67	3.67	

Population	2,580,000		
(*nationals* 24% *expatriates* 76%, of which Indian 30%, Pakistani 16%, other Arab 12%, other Asian 12%, European 1%)			
Age	13–17	18–22	23–32
Men	84,000	77,000	141,000
Women	82,000	70,000	92,000

Total Armed Forces

The Union Defence Force and the armed forces of the UAE (Abu Dhabi, Dubai, Ras Al Khaimah and Sharjah) were formally merged in 1976 and centred on Abu Dhabi. Dubai still maintains its independence, and other emirates a smaller degree of independence.

ACTIVE ε64,500 (perhaps 30% expatriates)

Army 59,000

(incl **Dubai** 15,000) **MoD** Dubai **GHQ** Abu Dhabi
INTEGRATED
1 Royal Guard 'bde' • 1 armd bde • 2 mech inf bde • 2 inf bde • 1 arty bde
NOT INTEGRATED
2 inf bde (Dubai)
EQUIPMENT
  MBT 45 AMX-30, 36 OF-40 Mk 2 (*Lion*), 150 *Leclerc*
  LT TK 76 *Scorpion*
  RECCE 49 AML-90, 20 *Saladin* (in store)
  AIFV 18 AMX-10P, 415 BMP-3
  APC 80 VCR (incl variants), 370 Panhard M-3, 120 EE-11 *Urutu*
  TOWED ARTY 105mm: 62 ROF lt; **130mm**: 20 PRC Type-59-1
  SP ARTY 155mm: 18 Mk F-3, 72 G-6, 85 M-109A3 (being upgraded before delivery in ε1999)
  MRL 70mm: 18 LAU-97; **122mm**: 48 FIROS-25 (ε24 op)
  MOR 81mm: 114 L16; **120mm**: 21 Brandt
  SSM 6 *Scud*-B (Dubai only)
  ATGW 230 *Milan, Vigilant*, 25 TOW, HOT (20 SP)
  RCL 84mm: *Carl Gustav*; **106mm**: 12 M-40
  AD GUNS 20mm: 42 M-3VDA SP; **30mm**: 20 GCF-BM2
  SAM 20+ *Blowpipe, Mistral*

Navy ε1,500

BASE Abu Dhabi
NAVAL FACILITIES Dalma, Mina Zayed, Ajman **Dubai** Mina Rashid, Mina Jabal, Al Fujairah **Ras al Khaimah** Mina Sakr **Sharjah** Mina Khalid, Khor Fakkan
PATROL AND COASTAL COMBATANTS 19
CORVETTES 2 *Muray Jip* (Ge Lürssen 62m) with 2 x 2 MM-40 *Exocet* SSM, plus 1 SA-316 hel

MISSILE CRAFT 8
  6 *Ban Yas* (Ge Lürssen TNC-45) with 2 x 2 MM-40 *Exocet* SSM
  2 *Mubarraz* (Ge Lürssen 45m) with 2 x 2 MM-40 *Exocet* SSM, plus 1 6 *Sadral* SAM
PATROL, INSHORE 9
  6 *Ardhana* (UK Vosper 33m) PFI
  3 *Kawkab* PCI< plus boats
AMPHIBIOUS craft only
  3 *Al Feyi* LCT, 1 LCM
SUPPORT AND MISCELLANEOUS 3
  1 div spt, 1 log spt, 1 tug

Air Force 4,000

(incl Police Air Wing) 108 cbt ac, 42 armed hel
Flying hours 110
FGA 3 sqn
  1 with 9 *Mirage* 2000E
  1 with 26 *Hawk* 102
  1 with 17 *Hawk* Mk 63/63A/63C (FGA/trg)
FTR 1 sqn with 22 *Mirage* 2000 EAD
CCT 1 sqn with 8 MB-326 (2 -KD, 6 -LD), 5 MB-339A
OCU *5 *Hawk* Mk 61, *2 MB-339A, *6 *Mirage* 2000 DAD
RECCE 8* *Mirage* 2000 RAD
TPT incl 1 BN-2, 4 C-130H, 2 L-100-30, 4 C-212, 7 CN-235M-100, 4 Il-76 (on lease)
HELICOPTERS
  ATTACK 5 AS-332F (anti-ship, 3 with *Exocet* AM-39), 10 SA-342K (with HOT), 7 SA-316/-319 (with AS-11/-12), 20 AH-64A
  TPT 2 AS-332 (VIP), 1 AS-350, 26 Bell (8 -205, 9 -206, 5 -206L, 4 -214), 10 SA-330, 2 *King Air* 350 (VIP)
  SAR 3 Bo-105, 3 *Agusta* -109 K2
TRG 30 PC-7, 5 SF-260 (4 -TP, 1 -W), 12 GROB G-115TA
MISSILES
  ASM HOT, AS-11/-12, *Exocet* AM-39, *Hellfire*, Hydra-70, PGM1, PGM2
  AAM R-550 *Magic*, AIM 9L
AIR DEFENCE
1 AD bde (3 bn)
5 bty I HAWK
12 *Rapier*, 9 *Crotale*, 13 RBS-70, 100 *Mistral* SAM

Paramilitary

COAST GUARD (Ministry of Interior)
some 40 PCI<, plus boats

Yemen, Republic of

The Republic of Yemen was formed in May 1990 by the Yemen Arab Republic (north) and the People's Democratic Republic of Yemen (south). Civil war broke out between the forces of the two former states in May 1994 and ended in victory for the north the following July

	1995	1996	1997	1998
GDP	Rn.k.	Rn.k.		
	($9.3bn)	($9.7bn)		
per capita	$1,300	$1,300		
Growth	6.2%	3.2%		
Inflation	ε55.0%	47.9%		
Debt	$6.2bn	$6.3bn		
Def exp	εR35bn	εR47bn		
	($345m)	($362m)		
Def bdgt			εR52bn	
			($400m)	
FMA (US)			$0.05m	$0.08m
$1 = rial[a]	40.8	50.0	50.0	

[a] Market rate **1997** $1 = R130

Population		15,342,000	
(*North* 79% *South* 21%)			
Age	*13–17*	*18–22*	*23–32*
Men	870,000	740,000	1,190,000
Women	843,000	700,000	1,079,000

Total Armed Forces

ACTIVE 66,3000

(incl conscripts)
Terms of service: conscription, 3 years

RESERVES perhaps 40,000

Army

Army 61,000

(incl conscripts)
The following is an IISS assessment after the 1994 civil war. Information on current structure after re-org is not yet available

7 armd bde • 1 SF bde • 18 inf bde • 4 arty bde • 5 mech bde • 1 SSM bde • 2 AB/cdo bde • 1 central guard force • 3 AD arty bn • 2 AD bn (1 with SA-2 SAM)

EQUIPMENT[a]
 MBT 1,125: 250 T-34, 675 T-54/-55, 150 T-62, 50 M-60A1
 RECCE 60 AML-245, 130 AML-90, 160 BRDM-2
 AIFV 270 BMP-1/-2
 APC 60 M-113, 500 BTR-40/-60/-152
 TOWED ARTY some 512: **76mm**: 200 M-194; **105mm**: 35 M-101; **122mm**: 30 M-1931/37, 40 M-1938, 125 D-30; **130mm**: 70 M-46; **152mm**: D-20; **155mm**: 12 M-114
 ASLT GUNS 100mm: 30 SU-100
 COASTAL ARTY 130mm: 36 SM-4-1
 MRL 122mm: 185 BM-21; **140mm**: BM-14

 MOR 81mm; 82mm; 120mm: 50 M-43; **160mm**
 SSM FROG-7, 12 SS-21 *Scud*-B
 ATGW 12 TOW, 24 *Dragon*, AT-3 *Sagger*
 RL 66mm: M72 LAW
 RCL 75mm: M-20; **82mm**: B-10; **107mm**: B-11
 ATK GUNS 85mm: D-44; **100mm**
 AD GUNS 20mm: 52 M-167, 20 M-163 *Vulcan* SP; **23mm**: 30 ZU-23, ZSU-23-4; **37mm**: 150 M-1939; **57mm**: 120 S-60; **85mm**: KS-12
 SAM SA-7/-9/-14

[a] Eqpt totals are of doubtful reliability, as is serviceability

Navy 1,800

BASES Aden, Hodeida
FACILITIES Al Mukalla, Perim Island, Socotra (these have naval support equipment)
PATROL AND COASTAL COMBATANTS 14
 MISSILE CRAFT 7
 3 *Hunan* with C-801 SSM (only 4 C-801 between the 4 craft)
 2 *Tarantul* 1 PFM with 4 SS-N-2C *Styx* SSM
 2 Sov *Osa* II with 4 SSN-2B *Styx* SSM, plus 6 boats
 PATROL, INSHORE 7
 3 *Sana'a* (US *Broadsword* 32m) PFI, 4 Sov *Zhuk* PFI<
MINE COUNTERMEASURES 5
 5 Sov *Yevgenya* MSI
AMPHIBIOUS 3
 2 Sov *Ondatra* LCU, 1 *Ropucha* LST, capacity 190tps

Air Force 3,500

61 cbt ac (plus some 40 in store), 6 attack hel
FGA 11 F-5E, 16 Su-20/-22
FTR 23 MiG-21, 5 MiG-29
TPT 1 An-12, 6 An-24, 4 An-26, 2 C-130H, 4 IL-14, 3 IL-76
HEL 1 AB-212, 1 AB-214, 11 Mi-8, 1 AB-47, 2 Ka-26, 6 Mi-24 (attack)
TRG 2* F-5B, 4* MiG-21U, 14 YAK-11

AIR DEFENCE
SAM some SA-2, -3, -5, -6
AAM AA-2 *Atoll*, AIM-9 *Sidewinder*

Paramilitary ε80,000

MINISTRY OF THE INTERIOR FORCES ε60,000
TRIBAL LEVIES at least 20,000
COASTAL GUARD
(slowly being established)
5 Fr *Interceptor* PCI<

REGIONAL DEVELOPMENTS

Civil wars continue in **Afghanistan** and **Sri Lanka**, although in **Tajikistan** the situation appears to be stabilising following a UN-brokered accord between the government and Islamic opposition groups in 1997. Relations between **India** and **Pakistan** have improved, due largely to internal political developments in both countries. In addition, internal security threats are the main pre-occupation of the Indian and Pakistani armed forces. In **Myanmar (Burma)**, the military regime maintains its grip on power and there is no serious armed opposition.

Central Asia

The major military development in the region was the peace accord signed in Moscow on 27 June 1997 by Tajik President Imomali Rakhmonov and Sayed Abdullo Nuri, the leader of the Islamic opposition. Russia, the UN and the Organisation for Security and Cooperation in Europe (OSCE) all played a role in bringing about the agreement. If the accord, known as the General Agreement of National Reconciliation and Peace Establishment, is successfully implemented, it will end five years of war which have reportedly left up to 50,000 people dead and forced 700,000 to flee to other parts of Tajikistan and into Afghanistan. By July 1997, the refugees in Afghanistan, which according to the UN High Commission for Refugees (UNHCR) numbered some 22,300, had begun returning home.

However, security will not be assured until parliamentary elections are held and the secular opposition, which was not included in the peace negotiations, is formally brought into the process. This group, known as the National Revival bloc and led by former Prime Minister Abdumalik Abdullojunov, has not been invited to join the National Reconciliation Commission which is to implement the peace accord. The National Revival bloc enjoys considerable support in the north. In other parts of the country tension remains betweeen local leaders of armed groups and the central government.

Although it is recognised that Russian troops are still needed in border areas, there is Tajik pressure to scale down their presence and make it less visible. An estimated 20,000 Russian troops, comprising regular forces and Border Troops, are present in the region. The main force is provided by the 201st Motor Rifle Division; although an integral part of the Russian forces, the Border Troops include a significant number of locally recruited personnel. Reports in July 1997 indicated that a 10% reduction in Russian troop strength was being considered; on 10 July, President Rakhmonov announced a plan to reduce the Tajik armed forces by 30%.

Other states in the region do not face military threats on the scale of those in Tajikistan. **Kazakstan**, **Kyrgyzstan**, **Turkmenistan** and **Uzbekistan** participate in the NATO Partnership for Peace (PFP) programme and are members of the Euro-Atlantic Partnership Council (EAPC), from which they are likely to gain more practical benefits, in terms of technical assistance and training, than from the Russian-led Commonwealth of Independent States (CIS). Apart from some border-protection agreements, CIS military agreements have little substance for these states, for whom economic relations with Russia, particularly over oil and other minerals, are more important.

The confidence-building measure (CBM) agreement between Russia, China, Kazakstan, Kyrgyzstan and Tajikistan, signed on 24 April 1997, is an important regional development. The agreement, which deals with all personnel and equipment of land forces, front-line aviation and air-defence aircraft, covers 100km either side of the states' borders and includes measures such as pre-notification of exercises and other military movements. The signatory states also agreed to reduce the number of regular forces along their borders with China.

South Asia

Terrorism, particularly in Assam and Kashmir, poses the main day-to-day challenge for India's regular armed forces and paramilitary security forces. Pakistan also has its share of terrorism, mainly in Karachi and Lahore.

Relations between India and Pakistan, however, have improved. Indian Prime Minister Inder Kumar Gujral has embarked on a policy to increase economic cooperation and improve relations with neighbouring countries. This aims to reduce external sources of tension to allow the government to concentrate on domestic policies, particularly economic liberalisation. Ministerial contacts between India and Pakistan have been renewed, although resolution of the Kashmir problem remains distant. However, the likelihood of conflict between the two countries over this or any other issue is becoming ever more remote.

Despite the reduced external threat, military force levels look set to remain at current strengths (for India, this means about 1.2 million personnel). Equipment-acquisition programmes in both India and Pakistan still involve conventional weapon systems best suited to major conflict rather than counter-guerrilla or counter-terrorist operations. Except in the missile and space area, Indian attempts at defence industrialisation to produce advanced conventional weapon systems continue to fall short of expectations (see below). A phase of flight testing for the *Agni* was completed in 1997, and it remains under development. Development of the shorter-range *Prithvi* SS150 with a conventional warhead is complete, but the missile is not yet in full production; it is not expected to be in full operational service until late 1998.

The civil war in Afghanistan continues, although by mid-1997 the *Taleban* controlled over two-thirds of the country. The Northern Group of opposition forces, mainly comprising Tajik, Uzbek and Turkmen groups, suffered a serious reverse when General Rashid Dostum was routed at Mazar-e-Sharif in March 1997. However, in a situation of shifting alliances, the *Taleban* quickly lost control of the town and has been unable to dislodge the well-organised and battle-hardened forces led by General Ahmad Shah Masoud in the north-east. These forces remain capable of threatening Kabul, and the *Taleban* is not fully secure. The Pashtun area in the south is relatively calm under authoritarian *Taleban* rule.

The civil war in Sri Lanka has entered its 14th year, with the death toll standing at around 43,000, mostly civilians. Despite some successes in the Jaffna peninsula, government forces are unlikely to inflict a decisive military defeat on the Liberation Tigers of Tamil Eelam (LTTE). The main Sinhalese political parties agreed in April 1997, with UK mediation, on a package of proposals for Tamil autonomy. The fruits of this effort are yet to be realised.

Myanmar's military rulers, through the State Law and Order Restoration Council (SLORC), remain in firm control, with the Karen National Liberation Army (KNLA) the only group in active armed opposition. As long as the regime receives support from China through trade and supplies of military equipment, the situation is unlikely to change. SLORC received further recognition on 23 July 1997 when the Association of South-east Asian Nations (ASEAN) accepted Myanmar as a member.

DEFENCE SPENDING

South Asian defence spending increased by 2% in 1996 in real terms. A lack of transparency in defence budgets makes it difficult to assess real expenditure in the five Central Asian republics but, although they have continued to build up their armed forces, International Monetary Fund (IMF) audits suggest that defence spending is a low priority. Further scrutiny shows that substantial military expenditure is funded by budgets for internal law enforcement.

The Central Asian Republics

The Central Asian republics retain Soviet and Russian accounting practices for Internal and Border Troops and other military and paramilitary forces. Under NATO definitions, funding for these organisations counts as military expenditure, even if they are financed under internal security, law enforcement or elsewhere in the government budget. *The Military Balance* figures include estimates of military and paramilitary funding under the defence expenditure heading. Official defence budgets (which *The Military Balance* also cites) are invariably small by comparison, even after allowing for the embryonic state of the armed forces in these countries. Uzbekistan's defence expenditure (narrowly defined) in 1996 came to just 4.3% of government spending, and the defence budget in 1997 (som 6.5 billion or about $113m) stands at similar levels. Kyrgyzstan's defence budget for 1997 is som 159m ($9m), compared to som 129m ($10m) in 1996. Kazakstan's defence budget for 1997 is tenge 16.3bn ($211m), with a further tenge 21.6bn ($280m) for law enforcement. Turkmenistan's defence budget for 1997 has increased to manat 577bn ($140m), over 11% of government spending.

India

India's defence budget increased markedly in 1996–97. The Congress Party government requested R278bn ($7.8bn) in 1996. Subsequent supplements added R9bn and R12bn, giving a provisional R299bn ($8.4bn). For 1997, the newly elected *Bharatiya Janata* (BJP)-led coalition government approved a R36bn pay rise for the armed forces, which helped to increase the defence budget to R356bn ($9.5bn). Around 25% of the budget is spent on equipment. For 1997, R89bn ($2.5bn) is allocated to the capital account (equipment and infrastructure), compared to R85bn ($2.4bn) in 1996. Not included in the defence budget are the allocations for paramilitary forces and the Indian Space Research Organisation (ISRO). Reports in 1997 concerning the prioritisation of internal security in Indian threat assessments indicate that paramilitary forces currently under the control of the Ministry of Home Affairs will revert within five years to their original policing or reserve roles, making way for a dedicated counter-insurgency force of 50–60,000 under Army control. Spending on paramilitary forces amounted to R44bn ($1.2bn) in 1996 under the Ministry of Home Affairs budget. Official defence budget figures, quoted in *The Military Balance*, exclude paramilitary funding. In its spending estimates, *The Military Balance* includes paramilitary and other extra-budgetary expenses.

Table 21 India's defence budget by service/department, 1994–1997

(1995 US$m)	1994	%	1995	%	1996	%	1997	%
Army	4,016	52.9	4,392	53.0	4,351	53.4	5,387	56.6
Air Force	2,102	27.7	2,138	25.8	2,087	25.6	2,348	24.7
Navy	980	12.9	1,171	14.1	1,104	13.5	1,111	11.7
Research and Development	406	5.3	426	5.1	403	4.9	448	4.7
DP&S[1]	93	1.2	155	1.9	208	2.6	226	2.4
Total	7,597	100	8,282	100	8,154	100	9,520	100

Note [1] Department of Defence Production and Supplies

India is placing renewed policy emphasis on domestic weapon development and production to reduce its dependence on foreign suppliers. India's efforts to build an indigenous defence-industrial capacity began in 1962 after the war with China, and the withdrawal of Soviet loan subsidies in the late 1980s gave impetus to this development. While India has resumed substantial defence trading with Russia, the cost of Russian and other foreign supplies has further encouraged domestic procurement.

Table 22 India's domestic research and production, 1994–1996			
(US$m)	1994	1995	1996
Production	1,489	1,299	1,692
of which defence	856	838	1,137
civil	633	461	555
research	406	426	403
Total defence	**1,262**	**1,264**	**1,540**

Several expensive weapon programmes have for some years appeared to be nearing serial production, only to be thwarted by technical problems. The first production-standard prototype of the advanced light helicopter (ALH) is due for delivery in December 1997, and the government has placed a firm order for 100 of the 300 required by the armed forces. The light combat aircraft (LCA), development of which started in 1983, is due for flight-testing (not for the first time) in November 1997, with a target in-service date of 2000, not 2002 as previously reported. The Air Force requires 220 LCAs. Development of the *Arjun* main battle tank (MBT) was reportedly completed in July 1996, and the Army has ordered 126, with delivery by 2002. The development of the 150km-range *Prithvi* SSM is complete, and that of a 250km *Prithvi* variant for the Air Force is near completion. According to government sources, the *Agni* development programme continues.

Pakistan

Pakistan's defence budget for 1997 is R135bn ($3.3bn), compared to R131bn ($3.8bn) in 1996, and accounts for a quarter of government spending. Before her departure from office in November 1996, Prime Minister Benazir Bhutto had promised an additional R16bn for defence in 1997. The Army is to take more direct responsibility for internal security, mirroring developments in India.

Sri Lanka

The cost of the civil war with the LTTE continues to rise. Defence outlays have increased from $521m in 1994 to $663m in 1995 and $867m in 1996. The government has allocated R44bn ($759m) for defence in 1997.

Myanmar

Myanmar's real defence spending is estimated at $2bn in 1996, taking into account government subsidies and off-budget funding. An IMF audit of 1994 government expenditure could not identify the application of some kyats 5.4bn (13% of the government's budget), and concluded that this represented military expenditure omitted from the accounts. The official defence budget for 1997 amounts to kyats19.3bn (an estimated $1.5bn at purchasing-power parity), or 39% of government spending. By comparison, in 1988, the year SLORC came to power, defence accounted for 23% of government spending. Through the Directorate of Defence Industries within the Ministry of Defence, the military also accumulates extra-budgetary funding via its control of state factories manufacturing weapons, commodities such as iron and steel, and civilian goods. Another agency, the Directorate of Defence Procurement, also raises income from businesses such as travel and tourism. Price subsidies on food and fuel are another source of off-budget income for the military. Apart from reducing the upkeep costs of the armed forces, these subsidies enable the military to run commercial food and fuel distribution businesses.

REGIONAL ARMS TRADE

Much attention on the regional arms trade over the past several years has focused on alleged nuclear- and missile-related transactions between India and Pakistan and their respective suppliers, Russia and China. Meanwhile, deliveries of conventional weapons, which fell from some $7bn in 1990 to a low of about $1bn in 1994 (at 1995 values), increased to some $1.7bn in 1996.

For India, the largest regional importer, technical challenges confronting its defence industry hamper the long-term build-up of domestic capacity, and procurement from foreign sources increased in 1996 and 1997. Russia has resumed its place as India's major supplier, notably with an order for 40 Su-30 ground-attack fighter variants in 1996, eight of which were delivered in early 1997. India is one of two beneficiaries of Russian export credits valued at $400m financed by the 1997 Russian Federal Budget. Other foreign orders in 1996–97 include two *Super Dvora* fast patrol boats and 12 *Searcher* unmanned aerial vehicles (UAVs) from Israel; 89 VT-72 armoured recovery vehicles (ARVs) from Slovakia; and four submarines (three *Kilo* variants from Russia and two Type 209 variants from Germany).

Some 60 of Pakistan's 1996 order for 320 T-80 MBTs from Ukraine had been delivered by June 1997, despite reports that Russia was refusing to cooperate as a sub-contractor because of Indian pressure. Pakistan is still claiming the refund of its payments for the embargoed F-16 aircraft purchase from the US. US supplies under the 1995 Brown Amendment – authorising deliveries worth $368m as part-compensation – include three PC-3 maritime patrol aircraft (MPA) equipped with *Harpoon* air-to-surface anti-ship missiles (ASSM).

Sri Lanka spent heavily on arms in 1996–97. In 1996, it took delivery of 15 T-55 MBTs from the Czech Republic. Other recent purchases include a second medium-sized landing ship (LSM) from China delivered in April 1997, 14 patrol craft (nine *Super Dvora*-type vessels built under licence from Israel, of which three were delivered by June 1996, and five *Trinity*-class ships from the US, three of which were delivered by the end of 1996). These replace losses caused by LTTE action. There are reports that ordnance from China (Sri Lanka's principal supplier) has been defective.

In 1990–94, China was Myanmar's dominant weapons supplier, reportedly financed on a long-term, soft-loan basis. Russia also became an important supplier in 1995–96. There have been unconfirmed reports that Russia supplied the northern opposition forces in Afghanistan with T-54 and T-55 MBTs, as well as MiG-21 combat aircraft, in early 1997.

Table 23 **UN Register of Conventional Arms imports, Central and South Asia, 1996**							
(as at 11 August 1997)	**MBT**	**ACV**	**Artillery**	**Combat aircraft**	**Attack helicopters**	**Warships**	**Missiles**
Bangladesh	–	–	18	–	–	–	–
India	–	–	1	–	–	–	12
Pakistan	3	–	24	3	–	1	530
Sri Lanka	15	–	–	–	3	–	–
Total	**18**	**0**	**43**	**3**	**3**	**1**	**542**

Table 24 Arms orders and deliveries, Central and South Asia, 1995–1997

Equipment	Type	Unit	Supplier	Order Date	Delivery Date	Comment
Bangladesh						
hel	Mi-17	8	RF	1995	1996	
tpt ac	AN-32	1	Ukr	1995	1996	
trg ac	L-39	8	Cz	1994	1995	
trg ac	T-37	12	US	1995	1996	EDA
MSI	*River*-class	4	UK	1993	1995	1 converted to AGOR 1997
MSO	T-43	4	PRC	1995	1997	Offshore minesweeper
India						
FGA	*Jaguar* GR1	15	Domestic	1993	1996	Ind to build 15 for 1997
FGA	LCA		Domestic	1983	2002	Development; possible order 220
FGA	MiG-29	10	RF	1994	1996	First deliveries 1995
FGA	MiG-21bis	125	RF	1996	1997	Upgrade; Fr, Il avionics
FGA	Su-30MK	40	RF	1996	1997	Licensed assembly; deliveries to 2000
hel	Mi-24	15	RF		1995	Ex-Kgz
hel	ALH	180	Domestic	1984		Development
arty	2S6M	12	RF	1995	1996	
MBT	*Arjun*	126	Domestic	1974		Order delayed for lack of funds
ARV	VT-72B	89	Slvk	1997		4 ordered since 1993; requirement 400
ATGW	*Trishul*		Domestic	1983		Atk missile first tested Dec 1996
IRBM	*Agni*		Domestic	1983		Development; first test Feb 1994
SSM	*Prithvi* SS150	75	Domestic	1983		20 delivered 1996; not deployed
SSM	*Prithvi* SS250	25	Domestic	1983		Longer-range SS350 flight-tested
UAV	*Searcher*	12	Il	1997		
OPV		4	Domestic			1 delivered, 3 under construction
AO	A-58	1	RF		1996	Tkr capable of resupplying at sea
DDG	*Project* 15	1	Domestic		1997	First of class
FF	*Leander*	1	UK		1995	Cadet training ship
LST	*Magyar*	1	Domestic		1997	Second of tank-landing ships class
PFM	*Tarantul* 1	1	RF		1997	Built in Goa under licence
submarine	*Kilo*	2	RF	1996	1998	First for late 1997, second 1998
submarine	HDW	2	Ge		2003	To be built in Ind
PFC	*Super Dvora*	6	Il	1997	1997	2 bought, 4 to be built locally 2000–2
Kazakstan						
FGA	MiG-29	19	RF		1996	8 delivered 1995
Myanmar						
FGA	A-5	24	PRC	1992	1996	
FGA	F-7	12	PRC	1993	1996	First deliveries 1994
hel	Mi-17	6	RF		1996	
hel	W-3	35	Pl	1996		13 delivered by Jan 1997
APC	Type-85	150	PRC	1991	1996	
MBT	Type-69	50	PRC	1993	1996	
FF	Mod *Jianghu*	2	PRC	1995	1997	1 delivered, 1 under construction
PFC	*Hainan*-class	6	PRC	1994	1996	
Pakistan						
FGA	*Mirage* III	40	Fr	1996	1998	Ex-LAR; to be upgraded in Fr
trg ac	K-8		Collaborative			With PRC; airframes delivered Jun 1997
MBT	T-80UD	320	Ukr	1996	1997	60 delivered by Jun 1997
MBT	T-85	51	PRC		1995	
MBT	*Al-Khalid*		Domestic			Prototype 1996
SSM	*Hatf* 2		Domestic		1996	
SSM	*Hatf* 3		Domestic			Development
SSM	M-11		PRC			Delivery of components unconfirmed
hel	Mi-17	12	RF	1995	1996	

Equipment	Type	Unit	Supplier	Order Date	Delivery Date	Comment
MSC	M-163	3	Fr	1992	1997	First delivered Jul 1989, second Feb 1997
PFM		1	Domestic		1997	
SS	*Agosta*-class	3	Fr	1994	1998	Deliveries 1998–2002; 2 built Fr, third Pak
MPA	PC-3C	3	US	1995	1996	With 28 *Harpoon*
Sri Lanka						
FGA	*Kfir*	3	Il	1995	1995	
hel	Mi-17	3	Ukr	1995	1996	
hel	Mi-24	6	Ukr	1995	1996	
MPA	*Beech* 200	4	US		1997	Procurement frozen early 1997
tpt	AN-32	4	Ukr		1996	
MBT	T-55	15	Cz	1995	1996	
AIFV	BMP-1	16	Ukr		1995	
UAV	*Super Hawk*	5	Il		1996	3 delivered 1996, 2 1997; 4 lost 1997
PFC	*Super Dvora*	9	Domestic	1995	1997	3 delivered
LSM	*Wuhu*-class	1	PRC		1995	
PFI	*Trinity*-class	5	US		1996	3 delivered Dec 1996; 2 more ordered 1997

Afghanistan

	1995	1996	1997	1998
GDP	ε$1.2bn	ε$1.3bn		
per capita	$500	$600		
Growth	ε6%	ε6%		
Inflation	ε14%	ε14%		
Debt	ε$5.6bn	ε$5.7bn		
Def exp	ε$200m	ε$200m		
$1 = afgani[a]	51	2,263	3,000	

[a] Market rate **1997** ε$1 = Afs4,750

Population[b]	ε23,196,000

(Pashtun 38%, Tajik 25%, Hazara 19%, Uzbek 12%, Aimaq 4%, Baluchi 0.5%)

Age	13–17	18–22	23–32
Men	1,306,000	1,130,000	1,894,000
Women	1,250,000	1,072,000	1,786,000

[b] Includes ε1,500,000 refugees in Pakistan, ε1,000,000 in Iran, ε150,000 in Russia and ε50,000 in Kyrgyzstan

Total Armed Forces

ACTIVE Nil

Taleban now controls two-thirds of Afghanistan, and continues to mount mil ops against an alliance of former Prime Minister Burhanuddin Rabbani's government troops, led by former Defence Minister Ahmad Shah Masoud and the National Islamic Alliance (NIA) of General Abdul Malik. The alliance appears to receive little support from Shi'a opposition groups

EQUIPMENT

It is impossible to show the division of ground force equipment among the different factions. The list below represents weapons known to be in the country in April 1992.

MBT 700 T-54/-55, 170 T-62
LT TK 60 PT-76
RECCE 250 BRDM-1/-2
AIFV 550 BMP-1/-2
APC 1,100 BTR-40/-60/-70/-80/-152
TOWED ARTY 1,000+: **76mm**: M-1938, M-1942; **85mm**: D-48; **100mm**: M-1944; **122mm**: M-30, D-30; **130mm**: M-46; **152mm**: D-1, D-20, M-1937 (ML-20)
MRL 185: **122mm**: BM-21; **140mm**: BM-14; **220mm**: 9P140 *Uragan*
MOR 1,000+ incl **82mm**: M-37; **107mm**; **120mm**: 100 M-43
SSM 30: *Scud*, FROG-7 launchers
ATGW AT-1 *Snapper*, AT-3 *Sagger*
RCL 73mm: SPG-9; **82mm**: B-10
AD GUNS 600+ incl **14.5mm; 23mm**: ZU-23, 20 ZSU-23-4 SP; **37mm**: M-1939; **57mm**: S-60; **85mm**: KS-12; **100mm**: KS-19
SAM SA-7/-13

Air Force

Only the former government–NIM alliance and *Taleban* have aircraft. These groups have an unknown quantity of SU-17/22 and MiG-21s and all have some Mi-8/17. The inventory shows ac in service in April 1992. Since then, an unknown number of fixed-wing ac and hel have either been shot down or destroyed on the ground.

FGA 30 MiG-23, 80 Su-7/-17/-22
FTR 80 MiG-21F

ARMED HEL 25 Mi-8, 35 Mi-17, 20 Mi-25
TPT ac 2 Il-18D; 50 An-2, An-12, An-26, An-32 **hel** 12 Mi-4
TRG 25 L-39*, 18 MiG-21*

AIR DEFENCE

SAM 115 SA-2, 110 SA-3, **37mm**, **85mm** and **100mm** guns

Opposition Groups

Afghan insurgency was a broad national movement, united only against the Najibullah government.

GROUPS ORIGINALLY BASED IN PESHAWAR

Traditionalist Moderate

ISLAMIC REVOLUTIONARY MOVEMENT (*Haraka't-Inqila'b-Isla'mi*) ε25,000 **Leader** Mohammed Nabi Mohammed **Area** Farah, Zabol, Paktika, southern Ghazni, eastern Lowgar, western Paktia, northern Nimruz, northern Helmand, northern Kandahar **Ethnic group** Pashtun. Has backed *Taleban*

NATIONAL ISLAMIC FRONT (*Mahaz-Millin Isla'mi*) ε15,000 **Leader** Sayyed Amhad Gailani **Area** eastern Paktia (Vardak–Lowgar border) **Ethnic group** Pashtun

NATIONAL LIBERATION FRONT[a] (*Jabha't-Nija't-Milli'*) ε15,000 **Leader** Sibghatullah Modjaddi **Area** enclaves in Kandahar, Zabol provinces, eastern Konar **Ethnic group** Pashtun

Islamic Fundamentalist

ISLAMIC SOCIETY (*Jamia't Isla'mi*) ε60,000 **Leader** Burhanuddin Rabbani **Area** eastern and northern Farah, Herat, Ghowr, Badghis, Faryab, northern Jowzjan, northern Balkh, northern Kondoz, Takhar, Baghlan, Kapisa, northern Laghman, Badakhshan **Ethnic groups** Turkoman, Uzbek, Tajik

ISLAMIC PARTY (*Hizbi-Isla'mi-Gulbuddin*)[a] ε50,000 **Leader** Gulbuddin Hekmatyar **Area** northern and southern Kabul, Parvan, eastern Laghman, northern Nangarhar, south-eastern Konar; large enclave at Badghis–Ghowr–Jowzjan junction, western Baghlan; enclaves in Farah, Nimruz, Kandahar, Oruzgan and Zabol **Ethnic groups** Pashtun, Turkoman, Tajik

ISLAMIC PARTY (*Hizbi-Isla'mi-Kha'lis*) ε40,000 **Leader** Yu'nis Kha'lis **Area** central Paktia, Nangarhar, south-east Kabul **Ethnic group** Pashtun

TALEBAN ε25,000 **Leaders** Maulewi Mohamed Omar, Maulewi Mohamed Rabbi **Area** southern Afghanistan **Ethnic group** Pashtun. Formed originally from religious students in Madrassahs (both Pashtun and non-Pashtun)

ISLAMIC UNION (*Ittiha'd-Isla'mi Barai Azadi*) ε18,000 **Leader** Abdul Rasul Sayyaf **Area** east of Kabul **Ethnic group** Pashtun

GROUPS ORIGINALLY BASED IN IRAN

HEZBI-WAHDAT (Unity Party)[a] umbrella party of Shi'a groups
Sazman-e-Nasr some 50,000 **Area** Bamian, northern Oruzgan, eastern Ghowr, southern Balkh, southern Samangan, south-western Baghlan, south-eastern Parvan, northern Vardak **Ethnic group** Hazara
Shura-Itifaq-Islami some 30,000+ **Area** Vardak, eastern Bamian **Ethnic group** Hazara
Harakat-e-Islami 20,000 **Area** west of Kabul; enclaves in Kandahar, Ghazni, Vardak, Samangan, Balkh **Ethnic groups** Pashtun, Tajik, Uzbek
Pasdaran-e-Jehad 8,000
Hizbollah 4,000
Nehzat 4,000

NATIONAL ISLAMIC MOVEMENT (NIM)[a]
Formed in March 1992, mainly from troops of former Afghan Army Northern Comd. Predominantly Uzbek, Tajik, Turkoman, Ismaeli and Hazara Shi'a. Str ε65,000 (120–150,000 in crisis). 2 Corps HQ, 5–7 inf div, some indep bde

[a] Form the Supreme Coordination Council

Bangladesh

	1995	1996	1997	1998
GDP	Tk1.2tr	Tk1.3tr		
	($29bn)	($31bn)		
per capita	$1,400	$1,500		
Growth	4.4%	5.3%		
Inflation	5.8%	2.7%		
Debt	$16.4bn	$16.5bn		
Def exp	Tk20.2bn	Tk22.2bn		
	($500m)	($528m)		
Def bdgt			Tk24.6bn	
			($563m)	
FMA (US)	$2.2m	$0.3m	$0.3m	$0.4m
$1 = taka	40.3	42.0	43.7	
Population	125,633,000 (Hindu 16%)			
Age	13–17	18–22	23–32	
Men	7,830,000	7,042,000	10,930,000	
Women	7,419,000	6,642,000	10,351,000	

Total Armed Forces

ACTIVE 121,000

Army 101,000

7 inf div HQ • 17 inf bde (some 26 bn) • 1 armd bde (2 armd regt) • 2 armd regt • 1 arty div (6 arty regt) • 1 engr bde • 1 AD bde

EQUIPMENT†
MBT some 80 PRC Type-59/-69, 60 T-54/-55
LT TK some 40 PRC Type-62
APC 20 BTR-80, some MT-LB
TOWED ARTY 105mm: 30 Model 56 pack, 50 M-101; **122mm:** 20 PRC Type-54; **130mm:** 40+ PRC Type-59
MRL 122mm: reported
MOR 81mm; 82mm: PRC Type-53; **120mm:** 50 PRC Type-53
RCL 106mm: 30 M-40A1
ATK GUNS 57mm: 18 6-pdr; **76mm:** 50 PRC Type-54
AD GUNS 37mm: 16 PRC Type-55; **57mm:** PRC Type-59
SAM some HN-5A

Navy† 10,500

BASES Chittagong (HQ), Dhaka, Khulna, Kaptai
FRIGATES 4
1 *Osman* (PRC *Jianghu I*) with 2 x 5 ASW mor, plus 2 x 2 CSS-N-2 *Hai Ying* 2 (*HY* 2) SSM, 2 x 2 100mm guns (second unit fitting out)
1 *Umar Farooq* (UK *Salisbury*) with 1 x 3 *Squid* ASW mor, 1 x 2 114mm guns
2 *Abu Bakr* (UK *Leopard*) with 2 x 2 114mm guns
PATROL AND COASTAL COMBATANTS 41
MISSILE CRAFT 10
5 *Durdarsha* (PRC *Huangfeng*) with 4 *HY* 2 SSM
5 *Durbar* (PRC *Hegu*) PFM< with 2 *HY* 2 SSM
TORPEDO CRAFT 4 PRC *Huchuan* PFT< with 2 533mm TT
PATROL, OFFSHORE 1 *Shaeed Ruhul Amin* (UK *Island*) PCO (trg role)
PATROL, COASTAL 3
1 *Durjoy* (PRC *Hainan*) with 4 x 5 ASW RL
2 *Meghna* fishery protection
PATROL, INSHORE 18
8 *Shahead Daulat* (PRC *Shanghai II*) PFI, 2 *Karnaphuli*, 1 *Bishkali* PCI, 1 *Bakarat* PCI, 4 Type 123K PFT, 2 *Akshay* PCI
PATROL, RIVERINE 5 *Pabna*<
MINE COUNTERMEASURES 5
3 *Shapla* (UK *River*) MSI, 1 *Sagar* MSO, 1 OH (PRC) MSI
AMPHIBIOUS 14
7 LCU, 4 LCM, 3 LCVP
SUPPORT AND MISCELLANEOUS 7
1 coastal tkr, 1 repair, 1 ocean tug, 1 coastal tug, 2 *Yuch'in* AGHS, 1 *Shaibal* AGOR (UK *River*)

Air Force† 9,500

49 cbt ac, no armed hel **Flying hours** 100–120
FGA/FTR 4 sqn with 12 A-5, 11 F-6, 14 F-7M, 4 FT-7B

TPT 3 An-32
HEL 3 sqn with 11 Bell 212, 7 Mi-8, 11 Mi-17
TRG 46 PT-6, 12 T-37B, 8 CM-170, 8* L-39ZA, 2 Bell 206L
AAM AA-2 *Atoll*

Forces Abroad

UN AND PEACEKEEPING
ANGOLA (UNOMA): 100 incl 10 Obs plus 23 civ pol. **BOSNIA** (UNMIBH): 31 civ pol. **CROATIA** (UNTAES): 6 Obs plus 40 civ pol; (UNMOP): 1 Obs. **FYROM** (UNPREDEP): 2 Obs. **GEORGIA** (UNOMIG): 10 Obs. **IRAQ/KUWAIT** (UNIKOM): 805 incl 5 Obs. **LIBERIA** (UNOMIL): 14. **TAJIKISTAN** (UNMOT): 2 Obs. **WESTERN SAHARA** (MINURSO): 6 Obs

Paramilitary 49,700

BANGLADESH RIFLES 30,000
border guard; 41 bn
ARMED POLICE 5,000
rapid action force (forming)
ANSARS (Security Guards) 14,500 in bn
A further 180,000 unembodied

COAST GUARD 200
2 *Padma* PCI
(force in its infancy and expected to expand)

Opposition

SHANTI BAHINI (Peace Force) ε5,000
Chakma tribe, Chittagong Hills

India

	1995	1996	1997	1998
GDP	Rs11tr	Rs13tr		
	($339bn)	($371bn)		
per capita	$1,400	$1,500		
Growth	6.2%	6.8%		
Inflation	10.3%	8.9%		
Debt	$93.8bn	$94.3bn		
Def expᵃ	Rs324bn	Rs363bn		
	($10.0bn)	($10.4bn)		
Def bdgt			Rs356bn	
			($9.9bn)	
FMAᵇ (US)	$0.2m	$0.4m	$0.4m	$0.5m
(Aus)	$0.2m	$0.3m		
$1 = rupee	32.4	35.0	36.0	

ᵃ Incl exp on paramil org
ᵇ UNMOGIP **1995** $6m **1996** $7m

Population	967,034,000		
(Muslim 14%, Christian 2%, Sikh 2%)			
Age	*13–17*	*18–22*	*23–32*
Men	51,331,000	47,262,000	82,695,000
Women	47,853,000	43,608,000	75,436,000

Total Armed Forces

ACTIVE 1,145,000 (incl 200 women)

RESERVES 528,400

Army 300,000 (first-line reserves within 5 years' full-time service, a further 500,000 have commitment until age 50) **Territorial Army** (volunteers) 33,400 **Air Force** 140,000 **Navy** 55,000

Army 980,000

HQ: 5 Regional Comd, 4 Fd Army, 11 Corps
3 armd div (each 2–3 armed, 1 SP arty (2 SP fd, 1 med regt) bde) • 4 RAPID div (each 2 inf, 1 mech bde) • 18 inf div (each 2–5 inf, 1 arty bde; some have armd regt) • 9 mtn div (each 3–4 bde, 1 or more arty regt) • 1 arty div • 15 indep bde: 7 armd, 5 inf, 2 mtn, 1 AB/cdo • 1 SSM regt (*Privthi*) • 4 AD bde (plus 14 cadre) • 3 engr bde
These formations comprise
  59 tk regt (bn) • 355 inf bn (incl 25 mech, 8 AB, 3 cdo) • 190 arty regt (bn) reported: incl 1 SSM, 2 MRL, 50 med (11 SP), 69 fd (3 SP), 39 mtn, 29 AD arty regt; perhaps 2 SAM gp (3–5 bty each) plus 15 SAM regt • 14 hel sqn: 6 atk, 8 air obs

EQUIPMENT

MBT ε3,314 (ε1,100 in store): some 700 T-55, 1,400 T-72/-M1, 1,200 *Vijayanta*, ε14 *Arjun*
LT TK ε90 PT-76
RECCE ε100 BRDM-2
AIFV 350 BMP-1, 1,000 BMP-2 (*Sarath*)
APC 157 OT-62/-64 (in store)
TOWED ARTY 4,175 (perhaps 600 in store) incl:
  75mm: 900 75/24 mtn, 215 FRY M-48; **105mm**: some 1,300 IFG Mk I/II, 50 M-56; **122mm**: some 550 D-30; **130mm**: 750 M-46; **155mm**: 410 FH-77B
SP ARTY 105mm: 80 *Abbot* (ε30 in store); **130mm**: 100 mod M-46 (ε70 in store)
MRL 122mm: 150 incl BM-21, LRAR; **214mm**: *Pinacha* (being deployed)
MOR 81mm: L16A1, E1; **120mm**: 500 Brandt AM-50, E1; **160mm**: 500 M-1943, 200 Tampella M-58 (150 in store)
SSM *Prithvi* (3–5 launchers)
ATGW *Milan*, AT-3 *Sagger*, AT-4 *Spigot*, AT-5 *Spandrel*
RCL 57mm: 500 M-18; **84mm**: *Carl Gustav*; **106mm**: 1,000+ M-40A1
AD GUNS some 2,400: **20mm**: Oerlikon (reported); **23mm**: 300 ZU 23-2, 100 ZSU-23-4 SP; **30mm**: 8

2S6 SP (reported); **40mm**: 1,200 L40/60, 800 L40/70
SAM 180 SA-6, 620 SA-7, 50 SA-8B, 400 SA-9, 45 SA-3, SA-13, 500 SA-16
SURV MUFAR, *Green Archer* (mor)
HEL 199 *Chetak*, *Cheetah*
LC 2 LCVP

RESERVES

Territorial Army 25 inf bn, plus 29 'departmental' units

DEPLOYMENT

North 2 Corps with 8 inf, 2 mtn div **West** 3 Corps with 1 armd, 5 inf div, 3 RAPID **Central** 1 Corps with 1 armd, 1 inf, 1 RAPID **East** 3 Corps with 1 inf, 7 mtn div **South** 2 Corps with 1 armd, 3 inf div

Navy 55,000

(incl 5,000 Naval Aviation and ε1,000 Marines)
PRINCIPAL COMMAND Western, Eastern, Southern
SUB-COMMAND Submarine, Naval Air
BASES Bombay (HQ Western Comd), Goa (HQ Naval Air), Karwar (under construction), Cochin (HQ Southern Comd), Visakhapatnam (HQ Eastern and submarines), Calcutta, Madras, Port Blair (Andaman Is), Arakonam (Naval Air)
FLEETS Western base Bombay **Eastern** base Visakhapatnam

SUBMARINES 17

  8 *Sindhughosh* (Sov *Kilo*) with 533mm TT
  4 *Shishumar* (Ge T-209/1500) with 533mm TT
  5 *Kursura* (Sov *Foxtrot*)† with 533mm TT (plus 3 in reserve)

PRINCIPAL SURFACE COMBATANTS 25

CARRIERS 1 *Viraat* (UK *Hermes*) (29,000t) CVV
  Air group typically **ac** 12 *Sea Harrier* ftr/attack **hel** 7 *Sea King* ASW/ASUW (*Sea Eagle* ASM)
DESTROYERS 6
  5 *Rajput* (Sov *Kashin*) with 2 x 2 SA-N-1 *Goa* SAM; plus 4 SS-N-2C *Styx* SSM, 5 533mm TT, 2 ASW RL, 1 Ka-25 or 28 hel (ASW)
  1 *Delhi* with 16 SS-N-25 SSM, 1 100mm gun, 6 324mm TT, 2 hel
FRIGATES 18
  3 *Godavari* FFH with 1 *Sea King* hel, 2 x 3 324mm ASTT; plus 4 SS-N-2C *Styx* SSM and 1 x 2 SA-N-4 SAM
  5 *Nilgiri* (UK *Leander*) with 2 x 3 ASTT, 4 with 1 x 3 *Limbo* ASW mor, 1 *Chetak* hel, 2 with 1 *Sea King*, 1 x 2 ASW RL; plus 2 114mm guns (plus 1 in reserve)
  1 *Krishna* (UK *Leander*) (trg role)
  4 *Kamorta* (Sov *Petya*) with 4 ASW RL, 3 533mm TT
  5 *Khukri* (ASUW) with 2 or 4 SS-N-2C *Styx* SSM, hel deck

PATROL AND COASTAL COMBATANTS 45

CORVETTES 19

3 *Vijay Durg* (Sov *Nanuchka* II) with 4 SS-N-2B *Styx* SSM

6 *Veer* (Sov *Tarantul*) with 4 *Styx* SSM

6 *Vibhuti* (similar to *Tarantul*) with 4 *Styx* SSM

4 *Abhay* (Sov *Pauk* II) (ASW) with 4 ASTT, 2 ASW mor

MISSILE CRAFT 6 *Vidyut*† (Sov *Osa* II) with 4 *Styx*

PATROL, OFFSHORE 9 *Sukanya* PCO

PATROL, INSHORE 11 SDB Mk 2/3

MINE WARFARE 20

MINELAYERS 0

none, but *Kamorta* FF and *Pondicherry* MSO have minelaying capability

MINE COUNTERMEASURES 20

12 *Pondicherry* (Sov *Natya*) MSO, 2 *Bulsar* (UK *Ham*) MSI, 6 *Mahé* (Sov *Yevgenya*) MSI<

AMPHIBIOUS 10

2 *Magar* LST, capacity 500 tps, 18 tk, 1 hel (plus 1 fitting out)

8 *Ghorpad* (Sov *Polnocny* C) LSM, capacity 140 tps, 6 tk

Plus craft: 7 *Vasco da Gama* LCU

SUPPORT AND MISCELLANEOUS 28

1 *Jyoti* AO, 5 small AO, 1 *Amba* (Sov *Ugra*) sub spt, 1 div spt , 2 ocean tugs, 6 *Sandhayak* and 4 *Makar* AGHS, 1 *Tir* trg , 1 *Sagardhwani* AGOR, 3 torpedo recovery vessels, 1 AH, 2 *Osa* 1 (special forces insertion)

NAVAL AVIATION (5,000)

68 cbt ac, 83 armed hel **Flying hours** some 180

ATTACK 2 sqn with 20 *Sea Harrier* FRS Mk-51, 2 T-60 trg

ASW 6 hel sqn with 26 *Chetak*, 7 Ka-25, 18 Ka-28, 32 *Sea King* Mk 42A/B

MR 3 sqn with 5 Il-38, 8 Tu-142M *Bear* F, 20 Do-228, 13 BN-2 *Defender*

COMMS 1 sqn with **ac** 5 BN-2 *Islander*, 10 Do-228 **hel** 3 *Chetak*

SAR 1 **hel** sqn with 6 *Sea King* Mk 42C

TRG 2 sqn with **ac** 6 HJT-16, 8 HPT-32 **hel** 2 *Chetak*, 4 Hughes 300

MISSILES

AAM R-550 *Magic* I and II

ASM *Sea Eagle*, *Sea Skua*

MARINES (ε1,000)

1 regt (3 gp)

Air Force 110,000

777 cbt ac, 34 armed hel. 5 Air Comd **Flying hours** 240

FGA 17 sqn

3 with 53 MiG-23 BN/UM, 4 with 88 *Jaguar* S(I), 6 with 148 MiG-27, 4 with 79 MiG-21 MF/PFMA

FTR 20 sqn

4 with 69 MiG-21 FL/U, 10 with 169 MiG-21 bis/U, 1 with 26 MiG-23 MF/UM, 3 with 64 MiG-29, 2 with 35 *Mirage* 2000H/TH, 8 SU-30MK

ECM 4 *Canberra* B(I) 58 (ECM/target towing, plus 2 *Canberra* TT-18 target towing)

ELINT 2 Boeing 707, 2 Boeing 737

AEW 4 HS-748

MARITIME ATTACK 7 *Jaguar* S(I) with *Sea Eagle*

ATTACK HEL 3 sqn with 32 Mi-25/35

RECCE 2 sqn

1 with 8 *Canberra* (6 PR-57, 2 PR-67)

1 with 6* MiG-25R, 2* MiG-25U

MR/SURVEY 2 *Gulfstream* IV SRA, 2 *Learjet* 29

TRANSPORT

ac 12 sqn

5 with 105 An-32 *Sutlej*, 2 with 43 Do-228, 2 with 28 BAe-748, 3 with 25 Il-76 *Gajraj*

hel 11 sqn with 74 Mi-8, 37 Mi-17, 10 Mi-26 (hy tpt)

VIP 1 HQ sqn with 2 Boeing 737-200, 7 BAe-748, 6 Mi-8

TRG ac 28 BAe-748 (trg/tpt), 120 *Kiran* I, 56 *Kiran* II, 88 HPT-32, 38 *Hunter* (20 F-56, 18 T-66), 14* *Jaguar* B(1), 9* MiG-29UB, 44 TS-11 *Iskara* **hel** 20 *Chetak*, 2 Mi-24, 2* Mi-35

MISSILES

ASM AS-7 *Kerry*, AS-11B (ATGW), AS-12, AS-20, *Sea Eagle*, AM 39 *Exocet*

AAM AA-7 *Apex*, AA-8 *Aphid*, AA-10 *Alamo*, AA-11 *Archer*, R-550 *Magic*, *Super* 530D

SAM 38 sqn with 280 *Divina* V75SM/VK (SA-2), *Pechora* (SA-3), SA-5, SA-10

Forces Abroad

UN AND PEACEKEEPING

ANGOLA (UNOMA): 390 incl 20 Obs plus 11 civ pol. **BOSNIA** (UNMIBH): 147 civ pol. **HAITI** (UNTMIH): 3 civ pol. **IRAQ/KUWAIT** (UNIKOM): 5 Obs. **LIBERIA** (UNOMIL): 14 Obs

Paramilitary 1,088,000 active

NATIONAL SECURITY GUARDS (Cabinet Secretariat) 7,400

Anti-terrorism contingency deployment force, comprising elements of the armed forces, CRPF and Border Security Force

SPECIAL PROTECTION GROUP 3,000

Protection of VVIP

SPECIAL FRONTIER FORCE (Cabinet Secretariat) 9,000

mainly ethnic Tibetans

RASHTRIYA RIFLES (Ministry of Defence) 40,000

36 bn in 12 Sector HQ

DEFENCE SECURITY CORPS 31,000

provides security at Defence Ministry sites

INDO-TIBETAN BORDER POLICE (Ministry of Home Affairs) 32,200

28 bn, Tibetan border security

ASSAM RIFLES (Ministry of Home Affairs) 52,500

7 HQ, 31 bn, security within north-eastern states, mainly Army-officered; better trained than BSF

RAILWAY PROTECTION FORCES 70,000

CENTRAL INDUSTRIAL SECURITY FORCE (Ministry of Home Affairs)[a] 88,600

guards public-sector locations

CENTRAL RESERVE POLICE FORCE (CRPF) (Ministry of Home Affairs) 165,300

130–135 bn incl 10 rapid action, 2 *Mahila* (women); internal security duties, only lightly armed, deployable throughout the country

BORDER SECURITY FORCE (BSF) (Ministry of Home Affairs) 185,000

some 150 bn, small arms, some lt arty, tpt/liaison air spt

HOME GUARD (R) 472,000

authorised, actual str 416,000 in all states except Arunachal Pradesh and Kerala; men on lists, no trg

STATE ARMED POLICE 400,000

For duty primarily in home state only, but can be moved to other states, incl 24 bn India Reserve Police (commando-trained)

CIVIL DEFENCE 394,000 (R)

in 135 towns in 32 states

COAST GUARD ε4,000

  PATROL CRAFT 56

  1 *Samar* OPV, 9 *Vikram* PCO, 11 *Tara Bai* PCC, 5 *Rajhans* PFI, 7 *Jija Bai* PCI, 11 *Mod Jija Bai* PCI, 12 PC

  AVIATION

  3 sqn with **ac** 20 Do-228, 2 Fokker F-27 **hel** 13 *Chetak*

[a] Lightly armed security guards only

Kazakstan

	1995	1996	1997	1998
GDP	εt1.1tr	εt1.2tr		
	($18bn)	($18bn)		
per capita	$3,200	$3,300		
Growth	ε-9.0%	ε1.1%		
Inflation	ε176%	ε29%		
Debt	$3.7bn	$4.4bn		
Def exp[a]	εt26bn	εt32bn		
	($427m)	($470m)		
Def bdgt			t16.3bn	
			($211m)	
contd	**1995**	**1996**	**1997**	**1998**
FMA[b] (US)	$0.1m	$0.4m	$0.4m	$0.6m
$1 = tenge	61	67	76	

[a] Incl exp on paramilitary forces
[b] Excl US Cooperative Threat Reduction funds for nuclear dismantlement and demilitarisation. In 1992–96, $35m of $173m budget was spent. Programme continues in 1997–98

Population	16,000,000		

(Kazak 51%, Russian 32%, Ukrainian 5%, German 2%, Tatar 2%, Uzbek 2%)

Age	*13–17*	*18–22*	*23–32*
Men	860,000	772,000	1,295,000
Women	842,000	760,000	1,261,000

Total Armed Forces

ACTIVE ε35,100

Terms of service 31 months

Army ε20,000

1 Corps HQ • 1 TD • 1 arty bde • 2 MRD (1 trg) • 1 arty regt • 1 indep MRR • 1 MRL bde • 1 air aslt bde

EQUIPMENT

  MBT 630 T-72 (plus some 470 in store)

  RECCE 140 BRDM

  ACV 1,000 incl BMP-1/-2, BRM AIFV, BTR-70/-80, MT-LB APC (plus some 1,000 in store)

  TOTAL ARTY 1,000

  TOWED ARTY 550: **122mm**: D-30; **152mm**: D-20, 2A65, 2A36

  SP ARTY 150: **122mm**: 2S1; **152mm**: 2S3

  MRL 170: **122mm**: BM-21; **220mm**: 9P140 *Uragan*

  MOR 130: **120mm**: 2B11, M-120

  ATK GUNS 100mm: 125 T-12

(In 1991, the former Soviet Union transferred some 2,680 T-64/-72s, 2,428 ACVs and 6,900 arty to storage bases in Kazakhstan. This eqpt is under Kazak control, but has deteriorated considerably)

Navy ε100

BASES Aktau

PATROL AND COASTAL COMBATANTS 6

  5 *Guardian* PCI, 1 *Dauntless* PCI

Air Force ε15,000

(incl Air Defence)

1 Air Force div, 113 cbt ac (plus some 40 in store)

Flying hours 25

FTR 1 regt with 12 MiG-29, 4 MiG-29UB, 12 MiG-23, 4 MiG-23UB

FGA 2 regt

  1 with 34 MiG-27, 9 MiG-23UB

  1 with 26 Su-24

RECCE 1 regt with 12 Su-24*
HEL 1 regt (tpt), 44 Mi-8
STORAGE some 75 MiG-27/MiG-23/MiG-23UB/
   MiG-25/MiG-29/SU-27
AD 1 regt, 32 cbt ac (plus 15 MiG-25 in store)
FTR 1 regt with 32 MiG-31
SAM 100 SA-2, SA-3, SA-5

Forces Abroad

TAJIKISTAN ε350 1 border gd bn

Paramilitary 34,500

INTERNAL SECURITY TROOPS (Ministry of Interior)
ε20,000

BORDER GUARDS (National Security Committee)
ε12,000

PRESIDENTIAL GUARD 2,000

GOVERNMENT GUARD 500

Kyrgyzstan

	1995	1996	1997	1998
GDP	εs17bn	εs24bn		
	($1.6bn)	($2.1bn)		
per capita	$1,800	$1,900		
Growth	ε1.3%	ε5.4%		
Inflation	ε43%	ε37%		
Debt	$610m	$707m		
Def exp*a*	εs610m	εs625m		
	($56m)	($54m)		
Def bdgt			s159m	
			($13m)	
FMA (US)	$0.1m	$0.2m	$0.3m	$0.3m
$1 = som	11	13	18	

a Incl exp on paramilitary forces

Population	4,530,000		
(Kyrgyz 56%, Russian 17%, Uzbek 13%, Ukrainian 3%)			
Age	*13–17*	*18–22*	*23–32*
Men	263,000	222,000	344,000
Women	259,000	219,000	339,000

Total Armed Forces

ACTIVE 12,200 (incl 11,000 conscripts)
Terms of service 18 months

RESERVES 57,000

Army 9,800

1 MRD (3 MR, 1 tk, 1 arty, 1 AA regt)

1 indep MR bde (mtn)
EQUIPMENT
  MBT 210 T-72
  RECCE 34 BRDM-2
  AIFV 98 BMP-1, 101 BMP-2, 20 BRM-1K
  APC 45 BTR-70
  TOTAL ARTY 227
  TOWED ARTY 161: **100mm**: 18 M-1944 (BS-3);
    122mm: 72 D-30, 37 M-30; **152mm**: 34 D-1
  COMBINED GUN/MOR 120mm: 12 2S9
  MOR 120mm: 6 2S12, 48 M-120
  ATGW 26 AT-3 *Sagger*
  AD GUNS 57mm: 24 S-60

Air Force 2,400

ac and hel assets inherited from Sov Air Force trg school;
Kgz failed to maintain pilot trg for foreign students
AC 67 L-39, plus 53 decommissioned MiG-21/MiG-
  21UB
HEL 15 Mi-24, 28 Mi-8, 2 Mi-17, 2 Mi-25/35
AIR DEFENCE
  SAM SA-2, SA-3, SA-7

Forces Abroad

TAJIKISTAN ε300 incl Army and Border Guards

Paramilitary ε5,000

BORDER GUARDS ε5,000

Myanmar

	1995	1996	1997	1998
GDP*a*	εK623bn	εK787bn		
	($25bn)	($26bn)		
per capita	$1,000	$1,000		
Growth	9.8%	7.0%		
Inflation	25.2%	20.0%		
Debt	$5.8bn	$5.6bn		
Def exp*a*	εK22bn	εK25bn		
	($1.9bn)	($2.0bn)		
Def bdgt*a*			K19.3bn	
			($1.5bn)	
$1 = kyat*b*	5.7	5.9	6.2	

a PPP est
b Market rate **1997** $1 = 250–300

Population	48,823,000		
(Burmese 68%, Shan 9%, Karen 7%, Rakhine 4%,			
Chinese 3+% *Other* Chin, Kachin, Kayan, Lahu,			
Mon, Palaung, Pao, Wa, 5%)			
Age	*13–17*	*18–22*	*23–32*
Men	2,549,000	2,359,000	4,043,000
Women	2,489,000	2,301,000	4,068,000

Total Armed Forces

ACTIVE some 429,000 reported

Army some 400,000 reported

10 lt inf div (each 3 tac op comd (TOC))
12 Regional Comd (each with 10 regt)
32 TOC with 145 garrison inf bn
Summary of cbt units
   245 inf bn • 7 arty bn • 4 armd bn • 2 AA arty bn
EQUIPMENT†
   MBT 30 *Comet*, ε80 PRC Type-69II, ε20 PRC Type-80
   LT TK ε105 Type-63
   RECCE 45 *Ferret*, 40 *Humber*, 30 *Mazda* (local
      manufacture)
   APC 20 *Hino* (local manufacture), 250 Type-85
   TOWED ARTY 76mm: 100 M-1948; **88mm**: 50 25-
      pdr; **105mm**: 96 M-101; **140mm**: 5.5in
   MRL 107mm: 30 Type-63
   MOR 81mm; 82mm: Type-53; **120mm**: Type-53, 80
      Soltam
   RCL 84mm: 500 *Carl Gustav*; **106mm**: M40A1
   ATK GUNS 60: **57mm**: 6-pdr; **76.2mm**: 17-pdr
   AD GUNS 37mm: 24 Type-74; **40mm**: 10 M-1;
      57mm: 12 Type-80
   SAM HN-5A (reported)

Navy† 20,000

(incl 800 Naval Infantry)
BASES Bassein, Mergui, Moulmein, Seikyi, Yangon
(Monkey Point), Sittwe
PATROL AND COASTAL COMBATANTS 65
CORVETTES 2
   1 *Yan Taing Aung* (US PCE-827)†
   1 *Yan Gyi Aung* (US *Admirable* MSF)†
MISSILE CRAFT 3 *Houxin* with 4 C-801 SSM
PATROL, COASTAL 16 *Yan Sit Aung* (PRC *Hainan*)
PATROL, INSHORE 15
   12 US PGM-401/412, 3 FRY PB-90 PFI<
PATROL, RIVERINE about 29
   2 *Nawarat*, 2 imp FRY Y-301 and 10 FRY Y-301, about
   15<, plus some 25 boats
AMPHIBIOUS 5
   5 LCU, plus craft: 10 LCM
SUPPORT 4
   1 coastal tpt, 2 AGHS, 1 PC/div spt

NAVAL INFANTRY (800) 1 bn

Air Force 9,000

91 cbt ac, 18 armed hel
FTR 3 sqn with 30 F-7, 6 FT-7
FGA 2 sqn with 24 A-5M

CCT 2 sqn with 15 PC-7, 4 PC-9, 12 *Super Galeb* G4
TPT 1 F-27, 4 FH-227, 5 PC-6A/-B, 2 Y-8D
LIAISON 6 Cessna 180, 1 Cessna *Citation* II
HEL 4 sqn with 12 Bell 205, 6 Bell 206, 9 SA-316, 10 Mi-
   2 (armed), 8 Mi-17 (armed), 25 PZL W-3 *Sokol*

Paramilitary ε85,250

PEOPLE'S POLICE FORCE 50,000

PEOPLE'S MILITIA 35,000

PEOPLE'S PEARL AND FISHERY MINISTRY ε250
11 patrol boats (3 *Indaw* (Dk *Osprey*) PCC, 3 US *Swift*
PGM PCI, 5 Aus *Carpentaria* PCI<)

Opposition and Former Opposition

GROUPS WITH CEASE-FIRE AGREEMENTS
UNITED WA STATE ARMY (UWSA) ε12,000 **Area**
   Wa hills between Salween river and Chinese border;
   formerly part of CPB
KACHIN INDEPENDENCE ARMY (KIA) some
   8,000 **Area** northern Myanmar, incl Kuman range,
   the Triangle. Reached cease-fire agreement with
   government in October 1993
MONG TAI ARMY (MTA) (formerly Shan United
   Army) ε3,000+ **Area** along Thai border and between
   Lashio and Chinese border
SHAN STATE ARMY (SSA) ε3,000 **Area** Shan state
**MYANMAR NATIONAL DEMOCRATIC ALLI-
   ANCE ARMY** (MNDAA) 2,000 **Area** north-east
   Shan state
MON NATIONAL LIBERATION ARMY (MNLA)
   ε1,000 **Area** on Thai border in Mon state
NATIONAL DEMOCRATIC ALLIANCE ARMY
   (NDAA) ε1,000 **Area** eastern corner of Shan state on
   China–Laos border; formerly part of CPB
PALAUNG STATE LIBERATION ARMY (PSLA)
   ε700 **Area** hill tribesmen north of Hsipaw
NEW DEMOCRATIC ARMY (NDA) ε500 **Area** along
   Chinese border in Kachin state; former Communist
   Party of Burma (CPB)
**DEMOCRATIC KAREN BUDDHIST
   ORGANISATION** (DKBO) ε100–500 armed
GROUPS STILL IN OPPOSITION
MONG TAI ε8,000
 KAREN NATIONAL LIBERATION ARMY (KNLA)
ε4,000 **Area** based in Thai border area; political wg is
   Karen National Union (KNU)
ALL BURMA STUDENTS DEMOCRATIC FRONT
   ε2,000
KARENNI ARMY (KA) >1,000 **Area** Kayah state,
   Thai border

Nepal

	1995	1996	1997	1998
GDP	NR220bn	NR250bn		
	($4.2bn)	($4.5bn)		
per capita	$1,300	$1,400		
Growth	5.8%	4.2%		
Inflation	7.6%	7.0%		
Debt	$2.4bn	$2.5bn		
Def exp	NR1.9bn	NR2.2bn		
	($37m)	($40m)		
Def bdgt			εNR2.4bn	
			($43.0m)	
FMA (US)	$0.1m	$0.1m	$0.2m	$0.2m
$1 = rupee	51.9	55.5	57.0	

Population		22,504,000	
(Hindu 90%, Buddhist 5%, Muslim 3%)			
Age	*13–17*	*18–22*	*23–32*
Men	1,340,000	1,102,000	1,681,000
Women	1,260,000	1,023,000	1,545,000

Total Armed Forces

ACTIVE 46,000 (to be 50,000)

Army 46,000

1 Royal Guard bde (incl 1 MP bn) • 7 inf bde (16 inf bn) • 43 indep inf coy • 1 SF bde (incl 1 AB bn, 2 indep SF coy, 1 cav sqn (*Ferret*)) • 1 arty bde (1 arty, 1 AD regt) • 1 engr bde (4 bn)

EQUIPMENT
  RECCE 40 *Ferret*
  TOWED ARTY† **75mm**: 6 pack; **94mm**: 5 3.7in mtn (trg); **105mm**: 14 pack (ε6 op)
  MOR **81mm**; **120mm**: 70 M-43 (ε12 op)
  AD GUNS **14.5mm**: 30 PRC Type 56; **37mm**: PRC **40mm**: 2 L/60

AIR WING (215)

no cbt ac, or armed hel
TPT **ac** 1 BAe-748, 2 *Skyvan* **hel** 2 SA-316B *Chetak*, 1 SA-316B, 1 AS-332L (*Puma*), 2 AS-332L-1 (*Super Puma*), 1 Bell 206, 2 Bell 206L, 2 AS-350 (*Ecureuil*)

Forces Abroad

UN AND PEACEKEEPING

BOSNIA (UNMIBH): 43 civ pol. **CROATIA** (UNTAES): 2 Obs plus 19 civ pol; (UNMOP): 1 Obs. **FYROM** (UNPREDEP): 1 Obs. **LEBANON** (UNIFIL): 597; 1 inf bn. **LIBERIA** (UNOMIL): 6 Obs

Paramilitary 40,000

POLICE FORCE 40,000

Pakistan

	1995	1996	1997	1998
GDP	Rs1.9tr	Rs2.2tr		
	($59bn)	($64bn)		
per capita	$2,200	$2,300		
Growth	4.4%	6.0%		
Inflation	12.4%	10.3%		
Debt	$30.2bn	$33.1bn		
Def exp	Rs115bn	Rs127bn		
	($3.6bn)	($3.7bn)		
Def bdgt			Rs135.0bn	
			($3.3bn)	
FMA[a] (US)	$2.5m	$2.5m	$2.5m	$2.5m
(Aus)	$0.05m	$0.02m		
$1 = rupee	31.6	34.8	40.4	
[a] UNMOGIP **1995** $6m **1996** $7m				

Population		137,027,000 (less than 3% Hindu)	
Age	*13–17*	*18–22*	*23–32*
Men	8,051,000	6,949,000	11,218,000
Women	7,478,000	6,236,000	9,984,000

Total Armed Forces

ACTIVE 587,000

RESERVES 513,000

Army ε500,000; obligation to age 45 (men) or 50 (officers), active liability for 8 years after service **Navy** 5,000 **Air Force** 8,000

Army 520,000

9 Corps HQ • 2 armd div • 9 Corps arty bde • 19 inf div • 7 engr bde • 1 area comd (div) • 3 armd recce regt • 7 indep armd bde • 1 SF gp (3 bn) • 9 indep inf bde • 1 AD comd (3 AD gp: 8 bde)
AVN 17 sqn
  7 ac, 8 hel, 1 VIP, 1 obs flt

EQUIPMENT
  MBT 2,120+: 15 M-47, 345 M-48A5, 50 T-54/-55, 1,200 PRC Type-59, 250 PRC Type-69, 200+ PRC Type-85, ε60 T-80UD
  APC 850 M-113
  TOWED ARTY 1,590: **85mm**: 200 PRC Type-56; **105mm**: 300 M-101, 50 M-56 pack; **122mm**: 200 PRC Type-60, 400 PRC Type-54; **130mm**: 200 PRC Type-59-1; **155mm**: 30 M-59, 60 M-114, 124 M-198; **203mm**: 26 M-115
  SP ARTY 240: **105mm**: 50 M-7; **155mm**: 150 M-109A2; **203mm**: 40 M-110A2
  MRL **122mm**: 45 *Azar* (PRC Type-83)
  MOR **81mm**: 500; **120mm**: 225 AM-50, M-61
  SSM 18 *Hatf* 1, *Hatf* 2 (under development)
  ATGW 800: incl *Cobra*, 200 TOW (incl 24 on M-901 SP), *Green Arrow* (PRC *Red Arrow*)
  RL **89mm**: M-20 3.5in

RCL 75mm: Type-52; **106mm**: M-40A1
AD GUNS 2,000+ incl: **14.5mm; 35mm**: 200 GDF-002; **37mm**: PRC Type-55/-65; **40mm**: M1, 100 L/60; **57mm**: PRC Type-59
SAM 350 *Stinger, Redeye,* RBS-70, 500 *Anza* Mk-1/-2
SURV RASIT (veh, arty), AN/TPQ-36 (arty, mor)
AIRCRAFT
    SURVEY 1 *Commander* 840
    LIAISON 1 Cessna 421, 2 *Commander* 690, 80 *Mashshaq,* 1 F-27
    OBS 40 O-1E, 50 *Mashshaq*
HELICOPTERS
    ATTACK 20 AH-1F (TOW)
    TPT 12 Bell 47G, 7 -205, 10 -206B, 16 Mi-8, 6 IAR/SA-315B, 23 IAR/SA-316, 35 SA-330, 5 UH-1H

Navy 22,000

(incl Naval Air, ε1,200 Marines and ε2,000 Maritime Security Agency (see Paramilitary))
BASE Karachi (Fleet HQ)
SUBMARINES 9
    2 *Hashmat* (Fr *Agosta*) with 533mm TT (F-17 HWT), *Harpoon* USGW
    4 *Hangor* (Fr *Daphné*) with 533mm TT (L-5 HWT), *Harpoon* USGW
    3 MG110 SSI SF *Midget* submarines
PRINCIPAL SURFACE COMBATANTS 11
DESTROYERS 3 *Alamgir* (US *Gearing*) (ASW) with 1 x 8 ASROC; plus 2 x 3 ASTT, 2 x 2 127mm guns, 3 x 2 *Harpoon* SSM and hel deck (1 trg) (1 with Maritime Security Agency)
FRIGATES 8
    6 *Tariq* (UK *Amazon*) with 2 x 3 324mm ASTT; 1 114mm gun (2 *Lynx* hel delivered)
    2 *Shamsher* (UK *Leander*) with SA-319B hel, 1 x 3 ASW mor, plus 2 114mm guns
PATROL AND COASTAL COMBATANTS 13
MISSILE CRAFT 8
    4 PRC *Huangfeng* with 4 *HY* 2 SSM
    4 PRC *Hegu<* with 2 *HY* 2
PATROL, COASTAL 1 *Larkana* PCO
PATROL, INSHORE 4
    2 *Quetta* (PRC *Shanghai*) PFI
    1 *Rajshahi* PCI
    1 *Larkana* PCI
MINE COUNTERMEASURES 4
    2 *Munsif* (Fr *Eridan*) MHC
    2 *Mahmood* (US-MSC 268) MSC
SUPPORT AND MISCELLANEOUS 4
    1 *Nasr* (PRC *Fuqing*) AO, 1 *Dacca* AO, 1 AGOR, 1 AOR

NAVAL AIR

7 cbt ac, 12 armed hel
ASW/MR 1 sqn with 4 *Atlantic* plus 3 in store, 3 P-3C (operated by Air Force)
ASW/SAR 2 hel sqn with 4 SA-319B (ASW), 6 *Sea King* Mk 45 (ASW), 2 *Lynx* HAS Mk-3 (ASW)
COMMS 3 Fokker F-27 **ac** (Air Force)
ASM *Exocet* AM-39

MARINES (ε1,200)

1 cdo/SF gp

Air Force 45,000

429 cbt ac, no armed hel **Flying hours** some 210
FGA 7 sqn
    1 with 18 *Mirage* (15 IIIEP (some with AM-39 ASM), 3 IIIDP (trg))
    3 (1 OCU) with 56 *Mirage* 5 (54 -5PA/PA2, 2-5DPA/DPA2)
    3 with 49 Q-5 (A-5 *Fantan*)
FTR 10 sqn
    4 with 99 J-6/JJ-6, (F-6/FT-6), 3 (1 OCU) with 34 F-16A/B, 2 (1 OCU) with 79 J-7 (F-7P), 1 with 30 *Mirage* 1110
RECCE 1 sqn with 12* *Mirage* IIIRP
ASW/MR 1 sqn with 4* *Atlantic,* 3* P-3C
SAR 1 hel sqn with 6 SA-319
TPT ac 12 C-130 (5 -B, 7 -E), 1 L-100, 3 Boeing 707, 3 *Falcon* 20, 2 F-27-200 (1 with Navy), 2 Beech (1 *Travel Air,* 1 *Baron*) **hel** 1 sqn with 12 SA-316, 4 SA-321, 12 SA-315B Lama
TRG 12 CJ-6A (PT-6A), 30 JJ-5 (FT-5), 45* MFI-17B *Mashshaq,* 6 MiG-15UTI, 10 T-33A, 44 T-37B/C, 6 K-8
AD 7 SAM bty
    6 each with 24 *Crotale,* 1 with 6 CSA-1 (SA-2)
MISSILES
    ASM AM-39 *Exocet,* AGM-65 *Maverick*
    AAM AIM-7 *Sparrow,* AIM-9 *Sidewinder,* R-530, R-550 *Magic*

Forces Abroad

UN AND PEACEKEEPING

ANGOLA (UNOMA): 14. **BOSNIA** (UNMIBH): 1 plus 80 civ pol. **CROATIA** (UNTAES): 990 incl 5 Obs; (UNMOP): 1 Obs. **FYROM** (UNPREDEP): 2 Obs. **GEORGIA** (UNOMIG): 7 Obs. **HAITI** (UNTMIH): 542. **IRAQ/KUWAIT** (UNIKOM): 6 Obs. **LIBERIA** (UNOMIL): 14 Obs. **WESTERN SAHARA** (MINURSO): 5 Obs

Paramilitary ε247,000 active

NATIONAL GUARD 185,000
incl *Janbaz* Force, *Mujahid* Force, National Cadet Corps, Women Guards
FRONTIER CORPS (Ministry of Interior) 35,000
11 regt (40 bn), 1 indep armd car sqn; 45 UR-416 APC
PAKISTAN RANGERS (Ministry of Interior) ε25,000
MARITIME SECURITY AGENCY ε2,000

1 *Alamgir* (US *Gearing* DD) (no ASROC or TT), 4 *Barakat* PCC, 4 (PRC *Shanghai*) PFI

COAST GUARD

some 23 PFI, plus boats

Sri Lanka

	1995	1996	1997	1998
GDP	Rs662bn	Rs743bn		
	($12.9bn)	($13.7bn)		
per capita	$3,400	$3,500		
Growth	5.6%	3.5%		
Inflation	7.7%	14.0%		
Debt	$8.2bn	$8.6bn		
Def exp	Rs34bn	Rs48bn		
	($663m)	($886m)		
Def bdgt			Rs44bn	
			($759m)	
FMA (US)	$0.1m	$0.2m	$0.2m	$0.2m
$1 = rupee	51.3	54.2	58.0	
Population		18,461,000		
(Tamil 18%, Moor 7%)				
Age	*13–17*	*18–22*		*23–32*
Men	928,000	871,000	1,554,000	
Women	891,000	840,000	1,532,000	

Total Armed Forces

ACTIVE some 112–117,000
(incl recalled reservists)

RESERVES 4,200
Army 1,100 **Navy** 1,100 **Air Force** 2,000
Obligation 7 years, post regular service

Army ε90–95,000

(incl 42,000 recalled reservists, ε1,000 women)
3 div, 4 task force HQ • 1 mech inf bde • 1 air mobile bde • 23 inf bde • 1 indep SF bde (1 cdo, 1 SF regt) • 1 armd regt • 3 armd recce regt (bn) • 4 fd arty (1 reserve) • 4 fd engr regt (1 reserve)

EQUIPMENT

MBT ε25 T-55 (perhaps 18 op)
RECCE 26 *Saladin*, 15 *Ferret*, 12 Daimler *Dingo*
AIFV 16 BMP (12 -1, 4 -2) (trg)
APC 35 PRC Type-85, 10 BTR-152, 31 *Buffel*, 30 *Unicorn*, 8 Shorland, 9 *Hotspur*, 30 *Saracen*
TOWED ARTY 76mm: 14 FRY M-48; **85mm**: 12 PRC Type-56; **88mm**: 12 25-pdr; **130mm**: 12 PRC Type-59-1
MRL 107mm: 1
MOR 81mm: 276; **82mm**: 19; **107mm**: 12; **120mm**: 36
M-43
RCL 105mm: 15 M-65; **106mm**: 34 M-40
AD GUNS 40mm: 7 L-40; **94mm**: 3 3.7in
UAV 1 I1

Navy 12,000

(incl 1,100 recalled reservists)
BASES Colombo (HQ), Trincomalee (main base), Karainagar, Tangalle, Kalpitiya, Galle, Welisara

PATROL AND COASTAL COMBATANTS 39

PATROL, COASTAL 1 *Jayesagara* PCC
PATROL, INSHORE 38
  6 *Sooraya*, 2 *Rana* (PRC MOD *Shanghai* II) PFI
  2 *Parakrambahu* (PRC *Houxin*) PFC
  7 Il *Dvora* PFI<
  3 Il *Super Dvora* PFI<
  3 ROK *Killer* PFI<
  17 PCI<, plus some 30 boats

AMPHIBIOUS 9

  2 *Wuhu* LSM, 3 LCM (1 non-op), 2 fast personnel carrier, 2 LCU

Air Force 10,000

22 cbt ac, 17 armed hel **Flying hours** 420
FGA 4 F-7M, 1 FT-7, 2 FT-5, 4 *Kfir*-C2, 1 *Kfir*-TC2
ARM AC 8 SF-260TP, 2 FMA IA58A *Pucara*
ATTACK HEL 12 Bell 212, 5 Mi-24V
TPT 1 sqn with **ac** 3 BAe 748, 1 Cessna 421C, 1 *Super King Air*, 1 Y-8, 7 Y-12, 4 AN-32B, 1 Cessna 150 **hel** 3 Bell 412 (VIP)
HEL 9 Bell 206, 5 Mi-17 (plus 6 in store)
TRG incl 4 DHC-1, 4 SF-260 W, 3 Bell 206
RESERVES Air Force Regt, 3 sqn; Airfield Construction Regt, 1 sqn
UAV 1 *Superhawk*

Paramilitary ε110,200

POLICE FORCE (Ministry of Defence) 80,000
incl reserves, 1,000 women and Special Task Force: 3,000-strong anti-guerrilla unit
NATIONAL GUARD ε15,000
HOME GUARD 15,200

Opposition

LIBERATION TIGERS OF TAMIL EELAM (LTTE) ε6,000
Leader Velupillai Prabhakaran

Tajikistan

	1995	1996	1997	1998
GDP[a]	εTr58bn	εTr309bn		
	($1.1bn)	($1.1bn)		
per capita	$900	$800		
Growth	ε-12.5%	ε-7.0%		
Inflation	ε610%	ε443%		
Debt	$665m	$667m		
Def exp[a]	ε$111m	ε$115m		
Def bdgt[a]			Tr n.k.	
			($70m)	
$1 = Tajik rouble	135	295	600	

[a] UNMOT 1995 $9m 1996 $7m

Population		6,100,000		
(Tajik 67%, Uzbek 25%, Russian 2%, Tatar 2%)				
Age	*13–17*	*18–22*	*23–32*	
Men	373,000	297,000	447,000	
Women	362,000	289,000	441,000	

Total Armed Forces

ACTIVE some 7–9,000

Terms of service: 24 months

A number of potential officers are being trained at the Higher Army Officers and Engineers College, Dushanbe. It is planned to form an Air Force sqn and to acquire Su-25 from Belarus, 5 Mi-24 and 10 Mi-8 have been procured

Army some 7,000

2 MR bde (incl 1 trg), 1 mtn bde
1 SF bde, 1 SF det (εbn+)
1 SAM regt

EQUIPMENT
MBT 40 T-72
AIFV 85 BMP-1/-2
APC 40 BTR-60/-70/-80
TOWED ARTY 122mm: 12 D-30
MOR 122mm: 12
SAM 20 SA-2/-3

Paramilitary ε1,200

BORDER GUARDS (Ministry of Interior) ε1,200
Russian controlled

Opposition

ISLAMIC MOVEMENT OF TAJIKISTAN some 5,000
Signed peace accord with government on 27 June 1997

Foreign Forces

UN (UNMOT) 20 mil obs from 7 countries

RUSSIA Frontier Forces ε25,000 (Tajik conscripts, Russian-controlled) **Army** ε 6,000+; 1 MRD
  EQUIPMENT
  MBT 190 T-72
  AIFV 165 BMP-2, 8 BRM-1K
  APC 130 BTR-80
  SP ARTY 122mm: 66 2S1; **152mm**: 54 2S3
  MRL 122mm: 12 BM-21; **220mm**: 12 9P140
  MOR 120mm: 36 PM-38
  AIR DEFENCE
  SAM 20 SA-8
KAZAKSTAN ε350; 1 border gd bn
KYRGYZSTAN ε300 incl Army and Border Guard
UZBEKISTAN 1 MR bn plus border gd

Turkmenistan

	1995	1996	1997	1998
GDP	εm1.1tr	εm6.0tr		
	($4.9bn)	($4.9bn)		
per capita	$2,600	$2,600		
Growth	ε-8.2%	ε-3.0%		
Inflation	ε1,005%	ε992%		
Debt	$393m	$427m		
Def exp	ε$135m	ε$138m		
Def bdgt			($140m)	
FMA (US)	$0.1m	$0.2m	$0.3m	$0.3m
$1 = manat	230	2,900	4,120	

Population		4,531,000		
(Turkmen 77%, Uzbek 9%, Russian 7%, Kazak 2%)				
Age	*13–17*	*18–22*	*23–32*	
Men	242,000	204,000	331,000	
Women	237,000	201,000	326,000	

Total Armed Forces

ACTIVE 16–18,000

Terms of service 24 months

Army 16–18,000

4 MRD (1 trg) • 1 arty bde • 1 MRL regt • 1 ATK regt • 1 SSM bde • 1 engr bde • 2 SAM bde • 1 indep air aslt bn

EQUIPMENT
MBT 570 T-72
RECCE 14 BRDM-2
AIFV 156 BMP-1, 405 BMP-2, 51 BRM
APC 728 BTR (-60/-70/-80)
TOWED ARTY 122mm: 197 D-30; **152mm**: 76 D-1, 72 2A65
SP ARTY 152mm: 16 2S3
COMBINED GUN/MOR 120mm: 12 2S9
MRL 122mm: 60 BM-21; **220mm**: 54 9P140

MOR 82mm: 31; **120mm**: 42 PM-38
SSM 12 *Scud*
ATGW AT-2 *Swatter*, AT-3 *Sagger*, AT-4 *Spigot*, AT-5 *Spandrel*
ATK GUNS 85mm: 6 D-44; **100mm**: 48 MT-12
AD GUNS 23mm: 28 ZSU-23-4 SP; **57mm**: 22 S-60
SAM 27 SA-4

Navy none

Has announced intention to form a Navy/Coast Guard. Caspian Sea Flotilla (see **Russia**) is operating as a joint RF, Kaz and Tkm flotilla under RF comd based at Astrakhan

Air Force 3,000

(incl Air Defence)
171 cbt ac (plus 218 in store)
FGA/FTR 1 composite regt with 22 MiG-29, 2 MiG-29U, 65 Su-17
TRG 1 unit with 3 Su-7B, 3 MiG-21, 2 L-39, 8 Yak-28, 3 An-12
TPT/GENERAL PURPOSE 1 composite sqn with 1 An-24, 10 Mi-24, 10 Mi-8
AIR DEFENCE
  FTR 2 regt with 48 MiG-23, 10 MiG-23U 24 MiG-25
  SAM 50 SA-2/-3/-5
  IN STORE 172 MiG-23, 46 Su-25

Uzbekistan

	1995	1996	1997	1998
GDP	εs302bn	εs560bn		
	($10bn)	($11bn)		
per capita	$2,400	$2,400		
Growth	ε-0.9%	ε1.6%		
Inflation	ε305%	ε54%		
Debt	$1.6bn	$1.9bn		
Def exp[a]	ε$385m	ε$420m		
Def bdgt			s6.5bn	
			($113.0m)	
FMA (US)	$0.1m	$0.3m	$0.3m	$0.4m
$1 = som	30	44	58	

[a] Incl exp on paramilitary forces

Population	24,064,000		

(Uzbek 73%, Russian 6%, Tajik 5%, Kazak 4%, Karakalpak 2%, Tatar 2%, Korean <1%, Ukrainian <1%)

Age	13–17	18–22	23–32
Men	1,368,000	1,139,000	1,792,000
Women	1,343,000	1,125,000	1,798,000

Total Armed Forces

ACTIVE ε65–70,000

(incl MoD staff and centrally controlled units)
Terms of service: conscription, 18 months

Army ε45,000 (to be 50,000)

2 Corps HQ • 2 tk, 4 MR, 1 lt mtn, 1 mot bde • 1 air aslt, 1 air-mobile bde • 3 arty, 1 MRL bde • 1 arty regt • 1 National Guard bde
EQUIPMENT
  MBT 370 incl T-54, T-62, T-64 plus some T-72
  RECCE 35 BRDM-2
  AIFV 273 BMP-2, 130 BMD-1
  APC 36 BTR-70, 290 BTR-80, 145 BTR-D
  TOTAL ARTY 501
  TOWED ARTY 199: **122mm**: 90 D-30; **152mm**: 28 D-1, 49 D-20, 32 2A36
  SP ARTY 83: **122mm**: 18 2S1; **152mm**: 17 2S3; **203mm**: 48 2S7
  COMBINED GUN/MOR 69: **120mm**: 69 2S9
  MRL 69: **122mm**: 33 BM-21; **220mm**: 36 9P140
  MOR 42: **120mm**: 18 PM-120, 19 2S12, 5 2B11
  ATK GUNS 100mm: 39 MT-12
(In 1991 the former Soviet Union transferred some 2,000 tanks (T-64), 1,200 ACV and 750 arty to storage bases in Uzbekistan. This eqpt is under Uzbek control, but has deteriorated considerably)

Air Force some 4,000

128 cbt ac, 43 attack hel
FGA 30 Su-17/Su-17UB, 4 Su-24
FTR 32 MiG-29/MiG-29UB, 32 Su-27/Su-27UB
RECCE 10* Su-24
TPT 30 An-2, plus 20 light tpt ac
TRG 15 L-39
HELICOPTERS
  ATTACK 43 Mi-24
  ASLT 43 Mi-8T
  TPT 23 Mi-6, 1 Mi-26
  RECCE 6 Mi-24K, 2 Mi-24 R
SAM 45 SA-2/-3/-5

Forces Abroad

TAJIKISTAN 1 MR bn plus border gd

Paramilitary 16,000

INTERNAL SECURITY TROOPS (Ministry of Interior) 15,300

NATIONAL GUARD (Ministry of Defence) 700
1 bde

MILITARY DEVELOPMENTS

Regional Trends

Military trends in East Asia and Australia in 1997 maintain the pattern of the preceding two years. Defence spending has increased in real terms and East Asia remains the world's second largest regional arms market, in financial terms, after the Middle East. Unless there is an economic recession, the trend looks set to persist. **China** continues to upgrade its military forces, while also participating in some major multilateral security arrangements. The **Japan**–US Security Alliance has been strengthened. Tension on the **Korean Peninsula** persists, and diplomacy on conflict resolution is complicated by the famine in the North. In South-east Asia, internal armed conflicts continue with the crisis in **Cambodia** in July 1997 posing a challenge to the Association of South-east Asian Nations (ASEAN)'s plans for expansion.

China

China continues to modernise its strategic and major conventional weapon systems, but its overall capability is little changed since 1996. Its main force elements, in terms of technology, remain well behind those of other major powers. It will take most of the next decade, and increasing defence expenditure, for China to reach the technological level of, for example, the major NATO powers. At present, China does not have the resources to project a major conventional force beyond its territory. Instead, it appears to give priority to improving strategic forces as a credible deterrent, and to enhancing the mobility and capability of the People's Liberation Army (PLA) to deal with border threats and major internal security problems. Despite being the last nuclear power to conduct a nuclear test (in May 1996), China was one of the original signatories to the Comprehensive Nuclear Test Ban Treaty (CTBT) the following September and, in April 1997, ratified the Chemical Weapons Convention (CWC). Under the latter, China has for the first time accepted an international inspection team on its territory. An important benefit for the country of this Convention is the disposal of the many thousands of chemical weapons abandoned by the Japanese Army in Manchuria during the Second World War. This major engineering and munitions disposal task, which will take a number of years, will be carried out at the expense of the Japanese government. In May 1997, China joined those UN member-states who have placed military forces on stand-by for UN peacekeeping operations (see pp. 274–84). On 1 July, China took back Hong Kong from the UK with no unexpected security problems. Relations with Taiwan, despite some major exercises by the navies of both China and Taiwan in June 1997, remain relatively calm as far as military activities are concerned.

Japan and the United States

Despite local opposition to US military bases on Okinawa, the US–Japan Security Alliance is as strong as ever and is perhaps even further reinforced by an interim agreement involving a Japanese commitment to supply more infrastructure support for US military deployments, participate more actively in maritime exercises and intelligence-gathering, and increase its role in peacekeeping operations. China's reaction to Japan's more active defence role is a cause for concern in the region. Both the Japanese and US governments have deliberately avoided any specific mention of the geographic areas where Japan may play its supporting role – particularly in relation to **Taiwan**. The US remains committed to maintaining forces in the region at a personnel strength of nearly 100,000, based for the most part in Japan and South Korea.

Korean Peninsula

While harrowing stories of famine and suffering emanate from North Korea, the military situation remains little changed in terms of the balance of forces with South Korea and its allies. The North still has armed forces with around one million troops on active duty and, while its equipment is outdated and training standards low, it still poses a serious threat to the South – Seoul is within field artillery range of the border zone. However, the 1994 US–North Korean Framework Agreement, under which North Korea receives assistance for its energy programmes in return for renouncing its nuclear-weapons programme, is progressing steadily but slowly. On 28 July 1997, the Korean Peninsula Energy Development Organisation (KEDO), which coordinates the consortium building the nuclear-power stations, opened, for the first time, an office at Kunho in North Korea, with some South Korean staff. This permanent presence in the North signalled an important stage in the project's development. In August 1997 at Sinpo, the ground was broken for the few nuclear power stations to be built in the North. The bilateral contacts between North and South have increased as a result, and the US is discussing other issues with the North, such as its missile programmes, in a bid to help allay proliferation concerns. Food aid to the North has also helped develop bilateral relations. In July 1997, there were more positive signs that formal four-party – North and South Korea, China and the US – talks may be held to try to negotiate a peace settlement for the Korean Peninsula. Preliminary discussions were held in New York in August 1997. Russia, while not a participant, supports the process.

South-east Asia

There have been no new outbreaks of armed conflict in the region in 1997, although the long-standing and intermittent internal conflicts in Cambodia, **Indonesia** and the **Philippines** continue. The most significant events occurred in Cambodia, where the Khmer Rouge continued to decline as a fighting force and, in July 1997, put their leader Pol Pot on public trial for his past atrocities. This did not, however, signal an early end to the violence as almost simultaneously then Second Prime Minister, Hun Sen, took power in what amounted to a military coup, pushing out First Prime Minister Prince Norodom Ranariddh. Troops loyal to Hun Sen quickly overcame Ranariddh's supporters. As a result of this overthrow of the UN-brokered peace plan, Cambodia was not invited to join ASEAN at the same time as **Laos** and, ironically, military-run Myanmar on 10 July 1997. In the Philippines, fighting continued in 1997 between government forces and the Moro Islamic Liberation Front on the island of Mindanao. The fighting was relatively low level, with cease-fire agreements being made and frequently broken. In Indonesia, resistance continues in East Timor, where separatist rebels battle against Indonesian government forces who also face a restive civilian population. Although President Suharto's supporters won the 29 May 1997 parliamentary elections with a large majority, over 200 people were killed in violent clashes with the security forces in Jakarta and elsewhere during the election campaign.

DEFENCE SPENDING

The underlying trend in regional defence spending continues to be upwards, rising by about 7% in real terms from $132 billion in 1994 to $141bn in 1996 after peaking at $144bn in 1995 (all at 1995 prices). The strength of the yen and other East Asian currencies against the US dollar in 1995 exaggerated the dollar values of regional defence spending in that year. The outlook for 1997 suggests defence spending at similar levels to 1996.

Japan

Japan's defence spending has shown modest growth since 1993 when measured in yen. Now that the yen has depreciated in value against the US dollar to below 1993 levels, the 1997 Japanese defence budget of ¥4,947bn ($43bn) is the lowest since 1992 in real terms when measured in US dollars, and well below the 1995 peak of $50bn.

The 1997 budget includes ¥6.1bn as the costs of transferring US military facilities on Okinawa to Japan, overseen by the Japan–US Special Action Committee on Okinawa (SACO). The budgets for Japan's host-nation support for US forces amounted to ¥274bn ($2.5bn) in 1997. Each year Japan pays around 15% towards the cost of UN peacekeeping operations ($482m in 1995).

Table 25 Japan's defence budget by function and selected other budgets, 1993–1997

(1995 US$bn)		1993	1994	1995	1996	1997
Personnel		18.3	20.0	22.0	18.7	17.7
Supplies		25.4	26.9	28.2	24.9	23.5
of which	Procurement	10.2	10.0	9.2	8.2	7.8
	R&D	1.2	1.3	1.5	1.4	1.3
	Maintenance	7.1	8.0	8.8	7.9	7.4
	Infrastructure and others	7.0	7.7	8.6	7.5	6.9
Total defence budget		**43.7**	**47.0**	**50.2**	**43.6**	**41.2**
Maritime Safety Agency		1.4	1.6	1.7	1.5	1.5
Veterans (Imperial Japanese Army)		14.5	15.4	16.1	13.1	11.7
Space		1.6	1.8	2.0	2.2	2.3

According to May 1997 government plans, the 1998 defence budget will fall in real terms. In addition, the 1996–2000 Mid-Term Defense Programme (MTDP) of ¥25,260bn is to be cut by nearly 4% (¥920bn or $8bn) in 1998–2000. The original plan allocated ¥4,280bn (17%) to front-line equipment. The previous 1991–95 MDTP amounted to ¥22,170bn, of which ¥4,440bn (20%) was for front-line equipment.

Table 26 Japan's defence budget by armed service, 1993–1996

(1995 US$bn)		1993	1994	1995	1996
Japanese Defense Agency		38.8	41.6	44.2	38.5
of which	Ground Self-Defense Force	15.7	17.1	19.0	16.1
	Maritime Self-Defense Force	10.2	11.1	11.2	10.2
	Air Self-Defense Force	11.1	11.4	11.7	10.1
	Other	1.8	2.0	2.2	2.0
Defense Facility Administration Agency		4.9	5.4	6.0	5.2
Total defence budget		**43.7**	**47.0**	**50.2**	**43.6**

Japan's procurement in 1997 includes eight F-2 fighters. Forty-seven will be purchased in the 1996–2000 MTDP, with a total programme buy of 130 expected to last to 2007–8. The first three OH-1 helicopters have been ordered; the Army has a requirement for 193 and the Japanese Defense Agency (JDA) programme buy is likely to be at least 250–300. With the expensive development of the F-2 and OH-1 now over, the JDA has scope to begin new programmes. Theatre Missile Defence (TMD) is currently the subject of preliminary feasibility studies conducted jointly with the US Department of Defense. The 1997 budget allocates $1.3m ($1.8m in 1996) to complete the two-year study. Other projects include the PC-3 maritime patrol aircraft

(MPA) replacement, a medium-range surface-to-air missile (SAM), a light armoured vehicle and a shoulder-firing anti-tank weapon.

Japan's weapons procurement continues to feature a mix of indigenous and licensed programmes with direct purchases from foreign sources. Japan's annual defence imports are worth over $1.5bn, mainly from the US. Imports from Western Europe were worth $63m in 1994 and $117m in 1995. At least 85% of the JDA's defence contracts are with domestic firms. The top ten firms accounted for nearly 64% of all JDA contracts in 1996. The majority of contracts (around 85% by value) are non-competitive, leaving 15% open to domestic and foreign competition.

China

China's official defence budget increased from Y71.5bn ($8.6bn) in 1996 to Y80.6bn ($9.7bn) in 1997. Real outlays grew from an estimated $33bn in 1995 to $35bn in 1996, largely because of increased spending on Operations and Maintenance (O&M) – notably the major exercise during the Taiwanese presidential election in March 1996 – and on procurement. China has an extensive range of indigenous development programmes, but their slow progress continues to provide opportunities for Russian exports. China took delivery of the second batch of 24 SU-27s during 1996; will take delivery of two 636-class *Kilo* submarines in 1997–98; and ordered two *Sovremenny*-class destroyers in late 1996. China's imported defence equipment was worth an estimated $1.5bn in 1996, but its arms exports continued to decline in 1996 from an estimated $630 million in 1995 to $584m (at 1995 prices). Despite these relatively low trade levels compared to 1980, China's arms-export policies remain a source of concern in terms of both weapon-of-mass-destruction (WMD) proliferation, and the supply of conventional and light weapons to belligerents.

South Korea

South Korean defence outlays increased to won 12,500bn($15.5bn) in 1996, up from $14.2bn in 1995. The 1997 budget is won 13,787bn($15.4bn); and the military has requested won 15,600bn ($17.3bn) for 1998, in part to counter the effects of the won's eroding purchasing power.

Table 27 **South Korea's defence budget by function, 1996–1997**

(US$bn)	1996	%	1997	%
Personnel	7.2	47.0	7.1	46.0
O&M	2.5	16.3	2.6	16.5
Procurement incl Research and Development (R&D)	4.3	28.0	4.5	28.9
Other	1.3	8.7	1.3	8.6
Total	**15.2**	**100.0**	**15.4**	**100.0**

Taiwan

Since 1993, Taiwan's defence budgets have been supplemented by special allocations to meet stage payments for exceptionally large contracts with the US (150 F-16C/D ordered in 1992 with deliveries commencing in early 1997) and France (six *La Fayette* frigates, four delivered by June 1997) and 60 *Mirage* 2000-5 combat aircraft (first five delivered in May 1997). Defence budgets including supplementary procurement allocations are NT$311bn($11.3bn) in 1997 and NT$308bn ($11.2bn) in 1998.

ASEAN

Defence-spending levels in ASEAN countries continue to rise on the back of high levels of economic growth. The combined defence spending of the nine existing and prospective ASEAN member-states amounted to over $19bn in 1996 (at 1995 prices), about 14% of regional spending. Thailand's 1997 defence budget of baht 109bn ($4.2bn) was cut by 4% in February 1997 to baht 104bn ($4.1bn). The government has set the armed forces a two-year spending cut target of baht 13bn, most of which will be deferred to 1998. The Interior Ministry has a budget of baht175bn ($6.8bn) in 1997 after a cut of baht 9.4bn, or around 19% of government spending, compared to 11% for defence.

Table 28 **Thailand's defence budget by service, 1997**			
	baht bn	US$m	%
Army	50,125	1,954	46.8
Navy	21,720	847	20.3
Air Force	21,838	851	20.4
Central Command	10,319	402	9.6
Defence Ministry	3,002	117	2.8
Other	1,566	61	1.5
Total	108,570	4,172	100.0

Indonesia's defence budget increases to Rp8,005bn ($3.3bn) in 1997, compared with Rp7,316bn ($3.1bn) in 1996. Actual military expenditures are uncertain because of procurement, paramilitary-military and defence-industrial funding outside the defence budget. *The Military Balance* estimates real military spending at 2.1–2.3% of gross domestic product (GDP) in 1992–96 (compared to the official figure of 1.4–1.5%). The Indonesian government's figure is almost certainly too low, while the IISS estimate is conservative. Real outlays may lie within the range of 3–5% of GDP. In the Philippines, defence funds have been switched to internal security since 1994. A 15-year P156bn ($6bn) defence-modernisation programme was approved by Congress in December 1996, of which P7bn ($270m) is available in the near term. Singapore's security spending accounts for a third of the government budget. The 1997 defence budget rises to S$6.1bn ($4.3bn) from S$5.7bn ($4bn) in 1996. In Malaysia, under the seventh Malaysian Five-Year Development Plan for 1996–2000, the Defence Ministry is to receive M$7bn ($2.8bn) for equipment and infrastructure over five years (down from the previous Plan's figure of M$9.2bn – $3.5bn), in addition to annual defence allocations.

Australasia
Australia's defence budget rises to A$10.4bn ($8.1bn) in 1997 from A$10bn ($7.8bn) in 1996. The government's Defence Efficiency Review, released in April 1997, is expected to generate one-time savings of A$441–674m ($340–530m) and recurrent savings of A$774–920m ($600–720m). Orders in 1997 include 40 *Hawk* training aircraft from the UK (of which 28 are to be built in Australia), and 11 SH-2G shipborne helicopters from the US for the new *Anzac*-class frigates. New Zealand also ordered four SH-2G in 1997 for its two *Anzac* frigates.

ARMS SALES
Arms sales to East Asia and Australasia were worth an estimated $9.3bn in 1995, making the region the most valuable defence trading market outside the Middle East. China, Japan, South Korea, Taiwan and Thailand are the largest regional importers of military equipment. Major transfers during 1997 include: the commissioning in March of Thailand's *Chakri Naruebet* aircraft carrier; deliveries to Taiwan of the first of 150 US F-16s and 60 French *Mirage* 2000 combat aircraft;

and first deliveries to Indonesia of a batch of 24 *Hawk* 109/209 advanced combat-capable trainers from the UK. New orders in 1997 include: Australia's purchase of 33 *Hawk* advanced trainers from the UK and 11 SH-2 ship-based helicopters from the US for the *Anzac*-class frigates (New Zealand also purchased four of the same type for two *Anzac*-class frigates); South Korea's purchase of 13 *Lynx* naval helicopters from the UK; and Vietnam's acquisition of six more SU-27 combat aircraft from Russia. In June 1997, Indonesia cancelled an order for F-16 aircraft following criticism of the government's human-rights record in the US Congress, in July 1997. In August 1997, Indonesia placed an order for 12 SU-30s as a replacement.

Table 29 UN Register of Conventional Arms imports, East Asia and Australasia, 1996

(as at 11 August 1997)	MBT	ACV	Artillery	Combat aircraft	Attack helicopters	Warships	Missiles
Australia	—	—	1	1	—	—	70
Brunei	—	—	26	—	—	3	20
China	—	—	—	22	—	—	—
Indonesia	—	16	20	17	—	4	—
Japan	—	—	9	—	—	—	288
Malaysia	—	—	8	—	—	—	37
Papua New Guinea	—	3	—	—	—	—	—
ROK	33	23	90	—	—	—	53
Singapore	—	—	—	—	—	—	1
Thailand	24	30	24	13	—	1	—
Vietnam	—	—	—	6	—	—	—
Total	57	72	178	59	0	8	469

Table 30 Arms orders and deliveries, East Asia and Australasia, 1995–1997

Equipment	Type	Unit	Supplier	Order Date	Delivery Date	Comment
Australia						
FGA	F-111	21	Domestic	1990	1999	Upgrade of F/RF-111C variants
MPA	P-3B *Orion*	4	US	1994	1995	EDA
tpt	C-130J	12	US	1996	1997	Deliveries late 1997–98
trg	*Hawk* 100	33	UK	1996	1999	12 operational by 2000
ASSM	*Harpoon*	12	US		1995	With 21 trg missiles
LAV	ASLAV	82	Ca	1992	1996	Customisation Aus; deliveries 1997
APC	M113	364	Domestic	1997		Upgrade; new turret and gun sight
FF	*Anzac*-class	6	Domestic	1989	1996	Ge design; first delivery 1996
MHC	*Gaeta*-class	6	Domestic	1994	1998	Deliveries to 2002
SS	*Collins*	6	Swe	1987	1996	Licensed production
hel	SH-2G	11	US	1997	2001	
Brunei						
trg	*Hawk* 100/200	10	UK	1997		Unconfirmed
hel	UH-60L	4	US	1996	1997	
trg	PC-7 *Pilatus*	4	CH	1995	1997	
APC	Renault VAB	26	Fr	1995	1996	
corvette		3	UK	1995	2000	First delivery 2000
MPA	CN-235	4	Indo	1995	1996	1 tpt
Cambodia						
FGA	MiG-21	8	Il	1995	1997	Upgrade; first 4 delivered Sep 1997
trg	L-39	6	Il	1994	1996	Upgraded before export

Equipment	Type	Unit	Supplier	Order Date	Delivery Date	Comment
APC	OT-64	30	Cz	1994	1995	
FAC	*Stenka*-class	2	RF	1994	1996	
China						
ICBM	DF-31/41		Domestic	1985	1998	Development begun 1985
SLBM	JL-2		Domestic	1985	2003	Development
MPA	radar	8	UK	1996		Searchwater to be fitted to Y-8
AEW	IL-76	4	Il	1997		
FGA	F-10		Domestic	1989	2003	Development; requirement for 300
FGA	SU-27	72	RF	1990	1995	Licensed production for ε150 more
trg	K-8		Collab.	1987		With Pak
MBT	Type-90-II		Domestic	1990	1997	Development of Type 85IIM; trials 1996
APC	Type-90	2,000	Domestic	1990	1995	Family of 12 AFVs; 400 delivered 1996
LPH		1	Domestic	1996	2000	
DDG	*Sovremenny*	2	RF	1997		
DMS		1	Domestic		1997	10,000ton Defence Mobilisation Ship
FF	*Luhu*-class	3	Domestic	1991	1996	Second of class commissioned in 1996
SS	*Song*-class	3	Domestic	1985	1996	
SS	*Ming*-class	6	Domestic	1992	1996	1 delivered 1996
SS	*Kilo* 636	4	RF	1993	1995	Deliveries to 1998
SSBN	Type 094	1	Domestic	1985	2000	Development; to carry JL-2 SLBM
SSGN	Type 093	1	Domestic	1985	2002	Similar to Russian *Victor* 3
Indonesia						
trg/FGA	*Hawk*	40	UK	1993	1996	Deliveries to 1999
FGA	Su-30K	12	RF	1997		
hel	Mi-17	8	RF	1997		
tpt	*Nomad*	20	Aus		1997	Delivered in three batches by Jun 1997
lt tk	*Scorpion*	100	UK	1993	1995	Deliveries to 1998
LAV	*Glover Webb*	16	UK	1993	1995	Delivered 1995–96; with water cannon
corvette	*Parchim*	16	Ge	1992	1996	
LST	*Frosch*	14	Ge	1992	1995	
SS	Type 206	5	Ge	1997	1998	2 late 1997, 2 1998, plus 1 for spares
tpt		1	RF	1997		Military personnel transport ship
MPA	CN-235MP	3	Domestic	1996		
Japan						
FGA	F-2	130	Domestic	1997		
trg	T-4	59	Domestic	1997		MTDP for 59; 9 ordered 1996
SAR	U-125	27	US	1997		Delivery to 2004
hel	S70	46	Domestic	1997		Licensed production
MPA	*Gulfstream* IV	10	US	1996	1997	Delivery to 2000
SAM	*Patriot*		US	1997		$179.4m for undisclosed number
hel	OH-1	193	Domestic	1992	1997	First 3 delivered 1997
hel	CH-47J	18	Domestic	1997		
MBT	Type-90	96	Domestic	1996		
MLRS		45	Domestic	1996		MTDP for total of 45
arty	FH70	45	Domestic	1996		155mm
DDG	*Kongo*	4	Domestic	1988	1998	3 early 1997; fourth to deliver 1998
DDG	DD-01	6	Domestic	1981	2000	Deliveries to 2000
LPD	*Osumi*	1	Domestic		1998	
MCM	*Hatsushima*	20	Domestic	1976	1996	
SS	*Harushio*-class	3	Domestic	1993	1998	
PCO	PM 15	1	Domestic		1995	
Laos						
hel	Mi-17	12	RF	1997		2 delivered 1998, 10 mid-1999
Malaysia						
FGA	MiG-29	18	RF	1993	1995	

Equipment	Type	Unit	Supplier	Order Date	Delivery Date	Comment
FGA	F/A-18C/D	8	US	1993	1997	First 4 delivered May 1997
msl	R27RI	131	Ukr	1993	1995	
tkr	KC-130H	2	UK	1995	1997	Conversion programme
trg/FGA	*Hawk*	28	UK	1990	1995	Deliveries completed 1995
tpt	C-130H	5	US	1993	1995	
trg	MD3-160	20	Domestic	1993	1995	Deliveries continued 1996
APC	KIFV	47	ROK		1995	Deliveries continued 1995
hel	S-70A	2	US	1996		
corvette	*Assad*-class	4	It	1995	1997	
FF	*Lekiu*-class	2	UK	1992	1996	Not fully operational
LST	*Newport*	1	US	1993	1995	EDA
New Zealand						
tpt	C-130J	8	US	1996	1998	Joint procurement with Aus
SAM	*Mistral*	12	Fr	1997		With 23 missiles
AK		1	De		1995	Military sea-lift ship
FF	*Anzac*-class	2	Aus	1990	1997	Option for 2 more
hel	SH-2G	4	US	1997	2001	
TAGOS	*Stalwart*	1	US	1996		Towed array ship
North Korea						
SSM	*Rodong*		Domestic			Production
SSM	*Nodong*		Domestic			Development
SS		4	Domestic			Production
Papua New Guinea						
mor	120mm mor	3	Sgp		1996	
LAV	CAV100	1	UK	1996	1996	
LAV	*Defender*	2	UK	1996	1996	
Philippines						
FGA	F-4A	3	ROK		1995	Surplus
tpt	C-130B	8	US	1991	1995	EDA; delivery unconfirmed
ACV	SINBA	61	UK		1995	
Singapore						
FGA	F-16	30	US	1994	1995	Deliveries to 1998
tkr	KC-130B/H	5	US		1996	4 -130B, 1 -130H
tkr	KC-135R	4	US	1996	1997	US surplus
tpt hel	CH-47	6	US	1997	1998	
OPV	*Fearless*	12	Domestic		1997	
PCI	PN 94	12	Domestic	1993	1998	
SS	*Sjobjornen*	4	Swe	1995	1997	First delivery 1997
South Korea						
FGA	F-16C/D	120	US	1992	1995	Deliveries to 1999
recce	HS 800	10	US	1996	1999	
trg	KTX-2	94	Domestic	1992	2005	Development recommenced 1997
trg	T-38	30	US	1996	1997	US surplus
SAM	*Stinger*	213	US	1997		213 launchers, 1,065 missiles
AIFV	BMP-3	30	RF	1995	1996	Deliveries to 1998, 23 delivered 1997
APC	BTR-80		RF	1995	1995	Deliveries to 1998
APC	KIFV		Domestic			Production continues; 1,700 by 1996
arty	M-109	90	US		1995	30 delivered
arty	M-110	13	US	1995	1995	EDA
MBT	K2			1997		Development
MBT	T-80U	33	RF	1995	1996	
MRL	227mm	29	US	1997		29 launch vehicles , 111 ATACMs
UAV	*Searcher*	100	Il	1997	1999	
hel	UH-60P	57	US		1999	Potential order for 60–80 more
FF	KDX-2000	3	Domestic		1998	Deliveries to 2000

Equipment	Type	Unit	Supplier	Order Date	Delivery Date	Comment
SS	Type-209	9	Ge	1989	1996	Licensed production; delivery to 2002
hel	*Super Lynx*	13	UK	1997		
Taiwan						
AEW	E-2T	4	US	1993	1995	
FGA	*Ching-Kuo*	130	Domestic	1982	1997	Deliveries to 2000
FGA	*Mirage* 2000-5	60	Fr	1992	1997	5 delivered May 1997, 5 Jul 1997
FGA	F-16C/D	150	US	1992	1997	6 delivered to May 1997
MPA	P-3		US	1996		With *Harpoon* missiles
tpt	C-130	12	US	1993	1995	8 delivered 1995, 4 more ordered 1996
trg	T-38	120	US	1993	1995	EDA
SAM	*Stinger*	1,299	US	1996	1998	
MBT	M-60A3	300	US	1995		US surplus; 160 delivered to 1996
lt tk	M41	50	US	1997		Upgrade to M41D standard
SAM	*Avenger*	74	US		1998	
SAM	*Patriot* PAC III	6	US	1994	1997	6 fire-control units, 200 missiles
SAM	*Mistral*	550	Fr	1995		
hel	OH-58D	28	US	1992	1996	
hel	AH-1W	81	US	1992	1995	Deliveries to 1999
hel	TH-67	30	US	1996		
FF	*Perry*-class	7	US	1979	1998	
FF	*La Fayette*	6	Fr	1992	1996	
FFG	*Knox*	9	US		1995	6 delivered 1995, order for 3 more
FFG	*Cheng Kung*	7	Domestic		1998	Fifth commissioned Jan 1997
LST	*Newport*	2	US	1994	1997	Commissioned May 1997
MSC	*Aggressive*	4	US	1994	1995	EDA
OPV	*Jin Chiang*	13	Domestic		1994	
Thailand						
FGA	F-16A/B	12	US	1992	1995	
SAM	RBS NS-70		Swe	1996	1997	To replace PRC-manufactured *Strela*
tpt	CN-235	2	Indo	1996		
trg	L-39	36	CZ	1994	1995	
MBT	M60A3	24	US	1995	1996	
ACV	*Condor*	18	Ge	1995	1996	
ACV	V-150	12	US	1995	1996	
APC	M113	82	US	1995	1996	US surplus
arty	*Canon* 105 LG1	24	Fr	1995	1996	Deliveries completed 1997
arty	155mm	72	CH	1995	1996	Deliveries to 1997
hel	AS-532	3	Fr	1995	1996	
CV	CV-911	1	Sp	1992	1997	
FF	Type 26-T	2	PRC	1991	1995	Second delivery late 1996–early 1997
FF	*Knox*-class	2	US		1996	US surplus
MCMV	*Gaeta*	2	It	1996	1998	Second delivery 1999
hel	S-70B	6	US	1993	1997	1 delivered Mar 1997, last by Jun 1997
FGA	A-7	18	US	1995	1997	EDA
FGA	AV-8S	9	Sp	1995	1997	
FGA	F/A-18C/D	8	US	1996	1999	4 -18C, 4 -18D; includes *Harpoon*
hel	S-76N	6	US		1996	
MPA	P-3	6	US	1993	1995	
Vietnam						
corvette	*Tarantul*-class	2	RF		1995	
PFC		3	RF		1996	
FGA	SU-27	12	RF	1993	1995	6 delivered 1995
FGA	MiG-21B	6	Ukr		1996	For trg
msl	R27RI (470-1)	14	Ukr		1995	
PFM	*Tarantul*	4	Domestic			2 being built in Vn

Australia

	1995	1996	1997	1998
GDP	A$473bn	A$502bn		
	($351bn)	($392bn)		
per capita	$19,000	$20,000		
Growth	3.7%	4.0%		
Inflation	4.7%	2.6%		
Publ Debt	43.4%	43.8%		
Def exp	A$11.3bn	A$11.0bn		
	($8.4bn)	($8.6bn)		
Def bdgt			A$10.0bn	A$10.4bn
			($7.8bn)	($8.1bn)
US$1 = A$	1.35	1.28	1.28	
Population		18,661,000		
(Asian 4%, Aborigines <1%)				
Age	*13–17*	*18–22*	*23–32*	
Men	675,000	691,000	1,519,000	
Women	636,000	658,000	1,467,000	

Total Armed Forces

ACTIVE 57,400

(incl 7,500 women)

RESERVES 33,650
GENERAL RESERVE
Army 25,100 **Navy** 4,700 **Air Force** 3,850

Army 25,400

(incl 2,600 women)
1 Land HQ, 1 northern comd • 1 inf div, 2 bde HQ • 1 armd regt HQ (1 active, 2 reserve sqn) • 1 recce regt (2 sqn) • 1 APC sqn • 5 inf bn (incl 1 AB, 1 mech) • 2 arty regt (1 fd, 1 med (each 2 bty)) • 1 AD regt (2 bty) • 2 cbt engr regt • 1 SAS regt (3 sqn) • 2 avn regt

RESERVES

GENERAL RESERVE 25,100
1 div HQ, 7 bde HQ, 1 armd sqn, 1 APC regt, 2 APC sqn, 2 recce regt, 1 recce sqn, 1 APC/recce regt, 14 inf bn, 1 cdo (2 coy), 4 arty regt (3 fd, 1 med), 4 indep arty bty, 5 engr regt (3 cbt, 2 construction), 4 indep engr sqn, 3 regional surv units

EQUIPMENT

MBT 71 *Leopard* 1A3 (excl variants)
AIFV 46 M-113 with **76mm** gun
APC 463 M-113 (excl variants, 364 to be upgraded, 119 in store), 111 ASLAV-25
TOWED ARTY 385: **105mm**: 246 M2A2/L5, 104 *Hamel*; **155mm**: 35 M-198
MOR 81mm: 296
RCL 84mm: 577 *Carl Gustav*; **106mm**: 74 M-40A1
SAM 19 *Rapier*, 17 RBS-70
AC 3 *King Air* 200, 1 DHC-6 (all on lease)

HEL 38 S-70 A-9, 43 Bell 206 B-1 *Kiowa* (to be upgraded), 25 UH-1H (armed), 18 AS-350B, 4 CH-47D
MARINES 15 LCM, 53 LARC-5 amph craft
SURV 14 RASIT (veh, arty), AN-TPQ-36 (arty, mor)

Navy 14,300

(incl 990 Fleet Air Arm, 2,200 women)
Maritime Comd, Support Comd, Training Comd
BASES Sydney, NSW (Maritime Comd HQ) 3 DDG, 3 FFG, 2 PFI, 1 LSH, 1 AO, 2 LCH, 2 MSI, 5 MSA **Garden Island, WA** 3 SS, 3 FFG, 1 DD, 1 FFH, 1 AO, 2 PFC, 1 AGS, 1 ASR **Cairns, Qld** 5 PFC, 5 AGS, 2 LCH **Darwin, NT** 6 PFC, 1 LCH

SUBMARINES 3

2 *Oxley* (mod UK *Oberon*) (incl 1 in refit) with Mk 48 HWT and *Harpoon* SSM (plus 1 alongside trg)
1 *Collins* with sub-*Harpoon* and MK48 HW7

PRINCIPAL SURFACE COMBATANTS 10

DESTROYERS 3 *Perth* (US *Adams*) DDG with 1 SM-1 MR SAM/*Harpoon* SSM launcher; plus 2 x 3 ASTT (Mk 46 LWT), 2 127mm guns
FRIGATES 7
6 *Adelaide* (US *Perry*), with S-70B-2 *Sea Hawk*, 2 x 3 ASTT; plus 1 SM-1 MR SAM/*Harpoon* SSM launcher
1 *Anzac* with *Sea Sparrow* VLS, 1 127mm gun, 6 324mm TT, plus hel

PATROL AND COASTAL COMBATANTS 15

PATROL, INSHORE 15 *Fremantle* PFI

MINE COUNTERMEASURES 7

2 *Rushcutter* MHI, 2 *Bandicoot*, 2 *Kooraaga* MSA, 1 *Brolga* MSI

AMPHIBIOUS 6

5 *Balikpapan* LCH, capacity 3 tk (plus 3 in store)
1 *Tobruk* LST
Plus 2 ex-US *Newport*-class LST under conversion, no beach-landing capability and equipping for 6 Army *Blackhawk* or *Sea King* hel

SUPPORT AND MISCELLANEOUS 9

1 *Success* (mod Fr *Durance*), 1 *Westralia* AO, 1 *Protector* sub trials and safety, 2 AGS, 4 small AGHS

FLEET AIR ARM (990)

no cbt ac, 16 armed hel
ASW 1 hel sqn with 16 S-70B-2 *Sea Hawk*
UTL/SAR 1 sqn with 6 AS-350B, 3 Bell 206B and 2 BAe-748 (EW trg), 1 hel sqn with 7 *Sea King* Mk 50/50A

Air Force 17,700

(incl 2,700 women); 126 cbt ac incl MR, no armed hel

Flying hours F-111, 200; F/A-18, 175
FGA/RECCE 2 sqn with 17 F-111C, 15 F-111G, 4 RF-111C
FTR/FGA 3 sqn with 52 F/A-18 (50 -A, 2 -B)
OCU 1 with 17* F/A-18B
TAC TRG 1 sqn with 16 MB-326H, 3 PC-9A
AIRCRAFT R&D 2* F/A-18, 4 C-47
MR 2 sqn with 19* P-3C
FAC 1 flt with 3 PC-9
TKR 4 Boeing 707
TPT 7 sqn
  2 with 24 C-130 (12 -E, 12 -H)
  1 with 5 Boeing 707 (4 fitted for AAR)
  2 with 14 DHC-4 (*Caribou*)
  1 VIP with 5 *Falcon* 900
  1 with 10 HS-748 (8 for navigation trg, 2 for VIP tpt)
TRG 59 PC-9, 14 MB-326
AD *Jindalee* OTH radar: 1 experimental, 3 planned
  3 control and reporting units (1 mobile)
MISSILES
  ASM AGM-84A, AGM-142
  AAM AIM-7 *Sparrow*, AIM-9M *Sidewinder*

Forces Abroad

Advisers in **Fji**, **Indo**, **Solomon Islands**, **Th**, **Vanuatu**, **Tonga**, **Western Samoa**, **Kiribati**
MALAYSIA Army ε115; 1 inf coy (on 3-month rotational tours) **Air Force** 33; det with 2 P-3C **ac**
PAPUA NEW GUINEA 38; trg unit
UN AND PEACEKEEPING
CYPRUS (UNFICYP): 20 plus 20 civ pol. **EGYPT** (MFO): 26 Obs. **MIDDLE EAST** (UNTSO): 12 Obs

Paramilitary

AUSTRALIAN CUSTOMS SERVICE
  ac 3 DHC-8, 3 *Reims* F406, 6 BN-2B-20, 1 *Strike Aerocommander* 500 **hel** 1 Bell 206L-4; about 6 boats

Foreign Forces

US Navy 35; joint facilities at NW Cape, Pine Gap and Nurrungar
NEW ZEALAND Air Force 47; 6 A-4K/TA-4K, (trg for Australian Navy); 10 navigation trg
SINGAPORE 160; Flying Training School with 27 S-211 **ac**

Brunei

	1995	1996	1997	1998
GDP	εB$6.9bn	εB$7.3bn		
	($4.8bn)	($5.2bn)		
per capita	$6,800	$7,100		

contd	1995	1996	1997	1998
Growth	ε3.0%	ε4.0%		
Inflation	ε2.5%	ε2.8%		
Debt	$0	$0		
Def exp	B$390m	εB$475m		
	($268m)	($337m)		
Def bdgt			εB$490m	
			($343m)	
US$1 = B$	1.45	1.41	1.43	
Population		310,000		

(Muslim 71%; also Malay 67%, Chinese 16%, non-Malay indigenous 6%)

Age	*13–17*	*18–22*	*23–32*
Men	15,000	13,000	28,000
Women	14,000	14,000	24,000

Total Armed Forces

ACTIVE 5,000
(incl 600 women)

RESERVES 700
Army 700

Army 3,900

(incl 250 women)
3 inf bn • 1 armd recce sqn • 1 SAM bty: 2 tps with *Rapier* • 1 engr sqn

EQUIPMENT
  LT TK 16 *Scorpion*
  APC 26 VAB, 2 *Sultan*, 24 AT-104 (in store)
  MOR 81mm: 24
  RL *Armbrust* (reported)
  SAM 12 *Rapier* (with *Blindfire*)

RESERVES
1 bn

Navy 700

BASE Muara
PATROL AND COASTAL COMBATANTS 9†
MISSILE CRAFT 3 *Waspada* PFM with 2 MM-38 *Exocet* SSM
PATROL, INSHORE 3 *Perwira* PFI<
PATROL, RIVERINE 3 *Rotork* Marine FPB plus boats
AMPHIBIOUS craft only
  4 LCU<; 1 SF sqn

Air Force 400

no cbt ac, 6 armed hel
HEL 2 sqn
  1 with 10 Bell 212, 1 Bell 214 (SAR), 4 UH-60L, 4 S-70
  1 with 6 Bo-105 armed hel (**81mm** rockets)

VIP TPT 2 S-70 hel, 2 Bell 412ST
TRG ac 2 SF-260W, 4 PC-7, 1 CN235 **hel** 2 Bell 206B

Paramilitary 4,050

GURKHA RESERVE UNIT 2,300+
2 bn
ROYAL BRUNEI POLICE 1,750
8 PCI<

Foreign Forces

UK Army some 900; 1 Gurkha inf bn, 1 hel flt
SINGAPORE ε500; trg school incl hel det (5 UH-1)

Cambodia

	1995	1996	1997	1998
GDP	r7.2tr	r8.5tr		
	($2.9bn)	($3.2bn)		
per capita	$600	$700		
Growth	7.5%	7.6%		
Inflation	7.8%	7.2%		
Debt	$2.0bn	$2.1bn		
Def exp	r309bn	r330bn		
	($126m)	($126m)		
Def bdgt			r372bn	
			($136m)	
FMA (US)	$0.3m	$1.4m	$1.5m	$1.6m
(Aus)	$3.0m	$2.0m	$2.0m	
(PRC)		$3.0m		
$1 = riel	2,451	2,624	2,738	
Population		10,205,000		
(Vietnamese 5%, Chinese 1%)				
Age	*13–17*	*18–22*	*23–32*	
Men	548,000	456,000	864,000	
Women	538,000	448,000	871,000	

Total Armed Forces

ACTIVE ε140,500
(incl Provincial Forces, perhaps only 19,000 cbt capable)
Terms of service: conscription authorised but not implemented since 1993

Army ε84,000

6 Mil Regions (incl 1 special zone for capital) • 12 inf div[a] • 3 indep inf bde • 1 protection bde (4 bn) • 9 indep inf regt • 3 armd bn • 1 AB/SF regt • 4 engr regt (3 fd, 1 construction) • some indep recce, arty, AD bn
EQUIPMENT

MBT 100 T-54/-55, plus PRC Type-59
LT TK 10 PT-76
APC 210 BTR-60/-152, M-113, 40 OT-64 (SKOT)
TOWED ARTY some 400: **76mm**: M-1942; **122mm**: M-1938, D-30; **130mm**: Type 59
MRL 107mm: Type-63; **122mm**: 8 BM-21; **132mm**: BM-13-16; **140mm**: 20 BM-14-16
MOR 82mm: M-37; **120mm**: M-43; **160mm**: M-160
RCL 82mm: B-10; **107mm**: B-11
AD GUNS 14.5mm: ZPU 1/-2/-4; **37mm**: M-1939; **57mm**: S-60
SAM SA-7

[a] Inf div established str 3,500, actual str some 1,500

Navy 5,000

(incl 1,500 Naval Infantry)
PATROL AND COASTAL COMBATANTS 13
PATROL, INSHORE 4
  2 Sov *Turya* PFI (no TT)
  2 Sov *Stenka* PFI (no TT), 1 x 2 23mm gun
RIVERINE 9
  4 Sov *Shmel* PCI< †, 2 Sov *Zhuk* PCI<, 3 Sov LCVP, plus boats

NAVAL INFANTRY (1,500)
  7 inf, 1 arty bn

Air Force ε1,500

23 cbt ac†; no armed hel
FTR 21† MiG-21
TPT 3 An-24, 1 An-26, Tu-134, 2 Y-12, 1 BN-2
HEL 2 Mi-8, 7 Mi-17, 2 Mi-26
TRG 2* L-39, 5 *Tecnam* P-92

Provincial Forces some 50,000

Reports of at least 1 inf regt per province, with varying numbers of inf bn with lt wpn

Paramilitary

MILITIA
org at village level for local defence: ε10–20 per village; not all armed

Opposition

KHMER ROUGE (National Army of Democratic Kampuchea) perhaps 3,500

FUNCINPEC/KHMER PEOPLE'S LIBERATION FRONT (KPNLF) ε10,000
alliance between Prince Ranariddh's party and the KPNLF

China

	1995	1996	1997	1998
GDP	Y5.8tr	Y6.8tr		
	($560bn)	($616bn)		
per capita	$2,800	$3,100		
Growth	10.2%	9.7%		
Inflation	16.9%	8.3%		
Debt	$118bn	$128bn		
Def exp[a]	ε$33bn	ε$38bn		
Def bdgt[b]	Y63.3bn	Y71.5bn	Y80.6bn	
	($7.6bn)	($8.6bn)	($9.7bn)	
$1 = yuan	8.35	8.33	8.30	

[a] PPP est incl extra-budgetary mil exp
[b] Def bdgt shows official figures at market rates

Population	1,221,621,000		

(Tibetan, Uighur and other non-Han 8% *Xinjiang*
Muslim ε60%; Uighur ε44% *Tibet* Chinese ε60%,
Tibetan ε40%)

Age	13–17	18–22	23–32
Men	49,858,000	53,657,000	121,823,000
Women	46,816,000	50,251,000	113,906,000

Total Armed Forces

ACTIVE some 2,840,000

(perhaps 1,275,000 conscripts, some 136,000 women),
being reduced
Terms of service: selective conscription
Army, Marines 3 years **Navy, Air Force** 4 years

RESERVES 1,200,000+

militia reserves being formed on a province-wide basis

Strategic Missile Forces

OFFENSIVE (125,000)

org in 6 bases (army level) with bde/regt incl 1 msl
testing and trg regt; org varies by msl type
ICBM 17+
  7 CSS-4 (DF-5); mod tested with MIRV
  10+ CSS-3 (DF-4)
IRBM ε46+
  38+ CSS-2 (DF-3), some updated
  ε8 CSS-5 (DF-21)
SLBM 1 *Xia* SSBN with 12 CSS-N-3 (J-1)
SSM 4 DF-15 (CSS-6/M-9) (range 600km), DF-11
  (CSS-7/M-11) (range 120–300+km)

DEFENSIVE

Tracking stations Xinjiang (covers Central Asia) and
  Shanxi (northern border)
Phased-array radar complex ballistic-missile early-
  warning

Army 2,090,000

(perhaps 1,075,000 conscripts) (reductions continue)
7 Mil Regions, 27 Mil Districts, 3 Garrison Comd
24 Integrated Group Armies (GA: 60–90,000, equivalent to Western corps), org varies, normally with 3
  inf div, 1 tk, 1 arty, 1 AAA bde or 3 inf, 1 tk div, 1
  arty, 1 AAA bde, cbt readiness category varies
Summary of cbt units
Group Army 73 inf div (e 2 mech inf) incl 3 with
  rapid-reaction role and 9 ready to mobilise in 24-48
  hours; 11 tk div, 13 tk bde, 5 arty div, 20 arty bde, 7
  hel regt
Independent 5 inf div, 1 tk, 2 inf bde, 1 arty div, 3 arty
  bde, 4 AAA bde
Local Forces (Garrison, Border, Coastal) 12 inf div, 1
  mtn bde, 4 inf bde, 87 inf regt/bn
AB (manned by Air Force) 1 corps of 3 div
Support Troops incl 50 engr, 50 sigs regt

EQUIPMENT

  MBT some 8,500: incl 700 T-34/85 (trg), 6,000 Type-
    59-I/-II, 200 Type-69-I/-II (mod Type-59), 800
    Type-69III/-79, 400 Type-80, 400 Type-85 IIM
  LT TK 1,200 Type-63 amph, 800 Type-62
  AIFV/APC 5,500 incl Type-63, some Type-77 (BTR-
    50PK), Type-90, WZ-523, WZ-551
  TOWED ARTY 14,500: **100mm**: Type-59 (fd/ATK);
    122mm: Type-54, Type-60, Type-83, Type-85;
    130mm: Type-59/-59-1; **152mm**: Type-54, Type-66,
    Type-83; **155mm**: WAC-21
  SP ARTY 122mm: Type-70 (Type-63 APC chassis),
    Type-85; **152mm**: Type-83
  MRL 122mm: Type-81, Type-89 SP; **130mm**: Type-70
    SP, Type-82, Type-85 SP; **273mm**: Type-83
  MOR 82mm: Type-53/-67/-W87/-82 (incl SP);
    100mm: Type-71 reported; **120mm**: Type-55 (incl
    SP); **160mm**: Type-56
  ATGW HJ-73 (*Sagger*-type), HJ-8 (TOW/*Milan*-type)
  RCL 75mm: Type-52, Type-56; **82mm**: Type-65;
    105mm: Type-75
  RL 90mm: Type-51
  ATK GUNS 57mm: Type-55; **76mm**: Type-54;
    100mm: Type-73, Type-86; **120mm**: Type-89 SP
  AD GUNS 23mm: Type-80; **37mm**: Type-55/-65/-
    74; **57mm**: Type-59, -80 SP; **85mm**: Type-56;
    100mm: Type-59
  SAM HN-5A/-C (SA-7 type), QW-1, HQ-61A
  SURV *Cheetah* (arty), Type-378 (veh), RASIT (veh,
    arty)
  HEL 28+ Mi-17, 25 Mi-8, Mi-6, 30 Z-9, 8 SA-342
    (with HOT), 20 S-70, some Z-9
  UAV *Chang Hong* 1, ASN-104/-105

RESERVES

(undergoing major re-org on provincial basis): perhaps
1,200,000; 120 inf div

DEPLOYMENT

(GA units only)
North-east Shenyang MR (Heilongjiang, Jilin,

Liaoning MD): 5 GA, 3 tk, 15 inf, 1 arty div

North Beijing MR (Beijing, Tianjin Garrison, Nei Mong-gol, Hebei, Shanxi MD): 6 GA, 3 tk, 19 inf, 1 arty div

West Lanzhou MR (incl Ningxia, Shaanxi, Gansu, Qing-hai, Xinjiang MD): 2 GA, 1 tk, 12 inf div

South-west Chengdu MR (incl Sichuan, Guizhou, Yunnan, Xizang MD): 2 GA, 7 inf, 1 arty div

South Guangzhou MR (Hubei, Hunan, Guangdong, Guangxi, Hainan MD): 2 GA, 6 inf, 2 AB (Air Force) div. Hong Kong: ε4,500: 1 inf bde (3 inf, 1 mot inf, 1 arty, 1 engr regt), 1 hel unit

Centre Jinan MR (Shandong, Henan MD): 4 GA, 2 tk, 13 inf, 1 AB (Air Force), 1 arty div

East Nanjing MR (Shanghai Garrison, Jiangsu, Zhejiang, Fujian, Jiangxi, Anhui MD): 3 GA, 2 tk, 11 inf, 1 arty div

Navy ε280,000

(incl 29,000 Coastal Regional Defence Forces, 27,000 Naval Air Force, some 5,000 Marines and some 40,000 conscripts)

SUBMARINES 61

(some may be armed with Russian wake-homing torpedoes)

STRATEGIC 1 SSBN

TACTICAL 59

SSN 5 *Han* with 533mm TT

SSG 1 mod *Romeo* (Type S5G), with 6 C-801 (YJ-6, *Exocet* derivative) SSM; plus 533mm TT (test platform)

SS 53

1 *Song* with YJ-82 SLCM (C802 derivative – submerged launch anti-ship op late 1998), 6 533mm TT

2 *Kilo*-class (Type EKM 877) with 533mm TT, prob wake-homing torpedo

1 *Kilo*-class (Type EKM 636) with 533mm TT, prob wake-homing torpedo

13 imp *Ming* (Type ES5E) with 533mm TT

36 *Romeo* (Type ES3B)† with 533mm TT (some 32 additional *Romeo*-class mothballed)

OTHER ROLES 1 *Golf* (SLBM trials)

PRINCIPAL SURFACE COMBATANTS 54

DESTROYERS 18

2 *Luhu* with 4 x 2 C-801 SSM, 1 x 2 100mm gun, 2 Z-9A (Fr *Dauphin*) hel, plus 2 x 3 ASTT, 1 x 8 *Crotale* SAM

1 *Luda* III with 4 x 2 C-801 SSM, 4 130mm gun, 6 324mm TT

1 mod *Luda*, 1 with 2 x 4 CSS-N-4 *Eagle Strike* SSM and 1 with 4 x 2 C-801 SSM, 1 x 2 130mm guns, 2 Z-9A (Fr *Dauphin*) hel (OTHT), 2 x 3 ASTT, 1 x 8 *Crotale* SAM

14 *Luda* (Type-051) (ASUW) with 2 x 3 HY 2 SSM, 2 x 2 130mm guns; plus 2 x 12 ASW RL

FRIGATES about 36

4 *Jiangwei* with 2 x 3 C-801 SSM, 2 x 5 ASW RL, 1 x 2 100mm gun, 1 Z-9A (Fr *Dauphin*) hel

About 30 *Jianghu*; 3 variants:

About 26 Type I, with 4 x 5 ASW RL, plus 2 x 2 HY 2 SSM, 2 100mm guns

About 1 Type II, with 2 x 5 ASW RL, plus 2 x 2 HY 2, 2 x 2 100mm guns

About 3 Type III, with 8 C-801 SSM, 2 x 2 100mm guns; plus 4 x 5 ASW RL

2 *Chengdu* with 1 x 2 HY 2 SSM, 3 100mm guns

PATROL AND COASTAL COMBATANTS about 830

MISSILE CRAFT about 188

1 *Huang* with 6 C-801 SSM

12 *Houxin* with 4 C-801 SSM

Some 100 *Huangfeng/Hola* (Sov *Osa* I-Type) with 6 or 8 C-801 SSM; some with 4 HY-2

About 75 *Hegu/Hema*< (*Komar*-Type) with 2 HY 2 or 4 C-801 SSM

TORPEDO CRAFT about 150

100 *Huchuan*

some 50 P-6, all < with 2 533mm TT

PATROL CRAFT about 495

COASTAL about 100

4 *Haijui* with 3 x 5 ASW RL

About 96 *Hainan* with 4 ASW RL

INSHORE about 350

300 *Shanghai*, 5 *Huludao* PFI, about 45 *Shantou*<, some *Huang Pu*

RIVERINE about 45<

(Some minor combatants have reportedly been assigned to paramilitary forces (People's Armed Police, border guards, the militia) to the Customs Service, or into store. Totals, therefore, may be high)

MINE WARFARE about 121

MINELAYERS 1 *Beleijan* reported

In addition, *Luda* and *Jiangnan*-class DD/FF, *Hainan*, *Shanghai* PC and T-43 MSO have minelaying capability

MINE COUNTERMEASURES about 120

35 Sov T-43 MSO

1 *Wosao* MSC

About 80 *Lienyun* aux MSC

3 *Wochang* and 1 *Shanghai* II MSI; plus about 60 drone MSI<

AMPHIBIOUS 71

7 *Yukan* LST, capacity about 200 tps, 10 tk

13 *Shan* (US LST-1) LST, capacity about 150 tps, 16 tk

5 *Yuting* LST, capacity 4 *Jingsah* ACV, 2 hel plus tps

31 *Yuliang*, 1 *Yuling*, 1 *Yudeng* LSM, capacity about 100 tps, 3 tk

9 *Wuhu-A* LSM capacity 250 tps, 2 tk

6 *Quonsha* shock tpt capacity 400 tps, 350 tons cargo

Plus about 140 craft: 90 LCU, 40 LCP, 10 LCT

SUPPORT AND MISCELLANEOUS about 165

2 *Fuqing* AO, 33 AOT, 14 AF, 10 submarine spt, 1 submarine rescue, 2 repair, 9 *Qiongsha* tps tpt, 30

tpt, 33 survey/research/experimental, 4 icebreakers, 1 DMS, 25 ocean tugs, 1 trg

COASTAL REGIONAL DEFENCE FORCES (29,000)

ε35 indep arty and SSM regt deployed in 25 coastal defence regions to protect naval bases, offshore islands and other vulnerable points
GUNS 85mm, 100mm, 130mm
SSM *HY* 2/CSS-C-3, *HY* 4/CSS-C-7

MARINES (some 5,000)

1 bde; special recce units
RESERVES on mob to total 8 div (24 inf, 8 tk, 8 arty regt), 2 indep tk regt. 3 Army div also have amph role

EQUIPMENT

MBT Type-59
LT TK Type-63 amph
APC Type-77-II
ARTY 122mm: Type-54, Type-70 SP
MRL 107mm: Type-63

NAVAL AIR FORCE (25,000)

535 shore-based cbt ac, 25 armed hel
BBR 7 H-6, 9 H-6D reported with two YJ anti-ship ALCM; about 60 H-5 torpedo-carrying lt bbr
FGA some 40 Q-5
FTR some 295 J-6, 66 J-7, 30 J-8
RECCE HZ-5
MR/ASW 4* ex-Sov Be-6 *Madge*, 4* PS-5 (SH-5)
HELICOPTERS
  ASW 9 SA-321, 4 Z-8, 12 Z-9
  TPT 76 Y-5, 4 Y-7, 6 Y-8, 2 YAK-42, 6 An-26, 8 Mi-8
  TRG 53 PT-6, 16* JJ-6, 4* JJ-7
ALCM YJ-6/C-601

(Naval ftr integrated into national AD system)

DEPLOYMENT AND BASES

NORTH SEA FLEET

coastal defence from Korean border (Yalu River) to south of Lianyungang (approx 35°10′N); equates to Shenyang, Beijing and Jinan MR, and to seaward
BASES Qingdao (HQ), Dalian (Luda), Huludao, Weihai, Chengshan, Yuchi; 9 coastal defence districts
FORCES 2 submarine, 3 escort, 1 mine warfare, 1 amph sqn; plus Bohai Gulf trg flotillas; about 300 patrol and coastal combatants

EAST SEA FLEET

coastal defence from south of Lianyungang to Dongshan (approx 35°10′N to 23°30′N); equates to Nanjing Military Region, and to seaward
BASES HQ Dongqian Lake (Ninbo), Shanghai Naval base, Dinghai, Hangzhou, Xiangshan; 7 coastal defence districts
FORCES 2 submarine, 2 escort, 1 mine warfare, 1 amph sqn; about 250 patrol and coastal combatants
  Naval Infantry 1 cadre div

Coastal Regional Defence Forces Nanjing Coastal District

SOUTH SEA FLEET

coastal defence from Dongshan (approx 23°30′N) to Vietnamese border; equates to Guangzhou MR, and to seaward (including Paracel and Spratly Islands)
BASE Hong Kong
  PATROL AND COASTAL COMBATANTS 8
    4 *Houjian* PGG with 6 C-801 SSM, 4 PCI
  SUPPORT AND MISCELLANEOUS 5
    2 *Yuliang* LSM capacity 60 tps 3 tk; 3 *Catamaran*
OTHER BASES Zhanjiang (HQ), Shantou, Guangzhou, Haikou, Dongguan city, Yulin, Beihai, Huangpu; plus outposts on Paracel and Spratly Islands; 9 coastal defence districts
FORCES 2 submarine, 2 escort, 1 mine warfare, 1 amph sqn; about 300 patrol and coastal combatants
  Naval Infantry 1 bde

Air Force 470,000

(incl strategic forces, 220,000 AD personnel and 160,000 conscripts); some 3,740 cbt ac, few armed hel
Flying hours H-6: 80; J-7 and J-8: 110; Su-27: 110+
7 Mil Air Regions, HQ Beijing
Combat elm org in armies of varying numbers of air div (each with 3 regt of 3 sqn of 3 flt of 3–4 ac, 1 maint unit, some tpt and trg ac); tpt ac in regt only
BBR med 100 H-6 (some may be nuclear-capable), some carry YJ-6/C-601 ASM **lt** some 200+ H-5 (some with YJ-8 ASM)
FGA 400+ Q-5
FTR ε2,748, some 60 regt with about 2,000 J-6/B/D/E, 500 J-7, 200 J-8, 40 Su-27, 8 Su-27B
RECCE ε290: ε40 HZ-5, 150 JZ-5, 100 JZ-6 ac
TPT incl 18 BAe *Trident* 1E/2E, 10 Il-18, 10 Il-76, 300 Y-5, 25 Y-7, 25 Y-8 (some tkr), 15 Y-11, 2 Y-12
HEL some 190: incl 6 AS-332, 4 Bell 214, 30 Mi-8, 100 Z-5, 50 Z-9
TRG incl HJ-5, JJ-6
MISSILES
  AAM PL-2/-2A, PL-5B, PL-7, PL-8, PL-9
  ASM YJ-1/2, C-801/802, YJ-6/C-601, C-601 subsonic ALCM (anti-ship, perhaps *HY* 2 SSM derivative); YJ-8 surface skimmer
AD ARTY 16 div: 16,000 **35mm, 57mm, 85mm** and **100mm** guns; 28 indep AD regts (100+ SAM units with HQ-2/-2B, -2J (CSA-1), SA-10)

Forces Abroad

UN AND PEACEKEEPING

MIDDLE EAST (UNTSO): 5 Obs. **IRAQ/KUWAIT** (UNIKOM): 11 Obs. **LIBERIA** (UNOMIL): 7 Obs. **WESTERN SAHARA** (MINURSO): 16 Obs

Paramilitary ε800,000 active

PEOPLE'S ARMED POLICE (Ministry of Defence) ε800,000 (to increase)

60 div incl **Internal security** ε500,000 **Border defence** 200,000 **Guards, Comms** ε69,000

Fiji

	1995	1996	1997	1998
GDP	F$2.8bn	F$3.0bn		
	($1.8bn)	($1.9bn)		
per capita	$5,300	$5,500		
Growth	2.2%	3.3%		
Inflation	2.2%	3.1%		
Debt	$253m	$232m		
Def exp	F$67m	F$68m		
	($48m)	($48m)		
Def bdgt			F$48m	
			($34m)	
FMA (Aus)	$4m	$3m	$3m	
US$1 = F$	1.41	1.41	1.40	
Population		790,000		

(Indian 49%, Fijian 46%, European/other 5%)

Age	*13–17*	*18–22*	*23–32*
Men	46,000	41,000	63,000
Women	44,000	39,000	61,000

Total Armed Forces

ACTIVE some 3,600
(incl recalled reserves)
RESERVES some 6,000
(to age 45)

Army 3,300

(incl 300 recalled reserves)
7 inf bn (incl 4 cadre) • 1 engr bn • 1 arty bty • 1 special ops coy
EQUIPMENT
 TOWED ARTY 88mm: 4 25-pdr (ceremonial)
 MOR 81mm: 12

Navy 300

BASES Walu Bay, Viti (trg)
PATROL AND COASTAL COMBATANTS 9
PATROL, INSHORE 9
 3 *Kulu* (*Pacific Forum*) PCI, 4 *Vai* (Il *Dabur*) PCI<, 2 *Levuka* PCI<
SUPPORT AND MISCELLANEOUS 1
 1 *Cagidonu* presidential yacht (trg)

Forces Abroad

UN AND PEACEKEEPING
CROATIA (UNTAES): 43 civ pol. **EGYPT** (MFO): 339; 1 inf bn(-). **IRAQ/KUWAIT** (UNIKOM): 5 Obs. **LEBANON** (UNIFIL): 596; 1 inf bn

Indonesia

	1995	1996	1997	1998
GDP	Rp452tr	Rp529tr		
	($201bn)	($226bn)		
per capita	$3,900	$4,200		
Growth	8.2%	7.8%		
Inflation	9.4%	8.0%		
Debt	$108bn	$120bn		
Def exp[a]	εRp9.9tr	εRp11.0tr		
	($4.4bn)	($4.7bn)		
Def bdgt			Rp8.0tr	
			($3.3bn)	
FMA (US)		$0.6m	$0.8m	
(Aus)	$4.0m	$4.0m		
$1 = rupiah	2,249	2,342	2,441	

[a] Incl mil exp on procurement and def industry

Population		198,011,000	

(Muslim 87%; also Javanese 45%, Sundanese 14%, Madurese 8%, Malay 8%, Chinese 3%, other 22%)

Age	*13–17*	*18–22*	*23–32*
Men	11,099,000	10,353,000	16,427,000
Women	10,615,000	9,999,000	17,270,000

Total Armed Forces

ACTIVE 461,000
(incl 177,000 Police (*POLRI*), see Paramilitary)
Terms of service: 2 years selective conscription authorised

RESERVES 400,000
Army cadre units; numbers, str n.k., obligation to age 45 for officers

Army 220,000

Strategic Reserve (KOSTRAD) (20,000)
 2 inf div HQ • 3 inf bde (9 bn) • 3 AB bde (9 bn) • 2 fd arty regt (6 bn) • 1 AD arty regt (2 bn) • 2 armd bn• 2 engr bn
10 Mil Area Comd (KODAM) (160–170,000)
(Provincial (KOREM) and District (KODIM) comd)
 2 inf bde (6 bn) • 67 inf bn (incl 4 AB) • 9 cav bn • 11 fd arty, 10 AD bn • 9 engr bn • 1 composite avn sqn, 1 hel sqn
Special Forces (KOPASSUS) (6–7,000 incl 4,800 cbt)
 subject to re-org; to be 5 SF gp (incl 2 cbt, 1 counter-

terrorist, 1 int, 1 trg)

EQUIPMENT

LT TK some 275 AMX-13 (to be upgraded), 30 PT-76, 50 *Scorpion* (incl 30 with **90mm**)

RECCE 69 *Saladin* (16 upgraded), 55 *Ferret* (13 upgraded), 18 VBL

APC 200 AMX-VCI, 55 *Saracen* (14 upgraded), 200 V-150 *Commando*, 22 *Commando Ranger*, 80 BTR-40, 14 BTR-50, 20 *Stormer* (incl variants)

TOWED ARTY 76mm: M48; **105mm**: 170 M-101, 10 M-56

MOR 875: **81mm**: 800; **120mm**: 75 Brandt

RCL 135: **90mm**: 90 M-67; **106mm**: 45 M-40A1

RL 89mm: 700 LRAC

AD GUNS 415: **20mm**: 125; **40mm**: 90 L/70; **57mm**: 200 S-60

SAM 93: 51 *Rapier*, 42 RBS-70

AC 1 BN-2 *Islander*, 2 C-47, 4 NC-212, 2 Cessna 310, 2 *Commander* 680, 18 *Gelatik* (trg), 3 DHC-5

HEL 9 Bell 205, 14 Bo-105, 7 NB-412, 10 Hughes 300C (trg)

Navy ε43,000 (increasing to 47,000)

(incl ε1,000 Naval Air and 12,000 Marines)

PRINCIPAL COMMAND

WESTERN FLEET HQ Teluk Ratai (Jakarta)
  BASES Primary Teluk Ratai, Belawan **Other** 10 plus minor facilities

EASTERN FLEET HQ Surabaya
  BASES Primary Surabaya, Ujung Pandang, Jaya Pura **Other** 13 plus minor facilities

MILITARY SEALIFT COMMAND (KOLINLAMIL)

controls some amph and tpt ships used for inter-island comms and log spt for Navy and Army (assets incl in Navy and Army listings)

SUBMARINES 2

2 *Cakra* (Ge T-209/1300) with 533mm TT (Ge HWT) (1 in long-term refit) (plus 2 Ge 206 late 1997)

FRIGATES 17

6 *Ahmad Yani* (Nl *Van Speijk*) with 1 *Wasp* hel (ASW) (Mk 44 LWT), 2 x 3 ASTT; plus 2 x 4 *Harpoon* SSM, 1 76mm gun

3 *Fatahillah* with 2 x 3 ASTT (not *Nala*), 1 x 2 ASW mor, 1 *Wasp* hel (*Nala* only); plus 2 x 2 MM-38 *Exocet*, 1 120mm gun

3 *M. K. Tiyahahu* (UK *Tribal*) with 1 *Wasp* hel, 1 x 3 *Limbo* ASW mor; plus 2 114mm guns

1 *Hajar Dewantara* (FRY) (trg) with 2 533mm TT, 1 ASW mor; plus 2 x 2 MM-38 *Exocet*, 1 57mm gun

4 *Samadikun* (US *Claud Jones*) with 2 x 3 ASTT

PATROL AND COASTAL COMBATANTS 59

CORVETTES 16 *Kapitan Patimura* (GDR *Parchim*)

MISSILE CRAFT 4 *Mandau* (Ko *Dagger*) PFM with 4 MM-38 *Exocet* SSM, 1 57mm gun

TORPEDO CRAFT 4 *Singa* (Ge Lürssen 57m (NAV I)) with 2 533mm TT and 1 57mm gun

PATROL CRAFT 35

  COASTAL 6
    2 *Pandrong* (Ge Lürssen 57m (NAV II)) PFC, with 1 57mm gun
    4 *Kakap* (Ge Lürssen 57m (NAV III)) PFC, with 40mm gun and hel deck

  INSHORE 29
    8 *Sibarau* (Aust *Attack*) PCI
    2 *Bima Samudera* PHT
    1 *Barabzuda* PCI
    18<

MINE COUNTERMEASURES 13

2 *Pulau Rengat* (mod Nl *Tripartite*) MCC (sometimes used for coastal patrol)

2 *Pulau Rani* (Sov T-43) MCC (mainly used for coastal patrol)

9 *Palau Rote* (Ge *Kondor* II)† MSC (mainly used for coastal patrol, 7 non-op)

AMPHIBIOUS 26

6 *Teluk Semangka* LST, capacity about 200 tps, 17 tk, 2 with 3 hel (1 fitted as hospital ship)

1 *Teluk Amboina* LST, capacity about 200 tps, 16 tk

7 *Teluk Langsa* (US LST-512) and 2 *Teluk Banten* (mod US LST-512) LST, capacity 200 tps, 16 tks)

12 *Teluk Gilimanuk* (Ge *Frosch* I/II) LST

Plus about 80 craft, incl 4 LCU, some 45 LCM

SUPPORT AND MISCELLANEOUS 15

1 *Sorong* AO, 1 *Arun* AOR (UK *Rover*), 2 Sov *Khobi* AOT, 1 cmd/spt/replenish, 1 repair, 2 ocean tug, 6 survey/research, 1 *Barakuda* (Ge *Lürsson Nav* IV) Presidental Yacht

NAVAL AIR (ε1,000)

40 cbt ac, 10 armed hel

ASW 6 *Wasp* HAS-1

MR 7 N-22 *Searchmaster* B, 7 *Searchmaster* L, 6 NC-212 (MR/ELINT), 14 N-22B, 6 N-24

TPT 4 *Commander*, 10 NC-212, 2 DHC-5, 20 *Nomad*

TRG 2 *Bonanza* F33, 6 PA-38

HEL 2 NAS-332F, *4 NBo-105, 4 Bell-412

MARINES (12,000)

2 inf bde (6 bn) • 1 SF bn(-) • 1 cbt spt regt (arty, AD)

EQUIPMENT

LT TK 100 PT-76†

RECCE 14 BRDM

AIFV 10 AMX-10 PAC-90

APC 24 AMX-10P, 60 BTR-50P

TOWED ARTY 48: **105mm**: 20 LG-1 Mk II; **122mm**: 28 M-38

MOR 81mm

MRL 140mm: 15 BM-14

AD GUNS 40mm, 57mm

Air Force 21,000

92 cbt ac, no armed hel; 2 Air Operations Areas
FGA 4 sqn
   1 with 20 A-4 (18 -E, 2 TA-4H)
   1 with 10 F-16 (6 -A, 4 -B)
   1 with 8 *Hawk* Mk 109 and 16 *Hawk* Mk 209 (FGA/
      ftr)
   1 with 14 *Hawk* Mk 53 (FGA/trg)
FTR 1 sqn with 12 F-5 (8 -E, 4 -F)
RECCE 1 sqn with 12* OV-10F
MR 1 sqn with 3 Boeing 737-200
TKR 2 KC-130B
TPT 19 C-130 (9 -B, 3 -H, 7 -H-30), 3 L100-30, 1 Boeing
   707, 4 Cessna 207, 5 Cessna 401, 2 C-402, 7 F-27-
   400M, 1 F-28-1000, 2 F-28-3000, 10 NC-212, 1 *Skyvan*
   (survey), 6 CN-235
HEL 10 S-58T, 10 Hughes 500, 12 NAS-330, 4 NBO-
   105CD
TRG 3 sqn with 31 AS-202, 2 Cessna 172, 18 T-34C, 2
   T-41D

Forces Abroad

UN AND PEACEKEEPING
BOSNIA (UNMIBH): 18 civ pol. **CROATIA** (UNTAES):
5 Obs plus 27 civ pol; (UNMOP): 2 Obs. **FYROM**
(UNPREDEP): 53 incl 2 Obs. **GEORGIA** (UNOMIG): 5
Obs. **IRAQ/KUWAIT** (UNIKOM): 6 Obs.

Paramilitary

POLICE (*POLRI*) some 177,000
incl 6,000 police 'mobile bde' (BRIMOB) org in 49 coy
(to be 56), incl counter-terrorism unit (*Gegana*)
   EQPT APC 34 *Tactica*; **ac** 3 *Commander*, 1 Beech 18, 2
      NC- 212 **hel** 19 NBO-105, 3 Bell 206
MARINE POLICE (12,000)
   about 10 PCC, 9 PCI and 6 PCI< (all armed)
KAMRA (People's Security) (R) 1,500,000
some 300,000 undergo 3 weeks' basic trg each year;
part-time police auxiliary
WANRA (People's Resistance) (R)
part-time local military auxiliary force under Regional
Military Comd (KOREM)
CUSTOMS
   about 72 PFI<, armed
SEA COMMUNICATIONS AGENCY (responsible to
Department of Communications)
   5 Kujang PCI, 4 Golok PCI (SAR), plus boats

Opposition

FRETILIN (Revolutionary Front for an Independent East
Timor) some 70 incl spt

FALINTIL mil wing; small arms
FREE PAPUA ORGANISATION (OPM) perhaps 200–
300
(100 armed)
FREE ACEH MOVEMENT (*Gerakan Aceh Merdeka*) 50
armed reported

Japan

	1995	1996	1997	1998
GDP	¥481tr	¥501tr		
	($5.1tr)	($4.6tr)		
per capita	$22,000	$23,200		
Growth	1.4%	3.6%		
Inflation	-0.1%	0.2%		
Publ Debt	80.7%	86.4%		
Def exp	¥4.7tr	¥4.9tr		
	($50.2bn)	($44.5bn)		
Def bdgt			¥5.0tr	¥5.0tr
			($42.9bn)	($43.3bn)
$1 = yen	94	109	115	
Population	125,864,000 (Korean <1%)			
Age	13–17	18–22		23–32
Men	3,955,000	4,539,000	9,268,000	
Women	3,762,000	4,318,000	8,870,000	

Total Armed Forces

ACTIVE some 235,600
(incl 1,300 Central Staffs, 9,900 women)

RESERVES 46,700
Army (GSDF) 44,800 **Navy** (MSDF) 1,100 **Air Force**
(ASDF) 800

Army (Ground Self-Defense Force) some 147,700

5 Army HQ (Regional Comds) • 1 armd div • 12 inf
div (7 at 7,000, 5 at 9,000 each) • 2 composite bde • 1
AB bde • 1 arty bde; 2 arty gp • 2 AD bde; 4 AD gp •
4 trg bde (incl 1 spt); 2 trg regt • 5 engr bde •1 hel bde
• 5 ATK hel sqn
EQUIPMENT
   MBT some 1,110: some 100 Type-61 (retiring), some
      870 Type-74, some 140 Type-90
   RECCE some 90 Type-87
   AIFV some 50 Type-89
   APC some 900: some 340 Type-60, some 340 Type-
      73, some 220 Type-82
   TOWED ARTY some 490: **105mm**: some 60 M2A1;
      155mm: some 430 FH-70
   SP ARTY some 310: **105mm**: some 20 Type-74;

155mm: some 200 Type-75; **203mm**: some 90 M-110A2

MRL some 100: **130mm**: some 70 Type-75 SP; **227mm**: some 30 MLRS

MOR some 1,400: incl **81mm**: some 770 (some SP); **107mm**: some 420 (some SP); **120mm**: some 210

SSM some 70 Type-88 coastal

ATGW some 680: some 220 Type-64, some 240 Type-79, some 220 Type-87

RL 89mm: some 2,350

RCL some 3,080: **84mm**: some 2,720 *Carl Gustav*; **106mm**: some 360 (incl Type 60 SP)

AD GUNS some 80: **35mm**: some 40 twin, some 40 Type-87 SP

SAM some 690: 320 *Stinger*, some 60 Type 81, some 80 Type 91, some 30 Type 93, some 200 I HAWK

AC some 20 LR-1

ATTACK HEL some 90 AH-1S

TPT HEL 3 AS-332L (VIP), some 40 CH-47J/JA, some 10 V-107, some 190 OH-6D/J, some 130 UH-1H/J

SURV Type-92 (mor), J/MPQ-P7 (arty)

Navy (Maritime Self-Defense Force) 42,500

(incl ε12,000 Air Arm and 1,800 women)

BASES Yokosuka, Kure, Sasebo, Maizuru, Ominato

FLEET Surface units org into 4 escort flotillas of 8 DD/FF each **Bases** Yokosuka, Kure, Sasebo, Maizuru

SS org into 2 flotillas **Bases** Kure, Yokosuka

Remainder assigned to 5 regional districts

SUBMARINES 16

7 *Harushio* with 533mm TT (J Type-89 HWT) with *Harpoon* USGW

9 *Yuushio* with 533mm TT (J Type-89 HWT), 7 with *Harpoon* USGW

PRINCIPAL SURFACE COMBATANTS 58

DESTROYERS 10

3 *Kongo* with 2 VLS for *Standard* SAM and ASROC SUGW (29 cells forward, 61 cells aft); plus 2 x 4 *Harpoon* SSM, 1 127mm gun, 2 x 3 ASTT and hel deck

2 *Murasame* with 8 *Harpoon* SSM, 1 VLS *Sea Sparrow* SAM, 1 VLS ASROC, 6 324mm TT, 1 SH-60J hel

2 *Hatakaze* with 1 SM-1-MR Mk 13 SAM; plus 2 x 4 *Harpoon* SSM, 1 x 8 ASROC SUGW (Mk 46 LWT) 2 x 3 ASTT, 2 127mm guns

3 *Tachikaze* with 1 SM-1-MR; plus 1 x 8 ASROC, 2 x 3 ASTT, 2 127mm guns

FRIGATES 48

FFH 24

2 *Shirane* with 3 SH-60J ASW hel, 1 x 8 ASROC, 2 x 3 ASTT; plus 2 127mm guns

2 *Haruna* with 3 SH-60J hel, 1 x 8 ASROC, 2 x 3 ASTT; plus 2 127mm guns

8 *Asagiri* with 1 SH-60J hel, 1 x 8 ASROC, 2 x 3 ASTT;

plus 2 x 4 *Harpoon* SSM

12 *Hatsuyuki* with 1 SH-60J, 1 x 8 ASROC, 2 x 3 ASTT; plus 2 x 4 *Harpoon* SSM

FF 24

6 *Abukuma* with 1 x 8 ASROC, 2 x 3 ASTT; plus 2 x 4 *Harpoon* SSM

2 *Takatsuki* with 1 x 8 ASROC, 2 x 3 ASTT, 1 x 4 ASW RL; plus 2 127mm gun

3 *Yamagumo* with 1 x 8 ASROC, 2 x 3 ASTT, 1 x 4 ASW RL

1 *Minegumo* with 1 x 8 ASROC, 2 x 3 ASTT, 1 x 4 ASW RL

2 *Yubari* with 2 x 3 ASTT, 1 x 4 ASW RL; plus 2 x 4 *Harpoon* SSM

1 *Ishikari* with 2 x 3 ASTT, 1 x 4 ASW RL; plus 2 x 4 *Harpoon* SSM

9 *Chikugo* with 1 x 8 ASROC, 2 x 3 ASTT

PATROL AND COASTAL COMBATANTS 6

MISSILE CRAFT 3 *Ichi-Go* Type PHM with 4 SSM-1B

PATROL CRAFT, INSHORE 3 *Jukyu-Go* PCI<

MINE COUNTERMEASURES 35

1 *Uraga* MCM spt with hel deck; can lay mines

1 *Hayase* MCM cmd with hel deck, 2 x 3 ASTT, plus minelaying capacity

18 *Hatsushima* MCC

9 *Uwajima* MCC

3 *Yaeyama* MSO

2 *Nana-go* MSB<

1 *Fukue* coastal MCM spt

AMPHIBIOUS 6

3 *Miura* LST, capacity 200 tps, 10 tk

3 *Atsumi* LST, capacity 130 tps, 5 tk

Plus craft: 2 *Yura* and 2 *Ichi-Go* LCM, 1 LCAC

SUPPORT AND MISCELLANEOUS 22

3 *Towada* AOE, 1 *Sagami* AOE (all with hel deck), 2 sub depot/rescue, 2 *Minegumo* trg, 1 *Uzushio* (trg), 1 *Kashima* (trg), 1 *Katori* (trg), 2 trg spt, 8 survey/experimental, 1 icebreaker

AIR ARM (ε12,000)

110 cbt ac, 99 armed hel **Flying hours** P-3: 500

7 Air Groups

MR 10 sqn (1 trg) with 100 P-3C

ASW 6 land-based hel sqn (1 trg) with 60 HSS-2B, 4 shipboard sqn with 40 SH-60J

MCM 1 hel sqn with 10 MH-53E

EW 1 sqn with 2 EP-3

TPT 1 sqn with 4 YS-11M

SAR 10 US-1A, 10 S-61 hel, 10 UH-60J

TRG 4 sqn with **ac** 30 KM-2, 30 T-5, 30 TC-90/UC-90, 10 YS-11T/M **hel** 10 HSS-2B, 10 OH-6D/J

Air Force (Air Self-Defense Force) 44,100

368 cbt ac, no armed hel, 7 cbt air wings

Flying hours 150
FGA 2 sqn with 50 F-I, 1 sqn with 20 F-4EJ
FTR 10 sqn
   8 with 179 F-15J/DJ
   2 with 49 F-4EJ
RECCE 1 sqn with 20* RF-4E/EJ
AEW 1 sqn with 10 E-2C
EW 1 fleet with 1 EC-1, 7 YS-11 E
AGGRESSOR TRG 1 sqn with 10 F-15DJ
TPT 8 sqn
   3 with 20 C-1, 10 C-130H, 10 YS-11
   1 with 2 747-400 (VIP)
   4 heavy-lift hel sqn with 10 CH-47J
SAR 1 wg (10 det) with **ac** 20 MU-2, 10 U-125 **hel** 20
   KV-107, 10 UH-60J
CAL 1 sqn with 1 YS-11, 10 U-125-800
TRG 6 wg, 12 sqn with 40 T-1A/B, 40* T-2, 40 T-3, 40
   T-4, 10 T-400
LIAISON 5 B-65, 10 T-33, 90 T-4, 2 U-4
TEST 1 wg with F-15J, T-4

AIR DEFENCE

ac control and warning: 4 wg, 28 radar sites
6 SAM gp (24 sqn) with 120 *Patriot*
Air Base Defence Gp with **20mm** *Vulcan* AA guns,
   Type 81, Type 91, *Stinger* SAM
ASM ASM-1, ASM-2
AAM AAM-3, AIM-9 *Sidewinder*, AIM-7 *Sparrow*

Forces Abroad

UN AND PEACEKEEPING
SYRIA/ISRAEL (UNDOF): 45

Paramilitary 12,000

MARITIME SAFETY AGENCY (Coast Guard) (Ministry
of Transport, no cbt role) 12,000
   PATROL VESSELS some 328
   Offshore (over 1,000 tons) 42, incl 1 *Shikishima* with
   2 *Super Puma* hel, 2 *Mizuho* with 2 Bell 212, 8 *Soya*
   with 1 Bell 212 hel, 2 *Izu*, 28 *Shiretok* and 1 *Kojima*
   (trg) **Coastal** (under 1,000 tons) 36 **Inshore** some 250
   patrol craft most<
   MISC about 90 service, 80 tender/trg vessels
   AC 5 NAMC YS-11A, 2 Short *Skyvan*, 16 *King Air*, 1
   Cessna U-206G
   HEL 32 Bell 212, 4 Bell 206, 2 Hughes 369

Foreign Forces

US 36,530: **Army** 1,530; 1 Corps HQ **Navy** 6,700; bases
at Yokosuka (HQ 7th Fleet) and Sasebo **Marines**
14,300; 1 MEF in Okinawa **Air Force** 14,000; 1 Air
Force HQ (5th Air Force), 90 cbt ac, 1 ftr wg, 2 sqn with
36 F-16, 1 wg, 3 sqn with 54 F-15C/D, 1 sqn with 15
KC-135, 1 SAR sqn with 8 HH-60, 1 sqn with 2 E-3

AWACS; 1 airlift wg with 16 C-130E/H, 4 C-21, 3 C-9;
1 special ops gp with 4 MC-130P, 4 MC-130E

Korea: Democratic People's Republic Of (North)

	1995	1996	1997	1998
GNP[a]	ε$20bn	ε$20bn		
per capita	$1,000	$1,000		
Growth	ε-4.5%	ε-3.6%		
Inflation	ε5%	ε5%		
Debt	ε$7.8bn	ε$7.9bn		
Def exp	ε$5.2bn	ε$5.4bn		
Def bdgt		εwon 5.3bn		
		($2.4bn)		
$1 = won[b]	2.2	2.2	2.2	

[a] GNP is larger than GDP because of remitted earnings of
DPRK expatriates in Japan and ROK
[b] Market rate **1997** $1 = 70–100 won

Population		24,681,000	
Age	*13–17*	*18–22*	*23–32*
Men	996,000	1,080,000	2,525,000
Women	1,014,000	1,119,000	2,395,000

Total Armed Forces

ACTIVE ε1,055,000

Terms of service: **Army** 5–8 years **Navy** 5–10 years **Air
Force** 3–4 years, followed by compulsory part-time
service to age 40. Thereafter service in the Worker/
Peasant Red Guard to age 60

RESERVES 4,700,000

Army 600,000 **Navy** 40,000 are assigned to units (see
Paramilitary)

Army ε923,000

20 Corps (1 armd, 4 mech, 12 inf, 2 arty, 1 capital
defence) • 26 inf div • 15 armd bde • 24 truck mobile
inf bde • 3 indep inf bde
Special Purpose Forces Comd (88,000): 10 *Sniper* bde
   (incl 2 amph, 2 AB), 14 lt inf bde (incl 3 AB) 17 recce,
   1 AB bn, 'Bureau of Reconnaissance SF' (8 bn)
Army tps: 6 hy arty bde (incl MRL), 1 *Scud* SSM bde, 1
   FROG SSM regt
Corps tps: 14 arty bde incl 122mm, 152mm SP, MRL

RESERVES

26 inf div, 18 inf bde
EQUIPMENT
   MBT some 3,000: T-34, T-54/-55, T-62, Type-59
   LT TK 500 PT-76, M-1985
   APC 2,500 BTR-40/-50/-60/-152, PRC Type-531,
   DPRK Type M-1973

TOTAL ARTY (excl mor) 10,600
TOWED ARTY 3,500: **122mm**: M-1931/-37, D-74, D-30; **130mm**: M-46; **152mm**: M-1937, M-1938, M-1943
SP ARTY 4,500: **122mm**: M-1977, M-1981, M-1985; **130mm**: M-1975, M-1991; **152mm**: M-1974, M-1977; **170mm**: M-1978, M-1989
MRL 2,600: **107mm**: Type-63; **122mm**: BM-21, BM-11, M-1977/-1985/-1992/-1993; **240mm**: M-1985/-1989/-1991
MOR 8,100: **82mm**: M-37; **120mm**: M-43; **160mm**: M-43
SSM 24 FROG-3/-5/-7; some 30 *Scud*-C
ATGW: AT-1 *Snapper*, AT-3 *Sagger*, AT-4 *Spigot*, AT-5 *Spandrel*
RCL 82mm: 1,700 B-10
AD GUNS 4,800 plus 3,000 in static positions: **14.5mm**: ZPU-1/-2/-4 SP, M-1983 SP; **23mm**: ZU-23, ZSU-23-4 SP; **37mm**: M-1939; **57mm**: S-60; **85mm**: KS-12; **100mm**: KS-19
SAM ε10,000+ SA-7/-16

Navy ε47,000

BASES East Coast Toejo (HQ), Changjon, Munchon, Songjon-pardo, Mugye-po, Mayang-do, Chaho Nodongjagu, Puam-Dong, Najin **West Coast** Nampo (HQ), Pipa Got, Sagon-ni, Chodo-ri, Koampo, Tasa-ri 2 Fleet HQ

SUBMARINES 26
22 PRC Type-031/Sov *Romeo* with 533mm TT
4 Sov *Whiskey*† with 533mm and 406mm TT
(Plus some 45 midget and 13 coastal submarines (incl 16 *Sang-O*) mainly used for SF ops, but some with 2 TT)

FRIGATES 3
1 *Soho* with 4 ASW RL, plus 4 SS-N-2 *Styx* SSM, 1 100mm gun and hel deck
2 *Najin* with 2 x 5 ASW RL, plus 2 SS-N-2 *Styx* SSM, 2 100mm guns

PATROL AND COASTAL COMBATANTS some 422
CORVETTES 3 *Sariwon* with 1 100mm gun
MISSILE CRAFT 47
15 *Soju*, 12 Sov *Osa*, 4 PRC *Huangfeng* PFM with 4 SS N-2 *Styx*, 6 *Sohung*, 10 Sov *Komar* PFM with 2 SS-N-2
TORPEDO CRAFT some 198
3 Sov *Shershen* with 4 533mm TT
Some 155 with 2 533mm TT
40 *Sin Hung* PHT
PATROL CRAFT 174
COASTAL 19
6 *Hainan* PFC with 4 ASW RL, 13 *Taechong* PFC with 2 ASW RL
INSHORE some 155
20 SO-1, 12 *Shanghai* II, 3 *Chodo*, some 120<
MINE COUNTERMEASURES about 25 MSI<

AMPHIBIOUS craft only
15 LCM, 15 LCU, about 100 Nampo LCVP, plus about 130 hovercraft
SUPPORT AND MISCELLANEOUS 7
2 ocean tugs, 1 AS, 1 ocean and 3 inshore survey

COASTAL DEFENCE
2 SSM regt: *Silkworm* in 6 sites, and probably some mobile launchers
GUNS 122mm: M-1931/-37; **130mm**: SM-4-1; **152mm**: M-1937

Air Force 85,000

607 cbt ac, armed hel **Flying hours** some 30
BBR 3 lt regt with 82 H-5 (Il-28)
FGA/FTR 15 regt
3 with 107 J-5 (MiG-17), 4 with 159 J-6 (MiG-19), 4 with 130 J-7 (MiG-21), 1 with 46 MiG-23, 1 with 30 MiG-29, 1 with 18 Su-7, 1 with 35 Su-25
TPT ac 282 An-2/Y-5, 6 An-24, 2 Il-18, 4 Il-62M, 2 Tu-134, 4 Tu-154 **hel** 80 Hughes 500D, 139 Mi-2, 15 Mi-8/-17, 48 Z-5
TRG incl 10 CJ-5, 7 CJ-6, 6 MiG-21, 170 Yak-18, 35 FT-2 (MiG-15UTI)
MISSILES
AAM AA-2 *Atoll*, AA-7 *Apex*
SAM 300+ SA-2, 36 SA-3, 24 SA-5

Forces Abroad

advisers in some 12 African countries

Paramilitary 189,000 active

SECURITY TROOPS (Ministry of Public Security) 189,000
incl border guards, public safety personnel
WORKER/PEASANT RED GUARD some 3,500,000
Org on a provincial/town/village basis; comd structure is bde – bn – coy – pl; small arms with some mor and AD guns (but many units unarmed)

Korea: Republic Of (South)

	1995	1996	1997	1998
GDP	won351tr	won390tr		
	($422bn)	($473bn)		
per capita	$11,400	$12,400		
Growth	9.0%	7.1%		
Inflation	4.5%	5.0%		
Debt	$78bn	$111bn		
Def exp	won10.9tr	won12.5tr		
	($14.2bn)	($15.5bn)		
Def bdgt			won13.8tr	
			($15.5bn)	

contd	1995	1996	1997	1998
$1 = won	771	804	892	
Population		45,990,000		
Age	*13–17*	*18–22*	*23–32*	
Men	1,918,000	2,104,000	4,383,000	
Women	1,787,000	1,962,000	4,099,000	

Total Armed Forces

ACTIVE 672,000

(ε159,000 conscripts)
Terms of service: conscription **Army** 26 months **Navy** and **Air Force** 30 months; First Combat Forces (Mobilisation Reserve Forces) or Regional Combat Forces (Homeland Defence Forces) to age 33

RESERVES 4,500,000

being re-org

Army 560,000

(140,000 conscripts)
HQ: 3 Army, 11 Corps
3 mech inf div (each 3 bde: 3 mech inf, 3 tk, 1 recce, 1 engr bn; 1 fd arty bde) • 19 inf div (each 3 inf regt, 1 recce, 1 tk, 1 engr bn; 1 arty regt (4 bn)) • 2 indep inf bde • 7 SF bde • 3 counter-infiltration bde • 3 SSM bn with NHK-I/-II (*Honest John*) • 3 AD arty bde • 3 I HAWK bn (24 sites), 2 *Nike Hercules* bn (10 sites) • 1 avn comd

RESERVES
1 Army HQ, 23 inf div
EQUIPMENT
  MBT 2,130: 800 Type 88, 80 T-80U, 400 M-47, 850 M-48
  APC some 2,490: incl 1,700 KIFV, 420 M-113, 140 M-577, 200 Fiat 6614/KM-900/-901, 30 BMP-3
  TOWED ARTY some 3,500: **105mm**: 1,700 M-101, KH-178; **155mm**: M-53, M-114, KH-179; **203mm**: M-115
  SP ARTY 155mm: 1,040 M-109A2; **175mm**: M-107; **203mm**: M-110
  MRL 130mm: 156 *Kooryong* (36-tube)
  MOR 6,000: **81mm**: KM-29; **107mm**: M-30
  SSM 12 NHK-I/-II
  ATGW TOW-2A, *Panzerfaust*, AT-7
  RCL 57mm, 75mm, 90mm: M67; **106mm**: M40A2
  ATK GUNS 58: **76mm**: 8 M-18; **90mm**: 50 M-36 SP
  AD GUNS 600: **20mm**: incl KIFV (AD variant), 60 M-167 *Vulcan*; **30mm**: 20 B1 HO SP; **35mm**: 20 GDF-003; **40mm**: 80 L60/70, M-1
  SAM 1,020: 350 *Javelin*, 60 *Redeye*, 130 *Stinger*, 170 *Mistral*, SA-16, 110 I HAWK, 200 *Nike Hercules*
  SURV RASIT (veh, arty), AN/TPQ-36 (arty, mor), AN/TPQ-37 (arty)

AC 5 O-1A
HELICOPTERS
  ATTACK 75 AH-1F/-J, 68 Hughes 500 MD.
  TPT 15 CH-47D
  UTL 170 Hughes 500, 130 UH-1H, 99 UH-60P

Navy 60,000

(incl 25,000 Marines and ε19,000 conscripts)
BASES Chinhae (HQ), Cheju, Inchon, Mokpo, Mukho, Pukpyong, Pohang, Pusan
FLEET COMMAND 3
SUBMARINES 6
  6 *Chang Bogo* (Ge T-209/1200) with 8 533 TT; plus 3 KSS-1 *Dolgorae* SSI (175t) with 2 406mm TT
PRINCIPAL SURFACE COMBATANTS 40
DESTROYERS 7 *Chung Buk* (US *Gearing*) with 2 or 3 x 2 127mm guns; plus 2 x 3 ASTT; 5 with 2 x 4 *Harpoon* SSM, 2 with 1 x 8 ASROC, 1 *Alouette* III hel (OTHT)
FRIGATES 33
  9 *Ulsan* with 2 x 3 ASTT (Mk 46 LWT); plus 2 x 4 *Harpoon* SSM
  24 *Po Hang* with 2 x 3 ASTT; some with 2 x 1 MM-38 *Exocet*
PATROL AND COASTAL COMBATANTS 105
CORVETTES 4 *Dong Hae* (ASW) with 2 x 3 ASTT
MISSILE CRAFT 11
  8 *Pae Ku*-52 (US *Asheville*), 3 with 4 *Standard* (boxed) SSM, 5 with 2 x 2 *Harpoon* SSM
  1 *Pae Ku*-51 (US *Asheville*), with 2 *Standard* SSM
  2 *Kilurki*-71 (*Wildcat*) with 2 MM-38 *Exocet* SSM
PATROL, INSHORE 90
  75 *Kilurki*-11 (*Sea Dolphin*) 37m PFI
  15 *Chebi*-51 (*Sea Hawk*) 26m PFI< (some with 2 MM-38 *Exocet* SSM)
MINE COUNTERMEASURES 14
  6 *Kan Keong* (mod It *Lerici*) MHC
  8 *Kum San* (US MSC-268/289) MSC
AMPHIBIOUS 17
  2 *Alligator* (RF) LST, capacity 700 tons vehicles
  8 *Un Bong* (US LST-511) LST, capacity 200 tps, 16 tk
  7 *Ko Mun* (US LSM-1) LSM, capacity 50 tps, 4 tk
  Plus about 36 craft; 6 LCT, 10 LCM, about 20 LCVP
SUPPORT AND MISCELLANEOUS 13
  2 AOE, 2 spt tankers, 2 ocean tugs, 2 salv/div spt, 1 ASR, about 4 survey (civil-manned, Ministry of Transport-funded)

NAVAL AIR
23 cbt ac; 47 armed hel
  ASW 3 sqn
    2 **ac** 1 with 15 S-2E, 1 with 8 P-3C
    1 **hel** with 25 Hughes 500MD
  1 flt with 8 SA-316 hel, 12 *Lynx* (ASW)

MARINES (25,000)

2 div, 1 bde

spt units

EQUIPMENT

MBT 60 M-47

APC 60 LVTP-7

TOWED ARTY 105mm, 155mm

SSM *Harpoon* (truck-mounted)

Air Force 52,000

461 cbt ac, no armed hel. 8 cbt, 2 tpt wg

FGA 8 sqn

2 with 60 F-16C/D

6 with 195 F-5E/F

FTR 4 sqn with 130 F-4D/E

CCT 1 sqn with 23* A-37B

FAC 10 O-2A

RECCE 1 sqn with 18* RF-4C, 10* RF-5A

SAR 1 hel sqn, 15 UH-60

TPT **ac** 2 BAe 748 (VIP), 1 Boeing 737-300 (VIP), 1 C-118, 10 C-130H, 15 CN-235M **hel** 16 UH-1H/N, 6 CH-47, 3 Bell-412, 3 AS-332, 3 VH-60

TRG 25* F-5B, 50 T-37, 30 T-38, 25 T-41B, 18 *Hawk* Mk-67

MISSILES

ASM AGM-65A *Maverick*, AGM-88 HARM (possibly AGM-130, AGM-142)

AAM AIM-7 *Sparrow*, AIM-9 *Sidewinder*, AIM-120 AMRAAM

SAM *Nike-Hercules*, I HAWK, *Javelin*, *Mistral*

Forces Abroad

UN AND PEACEKEEPING

GEORGIA (UNOMIG) 4 Obs: INDIA/PAKISTAN (UNMOGIP): 9 Obs. WESTERN SAHARA (MINURSO): 20

Paramilitary ε4,500 active

CIVILIAN DEFENCE CORPS (to age 50) 3,500,000

COAST GUARD ε4,500

PATROL CRAFT 77

OFFSHORE 10

3 *Mazinger* (HDP-1000) (1 CG flagship), 1 *Han Kang* (HDC-1150), 6 *Sea Dragon/Whale* (HDP-600)

COASTAL 29

22 *Sea Wolf/Shark*, 2 *Bukhansan*, 3 *Hyundai*-type, 2 *Bukhansan*

INSHORE 38

18 *Seagull*, about 20<, plus numerous boats

SUPPORT AND MISCELLANEOUS 2 salvage

HEL 9 Hughes 500

Foreign Forces

US 35,920: **Army** 27,260; 1 Army HQ, 1 inf div **Air Force** 8,660; 1 HQ (7th Air Force): 90 cbt ac, 2 ftr wg; 3 sqn with 72 F-16, 1 sqn with 6 A-10, 12 OA-10, 1 special ops sqn with 5MH -53J

Laos

	1995	1996	1997	1998
GDP	kip1.4tr ($1.7bn)	kip1.8tr ($1.9bn)		
per capita	$2,400	$2,500		
Growth	7.0%	7.5%		
Inflation	19.6%	7.5%		
Debt	$2.2bn	$2.3bn		
Def exp	εkip58bn ($73m)	εkip71bn ($77m)		
Def bdgt			εkip76bn ($79m)	
FMA (US)	$2.2m	$2.0m	$2.5m	$2.5m
$1 = kip	805	921	961	
Population		5,064,000		

(*lowland* Lao Loum 68% *upland* Lao Theung 22% *highland* Lao Soung incl Hmong and Yao 9%, Chinese and Vietnamese 1%)

Age	13–17	18–22	23–32
Men	277,000	226,000	354,000
Women	272,000	224,000	353,000

Total Armed Forces

ACTIVE ε29,000

Terms of service: conscription, 18 months minimum

Army 25,000

4 Mil Regions • 5 inf div • 7 indep inf regt • 5 arty, 9 AD arty bn • 3 engr (2 construction) regt • 65 indep inf coy • 1 lt ac liaison flt

EQUIPMENT

MBT 30 T-54/-55, T-34/85

LT TK 25 PT-76

APC 70 BTR-40/-60/-152

TOWED ARTY 75mm: M-116 pack; 105mm: 25 M-101; 122mm: 40 M-1938 and D-30; 130mm: 10 M-46; 155mm: M-114

MOR 81mm; 82mm; 107mm: M-2A1, M-1938; 120mm: M-43

RCL 57mm: M-18/A1; 75mm: M-20; 106mm: M-40; 107mm: B-11

AD GUNS 14.5mm: ZPU-1/-4; 23mm: ZU-23, ZSU-23-4 SP; 37mm: M-1939; 57mm: S-60

SAM SA-3, SA-7

Navy (Army Marine Section) ε500

PATROL AND COASTAL COMBATANTS some 16
PATROL, RIVERINE some 16
some 12 PCI<, 4 LCM, plus about 40 boats

Air Force 3,500

30 cbt ac; no armed hel
FGA 1 regt with some 28 MiG-21
TPT 1 sqn with 4 An-2, 5 An-24, 4 An-26, 4 Yak-12, 2 Yak-40
HEL 1 sqn with 2 Mi-6, 10 Mi-8, 3 SA-360
TRG *2 MiG-21U
AAM AA-2 *Atoll*

Paramilitary

MILITIA SELF-DEFENCE FORCES 100,000+
village 'home-guard' org for local defence

Opposition

Numerous factions/groups; total armed str: ε2,000
United Lao National Liberation Front (ULNLF) largest group

Malaysia

	1995	1996	1997	1998
GDP	r214bn	r252bn		
	($78bn)	($86bn)		
per capita	$9,100	$10,000		
Growth	9.6%	8.2%		
Inflation	5.3%	3.6%		
Debt	$34.4bn	$43.0bn		
Def exp[a]	r8.8bn	r9.1bn		
	($3.5bn)	($3.6bn)		
Def bdgt[b]			r6.5bn	
			($2.5bn)	
FMA (US)	$11.2m	$0.5m	$0.6m	$0.7m
(Aus)	$5.0m	$4.0m		
$1 = ringgit	2.50	2.52	2.50	

[a]Incl procurement and def industry exp
[b]Excl est procurement allocation

Population	24,100,000		

(Muslim 39%; also Malay and other indigenous 64%, Chinese 27%, Indian 9%; in *Sabah* and *Sarawak* non-Muslim Bumiputras form the majority of the population; 1,000,000+ Indonesian and Filipino illegal immigrants)

Age	*13–17*	*18–22*	*23–32*
Men	1,125,000	964,000	1,695,000
Women	1,071,000	925,000	1,656,000

Total Armed Forces

ACTIVE 111,500

RESERVES some 37,800
Army 35–40,000 Navy 2,200 Air Force 600

Army 85,000

(reducing to 80,000)
2 Mil Regions • 1 HQ fd comd, 4 area comd (div) • 1 mech inf, 10 inf bde • 1 AB bde (3 AB bn, 1 lt arty regt, 1 lt tk sqn – forms Rapid Deployment Force)
Summary of combat units
5 armd regt • 31 inf bn • 3 AB bn • 5 fd arty, 1 AD arty, 5 engr regt
1 SF regt (3 bn)
AVN 1 hel sqn

RESERVES
Territorial Army 1 bde HQ; 12 inf regt, 4 highway sy bn

EQUIPMENT
LT TK 26 *Scorpion* (**90mm**)
RECCE 162 SIBMAS, 140 AML-60/-90, 92 *Ferret* (60 mod)
APC 111 KIFV (incl variants), 184 V-100/-150 *Commando*, 25 *Stormer*, 459 *Condor*, 37 M-3 Panhard
TOWED ARTY 127: **105mm**: 75 Model 56 pack, 40 M-102A1 († in store); **155mm**: 12 FH-70
MOR 81mm: 300
ATGW SS-11
RL 89mm: M-20; **92mm**: FT5
RCL 84mm: *Carl Gustav*; **106mm**: 150 M-40
AD GUNS 35mm: 24 GDF-005; **40mm**: 36 L40/70
SAM 48 *Javelin, Starburst*, 12 *Rapier*
HEL 10 SA-316B
ASLT CRAFT 165 *Damen*

Navy 14,000

(incl 160 Naval Air)
Fleet Operations Comd (HQ Lumut)
Naval Area 1 Kuantan **Naval Area 2** Labuan
BASES Naval Area 1 Kuantan **Naval Area 2** Labuan, Sandakan (Sabah) **Naval Area 3** Lumut **Naval Area 4** Sungei Antu (Sarawak)

PRINCIPAL SURFACE COMBATANTS 4
FF 4
2 *Kasturi* (FS-1500) with 2 x 2 ASW mor, deck for *Wasp* hel; plus 2 x 2 MM-38 *Exocet* SSM, 1 100mm gun
1 *Hang Tuah* (UK *Mermaid*) with 1 x 3 *Limbo* ASW mor, hel deck for *Wasp*; plus 1 x 2 102mm gun (trg)
1 *Rahmat* with 1 x 3 ASW mor, 1 114mm gun hel

deck (trg)
CORVETTES 2 *Hang Nadim* (It *Assad*) armament n.k.
PATROL AND COASTAL COMBATANTS 37
MISSILE CRAFT 8
 4 *Handalan* (Swe *Spica*) with 4 MM-38 *Exocet* SSM
 4 *Perdana* (Fr *Combattante* II) with 2 *Exocet* SSM
PATROL CRAFT 29
 OFFSHORE 2 *Musytari* with 1 100mm gun, hel deck
 INSHORE 27
 6 *Jerong* PFI, 3 *Kedah*, 4 *Sabah*, 14 *Kris* PCI
MINE COUNTERMEASURES 5
 4 *Mahamiru* (mod It *Lerici*) MCO
 1 diving tender (inshore)
AMPHIBIOUS 3
 2 *Sri Banggi* (US LST-511) LST, capacity 200 tps, 16 tk
  (but usually employed as tenders to patrol craft)
 1 *Sri Inderapura* (US LST-1192) LST, capacity 400 tps, 10
  tk
 Plus 33 craft: 5 LCM, 13 LCU, 15 LCP
SUPPORT AND MISCELLANEOUS 3
 2 log/fuel spt, 1 survey

NAVAL AIR (160)
no cbt ac, 12 armed hel
 HEL 12 *Wasp* HAS-1

Air Force 12,500

94 cbt ac, no armed hel; 4 Air Div **Flying hours** 200
FGA 3 sqn
 2 with 8 *Hawk* 108, 17 *Hawk* 208
 1 with 8 F/A-18D
FTR 3 sqn
 1 with 11 F-5E, 2 F-5F, 2 RF-5E
 2 with 16 MiG-29, 2 MiG-29U
MR 2 sqn with 3* C-130H/MP, 4* B200T
TKR 6 A-4, 2 KC-130H
TRANSPORT
 AC 4 sqn
 2 with 5 C-130H, 6 C-130H-30, 1 with 13 DHC-4, 1
  with 2 BAe-125 (VIP), 2 *Falcon*-900 (VIP), 11
  Cessna 402B
 HEL 3 sqn with 30 S-61A, 20 SA-316A/B (liaison)
TRAINING
 AC 9* MB-339, 37 PC-7 (12* wpn trg), 15 MD3-160
 HEL 8 SA-316, 5 Bell 47G
AAM AIM-9 *Sidewinder*, AA-10 *Alamo*, AA-11 *Archer*

AIRFIELD DEFENCE
1 field sqn
SAM 1 sqn with *Starburst*

Forces Abroad

UN AND PEACEKEEPING
ANGOLA (UNOMA): 19 Obs plus 20 civ pol.
BOSNIA (SFOR): ε1,000; 1 armd inf bn gp, plus 14

Obs; (UNMIBH): 38 civ pol. **IRAQ/KUWAIT**
(UNIKOM): 5 Obs. **LIBERIA** (UNOMIL): 3 Obs.
WESTERN SAHARA (MINURSO): 13 Obs

Paramilitary ε20,100

POLICE FIELD FORCE 18,000
5 bde HQ: 21 bn (incl 2 Aboriginal, 1 cdo), 4 indep coy
 EQPT ε100 Shorland armd cars, 140 AT-105 *Saxon*,
  ε30 SB-301 APC
MARINE POLICE about 2,100
 BASES Kuala, Kemaman, Penang, Tampoi,
 Kuching, Sandalean
 PATROL CRAFT, INSHORE 48
 15 *Lang Hitam* (38m) PFI, 6 *Sangitan* (29m) PFI, 27
  PCI<, plus boats
POLICE AIR UNIT
 ac 6 Cessna *Caravan* I, 4 Cessna 206, 7 PC-6 **hel** 1 Bell
 206L, 2 AS-355F
AREA SECURITY UNITS (aux Police Field Force) 3,500
89 units
BORDER SCOUTS (in Sabah, Sarawak) 1,200
PEOPLE'S VOLUNTEER CORPS (RELA) 240,000
some 17,500 armed
CUSTOMS SERVICE
 PATROL CRAFT, INSHORE 56
  6 *Perak* (Vosper 32m) armed PFI, about 50 craft<

Foreign Forces

AUSTRALIA 148 **Army** 115; 1 inf coy **Air Force** 33;
det with 2 P-3C **ac**

Mongolia

	1995	1996	1997	1998
GDP	t391bn	t532bn		
	($796m)	($841m)		
per capita	$1,900	$2,000		
Growth	6.3%	2.3%		
Inflation	53.1%	53.2%		
Debt	$512m	$545m		
Def exp	t8.7bn	t7.9bn		
	($19.0m)	($14.0m)		
Def bdgt			t18.2bn	
			($22.0m)	
FMA (US)	$0.1m	$0.1m	$0.3m	$0.3m
$1 = tugrik	449	548	811	
Population		2,368,000		
(Kazak 5%, Russian 2%, Chinese 2%)				
Age	*13–17*	*18–22*	*23–32*	
Men	148,000	131,000	213,000	
Women	142,000	126,000	206,000	

Total Armed Forces

ACTIVE 11,000
(incl 6,100 conscripts; 1,500 construction tps and 500
Civil Defence – see Paramilitary)
Terms of service: conscription: males 18–28 years, 1 year

RESERVES 137,000
Army 137,000

Army 8,500 (5,300 conscripts)

7 MR bde (all under str) • 1 arty bde • 1 lt inf bn
(rapid-deployment forming) • 1 AB bn
EQUIPMENT
  MBT 650 T-54/-55/-62
  RECCE 120 BRDM-2
  AIFV 400 BMP-1
  APC 300 BTR-40/-60/-152
  TOWED ARTY 300: **122mm**: M-1938/D-30;
    130mm: M-46; **152mm**: ML-20
  MRL 122mm: 130+ BM-21
  MOR 140: **82mm, 120mm, 160mm**
  ATK GUNS 200 incl: **85mm**: D-44/D-48; **100mm**:
    BS-3, MT-12

Air Defence 500

9 cbt ac; 12 armed hel **Flying hours** 22
FTR 1 sqn with 8 MiG-21, 1 Mig-21U
ATTACK HEL 12 Mi-24
TPT (Civil Registration) 15 An-2, 16 An-24, 3 An-26, 3
  Boeing 727, 5 Y-12
AD GUNS: 150: **14.5mm**: ZPU-4, **23mm**: ZU-23, ZSU-
  23-4, **57mm**: S-60
SAM 250 SA-7

Paramilitary 5,900 active

BORDER GUARD 5,000 (incl 4,200 conscripts)
INTERNAL SECURITY TROOPS 900 (incl 500
conscripts) 4 gd units
CIVIL DEFENCE TROOPS (500)
CONSTRUCTION TROOPS (1,500) (incl 800 con-
scripts)

New Zealand

	1995	1996	1997	1998
GDP	NZ$91.1bn	NZ$92.6bn		
	($54bn)	($56bn)		
per capita	$16,600	$16,800		
Growth	2.7%	2.1%		
Inflation	3.8%	2.3%		
Publ debt	50.9%	47.0%		

contd	1995	1996	1997	1998
Def exp	NZ$1.6bn	NZ$1.1bn		
	($1,024m)	($744m)		
Def bdgt			NZ$1.1bn	NZ$1.2bn
			($757m)	($831m)
US$1 = NZ$	1.52	1.45	1.45	
Population		3,590,000		

(Maori 9%, Pacific Islander 3%)

Age	13–17	18–22	23–32
Men	130,000	136,000	294,000
Women	123,000	129,000	281,000

Total Armed Forces

ACTIVE 9,550
(incl some 1,340 women)

RESERVES some 6,960
Regular some 2,310 **Army** 1,500 **Navy** 800 **Air Force** 10
Territorial 4,650 **Army** 3,900 **Navy** 400 **Air Force** 350

Army 4,400

(incl 500 women)
1 Land Force Comd HQ • 2 Land Force Gp HQ • 1
APC/Recce regt (-) • 2 inf bn • 1 arty regt (2 fd bty) •
1 engr regt (-) • 1 AD tp (forming) • 2 SF sqn (incl 1
reserve)

RESERVES
Territorial Army 6 inf bn, 4 fd arty bty, 2 armd sqn
(incl 1 lt recce)
EQUIPMENT
  LT TK 20 *Scorpion*
  APC 78 M-113 (incl variants)
  TOWED ARTY 105mm: 19 M-101A1, 24 *Hamel*
  MOR 81mm: 50
  RL 94mm: LAW
  RCL 84mm: 63 *Carl Gustav*
  SURV *Cymbeline* (mor)

Navy 2,100

(incl 340 women)
BASE Auckland (Fleet HQ)
FRIGATES 4
  3 *Waikato* (UK *Leander*) with 1 SH-2F hel, 2 x 3 ASTT
    and 3 with 2 114mm guns (1 in long refit)
  1 *Anzac* with 8 *Sea Sparrow* SAM, 1 127mm gun, 6
    324mm TT, *Seasprite* hel
PATROL AND COASTAL COMBATANTS 4
  4 *Moa* PCI (reserve trg)
SUPPORT AND MISCELLANEOUS 6
  1 *Resolution* TAGOS (US *Tenacious*), 1 *Endeavour* AO,
    1 *Monowai* AGHS, 1 *Tui* AGOR, 1 *Manawanui*
    diving spt, 1 *Charles Upham* military sealift

East Asia and
Australasia

NAVAL AIR

no cbt ac, 4 armed hel
HEL 4 SH-2F *Sea Sprite* (see Air Force)

Air Force 3,050

(incl 500 women); 42 cbt ac, no armed hel
Flying hours A-4: 180

AIR COMMAND

FGA 2 sqn with 14 A-4K, 5 TA-4K
MR 1 sqn with 6* P-3K *Orion*
LIGHT ATTACK/TRG 1 sqn for *ab initio* and ftr lead-in trg with 17* MB-339C
ASW 4 SH-2F (Navy-assigned)
TPT 2 sqn
  ac 1 with 5 C-130H, 2 Boeing 727
  hel 1 with 13 UH-1H, 5 Bell 47G (trg)
TRG 2 sqn
  1 with 18 CT-4B, 1 with 4 *Andover*
MISSILES
  ASM AGM-65B/G *Maverick*
  AAM AIM-9L *Sidewinder*

Forces Abroad

AUSTRALIA 47; 3 A-4K, 3 TA-4K, 9 navigation trg
SINGAPORE 11; spt unit
UN AND PEACEKEEPING
ANGOLA (UNOMA): 13 incl 4 Obs. **CROATIA** (UNTAES): 5 incl 4 Obs; (UNMOP): 1 Obs. **EGYPT** (MFO): 25. **FYROM** (UNPREDEP): 1 Obs. **MIDDLE EAST** (UNTSO): 7 Obs

Total Armed Forces

ACTIVE ε4,300

Army ε3,800

2 inf bn • 1 engr bn
EQUIPMENT
  MOR 81mm; 120mm: 3

Navy 400

BASES Port Moresby (HQ), Lombrum (Manus Island) (patrol boat sqn); forward bases at Kieta and Alotau
PATROL AND COASTAL COMBATANTS 4
PATROL, INSHORE 4 *Tarangau* (Aust *Pacific Forum* 32-m) PCI
AMPHIBIOUS craft only
  2 *Salamaua* (Aust *Balikpapan*) LCH, plus 4 other landing craft, manned and operated by the civil administration

Air Force 100

no cbt ac, no armed hel
TPT 2 CN-235, 3 IAI-201 *Arava*
HEL †4 UH-1H

Opposition

BOUGAINVILLE REVOLUTIONARY ARMY ε1,000
Perhaps 200–300 armed

Foreign Forces

AUSTRALIA 100; trg unit, 2 engr unit, 75 advisers

Papua New Guinea

	1995	1996	1997	1998
GDP	K6.6bn	K7.2bn		
	($5.2bn)	($5.4bn)		
per capita	$2,600	$2,700		
Growth	-2.9%	2.3%		
Inflation	17.3%	11.6%		
Debt	$2.4bn	$2.3bn		
Def exp	εK84m	K104m		
	($66m)	($79m)		
Def bdgt			K71m	
			($51m)	
FMA (US)	$0.1m	$0.2m	$0.2m	$0.2m
(Aus)	$11.0m	$9.0m		
$1 = kina	1.28	1.32	1.39	
Population		4,552,000		
Age	*13–17*	*18–22*	*23–32*	
Men	259,000	234,000	393,000	
Women	244,000	218,000	353,000	

Philippines

	1995	1996	1997	1998
GDP	P1.9tr	P2.2tr		
	($69bn)	($74bn)		
per capita	$2,700	$2,900		
Growth	4.8%	5.5%		
Inflation	8.1%	8.4%		
Debt	$39.4bn	$41.9bn		
Def exp[a]	P35bn	P39bn		
	($1.4bn)	($1.5bn)		
Def bdgt[b]			P30.0bn	
			($1.1bn)	
FMA (US)	$1.2m	$1.2m	$1.3m	$1.4m
(Aus)	($3.0m)	($3.0m)		
$1 = peso	25.7	26.2	26.3	

[a] Incl paramil exp

[b] A five-year supplementary procurement budget of P50bn ($1.9bn) for 1996–2000 was approved in Dec 1996

Population	72,433,000		
(Muslim 45%; Chinese 2%)			
Age	*13–17*	*18–22*	*23–32*
Men	4,015,000	3,562,000	5,927,000
Women	3,876,000	3,432,000	5,753,000

Total Armed Forces

ACTIVE ε110,500

RESERVES 131,000

Army 100,000 (some 75,000 more have commitments)
Navy 15,000 **Air Force** 16,000 (to age 49)

Army 70,000

5 Area Unified Comd (joint service) • 8 inf div (each with 3 inf bde) • 1 special ops comd with 1 lt armd bde ('regt'), 1 scout ranger, 1 SF regt • 3 engr bde; 1 construction bn • 8 arty bn • 1 Presidential Security Group

EQUIPMENT
LT TK 41 *Scorpion*
AIFV 85 YPR-765 PRI
APC 100 M-113, 20 *Chaimite*, 165 V-150, some 90 *Simba*
TOWED ARTY 242: **105mm**: 230 M-101, M-102, M-26 and M-56; **155mm**: 12 M-114 and M-68
MOR 81mm: M-29; **107mm**: 40 M-30
RCL 75mm: M-20; **90mm**: M-67; **106mm**: M-40 A1

Navy† ε24,000 (incl Coast Guard)

(incl 9,500 Marines)
6 Naval Districts
BASES Sangley Point/Cavite, Zamboanga, Cebu
FRIGATES 1
1 *Rajah Humabon* (US *Cannon*) with ASW mor, 76mm gun
PATROL AND COASTAL COMBATANTS 63
PATROL, OFFSHORE 14
3 (ex-UK) *Peacock* with 1 76mm gun
2 *Rizal* (US *Auk*) with hel deck
8 *Miguel Malvar* (US PCE-827)
1 *Magat Salamat* (US-MSF)
PATROL, INSHORE 49
2 *Aguinaldo*, 3 *Kagitingan*, 18 *José Andrada* PCI<, 5 *Thomas Batilo* (ROK *Sea Dolphin*), and about 21 other PCI<
AMPHIBIOUS some 9
2 US *F. S. Beeson*-class LST, capacity 32 tk plus 150 tps, hel deck
Some 7 *Zamboanga del Sur* (US LST-1/511/542) LST,

capacity either 16tk or 10tk plus 200 tps
Plus about 39 craft: 30 LCM, 3 LCU, some 6 LCVP
SUPPORT AND MISCELLANEOUS 11
2 AOT (small), 1 repair ship, 3 survey/research, 3 spt, 2 water tkr

NAVAL AVIATION
8 cbt ac, no armed hel
MR/SAR ac 8 BN-2A *Defender*, 1 *Islander* **hel** 11 Bo-105 (SAR)

MARINES (9,000)
3 bde (10 bn) - to be 2 bde (6 bn)
EQUIPMENT
APC 30 LVTP-5, 55 LVTP-7, 24 LAV-300 (reported)
TOWED ARTY 105mm: 150 M-101
MOR 4.2in (107mm): M-30

Air Force 16,500

39 cbt ac, some 103 armed hel
FTR 1 sqn with 5 F-5 (3 -A, 2 -B)
ARMD HEL 3 sqn with 62 Bell UH-1H/M, 16 AUH-76 (S-76 gunship conversion), 25 Hughes 500/520MD
MR 2 F-27M
RECCE 6 RT-33A, 22* OV-10 *Broncos*
SAR ac 4 HU-16 **hel** 10 Bo-105C
PRESIDENTIAL AC WG ac 1 F-27, 1 F-28 **hel** 2 Bell 212, 2 S-70A, 2 SA-330
TPT 3 sqn
1 with 2 C-130B, 3 C-130H, 3 L-100-20, 5 C-47, 7 F-27
2 with 22 BN-2 *Islander*, 14 N-22B *Nomad Missionmaster*
HEL 2 sqn with 55 Bell 205, 17 UH-1H
LIAISON 10 Cessna (7 -180, 2 -210, 1 -310), 5 DHC-2, 12 U-17A/B
TRG 4 sqn
1 with 6 T-33A, 1 with 10 T-41D, 1 with 15 SF-260TP, 1 with 12* S-211
AAM AIM-9B *Sidewinder*

Paramilitary 42,500 active

PHILIPPINE NATIONAL POLICE (Department of Interior and Local Government) 40,500
62,000 active aux; 15 Regional, 73 Provincial Comd
COAST GUARD 2,000
(no longer part of Navy)
EQPT 1 *Kalinga* PCO, 4 *Basilan* (US PGM-39/42 PCI, 2 *Tirad Pass* PCI (SAR), 4 ex-US Army spt ships, plus some 50 patrol boats; 2 lt ac
CITIZEN ARMED FORCE GEOGRAPHICAL UNITS (CAFGU) 60,000
Militia, 56 bn; part-time units which can be called up for extended periods

Opposition and Former Opposition

Groups with Cease-fire Agreements

BANGSA MORO ARMY (armed wing of Moro National Liberation Front (MNLF); Muslim) ε5,000

Groups Still in Opposition

NEW PEOPLE'S ARMY (NPA; communist) ε8,000

MORO ISLAMIC LIBERATION FRONT (breakaway from MNLF; Muslim) ε6–10,000

MORO ISLAMIC REFORMIST GROUP (breakaway from MNLF; Muslim) 900

ABU SAYAF GROUP ε500

Singapore

	1995	1996	1997	1998
GDP	S$121bn	S$131bn		
	($67bn)	($74bn)		
per capita	$21,700	$23,400		
Growth	8.9%	7.0%		
Inflation	1.8%	1.3%		
Debt	$7bn	$8bn		
Def exp	S$5.6bn	S$5.7bn		
	($4.0bn)	($4.0bn)		
Def bdgt			S$6.1bn	
			($4.3bn)	
FMA (US)	$0.02m	$0.02m		
(Aus)	$1.0m	$1.0m		
US$1 = S$	1.42	1.41	1.43	
Population		3,031,000		

(Chinese 76%, Malay 15%, Indian 6%)

Age	*13–17*	*18–22*	*23–32*
Men	110,000	110,000	255,000
Women	104,000	104,000	248,000

Total Armed Forces

ACTIVE ε70,000

(39,800 conscripts)
Terms of service: conscription 24–30 months

RESERVES ε263,800

Army 250,000; annual trg to age 40 for men, 50 for officers **Navy** ε6,300 **Air Force** ε7,500

Army 55,000

(35,000 conscripts/active reserves)
3 combined arms div each with 2 inf bde (each 3 inf bn), 1 mech bde, 1 recce, 2 arty, 1 AD, 1 engr bn (mixed active/reserve formations)

1 Rapid Deployment (op reserve) div with 3 inf bde (incl 1 air mob, 1 amph, mixed active/reserve formations)
1 mech bde
Summary of active units
9 inf bn • 4 lt armd/recce bn • 4 arty bn • 1 cdo (SF) bn • 4 engr bn

RESERVES

1 op reserve div, some inf bde HQ; ε40 inf, ε8 lt armd recce, ε8 arty, ε1 cdo (SF), ε8 engr bn
People's Defence Force: some 30,000; org in 2 comd, 7+ bde gp, ε20+ bn

EQUIPMENT

MBT some 60 *Centurion* (reported)
LT TK ε350 AMX-13SM1
RECCE 22 AMX-10 PAC 90
AIFV 22 AMX-10P
APC 750+ M-113, 30 V-100, 250 V-150/-200 *Commando*
TOWED ARTY 105mm: 37 LG1; **155mm**: 38 Soltam M-71S, 16 M-114A1 (may be in store), M-68 (may be in store), 52 FH88, 17 FH2000
MOR 81mm (some SP); **120mm**: 50 (some SP in M-113); **160mm**: 12 Tampella
ATGW 30+ *Milan*
RL *Armbrust*; **89mm**: 3.5in M-20
RCL 84mm: ε200 *Carl Gustav*; **106mm**: 90 M-40A1 (in store)
AD GUNS 20mm: 30 GAI-CO1 (some SP)
SAM RBS-70 (some SP in V-200) (Air Force), *Mistral* (Air Force)
SURV AN/TPQ-36/-37 (arty, mor)

Navy ε9,000

incl 4,500 full time (2,700 regular and 1,800 national service) plus 4,500 operationally ready national service
COMMANDS Fleet (1st and 3rd Flotillas) **Coastal** and **Naval Logistic, Training Command**
BASES Pulau Brani, Tuas (Jurong)

PATROL AND COASTAL COMBATANTS 25

CORVETTES 6 *Victory* (Ge Lürssen 62m) with 8 *Harpoon* SSM, 2 x 3 ASTT (1 x 2 *Barak* SAM being fitted)
MISSILE CRAFT 13
6 *Sea Wolf* (Ge Lürssen 45m) PFM with 2 x 2 *Harpoon*, 4 x 2 *Gabriel* SSM, 1 x 2 *Sinbad/Mistral* SAM
7 *Fearless* OPV with 2 *Mistral Sadral* SAM, 1 76mm gun, 6 324mm TT
PATROL, INSHORE 6 *Independence/Sovereignty* (33m), plus boats

MINE COUNTERMEASURES 4

4 *Bedok* (SW *Landsort*) MHC (*Jupiter* diving spt has mine-hunting capability)

AMPHIBIOUS 3

1 *Perseverance* (UK *Sir Lancelot*) LSL with 1 x 2 *Simbad*

(navalised *Mistral*) SAM capacity: 340 tps, 16 tk, hel deck

2 *Excellence* (US LST-511) LST, capacity 200 tps, 16 tk, hel deck, 1 x 2 *Sinbad/Mistral* SAM (plus 3 in store)

Plus craft: 10 LCM, 1 hovercraft and boats

SUPPORT AND MISCELLANEOUS 2

1 *Jupiter* diving spt and salvage, 1 trg

Air Force 6,000

(incl 3,000 conscripts); 139 cbt ac, 20 armed hel

FGA 4 sqn

3 with 51 A-4S/SI, 24 TA-4S/SI

1 with 7 F-16 (3 -A, 4 -B) (with a further 12 F-16A/B in US)

FTR 2 sqn with 28 F-5E, 9 F-5F

RECCE 1 sqn with 8* RF-5E

AEW 1 sqn with 4 E-2C

ARMED HEL 2 sqn with 20 AS 550A2/C2

TRANSPORT 5 sqn

AC 2 sqn

1 with 4 KC-130B (tkr/tpt), 5 C-130H, 1 KC-130H

1 with tpt/MR, 4 *Fokker* 50, 5 *Fokker* 50 *Enforcer* Mk 2 MPA (MR)

HEL 3 sqn

1 with 19 UH-1H, 1 with 21 AS-332M (incl 5 SAR), 1 with 20 AS-532UL *Cougar*

TRG 2 sqn

1 with 27 SIAI S-211

1 with 26 SF-260

UAV 1 sqn with *Scout*

AIR DEFENCE SYSTEMS DIVISION

4 field def sqn

Air Defence Bde 1 bn with 1 sqn with **35mm** Oerlikon, 1 sqn with I HAWK, 1 sqn with blind fire *Rapier*

Air Force Systems Bde 1 bn with 1 sqn mobile RADAR, 1 sqn LORADS

Divisional Air Def Arty Bde (attached to Army Division) 1 bn with *Mistral* (SAM), 3 sqn RBS 70 (SAM)

MISSILES

AAM AIM-9 J/P *Sidewinder*

ASM AGM-65B *Maverick*, AGM-65G *Maverick*

Forces Abroad

AUSTRALIA 160; flying trg school with 27 S-211

BRUNEI 500; trg school, incl hel det (with 5 UH-1)

TAIWAN 4 trg camps (incl MBT, inf and arty)

THAILAND 2 trg camps (arty)

US 250; 150 6 CH-47D (ANG facility Grand Prairie, TX); 100 12 F-16A/B (leased from USAF at Luke AFB, AZ)

UN AND PEACEKEEPING

IRAQ/KUWAIT (UNIKOM): 6 Obs

Paramilitary ε108,000+ active

SINGAPORE POLICE FORCE

incl Police Coast Guard

12 *Swift* PCI< and about 80 boats

Singapore Gurkha Contingent (750)

CIVIL DEFENCE FORCE 108,000

(incl 1,500 regulars, 3,600 conscripts, 62,100 former Army reservists, 40,500+ volunteers); 1 construction bde (2,500 conscripts)

Foreign Forces

NEW ZEALAND 11; spt unit

US 140 **Navy** 100 **Air Force** 40

Taiwan (Republic Of China)

	1995	1996	1997	1998
GNP	NT$7.0tr	NT$7.6tr		
	($263bn)	($275bn)		
per capita	$11,300	$11,700		
Growth	6.0%	5.7%		
Inflation	3.7%	3.1%		
Debt	$26bn	$27bn		
Def exp°	NT$348bn	NT$357bn		
	($13.1bn)	($13.6bn)		
Def bdgt			NT$311bn	NT$308bn
			($11.3bn)	($11.3bn)
US$1 = NT$	26.5	26.3	27.8	

NT$ = New Taiwan dollar

° Incl special appropriations for procurement and infrastructure

Population	21,550,000		
(Taiwanese 84%, mainland Chinese 14%)			
Age	*13–17*	*18–22*	*23–32*
Men	1,039,000	952,000	1,929,000
Women	979,000	905,000	1,845,000

Total Armed Forces

ACTIVE ε376,000

Terms of service: 2 years

RESERVES 1,657,500

Army 1,500,000 with some obligation to age 30 **Navy** 32,500 **Marines** 35,000 **Air Force** 90,000

Army ε240,000

(incl mil police)

3 Army, 1 AB Special Ops HQ • 10 inf div • 2 mech inf div • 2 AB bde • 6 indep armd bde • 1 tk gp • 2 AD SAM gp with 6 SAM bn: 2 with *Nike Hercules*, 4 with I HAWK • 2 avn gp, 6 avn sqn

RESERVES

7 lt inf div

EQUIPMENT

MBT 100 M-48A5, 450+ M-48H, 169 M-60A3

LT TK 230 M-24 (**90mm gun**), 675 M-41/Type 64

AIFV 225 M-113 with **20–30mm** cannon

APC 650 M-113, 300 V-150 *Commando*

TOWED ARTY 105mm: 650 M-101 (T-64); **155mm**: M-44, 90 M-59, 250 M-114 (T-65); **203mm**: 70 M-115

SP ARTY 105mm: 100 M-108; **155mm**: 45 T-69, 110 M-109A2; **203mm**: 60 M-110

COASTAL ARTY 127mm: US Mk 30 (reported)

MRL: **117mm**: KF VI; **126mm**: KF III/IV towed and SP

MOR 81mm: M-29 (some SP); **107mm**

ATGW 1,000 TOW (some SP)

RCL 90mm: M-67; **106mm**: 500 M-40A1/Type 51

AD GUNS 40mm: 400 (incl M-42 SP, Bofors)

SAM 40 Nike *Hercules* (to be retired), 100 HAWK, *Tien Kung* (*Sky Bow*) -1/-2, 2 *Chaparral*, ε6 *Patriot*

AC 20 O-1

HEL 110 UH-1H, 45 AH-1W, 26 OH-58D, 12 KH-4, 7 CH-47, 5 Hughes 500

UAV *Mastiff* III

DEPLOYMENT

Quemoy 35–40,000; 4 inf div **Matsu** 8–10,000; 1 inf div

Navy 68,000

(incl 30,000 Marines)

3 Naval Districts

BASES Tsoying (HQ), Makung (Pescadores), Keelung (New East Coast fleet set up and based at Suo; 6 *Chin Yang*-class FF)

SUBMARINES 4

2 *Hai Lung* (Nl mod *Zwaardvis*) with 533mm TT

2 *Hai Shih* (US *Guppy* II) with 533mm TT (trg only)

PRINCIPAL SURFACE COMBATANTS 36

DESTROYERS 18

DDG 7 *Chien Yang* (US *Gearing*) (*Wu Chin* III conversion) with 10 SM-1 MR SAM (boxed), plus 1 x 8 ASROC, 2 x 3 ASTT, plus 1 *Hughes* MD-500 hel

DD 11

6 *Fu Yang* (US *Gearing*) (ASW); 5 with 1 *Hughes* MD 500 hel, 1 with 1 x 8 ASROC, all with 2 x 3 ASTT; plus 1 or 2 x 2 127mm guns, 3 or 5 *Hsiung Feng* I (*HF* 1) (Il *Gabriel*) SSM

2 *Po Yang* (US *Sumner*)† with 1 or 2 x 2 127mm guns; plus 2 x 3 ASTT; 5 or 6 *HF* 1 SSM, 1 with 1 *Hughes* MD-500 hel

3 *Kun Yang* (US *Fletcher*) with 2 or 3 127mm guns; 1 76mm gun; plus 2 x 3 ASTT with 5 *HF* 1 SSM†

FRIGATES 18

FFG 5 *Cheng Kung* with 1 SM-1 MR SAM, 2 x 3

ASTT plus 2 x 4 *HF* II, 1 or 2 S-70C hel

FF 13

4 *Kang Ding* (Fr *La Fayette*) with 8 *Harpoon* SSM, 1 x 8 ASROC, 1 127mm gun, 4 324mm TT, 1 SH-2F hel

3 *Tien Shan* (US *Lawrence/Crosley*), some with up to 6 40mm guns (fishing protection and tpt 160 tps)

6 *Chin Yang* (US *Knox*) with 1 x 8 ASROC, 1 SH-2F hel, 4 ASTT; plus *Harpoon* (from ASROC launchers), 1 127mm gun

PATROL AND COASTAL COMBATANTS 101

CORVETTES 3 *Ping Ching* (US *Auk*) with 4 40mm gun

MISSILE CRAFT 53

2 *Lung Chiang* PFM with 2 *HF* 1 SSM

1 *Jinn Chiang* PFM with 4 *HF* 1 SSM

50 *Hai Ou* (mod Il *Dvora*)< with 2 *HF* 1 SSM

PATROL, INSHORE 45 (op by Maritime Police)

22 Vosper-type 32m PFI, 7 PCI, about 16 PCI<

MINE COUNTERMEASURES 13

5 *Yung Chou* (US *Adjutant*) MSC

4 (ex-US) *Aggressive* ocean-going minesweepers

4 MSC converted from oil rig spt ships

AMPHIBIOUS 23

2 *Newport* LST capacity 400 troops, 500 tons vehicles, 4 LCVP

1 *Kao Hsiung* (US LST 511) amph comd

14 *Chung Hai* (US LST 511) LST, capacity 16 tk, 200 tps

4 *Mei Lo* (US LSM-1) LSM, capacity about 4 tk

1 *Cheng Hai* (US *Cabildo*) LSD, capacity 3 LCU or 18 LCM

1 *Chung Cheng* (US *Ashland*) LSD, capacity 3 LCU or 18 LCM

Plus about 400 craft: 22 LCU, some 260 LCM, 120 LCVP

SUPPORT AND MISCELLANEOUS 20

3 spt tkr, 2 repair/salvage, 1 *Wu Yi* combat spt with hel deck, 2 *Yuen Feng* and 2 *Wu Kang* attack tpt with hel deck, 2 tpt, 7 ocean tugs, 1 *Te Kuan* (research)

COASTAL DEFENCE 1

1 SSM coastal def bn with *Hsiung Feng* (*Gabriel*-type)

NAVAL AIR

31 cbt ac; 21 armed hel

MR 1 sqn with 31 S-2 (24 -E, 7 -G) (Air Force-operated)

HEL 12* Hughes 500MD, 9* S-70C ASW *Defender*, 9 S-70C(M)-1

MARINES (30,000)

2 div, spt elm

EQUIPMENT

AAV LVTP-4/-5

TOWED ARTY 105mm, 155mm

RCL 106mm

Air Force 68,000

402 cbt ac, no armed hel **Flying hours** 180
FGA/FTR 13 sqn
 10 with 274 F-5 (7 -B, 214 -E, 53 -F)
 3 with 70 *Ching-Kuo* (plus 10 test)
(First deliveries of 60 *Mirage* 2000-5 and 150 F-16C/D May 1997)
AEW 4 E-2T
SAR 1 sqn with 14 S-70C
TPT 7 ac sqn
 2 with 8 C-47, 1 C-118B, 1 DC-6B
 3 with 30 C-119G
 1 with 13 C-130H (1 EW)
 1 VIP with 4 -727-100, 12 Beech 1900
HEL 5 CH-34, 1 S-62A (VIP), 14 S-70
TRG ac incl 58* AT-3A/B, 60 T-38A, 42 T-34C
MISSILES
 ASM AGM-65A *Maverick*
 AAM AIM-4D *Falcon*, AIM-9J/P *Sidewinder*, *Shafrir*, *Sky Sword* I and II, R550 *Magic*, *Mica*

Paramilitary ε26,650

SECURITY GROUPS 25,000
National Police Administration (Ministry of Interior); **Bureau of Investigation** (Ministry of Justice); **Military Police** (Ministry of Defence)
MARITIME POLICE ε1,000
about 38 armed patrol boats; also man many of the patrol craft listed under Navy
CUSTOMS SERVICE (Ministry of Finance) 650
5 PCO, 2 PCC, 1 PCI, 5 PCI<; most armed

Foreign Forces

SINGAPORE 4 trg camps

Thailand

	1995	1996	1997	1998
GDP	b4.2tr	b4.4tr		
	($167bn)	($174bn)		
per capita	$7,700	$8,200		
Growth	8.6%	6.7%		
Inflation	5.7%	5.9%		
Debt	$56.8bn	$69.9bn		
Def exp	b100bn	b109bn		
	($4.0bn)	($4.3bn)		
Def bdgt			b104bn	
			($4.1bn)	
FMA (US)	$3.4m	$2.9m	$4.5m	$4.6m
(Aus)	$3.0m	$3.0m		
$1 = baht	25.0	25.3	25.7	

Population	62,093,000		

(Thai 75%, Chinese 14%, Muslim 4%)

Age	*13–17*	*18–22*	*23–32*
Men	3,181,000	3,159,000	5,965,000
Women	3,077,000	3,062,000	5,807,000

Total Armed Forces

ACTIVE 266,000
Terms of service: conscription, 2 years (ends Oct 1997)

RESERVES 200,000

Army 150,000

(80,000 conscripts)
4 Regional Army HQ, 2 Corps HQ • 2 cav div • 3 armd inf div • 3 mech inf div • 1 lt inf div • 2 SF div • 1 arty div, 1 AD arty div (6 AD arty bn) • 1 engr div • 4 economic development div • 1 indep cav regt • 8 indep inf bn • 4 recce coy • armd air cav regt with 3 air-mobile coy • Some hel flt

RESERVES
4 inf div HQ

EQUIPMENT
 MBT 50+ PRC Type-69 (in store), 150 M-48A5, 77 M-60A1
 LT TK 154 *Scorpion*, 250 M-41, 106 *Stingray*
 RECCE 32 Shorland Mk 3
 APC 340 M-113, 162 V-150 *Commando*, 18 *Condor*, 450 PRC Type-85 (YW-531H)
 TOWED ARTY 105mm: 24 LG1 Mk 2, 200 M-101/-101 mod, 12 M-102, 32 M-618A2 (local manufacture); **130mm**: 15 PRC Type-59; **155mm**: 56 M-114, 62 M-198, 32 M-71
 SP ARTY 155mm: 20 M-109A5 (reported)
 MOR 81mm, 107mm
 ATGW TOW, 300 *Dragon*
 RL M-72 LAW
 RCL 75mm: M-20; **106mm**: 150 M-40
 AD GUNS 20mm: 24 M-163 *Vulcan*, 24 M-167 *Vulcan*; **37mm**: 122 Type-74; **40mm**: 80 M-1/M-42 SP, 28 L/70; **57mm**: 24+ PRC Type-59
 SAM *Redeye*, some *Aspide*
 AIRCRAFT
  TPT 2 C-212, 2 Beech 1900C-1, 4 C-47, 10 Cessna 208, 2 Short 330UTT, 1 *Beech King Air*, 2 *Jetstream* 41
  LIAISON 60 O-1A, 17 -E, 5 T-41A, 13 U-17A
  TRG 16 T-41D
 HELICOPTERS
  ATTACK 4 AH-1F
  TPT 12 CH-47, 10 Bell 206, 9 B-212, 6 B-214, 69 UH-1H
  TRG 36 Hughes 300C, 3 OH-13, 7 TH-55

SURV RASIT (veh, arty), AN-TPQ-36 (arty, mor)

Navy 73,000

(incl 1,700 Naval Air, 22,000 Marines, 7,000 Coastal
Defence, 28,000 conscripts)
FLEETS 1st North Thai Gulf **2nd** South Thai Gulf
1 Naval Air Division
BASES Bangkok, Sattahip (Fleet HQ), Songkhla,
Phang Nga, Nakhon Phanom (HQ Mekong River
Operating Unit)

PRINCIPAL SURFACE COMBATANTS 15

AIRCRAFT CARRIER 1 *Chakri Naruebet* with 8 AV-8S
Matador (*Harrier*), 6 S-70B *Seahawk* hel, 3 x 6 *Sadral*
SAM

FRIGATES 14

FFG 8

2 *Naresuan* with 2 x 4 *Harpoon* SSM, 8 cell *Sea Sparrow*
SAM, 1 127mm gun, 6 324mm TT, 1 SH-2F hel
2 *Chao Phraya* (PRC *Jianghu* III) with 8 C-801 SSM, 2
x 2 100mm guns; plus 2 x 5 ASW RL (plus 1
undergoing weapons fit)
2 *Kraburil* (PRC *Jianghu* IV type) with 8 C-801 SSM, 1
x 2 100mm guns; plus 2 x 5 ASW RL and *Bell* 212
hel
2 *Phutthayotfa Chulalok* (US *Knox*) (to be leased) with
8 *Harpoon* SSM, 8 ASROC ASTT, 1 127mm gun, 1
Bell 212 hel

FF 6

1 *Makut Rajakumarn* with 2 x 3 ASTT (*Sting Ray*
LWT); plus 2 114mm guns
2 *Tapi* (US PF-103) with 2 x 3 ASTT (Mk 46 LWT)
2 *Tachin* (US *Tacoma*) with 2 x 3 ASTT (trg)
1 *Pin Klao* (US *Cannon*) with 1 76mm gun, 6 324mm
TT

PATROL AND COASTAL COMBATANTS 75

CORVETTES 5

2 *Rattanakosin* with 2 x 3 ASTT (*Sting Ray* LWT); plus
2 x 4 *Harpoon* SSM, 8 *Aspide* SAM
3 *Khamronsin* with 2 x 3 ASTT; plus 1 76mm gun

MISSILE CRAFT 6

3 *Ratcharit* (It Breda 50m) with 4 MM-38 *Exocet* SSM
3 *Prabparapak* (Ge Lürssen 45m) with 5 *Gabriel* SSM

PATROL CRAFT 64

COASTAL 12

3 *Cholburi* PFC, 6 *Sattahip*, 3 PCD

INSHORE 52

10 T-11 (US PGM-71), 9 T-91, about 33 PCF

MINE COUNTERMEASURES 5

2 *Bang Rachan* (Ge Lürssen T-48) MCC
2 *Ladya* (US *Bluebird*) MSC
1 *Thalang* MCM spt with minesweeping capability
(Plus some 12 MSB)

AMPHIBIOUS 9

2 *Sichang* (Fr PS-700) LST, capacity 14 tk, 300 tps
with hel deck (trg)
5 *Angthong* (US LST-511) LST, capacity 16 tk, 200 tps

2 *Kut* (US LSM-1) LSM, capacity about 4 tk
Plus about 51 craft: 9 LCU, about 24 LCM, 1 LCG, 2
LSIL, 3 hovercraft, 12 LCVP

SUPPORT AND MISCELLANEOUS 16

1 *Similan* AO (1 hel) , 1 *Chula* AO, 5 small tkr, 3
survey, 6 trg

NAVAL AIR (1,700)

(300 conscripts); 56 cbt ac; 6 armed hel
FTR 9 *Harrier* (7 AV-8, 2 TAV-8)
MR/ATTACK 11 Cessna T-337 *Skymasters*, 14 A-7E, 4 TA-
7C
MR/ASW 2 P-3T *Orion*, 1 UP-3T, 6 Do-228, 5 F-27
MPA, 4 S-2F (plus 2 P-3A in store)
ASW HEL 6 S-70B
UTILITY 2 CL-215, 5 N-24A *Nomad*
SAR/UTILITY 7 Bell 212, 4 Bell 214, 4 UH-1H, 6 S-76N
ASM AGM-84 *Harpoon* (for F-27MPA, P-3T)

MARINES (22,000)

1 div HQ, 2 inf regt, 1 arty regt (3 fd, 1 AA bn); 1 amph
aslt bn; recce bn

EQUIPMENT

APC 33 LVTP-7
TOWED ARTY 155mm: 18 GC-45, 18 GHN-45
ATGW TOW, *Dragon*

Air Force 43,000

210 cbt ac, no armed hel **Flying hours** 100
FGA 3 sqn
    1 with 7 F-5A, 4 -B
    2 with 36 F-16 (26 -A, 10 -B)
FTR 2 sqn with 35 F-5E, 6 -F
ARMED AC 5 sqn
    1 with 7 AC-47,
    3 with 24 AU-23A
    1 with 20* N-22B *Missionmaster* (tpt/armed)
ELINT 1 sqn with 3 IAI-201
RECCE 2 sqn with 30* OV-10C, 4* RF-5A, 3*RT-33A
SURVEY 2 *Learjet* 35A, 3 *Merlin* IVA, 3 GAF N-22B
    Nomads
TPT 3 sqn
    1 with 6 C-130H, 6 C-130H-30, 3 DC-8-62F
    1 with 3 C-123-K, 4 BAe-748
    1 with 6 G-222
VIP Royal flight **ac** 1 Airbus A-310-324, 1 Boeing 737-
    200, 1 *King Air* 200, 2 BAe-748, 3 *Merlin* IV **hel** 2 Bell
    412
TRG 24 CT-4, 30 *Fantrainer*-400, 16 *Fantrainer*-600, 16
    SF-260, 10 T-33A, 20 PC-9, 6 -C, 11 T-41, 34* L-
    39ZA/MP
LIAISON 3 *Commander*, 2 *King Air* E90, 30 O-1 *Bird
    Dog*, 2 *Queen Air*, 3 *Basler Turbo*-67
HEL 2 sqn:
    1 with 18 S-58T, 1 with 21 UH-1H
AAM AIM-9B/J *Sidewinder*, *Python* 3

AIR DEFENCE

1 AA arty bty: 4 *Skyguard*, 1 *Flycatcher* radars, each
with 4 fire units of 2 30mm Mauser guns
SAM *Blowpipe*, *Aspide*, RBS-70

Forces Abroad

UN AND PEACEKEEPING

IRAQ/KUWAIT (UNIKOM): 5 Obs

Paramilitary ε71,000 active

THAHAN PHRAN (Hunter Soldiers) 18,500
volunteer irregular force; 27 regt of some 200 coy
NATIONAL SECURITY VOLUNTEER CORPS
50,000
MARINE POLICE 2,500
3 PCO, 3 PCC, 8 PFI, some 110 PCI<
POLICE AVIATION 500
ac 1 *Airtourer*, 6 AU-23, 2 Cessna 310, 1 Fokker 50, 1
CT-4, 1 CN 235, 8 PC-6, 2 Short 330 **hel** 27 Bell 205A,
14 Bell 206, 3 Bell 212, 6 UH-12, 5 KH-4
BORDER PATROL POLICE 18,000
PROVINCIAL POLICE ε50,000
incl ε500 Special Action Force

Foreign Forces

SINGAPORE 2 trg camps (arty)

Vietnam

	1995	1996	1997	1998
GDP	d210tr	d260tr		
	($21.3bn)	($23.6bn)		
per capita	$900	$1,000		
Growth	9.5%	9.5%		
Inflation	12.7%	6.0%		
Debt	$26.5bn	$27.4bn		
Def exp	d21tr	d24tr		
	($910m)	($950m)		
Def bdgt			εd26.0tr	
			($1.1bn)	
$1 = dong	11,000	11,000	11,659	
Population		77,271,000 (Chinese 3%)		
Age	*13–17*	*18–22*	*23–32*	
Men	4,246,000	3,843,000	6,663,000	
Women	4,097,000	3,729,000	6,574,000	

Total Armed Forces

ACTIVE ε492,000

(referred to as 'Main Force')
Terms of service: 2 years, specialists 3 years, some ethnic
minorities 2 years

RESERVES some 3–4,000,000
'Strategic Rear Force' (see also Paramilitary)

Army ε420,000

8 Mil Regions, 2 special areas • 14 Corps HQ • 58 inf
div[a] • 4 mech inf div • 10 armd bde • 15 indep inf regt
• SF incl AB bde, demolition engr regt • Some 10 fd
arty bde • 8 engr div • 10–16 economic construction
div • 20 indep engr bde

EQUIPMENT

MBT 1,315: 45 T-34, 850 T-54/-55, 70 T-62, 350 PRC
Type-59
LT TK 300 PT-76, 320 PRC Type-62/63
RECCE 100 BRDM-1/-2
AIFV 300 BMP
APC 1,100 BTR-40/-50/-60/-152, YW-531, M-113
TOWED ARTY 2,300: **76mm; 85mm; 100mm**: M-
1944, T-12; **105mm**: M-101/-102; **122mm**: Type-54,
Type-60, M-1938, D-30, D-74; **130mm**: M-46;
152mm: D-20; **155mm**: M-114
SP ARTY 152mm: 30 2S3; **175mm**: M-107
COMBINED GUN/MOR 120mm: 2S9 reported
ASLT GUNS 100mm: SU-100; **122mm**: ISU-122
MRL 107mm: 360 Type 63; **122mm**: 350 BM-21;
140mm: BM-14-16
MOR 82mm, 120mm: M-43; **160mm**: M-43
ATGW AT-3 *Sagger*
RCL 75mm: PRC Type-56; **82mm**: PRC Type-65, B-
10; **87mm**: PRC Type-51
AD GUNS 12,000: **14.5mm; 23mm**: incl ZSU-23-4
SP; **30mm; 37mm; 57mm; 85mm; 100mm**
SAM SA-7/-16

[a] Inf div str varies from 5,000 to 12,500

Navy ε42,000

(incl 30,000 Naval Infantry)
Four Naval Regions
BASES Hanoi (HQ), Cam Ranh Bay, Da Nang,
Haiphong, Ha Tou, Ho Chi Minh City, Can Tho, plus
several smaller bases

FRIGATES 7

1 *Barnegat* (US *Cutter*) with 2 SS-N-2A *Styx* SSM, 1
127mm gun
3 Sov *Petya* II with 2 ASW RL, 10 406mm TT, 4
76mm gun
2 Sov *Petya* III with 2 ASW RL, 3 533mm TT, 4 76mm
gun
1 *Dai Ky* (US *Savage*) with 2 x 3 ASTT (trg)

PATROL AND COASTAL COMBATANTS 55

MISSILE CRAFT 9

7 Sov *Osa* II with 4 SS-N-2 SSM
2 Sov *Tarantul* with 4 SS-N-2D *Styx* SSM
TORPEDO CRAFT 23
7 Sov *Turya* PHT with 4 533mm TT
16 Sov *Shershen* PFT with 4 533mm TT
PATROL, INSHORE 23
4 Sov SO-1, 3 US PGM-59/71, 10 *Zhuk*<, 2 Sov
Turya< (no TT), 4 PCI<
MINE COUNTERMEASURES 11
2 *Yurka* MSC, 4 *Sonya* MSC, 2 PRC *Lienyun* MSC, 1
Vanya MSI, 2 *Yevgenya* MSI, plus 5 K-8 boats
AMPHIBIOUS 7
3 US LST-510-511 LST, capacity 200 tps, 16 tk
3 Sov *Polnočny* LSM, capacity 180 tps, 6 tk
1 US LSM-1 LSM, capacity about 50 tps, 4 tk
Plus about 30 craft: 12 LCM, 18 LCU
SUPPORT AND MISCELLANEOUS 30+
incl 1 trg, 1 survey, 4 small tkr, about 12 small tpt, 2
ex-Sov floating docks and 3 div spt. Significant
numbers of small merchant ships and trawlers are
taken into naval service for patrol and resupply
duties. Some of these may be lightly armed

NAVAL INFANTRY (30,000)
(amph, cdo)

Air Force 15,000

201 cbt ac, 32 armed hel (plus many in store). 4 Air Div
FGA 2 regt with 65 Su-22, 6 Su-27
FTR 5 regt with 124 MiG-21bis/PF
ATTACK HEL 24 Mi-24

MR 4 Be-12
ASW HEL 8 Ka-25
SURVEY 2 An-30
TPT 3 regt incl 12 An-2, 4 An-24, 30 An-26, 8 Tu-134, 14
Yak-40
HEL some 70 incl Mi-4, Mi-6, Mi-8
TRG 3 regt with 52 **ac**, incl L-39, MiG-21U, Yak-18
AAM AA-2 *Atoll*, AA-8 *Aphid*, AA-10 *Allamo*

Air Defence Force 15,000

14 AD div
SAM some 66 sites with SA-2/-3/-6
AD 4 arty bde: **37mm, 57mm, 85mm, 100mm, 130mm**
People's Regional Force: ε1,000 units, 6 radar bde: 100
sites

Paramilitary ε65,000 active

LOCAL FORCES some 4–5,000,000 (incl 1.5,000,000
reserves)
incl **People's Self-Defence Force** (urban units)
People's Militia (rural units); these comprise
static and mobile cbt units, log spt and village
protection pl; some arty, mor and AD guns; acts as
reserve
BORDER DEFENCE CORPS ε65,000

Foreign Forces

RUSSIA 700; naval facilities; ELINT station

MILITARY DEVELOPMENTS

The main challenge facing the security forces in a number of states in the Caribbean and Latin America remains guerrilla groups with a less ideologically driven agenda, but one more linked to organised crime and drug trafficking. Inter-state disputes remain at a low level and are unlikely to provoke more than skirmishes over borders and illegal migration. While political control of the military in the region is in the ascendancy, much remains to be done in reforming the armed forces; many are still organised and equipped to deal with diminishing external threats. Regional military spending has more to do with maintaining the military's position and prestige than with organising and equipping it to face the daunting challenge of operations against politically inspired armed groups and organised crime, in particular related to narcotics. Successful operations against these threats demand a high level of training, morale and good intelligence rather than expensive weapon systems. Too many resources still seem to be spent on sustaining pay and pensions for active and retired personnel, and on major weapons systems not best suited to the military operations most likely to be conducted. This misallocation of military resources means that forces facing internal threats from non-state armed groups are over-stretched. The situation is exacerbated, in some cases, by corruption among both the police and security forces.

An important development in the region was the US decision on 31 July 1997 to relax restrictions on sales of advanced conventional-weapon systems to Central and South America.

There have been positive developments in security policy in **Brazil**, the largest country in the region. On 20 June 1997, President Fernando Henrique Cardoso announced that he was formally requesting the National Congress to ratify accession to the Treaty on the Non-Proliferation of Nuclear Weapons (NPT). At the beginning of the year, Brazil began implementing its new National Defence Plan, announced on 17 November 1996, which recognised that the main national-security threats are drug trafficking and international organised crime. The traditional military doctrine that Brazil's major security threat comes from the south was finally dropped. However, the recent order of 87 *Leopard* 1A1 tanks from Belgium and 91 M60A3 tanks from the US, being delivered in 1997, does not seem consistent with that policy.

In **Colombia**, where *Plan Horizonte* for re-organising the armed forces to deal with the formidable internal security threat has been under way since the beginning of 1995, progress has been disappointing. The plan was intended to develop better-trained and more mobile formations to deal with the increasing guerrilla threat and to carry out anti-drug operations. Only two of four planned mobile assault brigades, to be attached to the existing four divisions, have been formed. There have also been serious military failures, in particular one which resulted in 60 members of the armed forces being captured and held hostage in August 1996. The soldiers were eventually released in June 1997, but at the high price of formally ceding control of a large swathe of territory to the Revolutionary Armed Forces of Colombia (FARC). This step confirms their combatant status under the laws of armed conflict. FARC and the other main guerrilla group, the National Liberation Army (ELN), have for some time held sway over significant portions of the country's rural areas, but do not enjoy sufficient public support to overthrow the central government.

The inability of the Colombian Armed Forces to contain rebel activity has had an effect on all neighbouring countries, in particular **Venezuela**. Tensions between Venezuela and Colombia have risen as the conflict has spilled over their common border, resulting in clashes between the ELN and the Venezuelan Army. In April 1997, Venezuela increased its forces in the border region by some 10,000 personnel.

Argentina and **Chile** have continued their modest equipment-modernisation programmes and both remain Latin America's leading troop suppliers to UN peacekeeping operations. Argentina runs a Joint Peacekeeping Operations Training Centre which has become, in effect, a training facility for the entire region. As in many other neighbouring countries, an inordinate portion – more than three-quarters – of the two countries' defence budgets is spent on personnel costs for both those serving and retired, leaving insufficient funds for operations, maintenance, equipment acquisition and upgrading. This is hampering efforts to develop more mobile and capable armed forces better suited to current security threats. Relations between **Ecuador** and **Peru** are improving as talks on their border dispute continue, and the likelihood of further conflict is receding. In Peru, the standing of the armed forces was enhanced as a result of the successful operation to end the hostage crisis at the Japanese Embassy in Lima in which 16 of the *Movimento Revolucionario Túpac Amaru* (MRTA) were killed. While the MRTA and the other main guerrilla group, the *Sendero Luminoso* (Shining Path), continue to decline, they still pose a challenge to the security forces from time to time.

In **Guatemala**, major reductions in the armed forces are in hand following the final peace settlement between the government and the *Unidad Revolucionara Nacional* (URNG) in December 1996. In May 1997, the government announced that 5,000 troops will be demobilised and up to 11,500 posts cut from the armed forces organisation. In **Mexico**, a settlement between the government and the *Ejercito Zapatista de Liberacion Nacional* (EZLN) is still to be agreed. However, violence has dropped to a low level. Military officers continue to play an important role in strengthening the morale and organisation of the civil police.

DEFENCE SPENDING

The general lack of transparency in military financial accounting makes analysing regional defence economics difficult. This situation is inconsistent with Latin America's growing role in the global economy and the ease with which other economic and financial data can be obtained. However, there are encouraging developments in the region's commitment to confidence-building measures (CBMs) related to openness in military matters. For example, more countries are reporting their major weapons acquisitions to the United Nations Register of Conventional Arms. This trend has been encouraged by the Organisation of American States (OAS) and the series of annual Defense Ministerial Meetings which has been urging members to participate in CBMs. In its session in Lima in June 1997, the OAS passed a resolution calling for the establishment of a 'legal regime' to give advance notification of major arms acquisitions. Such a complementary measure would be a major improvement on the UN Register, which requires only retrospective reports. The trend towards greater responsibility and transparency in arms acquisitions helped ease the US policy of barring exports of advanced weapon systems to Latin American countries. US companies are already being allowed to enter the competition in Chile for replacement combat aircraft (see below).

The lack of transparency accounts for the variations in independent estimates of regional defence expenditure. According to the International Monetary Fund (IMF), defence expenditure in individual countries of the region on average accounted for 1.3% of gross domestic product (GDP) in 1995, falling to 1.2% in 1996. By comparison, the IISS estimates average defence expenditures at 1.9% of GDP in 1995 and 1.8% in 1996.

Although the region currently uses more IMF credit and loans than any other part of the world (some $15 billion out of a total of $41bn as of March 1997), the IMF is generally unable to count on timely reporting of defence expenditure from many of its clients. In the 1996 edition of the annual

Table 31 Countries reporting defence expenditures to the UN, 1995

(US$m)

By function	Argentina	Brazil	Chile	Colombia	El Salvador
Personnel	3,044	5,560	n.a.	379	8
Operations & Maintenance	449	918	n.a.	237	81
Procurement	82	690	n.a.	73	0
Research & Development	13	33	n.a.	1	0
Infrastructure	14	144	n.a.	17	1
Other	n.a.	n.a.	n.a.	n.a.	11
Total	3,602	7,345	1,057	708	101
By service					
Army	734	3,178	n.a.	691	n.a.
Navy	493	2,133	n.a.	0	n.a.
Air Force	498	1,864	n.a.	17	n.a.
Central Command	1,377	64	n.a.	n.a.	11
Paramilitary	499	n.a.	n.a.	n.a.	n.a.
Total	3,602	7,240	1,057	708	101

Source United Nations, 1996

Table 32 Chile's defence-related expenditure, 1996–1997

(US$m)	1996	1997
Defence budget	1,057	1,158
Codelco Copper Fund (for equipment)	285	260
Pensions for retired military personnel	545	591
Other	108	119
Total	1,995	2,128

Government Finance Statistics Yearbook, the IMF published 1995 defence expenditure figures for just five of the 28 countries covered in *The Military Balance.* Excessive reporting lags apart, difficulties also arise in classifying military expenditures under other budget headings and the lack of adherence by reporting states to a standardised method.

The lack of transparency is particularly evident in funding for paramilitary forces, pensions for retired military personnel, defence-industrial subsidies and extra-budgetary sources of military revenue. The funding of paramilitary forces, for example, may be listed under the Defence or the Public Order and Safety budget. While it is reasonable to expect some variance in the relative priority of the Defence and Public Order and Safety budgets, the IMF figures imply that there may be reporting inconsistencies. The regional response to the annual UN survey on military expenditures is equally poor (just five countries reported for 1995) and reproduces the inconsistencies apparent in IMF figures.

In some respects, Chile is an example of improved transparency in the region (despite its incomplete reporting to the IMF and UN). Details of defence spending are published in the national press. The defence budget is acknowledged to exclude some extra-budgetary military funding for equipment (from the state-owned Codelco copper fund) as well as pensions for retired military personnel which are funded from the Social Security budget. The positive effects of this transparency have been offset by the government's over-reaction to accusations of excessive military spending levelled by regional neighbours (none of which can near match Chile's efforts in respect of transparency, and all of which spend considerably more on their military than their budgets indicate).

THE REGIONAL ARMS TRADE

The US Arms Control and Disarmament Agency (ACDA) reported that the value of the regional arms trade (deliveries) doubled in 1995 to around $1.5bn. The IISS estimates that regional arms deliveries increased again in 1996 to some $1.6bn. Although this was the highest level since 1991, Latin America in general remains one of the smallest regional arms markets.

Recent major developments in the regional arms trade include: a shift in US arms-sales policy to allow US defence firms to take part in a 1997 international competition to supply Chile with combat aircraft; the sale of Belarus-supplied MiG-29s (now delivered) and SU-25s (on order) to Peru in 1996; purchases by Colombia and Mexico of Russian Mi-17s, another indication of the revival of Russian arms sales to the region; and Chile's possible purchase of two Franco-Spanish *Scorpene* submarines.

Table 33 UN Arms Register of Conventional Arms transfers, Caribbean and Latin America, 1996

(as at 11 August 1997)	MBT	ACV	Artillery	Combat Aircraft	Attack Helicopters	Warships	Missiles
Argentina	–	–	–	4	–	–	–
Brazil	7	–	18	–	7	2	–
Chile	11	128		10	10		8
Ecuador	–	–	–	–	–	2	4
Mexico	–	136	–	–	38	–	–
Peru	–	37	–	11	–	–	268
Uruguay	–	10	2	–	–	–	–
Total	8	311	20	21	55	4	280

Table 34 Arms orders and deliveries, Caribbean and Latin America, 1995–1997

Equipment	Type	Unit	Supplier	Order Date	Delivery Date	Comment
Argentina						
AIFV	TAM IFV	213	Domestic	1994	1995	50 delivered 1995
APC	*Grenadier*	111	Domestic	1994	1995	88 delivered to mid-1997
arty	155mm		Domestic	1995	1996	Development
FGA	A-4	8	US	1997		Further 11 for parts
hel	UH-1H	26	US	1995	1997	EDA
MBT	TAM	200	Domestic	1994	1995	30 delivered 1995
tpt	C-130B	5	US	1995	1997	EDA
Bahamas						
OPV	*Bahamas*-class	2	US	1997		

Equipment	Type	Unit	Supplier	Order Date	Delivery Date	Comment
Belize						
OPV	*Daphne*-class	1	UK	1996	1996	Ex-Da; refurbishment
Brazil						
AEW	EMB-145	8	Domestic			8 EMB-145 recce variants
arty	105mm	18	It		1995	*Otobreda* 105mm Pack howitzer
arty	M-114 155mm	15	It	1996	1997	
arty	L118 105mm	50	UK	1994	1995	
ATGW	MSS-1.2		Domestic			Development
FF	Type-22	4	UK	1994	1997	*Battleaxe* deliveries completed
FGA	AMX	56	Collab	1985	1997	With Italy; 32 delivered
hel	AS 550	2	Fr	1993	1995	
hel	*Lynx*	9	UK	1993	1996	Also upgrades for 5 of existing fleet
hel	UH-1H	20	US	1995	1995	
hel	UH-60	4	US	1997	1997	For MOMEP operation
MBT	M-60A3	91	US	1995	1996	
MBT	*Leopard* 1A1	87	Be	1995		Delayed order
MRL	SS-80		Domestic			Development
mor	81mm		UK	1994	1995	
MSC	*River*-class	3	UK	1994		Ex-UK; none in service by Apr 1997
PCI	*Grauna*	10	Ge		1997	8 in service
SAM	*Mistral*		Fr	1995		
SAM	SA-18	56	RF	1995		
SS	Type 209/1400	6	Domestic	1985	1995	Fourth launched 1996
trg	EMB-312H		Domestic	1994		*Tucano* development
Chile						
AEW	B-707 *Condor*	1	Il		1995	Modified to AEW
APC	M-113	220	US	1996	1997	
APC	*Piranha* APC	180	Domestic	1993	1995	CH licence; 100 delivered 1995
FAC	*Saar* 4.5	2	Il		1997	2-*Aliyah*, *Geoula* delivered
FAC	Type 148	4	Ge		1997	
FGA	F-5 E/F	14	Domestic	1997	1998	Upgrade for aerial refuelling
FGA	*Mirage* 5M	25	Be	1994	1995	Ex-Be; upgrade
lt tk	*Scorpion*	30	UK	1993	1995	12 delivered
arty	G-5	28	RSA	1997		
MBT	*Leopard* 1A5	67	Be	1997		
PCC	Type 1200	1	Ca		1995	Icebreaker
PCI	*Dabur*	10	Il		1995	
PFC	*Saar*-class	6	Il	1996	1996	Ex-Il; 4 delivered
SS	*Scorpene*	2	Fr			Unconfirmed; Fr/Sp venture
tkr	B-707	1	Il	1995	1996	
tpt	C-130B	4	US	1995	1996	
Colombia						
hel	Mi-17	10	RF	1996	1997	To complete 1998
hel	UH-60	12	US	1992	1995	Deliveries 1994–95
hel	UH1-H	12	US		1997	EDA
tpt	C-130B	7	US		1997	Deliveries completed
tpt	CN-235	3	Sp	1997	1998	
Ecuador						
arty	ZU-23	34	Nic		1997	
FGA	Kfir	4	Il	1995	1996	Unconfirmed
MBT	T-55	3	Nic		1997	
MRL	122MM	6	Slvk		1995	
tpt	C-130B	4	US	1993	1997	4 delivered

Equipment	Type	Unit	Supplier	Order Date	Delivery Date	Comment
Mexico						
APC	AMX 13	97	Be	1994	1995	
hel	UH-1H	73	US	1995	1997	
hel	UH-60	4	US	1992	1995	
PFC	*Mako* 295	10	US	1994	1995	4 delivered, rest by end-1996
Nicaragua						
PFC	*Dabur*-class	3	Il	1996		
Paraguay						
PCI	*Rodman* 101/55	7	Sp		1995	2 *Rodman* 101, 1 *Rodman* 55
Peru						
FGA	A-37	11	US	1995	1996	
FGA	Su-25	14	Bel	1996		Delivery unconfirmed
FGA	MiG-29	12	Bel	1996	1996	
SAM	*Javelin*	28	UK		1995	
tpt	B-737	2	US		1996	Ex-Fr
Uruguay						
APC	OT-64	60	Cz	1994	1995	
hel	*Wessex*	6	UK	1996	1997	
FGA	F-5	8	ROC	1997	1997	Surplus
Venezuela						
tpt	PZL-An-28	24	Pl	1995	1997	Deliveries to 1998
arty	105mm	18	Arg	1995	1995	Reconditioned
hel	AS-332	6	Fr	1997		For border patrols
hel	Mi-17	18	RF	1995	1996	Deliveries to 1997; refurbished in Pl
PCI	*Integnidad*-class	10	Domestic		1997	First delivered
hel	UH-1H	5	US	1997		

Dollar GDP figures for several countries in Latin America are based on Inter-American Development Bank estimates. In some cases, the dollar conversion rates are different from the average exchange rate values shown under the country entry. Dollar GDP figures may vary from those cited in *The Military Balance* in previous years. Defence budgets and expenditures have been converted at the dollar exchange rate used to calculate GDP.

Antigua and Barbuda

	1995	1996	1997	1998
GDP	EC$1.2bn	EC$1.1bn		
	($436m)	($419m)		
per capita	$4,800	$4,600		
Growth	-3.8%	-6.0%		
Inflation	2.9%	1.7%		
Ext Debt	$275m	$274m		
Def exp	εEC$8.9m	εEC$9.0m		
	($3.2m)	($3.2m)		
Def bdgt			εEC$9.0m	
			($3.2m)	
US$1 = EC$*	2.70	2.70	2.70	

*East Caribbean dollar

Population		70,000		
Age	*13–17*	*18–22*	*23–32*	
Men	5,000	4,000	5,000	
Women	5,000	5,000	7,000	

Total Armed Forces

ACTIVE (all services form combined Antigua and Barbuda Defence Force) 150

RESERVES 75

Army 125

Navy 25

BASE St Johns
PATROL CRAFT 2
  PATROL, INSHORE 2
  1 *Swift* PCI with 1 12.7mm, 2 7.62mm gun
  1 *Dauntless* PCI with 1 7.62mm gun

Argentina

	1995	1996	1997	1998
GDP	P280bn	P299bn		
	($232bn)	($248bn)		
per capita	$8,500	$8,900		

contd	1995	1996	1997	1998
Growth	-4.6%	4.7%		
Inflation	3.3%	0.2%		
Debt	$89bn	$101bn		
Def exp	P4.7bn	P4.6bn		
	($3.9bn)	($3.8bn)		
Def bdgt			P4.7bn	εP4.9bn
			($3.9bn)	($4.0bn)
FMA (US)	$1.6m	$0.6m	$0.6m	$0.6m
$1 = Peso	1.0	1.0	1.0	

Population		34,860,000		
Age	*13–17*	*18–22*	*23–32*	
Men	1,632,000	1,545,000	2,594,000	
Women	1,579,000	1,499,000	2,533,000	

Total Armed Forces

ACTIVE 73,000

RESERVES 375,000

Army 250,000 (National Guard 200,000 **Territorial Guard** 50,000 **Navy** 75,000**Air Force** 50,000

Army 41,000

3 Corps
  1 with 1 armd, 1 mech bde, 1 trg bde
  1 with 1 inf, 1 mtn bde
  1 with 1 armd, 2 mech, 1 mtn bde
Corps tps: 1 lt armd cav regt (recce), 1 arty, 1 AD arty, 1 engr bn in each Corps

STRATEGIC RESERVE
1 AB bde
1 mech bde (4 mech, 1 armd cav, 2 SP arty bn)
Army tps
  1 mot inf bn (Army HQ Escort Regt) • 1 mot cav regt (Presidential Escort) • 1 SF coy, 3 avn bn • 1 AD arty bn, 2 engr bn

EQUIPMENT
  MBT 96 M-4 *Sherman* (in store), 230 TAM
  LT TK 56 AMX-13, 106 SK-105 *Kuerassier*
  RECCE 48 AML-90
  AIFV 30 AMX-VCI, 88 TAM VCTP
  APC 129 M-3 half-track, 319 M-113, 70 MOWAG *Grenadier* (mod *Roland*)
  TOWED ARTY 193: **105mm**: 84 M-56; **155mm**: 109 CITEFA Models 77/-81
  SP ARTY 155mm: 24 Mk F3
  MRL 50: **105mm**: 30 SLAM *Pampero*; **127mm**: 20 SLAM SAPBA-1
  MOR 1,309: **81mm**: 1,000; **120mm**: 309 Brandt (37 SP in VCTM AIFV)
  ATGW 2,700: 600 SS-11/-12, *Cobra* (*Mamba*), 2,100 *Mathogo*
  RCL 1,105: **75mm**: 75 M-20; **90mm**: 100 M-67;

105mm: 930 M-1968

AD GUNS 275: **20mm**: 30; **30mm**: 30; **35mm**: 100 GDF-001; **40mm**: 95 L/60/-70 (in store); **90mm**: 20

SAM *Tigercat*, *Blowpipe*, 6 *Roland*

SURV RASIT (veh, arty), *Green Archer* (mor)

AC 1 C212-200, 5 Cessna 207, 5 *Commander* 690, 2 DHC-6, 3 G-222, 1 *Merlin* IIIA, 5 *Merlin* IV, 3 *Queen Air*, 1 *Sabreliner*, 5 T-41, 23 OV-1D

HEL 6 A-109, 3 AS-332B, 5 Bell 205, 4 FH-1100, 4 SA-315B, 1 SA-330, 9 UH-1H, 8 UH-12

Navy 20,000

(incl 2,500 Naval Aviation and 3,500 Marines)

NAVAL AREAS Centre from River Plate to 42° 45' S **South** from 42° 45' S to Cape Horn **Antarctica**

BASES Buenos Aires, Ezeiza (Naval Air), La Plata, Rio Santiago (submarine base), Puerto Belgrano (HQ Centre), Punta Indio (Naval Air), Mar del Plata (submarine base), Ushuaia (HQ South)

SERVICEABILITY very poor throughout Navy

SUBMARINES 3

2 *Santa Cruz* (Ge TR-1700) with 533mm TT (SST-4 HWT)

1 *Salta* (Ge T-209/1200) with 533mm TT (SST-4 HWT) (plus 1 in major refit/mod)

PRINCIPAL SURFACE COMBATANTS 13

DESTROYERS 6

2 *Hercules* (UK Type 42) with 1 x 2 *Sea Dart* SAM; plus 1 SA-319 hel (ASW), 2 x 3 ASTT, 2 MM-38 *Exocet* SSM, 1 114mm gun (incl 1 in reserve)

4 *Almirante Brown* (Ge MEKO 360) ASW with 2 SA-316 hel, 2 x 3 ASTT; plus 8 MM-40 *Exocet* SSM, 1 127mm gun

FRIGATES 7

4 *Espora* (Ge MEKO 140) with 2 x 3 ASTT, hel deck; plus 4 MM-38 *Exocet* SSM

3 *Drummond* (Fr A-69) with 2 x 3 ASTT; plus 4 MM-38 *Exocet*, 1 100mm gun

PATROL AND COASTAL COMBATANTS 18

TORPEDO CRAFT 2 *Intrepida* (Ge Lürssen 45m) PFT with 2 533mm TT (SST-4 HWT) (one poss with 2 MM-38 SSM)

PATROL, OFFSHORE 12

1 *Teniente Olivieri* (ex-US oilfield tug)

3 *Irigoyen* (US *Cherokee* AT)

2 *King* (trg) with 3 105mm guns

2 *Sorbral* (US *Sotoyomo* AT)

PATROL, INSHORE 4 *Baradero* PCI<

MINE COUNTERMEASURES 2

2 *Chaco* (UK *Ton*) MHC

AMPHIBIOUS 20 (craft only)

4 LCM, 16 LCVP

SUPPORT AND MISCELLANEOUS 9

1 AGOR, 3 tpt, 1 ocean tug, 1 icebreaker, 2 trg, 1 research

NAVAL AVIATION (2,500)

30† cbt ac, 11† armed hel

Carrier air crew training on Brazilian CV *Minas Gerais*

ATTACK 1 sqn with 2 *Super Etendard*

MR/ASW 1 sqn with 2 L-188, 5 S-2E/T

EW 2 L-188E

HEL 2 sqn

1 ASW/tpt with 7 ASH-3H (ASW) and 4 AS-61D (tpt), 4 AS-555

1 spt with 6 SA-316

TPT 1 sqn with 3 F-28-3000, 3 L-188, 4 *Queen Air* 80, 9 *Super King Air*

SURVEY 3 PC-6B (Antarctic flt)

TRG 2 sqn with 7* EMB-326, 9* MB-326 *Xavante*, 5* MB-339A, 10 T-34C

MISSILES

ASM AGM-12 *Bullpup*, AM-39 *Exocet*, AS-12, *Martín Pescador*

AAM R-550 *Magic*

MARINES (3,500)

FLEET FORCES 2, each with 2 bn, 1 amph recce coy, 1 fd arty bn, 1 atk, 1 engr coy

AMPH SPT FORCE 1 marine inf bn

1 AD arty regt (bn)

2 SF bn

EQUIPMENT

RECCE 12 ERC-90 *Lynx*

AAV 21 LVTP-7

APC 6 MOWAG *Grenadier*, 35 Panhard VCR

TOWED ARTY 21: **105mm**: 15 M-101/M-56; **155mm**: 6 M-114

MOR 81mm: 70

ATGW 50 *Bantam*, *Cobra* (*Mamba*)

RL 89mm: 60 M-20

RCL 105mm: 30 1974 FMK1

AD GUNS 30mm: 10 HS-816; **35mm**: GDF-001

SAM *Blowpipe*, *Tigercat*

Air Force 12,000

202 cbt ac, 14 armed hel, 9 air bde, 10 AD arty bty, 1 SF (AB) coy

AIR OPERATIONS COMMAND (9 bde)

FGA/FTR 7 sqn

1 with 7 *Mirage* 5P, 22 *Dagger Nesher* (19 -A, 3 -B)

4 with 16 A-4B/C, 32 A-4M, 4 OA-4M

2 with 45 IA-58A, 30 MS-760

MR 1 Boeing 707

SURVEY 3 *Learjet* 35A, 4 1A-50

TKR 2 Boeing 707, 2 KC-130H

SAR 4 SA-315 hel

TPT 5 sqn

ac 4 Boeing 707, 2 C-130E, 5 C-130B, 5 -H, 1 L-100-30, 6 DHC-6, 9 F-27, 4 F-28, 15 IA-50, 2 *Merlin* IVA, 1 S-70A (VIP); Antarctic spt unit with 1 DHC-6

hel 5 Bell 212, 2 CH-47C, 1 S-61R (*Sea King*), 11 MD-

500 (armed), 3 UH-1H (armed)
CAL 1 sqn with 2 Boeing 707, 3 IA-50, 2 *Learjet* 35, 1 PA-31
LIAISON 1 sqn with 20 Cessna 182, 1 C-320, 7 *Commander*, 1 *Sabreliner*

AIR TRAINING COMMAND

AC 28 EMB-312, 16* IA-63, 30* MS-760, 28 T-34B, 8 Su-29
HEL 3 Hughes 500D

MISSILES

ASM ASM-2 *Martín Pescador*
AAM AIM-9B *Sidewinder*, R-530, R-550, *Shafrir*

Forces Abroad

UN AND PEACEKEEPING

BOSNIA (UNMIBH): 48 civ pol. **CROATIA** (UNTAES): 75 incl 2 Obs plus 16 civ pol; (UNMOP): 1 Obs. **CYPRUS** (UNFICYP): 383; 1 inf bn. **ECUADOR/PERU** (MOMEP): some Obs. **FYROM** (UNPREDEP): 1 Obs. **IRAQ/KUWAIT** (UNIKOM): 42 engr plus 3 Obs. **MIDDLE EAST** (UNTSO): 3 Obs. **WESTERN SAHARA** (MINURSO): 1 Obs

Paramilitary 31,240

GENDARMERIE (Ministry of Interior) 18,000

5 Regional Comd, 16 bn
  EQPT Shorland recce, 40 UR-416; **81mm** mor; **ac** 3 *Piper*, 5 PC-6 **hel** 5 SA-315

PREFECTURA NAVAL (Coast Guard) 13,240

7 comd
  SERVICEABILITY much better than Navy
  EQPT 5 *Mantilla*, 1 *Delfin* PCO; 4 PCI, 19 PCI<; **ac** 5 C-212 **hel** 2 SA-330, 1 AS-365, 3 AS-565MA, 2 Bell-47, 2 Schweizer-300C

Bahamas

	1995	1996	1997	1998
GDP	B$3.5bn	B$3.6bn		
	($3.5bn)	($3.6bn)		
per capita	$12,300	$12,700		
Growth	0.8%	2.0%		
Inflation	2.0%	1.4%		
Debt	$0m	$0m		
Def exp	B$18m	B$19m		
	($18m)	($19m)		
Def bdgt			εB$29m	εB$35m
			($29m)	($35m)
FMA (US)	$0.7m	$0.8m	$1.1m	$1.1m
US$1 = B$	1.00	1.00	1.00	
Population		284,000		
Age	*13–17*	*18–22*	*23–32*	
Men	15,000	16,000	30,000	
Women	13,000	15,000	28,000	

Total Armed Forces

ACTIVE 860

Navy (Royal Bahamian Defence Force) 860

(incl 70 women)
BASE Coral Harbour, New Providence Island
MILITARY OPERATIONS PLATOON 1
  ε120; Marines with internal and base sy duties
PATROL AND COASTAL COMBATANTS 7
PATROL, INSHORE 7
  3 *Yellow Elder* PFI, 1 *Marlin*, 2 *Cape* PFI, 1 *Kieth Nelson* PFI
SUPPORT AND MISCELLANEOUS 9
  2 *Fort Montague* (aux), 2 *Dauntless* (aux), 2 converted fishing vessels, 1 diving boat, 1 LCM, 1 small auxiliary
HARBOUR PATROL UNITS 6
  4 *Boston* whaler, 2 *Wahoo*
AIRCRAFT 2
  1 Cessna 404, 1 C-421C

Barbados

	1995	1996	1997	1998
GDP	B$3.7bn	B$4.1bn		
	($1.9bn)	($2.1bn)		
per capita	$5,600	$5,900		
Growth	2.3%	4.8%		
Inflation	1.8%	2.4%		
Debt	$597m	$597m		
Def exp	B$26m	εB$27m		
	($13m)	($13m)		
Def bdgt			εB$28m	
			($14m)	
US$1 = B$	2.01	2.01	2.01	
Population		263,000		
Age	*13–17*	*18–22*	*23–32*	
Men	11,000	12,000	24,000	
Women	11,000	11,000	22,000	

Total Armed Forces

ACTIVE 610

RESERVES 430

Army 500

Navy 110

BASES St Ann's Fort Garrison (HQ), Bridgetown
PATROL AND COASTAL COMBATANTS 5
PATROL, OFFSHORE 2
  1 *Kebir* PCO with 2 12.7mm gun
  1 *Enterprise* PCO< with 1 12.7mm gun
PATROL, INSHORE 3 *Guardian* II PCI<

Belize

	1995	1996	1997	1998
GDP	BZ$1.1bn	BZ$1.2bn		
	($560m)	($580m)		
per capita	$2,500	$2,600		
Growth	3.8%	2.4%		
Inflation	2.8%	6.4%		
Debt	$261m	$263m		
Def exp	εBZ$27m	εBZ$29m		
	($13m)	($14m)		
Def bdgt			εBZ$20m	
			($10m)	
FMA (US)	$0.05m	$0.20m	$0.25m	$0.25m
US$1 = BZ$	2.00	2.00	2.00	
Population		226,000		
Age	*13–17*	*18–22*	*23–32*	
Men	13,000	12,000	18,000	
Women	13,000	12,000	18,000	

Total Armed Forces

ACTIVE 1,050

RESERVES 700

Army 1,000

1 inf bn (3 inf, 1 spt, 1 trg, 3 Reserve coy)
EQUIPMENT
  MOR 81mm: 6
  RCL 84mm: 8 *Carl Gustav*

MARITIME WING 50
  PATROL CRAFT 1 *Sharan* (*Da Daphne*) PCI, plus
    some 11 armed boats and 3 LCU

AIR WING
2 cbt ac, no armed hel
  MR/TPT 2 BN-2B *Defender*
  TRG 1 T 67-200 *Firefly*

Bolivia

	1995	1996	1997	1998
GDP	B33.5bn	B37.7bn		
	($7.0bn)	($7.4bn)		
per capita	$2,500	$2,600		
Growth	3.8%	3.9%		
Inflation	10.2%	9.7%		
Debt	$5.3bn	$5.6bn		
Def exp	B702m	B745m		
	($146m)	($155m)		
Def bdgt			B670m	
			($140m)	
FMA (US)	$14.6m	$15.5m	$45.5m	$45.6m
$1 = Boliviano	4.8	5.1	5.2	
Population		8,485,000		
Age	*13–17*	*18–22*	*23–32*	
Men	477,000	420,000	642,000	
Women	473,000	422,000	663,000	

Total Armed Forces

ACTIVE 33,500 (to be 35,000)
(some 21,800 conscripts)
Terms of service: 12 months, selective

Army 25,000

(some 18,000 conscripts)
HQ: 6 Mil Regions
Army HQ direct control
  2 armd bn • 1 mech cav regt • 1 Presidential Guard
  inf regt
10 'div'; org, composition varies; comprise
  8 cav gp (5 horsed, 2 mot, 1 aslt) • 1 mot inf 'regt'
  with 2 bn • 22 inf bn (incl 5 inf aslt bn) • 10 arty
  'regt' (bn) • 1 AB 'regt' (bn) • 6 engr bn
EQUIPMENT
  LT TK 36 SK-105 *Kuerassier*
  RECCE 24 EE-9 *Cascavel*
  APC 108: 50 M-113, 10 V-100 *Commando*, 24
    MOWAG *Roland*, 24 EE-11 *Urutu*
  TOWED ARTY ε146: **75mm**: 70 incl M-116 pack, ε10
    Bofors M-1935; **105mm**: 30 incl M-101, FH-18;
    122mm: 36 PRC Type-54
  MOR 81mm: 50; **107mm**: M-30
  AC 2 C-212, 1 *King Air* B90, 1 *Cheyenne* II, 1 *Seneca*
    III, 5 Cessna (4 -206, 1 -421B)

Navy 4,500

(incl Naval Aviation, 2,000 Marines and 1,800
conscripts)
NAVAL DISTRICTS 6, covering Lake Titicaca and the
rivers; each 1 flotilla
BASES Riberalta (HQ), Tiquina (HQ), Puerto Busch,

Puerto Guayaramerín (HQ), Puerto Villaroel, Trinidad (HQ), Puerto Suárez (HQ), Cobija (HQ)

PATROL CRAFT, RIVERINE some 17

some 17 riverine craft/boats, plus 11 US *Boston* whalers)

SUPPORT AND MISCELLANEOUS 30

some 30 logistic support and patrol craft

NAVAL AVIATION

AC 1 Cessna U206G, 1 Cessna 402C

MARINES (2,000)

6 bn (1 in each District)

Air Force 4,000

(perhaps 2,000 conscripts); 33 cbt ac, 10 armed hel
FTR 1 sqn with 6 AT-33N
ARMED HEL 1 sqn with 10 Hughes 500M hel
SAR 1 hel sqn with 4 HB-315B, 2 SA-315B, 1 UH-1
SURVEY 1 sqn with 5 Cessna 206, 1 C-210, 1 C-402, 3 *Learjet* 25/35
TPT 3 sqn
1 VIP tpt with 1 L-188, 1 *Sabreliner*, 2 *Super King Air*
2 tpt with 14 C-130A/B/H, 4 F-27-400, 1 IAI-201, 2 *King Air*, 2 C-47, 1 *Convair* 580
LIAISON ac 9 Cessna 152, 2 C-185, 13 C-206, 1 C-208, 2 C-402, 2 Beech *Bonanza*, 2 Beech *Barons*, PA-31, 4 PA-34 **hel** 2 Bell 212, 22 UH-1H
TRG 1 Cessna 152, 2 C-172, 15* PC-7, 4 SF-260CB, 15 T-23, 12* T-33A, 1 *Lancair* 320
AD 1 air-base def regt (Oerlikon twin **20mm**, 18 PRC Type-65 **37mm**, some truck-mounted guns)

Paramilitary 37,100

NATIONAL POLICE some 31,100
9 bde, 2 rapid action regt, 27 frontier units

NARCOTICS POLICE some 6,000

Brazil

	1995	1996	1997	1998
GDP	R658bn	R n.k.		
	($497bn)	($507bn)		
per capita	$5,700	$5,900		
Growth	5.2%	2.9%		
Inflation	84.4%	18.2%		
Debt	$159bn	$161bn		
Def exp	R13.0bn	R14.0bn		
	($9.8bn)	($10.6bn)		
Def bdgt			R15.9bn	
			($12.0bn)	
FMA (US)	$2.2m	$0.5m	$0.7m	$1.2m
$1 = real	0.9	1.0	1.1	

Population		165,716,000	
Age	*13–17*	*18–22*	*23–32*
Men	8,570,000	7,937,000	14,076,000
Women	8,509,000	7,941,000	14,162,000

Total Armed Forces

ACTIVE 314,700

(132,000 conscripts)
Terms of service: 12 months (can be extended to 18)

RESERVES

Trained first-line 1,115,000; 400,000 subject to immediate recall **Second-line** 225,000

Army 200,000

(incl 125,000 conscripts)
HQ: 7 Mil Comd, 11 Mil Regions; 8 div (3 with Regional HQ)
1 armd cav bde (2 mech, 1 armd, 1 arty bn), 3 armd inf bde (each 2 inf, 1 armd, 1 arty bn), 4 mech cav bde (each 3 inf, 1 arty bn) • 13 motor inf bde (26 bn) • 1 mtn bde • 4 jungle bde • 1 frontier bde (6 bn) • 1 AB bde (3 AB, 1 SF bn) • 2 coast and AD arty bde • 3 cav guard regt • 28 arty gp (4 SP, 6 med, 18 fd) • 2 engr gp each 4 bn • 10 bn (incl 2 railway) (to be increased to 34 bn)
AVN 2 hel bn (bde forming, to comprise 52 hel per bn)
EQUIPMENT
LT TK 287 M-41B/C
RECCE 409 EE-9 *Cascavel*, 30 M-8
APC 823: 219 EE-11 *Urutu*, 20 M-59, 584 M-113
TOWED ARTY 451: **105mm**: 353 incl M-101/-102, Model 56 pack; **155mm**: 98 M-114
SP ARTY 105mm: 74 M-7/-108
COASTAL ARTY some 240 incl **57mm**, **75mm**, **120mm**, **150mm**, **152mm**, **305mm**
MRL 108mm: SS-06; 4 ASTROS II
MOR 81mm; **107mm**: 217 M-30; **120mm**: 85 Brandt
ATGW 300 *Cobra* (in store)
RCL 57mm: 240 M-18A1; **75mm**: 20 M-20; **105mm**; **106mm**: M-40A1
AD GUNS 200 incl **20mm**; **35mm**: GDF-001; **40mm**: L-60/-70 (some with BOFI)
SAM 4 *Roland* II, SA-18 (reported)
AC ε3 C-95
HEL 4 S-70A (being delivered), 36 SA-365, 15 AS-550 *Fennec*, 26 AS-350 (armed), 16 AS-355

Navy 64,700

(incl 1,300 Naval Aviation, 14,600 Marines and 2,000 conscripts)
OCEANIC NAVAL DISTRICTS 5 plus 1 Riverine; 1 Comd

BASES Ocean Rio de Janeiro (*HQ I Naval District*), Salvador (*HQ II District*), Recife (*HQ III District*), Belém (*HQ IV District*), Floricholis (*HQ V District*) **River** Ladario (*HQ VI District*), Manaus

SUBMARINES 6

3 *Tupi* (Ge T-209/1400) with 533mm TT (UK *Tigerfish* HWT)

3 *Humaitá* (UK *Oberon*) with 533mm TT (UK *Tigerfish* HWT) (1 in refit)

PRINCIPAL SURFACE COMBATANTS 22

CARRIERS 1 *Minas Gerais* (UK *Colossus*) CV (ASW), typically **ac** 6 S-2E ASW **hel** 4–6 ASH-3H, 3 AS-332 and 2 AS-355; has been used by Argentina for embarked aircraft training (S-2E to be withdrawn)

DESTROYERS 3

1 *Marcilio Dias* (US *Gearing*) ASW with 1 *Jetranger* hel (Mk 46 LWT), 1 x 8 ASROC, 2 x 3 ASTT; plus 2 x 2 127mm guns

2 *Sergipe* (US *Sumner*) ASW with 1 wasp hel, 2 x 3 ASTT plus 3 x 2 127mm gun

FRIGATES 18

4 *Greenhaigh* (ex-UK *Broadsword*) with 4 MM-38 *Exocet* SSM, *Seawolf* MOD 4 SAM

4 *Para* (US *Garcia*) with 1 x 8 ASROC, 2 x 3 ASTT, 1 *Lynx* hel; plus 2 127mm guns

2 *Constituição* ASW with 1 *Lynx* hel, 2 x 3 ASTT, *Ikara* SUGW, 1 x 2 ASW mor; plus 2 MM-40 *Exocet* SSM, 1 114mm gun

4 *Niteroi*; weapons as ASW, except 4 MM-40 *Exocet*, 2 114mm guns, no *Ikara*

4 *Inhauma*, with 1 *Lynx* hel, 2 x 3 ASTT, plus 4 MM-40 *Exocet*, 1 114mm gun

PATROL AND COASTAL COMBATANTS 35

PATROL, OFFSHORE 16

8 *Imperial Marinheiro* PCO, 8 *Grajaü* PCC

PATROL, INSHORE 13

6 *Piratini* (US PGM) PCI, 3 *Aspirante Nascimento* PCI (trg), 4 *Tracker* PCI<

PATROL, RIVERINE 6

3 *Roraima* and 2 *Pedro Teixeira*, 1 *Parnaiba*

MINE COUNTERMEASURES 6

6 *Aratü* (Ge *Schütze*) MSI

AMPHIBIOUS 4

2 *Ceara* (US *Thomaston*) LSD capacity 350 tps, 38 tk

1 *Duque de Caxais* (US *de Soto County* LST), capacity 600 tps, 18 tk

1 *Mattoso Maia* (US *Newport* LST) capacity 400 tps, 500 tons veh, 3 LCVP, 1 LCPL

Plus some 49 craft: 3 LCU, 11 LCM, 35 LCVP (12 AAVC-7-A1 amph ships due late 1997)

SUPPORT AND MISCELLANEOUS 26

1 *Marajo* AO, 1 *Almirante G. Motta* AO, 1 repair ship, 1 submarine rescue, 4 tpt, 9 survey/oceanography, 1 *Brasil* trg, 5 ocean tugs, 3 buoy tenders (UK *River*)

NAVAL AVIATION (1,300)

54 armed hel

ASW 6 SH-3B, 7 SH-3D, 6 SH-3G/H

ATTACK 5 *Lynx* HAS-21, 9 *Lynx* MK-21A

UTL 2 sqn with 5 AS-332, 12 AS-350 (armed), 9 AS-355 (armed)

TRG 1 hel sqn with 13 TH-57

ASM AS-11, AS-12, *Sea Skua*

MARINES (14,600)

FLEET FORCE 1 amph div (1 comd, 3 inf bn, 1 arty gp)

REINFORCEMENT COMD 5 bn incl 1 engr, 1 SF

INTERNAL SECURITY FORCE 8+ regional gp

EQUIPMENT

RECCE 6 EE-9 Mk IV *Cascavel*

AAV 11 LVTP-7A1

APC 28 M-113, 5 EE-11 *Urutu*

TOWED ARTY 39: **105mm**: 15 M-101, 18 L118; **155mm**: 6 M-114

MOR 81mm; **120mm**: 8 K 6A3

RL 89mm: 3.5in M-20

RCL 106mm: 8 M-40A1

AD GUNS 40mm: 6 L/70 with BOFI

Air Force 50,000

(5,000 conscripts); 269 cbt ac, 29 armed hel

AIR DEFENCE COMMAND 1 gp

FTR 2 sqn with 16 F-103E/D (*Mirage* IIIE/DBR)

TACTICAL COMMAND 10 gp

FGA 3 sqn with 46 F-5E/-B/-F, 32 AMX

CCT 2 sqn with 58 AT-26 (EMB-326)

RECCE 2 sqn with 4 RC-95, 10 RT-26, 12 *Learjet* 35 recce/VIP, 3 RC-130E

LIAISON/OBS 7 sqn

1 with **ac** 8 T-27

5 with **ac** 31 U-7

1 with **hel** 29 UH-1H (armed)

MARITIME COMMAND 4 gp

ASW (afloat) 1 sqn with 4† S-2 (4 -A, 1 -ET)

MR/SAR 3 sqn with 10 EMB-110B, 20 EMB-111

TRANSPORT COMMAND

6 gp (6 sqn)

1 with 9 C-130H, 2 KC-130H • 1 with 4 KC-137 (tpt/tkr) • 1 with 12 C-91 • 1 with 18 C-95A/B/C • 1 with 17 C-115 • 1 (VIP) with **ac** 1 VC-91, 12 VC/VU-93, 2 VC-96, 5 VC-97, 5 VU-9, 2 Boeing 737-200 **hel** 3 VH-4

7 regional sqn with 7 C-115, 86 C-95A/B/C, 6 EC-9 (VU-9)

HEL 6 AS-332, 8 AS-355, 4 Bell 206, 27 HB-350B

LIAISON 50 C-42, 3 Cessna 208, 30 U-42

TRAINING COMMAND

AC 38* AT-26, 97 C-95 A/B/C, 25 T-23, 98 T-25, 61* T-27 (*Tucano*), 14* AMX-T

HEL 4 OH-6A, 25 OH-13
CAL 1 unit with 2 C-95, 1 EC-93, 4 EC-95, 1 U-93
MISSILES
    AAM AIM-9B *Sidewinder*, R-530, *Magic* 2

Forces Abroad

UN AND PEACEKEEPING
ANGOLA (UNOMA): 454 incl 20 Obs plus 14 civ pol.
CROATIA (UNTAES): 6 Obs; (UNMOP): 1 Obs.
ECUADOR/PERU (MOMEP): Obs plus log spt.
FYROM (UNPREDEP): 2 Obs

Paramilitary

PUBLIC SECURITY FORCES (R) some 385,600

in state mil pol org (state militias) under Army control
and considered Army Reserve

Chile

	1995	1996	1997	1998
GDP	pCh26.7tr	pCh29.7tr		
	($52.5bn)	($57.5bn)		
per capita	$9,700	$10,500		
Growth	7.9%	7.2%		
Inflation	7.9%	7.3%		
Debt	$25.6bn	$27.5bn		
Def exp	pCh0.9tr	pCh1.0tr		
	($1.9bn)	($2.0bn)		
Def bdgt			pCh1.1tr	
			($2.1bn)	
FMA (US)	$0.2m	$0.3m	$0.4m	$0.5m
$1 = pCh*	397	412	418	

*Chilean peso

Population		14,580,000	
Age	*13–17*	*18–22*	*23–32*
Men	669,000	623,000	1,228,000
Women	644,000	603,000	1,201,000

Total Armed Forces

ACTIVE 94,300

(32,800 conscripts)
Terms of service: **Army** 1 year **Navy** and **Air Force** 22
months

RESERVES 50,000
Army

Army 51,000

(28,000 conscripts)
7 Mil Regions, 2 Corps HQ

7 div; org, composition varies; comprise
    14 mot inf, 9 mtn inf, 10 armd cav, 8 arty, 7 engr regt
1 bde with 1 armd cav, 1 mtn regt
1 bde with 1 mot inf, 1 cdo regt
Army tps: 1 avn bde, 1 engr, 1 AB regt (1 AB, 1 SF bn)
EQUIPMENT
    MBT 130: 100 M-4A3, 30 AMX-30
    LT TK 81: 21 M-24, 60 M-41
    RECCE 50 EE-9 *Cascavel*
    AIFV 20 MOWAG *Piranha* with **90mm** gun
    APC 438: 228 M-113, 180 Cardoen/MOWAG
      Piranha, 30 EE-11 *Urutu*
    TOWED ARTY 114: **105mm**: 66 M-101, 36 Model
      56; **155mm**: 12 M-71, 28 G5 (being delivered)
    SP ARTY 155mm: 12 Mk F3
    MOR 440: **81mm**: 300 M-29; **107mm**: 15 M-30;
      120mm: 125 FAMAE (incl 50 SP)
    ATGW *Milan/Mamba, Mapats*
    RL 89mm: 3.5in M-20
    RCL 150 incl: **57mm**: M-18; **106mm**: M-40A1
    AD GUNS 20mm: 60 incl some SP (*Cardoen/*
      MOWAG)
    SAM 50 *Blowpipe, Javelin*
    AIRCRAFT
    TPT 9 C-212, 1 *Citation* (VIP), 4 CN-235, 4 DHC-6, 3
      PA-31, 8 PA-28 Piper *Dakota*
    TRG 16 Cessna R-172
    HEL 2 AB-206, 3 AS-332, 15 Enstrom 280 FX, 15
      Hughes MD-530F (armed trg), 10 SA-315, 9 SA-
      330

Navy 29,800

(incl 800 Naval Aviation, 3,200 Marines, 1,800 Coast
Guard and 3,800 conscripts)
DEPLOYMENT AND BASES
MAIN COMMAND Fleet (includes DD and FF),
submarine flotilla, tpt. Remaining forces allocated to 4
Naval Zones **1st** 26°S–36°S approx: Valparaiso (HQ),
Vina Del Mar **2nd** 36°S–43°S approx: Talcahuano (HQ),
Puerto Montt **3rd** 43°S to Cape Horn: Punta Arenas
(HQ), Puerto Williams **4th** north of 26°S approx:
Iquique (HQ)
SUBMARINES 4
    2 *O'Brien* (UK *Oberon*) with 8 533mm TT (Ge HWT)
    2 *Thompson* (Ge T-209/1300) with 8 533mm TT (HWT)
PRINCIPAL SURFACE COMBATANTS 10
DESTROYERS 4
    2 *Prat* (UK *Norfolk*) DDG with 1 x 2 *Seaslug* 2 SAM, 4
      MM-38 *Exocet* SSM, 1 x 2 114mm guns, 1 AB-206B
      hel plus 2 x 3 ASTT (Mk 44)
      (1 unit retains *Seaslug*, both have *Barak* SAM)
    2 *Blanco Encalada* (UK *Norfolk*) DDH with 4 MM-38,
      Exocet SSM, 1 x 2 114 mm guns, 2 AS-332F hel;
      plus 2 x 3 ASTT (Mk 44), 2 x 8 *Barak* 1 SAM, 1 with
      1 x 2 *Seaslug* SAM in addition

FRIGATES 4 *Condell* (mod UK *Leander*), 2 with 2 x 3 ASTT (Mk 44), 1 hel; plus 1 with 2 x 2 MM-40 *Exocet* SSM, 1 with 2 MM-38 *Exocet* SSM, 1 x 2 114mm guns

PATROL AND COASTAL COMBATANTS 30

MISSILE CRAFT 8
  4 *Casma* (Il *Sa'ar* 4) PFM with 4 *Gabriel* SSM, 2 76mm gun
  2 *Iquique* (Il *Sa'ar* 3) with 6 *Gabriel* SSM, 1 76mm gun
  2 *Tiger* (Ge Type 148) PFM with 4 *Exocet* SSM, 1 76mm gun

TORPEDO CRAFT 2 *Guacola* (Ge Lürssen 36-M) with 4 533mm TT

PATROL, OFFSHORE 4
  1 PCO (ex-US tug), 2 *Taito* OPV, 1 *Viel* (ex-Ca) icebreaker

PATROL, INSHORE 16
  6 *Micalvi* PCC, 10 *Grumete Diaz* (Il *Dabur*) PCI<

AMPHIBIOUS 4
  3 *Maipo* (Fr *Batral*) LSM, capacity 140 tps, 7 tk
  1 *Valdivia†* (US *Newport*) LST, capacity 400 tps, 500t vehicles
  Plus craft: 2 *Elicura* LCT, 1 *Pisagua* LCU

SUPPORT AND MISCELLANEOUS 12
  1 *Almirante Jorge Montt* (UK *Tide*) AO, 1 *Araucano* AO, 1 tpt, 1 survey, 1 *Uribe* trg, 1 Antarctic patrol, 1 *Alvsborg* submarine depot ship with minelaying capability, 5 tugs/spt

NAVAL AVIATION (800)
  12 cbt ac, 12 armed hel
  MR 1 sqn with 6 EMB-111N, 2 *Falcon* 200, 4 P-3 *Orion* (4 in store)
  ASW HEL 6 AS-532 (4 with AM-39 *Exocet*, 2 with torpedoes), 6 AS-332
  LIAISON 1 sqn with 3 C-212A, 3 EMB-110CN
  HEL 1 sqn with 6 AB-206-B, 8 BO-105, 1 AS-332
  TRG 1 sqn with 7 PC-7

MARINES (3,200)
4 gp each with 1 inf bn (+), 1 cdo coy, 1 fd arty, 1 AD arty bty • 1 amph bn
  EQUIPMENT
  LT TK 12 *Scorpion* (+ 18 to be delivered)
  AAV 20 LVTP-5 (in store)
  APC 40 MOWAG *Roland*
  TOWED ARTY 105mm: 25 M-101, 155mm: 36 M-114
  COASTAL GUNS 155mm: 20 GPFM-3
  MOR 81mm: 50
  SSM *Excalibur* (reported)
  RCL 106mm: ε30 M-40A1
  SAM *Blowpipe*

COAST GUARD (1,800)
(integral part of the Navy)
  PATROL CRAFT 22
  2 PCC (buoy tenders), 1 *Castor* PCI, 2 *Alacalufe*, 2 *Guacola* PCI, 15 *Rodman* PCI, plus about 12 boats

Air Force 13,500

(1,000 conscripts); 92 cbt ac, no armed hel
5 Air Bde, 5 wg
FGA 2 sqn
  1 with 15 *Mirage* 5BA (MRIS), 6 *Mirage* BD (MRIS)
  1 with 16 F-5 (13 -E, 3 -F)
CCT 2 sqn with 24 A-37B, 12 A-36
FTR/RECCE 1 sqn with 15 *Mirage* 50 (8 -FCH, 6 -CH, 1 -DCH), 4 *Mirage* 5-BR
RECCE 2 photo units with 1 *King Air* A-100, 2 *Learjet* 35A
AEW 1 IAI-707 *Phalcon*
TPT ac 3 Boeing 707(tkr), 1 Boeing 737-300 (VIP), 2 C-130H, 4 C-130B, 4 C-212, 9 Beech 99 (ELINT, tpt, trg), 14 DHC-6 (5 -100, 9 -300), 1 *Gulfstream* III (VIP), 1 *Beechcraft* 200 (VIP) **hel** 5 SA-315B
TRG 1 wg, 3 flying schools **ac** 16 PA-28, 49 T-35A/B, 20 T-36, 15 T-37B/C, 6 *Extra* 300 **hel** 10 UH-1H
MISSILES
  ASM AS-11/-12
  AAM AIM-9B *Sidewinder*, *Shafrir*, *Python* III
  AD 1 regt (5 gp) with **20mm**: S-639/-665, GAI-CO1 twin; **35mm**: Oerlikon GDF-005, MATRA *Mistral*, *Mygalle*

Forces Abroad

UN AND PEACEKEEPING
BOSNIA (UNMIBH): 14 civ pol. **ECUADOR/CHILE** (MOMEP): some Obs. **INDIA/PAKISTAN** (UNMOGIP): 3 Obs. **MIDDLE EAST** (UNTSO): 3 Obs

Paramilitary 31,200

CARABINEROS (Ministry of Defence) 31,200
8 zones, 38 districts
  APC 20 MOWAG *Roland*
  MOR 60mm, 81mm
  AC 22 Cessna (6 C-150, 10 C-182, 6 C-206), 1 *Metro*
  HEL 2 Bell 206, 12 Bo-105

Opposition

FRENTE PATRIOTICO MANUEL RODRIGUEZ –
AUTONOMOUS FACTION (FPMR-A) ε800
leftist

Colombia

	1995	1996	1997	1998
GDP	pC72.4tr	pC88.9tr		
	($68.3bn)	($72.0bn)		
per capita	$5,700	$5,900		
Growth	5.9%	3.2%		

contd	1995	1996	1997	1998
Inflation	21.0%	20.2%		
Debt	$20.8bn	$23.4bn		
Def exp	εpC1.9tr	εpC2.0tr		
	($1.8bn)	($1.9bn)		
Def bdgt			εpC2.2tr	
			($2.1bn)	
FMA (US)	$27.0m	$16.1m	$30.6m	$30.9m
$1 = pC*	913	1,037	1,074	

*Colombian peso

Population		36,050,000		
Age	*13–17*	*18–22*	*23–32*	
Men	1,927,000	1,778,000	3,277,000	
Women	1,841,000	1,715,000	3,239,000	

Total Armed Forces

ACTIVE 146,300

(some 67,300 conscripts)
Terms of service: 12–18 months, varies (all services)

RESERVES 60,700

(incl 2,000 first-line) **Army** 54,700 **Navy** 4,800 **Air Force** 1,200

Army 121,000

(63,800 conscripts)
5 div HQ
18 regional bde
  7 mech each with 3 inf, 1 mech cav, 1 arty, 1 engr bn
  2 air-portable each with 2 inf bn
  8 inf (7 with 2 inf bn, 1 with 4 inf bn)
2 arty bn
Army tps
  2 Mobile Counter Guerilla Force (bde) (each with 1 cdo unit, 4 bn) (3rd bde forming)
  1 trg bde with 1 Presidential Guard, 1 SF, 1 AB, 1 mech, 1 arty, 1 engr bn
  1 AD arty bn
  army avn (forming)
EQUIPMENT
  LT TK 12 M-3A1 (in store)
  RECCE 12 M-8, 120 EE-9 *Cascavel*
  APC 80 M-113, 76 EE-11 *Urutu*, 4 RG-31 *Nyala*
  TOWED ARTY 105mm: 130 M-101
  MOR 245: 81mm: 125 M-1; **120mm**: 120 Brandt
  ATGW TOW
  RCL 106mm: M-40A1
  AD GUNS 40mm: 30 Bofors
  HEL 10 Mi-17 (reported)

Navy (incl Coast Guard) 18,000

(incl 9,000 Marines and 100 Naval Aviation)
BASES Ocean Cartagena (main), Buenaventura,

Málaga (Pacific) **River** Puerto Leguízamo, Barrancabermeja, Puerto Carreño (tri-Service Unified Eastern Command HQ), Leticia, Puerto Orocue, Puerto Inirida

SUBMARINES 2
  2 *Pijao* (Ge T-209/1200) with 8 533mm TT (Ge HWT) (Plus 2 *Intrepido* (It SX-506) SSI (SF delivery))

FRIGATES 4
  4 *Almirante Padilla* with 1 Bo-105 hel (ASW), 2 x 3 ASTT; plus 8 MM-40 *Exocet* SSM

PATROL AND COASTAL COMBATANTS 39
PATROL, OFFSHORE 4
  3 *Pedro de Heredia* (ex-US tugs), 1 *Esperanta* (Sp *Cormoran*) PCO
PATROL, INSHORE 10
  2 *Quito Sueno* (US *Asheville*) PFI, 2 *Castillo Y Rada* (*Swiftship* 32m) PCI, 2 *José Palas* PCI<, 2 *José Garcia* PCI<, 2 *Jaime Gomez* PCI
PATROL, RIVERINE 25
  3 *Arauca*, 16 *Juan Lucioá*, 6 *Capitan* tugs, plus boats
SUPPORT AND MISCELLANEOUS 4
  1 tpt, 2 research, 1 trg

MARINES (9,000)
2 bde (each of 2 bn), 1 amph aslt, 1 river ops (15 amph patrol units), 1 SF, 1 sy bn
No hy eqpt (to get EE-9 *Cascavel* recce, EE-11 *Urutu* APC)

NAVAL AVIATION (100)
  AC 2 *Commander*, 2 PA-28, 2 PA-31
  HEL 2 Bo-105

Air Force 7,300

(some 3,500 conscripts); 72 cbt ac, 63 armed hel
AIR COMBAT COMMAND
FGA 2 sqn
  1 with 12 *Mirage* 5, 1 with 13 *Kfir* (11 -C2, 2 -TC2)
TACTICAL AIR SUPPORT COMMAND
CBT ac 1 AC-47, 2 AC-47T, 3 IA-58A, 22 A-37B, 6 AT-27
ARMED HEL 12 Bell 205, 5 Bell 212, 2 Bell 412, 2 UH-1B, 16 UH-60, 11 MD-500ME, 2 MD-500D, 3 MD-530F, 10 Mi-17
RECCE 8 *Schweizer* SA 2-37A, 13* OV-10
MILITARY AIR TRANSPORT COMMAND
  AC 1 Boeing 707, 2 Boeing 727, 14 C-130B, 2 C-130H, 1 C-117, 2 C-47, 2 CASA 212, 2 *Bandeirante*, 1 F-28
  HEL 20 UH-1H
AIR TRAINING COMMAND
  AC 14 T-27 (*Tucano*), 6 T-34M, 13 T-37, 8 T-41
  HEL 2 UH-1B, 4 UH-1H, 12 F-28F
MISSILES
  AAM AIM-9 *Sidewinder*, R-530

Forces Abroad

UN AND PEACEKEEPING
EGYPT (MFO): 358; 1 inf bn

Paramilitary 87,000

NATIONAL POLICE FORCE 87,000
ac 2 C-47, 2 DHC-6, 9 Cessna (2 C-152, 6 C-206G, 1 C-208), 1 Beech C-99, 5 *Turbo Thrush* **hel** 7 Bell-206L, 5 Bell-212, 3 Hughes 500D, 12 UH-1H

COAST GUARD
integral part of Navy

Opposition

COORDINADORA NACIONAL GUERRILLERA SIMON BOLIVAR (CNGSB) loose coalition of guerrilla gp incl **Revolutionary Armed Forces of Colombia (FARC)** ε5,700 active; **National Liberation Army (ELN)** ε2,500, pro-Cuban; **People's Liberation Army (EPL)** ε500

Costa Rica

	1995	1996	1997	1998
GDP	C1.7tr	C1.9tr		
	($8.2bn)	($8.3bn)		
per capita	$6,400	$6,400		
Growth	2.3%	-0.6%		
Inflation	23.2%	17.5%		
Debt	$3.8bn	$3.6bn		
Sy exp[a]	εC9.6bn	εC10.2bn		
	($48m)	($51m)		
Sy bdgt			C5.8bn	
			($29m)	
FMA (US)	$1.1m	$0.2m	$0.2m	$0.2m
$1 = colon	180	208	229	

[a] No defence forces. Budgetary data are for border and maritime policing and internal security

Population		3,532,000		
Age	*13–17*	*18–22*	*23–32*	
Men	184,000	164,000	296,000	
Women	177,000	157,000	286,000	

Total Armed Forces

ACTIVE Nil

Paramilitary 7,000

CIVIL GUARD 3,000
7 urban *comisaria*[a] • 1 tac police *comisaria* • 1 special ops unit • 6 provincial *comisaria*

BORDER SECURITY POLICE 2,000
2 Border Sy Comd (7 *comisaria*)
MARINE ELEMENT (ε400)
  BASES Pacific Golfito, Punt Arenas, Cuajiniquil, Quepos **Atlantic** Limon, Moin
  PATROL CRAFT, INSHORE 7
    1 *Isla del Coco* (US *Swift* 32m) PFI
    1 *Astronauta Franklin Chang* (US *Cape Higgon*) PCI
    5 PCI<; plus about 10 boats
AIR SECTION
  ac 4 Cessna 206, 1 *Commander* 680, 3 O-2 (surv), 2 PA-23, 3 PA-28, 1 PA-32, 1 PA-34 **hel** 2 *Hughes* 500E, 1 Mi-8, 1 FH-1100

RURAL GUARD (Ministry of Government and Police) 2,000
8 comd; small arms only

[a] *comisaria* = reinforced coy

Cuba

	1995	1996	1997	1998
GDP	$12bn	$13bn		
per capita	$1,900	$2,100		
Growth	2.5%	7.8%		
Inflation	30%	n.k.		
Debt	$10.5bn	$12.0bn		
Def exp	ε$700m	ε$700m		
Def bdgt			ε$700m	
$1 = Cuban peso	1	22	21	
Population		11,123,000		
Age	*13–17*	*18–22*	*23–32*	
Men	397,000	446,000	1,099,000	
Women	373,000	419,000	1,042,000	

Total Armed Forces

ACTIVE ε50–60,000
(incl Ready Reserves, conscripts)
Terms of service: 2 years

RESERVES
Army 39,000 **Ready Reserves** (serve 45 days per year) to fill out Active and Reserve units; see also Paramilitary

Army ε38,000

(incl conscripts and Ready Reservists)
HQ: 3 Regional Comd, 3 Army
  4–5 armd bde • 9 mech inf bde (3 mech inf, 1 armd, 1 arty, 1 AD arty regt) • 1 AB bde • 14 reserve bde • 1 frontier bde

AD AD arty regt and SAM bde
EQUIPMENT † (some 75% in store)
  MBT ε1,500 incl: T-34, T-54/-55, T-62
  LT TK some PT-76
  RECCE some BRDM-1/-2
  AIFV 400 BMP-1
  APC ε700 BTR-40/-50/-60/-152
  TOWED ARTY 700: **76mm**: M-1942; **122mm**: M-1938, D-30; **130mm**: M-46; **152mm**: M-1937, D-1
  SP ARTY 40: **122mm**: 2S1; **152mm**: 2S3
  MRL 300: **122mm**: BM-21; **140mm**: BM-14
  MOR 1,000: **82mm**: M-41/-43; **120mm**: M-38/-43
  STATIC DEF ARTY JS-2 (**122mm**) hy tk, T-34 (**85mm**), SU-100 (**100mm**) SP guns
  ATGW AT-1 *Snapper*, AT-3 *Sagger*
  ATK GUNS 85mm: D-44; **100mm**: SU-100 SP, T-12
  AD GUNS 255 incl: **23mm**: ZU-23, ZSU-23-4 SP; **30mm**: M-53 (twin)/BTR-60P SP; **37mm**: M-1939; **57mm**: S-60 towed, ZSU-57-2 SP; **85mm**: KS-12; **100mm**: KS-19
  SAM SA-6/-7/-8/-9/-13/-14/-16

Navy ε5,000

(incl 550+ Naval Infantry, ε3,000 conscripts), 4 op flotillas
NAVAL DISTRICTS Western HQ Cabanas **Eastern** HQ Holquin
BASES Cienfuegos, Cabanas, Havana, Mariel, Punta Movida, Nicaro
SUBMARINES 2
  2 Sov *Foxtrot* with 533mm and 406mm TT (non-op)
FRIGATES I
  1 Sov *Koni* with 2 ASW RL (non-op)
PATROL AND COASTAL COMBATANTS 5
MISSILE CRAFT 4 Sov *Osa* I/II with 4 SS-N-2 *Styx* SSM†
PATROL, COASTAL 1 Sov *Pauk* II PFC with 2 ASW RL, 4 ASTT
MINE COUNTERMEASURES 10
  4 Sov *Sonya* MSC, 6 Sov *Yevgenya* MSI
AMPHIBIOUS I
  1 Sov *Polnocny* LSM, capacity 180 tps, 6 tk (non-op)
SUPPORT AND MISCELLANEOUS 2
  1 AGI, 1 survey
NAVAL INFANTRY (550+)
2 amph aslt bn
COASTAL DEFENCE
  ARTY 122mm: M-1931/37; **130mm**: M-46; **152mm**: M-1937
  SSM 2 SS-C-3 systems, some mobile *Bandera* IV (reported)

Air Force ε10,000

(incl AD and conscripts); 130† cbt ac, 45 armed hel

Flying hours less than 50
FGA 2 sqn with 10 MiG-23BN
FTR 4 sqn
  2 with 30 MiG-21F, 1 with 50 MiG-21bis, 1 with 20 MiG-23MF, 6 MiG-29
  (Probably only some 3 MiG-29, 10 MiG-23, 5 MiG-21bis in operation)
ATTACK HEL 45 Mi-8/-17, Mi-25/35
ASW 5 Mi-14 hel
TPT 4 sqn with 8 An-2, 1 An-24, 15 An-26, 1 An-30, 2 An-32, 4 Yak-40, 2 Il-76 (Air Force ac in civilian markings)
HEL 40 Mi-8/-17
TRG 25 L-39, 8* MiG-21U, 4* MiG-23U, 2* MiG-29UB, 20 Z-326
MISSILES
  ASM AS-7
  AAM AA-2, AA-7, AA-8, AA-10, AA-11
  SAM 13 active SA-2, SA-3 sites
CIVIL AIRLINE
  10 Il-62, 7 Tu-154, 12 Yak-42, 1 An-30 used as troop tpt

Forces Abroad

UN AND PEACEKEEPING
GEORGIA (UNOMIG): 4 Obs

Paramilitary 19,000 active

YOUTH LABOUR ARMY 65,000

CIVIL DEFENCE FORCE 50,000

TERRITORIAL MILITIA (R) ε1,000,000

STATE SECURITY (Ministry of Interior) 15,000

BORDER GUARDS (Ministry of Interior) 4,000
  about 20 Sov *Zhuk* and 3 Sov *Stenka* PFI<, plus boats

Foreign Forces

US 1,640: **Navy** 1,000 **Marines** 640
RUSSIA 810: 800 SIGINT, ε10 mil advisers

Dominican Republic

	1995	1996	1997	1998
GDP	pRD161bn	pRD182bn		
	($8.3bn)	($9.1bn)		
per capita	$4,000	$4,300		
Growth	4.8%	7.3%		
Inflation	12.5%	5.0%		
Debt	$4.3bn	$4.1bn		

contd	1995	1996	1997	1998
Def exp	pRD2.1bn	pRD2.0bn		
	($109m)	($104m)		
Def bdgt			εpRD1.3bn	
			($68m)	
FMA (US)	$0.2m	$0.5m	$0.5m	$0.5m
$1 = pRD*	13.6	13.8	14.1	

*peso República Dominicana

Population		7,928,000		
Age	*13–17*	*18–22*	*23–32*	
Men	437,000	396,000	700,000	
Women	426,000	388,000	687,000	

Total Armed Forces

ACTIVE 24,500

Army 15,000

3 Defence Zones • 4 inf bde (with 8 inf, 1 arty bn, 2 recce sqn) • 1 armd, 1 Presidential Guard, 1 SF, 1 arty, 1 engr bn

EQUIPMENT
LT TK 12 AMX-13 (**75mm**), 12 M-41A1 (**76mm**)
RECCE 8 V-150 *Commando*
APC 20 M-2/M-3 half-track
TOWED ARTY 105mm: 22 M-101
MOR 81mm: M-1; **120mm**: 24 ECIA

Navy 4,000

(incl marine security unit and 1 SEAL unit)
BASES Santo Domingo (HQ), Las Calderas

PATROL AND COASTAL COMBATANTS 17
PATROL, OFFSHORE 8
1 *Mella* (Ca *River*) (comd/trg), 3 *Cambiaso* (US *Cohoes*), 2 *Canopus* PCO, 2 *Prestol* (US *Admirable*)
PATROL, INSHORE 9
1 *Betelgeuse* (US PGM-71), 1 *Capitan Alsina* (trg), 1 *Balsam* PCI, some 6 PCI<
AMPHIBIOUS craft only
2 LCU
SUPPORT AND MISCELLANEOUS 4
1 AOT (small harbour), 3 ocean tugs

Air Force 5,500

10 cbt ac, no armed hel
Flying hours probably less than 60
CCT 1 sqn with 8 A-37B
TPT 1 sqn with 3 C-47, 1 *Commander* 680
LIAISON 1 Cessna 210, 2 PA-31, 3 *Queen Air* 80, 1 *King Air*
HEL 8 Bell 205, 2 SA-318C, 1 SA-365 (VIP)
TRG 2* AT-6, 6 T-34B, 3 T-41D

AB 1 SF (AB) bn
AD 1 bn with 4 **20mm** guns

Paramilitary 15,000

NATIONAL POLICE 15,000

Ecuador

	1995	1996	1997	1998
GDP	ES46.0tr	ES57.6tr		
	($15.6bn)	($15.9bn)		
per capita	$4,300	$4,400		
Growth	7.9%	2.5%		
Inflation	22.9%	24.4%		
Debt	$14.0bn	$14.0bn		
Def expᵃ	εES1.6tr	εES1.6tr		
	($531m)	($538m)		
Def bdgtᵃ			εES1.6tr	
			($542m)	
FMAᵇ (US)	$0.8m	$1.0m	$0.8m	$0.85m
$1 = ES*	2,565	3,190	3,894	

*Ecuadorean sucre
ᵃ incl extra-budgetary funding
ᵇ MOMEP 1995ε $3m 1996ε $3m

Population		12,186,000		
Age	*13–17*	*18–22*	*23–32*	
Men	682,000	623,000	1,047,000	
Women	663,000	608,000	1,027,000	

Total Armed Forces

ACTIVE 57,100
Terms of service: conscription 1 year, selective

RESERVES 100,000
Ages 18–55

Army 50,000

4 Defence Zones
1 div with 2 inf bde (each 3 inf, 1 armd, 1 arty bn) •
1 armd bde (3 armd, 1 mech inf, 1 SP arty bn) • 2 inf
bde (5 inf, 3 mech inf, 2 arty bn) • 3 jungle bde (2
with 3, 1 with 4 jungle bn)
Army tps: 1 SF (AB) bde (4 bn), 1 AD arty gp, 1 avn gp
(4 bn), 3 engr bn
EQUIPMENT
MBT 3 T-55 (reported)
LT TK 45 M-3, 108 AMX-13
RECCE 27 AML-60/-90, 22 EE-9 *Cascavel*, 10 EE-3 *Jararaca*
APC 20 M-113, 60 AMX-VCI, 20 EE-11 *Urutu*
TOWED ARTY 128: **105mm**: 50 M2A2, 30 M-101, 24

Model 56; **155mm**: 12 M-198, 12 M-114
SP ARTY 155mm: 10 Mk F3
MRL 122mm: 6 RM-70
MOR 300: 81mm: M-29; **107mm**: 4.2in M-30;
160mm: 12 Soltam
RCL 90mm: 380 M-67; **106mm**: 24 M-40A1
AD GUNS 14.5mm: 128 ZPU-1/-2; **20mm**: 20 M-
1935; **23mm**: 34 ZU-23; **35mm**: 30 GDF-002 twin;
37mm: 18 Ch; **40mm**: 30 L/70
SAM 75 *Blowpipe*, 90 SA-18 (reported), SA-8 (being
delivered)

AIRCRAFT
SURVEY 1 Cessna 206, 1 *Learjet* 24D
TPT 1 CN-235, 1 DHC-5, 3 IAI-201, 1 *King Air* 200, 2
PC-6
LIAISON/TRG/OBS 1 Cessna 172, 1 -182
HELICOPTERS
SURVEY 3 SA-315B
TPT/LIAISON 10 AS-332, 4 AS-350B, 1 Bell 214B, 3
SA-315B, 3 SA-330, 30 SA-342

Navy 4,100

(incl 250 Naval Aviation and 1,500 Marines)
BASES Guayaquil (main base), Jaramijo, Galápagos
Islands
SUBMARINES 2
2 *Shyri* (Ge T-209/1300) with 533mm TT (Ge SUT
HWT)
FRIGATES 2
2 *Presidente Eloy Alfaro* (ex-UK *Leander Batch* II) with
1 206B hel; plus 4 MM-38 *Exocet* SSM
PATROL AND COASTAL COMBATANTS 12
CORVETTES 6 *Esmeraldas* with 2 x 3 ASTT, hel deck;
plus 2 x 3 MM-40 *Exocet* SSM
MISSILE CRAFT 6
3 *Quito* (Ge Lürssen 45m) with 4 MM-38 *Exocet*
3 *Manta* (Ge Lürssen 36m) with 4 *Gabriel* II SSM
AMPHIBIOUS 1
1 *Hualcopo* (US LST-511) LST, capacity 200 tps, 16 tk
SUPPORT AND MISCELLANEOUS 8
1 survey, 1 ex-GDR depot ship, 1 AOT (small), 1
Calicuchima (ex-UK *Throsk*) armament carrier, 1
water carrier, 2 armed ocean tugs, 1 trg

NAVAL AVIATION (250)
LIAISON 1 *Super King Air* 200, 1 *Super King Air* 300, 1
CN-235
TRG 3 T-34C
HEL 2 Bell 230, 4 Bell 206, 4 TH-57

MARINES (1,500)
3 bn: 2 on garrison duties, 1 cdo (no hy weapons/veh)

Air Force 3,000

58 cbt ac, no armed hel

OPERATIONAL COMMAND
2 wg, 5 sqn
FGA 3 sqn
1 with 8 *Jaguar* S (6 -S(E), 2 -B(E))
1 with 12 *Kfir* C-2, 5 TC-2
1 with 8 A-37B
FTR 1 sqn with 13 *Mirage* F-1JE, 1 F-1JB
CCT 1 sqn with 2 *Strikemaster* Mk 89, 7 *Strikemaster*
Mk 89A
MILITARY AIR TRANSPORT GROUP
2 civil/military airlines:
TAME 6 Boeing 727, 2 BAe-748, 4 C-130B, 2 C-130H,
3 DHC-6, 1 F-28, 1 L-100-30
ECUATORIANA 3 Boeing 707-320, 1 DC-10-30, 2
Airbus A-310
LIAISON 1 *King Air* E90, 1 *Sabreliner*
LIAISON/SAR hel 2 AS-332, 1 Bell 212, 6 Bell-206B, 5
SA-316B, 1 SA-330, 2 UH-1B, 24 UH-1H
TRG incl 20 Cessna 150, 5 C-172, 17 T-34C, 1 T-41
MISSILES
AAM R-550 *Magic*, *Super* 530, *Shafrir*
AB 1 AB sqn

Paramilitary 270

COAST GUARD 270
PATROL, INSHORE 6
2 25 *De Julio* PCI, 2 5 *De Agosto* PCI, 2 10 *De Agosto*
PCI<, plus some 20 boats

El Salvador

	1995	1996	1997	1998
GDP	C83.7bn	C92.6bn		
	($8.2bn)	($8.6bn)		
per capita	$2,600	$2,700		
Growth	6.3%	3.0%		
Inflation	10.0%	9.8%		
Debt	$2.6bn	$2.7bn		
Def exp	εC1.5bn	εC1.3bn		
	($145m)	($125m)		
Def bdgt			C910m	
			($89m)	
FMA[a] (US)	$0.40m	$0.54m	$0.45m	$0.50m
$1 = colon	8.8	8.8	8.8	

[a] ONUSAL **1995** $10m

Population		5,873,000		
Age	13–17	18–22	23–32	
Men	367,000	335,000	464,000	
Women	354,000	328,000	494,000	

Total Armed Forces

ACTIVE 28,400

Terms of service: selective conscription, 1 year

RESERVES
Ex-soldiers registered

Army 25,700

(4,000 conscripts)
6 Mil Zones • 6 inf bde (each of 2 inf bn) • 1 special sy bde (2 MP, 2 border gd bn) • 8 inf det (bn) • 1 engr comd (3 engr bn) • 1 arty bde (3 fd, 1 AD bn) • 1 mech cav regt (2 bn) • 2 indep bn (1 Presidential Guard, 1 sy) • 1 special ops gp (1 para bn, 1 naval inf, 1 SF coy)

EQUIPMENT
RECCE 10 AML-90
APC 40 M-37B1 (mod), 14 M-113, 8 UR-416
TOWED ARTY 78: **105mm**: 24 M-101, 36 M-102, 18 M-56 (in store)
MOR some 360: **81mm**: incl 300 M-29; **120mm**: 60 UB-M52, M-74 (all in store)
RL 94mm: LAW; **82mm**: B-300
RCL 420+: **90mm**: 400 M-67; **106mm**: 20+ M-40A1 (in store)
AD GUNS 40: **20mm**: 36 FRY M-55, 4 TCM-20
SAM some captured SA-7 may be in service

Navy 1,100

(incl some 150 Naval Infantry and spt forces)
BASES La Unión, La Libertad, Acajutla, El Triunfo, Guija Lake

PATROL AND COASTAL COMBATANTS 5
PATROL, INSHORE 5
3 *Camcraft* 30m, 2 PCI<, plus 16 boats
AMPHIBIOUS craft only
2 LCM

NAVAL INFANTRY (Marines) (some 150)
1 Marine coy

Air Force 1,600

(incl AD and ε200 conscripts); 20 cbt ac, 25 armed hel
Flying hours A-37: 90
CBT AC 1 sqn with 10 A-37B, 2 AC-47
ARMED HEL 1 sqn with 10 Hughes 500D/E, 15 UH-1M
RECCE 8* O-2A
TPT 1 sqn with **ac** 1 C-47, 4 C-47 Turbo-67, 1 C-123K, 1 *Commander*, 1 DC-6B, 1 *Merlin* IIIB, 9 *Rallye* **hel** 1 sqn with 24 UH-1H tpt hel (incl 4 SAR)
LIAISON 2 Cessna-210
TRG 6 CM-170, 3 T-41C/D, 6 TH-300, 3 O-2A

Forces Abroad

UN AND PEACEKEEPING
WESTERN SAHARA (MINURSO): 2 Obs

Paramilitary 12,000

NATIONAL CIVILIAN POLICE (Ministry of Public Security) some 12,000 (to be 16,000)
small arms; **ac** 1 Cessna **hel** 1 UH-1H, 2 MD-500 *Notar*

Guatemala

	1995	1996	1997	1998
GDP	q84.1bn	q95.1bn		
	($11.0bn)	($11.6bn)		
per capita	$3,600	$3,700		
Growth	4.9%	3.1%		
Inflation	8.7%	11.1%		
Debt	$3.3bn	$3.3bn		
Def exp	εq1.2bn	εq1.2bn		
	($147m)	($154m)		
Def bdgt			q729m	
			($93m)	
FMA^a (US)	$2.1m	$2.0m	$2.2m	$2.2m
$1 = quetzal	5.8	6.1	6.0	
^aMINUGUA **1997** ε$4m				
Population		11,251,000		
Age	*13–17*	*18–22*	*23–32*	
Men	674,000	570,000	847,000	
Women	656,000	557,000	837,000	

Total Armed Forces

(National Armed Forces are combined; the Army provides log spt for Navy and Air Force)

ACTIVE 40,700

(30,000 conscripts)
Terms of service: conscription; selective, 30 months

RESERVES
Army ε35,000 (trained) **Navy** (some) **Air Force** 200

Army 38,500 (to be 33,500)

(30,000 conscripts)
19 Mil Zones (39 inf, 1 trg bn, 6 armd sqn) • 2 strategic bde (6 inf, 1 lt armd bn, 1 recce sqn, 2 arty bty) • 1 SF gp (3 coy incl 1 trg) • 2 AB bn • 5 inf bn gp (each 1 inf bn, 1 recce sqn, 1 arty bty) • 1 MP bn • 1 Presidential Guard bn • 1 engr bn
RESERVES ε19 inf bn
EQUIPMENT

LT TK 10 M-41A3
RECCE 8 M-8, 5 RBY-1
APC 54: 15 M-113, 4 V-100 *Commando*, 35 *Armadillo*
TOWED ARTY 84: **75mm**: 8 M-116; **105mm**: 12 M-101, 8 M-102, 56 M-56
MOR 85: **81mm**: 55 M-1; **107mm**: 12 M-30; **120mm**: 18 ECIA
RL 89mm: 3.5in M-20
RCL 57mm: M-20; **105mm**: 64 Arg M-1974 FMK-1; **106mm**: 20 M-40A1
AD GUNS 20mm: 16 M-55

Navy ε1,500

(incl some 650 Marines)
BASES Atlantic Santo Tomás de Castilla **Pacific** Puerto Quetzal
PATROL CRAFT, INSHORE 15
  1 *Kukulkan* (US *Broadsword* 32m) PFI, 2 *Stewart* PCI, 6 *Cutlas* PCI, 6 *Vigilante* PCI (plus 20 river patrol craft and 2 LCP)

MARINES (some 650)
2 under-str bn

Air Force 700

14† cbt ac, 7 armed hel. Serviceability of ac is less than 50%
CBT AC 1 sqn with 2 Cessna A-37B, 8 PC-7, 4 IAI-201
ARMED HEL 6 Bell 212, 1 Bell 412
TPT 1 sqn with 1 C-47, 3 T-67 (mod C-47 *Turbo*), 2 F-27, 1 *Super King Air* (VIP), 1 DC-6B
LIAISON 1 sqn with 3 Cessna 206, 1 Cessna 310
HEL 1 sqn with 9 Bell 206, 5 UH-1D/-H, 3 S-76
TRG 6 T-41
TACTICAL SECURITY GROUP
  3 CCT coy, 1 armd sqn, 1 AD bty (Army units for air-base sy)

Paramilitary 9,800 active

NATIONAL POLICE 9,800
21 departments, 1 SF bn, 1 integrated task force (incl mil and treasury police)
TREASURY POLICE (2,500)
TERRITORIAL MILITIA (R) (CVDC) ε300,000

Opposition

UNIDAD REVOLUCIONARIA NACIONAL GUATEMALTECA (URNG): all groups demobilised (ε3,600) under UN supervision

Guyana

	1995	1996	1997	1998
GDP	G$91bn	G$104bn		
	($660m)	($730m)		
per capita	$2,900	$3,200		
Growth	5.4%	7.3%		
Inflation	8.1%	7.0%		
Debt	$2.1bn	$2.1bn		
Def exp	G$1.0bn	G$1.0bn		
	($7.0m)	($7.0m)		
Def bdgt			G$1.0bn	
			($7.0m)	
FMA (US)	$0.10m	$0.22m	$0.18m	$0.18m
US$1 = G$	142	140	142	
Population		833,000		
Age	*13–17*	*18–22*	*23–32*	
Men	42,000	41,000	79,000	
Women	40,000	39,000	77,000	

Total Armed Forces

ACTIVE (combined Guyana Defence Force) some 1,600
RESERVES some 1,500
People's Militia (see Paramilitary)

Army 1,400

(incl 500 Reserves)
1 inf bn, 1 SF, 1 spt wpn, 1 engr coy
EQUIPMENT
  RECCE 3 Shorland
  TOWED ARTY 130mm: 6 M-46
  MOR 48: **81mm**: 12 L16A1; **82mm**: 18 M-43; **120mm**: 18 M-43

Navy

Authorised 30 plus 300 reserves **Actual** 17 plus 170 reserves
BASES Georgetown, New Amsterdam
2 boats

Air Force 100

no cbt ac, no armed hel
TPT ac 1 BN-2A, 1 *Skyvan* 3M **hel** 1 Bell 206, 1 Bell 412

Paramilitary

GUYANA PEOPLE'S MILITIA (GPM) some 1,500

Caribbean *and* Latin America

Haiti

	1995	1996	1997	1998
GDP	G41.6bn	G43.5bn		
	($1.7bn)	($1.8bn)		
per capita	$1,000	$1,000		
Growth	4.5%	2.0%		
Inflation	25.5%	17.1%		
Debt	$806m	$941m		
Sy exp	εG1.4bn	εG1.5bn		
	($59m)	($63m)		
Sy bdgt			G0.8bn	
			($32m)	
FMA[a] (US)	$28.3m	$0.3m	$0.3m	$0.3m
$1 = gourde	16.2	15.1	16.7	

[a] UNMIH **1995** $258m **1996** $243m

Population		7,928,000		
Age	*13–17*	*18–22*	*23–32*	
Men	404,000	359,000	581,000	
Women	396,000	355,000	584,000	

Total Armed Forces

ACTIVE Nil

Paramilitary

In 1994, the military government of Haiti was replaced by a civilian administration. The armed forces and police have been disbanded and an Interim Public Security Force (IPSF) of 3,000 formed. A National Police Force of some 4,000 personnel is being formed, and all Army equipment has been destroyed.

The United Nations Transition Mission in Haiti (UNTMIH) has maintained some 1,296 troops and 227 civ pol to ensure a secure and stable environment and to supervise the creation of a separate national police force.

NAVY (Coast Guard) 30 (being developed)
BASE Port-au-Prince
　PATROL CRAFT boats only

AIR FORCE (disbanded in 1995)

Honduras

	1995	1996	1997	1998
GDP	L37.6bn	L47.0bn		
	($4.1bn)	($4.4bn)		
per capita	$2,000	$2,000		
Growth	3.7%	2.9%		
Inflation	29.5%	23.8%		
Debt	$4.6bn	$4.5bn		
Def exp	L486m	L530m		
	($54m)	($59m)		

contd	1995	1996	1997	1998
Def bdgt			L348m	
			($38m)	
FMA (US)	$0.3m	$0.5m	$0.4m	$0.5m
$1 = lempira	10.3	12.9	12.8	

Population		6,272,000		
Age	*13–17*	*18–22*	*23–32*	
Men	370,000	322,000	502,000	
Women	358,000	313,000	494,000	

Total Armed Forces

ACTIVE 18,800

(13,200 conscripts)
Terms of service: conscription, 24 months (ended 1995)

RESERVES 60,000
Ex-servicemen registered

Army 16,000

(12,000 conscripts)
6 Mil Zones
4 inf bde
　2 with 3 inf, 1 arty bn • 1 with 2 inf, 1 arty bn • 1 with 2 inf, 1 engr bn
1 special tac gp with 1 inf, 1 ranger bn, 2 trg units
1 territorial force (2 inf, 1 SF, 1 AB bn)
1 armd cav regt (2 bn)
1 Presidential Guard bn

RESERVES

3 inf bde

EQUIPMENT

　LT TK 12 *Scorpion*
　RECCE 3 *Scimitar*, 1 *Sultan*, 50 *Saladin*
　TOWED ARTY 28: **105mm**: 24 M-102; **155mm**: 4 M-198
　MOR 400: **60mm**; **81mm**; **120mm**: 60 Brandt; **160mm**: 30 *Soltam*
　RL 84mm: 120 *Carl Gustav*
　RCL 106mm: 80 M-40A1

Navy 1,000

(incl 400 Marines and 500 conscripts)
BASES Atlantic Puerto Cortés, Puerto Castilla **Pacific** Amapala
PATROL CRAFT, INSHORE 11
　3 *Guaymuras* (US *Swiftship* 31m) PFI
　2 *Copan* (US *Lantana* 32m) PFI<
　6 PCI<, plus 33 riverine boats
AMPHIBIOUS craft only
　1 *Punta Caxinas* LCT; plus some 3 ex-US LCM

MARINES (400)
1 bn

Air Force some 1,800

(700 conscripts); 40 cbt† ac plus 8 in store, no armed hel
FGA 2 sqn
1 with 13 A-37B
1 with 10 F-5E, 2 -F
FTR 8 *Super Mystère* B2 (in store)
TPT 5 C-47, 4 C-130A, 1 L-188, 2 IAI-201, 2 IAI-1123
LIAISON 1 sqn with 3 Cessna 172, 2 C-180, 2 C-185, 3 *Commander*, 1 PA-31, 1 PA-34
HEL 9 Bell 412, 4 Hughes 500, 6 UH-1B/H, 1 S-76
TRG 4* C-101BB, 6 U-17A, 11* EMB-312, 5 T-41A

Forces Abroad

UN AND PEACEKEEPING
WESTERN SAHARA (MINURSO): 12 Obs

Paramilitary 5,500

PUBLIC SECURITY FORCES (Ministry of Public Security and Defence) 5,500
11 regional comd

Foreign Forces

US 53 Army 6 Air Force 47

Jamaica

	1995	1996	1997	1998
GDP	J$169bn	J$193bn		
	($4.9bn)	($5.0bn)		
per capita	$3,400	$3,400		
Growth	0.5%	-1.4%		
Inflation	19.9%	16.0%		
Debt	$4.3bn	$4.0bn		
Def exp	J$965m	J$990m		
	($34m)	($35m)		
Def bdgt			εJ$1.0bn	
			($35m)	
FMA (US)	$0.8m	$1.2m	$1.3m	$1.3m
US$1 = J$	35.1	37.1	34.2	
Population		2,477,000		
Age	*13–17*	*18–22*	*23–32*	
Men	125,000	124,000	227,000	
Women	122,000	120,000	231,000	

Total Armed Forces

ACTIVE (combined Jamaican Defence Force) some 3,320

RESERVES some 950

Army 877 Coast Guard 60 Air Wing 16

Army 3,000

2 inf bn, 1 spt bn
EQUIPMENT
APC 13 V-150 *Commando*
MOR 81mm: 12 L16A1

RESERVES 877
1 inf bn

Coast Guard ε150

BASE Port Royal
PATROL CRAFT, INSHORE 5
1 *Fort Charles* PFI (US 34m), 1 *Paul Bogle* (US-31m), 3 PFI<, plus 8 boats

Air Wing 170

no cbt ac, no armed hel
AC 2 BN-2A, 1 Cessna 210, 1 *King Air*
HEL 4 Bell 206, 3 Bell 212, 4 UH-1H

Mexico

	1995	1996	1997	1998
GDP	Np1.8tr	Np2.5tr		
	($292bn)	($315bn)		
per capita	$6,600	$7,000		
Growth	-6.7%	5.4%		
Inflation	35.0%	27.7%		
Debt	$166bn	$173bn		
Def exp	Np16.9bn	Np19.1bn		
	($2.8bn)	($3.1bn)		
Def bdgt			Np18.0bn	
			($2.9bn)	
FMA (US)	$0.4m	$3.2m	$9.0m	$9.0m
$1 = new peso	6.4	7.6	7.9	
Population		93,793,000 (Chiapas region 4%)		
Age	*13–17*	*18–22*	*23–32*	
Men	5,103,000	4,865,000	8,372,000	
Women	4,966,000	4,776,000	8,400,000	

Total Armed Forces

ACTIVE 175,000
(60,000 conscripts)
Terms of service: 1 year conscription (4 hours per week) by lottery

RESERVES 300,000

Army 130,000

(incl ε60,000 conscripts)
12 Mil Regions
ε39 Zonal Garrisons incl 1 armd, 19 mot cav, 1 mech inf, 7 arty regt, plus 3 arty, 8 inf bn • 1 armd bde (3 armd, 1 mech inf regt) • 1 Presidential Guard bde (3 inf, 1 SF, 1 arty bn) • 1 mot inf bde (3 mot inf regt) • 2 inf bde (each 3 inf bn, 1 arty bn) • 1 AB bde (3 bn) • 1 MP, 1 engr bde • AD, engr and spt units

EQUIPMENT
RECCE 40 M-8, 119 ERC-90F *Lynx*, 40 VBL, 25 MOWAG, 15 MAC-1, 41 Mex-1
APC 40 HWK-11, 34 M-2A1 half-track, 36 VCR/TT, 40 DN-4 *Caballo*, 40 DN-5 *Toro*, 409 AMX-VCI, 95 BDX, 26 LAV-150 ST
TOWED ARTY 118: **75mm**: 18 M-116 pack; **105mm**: 16 M-2A1/M-3, 60 M-101, 24 M-56
SP ARTY 75mm: 5 DN-5 *Bufalo*
MOR 81mm: 1,500; **120mm**: 75 Brandt
ATGW *Milan* (incl 8 VBL)
RL 82mm: B-300
ATK GUNS 37mm: 30 M-3
AD GUNS 12.7mm: 40 M-55
SAM RBS-70

Navy 37,000

(incl 1,100 Naval Aviation and 8,600 Marines)
NAVAL REGIONS Gulf 6 **Pacific** 11
BASES Gulf Vera Cruz (HQ), Tampico, Chetumal, Ciudad del Carmen, Yukalpetén, Lerna, Frontera, Coatzacoalcos, Isla Mujéres **Pacific** Acapulco (HQ), Ensenada, La Paz, San Blas, Guaymas, Mazatlán, Manzanillo, Salina Cruz, Puerto Madero, Lázaro Cárdenas, Puerto Vallarta

PRINCIPAL AND SURFACE COMBATANTS 7
DESTROYERS 3
2 *Ilhuicamina* (ex-*Quetzalcoatl*) (US *Gearing*) ASW with 1 x 8 ASROC, 2 x 3 ASTT; plus 2 x 2 127mm guns and 1 Bo-105 hel
1 *Cuitlahuac* (US *Fletcher*) with 5 533mm TT, 5 127mm guns
FRIGATES 4
2 *H. Galeana* (US *Bronstein*) with 1 x 8 ASROC, 2 x 3 ASTT, 1 x 2 76mm guns
1 *Comodoro Manuel Azueta* (US *Edsall*) (trg)
1 *Zacatecas* (US *Lawrence/Crosley*) with 1 127mm gun
PATROL AND COASTAL COMBATANTS 106
PATROL, OFFSHORE 39
4 *S. J. Holzinger* (ex-*Uxmal*) (imp *Uribe*) with Bo-105 hel
6 *Cadete Virgilio Uribe* (Sp '*Halcon*') with Bo-105 hel
16 *Leandro Valle* (US *Auk* MSF)
1 *Guanajuato* with 2 102mm gun
12 D-01 (US *Admirable* MSF), 3 with hel deck

PATROL, INSHORE 47
4 *Isla* (US *Halter*) XFPB
31 *Quintana Roo* (UK *Azteca*) PCI
3 *Cabo* (US *Cape Higgon*) PCI
2 *Punta* (US *Point*) PCI
7 *Tamiahua* (US *Polimar*)
PATROL, RIVERINE 20<, plus boats
AMPHIBIOUS 2
2 *Panuco* (US-511) LST
SUPPORT AND MISCELLANEOUS 22
3 AOT, 1 PCI spt, 4 log spt, 6 ocean tugs, 5 survey, 1 *Durango* tpt, plus 2 other tpt

NAVAL AVIATION (1,100)
9 cbt ac, no armed hel
MR 1 sqn with 9 C-212-200M
MR HEL 12 Bo-105 (8 afloat)
TPT 1 C-212, 2 C-180, 3 C-310, 1 DHC-5, 1 FH-227, 1 *King Air* 90, 1 *Learjet* 24, 1 *Commander*, 2 C-337, 2 C-402
HEL 3 Bell 47, 4 SA-319, 2 UH-1H, 4 MD-500 (trg), 8 Mi-8/17, 4 AS-335
TRG 8 Cessna 152, 10 F-33C *Bonanza*, 12 L-90 *Redigo*, 4 MD-500E

MARINES (8,600)
1 AB regt (2 bn) • 1 sy, 1 Presidential Guard bn • 22 regional bn
EQUIPMENT
AAV 25 VAP-3550
TOWED ARTY 105mm: 8 M-56
MRL 51mm: 6 *Firos*
MOR 100 incl **60mm**, **81mm**
RCL 106mm: M-40A1
AD GUNS 20mm: Mk 38; **40mm**: Bofors

Air Force 8,000

(incl 1,500 AB bde); 125 cbt ac, 95 armed hel
FTR 1 sqn with 8 F-5E, 2 -F
CCT 10 sqn
7 with 74 PC-7
3 with 27 AT-33
ARMED HEL 1 sqn with 1 Bell 205, 27 Bell 206, 25 Bell 212, 20 UH-1H
RECCE 2 photo sqn with 14* *Commander* 500S, 1 SA 2-37A, 4 C-26
TPT 5 sqn with 2 BN-2, 12 C-47, 1 C-54, 10 C-118, 9 C-130A, 5 *Commander* 500, 1 -680, 5 DC-6 *Skytrain*, 2 F-27, 5 Boeing 727, 1 sqn with 12 IAI-201 (tpt/SAR)
HEL 4 Bell 205, 3 SA-332, 2 UH-60, 6 S-70A
PRESIDENTIAL TPT ac 1 Boeing 757, 2 Boeing 737, 1 L-188, 3 FH-227, 2 *Merlin*, 4 *Sabreliners* **hel** 1 AS-332, 2 SA-330, 2 UH-60
LIAISON/UTL 2 *King Air*, 1 *Musketeer*, 40 Beech *Bonanza* F-33A, 10 Beech *Musketeer*
TRG ac 20 CAP-10, 5 T-39 *Sabreliner* **hel** 22* MD 530F (SAR/paramilitary/trg)

Paramilitary

RURAL DEFENCE MILITIA (R) 14,000

COAST GUARD
4 *Mako* 295 PCI

Nicaragua

	1995	1996	1997	1998
GDP	Co14.4bn	Co17.3bn		
	($2.2bn)	($2.4bn)		
per capita	$1,900	$2,000		
Growth	4.8%	6.1%		
Inflation	10.9%	11.6%		
Debt	$9.3bn	$6.0bn		
Def exp	Co260m	Co240m		
	($39m)	($36m)		
Def bdgt			Co258m	
			($39m)	
FMA (US)			$0.2m	$0.2m
$1 = Co*	7.6	8.4	9.3	
* Cordoba oro				
Population		4,454,000		
Age	*13–17*	*18–22*	*23–32*	
Men	297,000	235,000	269,000	
Women	266,000	225,000	353,000	

Total Armed Forces

ACTIVE ε17,000

Terms of service: voluntary, 18–36 months

Army 15,000

Reorganisation in progress
5 Regional Comd (10 inf, 1 tk bn) • 2 mil det (2 inf bn)
• 1 lt mech bde (1 mech inf, 1 tk, 1 recce bn, 1 fd arty
gp (2 bn), 1 atk gp), 1 comd regt (1 inf, 1 sy bn) • 1 SF
bde (3 SF bn) • 1 engr bn
EQUIPMENT
  MBT some 127 T-55 (63 in store)
  LT TK 10 PT-76
  RECCE 20 BRDM-2
  APC 102 BTR-152, 64 BTR-60
  TOWED ARTY 142: **122mm**: 12 D-30, 100 *Grad* 1P
  (single-tube rocket launcher); **152mm**: 30 D-20 (in
  store)
  MRL 51: **107mm**: 33 Type-63; **122mm**: 18 BM-21
  MOR 607: **82mm**: 579; **120mm**: 24 M-43; **160mm**: 4
  M-160 (in store)
  ATGW AT-3 *Sagger* (12 on BRDM-2)
  RCL 82mm: B-10
  ATK GUNS 461: **57mm**: 354 ZIS-2 (90 in store);

76mm: 83 Z1S-3; **100mm**: 24 M-1944
SAM 200+ SA-7/-14/-16

Navy ε800

BASES Corinto, Puerto Cabezzas, El Bluff

PATROL AND COASTAL COMBATANTS 15
PATROL, INSHORE 15†
  2 Sov *Zhuk* PFI<, 4 DPRK *Sin Hung* PFI<, 3 *Dabur*
  PCI, 6 PCI< plus boats

MINECOUNTERMEASURES 3
  3 *Yevgenya* MCI

Air Force 1,200

no cbt ac, 16 armed hel
TPT 6 An-2, 5 An-26
HEL 16 Mi-17 (tpt/armed)
UTL/TRG ac 1 Cessna 180, 1 Cessna-T-41D, 2 Cessna-
U-17
ASM AT-2 *Swatter* ATGW
AD GUNS 1 air def gp, 18 ZU-23, 18 C3-*Morigla* M1

Panama

	1995	1996	1997	1998
GDP	B7.9bn	B8.0bn		
	($8.0bn)	($8.2bn)		
per capita	$5,900	$6,100		
Growth	2.0%		2.5%	
Inflation	1.0%	1.3%		
Debt	$7.2bn	$6.8bn		
Sy bdgt	B106m	B110m	B114m	
	($108m)	($112m)	($116m)	
FMA (US)	$0.15			
$1 = balboa	1.0	1.0	1.0	
Population		2,748,000		
Age	*13–17*	*18–22*	*23–32*	
Men	141,000	136,000	245,000	
Women	135,000	130,000	240,000	

Total Armed Forces

ACTIVE Nil

Paramilitary ε11,800

NATIONAL POLICE FORCE 11,000

Presidential Guard bn (-), 1 MP bn plus 8 coys, 18
Police coy, 1 SF unit (reported); no hy mil eqpt, small
arms only

NATIONAL MARITIME SERVICE ε400

BASES Amador (HQ), Balboa, Colón
PATROL CRAFT, INSHORE 5
2 *Panquiaco* (UK *Vosper* 31.5m), 1 *Tres de Noviembre*
(ex-USCG *Cape Higgon*), 2 ex-US MSB 5-class
(plus about 6 other ex-US patrol/spt craft and
boats)
AMPHIBIOUS craft only
1 LCM

NATIONAL AIR SERVICE 400

TPT 1 CN-235-2A, 1 BN-2B, 1 PA-34, 3 CASA-212M
Aviocar
TRG 6 T-35D
HEL 2 Bell 205, 3 Bell 212, 1 UH-H

Foreign Forces

US 6,230: **Army** 3,370; 1 inf bde (1 inf bn), 1 avn bde
Navy 700 **Marines** 200 **Air Force** 1,960; 1 wg (1 C-21, 9
C-27, 1 CT-43)

Paraguay

	1995	1996	1997	1998
GDP	Pg17.7tr	Pg19.7tr		
	($8.3bn)	($8.5bn)		
per capita	$3,700	$3,700		
Growth	4.6%	1.1%		
Inflation	15.4%	8.2%		
Debt	$2.3bn	$2.4bn		
Def exp[a]	Pg239bn	Pg240bn		
	($112m)	($112m)		
Def bdgt			εPg260bn	
			($122m)	
FMA (US)	$0.1m	$0.2m	$0.2m	$0.2m
$1 = Pg*	1,970	2,064	2,156	
* Paraguayan guarani				
Population		5,220,000		
Age	*13–17*	*18–22*	*23–32*	
Men	283,000	246,000	416,000	
Women	273,000	237,000	400,000	

Total Armed Forces

ACTIVE 20,200

(12,900 conscripts)
Terms of service: 12 months **Navy** 2 years

RESERVES some 164,500

Army 14,900

(10,400 conscripts)
3 corps HQ • 9 div HQ (6 inf, 3 cav) • 9 inf regt (bn) •
3 cav regt (horse) • 3 mech cav regt • Presidential
Guard (1 inf, 1 MP bn, 1 arty bty) • 20 frontier det • 3
arty gp (bn) • 1 AD arty gp • 4 engr bn
EQUIPMENT
MBT 5 M-4A3
RECCE 8 M-8, 5 M-3, 30 EE-9 *Cascavel*
APC 10 EE-11 *Urutu*
TOWED ARTY 41: **75mm**: 20 Model 1927/1934;
105mm: 15 M-101; **152mm**: 6 Vickers 6in (coast)
MOR 81mm: 80
RCL 75mm: M-20
AD GUNS 30: **20mm**: 20 Bofors; **40mm**: 10 M-1A1

Navy 3,600

(incl 900 Marines, 800 Naval Aviation, Harbour and
River Guard, and ε1,900 conscripts)
BASES Asunción (Puerto Sajonia), Bahía Negra,
Ciudad Del Este
PATROL AND COASTAL COMBATANTS 13
PATROL, COASTAL 13
2 *Paraguais* with 4 120mm guns
2 *Nanawa* PCO with 4 40mm and 2 12.7mm guns
1 *Itapu* PCR with 1 40mm, 6 12.7mm guns, 2 81mm
mor
1 *Capitan Cabral* PCR with 1 40mm, 2 20mm, 2
12.7mm guns
7 *Rodman* SS/101 PCI (plus 13 riverine boats)
SUPPORT AND MISCELLANEOUS 6
1 tpt, 1 *Boqueron* spt (ex-US LSM with hel deck), 1
trg/tpt, 1 survey<, 2 LCT
MARINES (900)
(incl 200 conscripts); 2 bn
NAVAL AVIATION (800)
2 cbt ac, no armed hel
CCT 2 AT-6G
LIAISON 2 Cessna 150, 2 C-206, 1 C-210
HEL 2 HB-350, 1 OH-13

Air Force 1,700

(600 conscripts); 21 cbt ac, no armed hel
CCT 5 AT-6, 7 EMB-326, 4 T-27
LIAISON 1 Cessna 185, 4 C-206, 2 C-402, 2 T-41
HEL 3 HB-350, 1 UH-1B, 2 UH-1H, 4 UH-12, 4 Bell
47G
TPT 1 sqn with 5 C-47, 4 C-212, 3 DC-6B, 1 DHC-6
(VIP), 1 C-131D
TRG 5* EMB-312, 6 T-6, 10 T-23, 5 T-25, 10 T-35, 1 T-
41

Paramilitary 14,800

SPECIAL POLICE SERVICE 14,800

(incl 4,000 conscripts)

Peru

	1995	1996	1997	1998
GDP	NS133bn	NS149bn		
	($55.4bn)	($57.8bn)		
per capita	$3,900	$4,000		
Growth	7.6%	2.0%		
Inflation	11.1%	12.0%		
Debt	$30.8bn	$30.7bn		
Def exp	εNS2.1bn	εNS2.6bn		
	($0.9bn)	($1.1bn)		
Def bdgt			εNS2.7bn	
			($1.1bn)	
FMA[a] (US)	$15.3m	$15.9m	$23.5m	$40.5m
$1 = new sol	2.3	2.5	2.7	
[a] MOMEP **1995** ε$3m **1996** ε$3m				
Population		24,575,000		
Age	*13–17*	*18–22*	*23–32*	
Men	1,326,000	1,243,000	2,125,000	
Women	1,314,000	1,234,000	2,117,000	

Total Armed Forces

ACTIVE 125,000

(74,500 conscripts)
Terms of service: 2 years, selective

RESERVES 188,000
Army only

Army 85,000

(60,000 conscripts)
6 Mil Regions
Army tps
  1 AB div (3 cdo, 1 para bn, 1 arty gp) • 1 Presidential Escort regt • 1 AD arty gp
Regional tps
  3 armd div (each 2 tk, 1 armd inf bn,1 arty gp, 1 engr bn) • 1 armd gp (3 indep armd cav, 1 fd arty, 1 AD arty, 1 engr bn) • 1 cav div (3 mech regt, 1 arty gp) • 7 inf div (each 3 inf bn, 1 arty gp) • 1 jungle div • 2 med arty gp; 2 fd arty gp • 1 indep inf bn • 1 indep engr bn • 3 hel sqn

EQUIPMENT

MBT 300 T-54/-55 (ε50 serviceable)
LT TK 110 AMX-13 (ε30 serviceable)
RECCE 60 M-8/-20, 10 M-3A1, 50 M-9A1, 15 Fiat 6616, 30 BRDM-2
APC 130 M-113, 12 BTR-60, 130 UR-416, Fiat 6614, *Casspir*, 4 *Repontec*
TOWED ARTY 252: **105mm**: 20 Model 56 pack, 130 M-101; **122mm**: 36 D-30; **130mm**: 30 M-46; **155mm**: 36 M-114
SP ARTY 24: **155mm**: 12 M-109A2, 12 Mk F3

MRL 122mm: 14 BM-21
MOR 81mm: incl some SP; **107mm**: incl some SP; **120mm**: 300 Brandt, ECIA
ATGW 400 SS-11
RCL 106mm: M40A1
AD GUNS 240: **23mm**: 80 ZSU-23-2, 35 ZSU-23-4 SP; **40mm**: 45 M-1, 80 L60/70
SAM SA-7, 236 SA-16, 10 SA-19 (2S6 SP) (8 SAM, plus twin **30mm** gun), *Javelin*
AC 13 Cessna incl 1 C-337, 1 *Queen Air* 65, 5 U-10, 3 U-17, 1 U-150, 2 U-206
HEL 2 Bell 47G, 2 Mi-6, 26 Mi-8, 13 Mi-17, 6 SA-315, 5 SA-316, 3 SA-318, 2 *Agusta* A-109

Navy 25,000

(incl some 800 Naval Aviation, 3,000 Marines and 12,500 conscripts)
NAVAL AREAS Pacific, Lake Titicaca, Amazon River
BASES Ocean Callao, San Lorenzo Island, Paita, Talara **Lake** Puno **River** Iquitos, Puerto Maldonado

SUBMARINES 8

6 *Casma* (Ge T-209/1200) with 533mm TT (It A184 HWT) (2 in refit)
2 *Abato* with 533mm TT, 1 127mm gun
  (Plus 1 *Pedrera* (US *Guppy* I) with 533mm TT (Mk 37 HWT) alongside trg only)

PRINCIPAL SURFACE COMBATANTS 7

CRUISERS 2
  1 *Almirante Grau* (Nl *De Ruyter*) with 4 x 2 152mm guns, 8 *Otomat* SSM
  1 *Aguirre* (Nl *De 7 Provincien*) with 3 SH-3D *Sea King* hel (ASW/ASUW) (Mk 46 LWT/AM-39 *Exocet*), 2 x 2 152mm guns
DESTROYERS 1 *Ferre* (UK *Daring*) with 4 x 2 MM-38 *Exocet*, 3 x 2 114mm guns, hel deck
FRIGATES 4 *Carvajal* (mod It *Lupo*) with 1 AB-212 hel (ASW OTHT), 2 x 3 ASTT; plus 8 *Otomat* Mk 2 SSM, 1 127mm gun (2 non-op)

PATROL AND COASTAL COMBATANTS 7

MISSILE CRAFT 6 *Velarde* PFM (Fr PR-72 64m) with 4 MM-38 *Exocet*
PATROL CRAFT 1 *Unanue* (ex-US *Sotoyomo*) PCC (Antarctic ops)

MINE COUNTERMEASURES 1

1 *Dokkum* (Nl *Abcoude*)

AMPHIBIOUS 3

3 *Paita* (US *Terrebonne Parish*) LST, capacity 395 tps, 16 tk

SUPPORT AND MISCELLANEOUS 8

3 AO, 1 AOT, 1 tpt, 2 survey, 1 ocean tug (SAR)

RIVER AND LAKE FLOTILLAS 7

some 4 gunboats, 3 patrol<

NAVAL AVIATION (some 800)

7 cbt ac, 13 armed hel

  ASW/MR 4 sqn with **ac** 7* S-2, 3 *Super King Air* B
    200T, 3 EMB-111A **hel** 5 AB-212 ASW, 8 ASH-3D
    (ASW)

  TPT 2 An-32

  LIAISON 4 Bell 206B, 6 UH-1D hel, 2 SA-319, 3 Mi-
    8

  TRG 1 Cessna 150, 5 T-34C

  ASM *Exocet* AM-39 (on SH-3 hel)

MARINES (3,000)

1 Marine bde (5 bn, 1 recce, 1 cdo coy)

EQUIPMENT

  RECCE V-100

  APC 15 V-200 *Chaimite*, 20 BMR-600

  MOR 81mm; **120mm** ε18

  RCL 84mm: *Carl Gustav*; **106mm**: M-40A1

  AD GUNS twin 20mm SP

COASTAL DEFENCE 3 bty with 18 **155mm** how

Air Force 15,000

(2,000 conscripts); 101 cbt ac, 23 armed hel

BBR 1 gp (2 sqn) with 15 *Canberra* (4 -B(1) 12, 8 -B1(68),
  1 T-4, 2 -T54)

FGA 2 gp, 6 sqn

  3 with 28 Su-22 (incl 4* Su-22U), 12 MiG-29

  3 with 23 Cessna A-37B

FTR 3 sqn

  1 with 10 *Mirage* 2000P, 2 -DP

  2 with 9 *Mirage* 5P, 2 -DP

ATTACK HEL 1 sqn with 23 Mi-24/-25

RECCE 1 photo-survey unit with 2 *Learjet* 25B, 2 -36A

TKR 1 Boeing KC 707-323C

TPT 3 gp, 7 sqn

  ac 18 An-32, 3 AN-72, 4 C-130A, 6 -D, 5 L-100-20, 2
  DC-8-62F, 12 DHC-5, 8 DHC-6, 1 FH-227, 9 PC-6, 6
  Y-12, 2 Boeing 737 **hel** 3 sqn with 8 Bell 206, 14 B-
  212, 5 B-214, 1 B-412, 10 Bo-105C, 5 Mi-6, 3 Mi-8, 35
  Mi-17, 5 SA-316

PRESIDENTIAL FLT 1 F-28, 1 *Falcon* 20F

LIAISON ac 2 Beech 99, 3 Cessna 185, 1 Cessna 320,
  15 *Queen Air* 80, 3 *King Air* 90, 1 PA-31T **hel** 8 UH-
  1D

TRG ac 2 Cessna 150, 25 EMB-312, 13 MB-339A, 20 T-
  37B/C, 15 T-41A/-D **hel** 12 Bell 47G

MISSILES

  ASM AS-30

  AAM AA-2 *Atoll*, R-550 *Magic*

  AD 3 SA-2, 6 SA-3 bn with 18 SA-2, 24 SA-3
    launchers

Paramilitary 78,000

NATIONAL POLICE 77,000

General Police 43,000 Security Police 21,000
Technical Police 13,000

  100+ MOWAG *Roland* APC

COAST GUARD 1,000

  5 *Rio Nepena* PCC, 3 PCI, 10 riverine PCI<

RONDAS CAMPESINAS (peasant self-defence force)

perhaps 2,000 *rondas* 'gp', up to pl strength, some with
small arms. Deployed mainly in emergency zone

Opposition

SENDERO LUMINOSO (Shining Path) ε1,500
Maoist

MOVIMIENTO REVOLUCIONARIO TUPAC AMARU
(MRTA) ε200
mainly urban gp

Suriname

	1995	1996	1997	1998
GDP	gld n.k.	gld n.k.		
	($362m)	($403m)		
per capita	$3,800	$4,300		
Growth	9.6%	9.1%		
Inflation	236%	-0.8%		
Debt	$95m	$99m		
Def exp	εgld n.k.	εgld n.k.		
	($14m)	($14m)		
Def bdgt			εgld n.k.	
			($14m)	
FMA (US)	$0.03m	$0.08m	$0.10m	$0.10m
$1 = guilder	442	401	401	
Population		413,000		
Age	13–17	18–22	23–32	
Men	21,000	19,000	37,000	
Women	21,000	18,000	37,000	

Total Armed Forces

ACTIVE (all services form part of the Army) ε1,800

Army 1,400

1 inf bn (4 inf coy) • 1 mech cav sqn • 1 MP 'bde' (bn)

EQUIPMENT

  RECCE 6 EE-9 *Cascavel*

  APC 9 YP-408, 15 EE-11 *Urutu*

  MOR 81mm: 6

  RCL 106mm: M-40A1

Navy 240

BASE Paramaribo

PATROL CRAFT, INSHORE 5
   3 S-401 (Nl 32m), 2<, plus boats

Air Force ε160

5 cbt ac, no armed hel
TPT/TRG 4* BN-2 *Defender*, 1* PC-7
LIAISON 1 Cessna U206
HEL 2 SA-319, 1 AB-205

Trinidad and Tobago

	1995	1996	1997	1998
GDP	TT$33bn	TT$38bn		
	($6.1bn)	($6.4bn)		
per capita	$9,000	$9,400		
Growth	2.4%	2.6%		
Inflation	5.2%	3.2%		
Debt	$2.6bn	$2.7bn		
Def exp	εTT$390m	εTT$395m		
	($72m)	($73m)		
Def bdgt			εTT$400m	
			($73m)	
FMA (US)			$0.1m	$0.1m
US$1 = TT$	5.9	6.0	6.2	
Population		1,327,000		
Age	*13–17*	*18–22*	*23–32*	
Men	69,000	61,000	105,000	
Women	68,000	61,000	109,000	

Total Armed Forces

ACTIVE (all services form part of the Army) 2,100

Army 1,400

2 inf bn • 1 spt bn
EQUIPMENT
   MOR ε46: **60mm**: ε40; **81mm**: 6 L16A1
   RL 82mm: 13 B-300
   RCL 84mm: *Carl Gustav*

Coast Guard 700

(incl 50 Air Wing)
BASE Staubles Bay (HQ), Hart's Cut, Point Fortin, Tobago
PATROL CRAFT, INSHORE 7 (some non-op)
   2 *Barracuda* PFI (Sw *Karlskrona* 40m)
   5 *Plymouth* PCI< (plus 13 boats and 2 auxiliary vessels)

AIR WING
   1 Cessna 310, 1 C-402, 1 C-172

Paramilitary 4,800

POLICE 4,800

Uruguay

	1995	1996	1997	1998
GDP	pU112bn	pU151bn		
	($11.3bn)	($12.1bn)		
per capita	$7,700	$8,200		
Growth	-2.3%	4.8%		
Inflation	42.2%	28.3%		
Debt	$5.3bn	$5.0bn		
Def exp	pU2.1bn	εpU2.2bn		
	($331m)	($276m)		
Def bdgt			εpU2.8bn	
			($301m)	
FMA (US)	$0.1m	$0.4m	$0.3m	$0.3m
$1 = pU*	6.3	8.0	9.3	
Uruguayan peso				
Population		3,213,000		
Age	*13–17*	*18–22*	*23–32*	
Men	135,000	135,000	237,000	
Women	129,000	130,000	235,000	

Total Armed Forces

ACTIVE 25,600

Army 17,600

4 Mil Regions/div HQ • 5 inf bde (4 of 3 inf bn, 1 of 1 mech, 1 mot, 1 para bn) • 3 cav bde (10 cav bn (4 horsed, 3 mech, 2 mot, 1 armd)) • 1 arty bde (2 arty, 1 AD arty bn) • 1 engr bde (3 bn) • 3 arty, 4 cbt engr bn
EQUIPMENT
   LT TK 17 M-24, 29 M-3A1, 22 M-41A1
   RECCE 16 EE-3 *Jararaca*, 10 EE-9 *Cascavel*
   AIFV 10 BMP-1
   APC 15 M-113, 50 *Condor*, 60 OT-64 SKOT
   TOWED ARTY 65: **75mm**: 12 Bofors M-1902; **105mm**: 48 M-101A/M-102; **155mm**: 5 M-114A1
   MRL 122mm: 2 RM-70
   MOR 149: **81mm**: 97; **107mm**: 8 M-30; **120mm**: 44
   ATGW 5 *Milan*
   RCL 60: **57mm**: 30 M-18; **106mm**: 30 M-40A1
   AD GUNS 14: **20mm**: 6 M-167 *Vulcan*; **40mm**: 8 L/60

Navy 5,000

(incl 280 Naval Aviation, 400 Naval Infantry, 1,600
Prefectura Naval (Coast Guard))
BASES Montevideo (HQ), La Paloma, Fray Bentos
FRIGATES 3
   3 *General Artigas* (Fr *Cdt Rivière*) with 2 x 3 ASTT, 1 x
   2 ASW mor, 2 100mm guns
PATROL AND COASTAL COMBATANTS 10
PATROL, INSHORE 10
   2 *Colonia* PCI (US *Cape*), 3 *15 de Noviembre* PFI (Fr
   Vigilante 42m), 1 *Salto* PCI, 1 *Paysandu* PCI<, 3
   other<
MINE COUNTERMEASURES 4
   4 *Temerario* MSC (Ge *Kondor* II)
AMPHIBIOUS craft only
   4 LCM, 2 LCVP
SUPPORT AND MISCELLANEOUS 5
   1 *Presidente Rivera* AOT, 1 *Vanguardia* Salvage, 1
   Campbell (US *Auk* MSF) PCO (Antarctic patrol/
   research), 1 tug (ex-GDR *Elbe*-Class), 1 trg

NAVAL AVIATION (280)
1 cbt ac, no armed hel
   ASW 1 *Super King Air* 200T
   TRG/LIAISON 2 T-28, 2 T-34B, 2 T-34C, 2 PA-34-
   200T, 3 C-182
   HEL 3 Wessex Mk60, 2 Bell 47G, 2 SH-34J

NAVAL INFANTRY (400)
1 bn

Air Force 3,000

33 cbt ac, no armed hel **Flying hours** 120
CBT AC 2 sqn
   1 with 10 A-37B, 6 T-33A, 1 with 5 IA-58B)
SURVEY 1 EMB-110B1
SAR 1 sqn with 2 Bell 212, 3 UH-1H hel, 6 *Wessex* HC2
TPT 3 sqn with 3 C-212 (tpt/SAR), 3 EMB-110C, 1 F-
   27, 3 C-130B, 1 Cessna 310 (VIP), 1 Cessna 206
LIAISON 2 Cessna 182, 2 *Queen Air* 80, 5 U-17, 1 T-34A
TRG *12 T-34A/B, 5 T-41D, 5 PC-7U

Forces Abroad

UN AND PEACEKEEPING
ANGOLA (UNOMA): 10 incl 3 Obs plus 15 civ pol.
EGYPT (MFO): 60. **GEORGIA** (UNOMIG): 4 Obs.
INDIA/PAKISTAN (UNMOGIP): 3 Obs. **IRAQ/
KUWAIT** (UNIKOM): 5 Obs. **LIBERIA** (UNOMIL): 2
Obs. **TAJIKISTAN** (UNMOT): 3 Obs. **WESTERN
SAHARA** (MINURSO): 13 Obs plus 2 civ pol

Paramilitary 920

GUARDIA DE GRANADEROS 450

GUARDIA DE CORACEROS 470

COAST GUARD (1,600)
Prefectura Naval (PNN) is part of the Navy

Venezuela

	1995	1996	1997	1998
GDP	Bs13.5bn	Bs28.1bn		
	($78.9bn)	($79.9bn)		
per capita	$8,000	$7,900		
Growth	3.0%	-1.1%		
Inflation	59.9%	99.9%		
Debt	$35.8bn	$35.3bn		
Def exp	Bs151bn	Bs325bn		
	($882m)	($922m)		
Def bdgt			Bs470bn	Bs718bn
			($981m)	($1,100m)
FMA (US)	$0.8m	$0.9m	$1.0m	$1.0m
$1 = bolivar	177	417	490	
Population		22,825,000		
Age	*13–17*	*18–22*	*23–32*	
Men	1,207,000	1,113,000	1,926,000	
Women	1,163,000	1,076,000	1,874,000	

Total Armed Forces

ACTIVE 79,000
(incl National Guard and ε31,000 conscripts)
Terms of service: 30 months selective, varies by region
for all services

RESERVES ε8,000
Army

Army 34,000

(incl 27,000 conscripts)
6 inf div • 1 armd bde • 1 cav bde • 7 inf bde (18 inf, 1
mech inf, 4 fd arty bn) • 1 AB bde • 1 Ranger bde (6
Ranger bn) • 1 avn regt
RESERVES ε6 inf, 1 armd, 1 arty bn
EQUIPMENT
   MBT 70 AMX-30
   LT TK 75 M-18, 36 AMX-13, 80 *Scorpion* 90
   RECCE 10 AML-60/-90, 30 M-8
   APC 25 AMX-VCI, 100 V-100, 30 V-150, 100 *Dragoon*
   (some with **90mm** gun), 35 EE-11 *Urutu*
   TOWED ARTY 92: **105mm**: 40 Model 56, 40 M-101;
   155mm: 12 M-114
   SP ARTY 15: **155mm**: 5 M-109, 10 Mk F3
   MRL 160mm: 20 LAR SP
   MOR 230: **81mm**: 165; **120mm**: 65 Brandt
   ATGW AT-4, AS-11, 24 *Mapats*

RCL 84mm: *Carl Gustav*; **106mm**: 175 M-40A1
SURV RASIT (veh, arty)
AC 3 IAI-202, 2 Cessna 182, 2 C-206, 2 C-207
ATTACK HEL 5 A-109 (atk)
TPT HEL 4 AS-61A, 3 Bell 205, 6 UH-1H
LIAISON 2 Bell 206

Navy 15,000

(incl 1,000 Naval Aviation, 5,000 Marines, 1,000 Coast
Guard and ε4,000 conscripts)
NAVAL COMMANDS Fleet, Marines, Naval Avn,
Coast Guard, Fluvial (River Forces)
NAVAL FLEET SQN submarine, frigate, patrol, amph,
service
BASES Main bases Caracas (HQ), Puerto Cabello
(submarine, frigate, amph and service sqn), Punto Fijo
(patrol sqn) **Minor bases** Puerto de Hierro, Puerto La
Cruz, El Amparo (HQ Arauca River), Maracaibo, La
Guaira, Ciudad Bolivar (HQ Fluvial Forces)
SUBMARINES 2
2 *Sabalo* (Ge T-209/1300) with 533mm TT (SST-4
HWT)
FRIGATES 6
6 *Mariscal Sucre* (It Lupo) with 1 AB-212 hel (ASW/
OTHT), 2 x 3 ASTT (A-244S LWT); plus 8 *Teseo*
SSM, 1 127mm gun, 1 x 8 *Aspide* SAM
PATROL AND COASTAL COMBATANTS 6
MISSILE CRAFT 6
3 *Constitución* PFM (UK Vosper 37m), with 2 *Teseo*
3 *Constitución* PFI with 4 *Harpoon* SSM
AMPHIBIOUS 4
4 *Capana* LST (Sov *Alligator*), capacity 200 tps, 12 tk
Plus craft: 2 LCU (river comd), 12 LCVP
SUPPORT AND MISCELLANEOUS 5
1 log spt, 1 trg, 1 *Punta Brava* AGHS, 2 survey

NAVAL AVIATION (1,000)
4 cbt ac, 8 armed hel
ASW 1 hel sqn (afloat) with 8 AB-212
MR 1 sqn with 4 C-212
TPT 2 C-212, 1 DHC-7, 1 *Rockwell Commander* 680
LIAISON 1 Cessna 310, 1 C-402, 1 *King Air* 90
HEL 2 Bell 412

MARINES (5,000)
4 inf bn • 1 arty bn (3 fd, 1 AD bty) • 1 amph veh bn •
1 river patrol, 1 engr, 2 para/cdo unit
EQUIPMENT
AAV 11 LVTP-7 (to be mod to -7A1)
APC 25 EE-11 *Urutu*, 10 *Fuchs/Transportpanzer* 1
TOWED ARTY 105mm: 18 Model 56
AD GUNS 40mm: 6 M-42 twin SP

COAST GUARD (1,000)
BASE La Guaira; operates under Naval Command
and Control, but organisationally separate

PATROL, OFFSHORE 3
2 *Almirante Clemente* (It FF type)
1 *Miguel Rodriguez* (ex-US ocean tug)
PATROL, INSHORE 6
2 *Petrel* (USCG *Point*-class) PCI<
4 riverine PCI<
plus 28 river patrol craft and boats

Air Force 7,000

(some conscripts); 114 cbt ac, 27 armed hel
Flying hours 155
FTR/FGA 6 air gp
1 with 15 CF-5A/B, 7 NF-5A/B • 1 with 2 *Mirage*
IIIEV, 5 *Mirage* 50EV • 2 with 21 F-16A/B • 2 with
20 EMB-312
RECCE 15* OV-10A
ECM 3 *Falcon* 20DC
ARMED HEL 1 air gp with 10 SA-316, 12 UH-1D, 5 UH-
1H
TPT ac 7 C-123, 5 C-130H, 8 G-222, 2 HS-748, 2 B-707
(tkr) **hel** 2 Bell 214, 4 Bell 412, 8 AS-332B, 2 UH-1N,
18 Mi-8/17
PRESIDENTIAL FLT 1 Boeing 737, 1 *Gulfstream* III, 1
Gulfstream IV, 1 *Learjet* 24D **hel** 1 Bell 412
LIAISON 9 Cessna 182, 1 *Citation* I, 1 *Citation* II, 2
Queen Air 65, 5 *Queen Air* 80, 5 *Super King Air* 200, 9
SA-316B *Alouette* III
TRG 1 air gp: 12* EMB-312, 20 T-34, 17* T-2D
MISSILES
AAM R-530 *Magic*, AIM-9L *Sidewinder*, AIM-9P
Sidewinder
ASM *Exocet*
AD GUNS 20mm: some Panhard M-3 SP; **35mm**;
40mm: 114: Bofors L/70 towed, Breda towed
SAM 10 *Roland*

National Guard (*Fuerzas Armadas de Cooperación*) 23,000

(internal sy, customs)
8 regional comd
EQUIPMENT
20 UR-416 AIFV, 24 Fiat-6614 APC, 100 **60mm** mor,
50 **81mm** mor **ac** 1 *Baron*, 1 BN-2A, 2 Cessna 185, 5
-U206, 4 IAI-201, 1 *King Air* 90, 1 *King Air* 200C, 2
Queen Air 80, 6 M-28 *Skytruck* **hel** 4 A-109, 20 Bell
206, 2 Bell 212
PATROL CRAFT, INSHORE 22; some 60 boats

Forces Abroad

UN AND PEACEKEEPING
IRAQ/KUWAIT (UNIKOM): 3 Obs. **WESTERN
SAHARA (MINURSO):** 3 Obs

MILITARY DEVELOPMENTS

The most striking military development in Sub-Saharan Africa in 1997 was the successful campaign conducted by Laurent Kabila and his Alliance of Democratic Forces for the Liberation of Congo-Zaire (ADFL) to seize control of what is now known as the **Democratic Republic of Congo** (DROC), formerly Zaire. The rapid advance of Kabila's small force from east to west across the country was a remarkable achievement. However, apart from the very early stages of the campaign, there was little more than token resistance from then President Mobutu Sese Seko's forces, who were ill equipped, badly paid and demoralised.

Kabila's success has formed an axis of shared politico-military interests and mutual support stretching from **Eritrea** and **Ethiopia** in the Horn of Africa through **Uganda** and **Rwanda** in central Africa to the DROC's Atlantic coast. Support from President Yoweri Museveni of Uganda, and the provision of soldiers from the Rwandan government, were important factors in Kabila's success. The pressure for change is also being felt in **Kenya**, where President Daniel arap Moi represents one of the few remaining autocrats from the old guard of the 1960s independence movements.

Major civil wars, such as in southern **Sudan**, continue, along with army mutinies, as in the **Central African Republic** (CAR), **Congo** and **Sierra Leone**. Hopes for progress towards peace in Sudan were raised by the government's acceptance of a 'framework for peace' in July 1997 which opened the way for negotiations with the Sudanese People's Liberation Army (SPLA) which had been in abeyance since 1994. Neighbouring states, in particular Ethiopia, Eritrea and Uganda, were directly involved in mediating this effort. In **Angola**, the incomplete demilitarisation of *União Nacional para a Independencia Total de Angola* (UNITA) forces means that conflict with government troops continues in the DROC border region. The situation there is further complicated by the struggle for control of high-value mineral resources.

DEVELOPMENTS IN PEACEKEEPING FORCES

In 1997, efforts to deploy African peacekeeping forces in attempts to re-establish security and oversee cease-fire and peace agreements have continued. On 27 May 1997, the West African Cease-Fire Monitoring Group (ECOMOG) of the Economic Community of West African States (ECOWAS) reinforced their troops in Sierra Leone. In the CAR, a peacekeeping force of Francophone African states has been deployed since January 1997 to help oversee an agreement between the government and rebellious soldiers. This force, on a renewable three-month mandate, comprises 800 troops from **Burkina Faso**, **Chad**, **Gabon**, **Mali**, **Senegal** and **Togo** and is known as the *Mission Interafricaine de Surveillance des Accords de Bangui* (MISAB). The Congo government, faced with an army mutiny, requested a similar force in July 1997 to help reinforce attempts to maintain cease-fire agreements between warring parties in and around the capital, Brazzaville.

While troops from outside Sub-Saharan Africa have been involved in many of the region's conflicts, their presence has been small and principally designed to assist in evacuating foreign nationals. France, in the process of reducing the size of its permanent troop presence in Africa, found its forces over-stretched in 1997, mainly supporting evacuation operations. The US has contributed financial and logistic support to African peacekeeping forces, most notably ECOMOG in **Liberia**. In Sierra Leone, a US amphibious squadron, with a Marine amphibious unit on board, played an important role in evacuating nearly 1,000 foreign nationals in June 1997. This trend marks a move away from the direct foreign military intervention of previous years in **Somalia**, Rwanda and former Zaire.

REGIONAL ORGANISATIONS

In dealing with regional security problems, the focus for direct action at the security-policy level has been with sub-regional groupings, but under the aegis of the pan-regional Organisation of African Unity (OAU). For example, six West African states – Burkina Faso, **Guinea**, **Liberia**, Mali, **Mauritania** and Senegal (Algeria also participated) – banded together in 1997, with UN support, to propose a moratorium on exports and imports of small arms and light weapons. The proposal was adopted at a ministerial-level meeting at Bamako in Mali on 26 March 1997. In addition to setting in train the political and technical processes necessary to implement the moratorium, the proposal sets out a Programme for Coordination and Assistance on Disarmament and Security (PCADIS). Among other things, PCADIS includes a programme to support updating and harmonising national legislation on light weapons, to establish a regional register of these weapons, and technical support for more effective border controls. It is envisaged that the PCADIS will be a five-year technical programme covering the implementation of the moratorium for three years, plus two years to consolidate a post-moratorium regime. Ahead of the implementation of this regime, practical steps have been taken to collect illegally held weapons in the region. In 1997, thousands of light weapons were collected and destroyed in Mali, which is taking a leading role in these activities. This encouraging development is reflected in a less mature form through sub-regional organisations in central and southern Africa.

DEFENCE SPENDING

Regional defence spending in 1996 was slightly lower than in 1995, representing a median of 3% of gross domestic product (GDP) for the 44 countries covered by *The Military Balance,* and around 1% of global military expenditure. By comparison, the latest International Monetary Fund (IMF) survey (April 1997) estimates that in 1996 defence accounted on average for some 2% of the GDP of Sub-Saharan countries. The discrepancy between estimates is testimony to the very low levels of transparency in government accounting in the region compared to elsewhere.

Most of the fall in regional defence spending is the result of a reduction in South Africa's military budget, achieved largely by switching defence funds to internal policing. The overall regional effect of this reduction would have been much greater but for increased military outlays elsewhere, notably in response to the spillover of civil wars in the DROC, Somalia and Sudan into Angola, Eritrea, Ethiopia and Uganda. In particular, Uganda's widening commitments have caused its military expenditure to rise from $81 million in 1994 to some $131m in 1996 (at 1995 prices). In addition to counter-insurgency operations in northern Uganda against the Sudan-backed Lord's Resistance Army, Uganda (along with the Tutsi government in Rwanda) provided military equipment and financial backing to Tutsi supporting Kabila in the DROC, and continues to support (along with Ethiopia and Eritrea) the National Democratic Alliance (NDA) in the civil war in southern Sudan.

In southern Africa, sustained investment in national security continues in **Botswana**, **Namibia** and **Zimbabwe**. This may in time provide the infrastructure for sub-regional peacekeeping. In contrast, governments actively or recently engaged in civil war face enormous difficulties in raising revenue to meet the escalating cost of hostilities and have little scope to invest in security beyond their borders. Although cease-fires in the civil wars in Liberia and Sierra Leone added to the fragile (and frequently breached) cease-fires in Angola, **Burundi** and Rwanda, military expenditure in these countries is likely to remain relatively high for some time, but more or less closed to public scrutiny. For those countries not engaged in civil war, but which choose not to invest in security, mutinies in the CAR, Congo, **Lesotho** and **Niger** in 1996–97 are reminders that too-low levels of defence expenditure are dangerous. The discontent over pay and poor training prevalent in several of the region's armed forces is often a function of very low defence spending, even by regional standards.

With few exceptions, government failure remains a common feature within the region. Inadequate security provision is the dominant symptom of this failure. The region is the least transparent in the world in terms of public reporting of military accounting. Given the political, security and economic difficulties within the region, this is hardly surprising. With the exception of South Africa, defence budgets are released as totals only, with no functional or service breakdown. No Sub-Saharan country reported military expenditures to the UN for the 1995 calendar year, and of the seven submitting returns in 1996 for the 1995 UN Register of Conventional Arms report, only one provided an explanatory note or background information (Ethiopia reported its military spending as 7% of the government budget).

The IMF and the World Bank, despite their influence, fare little better in persuading client countries to account for military expenditures. Since IMF programmes target unproductive expenditures, which may include military spending, it is reasonable to assume that the Fund gains access to the military spending figures of its numerous African client states. Yet the latest published IMF estimates show 1995 defence spending figures for **Madagascar, Mauritius**, the **Seychelles** and former Zaire only. This low level of reporting should be seen in the context of IMF loans and credits to the region, which in 1996 amounted to over $7 billion (or a fifth of the IMF's global commitments). The World Bank, which coordinates the global Official Development Assistance (ODA) programmes, reported that the region accounted for 34% of global ODA ($14bn) in 1996. Only in the case of the World Bank's demobilisation programmes, which it has helped to sponsor in Angola, Chad, **Djibouti, Mozambique**, Namibia, Uganda and Zimbabwe, is there any evidence that such support promotes improved transparency in military spending.

South Africa

South Africa's defence budget for 1997 was originally R10.2bn ($2.3bn), but it was reduced in February 1997 to R9.5bn ($2.1bn). The revised defence budget is thus R1.5bn ($340m) below the 1996 outlay of R11bn ($2.6bn). In June 1997, the Finance Ministry reportedly pressed for a further cut of R700m. The declining budget means that several modernisation programmes are uncertain. The police budget (around 7% of government expenditure) now exceeds the defence budget (6%).

Table 35 **South Africa's defence budget by function, 1995**

	Rm	US$m	%
Personnel	4,534	1,250	39.4
Administration	463	128	4.0
Equipment and stores	1,408	388	12.2
Infrastructure	32	9	0.3
Intelligence and other services	1,309	361	11.4
Pensions	3,715	1,024	32.2
Other	59	16	0.5
Total	**11,521**	**3,176**	*100.0*

The South African government alone in Sub-Saharan Africa releases detailed statistical information on its defence activities. Army restructuring is in progress, in particular reducing the number of divisions in the part-time force from three to one (which has three brigades). The full-time force now consists of one mechanised brigade, one airborne brigade and one special forces brigade. The integration of the so-called 'non-statutory' forces (such as the former African National Congress (ANC) and *Inkatha* Freedom Party (IFP) guerrilla forces) into the South African National Defence Forces (SANDF) was completed in 1997. However, the SANDF continues to have difficulty retaining its long-term professonals, particularly air crew. By the end of the 1997 financial year, it is predicted that there will be 275 trained pilots against a requirement of 486.

Table 36 **South Africa's defence budget by programme, 1995**		
(US$m)	**Budget**	**Outlay**
Command and Control	123	101
Land Defence	1,149	1,097
Air Defence	515	483
Maritime Defence	224	215
Medical Support	213	204
General Support	103	101
Sub-total: General Defence Vote	2,326	2,202
Special Defence Account	972	972
Authorised losses		3
Total authorisation	**3,298**	**3,176**

Nigeria

Nigeria's defence budget for 1997 amounts to N17.5bn ($800m at the official exchange rate), up from N15.5bn ($710m) in 1996. Defence now accounts for 12% of government spending (11% in 1996), while police allocations have increased from N9.8bn (7% of government spending) to N12.3bn (8%). The combined security spend for 1997 is nearly N30bn (more than $1.3bn), but real military expenditure is likely to be higher as the presidential budget certainly contains military-related funding.

Nigeria's military imports are subsidised by its over-valued official exchange rate. Foreign procurement may be largely funded outside the defence budget, either through the external debt repayment allocation in the federal budget or through off-budget accounts. While a US and European arms embargo remains in place, Nigeria ordered 1,500 military vehicles from Indian defence factories in May 1997.

Between them, South Africa and Nigeria account for around half of budgetary defence spending in the region. The outlays of former Zaire and Angola, the most prolific regional military spenders of the 1990s, are uncertain. The US Arms Control and Disarmament Agency (ACDA) reports 1993 Zairean outlays of $524m, falling to $37m in 1994 and $17m in 1995 (in 1995 US dollars), indicating a very low level of funding. Arms purchases suggest spending more in line with the budgetary allocations cited in *The Military Balance*. When the civil war broke out in late 1996, Portugal was among those countries that suspended the former Zairean government's orders for military equipment and ordnance, while the Czech Republic reported delivering a large consignment of light weapons and ammunition to former Zairean government forces in spring 1996.

Arms Transfers

In a region short of modern combat aircraft, Botswana in 1996 began taking delivery of 13 surplus F-5 aircraft from Canada; Eritrea is to receive six new MB-339D combat-capable training aircraft from Italy. Botswana's purchase of 54 ex-Netherlands *Leopard* 1 Main Battle Tanks (MBTs) remains blocked by the German government. Under US emergency draw-down authorities, military equipment was supplied by the US to Liberia ($15m) for ECOMOG in 1996, and to Eritrea ($4m), Ethiopia ($7m) and Uganda ($4m) in 1996–97. There have been reports in 1997 that South Africa is supplying Uganda with light armoured vehicles (*Casspir* series) and artillery (G-5 155mm), and assisting in assembling and modifying armoured vehicles in Uganda. Botswana, South Africa and Zimbabwe are taking delivery of a small number of C-130 *Hercules* under the US Excess Defense Articles (EDA) programme. In February 1997, the Belgian government suspended the export licence for constructing a munitions plant in Eldoret (Kenya) by the Belgian company FN Herstal (owned by the French GIAT) pending Kenyan government guarantees that no materiel, machines or technology would be transferred to the Central African Great Lakes region.

Although no recipient country reported deliveries in 1995 to the UN Register of Conventional Arms, supplier data show some of the major transactions. Angola took delivery of 52 BMP-2 Armoured Personnel Carriers (APCs) from Poland and three from South Africa; Botswana received ten of 36 *Scorpion* light tanks from the UK; and Uganda received 60 MBTs (T-54/55) from Ukraine and ten APCs from South Africa. The first returns for the UN Register for 1996 feature supplier data on just three countries – Botswana, which has taken delivery of the first three of 13 F-5 aircraft on order from Canada, and ten more *Scorpion* tanks and 12 L118 105mm field artillery from the UK; Romania reported delivering 20 GRAD 122mm rocket launchers to **Cameroon**; and South Africa delivered six RG-31 light armoured vehicles to Rwanda.

Table 37 UN Register of Conventional Arms imports, Sub-Saharan Africa, 1996

(as at 11 August 1997)	MBT	ACVs	Artillery	Combat aircraft	Attack helicopters	Warships	Missiles
Botswana	—	10	12	3	—	—	—
Cameroon	—	—	20	—	—	—	—
Rwanda	—	6	—	—	—	—	—
Total	0	16	32	3	0	0	0

The UN Register of Conventional Arms deals only with major conventional weapon systems. Light weapons account for the majority of the regional arms trade. Great difficulties arise in regulating this trade, particularly when it is associated with an area of conflict. There are reports that Chad is a large distributor of Chinese weapons to the CAR, DROC and Sudan. Iran and the Czech Republic have reportedly been supplying light weapons to Sudan and the DROC respectively, as well as ammunition to civil war zones. There are also reports that the Former Republic of Yugoslavia (FRY) supplied military equipment to former Zaire in early 1997. South Africa suspended arms sales to Rwanda in late 1996, adopting the position taken by Israel, the EU and the US; sales were resumed in July 1997. It remains to be seen if the moratorium on the export and import of light weapons declared by a group of West African states in March 1997 (see above) comes to fruition.

Table 38 Arms orders and deliveries, Sub-Saharan Africa, 1995–1997

Equipment	Type	Unit	Supplier	Order Date	Delivery Date	Comment
Angola						
APC	*Casspir* Mk2B	3	RSA	1994	1995	
APC	BMP-2	52	Pl	1994	1995	Ex-Pl Army
Botswana						
lt tk	*Scorpion*	36	UK	1994	1995	10 delivered 1995, 10 1996
arty	L118 (105mm)	15	UK	1994	1995	3 delivered 1995, 12 1996
FGA	F-5	13	Ca	1996	1996	Ex-Ca Air Force; 10 CF-As, 3 CF-5Bs
tpt	CN-212	2	Indo	1994	1996	
tpt	C-130B	2	US	1995	1995	EDA
Cameroon						
FGA	MB-326	6	RSA	1996	1997	Second-hand
MRL	*Grad*	20	R	1995	1996	122mm
Chad						
hel	SA-316B	2	Nl	1995	1995	Ex-Nl Army
Côte d'Ivoire						
APC	*Mamba* Mk2	10	RSA	1994	1995	
APC	RG12	3	RSA	1994	1995	
Eritrea						
trg	MB-339	6	It	1996	1997	
Ethiopia						
FGA	MiG-21		Il	1996		Upgrade; reported Il/Ukr programme
tpt	C-130B	2	US	1995	1995	EDA; further 4 for delivery 1997
Kenya						
ammo	plant	1	Be	1989	1996	Ammunition plant in Eldoret
Rwanda						
APC	*Mamba* Mk2		RSA	1995	1997	
APC	RG-31 *Nyala*	6	RSA	1995	1996	
Sierra Leone						
APC	OT-64	10	Slvk		1996	
MBT	T-72	2	Ukr	1994	1995	Ex-Pl Army
South Africa						
hel	CSH-2 *Rooivalk*	12	Domestic	1981	1998	Deliveries to 2001
tpt	C-130	12	US	1996	2002	Upgrade of 12 C-130s
trg	PC-7	60	CH	1993	1996	Pilatus Mk II *Astra*; assembled in RSA
Sudan						
FGA		10	Bel	1995	1995	Unconfirmed
FGA	F-7	6	PRC	1995	1996	Unconfirmed
hel		12	Ye	1995	1995	Unconfirmed
hel	Z-6	50	PRC	1995	1996	Unconfirmed
MBT		60	Ir		1997	Unconfirmed
mor	82, 120mm	100	PRC	1995	1996	Unconfirmed
Uganda						
APC	*Ferret*	60	US		1996	Surplus; unconfirmed
APC	*Eland* Mk7	40	RSA			Unconfirmed
APC	*Casspir*	70	RSA	1996	1997	
APC	*Mamba* Mk2	10	RSA	1994	1995	
arty	G-5		RSA	1996	1997	
MBT	T-54/T-55	60	Ukr	1994	1995	Surplus
ACV	BTC-4	2	Ukr	1994	1995	
Zimbabwe						
tpt	C-130B	2	US	1995	1997	EDA
hel	AS-532	2	Fr	1997		
trg	SF-260F	6	It	1997		Aeromacchi primary trainers

Dollar GDP figures in Sub-Saharan Africa are usually based on African Development Bank estimates. In several cases, the dollar GDP values do not reflect the exchange rates shown in the country entry.

Angola

	1995	1996	1997	1998
GDP	$6.3bn	$7.0bn		
per capita	$1,200	$1,300		
Growth	12.0%	8.6%		
Inflation	2,672%	4,182%		
Debt	$11.5bn	$11.4bn		
Def exp[a]	ε$400m	ε$450m		
Def bdgt			$295m	
FMA[b] (Fr)	$0.04m	$0.02m	$0.02m	
(US)		$0.10m	$0.13m	$0.2m
$1 = kwanza				
	1,212,600	31,784	266,000	

[a] FAA mil exp only, excl UNITA mil exp
[b] UNAVEM III **1995** $311m **1996** $344m

Population	11,346,000		
Age	*13–17*	*18–22*	*23–32*
Men	620,000	523,000	791,000
Women	621,000	527,000	808,000

Total Armed Forces

ACTIVE ε110,500

A unified national army, including 18,500 UNITA troops, is to form with a str of ε90,000. As of early May 1997, about 10,600 UNITA soldiers had been integrated into the army

Army ε98,000

25 regts (armd and inf – str vary)

EQUIPMENT†
  MBT 100 T-54/-55, ε150 T-62, ε50 T-72
  AIFV 50+ BMP-1, ε100 BMP-2
  RECCE some 40+ BRDM-2
  APC 100 BTR-60/-152
  TOWED ARTY 300: incl **76mm**: M-1942 (ZIS-3);
    85mm: D-44; **122mm**: D-30; **130mm**: M-46
  ASLT GUNS 100mm: SU-100
  MRL 122mm: 50 BM-21, 40 RM-70; **240mm**: some
    BM-24
  MOR 82mm: 250; **120mm**: 40+ M-43
  ATGW AT-3 *Sagger*
  RCL 500: **82mm**: B-10; **107mm**: B-11
  AD GUNS 200+: **14.5mm**: ZPU-4; **23mm**: ZU-23-2,
    20 ZSU-23-4 SP; **37mm**: M-1939; **57mm**: S-60
    towed, 40 ZSU-57-2 SP
  SAM SA-7/-14

Navy ε1,500–2,000

BASES Luanda (HQ), Lobito, Namibe (not usually occupied)
PATROL, INSHORE 7
  4 *Mandume* Type 31.6m PCI, 3 *Patrulheiro* PCI
MINE COUNTERMEASURES 1
  1 Sov *Yevgenya* MHC
AMPHIBIOUS 1
  1 Sov *Polnochny* LSM, capacity 100 tps, 6 tk
  Plus craft

COASTAL DEFENCE
  SS-C-1 *Sepal* at Luanda

Air Force/Air Defence 11,000†

27 cbt ac, 26 armed hel
FGA 6 MiG-23, 4 Su-22, 4 Su-25
FTR 4 MiG-21 MF/bis
CCT/RECCE 9* PC-7/9
MR 2 EMB-111, 1 F-27MPA
ATTACK HEL 15 Mi-25/35, 5 SA-365M (guns), 6 SA-
  342 (HOT)
TPT 5 Am-2, 4 An-26, 6 BN-2, 8 C-212, 4 PC-6B, 2 L-100-
  20
HEL 8 AS-565, 30 IAR-316
TRG 3 Cessna 172, 6 Yak-11
AD 5 SAM bn†, 10 bty with 40 SA-2, 12 SA-3, 25 SA-6,
  15 SA-8, 20 SA-9, 10 SA-13
MISSILES
  ASM HOT
  AAM AA-2 *Atoll*

Paramilitary 15,000

RAPID-REACTION POLICE 15,000

Opposition

UNITA (Union for the Total Independence of Angola)
Some 10,600 of ε18,500 tps have been integrated into the national army. A further ε24,000 fully equipped tps plus an additional 35,000 are awaiting demobilisation.
FLEC (Front for the Liberation of the Cabinda Enclave)
ε600 (claims 5,000)
small arms only

Foreign Forces

UN (UNOMA): 3,025 tps, 253 mil obs and 289 civ pol from 31 countries

Benin

	1995	1996	1997	1998
GDP	fr1.1tr	fr1.2tr		
	($1.7bn)	($1.9bn)		
per capita	$1,700	$1,800		
Growth	4.8%	5.5%		
Inflation	14.5%	4.9%		
Debt	$1.6bn	$1.7bn		
Def exp	εfr12bn	εfr14bn		
	($24m)	($26m)		
Def bdgt			εfr16bn	
			($28m)	
FMA (Fr)	$2.0m	$1.0m	$1.0m	
(US)	$0.2m	$0.3m	$0.4m	$0.4m
$1 = CFA fr	499	512	570	
Population		5,800,000		
Age	*13–17*	*18–22*	*23–32*	
Men	340,000	273,000	394,000	
Women	351,000	289,000	429,000	

Total Armed Forces

ACTIVE ε4,800

Terms of service: conscription (selective), 18 months

Army 4,500

3 inf, 1 AB/cdo, 1 engr bn, 1 armd sqn, 1 arty bty
EQUIPMENT
  LT TK 20 PT-76 (op status uncertain)
  RECCE 9 M-8, 14 BRDM-2, 10 VBL
  TOWED ARTY 105mm: 4 M-101, 12 L-118
  MOR 81mm
  RL 89mm: LRAC

Navy† ε150

BASE Cotonou
PATROL, INSHORE 1
  1 *Patriote* PFI (Fr 38m)<, 4 Sov *Zhuk*< PFI† in store

Air Force† 150

no cbt ac
AC 2 An-26, 2 C-47, 1 *Commander* 500B, 2 Do-128, 1
  Boeing 707-320 (VIP), 1 F-28 (VIP), 1 DHC-6
HEL 2 AS-350B, 1 SE-3130

Forces Abroad

PEACEKEEPING
HAITI (UNTMIH): 10 civ pol. **LIBERIA** (ECOMOG)

Paramilitary 2,500

GENDARMERIE 2,500
4 mobile coy

Botswana

	1995	1996	1997	1998
GDP	P12.5bn	P14.6bn		
	($3.2bn)	($3.4bn)		
per capita	$5,200	$5,400		
Growth	3.1%	7.0%		
Inflation	10.3%	10.3%		
Debt	$699m	$678m		
Def exp[a]	εP625m	εP760m		
	($226m)	($229m)		
Def bdgt[a]			P879m	
			($248m)	
FMA (US)	$0.4m	$0.5m	$0.5m	$0.5m
$1 = pula	2.77	3.32	3.54	

[a] Incl mil funding in presidential bdgt

Population		1,570,000		
Age	*13–17*	*18–22*	*23–32*	
Men	95,000	80,000	120,000	
Women	97,000	81,000	126,000	

Total Armed Forces

ACTIVE 7,500

Army 7,000 (to be 10,000)

2 bde: 4 inf bn, 1 armd recce, 2 fd arty, 2 AD arty, 1
engr regt, 1 cdo unit

EQUIPMENT
  LT TK 36 *Scorpion* (incl variants, being delivered)
  RECCE 12 V-150 *Commando* (some with **90mm** gun),
    RAM-V
  APC 30 BTR-60 (15 serviceable)
  TOWED ARTY 105mm: 12 lt, 4 Model 56 pack
  MOR 81mm: 10; **120mm**: 6 M-43
  ATGW 6 TOW (some SP on V-150)
  RCL 84mm: 88 *Carl Gustav*
  AD GUNS 20mm: 7 M-167
  SAM 12 SA-7, 10 SA-16, 5 *Javelin*

Air Wing 500

38 cbt ac, no armed hel
FTR/FGA 10 F-5A, 3 F-5B
TPT 1 sqn with 2 CN-235, 2 *Skyvan* 3M, 1 BAe 125-800,
  2 CN-212 (VIP), 1 *Gulfstream* IV, 11* BN-2 *Defender*
TRG 3 sqn
  2 with 2 Cessna 152, 7* PC-7

1 with 7* BAC-167 Mk 90
HEL 1 sqn with 2 AS-350L, 5 Bell 412 (VIP)

Paramilitary 1,000

POLICE MOBILE UNIT 1,000
(org in territorial coy)

Burkina Faso

	1995	1996	1997	1998
GDP	fr1.5tr	fr1.7tr		
	($2.6bn)	($2.8bn)		
per capita	$800	$900		
Growth	3.9%	5.5%		
Inflation	7.4%	6.2%		
Debt	$1.3bn	$1.3bn		
Def exp	εfr34bn	εfr34bn		
	($68m)	($67m)		
Def bdgt			εfr39bn	
			($69m)	
FMA (Fr)	$1.6m	$1.1m	$1.0m	
$1 = CFA fr	499	512	570	
Population		11,124,000		
Age	*13–17*	*18–22*	*23–32*	
Men	638,000	519,000	789,000	
Women	617,000	512,000	807,000	

Total Armed Forces

ACTIVE 10,000
(incl *Gendarmerie*)

Army 5,600

6 Mil Regions • 5 inf 'regt': HQ, 3 'bn' (each 1 coy of 5
pl) • 1 AB 'regt': HQ, 1 'bn', 2 coy • 1 tk 'bn': 2 pl • 1
arty 'bn': 2 tp • 1 engr 'bn'
EQUIPMENT
  RECCE 15 AML-60/-90, 24 EE-9 *Cascavel*, 10 M-8, 4
    M-20, 30 *Ferret*
  APC 13 M-3
  TOWED ARTY 105mm: 8 M-101; **122mm:** 6
  MRL 107mm: PRC Type-63
  MOR 81mm: Brandt
  RL 89mm: LRAC, M-20
  RCL 75mm: PRC Type-52
  AD GUNS 14.5mm: 30 ZPU
  SAM SA-7

Air Force 200

5 cbt ac, no armed hel
TPT 1 *Beech Super King*, 1 *Commander* 500B, 2 HS-748, 2

N-262, 1 Boeing 727 (VIP)
LIAISON 2 Cessna 150/172, 1 SA-316B, 1 AS-350, 3
  Mi-8/17
TRG 5* SF-260W/WL

Forces Abroad

PEACEKEEPING
CAR (MISAB). **LIBERIA** (ECOMOG)

Paramilitary

GENDARMERIE 4,200
SECURITY COMPANY (CRG) 250
PEOPLE'S MILITIA (R) 45,000 trained

Burundi

	1995	1996	1997	1998
GDP	fr310bn	fr310bn		
	($1.2bn)	($1.2bn)		
per capita	$700	$600		
Growth	-3.7%	-3.6%		
Inflation	19.2%	12.0%		
Debt	$1.2bn	$1.2bn		
Def exp	εfr12bn	εfr15bn		
	($46m)	($50m)		
Def bdgt			fr21bn	
			($60m)	
FMA (US)	$0.04m	$0.07m	$0.10m	$0.10m
(Fr)	$1.2m	$1.0m		
$1 = franc	250	303	341	
Population		ε6,673,000 (Hutu 85%, Tutsi 14%)		
Age	*13–17*	*18–22*	*23–32*	
Men	396,000	321,000	505,000	
Women	361,000	295,000	470,000	

Total Armed Forces

ACTIVE ε22,000
(incl *Gendarmerie*)

Army 18,500 (to be 40,000 reported)

5 inf bn • 2 lt armd 'bn' (sqn) • 1 engr bn • some indep
inf coy • 1 arty, 1 AD bty
EQUIPMENT
  RECCE 18 AML (6-60, 12-90), 7 Shorland, BRDM-2
  APC 9 Panhard M-3, 20 BTR-40 and *Walid*
  TOWED ARTY 122mm: D-30
  MRL 122mm: BM-21
  MOR 82mm: 18 M-43; **120mm**
  RL 83mm: *Blindicide*

RCL **75mm**: 15 PRC Type-52
AD GUNS 150: **14.5mm**: 15 ZPU-4; **23mm**: ZU-23;
  37mm: Type 54
SAM SA-7

AIR WING (100)

6 cbt ac, no armed hel
TRG 6* SF-260W/TP
HEL 2 SA-342L

Paramilitary

GENDARMERIE ε3,500 (incl ε50 Marine Police)
BASE Bujumbura
  4 *Huchuan* (PRC Type 026) PHT† plus 4 boats

Opposition

FORCES FOR THE DEFENCE OF DEMOCRACY
(FDD) str n.k.

Cameroon

	1995	1996	1997	1998
GDP	fr4.3bn	fr4.7bn		
	($8.6bn)	($9.2bn)		
per capita	$2,000	$2,100		
Growth	3.3%	5.0%		
Inflation	26.9%	6.4%		
Debt	$9.4bn	$9.5bn		
Def exp	εfr101bn	εfr114bn		
	($202m)	($223m)		
Def bdgt			εfr130bn	
			($228m)	
FMA (US)		$0.08m	$0.10m	$0.13m
(Fr)	$0.8m	$1.3m	$1.6m	
$1 = CFA fr	499	512	570	
Population		14,240,000		
Age	*13–17*	*18–22*	*23–32*	
Men	803,000	679,000	1,013,000	
Women	801,000	682,000	1,031,000	

Total Armed Forces

ACTIVE ε22,100
(incl *Gendarmerie*)

Army 11,500

8 Mil Regions each 1 inf bn under comd • Presidential
Guard: 1 guard, 1 armd recce bn, 3 inf coy • 1 AB/cdo
bn • 1 arty bn (5 bty) • 5 inf bn (1 trg) • 1 AA bn (6
bty) • 1 engr bn

EQUIPMENT
RECCE 8 M-8, *Ferret*, 8 V-150 *Commando* (**20mm**
  gun), 5 VBL
AIFV 14 V-150 *Commando* (**90mm** gun)
APC 21 V-150 *Commando*, 12 M-3 half-track
TOWED ARTY **75mm**: 6 M-116 pack; **105mm**: 16
  M-101; **130mm**: 12 Type-59
MRL **122mm**: 20 BM-21
MOR **81mm** (some SP); **120mm**: 16 Brandt
ATGW *Milan*
RL **89mm**: LRAC
RCL **57mm**: 13 PRC Type-52; **106mm**: 40 M-40A2
AD GUNS **14.5mm**: 18 PRC Type-58; **35mm**: 18
  GDF-002; **37mm**: 18 PRC Type-63

Navy ε1,300

BASES Douala (HQ), Limbe, Kribi
PATROL AND COASTAL COMBATANTS 30
MISSILE CRAFT 1 *Bakassi* (Fr P-48) PFM with 2 x 4
  MM-40 *Exocet* SSM
PATROL, INSHORE 3
  1 *L'Audacieux* (Fr P-48) PFI, 1 *Bizerte* (Fr PR-48) PCI†,
  1 *Quartier* PCI
PATROL, RIVERINE 26
  20 US *Swift*-38, 6 *Simonneau* (not all op)
AMPHIBIOUS craft only
  2 LCM

Air Force 300

15 cbt ac, 4 armed hel
1 composite sqn, 1 Presidential Fleet
FGA 4† *Alpha Jet*, 5 CM-170, 6 MB-326
MR 2 Do-128D-6
ATTACK HEL 4 SA-342L (with HOT)
TPT **ac** 3 C-130H/-H-30, 1 DHC-4, 4 DHC-5D, 1 IAI-
  201, 2 PA-23, 1 *Gulfstream* III, 1 Do-128, 1 Boeing 707
  hel 3 Bell 206, 3 SE-3130, 1 SA-318, 3 SA-319, 2 AS-
  332, 1 SA-365

Paramilitary

GENDARMERIE 9,000
10 regional groups; about 10 US *Swift*-38 (see Navy)

Cape Verde

	1995	1996	1997	1998
GDP	E17bn	E18bn		
	($202m)	($215m)		
per capita	$2,000	$2,100		
Growth	4.7%	4.0%		
Inflation	8.4%	5.0%		
Debt	$216m	$252m		

contd	1995	1996	1997	1998
Def exp	εE305m	εE310m		
	($4m)	($4m)		
Def bdgt			εE350m	
			($4m)	
FMA (US)	$0.08m	$0.06m	$0.10m	$0.10m
(Fr)	$0.7m	$0.2m	$0.1m	
$1 = Escudo	77	83	93	
Population			438,000	
Age	*13–17*	*18–22*	*23–32*	
Men	26,000	21,000	36,000	
Women	26,000	23,000	40,000	

Total Armed Forces

ACTIVE ε1,100

Terms of service: conscription (selective)

Army 1,000

2 inf bn gp
EQUIPMENT
RECCE 10 BRDM-2
TOWED ARTY 75mm: 12; 76mm: 12
MOR 82mm: 12; 120mm: 6 M-1943
RL 89mm: 3.5in
AD GUNS 14.5mm: 18 ZPU-1; 23mm: 12 ZU-23
SAM 50 SA-7

Coast Guard ε50

1 *Zhuk* PCI<, 1 *Espadarte* PCI<

Air Force under 100

no cbt ac
MR 1 Do-228

Central African Republic

	1995	1996	1997	1998
GDP	fr551bn	fr565bn		
	($1.2bn)	($1.3bn)		
per capita	$1,200	$1,200		
Growth	2.4%	-0.9%		
Inflation	9.5%	3.5%		
Debt	$937m	$957m		
Def exp	εfr12bn	εfr15bn		
	($24m)	($30m)		
Def bdgt			εfr19bn	
			($33m)	
FMA (US)	$0.2m	$0.1m	$0.1m	$0.2m
(Fr)	$2.5m	$1.8m	$2.0m	
$1 = CFA fr	499	512	570	

Population	3,589,000		
Age	*13–17*	*18–22*	*23–32*
Men	189,000	168,000	270,000
Women	192,000	170,000	266,000

Total Armed Forces

ACTIVE 4,950

(incl *Gendarmerie*)
Terms of service: conscription (selective), 2 years; reserve obligation thereafter, term n.k.

Army 2,500

1 Republican Guard regt (2 bn) • 1 territorial defence regt (bn) • 1 combined arms regt (1 mech, 1 inf bn) • 1 spt/HQ regt • 1 Presidential Guard bn
EQUIPMENT†
MBT 4 T-55
RECCE 10 *Ferret*
APC 4 BTR-152, some 10 VAB, 25+ ACMAT
MOR 81mm; 120mm: 12 M-1943
RL 89mm: LRAC
RCL 106mm: 14 M-40
RIVER PATROL CRAFT 9<

Air Force 150

no cbt ac, no armed hel
TPT 1 Cessna 337, 1 *Mystère Falcon* 20, 1 *Caravelle*
LIAISON 6 AL-60, 6 MH-1521
HEL 1 AS-350, 1 SE-3130

Paramilitary

GENDARMERIE 2,300
3 regional legions, 8 'bde'

Foreign Forces

FRANCE 1,300; 1 inf bn gp, 1 armd cav sqn, 1 arty bty; 3 F-1CT, 2 F-1CR, 2 C-160, 4 SA-330
PEACEKEEPING
MISAB: some 800 tps from **BF, Cha, Gbn, RMM, Sen** and **Tg** plus **Fr** log spt

Chad

	1995	1996	1997	1998
GDP	r493bn	fr530bn		
	($1.3bn)	($1.4bn)		
per capita	$700	$800		
Growth	2.8%	6.0%		

contd	1995	1996	1997	1998
Inflation	9.5%	10.0%		
Debt	$908m	$1,010m		
Def exp	εfr17bn	εfr20bn		
	($34m)	($39m)		
Def bdgt			εfr25bn	
			($44m)	
FMA[a] (Fr)	$8.0m	$4.0m	$3.0m	
(US)	$0.06m		$0.03m	$0.05m
$1 = CFA fr	499	512	570	

[a] excl $10m for demob in 1996 (World Bank)

Population		6,810,000		
Age	*13–17*	*18–22*	*23–32*	
Men	358,000	299,000	476,000	
Women	358,000	301,000	485,000	

Total Armed Forces

ACTIVE ε30,350

(incl Republican Guard)
Terms of service: conscription authorised

Army ε25,000

(being re-organised)
7 Mil Regions
EQUIPMENT
  MBT 60 T-55
  AFV 4 ERC-90, some 50 AML-60/-90, 9 V-150 with
    90mm, some EE-9 *Cascavel*
  TOWED ARTY 105mm: 5 M-2
  MOR 81mm; 120mm: AM-50
  ATGW *Milan*
  RL 89mm: LRAC
  RCL 106mm: M-40A1; **112mm**: APILAS
  AD GUNS 20mm, 30mm

Air Force 350

4 cbt ac, no armed hel
TPT ac 1 C-130A, 2 -B, 2 -H, 1 C-212, 2 PC-6B **hel** 2
  SA-316
LIAISON 2 PC-6B, 5 Reims-Cessna FTB 337
TRG 2* PC-7, 2* SF-260W

Forces Abroad

PEACEKEEPING
CAR (MISAB)

Paramilitary 4,500 active

REPUBLICAN GUARD 5,000

GENDARMERIE 4,500

Opposition

WESTERN ARMED FORCES str n.k.

Foreign Forces

FRANCE 800; 2 inf coy, 1 AML sqn(-); 2 C-160 **ac**

Congo

	1995	1996	1997	1998
GDP	fr1.0tr	fr1.2tr		
	($2.6bn)	($2.8bn)		
per capita	$1,900	$2,000		
Growth	2.2%	4.8%		
Inflation	14.5%	10.6%		
Debt	$6.0bn	$5.7bn		
Def exp	εfr24bn	εfr28bn		
	($49m)	($55m)		
Def bdgt			εfr32bn	
			($56m)	
FMA (US)	$0.2m	$0.2m	$0.2m	$0.2m
(Fr)	$2.1m	$1.0m	$1.0m	
$1 = CFA fr	499	512	570	

Population		2,859,000		
Age	*13–17*	*18–22*	*23–32*	
Men	162,000	134,000	212,000	
Women	153,000	128,000	204,000	

Total Armed Forces

ACTIVE ε10,000

Army 8,000

2 armd bn • 2 inf bn gp (each with lt tk tp, 76mm gun
bty) • 1 inf bn • 1 arty gp (how, MRL) • 1 engr bn • 1
AB/cdo bn
EQUIPMENT†
  MBT 25 T-54/-55, 15 PRC Type-59 (some T-34 in
    store)
  LT TK 10 PRC Type-62, 3 PT-76
  RECCE 25 BRDM-1/-2
  APC M-3, 50 BTR (30 -60, 20 -152)
  TOWED ARTY 76mm: M-1942; **100mm**: 10 M-1944;
    122mm: 10 D-30; **130mm**: 5 M-46; **152mm**: some
    D-20
  MRL 122mm: 8 BM-21; **140mm**: BM-14-16
  MOR 82mm; 120mm: 10 M-43
  RCL 57mm: M-18
  ATK GUNS 57mm: 5 M-1943
  AD GUNS 14.5mm: ZPU-2/-4; **23mm**: ZSU-23-4 SP;
    37mm: 28 M-1939; **57mm**: S-60; **100mm**: KS-19

Navy† ε800

BASE Pointe Noire
PATROL AND COASTAL COMBATANTS ε6
PATROL, INSHORE 6
   3 *Marien N'gouabi* PFI (Sp *Barcelo* 33m)†
   3 Sov *Zhuk* PFI<
PATROL, RIVERINE n.k.
   boats only

Air Force† 1,200

12 cbt ac, no armed hel
FGA 12 MiG-21
TPT 5 An-24, 1 An-26, 1 Boeing 727, 1 N-2501
TRG 4 L-39, 1 MiG-15UTI
HEL 2 SA-316, 2 SA-318, 1 SA-365, 2 Mi-8

Forces Abroad

UN AND PEACEKEEPING
ANGOLA (UNOMA): 4 Obs

Paramilitary 2,000 active

GENDARMERIE 2,000
20 coy
PEOPLE'S MILITIA 3,000
being absorbed into national army
PRESIDENTIAL GUARD
(forming)

Côte D'Ivoire

	1995	1996	1997	1998
GDP	fr5.0tr	fr5.5tr		
	($9.8bn)	($10.7bn)		
per capita	$1,400	$1,500		
Growth	7.0%	6.5%		
Inflation	14.3%	2.5%		
Debt	$19.0bn	$19.1bn		
Def exp	εfr49bn	εfr48bn		
	($98m)	($94m)		
Def bdgt			εfr59bn	
			($104m)	
FMA (US)	$0.1m	$0.2m	$0.2m	$0.2m
(Fr)	$2.4m	$2.5m	$2.1m	
$1 = CFA fr	499	512	570	
Population		15,425,000		
Age	*13–17*	*18–22*	*23–32*	
Men	901,000	713,000	1,053,000	
Women	901,000	716,000	1,042,000	

Total Armed Forces

ACTIVE ε13,900
(incl Presidential Guard, *Gendarmerie*)
Terms of service: conscription (selective), 6 months

RESERVES 12,000

Army 6,800

4 Mil Regions • 1 armd, 3 inf bn, 1 arty gp • 1 AB, 1
AA, 1 engr coy
EQUIPMENT
   LT TK 5 AMX-13
   RECCE 7 ERC-90 *Sagaie*, 16 AML-60/-90, 10 *Mamba*
   APC 16 M-3, 13 VAB
   TOWED ARTY 105mm: 4 M-1950
   MOR 81mm; 120mm: 16 AM-50
   RL 89mm: LRAC
   RCL 106mm: M-40A1
   AD GUNS 20mm: 16, incl 6 M-3 VDA SP; **40mm:** 5
   L/60

Navy ε900

BASE Locodjo (Abidjan)
PATROL AND COASTAL COMBATANTS 4
MISSILE CRAFT 2 *L'Ardent* (Fr *Auroux* 40m) with 4
   SS 12M SSM
PATROL, INSHORE 2 *Le Vigilant* (Fr SFCN 47m) PCI
AMPHIBIOUS 1
   1 *L'Eléphant* (Fr *Batral*) LSM, capacity 140 tps, 7 tk,
   hel deck, plus some 8 craft

Air Force 700

5† cbt ac, no armed hel
FGA 1 sqn with 5† *Alpha Jet*
TPT 1 hel sqn with 1 SA-318, 1 SA-319, 1 SA-330, 4 SA
   365C
PRESIDENTIAL FLT ac 1 F-28, 1 *Gulfstream* IV, 3
   Fokker 100 **hel** 1 SA-330
TRG 3 Beech F-33C, 2 Reims Cessna 150H
LIAISON 1 Cessna 421, 1 *Super King Air* 200

Paramilitary

PRESIDENTIAL GUARD 1,100
GENDARMERIE 4,400
VAB APC, 4 patrol boats
MILITIA 1,500

Foreign Forces

FRANCE 500; 1 marine inf bn; 1 AS-555 hel

Democratic Republic of Congo

	1995	1996	1997	1998
GDP	$5.8bn	$6.0bn		
per capita	$500	$500		
Growth	-4.0%	1.3%		
Inflation	542%	611%		
Debt	$13.1bn	$13.1bn		
Def exp	ε$185m	ε$170m		
Def bdgt			ε$250m	
$1 = new zaire				
	7,024	49,900	137,000	
Population		46,307,000		
Age	*13–17*	*18–22*	*23–32*	
Men	2,713,000	2,176,000	3,203,000	
Women	2,690,000	2,174,000	3,231,000	

Total Armed Forces

Following the overthrow of the Mobutu regime in May 1997, the former Zairean armed forces have been disbanded. The insurgent Congo Liberation Army comprises 20–40,000 fighters from the Alliance of Democratic Forces for the Liberation of Congo-Zaire, the descendants of Katangan *Gendarmes* returned from Angola, Zairean Tutsi trained in Uganda and Rwanda, and recent recruits from other Zairean tribes. These forces are mainly equipped with small arms and some SA-7 SAM. Eqpt details represent the inventory prior to the civil war. Much of this equipment is believed to be non-op, although some key weapons (incl BM-21) and hels remain in service

EQUIPMENT
MBT 20 PRC Type-59, some 40 PRC Type-62
RECCE† 60 AML (30 -60, 30 -90)
APC 12 M-113, 12 YW-531, 60 Panhard M-3
TOWED ARTY 75mm: 30 M-116 pack; **85mm**: 20 Type 56; **122mm**: 20 M-1938/D-30, 15 Type 60; **130mm**: 8 Type 59
MRL 107mm: 20 Type 63; **122mm**: 10 BM-21
MOR 81mm; 107mm: M-30; **120mm**: 50 Brandt
RCL 57mm: M-18; **75mm**: M-20; **106mm**: M-40A1
AD GUNS 14.5mm: ZPU-4; **37mm**: 40 M-1939/Type 63; **40mm**: L/60
SAM SA-7

Navy†

(incl 600 Marines)
BASES Coast Banana **River** Boma, Matadi, Kinshasa **Lake Tanganyika** (4 boats) Kalémié
PATROL AND COASTAL COMBATANTS ε9
PATROL, INSHORE ε9
5 PRC *Shanghai* II PFI
about 4 *Swiftships*<, plus about 6 armed boats

MARINES (600)

Paramilitary

GENDARMERIE details n.k.
CIVIL GUARD details n.k.

Djibouti

	1995	1996	1997	1998
GDP	fr70bn	fr72bn		
	($396m)	($404m)		
per capita	$1,000	$1,000		
Growth	-4.0%	-1.2%		
Inflation	4.9%	4.0%		
Debt	$260m	$271m		
Def exp	εfr3.9bn	εfr3.7bn		
	($22m)	($21m)		
Def bdgt			εfr4.0bn	
			($23m)	
FMA (US)	$0.1m	$0.2m	$0.2m	$0.1m
(Fr)	$1.4m	$1.2m	$1.1m	
$1 = franc	178	178	178	
Population		683,000 (Somali 60%, Afar 35%)		
Age	*13–17*	*18–22*	*23–32*	
Men	37,000	31,000	50,000	
Women	36,000	32,000	54,000	

Total Armed Forces

ACTIVE ε9,600
(incl *Gendarmerie*)

Army ε8,000

3 Comd (North, Central, South) • 1 inf bn, incl mor, ATK pl • 1 arty bty • 1 armd sqn • 1 border cdo bn • 1 AB coy • 1 spt bn
EQUIPMENT
RECCE 15 M-11 VBL, 4 AML-60†
APC 12 BTR-60 (op status uncertain)
TOWED ARTY 122mm: 6 D-30
MOR 81mm: 25; **120mm**: 20 Brandt
RL 73mm; 89mm: LRAC
RCL 106mm: 16 M-40A1
AD GUNS 20mm: 5 M-693 SP; **23mm**: 5 ZU-23; **40mm**: 5 L/70

Navy ε200

BASE Djibouti
PATROL CRAFT, INSHORE 8
5 *Sawari* PCI<, 2 *Moussa Ali* PCI<, 1 *Zena* PCI<†; plus boats

Air Force 200

no cbt ac or armed hel
TPT 2 C-212, 2 N-2501F, 2 Cessna U206G, 1 *Socata*
   235GT
HEL 3 AS-355, 1 AS-350; Mi-8, Mi-24 hel from **Eth**

Forces Abroad

UN AND PEACEKEEPING
HAITI (UNTMIH): 19 civ pol

Paramilitary ε3,000 active

GENDARMERIE (Ministry of Defence) 1,200
1 bn, 1 patrol boat
NATIONAL SECURITY FORCE (Ministry of Interior)
ε3,000

Foreign Forces

FRANCE 3,900; incl 1 marine inf, 1 Foreign Legion
regt, 1 sqn: **ac** 6 *Mirage* F-1C (plus 4 in store), 1 C-160
hel 3 SA-319

Equatorial Guinea

	1995	1996	1997	1998
GDP	fr79bn	fr118bn		
	($164m)	($230m)		
per capita	$1,100	$1,500		
Growth	14.9%	37.3%		
Inflation	11.4%	6.0%		
Debt	$293m	$301m		
Def exp	εfr1.2bn	εfr1.2bn		
	($2.4m)	($2.3m)		
Def bdgt			εfr1.3bn	
			($2.3m)	
FMA (Fr)	$0.2m	$0.2m	$0.1m	
$1 = CFA fr	499	512	570	
Population		490,000		
Age	*13–17*	*18–22*	*23–32*	
Men	25,000	21,000	35,000	
Women	25,000	22,000	35,000	

Total Armed Forces

ACTIVE 1,320

Army 1,100

3 inf bn
EQUIPMENT
   RECCE 6 BRDM-2

APC 10 BTR-152

Navy† 120

BASES Malabo (Santa Isabel), Bata
PATROL CRAFT, INSHORE 2 PCI<

Air Force 100

no cbt ac or armed hel
TPT ac 1 Yak-40, 3 C-212, 1 Cessna-337 **hel** 2 SA-316

Paramilitary

GUARDIA CIVIL
2 coy
COAST GUARD
1 PCI<

Foreign Forces

MOROCCO 360; 1 bn

Eritrea

	1995	1996	1997	1998
GDP	εB4.4bn	εB4.5bn		
	($700m)	($714m)		
per capita	$400	$400		
Growth	ε5%	ε12%		
Inflation	ε11%	ε1%		
Debt	ε$75m	ε$150m		
Def exp	ε$40m	ε$60m		
Def bdgt			ε$80m	
FMA (US)	$0.2m	$4.3m	$0.4m	$0.4m
$ = Birr	6.32	6.35	6.47	
Population		3,784,000		
(Tigray 50%, Tigre and Kunama 40%, Afar 4%)				
Age	*13–17*	*18–22*	*23–32*	
Men	224,000	187,000	285,000	
Women	222,000	186,000	283,000	

Total Armed Forces

ACTIVE ε46,000 (to be 35,000)

Eritrea declared itself independent from Ethiopia on 27 April
1993. A conscription period of 2 years is authorised to incl 6
months mil trg. No info on div of mil assets between Ethiopia
and Eritrea is available. Eritrea holds some air and naval
assets, but holdings of army assets n.k. Close cooperation with
Ethiopia is likely to continue to the possible extent of sharing
mil assets. Numbers given should be treated with caution.

Navy

BASES Massawa, Assab, Dahlak
FRIGATES 1
  1 *Zerai Deres* (Sov *Petya* II) with 2 ASW RL, 5 406mm TT†
PATROL AND COASTAL COMBATANTS 8
TORPEDO CRAFT 1 *Mol* PFT† with 4 533mm TT
PATROL, INSHORE 7
  2 Sov Zhuk<, 4 *Super Dvora* PCF<, 1 *Osa* II PFM
AMPHIBIOUS 11
  3 LCT (1 *Fredic* and 2 *Chamo* (Ministry of Transport)), 1 *Polnocny* LCM, 4 LCM, 3 LPC
SUPPORT AND MISCELLANEOUS 1
  1 AOT
AIR WING
  ac 8 *Redigo*, 6* MB-339CE, 4 Y-11, 1 IAI-1125 *Astra*
  hel 4 Mi-17

Ethiopia

	1995	1996	1997	1998
GDP	EB34.1bn	EB38.8bn		
	($5.4bn)	($6.2bn)		
per capita	$400	$400		
Growth	5.4%	12.4%		
Inflation	13.4%	0.9%		
Debt	$5.2bn	$5.3bn		
Def exp	EB750m	EB790m		
	($119m)	($124m)		
Def bdgt			EB823m	
			($127m)	
FMA (US)	$0.2m	$7.3m	$0.4m	$0.5m
$1 = Eth birr	6.32	6.35	6.47	
Population	ε53,000,000			

(Oromo 40%, Amhara and Tigrean 32%, Sidamo 9%, Shankella 6%, Somali 6%, Afar 4%)

Age	*13–17*	*18–22*	*23–32*
Men	3,436,000	2,813,000	4,246,000
Women	3,294,000	2,680,000	4,085,000

Total Armed Forces

ACTIVE ε120,000

Following Eritrea's declaration of independence in April 1993, the Ethiopian armed forces were formed from former members of the Tigray People's Liberation Front (TPLF) with maybe 10–15,000 from the Oromo Liberation Front. Ethiopia auctioned off its naval assets in Sep 1996. Reports indicate that large quantities of eqpt are in preservation. Numbers in service should be treated with caution.

Army ε100,000

Being re-org to consist of 3 mil regions each with a corps HQ (each corps 2 divs, 1 reinforced mech bde); a strategic reserve div of 6 bde will be located at Addis Ababa
  MBT ε350 T-54/-55, T-62
  RECCE/AIFV/APC ε200, incl BRDM, BMP, BTR-60/-152
  TOWED ARTY 76mm: ZIS-3; **85mm**: D-44; **122mm**: D-30/M-30; **130mm**: M-46
  MRL BM-21
  MOR 81mm: M-1/M-29; **82mm**: M-1937; **120mm**: M-1938
  ATGW AT-3 *Sagger*
  RCL 82mm: B-10; **107mm**: B-11
  AD GUNS 23mm: ZU-23, ZSU-23-4 SP; **37mm**: M-1939; **57mm**: S-60
  SAM 20 SA-2, 30 SA-3, 300 SA-7, SA-9

Air Force

† 85 cbt ac, 18 armed hel
Most of the Air Force is grounded. Air Force activity is believed to be limited to re-org, ground-crew trg and maint. Types and numbers of ac are assessed as follows:
FGA 40 MiG-21MF, 20 MiG-23BN, 5 MiG-27, 20 F-5
TPT 2 C-130B, 4 An-12, 2 DH-6, 1 Yak-40 (VIP), 2 Y-12
TRG 14 L-39
ATTACK HEL 18 Mi-24
TPT HEL 21 Mi-8, 2 UH-1, 2 Mi-14

Gabon

	1995	1996	1997	1998
GDP	fr2.5tr	fr2.6tr		
	($5.3bn)	($5.6bn)		
per capita	$5,200	$5,300		
Growth	3.7%	3.2%		
Inflation	10.0%	5.1%		
Debt	$4.5bn	$4.4bn		
Def exp	εfr51bn	εfr57bn		
	($102m)	($111m)		
Def bdgt			εfr67bn	
			($118m)	
FMA (Fr)	$0.6m	$1.2m	$1.0m	
$1 = CFA fr	499	512	570	
Population	1,390,000			

Age	*13–17*	*18–22*	*23–32*
Men	66,000	55,000	92,000
Women	67,000	57,000	95,000

Total Armed Forces

ACTIVE ε4,700

Army 3,200

Presidential Guard bn gp (1 recce/armd, 3 inf coy, arty,
AA bty), under direct Presidential control
  8 inf, 1 AB/cdo, 1 engr coy

EQUIPMENT
  RECCE 14 EE-9 *Cascavel*, 24 AML, 6 ERC-90 *Sagaie*,
    12 EE-3 *Jararaca*, 14 VBL
  AIFV 12 EE-11 *Urutu* with **20mm** gun
  APC 9 V-150 *Commando*, Panhard M-3, 12 VXB-170
  TOWED ARTY 105mm: 4 M-101
  MRL 140mm: 8 *Teruel*
  MORS 81mm: 35; **120mm**: 4 Brandt
  ATGW 4 *Milan*
  RL 89mm: LRAC
  RCL 106mm: M40A1
  AD GUNS 20mm: 4 ERC-20 SP; **23mm**: 24 ZU-23-2;
    37mm: 10 M-1939; **40mm**: 3 L/70

Navy ε500

BASE Port Gentil (HQ)
PATROL AND COASTAL COMBATANTS 3
MISSILE CRAFT 1 *General Nazaire Boulingu* PFM (Fr
  42m) with 4 SS 12M SSM
PATROL, COASTAL 2 *General Ba'Oumar* (Fr P-400 55m)
AMPHIBIOUS I
  1 *President Omar Bongo* (Fr *Batral*) LST, capacity 140
  tps, 7 tk; plus craft: 1 LCM

Air Force 1,000

16 cbt ac, 5 armed hel
FGA 9 *Mirage* 5 (2 -G, 4 -GII, 3 -DG)
MR 1 EMB-111
TPT 1 C-130H, 3 L-100-30, 1 EMB-110, 2 YS-11A, 1
  CN-235
HELICOPTERS
  ATTACK 5 SA-342
  TPT 3 SA-330C/-H
  LIAISON 3 SA-316/-319
PRESIDENTIAL GUARD
  CCT 4 CM-170, 3 T-34
  TPT ac 1 ATR-42F, 1 EMB-110, 1 *Falcon* 900 **hel** 1 AS-
  332

Forces Abroad

CAR (MISAB)

Paramilitary 4,800

COAST GUARD ε2,800
boats only
GENDARMERIE 2,000
3 'bde', 11 coy, 2 armd sqn, air unit with 1 AS-355, 2
AS-350

Foreign Forces

FRANCE 600; 1 marine inf bn **ac** 1 C-160, 1 *Atlantic*
hel 1 AS-555

The Gambia

	1995	1996	1997	1998
GDP	D3.4bn	D3.7bn		
	($355m)	($374m)		
per capita	$1,100	$1,100		
Growth	-4.0%	3.2%		
Inflation	2.6%	5.5%		
Debt	$426m	$434m		
Def exp	εD139m	εD143m		
	($15m)	($15m)		
Def bdgt			εD150m	
			($15m)	
FMA (Fr)	$0.1m			
$1 = dalasi	9.5	9.8	9.9	
Population		1,135,000		
Age	*13–17*	*18–22*	*23–32*	
Men	61,000	49,000	77,000	
Women	60,000	49,000	78,000	

Total Armed Forces

ACTIVE 800

Gambian National Army 800

Presidential Guard (reported) • 2 inf bn • engr sqn

MARINE UNIT (about 70)
BASE Banjul
PATROL CRAFT, INSHORE 5
  2 *Gonjur* (PRC *Shanghai* II) PFI, 3 PFI<, boats

Ghana

	1995	1996	1997	1998
GDP	C7.4tr	C10.5tr		
	($7.9bn)	($8.5bn)		
per capita	$2,100	$2,200		
Growth	4.5%	5.0%		
Inflation	74.3%	34.0%		
Debt	$5.9bn	$6.6bn		
Def exp	εC145bn	εC197bn		
	($120m)	($120m)		
Def bdgt			εC275bn	
			($138m)	
FMA (US)	$0.2m	$0.3m	$0.3m	$0.3m
$1 = cedi	1,200	1,637	2,000	

Population		18,345,000	
Age	*13–17*	*18–22*	*23–32*
Men	1,079,000	890,000	1,327,000
Women	1,072,000	888,000	1,340,000

Total Armed Forces

ACTIVE 7,000

Army 5,000

2 Comd HQ • 2 bde (6 inf bn (incl 1 trg, 1 UNIFIL, 1 ECOMOG), spt unit) • 1 recce regt (2 sqn) • 1 arty 'regt' (mor bn) • 1 AB force (incl 1 para coy) • 1 fd engr regt (bn)

EQUIPMENT
  RECCE 3 EE-9 *Cascavel*
  AIFV 50 MOWAG *Piranha*
  MOR 81mm: 50; **120mm**: 28 Tampella
  RCL 84mm: 50 *Carl Gustav*
  AD GUNS 14.5mm: 4 ZPU-2, ZPU-4; **23mm**: 4 ZU-23-2
  SAM SA-7

Navy 1,000

COMMANDS Western and **Eastern**
BASES HQ Western Sekondi **HQ Eastern** Tema
PATROL AND COASTAL COMBATANTS 4
PATROL, COASTAL 2 *Achimota* (Ge Lürssen 57m) PFC
PATROL, INSHORE 2 *Dzata* (Ge Lürssen 45m) PCI

Air Force 1,000

15 cbt ac, no armed hel
TPT 5 Fokker (4 F-27, 1 F-28 (VIP)); 1 C-212, 6 *Skyvan*
HEL 2 Bell 212 (VIP), 2 Mi-2, 4 SA-319
TRG 1 sqn with 12* L-29, 2 MB 339F, 1 sqn with 3* MB-326K

Forces Abroad

UN AND PEACEKEEPING
BOSNIA (UNMIBH): 87 civ pol. **CROATIA** (UNTAES): 6 Obs; (UNMOP): 2 Obs. **FYROM** (UNPREDEP): 1 Obs. **LEBANON** (UNIFIL): 651; 1 inf bn. **LIBERIA** (ECOMOG): about 900 **IRAQ/KUWAIT** (UNIKOM): 6 Obs. **SIERRA LEONE** (ECOMOG) **WESTERN SAHARA** (MINURSO): 13 incl 6 Obs

Paramilitary ε800

PRESIDENTIAL GUARD ε800–1,000 (increasing)
1 inf bn

Guinea

	1995	1996	1997	1998
GDP	fr3.6tr	fr4.0tr		
	($2.8bn)	($3.0bn)		
per capita	$800	$800		
Growth	4.4%	4.5%		
Inflation	5.6%	5.0%		
Debt	$3.2bn	$3.2bn		
Def exp	εfr51bn	εfr56bn		
	($51m)	($57m)		
Def bdg			εfr59bn	
			($55m)	
FMA (US)	$0.20m	$0.04m	$0.15m	
(Fr)	$1.1m	$1.3m	$1.1m	$0.2m
$1 = franc	991	1,004	1,083	
Population		7,022,000		
Age	*13–17*	*18–22*	*23–32*	
Men	397,000	328,000	493,000	
Women	404,000	333,000	501,000	

Total Armed Forces

ACTIVE 9,700
(perhaps 7,500 conscripts).
Terms of service: conscription, 2 years

Army 8,500

1 armd bn • 1 arty bn • 1 cdo bn • 1 engr bn • 5 inf bn • 1 AD bn • 1 SF bn
EQUIPMENT†
  MBT 30 T-34, 8 T-54
  LT TK 20 PT-76
  RECCE 25 BRDM-1/-2, 2 AML-90
  APC 40 BTR (16 -40, 10 -50, 8 -60, 6 -152)
  TOWED ARTY 76mm: 8 M-1942; **85mm**: 6 D-44; **122mm**: 12 M-1931/37
  MOR 82mm: M-43; **120mm**: 20 M-1938/43
  RCL 82mm: B-10
  ATK GUNS 57mm: M-1943
  AD GUNS 30mm: twin M-53; **37mm**: 8 M-1939; **57mm**: 12 S-60, PRC Type-59; **100mm**: 4 KS-19
  SAM SA-7

Navy 400

BASES Conakry, Kakanda
PATROL AND COASTAL COMBATANTS 10
  PATROL, INSHORE 10
  Some 3 Sov *Bogomol* PFI, 2 Sov *Zhuk*, 1 US *Swiftships* 77, 4 other PCI<

Air Force† 800

8 cbt ac, no armed hel

FGA 4 MiG-17F, 4 MiG-21
TPT 4 An-14, 1 An-24
TRG 2 MiG-15UTI
HEL 1 IAR-330, 1 Mi-8, 1 SA-316B, 1 SA-330, 1 SA-342K

Forces Abroad

UN AND PEACEKEEPING
LIBERIA (ECOMOG): some 1,000. SIERRA LEONE (ECOMOG): ε700. WESTERN SAHARA (MINURSO): 3 Obs

Paramilitary 2,600 active

PEOPLE'S MILITIA 7,000
GENDARMERIE 1,000
REPUBLICAN GUARD 1,600

Guinea-Bissau

	1995	1996	1997	1998
GDP	εpG4.4tr	εpG6.9tr		
	($263m)	($285m)		
per capita	$800	$900		
Growth	4.4%	6.2%		
Inflation	45.3%	50.7%		
Debt	$894m	$914m		
Def exp	ε$8m	ε$8m		
Def bdgt			ε$8m	
FMA (Fr)	$0.1m	$0.1m	$0.1m	
(US)	$0.1m	$0.1m	$0.1m	$0.1m
$1 = peso	18,073	26,373	35,001	
Population		1,129,000		
Age	*13–17*	*18–22*	*23–32*	
Men	64,000	56,000	86,000	
Women	61,000	52,000	82,000	

Total Armed Forces

ACTIVE (all services, incl *Gendarmerie*, form part of the armed forces) ε9,250

Terms of service: conscription (selective)

Army 6,800

1 armd 'bn' (sqn) • 5 inf, 1 arty bn • 1 recce, 1 engr coy
EQUIPMENT
MBT 10 T-34
LT TK 20 PT-76
RECCE 10 BRDM-2
APC 35 BTR-40/-60/-152, 20 PRC Type-56

TOWED ARTY 85mm: 8 D-44; 122mm: 18 M-1938/D-30
MOR 82mm: M-43; 120mm: 8 M-1943
RL 89mm: M-20
RCL 75mm: PRC Type-52; 82mm: B-10
AD GUNS 23mm: 18 ZU-23; 37mm: 6 M-1939; 57mm: 10 S-60
SAM SA-7

Navy ε350

BASE Bissau
PATROL AND COASTAL COMBATANTS 9
PATROL, INSHORE 9
2 *Alfeite* PCC<, 1 ex-Ge *Kondor* I PCI†, 2 Sov *Bogomol*, 1 Indian SDB Mk III PCI, some 3 PCI†< (incl 1 customs service)
AMPHIBIOUS 1
1 LCM

Air Force 100

3 cbt ac, no armed hel
FTR 3 MiG-17
HEL 1 SA-318, 2 SA-319

Forces Abroad

UN AND PEACEKEEPING
ANGOLA (UNOMA): 4 Obs plus 4 civ pol

Paramilitary

GENDARMERIE 2,000

Kenya

	1995	1996	1997	1998
GDP	sh461bn	sh544bn		
	($8.9bn)	($9.5bn)		
per capita	$1,400	$1,400		
Growth	4.9%	4.6%		
Inflation	3.1%	6.4%		
Debt	$7.4bn	$7.2bn		
Def exp	εsh10.6bn	εsh12.1bn		
	($206m)	($212m)		
Def bdgt			εsh12.5bn	
			($205m)	
FMA (US)	$0.3m	$0.3m	$0.3m	$0.4m
$1 = shilling	51.4	57.1	53.6	
Population		29,214,000		
Age	*13–17*	*18–22*	*23–32*	
Men	1,867,000	1,554,000	2,212,000	
Women	1,863,000	1,558,000	2,232,000	

Total Armed Forces

ACTIVE 24,200

Army 20,500

1 armd bde (3 armd bn) • 2 inf bde (1 with 2, 1 with 3 inf bn) • 1 indep inf bn • 1 arty bde (2 bn) • 1 AD arty bn • 1 engr bde • 2 engr bn • 1 AB bn • 1 indep air cav bn

EQUIPMENT
MBT 76 Vickers Mk 3
RECCE 72 AML-60/-90, 12 *Ferret*, 8 Shorland
APC 52 UR-416, 10 Panhard M-3 (in store)
TOWED ARTY 105mm: 40 lt, 8 pack
MOR 81mm: 50; **120mm:** 12 Brandt
ATGW 40 *Milan*, 14 *Swingfire*
RCL 84mm: 80 *Carl Gustav*
AD GUNS 20mm: 50 TCM-20, 11 Oerlikon; **40mm:** 13 L/70

Navy 1,200

BASE Mombasa
PATROL AND COASTAL COMBATANTS 7
MISSILE CRAFT 6
2 *Nyayo* (UK Vosper 57m) PFM with 4 *Ottomat* SSM, 1 *Mamba*, 3 *Madaraka* (UK *Brooke Marine* 37m/32m), PFM with 4 *Gabriel* II SSM
PATROL, INSHORE 1 *Simba* with 2 40mm gun
AMPHIBIOUS 2
2 *Galana* LCM
SUPPORT AND MISCELLANEOUS 1
1 tug

Air Force 2,500

30 cbt ac, 34 armed hel
FGA 10 F-5 (8 -E, 2 -F)
TPT 7 DHC-5D, 6 Do-28D-2, 1 PA-31, 3 DHC-8, 1 Fokker 70 (VIP)
TRG 12 *Bulldog* 103/127
ATTACK HEL 11 Hughes 500MD (with TOW), 8 Hughes 500ME, 15 Hughes 500M
TPT HEL 9 IAR-330, 3 SA-330, 1 SA-342
TRG 2 Hughes 500D, 8* *Hawk* Mk 52, 12* *Tucano*
MISSILES
ASM AGM-65 *Maverick*, TOW
AAM AIM-9 *Sidewinder*

Forces Abroad

UN AND PEACEKEEPING
ANGOLA (UNOMA): 10 Obs. **CROATIA** (UNTAES): 6 Obs plus 25 civ pol; (UNMOP): 2 Obs. **FYROM** (UNPREDEP): 2 Obs. **IRAQ/KUWAIT** (UNIKOM): 6 Obs. **LIBERIA** (UNOMIL): 13 Obs. **WESTERN SAHARA** (MINURSO): 8 Obs

Paramilitary 5,000

POLICE GENERAL SERVICE UNIT 5,000
AIR WING ac 7 Cessna lt **hel** 3 Bell (1 206L, 2 47G)
POLICE NAVAL SQN/CUSTOMS about 5 PCI< (2 Lake Victoria), some 12 boats

Lesotho

	1995	1996	1997	1998
GDP	M3.3bn	M4.1bn		
	($552m)	($637m)		
per capita	$1,900	$2,100		
Growth	9.3%	13.1%		
Inflation	9.3%	8.9%		
Debt	$659m	$843m		
Def exp	εM120m	εM137m		
	($33m)	($32m)		
Def bdgt			εM148m	
			($33m)	
FMA (US)	$0.03m	$0.07m	$0.08m	$0.08m
$1 = maloti	3.63	4.30	4.47	
Population		2,083,000		
Age	*13–17*	*18–22*	*23–32*	
Men	120,000	102,000	154,000	
Women	119,000	101,000	156,000	

Total Armed Forces

ACTIVE 2,000

Army 2,000

7 inf coy • 1 spt coy (incl recce/AB, 81mm mor) • 1 air sqn
EQUIPMENT
RECCE 10 Il *Ramta*, 8 Shorland, AML-90
MOR 81mm: some
RCL 106mm: M-40
AC 3 C-212 *Aviocar* 300, 1 Cessna 182Q
HEL 2 Bo-105 CBS, 1 Bell 47G, 2 Bell 412 SP

Liberia

	1995	1996	1997	1998
GDP	ε$1.3bn	ε$1.3bn		
per capita	$1,000	$1,000		
Growth	ε2.7%	ε2.7%		
Inflation	ε10%	ε10%		

contd	1995	1996	1997	1998
Debt	$2.1bn	$2.2bn		
Def exp	ε$45m	ε$45m		
FMA[a] (US)		$15m		
US$1 = L$	1.0	1.0	1.0	

[a] UNOMIL **1995** $17m **1996** $34m

ECOMOG **1994–97**ε$30m annually. Funded by voluntary contributions from the US, other non-participating countries and participating ECOMOG countries

Population		ε3,201,000		
(Americo-Liberians 5%)				
Age	*13–17*	*18–22*	*23–32*	
Men	155,000	125,000	171,000	
Women	151,000	119,000	161,000	

Total Armed Forces

ACTIVE Nil

On 19 August 1995, the warring factions signed a peace accord. Under a transitional plan negotiated in 1996 between the principal armed factions, it was agreed to disarm and demobilise all militias. Implementation of the plan is being supervised by ECOMOG with forces from Bn, BF, Gam, Gha (1,400), Gui (1,000), RMM (600), Ngr (200+), Nga (ε9,000), Sen and SL (ε250). UNOMIL has deployed some 92 military obs and spt tps.

Madagascar

	1995	1996	1997	1998
GDP	fr13.6tr	fr17.7tr		
	($4.2bn)	($4.4bn)		
per capita	$600	$700		
Growth	1.8%	2.0%		
Inflation	49.0%	19.7%		
Debt	$4.3bn	$4.3bn		
Def exp	εfr140bn	εfr150bn		
	($33m)	($37m)		
Def bdgt			εfr140bn	
			($33m)	
FMA (US)		$0.1m	$0.1m	$0.1m
(Fr)	$2.7m	$1.5m	$1.2m	
$1 = franc	4,294	4,061	4,300	
Population		14,291,000		
Age	*13–17*	*18–22*	*23–32*	
Men	819,000	678,000	1,033,000	
Women	799,000	665,000	1,026,000	

Total Armed Forces

ACTIVE some 21,000

Terms of service: conscription (incl for civil purposes), 18 months

Army some 20,000

2 bn gp • 1 engr regt
EQUIPMENT
LT TK 12 PT-76
RECCE 8 M-8, ε20 M-3A1, 10 *Ferret*, ε35 BRDM-2
APC ε30 M-3A1 half-track
TOWED ARTY 76mm: 12 ZIS-3; **105mm**: some M-101; **122mm**: 12 D-30
MOR 82mm: M-37; **120mm**: 8 M-43
RL 89mm: LRAC
RCL 106mm: M-40A1
AD GUNS 14.5mm: 50 ZPU-4; **37mm**: 20 Type 55

Navy† 500

(incl some 100 Marines)
BASES Diégo-Suarez, Tamatave, Fort Dauphin, Tuléar, Majunga
PATROL CRAFT 1
1 *Malaika* (Fr PR48m) PCI†
AMPHIBIOUS 1
1 *Toky* (Fr *Batram*) LSM, capacity 30 tps, 4 tk
Plus craft: 1 LCT (Fr *Edic*), 1 LCA
SUPPORT AND MISCELLANEOUS 1
1 tpt/trg

Air Force 500

12 cbt ac, no armed hel
FGA 1 sqn with 4 MiG-17F, 8 MiG-21FL
TPT 4 An-26, 1 BN-2, 2 C-212, 2 Yak-40 (VIP)
HEL 1 sqn with 6 Mi-8
LIAISON 1 Cessna 310, 2 Cessna 337, 1 PA-23
TRG 4 Cessna 172

Paramilitary 7,500

GENDARMERIE 7,500
incl maritime police with some 5 PCI<

Malawi

	1995	1996	1997	1998
GDP	K22.5bn	K28.9bn		
	($1.7bn)	($1.9bn)		
per capita	$700	$800		
Growth	9.6%	10.4%		
Inflation	83.1%	37.7%		
Debt	$2.1bn	$2.2bn		
Def exp	εK320m	εK360m		
	($21m)	($24m)		
Def bdgt			εK420m	
			($28m)	
FMA (US)	$0.10m	$0.15m	$0.23m	$0.23m

contd	1995	1996	1997	1998
FMA (ROC)			$2.0m	
$1 = kwacha	15.3	15.3	15.3	
Population		10,273,000		
Age	*13–17*	*18–22*	*23–32*	
Men	588,000	478,000	717,000	
Women	583,000	482,000	756,000	

Total Armed Forces

ACTIVE (all services form part of the Army) 5,000

Army 5,000

2 bde HQ, 3 inf, 1 spt, 1 AB bn

EQUIPMENT (less than 50% serviceability)
  RECCE 20 *Fox*, 8 *Ferret*, 12 *Eland*
  TOWED ARTY 105mm: 9 lt
  MOR 81mm: 8 L16
  SAM 15 *Blowpipe*

MARITIME WING (220)
BASE Monkey Bay (Lake Nyasa)
  PATROL CRAFT 2
  1 *Kasungu* PCI†, 1 *Namacurra* PCI<, some boats

AIR WING (80)
no cbt ac, no armed hel
  TPT AC 1 sqn with 3 Do-228, 1 Do-28D, 1 *King Air* C90, 1 HS-125-800
  TPT HEL 2 SA-330F, 4 AS-350L

Paramilitary 1,000

MOBILE POLICE FORCE (MPF) 1,000
8 Shorland armd car **ac** 3 BN-2T *Defender* (border patrol), 1 *Skyvan* 3M, 4 Cessna **hel** 2 AS-365

Mali

	1995	1996	1997	1998
GDP	fr1.2tr	fr1.2tr		
	($2.2bn)	($2.3bn)		
per capita	$600	$600		
Growth	6.4%	4.0%		
Inflation	12.4%	6.5%		
Debt	$3.1bn	$3.1bn		
Def exp	εfr25bn	εfr21bn		
	($50m)	($41m)		
Def bdgt			εfr25bn	
			($44m)	
FMA (US)	$0.16m	$0.16m	$0.15m	$0.18m
(Fr)	$1.6m	$0.7m	$1.0m	
$1 = CFA fr	499	512	570	

Population	10,517,000 (Tuareg 6–10%)		
Age	*13–17*	*18–22*	*23–32*
Men	580,000	475,000	713,000
Women	602,000	495,000	753,000

Total Armed Forces

ACTIVE (all services form part of the Army) about 7,350
Terms of service: conscription (incl for civil purposes), 2 years (selective)

Army about 7,350

2 tk • 4 inf • 1 AB, 2 arty, 1 engr, 1 SF bn • 2 AD, 1 SAM bty

EQUIPMENT†
  MBT 21 T-34, T-54/-55 reported
  LT TK 18 Type 62
  RECCE 20 BRDM-2
  APC 30 BTR-40, 10 BTR-60, 10 BTR-152
  TOWED ARTY 85mm: 6 D-44; **100mm**: 6 M-1944; **122mm**: 8 D-30; **130mm**: M-46 reported
  MRL 122mm: 2 BM-21
  MOR 82mm: M-43; **120mm**: 30 M-43
  AD GUNS 37mm: 6 M-1939; **57mm**: 6 S-60
  SAM 12 SA-3

NAVY† (about 50)
BASES Bamako, Mopti, Segou, Timbuktu
PATROL CRAFT, RIVERINE 3<

AIR FORCE (400)
16† cbt ac, no armed hel
FGA 5 MiG-17F
FTR 11 MiG-21
TPT 2 An-24, 1 An-26
TRG 6 L-29, 1 MiG-15UTI, 4 Yak-11, 2 Yak-18
HEL 2 Mi-4, 1 Mi-8, 1 AS-350

Forces Abroad

UN AND PEACEKEEPING
ANGOLA (UNOMA): 9 Obs plus 15 civ pol. **CAR** (MISAB). **HAITI** (UNTMIH): 38 civ pol

Paramilitary 4,800

GENDARMERIE 1,800
8 coy
REPUBLICAN GUARD 2,000
MILITIA 3,000
NATIONAL POLICE 1,000

Mauritius

	1995	1996	1997	1998
GDP	R68.5bn	R76.5bn		
	($2.5bn)	($2.7bn)		
per capita	$13,300	$14,100		
Growth	3.3%	4.4%		
Inflation	6.0%	6.5%		
Debt	$1.8bn	$1.8bn		
Def exp	R0.2bn	εR1.1bn		
	($14m)	($61m)		
Def bdgt			εR320m	
			($16m)	
FMA (US)			$0.03m	$0.05m
$1 = rupee	17.4	18.0	20.4	
Population		1,157,000		
Age	*13–17*	*18–22*	*23–32*	
Men	54,000	53,000	102,000	
Women	53,000	52,000	102,000	

Total Armed Forces

ACTIVE Nil

Paramilitary ε1,800

SPECIAL MOBILE FORCE 1,300
6 rifle, 2 mob, 1 engr coy, spt tp
  APC 10 VAB
  MOR 81mm: 2
  RL 89mm: 4 LRAC

COAST GUARD ε500
  PATROL CRAFT 9
  1 *Vigilant* (Ca *Guardian* design) OPV, capability for 1 hel
  5 *Marlin* (Ind *Mandovi*) PCI
  1 SDB-3 PFI
  2 Sov *Zhuk* PCI<, plus 26 boats
  MR 2 Do-228-101, 1 BN-2T *Defender*, 3 SA-316B

POLICE AIR WING
  2 *Alouette* III

Mozambique

	1995	1996	1997	1998
GDP	M1.4tr	M1.9tr		
	($1.6bn)	($1.7bn)		
per capita	$900	$900		
Growth	1.5%	6.4%		
Inflation	54.4%	44.6%		
Debt	$5.8bn	$6.0bn		

contd	1995	1996	1997	1998
Def exp	M520bn	M704bn		
	($58m)	($62m)		
Def bdgt			M830bn	
			($72m)	
FMA (US)	$0.1m	$0.2m	$0.2m	$0.2m
(Fr)	$0.1m			
$1 = metical	9,024	11,294	1,545	
Population		18,755,000		
Age	*13–17*	*18–22*	*23–32*	
Men	1,052,000	872,000	1,347,000	
Women	1,066,000	887,000	1,385,000	

Total Armed Forces

ACTIVE ε5,100–6,100

Army ε4–5,000 (to be 12–15,000)

5 inf, 3 SF, 1 log bn • 1 engr coy

EQUIPMENT† (ε10% or less serviceability)
  MBT some 80 T-54/-55 (300+ T-34, T-54/-55 non-op)
  RECCE 30 BRDM-1/-2
  AIFV 40 BMP-1
  APC 150+ BTR-60, 100 BTR-152
  TOWED ARTY 100+: **76mm**: M-1942; **85mm**: 150+: D-44, D-48, Type-56; **100mm**: 24 M-1944; **105mm**: M-101; **122mm**: M-1938, D-30; **130mm**: 24 M-46; **152mm**: 20 D-1
  MRL 122mm: 30 BM-21
  MOR 82mm: M-43; **120mm**: M-43
  RCL 75mm; 82mm: B-10; **107mm**: B-11
  AD GUNS 400: **20mm**: M-55; **23mm**: 90 ZU-23-2; **37mm**: 100 M-1939; **57mm**: 90: S-60 towed, ZSU-57-2 SP
  SAM SA-7

Navy 100

BASES Maputo (HQ), Beira, Nacala, Pemba, Inhambane **Ocean** Quelimane **Lake Nyasa** Metangula
PATROL AND COASTAL COMBATANTS 3
  PATROL, INSHORE 3 PCI< (non-op) Lake Malawi

Air Force 1,000

(incl AD units); 43† cbt ac, 4† armed hel
FGA 5 sqn with 43† MiG-21
TPT 1 sqn with 5 An-26, 2 C-212
HELICOPTERS
  ATTACK 4† Mi-24
  TPT 5 Mi-8
  TRG 4 PA-32, 1 Cessna 182, 7 ZLIN-326
  AD SAM †SA-2, 10 SA-3

Namibia

	1995	1996	1997	1998
GDP	N$11.3bn	N$12.1bn		
	($2.3bn)	($2.4bn)		
per capita	$4,400	$4,500		
Growth	2.6%	2.0%		
Inflation	10.0%	8.0%		
Debt	$63m	$64m		
Def exp	N$234m	N$312m		
	($65m)	($73m)		
Def bdgt			εN$340m	
			($76m)	
FMA (US)	$0.1m	$0.2m	$0.2m	$0.2m
US$1 = N$	3.63	4.30	4.47	
Population		1,741,000		
Age	13–17	18–22	23–32	
Men	101,000	84,000	127,000	
Women	100,000	80,000	127,000	

Total Armed Forces

ACTIVE ε5,800

Army 5,700

1 Presidential Guard bn • 4 inf bn • 1 cbt spt bde with 1 arty, 1 AD, 1 ATK regt

EQUIPMENT
MBT some T-34, T-54/-55 (serviceability doubtful)
RECCE BRDM-2
APC some Casspir, Wolf, BTR-152
MRL 122mm: 5 BM-21
MOR 81mm; 82mm
RCL 82mm: B-10
ATK GUNS 57mm; 76mm: M-1942 (ZIS-3)
AD GUNS 14.5mm: 50 ZPU-4; 23mm: 15 ZU-23-2 SP
SAM SA-7

AIR WING
ac 1 Falcon 900, 1 Learjet 36, 6 Cessna 337/02-A hel 4 SA-319

Coast Guard ε100 (fishery protection)

BASE Walvis Bay
PATROL CRAFT 3
1 Osprey, 1 Oryx, 1 Cuito Cuanavale PCO

Forces Abroad

UN AND PEACEKEEPING
ANGOLA (UNOMA): 196

Niger

	1995	1996	1997	1998
GDP	fr921bn	fr970bn		
	($2.3bn)	($2.4bn)		
per capita	$800	$800		
Growth	3.0%	3.6%		
Inflation	10.9%	5.3%		
Debt	$1.6bn	$1.6bn		
Def exp	εfr11bn	εfr11bn		
	($21m)	($21m)		
Def bdgt			εfr13bn	
			($23m)	
FMA (US)	$0.20m	$0.01m		
(Fr)	$2.0m	$1.9m	$1.1m	
(LAR)			$4.0m	
$1 = CFA fr	499	512	570	
Population		9,687,000 (Tuareg 10%)		
Age	13–17	18–22	23–32	
Men	538,000	433,000	642,000	
Women	542,000	441,000	655,000	

Total Armed Forces

ACTIVE 5,300
Terms of service: selective conscription (2 years)

Army 5,200

3 Mil Districts • 4 armd recce sqn • 7 inf, 2 AB, 1 engr coy

EQUIPMENT
RECCE 90 AML-90, 35 AML-60/20, 7 VBL
APC 22 M-3
MOR 81mm: 19 Brandt; 82mm: 17; 120mm: 4 Brandt
RL 89mm: 36 LRAC
RCL 75mm: 6 M-20; 106mm: 8 M-40
ATK GUNS 85mm; 90mm
AD GUNS 20mm: 39 incl 10 M-3 VDA SP

Air Force 100

no cbt ac or armed hel
TPT 1 C-130H, 1 Do-28, 1 Do-228, 1 Boeing 737-200 (VIP), 1 An-26
LIAISON 2 Cessna 337D

Forces Abroad

PEACEKEEPING
LIBERIA (ECOMOG): 200+

Paramilitary 5,400

GENDARMERIE 1,400

REPUBLICAN GUARD 2,500

NATIONAL POLICE 1,500

Nigeria

	1995	1996	1997	1998
GDP	εN1.1tr	εN1.2tr		
	($43bn)	($45bn)		
per capita	$1,200	$1,200		
Growth	2.5%	2.1%		
Inflation	72.9%	29.2%		
Debt	$35.0bn	$34.9bn		
Def exp[a]	εN33bn	εN34bn		
	($1.5bn)	($1.6bn)		
Def bdgt			N17.5bn	
			($800m)	
$1 = naira[b]	21.9	21.9	21.9	

[a] Incl extra-budgetary mil and paramil funding
[b] Market rate **1997** N75 = $1

Population	ε107,000,000		

(*North* Hausa and Fulani *South-west* Yoruba *South-east* Ibos; these tribes make up ε65% of population)

Age	*13–17*	*18–22*	*23–32*
Men	6,961,000	5,886,000	8,762,000
Women	6,978,000	6,003,000	9,115,000

Total Armed Forces

ACTIVE 77,000

RESERVES

planned, none organised

Army 62,000

1 armd div (2 armd bde) • 1 composite div (1 mot inf, 1 amph bde, 1 AB bn) • 2 mech div (each 1 mech, 1 mot inf bde) • 1 Presidential Guard bde (2 bn) • 1 AD bde • each div 1 arty, 1 engr bde, 1 recce bn

EQUIPMENT

MBT 50 T-55†, 150 Vickers Mk 3

LT TK 140 *Scorpion*

RECCE ε120 AML-60, 60 AML-90, 55 *Fox*, 75 EE-9 *Cascavel*

APC 10 *Saracen*, 300 Steyr 4K-7FA, 70 MOWAG *Piranha*, EE-11 *Urutu* (reported)

TOWED ARTY 105mm: 200 M-56; **122mm**: 200 D-30/-74; **130mm**: 7 M-46; **155mm**: 24 FH-77B (in store)

SP ARTY 155mm: 27 *Palmaria*

MRL 122mm: 11 APR-21

MOR 81mm: 200; **82mm**: 100; **120mm**: 30+

RCL 84mm: *Carl Gustav*; **106mm**: M-40A1

AD GUNS 20mm: some 60; **23mm**: ZU-23, 30 ZSU-23-4 SP; **40mm**: L/60

SAM 48 *Blowpipe*, 16 *Roland*

SURV RASIT (veh, arty)

Navy 5,500

(incl Coast Guard)

BASES Lagos, **HQ Western Comd** Apapa **HQ Eastern Comd** Calabar **Akwa Ibom state** Warri, Port Harcourt, Ibaka

FRIGATES 1

1 *Aradu* (Ge MEKO 360) with 1 *Lynx* hel, 2 x 3 ASTT; plus 8 *Otomat* SSM, 1 127mm gun (non-op)

PATROL AND COASTAL COMBATANTS 51

CORVETTES 1† *Erinomi* (UK Vosper Mk 9) with 1 x 3 *Seacat*, 1 76mm gun, 1 x 2 ASW mor† (plus 1 non-op)

MISSILE CRAFT 5

3 *Ekpe* (Ge Lürssen 57m) PFM with 4 *Otomat* SSM (non-op)

2† *Ayam* (Fr *Combattante*) PFM with 2 x 2 MM-38 *Exocet* SSM

PATROL, INSHORE 45

4 *Makurdi* (UK *Brooke Marine* 33m) (non-op)
some 41 PCI<†

MINE COUNTERMEASURES 2

2 *Ohue* (mod It *Lerici*) MCC (non-op)

AMPHIBIOUS 1

1 *Ambe* (Ge) LST (1 non-op), capacity 220 tps 5 tk

SUPPORT AND MISCELLANEOUS 6

1 *Lana* AGHS, 4 tugs, 1 nav trg

NAVAL AVIATION

HEL 2† *Lynx* Mk 89 MR/SAR

Air Force 9,500

92† cbt ac, 15† armed hel

FGA/FTR 3 sqn

1 with 20 *Alpha Jet* (FGA/trg)

1 with 6† MiG-21MF, 4† MiG-21U, 12† MiG-21B/FR

1 with 15† *Jaguar* (12 -SN, 3 -BN)

ARMED HEL †15 Bo-105D

TPT 2 sqn with 5 C-130H, 3 -H-30, 17 Do-128-6, 3 Do-228 (VIP), 5 G-222

PRESIDENTIAL FLT ac 1 Boeing 727, 1 *Falcon*, 2 *Gulfstream*, 1 BAe 125-700, 1 BAe 125-1000 **hel** 4 AS-332, 2 SA-330

TRG ac† 23* L-39MS, 12* MB-339AN, 25† *Bulldog*, 3 Air *Beetle* **hel** 14 Hughes 300

AAM AA-2 *Atoll*

Forces Abroad

UN AND PEACEKEEPING

ANGOLA (UNOMA): 19 Obs plus 21 civ pol.

BOSNIA (UNMIBH): 16 civ pol. **CROATIA**

(UNTAES): 3 Obs plus 5 civ pol; (UNMOP): 1 Obs. **FYROM** (UNPREDEP): 1 Obs plus 4 civ pol. **IRAQ/KUWAIT** (UNIKOM): 6 Obs. **LIBERIA** (ECOMOG): ε9,000; 2 inf bde. **SIERRA LEONE** some 3,000 reported. **WESTERN SAHARA** (MINURSO): 3 Obs

Paramilitary

COAST GUARD

incl in Navy

PORT SECURITY POLICE ε2,000

about 60 boats and some 5 hovercraft

SECURITY AND CIVIL DEFENCE CORPS (Ministry of Internal Affairs)

    POLICE UR-416, 70 AT-105 *Saxon*† APC **ac** 1 Cessna 500, 3 Piper (2 *Navajo*, 1 *Chieftain*) **hel** 4 Bell (2 - 212, 2 -222)

Rwanda

	1995	1996	1997	1998
GDP	fr324bn	εfr461bn		
	($1.3bn)	($1.5bn)		
per capita	$400	$500		
Growth	24.6%	13.3%		
Inflation	22.0%	7.4%		
Debt	$1bn	$1bn		
Def exp	εfr27bn	εfr29bn		
	($90m)	($95m)		
Def bdgt			εfr31bn	
			($103m)	
FMA (US)	$0.1m	$0.2m	$0.3m	$0.3m
(Fr)	$2.4m			
$1 = franc	300	307	300	
Population	ε8,137,000 (Hutu 90%, Tutsi 9%)			
Age	*13–17*	*18–22*	*23–32*	
Men	507,000	409,000	592,000	
Women	523,000	424,000	619,000	

Total Armed Forces

ACTIVE (all services, incl *Gendarmerie*, form part of the Army) 62,000

Army 55,000

6 inf bde

EQUIPMENT

    RECCE AML-245, 15 AML-60, AML-90

    APC some BTR, Panhard, 6 RG-31 *Nyala*

    TOWED ARTY 105mm; 122mm

    MOR 81mm: 8; 120mm

    AD GUNS 14.5mm; 23mm; 37mm

SAM SA-7

HEL 2 Mi-24

Paramilitary 7,000

GENDARMERIE 7,000

Opposition

ε6,000 former govt tps dispersed in recent fighting in the Democratic Republic of Congo. Some have returned to Rwanda with associated *Interahamwe* militia

Senegal

	1995	1996	1997	1998
GDP	fr2.4tr	fr2.6tr		
	($4.0bn)	($4.3bn)		
per capita	$1,600	$1,700		
Growth	4.8%	5.2%		
Inflation	8.1%	2.9%		
Debt	$3.8bn	$3.9bn		
Def exp	εfr37bn	εfr38bn		
	($74m)	($74m)		
Def bdgt			εfr47bn	
			($83m)	
FMA (US)	$0.6m	$0.6m	$0.7m	$0.7m
(Fr)	$3.6m	$2.8m	$2.1m	
$1 = CFA fr	499	512	570	
Population	8,955,000			
Age	*13–17*	*18–22*	*23–32*	
Men	539,000	440,000	642,000	
Women	533,000	438,000	649,000	

Total Armed Forces

ACTIVE 13,350

Terms of service: conscription, 2 years selective

RESERVES n.k.

Army 12,000 (mostly conscripts)

4 Mil Zone HQ • 1 armd bn • 1 engr bn • 6 inf bn • 1 Presidential Guard (horsed) • 1 arty bn • 3 construction coy • 1 cdo bn • 1 AB bn • 1 engr bn

EQUIPMENT

    RECCE 10 M-8, 4 M-20, 30 AML-60, 27 AML-90

    APC some 16 Panhard M-3, 12 M-3 half-track

    TOWED ARTY 18: **75mm:** 6 M-116 pack; **105mm:** 6 M-101/HM-2; **155mm:** ε6 Fr Model-50

    MOR 81mm: 8 Brandt; **120mm:** 8 Brandt

    ATGW 4 *Milan*

    RL 89mm: 31 LRAC

AD GUNS 20mm: 21 M-693; 40mm: 12 L/60

Navy 700

BASES Dakar, Casamance
PATROL AND COASTAL COMBATANTS 10
PATROL, COASTAL 2
  1 *Fouta* (Dk *Osprey*) PCC
  1 *Njambuur* (Fr SFCN 59m) PFC
PATROL, INSHORE 8
  3 *Saint Louis* (Fr 48m) PCI, 3 *Senegal* II PFI<, 2
    Alioune Samb PCI<
AMPHIBIOUS craft only
  2 LCT

Air Force 650

8 cbt ac, no armed hel
MR/SAR 1 EMB-111
TPT 1 sqn with 6 F-27-400M, 1 Boeing 727-200 (VIP)
HEL 2 SA-318C, 2 SA-330, 1 SA-341H
TRG 4* CM-170, 4* R-235 *Guerrier*, 2 *Rallye* 160, 2 R-235A

Forces Abroad

UN AND PEACEKEEPING
ANGOLA (UNOMA): 10 Obs. BOSNIA (UNMIBH):
32 civ pol. CAR (MISAB). IRAQ/KUWAIT
(UNIKOM): 5 Obs

Paramilitary 4,000

GENDARMERIE 4,000
12 VXB-170 APC
CUSTOMS
2 PCI<, boats

Opposition

**CASAMANCE MOVEMENT OF DEMOCRATIC
FORCES** str n.k.

Foreign Forces

FRANCE 1,500; 1 marine inf bn; **ac** MR *Atlantic*, 1 C-
160 **hel** 1 SA-319

Seychelles

	1995	1996	1997	1998
GDP	SR2.4bn	SR2.5bn		
	($325m)	($342m)		
per capita	$3,900	$4,100		

contd	1995	1996	1997	1998
Growth	-1.8%	3.2%		
Inflation	0.2%	-1.0%		
Debt	$164m	$162m		
Def exp	SR55m	SR52m		
	($12m)	($11m)		
Def bdgt			SR51m	
			($10m)	
FMA (US)	$0.01m	$0.03m	$0.08m	$0.08m
$1 = rupee	4.8	5.0	5.0	
Population		72,000		
Age	13–17	18–22	23–32	
Men	4,000	4,000	7,000	
Women	4,000	4,000	7,000	

Total Armed Forces

ACTIVE (all services, incl Coast Guard, form part of the
Army) 400

Army 200

1 inf coy
1 sy unit
EQUIPMENT†
  RECCE 6 BRDM-2
  MOR 82mm: 6 M-43
  RL RPG-7
  AD GUNS 14.5mm: ZPU-2/-4; 37mm: M-1939
  SAM 10 SA-7

Paramilitary 250 active

NATIONAL GUARD 250

  COAST GUARD (200)
  (incl 20 Air Wing and ε80 Marines)
  BASE Port Victoria
  PATROL, INSHORE 4
  1 *Andromache* (It *Pichiotti* 42m) PFI, 1 *Gemini* PCI, 2
    Zhuk PFI< (1 non-op)

  AIR WING (20)
  No cbt ac, no armed hel
  MR 1 BN-2 *Defender*
  TPT 1 Reims-Cessna F-406/*Caravan* 11
  TRG 1 Cessna 152

Sierra Leone

	1995	1996	1997	1998
GDP	Le710bn	Le857bn		
	($725m)	($776m)		
per capita	$700	$700		
Growth	-10.0%	4.9%		

contd	1995	1996	1997	1998
Inflation	26.0%	23.2%		
Debt	$1.2bn	$1.3bn		
Def exp	εLe31bn	εLe42bn		
	($41m)	($45m)		
Def bdgt			Le9bn	
			($11m)	
FMA (US)	$0.05m	$0.13m	$0.12m	$0.12m
$1 = leone	755	921	850	
Population		ε4,972,000		
Age	*13–17*	*18–22*	*23–32*	
Men	265,000	224,000	347,000	
Women	264,000	223,000	351,000	

Total Armed Forces

ACTIVE n.k.

Following the civil war of May–June 199,7 the Armed Forces Revolutionary Council (AFRC) have formed an alliance with their former opponents, the Revolutionary United Front (RUF). Str are reported as **AFRC** 8–10,000 **RUF** 3–5,000 with perhaps 1,000 armed. Details of force structure are not available. Eqpt details should be treated with caution.

EQUIPMENT

MOR 81mm: 3; **82mm**: 2; **120mm**: 2
RCL 84mm: *Carl Gustav*
AD GUNS 12.7mm: 4; **14.5mm**: 3
SAM SA-7
HEL 1 Mi-24

Navy ε200

BASE Freetown
PATROL AND COASTAL COMBATANTS 6
2 PRC *Shanghai* II PFI, 1 *Swiftship 32m†* PFI, 2 CAT 900S PC<, 1 *Fairy Marine Tracker* II

Forces Abroad

LIBERIA (ECOMOG): ε250

Opposition

KAMAJORS (tribal militia) ε17,000
armed str n.k.

Foreign Forces

PEACEKEEPING
ECOMOG: tps from **Gui** ε700, **Gha**, **Nga** some 3,000 reported

Somali Republic

	1995	1996	1997	1998
GDP	ε$810m	ε$826m		
per capita	$800	$800		
Growth	ε-3.0%	ε-1.0%		
Inflation	ε16%	ε17%		
Debt	$2.7bn	$2.7bn		
Def exp	ε$40m	ε$40m		
Def bdgt			ε$40m	
$1 = shilling[a]	2,620	2,620	2,620	
[a] Market rate June **1997** $1 = 8,000 shillings				
Population		ε6,000,000 (Somali 85%)		
Age	*13–17*	*18–22*	*23–32*	
Men	547,000	442,000	648,000	
Women	545,000	439,000	653,000	

Total Armed Forces

ACTIVE Nil

Following the 1991 revolution, no national armed forces have yet been formed. The Somali National Movement has declared northern Somalia the independent 'Republic of Somaliland', while insurgent groups compete for local supremacy in the south. Heavy military equipment is in poor repair or inoperable.

Clan/Movement Groupings

'SOMALILAND' (northern Somalia)
UNITED SOMALI FRONT clan Issa
SOMALI DEMOCRATIC ALLIANCE clan Gadabursi
SOMALI NATIONAL MOVEMENT 5–6,000 **clan** Issaq, 3 factions (Tur, Dhegaweyne, Kahin)
UNITED SOMALI PARTY clan Midigan/Tumaal **leader** Ahmed Guure Adan

SOMALIA
SOMALI SALVATION DEMOCRATIC FRONT 3,000 **clan** Darod **leaders** Abdullah Yusuf Ahmed
UNITED SOMALI CONGRESS clan Hawiye **sub-clan** Habr Gidir **leadership** in dispute
Ali Mahdi Faction 10,000(-) **clan** Abgal **leader** Mohammed Ali Mahdi
SOMALI NATIONAL FRONT 2–3,000 **clan** Darod **leader** General Omar Hagi Mohammed Hersi
SOMALI DEMOCRATIC MOVEMENT clan Hawiye
SOMALI PATRIOTIC MOVEMENT 203,000 **clan** Darod **leader** Ahmed Omar Jess

Sub-Saharan Africa

South Africa

	1995	1996	1997	1998
GDP	R486bn	R543bn		
	($134bn)	($141bn)		
per capita	$5,300	$5,500		
Growth	3.4%	3.1%		
Inflation	8.6%	7.4%		
Debt	$22.2bn	$29.4bn		
Def exp	R11.5bn	R11.0bn		
	($3.2bn)	($2.6bn)		
Def bdgt[a]			R9.5bn	
			($2.1bn)	
FMA (US)	$0.3m	$0.5m	$0.7m	$0.8m
$1 = rand	3.63	4.30	4.47	

[a] The gov proposes to cut 1997 def bdgt by R700m ($157m)

Population	44,411,000		
Age	*13–17*	*18–22*	*23–32*
Men	2,397,000	2,155,000	3,493,000
Women	2,365,000	2,138,000	3,487,000

Total Armed Forces

ACTIVE 79,440

(incl 6,000 Medical Services; 8,000 women)
Terms of service: Voluntary service in 3 categories (full career, up to 10 yrs, up to 6 yrs)
Up to 28,000 personnel from non-statutory forces, incl MK, plus some 10,000 from the Homelands, were to be absorbed into the new South African National Defence Force (SANDF). Only 19,000 did so, of whom 3,000 have since resigned. Some 16,000 are now SANDF members. The process is complete.

RESERVES 386,000

Army 312,500 Navy 17,000 Air Force 20,500 Medical Service 36,000

Army 54,300

(12,000 White, 38,300 Black, 4,000 Coloured/Asian; ε4,000 women)

FULL-TIME FORCE (FTF) (52,000)

9 regional comd (each consists of HQ and a number of group HQ, but no tps which are provided when necessary by FTF and PTF units)
1 mech inf bde HQ (designated units 1 tk, 1 armd car, 1 mech inf bn gp, 5 inf, 1 arty, 1 AD, 1 engr bn)
1 AB bde (1 AB bn, AB trg school)
1 SF bde (2 bn)

PART-TIME FORCE (PTF)

1 div (3 bde each 1 tk, 1 armd recce, 2 mech inf, 1 SP arty, 1 AD, 1 engr bn)
div tps incl: 1 armd recce, 1 mech inf, 1 mot inf, 1 arty, 1 MRL, 1 AD bn
30 Group HQ
some 50 inf coy home defence units

EQUIPMENT

MBT some 224 *Olifant* 1A/-B
RECCE 1,600 *Eland*-90, 176 *Rooikat*-76
AIFV 1,243 *Ratel*-20/-60/-90
APC 2,400 *Buffel*, 390 *Casspir*, 440 *Mamba*
TOWED ARTY 350: **88mm**: incl 25-pdr, 30 G-1 (in store); **140mm**: 5.5in, 75 G-2; **155mm**: 72 G-5
SP ARTY 155mm: 43 G-6
MRL 127mm: 120 *Bataleur* (40 tube)
MOR 81mm: 1,110 (incl some SP)
ATGW ZT-3 *Swift* (53 SP), *Milan*
RL 92mm: FT-5
RCL 106mm: 150 M-40A1 (some SP)
AD GUNS 600: **20mm**: GAI, *Ystervark* SP; **23mm**: 36 *Zumlac* (ZU-23-2) SP; **35mm**: 150 GDF-002 twin, some ZA-35 twin; **40mm**: L/60 (in store)
SAM SA-7/-14
SURV *Green Archer* (mor), *Cymbeline* (mor)

Navy 8,000

(ε500 women)
NAVAL HQ Pretoria
FLOTILLAS submarine, strike, MCM
BASES Simon's Town, Durban (Salisbury Island)

SUBMARINES 3

3 *Maria van Riebeek* (Mod Fr *Daphné*) with 550mm TT (2 in refit)

PATROL AND COASTAL COMBATANTS 9

MISSILE CRAFT 6 *Warrior* (Il *Reshef*) with 6–8 *Skerpioen* (Il *Gabriel*) SSM (incl 3 non-op), class being modernised
PATROL, INSHORE 3 PFI< plus boats

MINE COUNTERMEASURES 6

2 *Kimberley* (UK *Ton*) MSC (incl 1 in refit) plus 2 in reserve
4 *River* (Ge *Navors*) MHC (incl 1 i refit)

SUPPORT AND MISCELLANEOUS 8

1 *Drakensberg* AO with 2 hel and extempore amph capability (perhaps 60 tps and 2 small landing craft)
1 *Outeniqua* AO with similar capability as *Drakensberg*
1 AGHS
1 diving spt
1 Antarctic tpt with 2 hel (operated by Ministry of Environmental Affairs)
3 tugs

Air Force 11,140

(800 women); 114 cbt ac, 14+ armed hel
2 Territorial Area Comd, log, trg comds
FTR/FGA 2 sqn
1 with 25 *Impala* II, 20 *Mirage* F-1AZ
1 with 32 *Cheetah* C

TPT/TKR/EW 1 sqn with 5 Boeing 707-320 (EW/tkr)
MR 1 sqn with 8 C-47TP
TPT 3 sqn
  1 with 9 C-130B, 2 C-130F, 4 C-160, 2 C-212-200, 2 C-212-300, 1 CN-235M
  1 (VIP) with 4 HS-125 -400B (civil registration), 1 HS-125-403B *Super King Air* 200, 1 *King Air* 300, 2 *Citation* II, 2 *Falcon* 50, 1 *Falcon* 900, 12 Cessna *Caravan*
  1 with 19 C-47 (being modified to C-4 TP)
LIAISON/FAC 24 Cessna 185A/D/E, 1 PC-12
HEL 4 sqn with 53 SA-316/-319 (some armed), 9 BK-117, 1 SA-365 (VIP)
TRG COMD (incl OCU) 5 schools
  ac 12 C-47TP, 12* *Cheetah* D, 25* *Impala* I, 58 PC-7 **hel** 37 SA-316/SA-330
UAV *Seeker, Scout*
MISSILES
  ASM AS-11/-20/-30
  AAM R-530, R-550 *Magic*, AIM-9 *Sidewinder*, V-3C *Darter*, V-3A/B *Kukri*, *Python* 3
GROUND DEFENCE
1 regt (South African Air Force Regt) *Rhino* APC
RADAR 2 Air Control Sectors, 3 fixed and some mob radars
SAM 2 wg (2 sqn each), 20 *Cactus* (*Crotale*), SA-8/-9/-13

Medical Service 6,000

(2,500 women); a separate service within the SANDF

Paramilitary 138,000

SOUTH AFRICAN POLICE SERVICE 138,000
  AIR WING
    ac 1 Cessna 402, 1 Beech 400, 8 PC-6 **hel** 2 BK-117, 15 Bo-105 CBS, 2 *Hughes* 500E
  MARINE WING
    20 PC

Sudan

	1995	1996	1997	1998
GDP	$9.1bn	$9.7bn		
per capita	$1,200	$1,300		
Growth	4.5%	4.0%		
Inflation	57.0%	85.0%		
Debt	$17.6bn	$17.8bn		
Def exp	ε$389m	ε$405m		
Def bdgt			ε$160m	
$1 = pound	501	1,251	1,460	
Population	ε30,485,000			

(Sunni Muslim 70% *mainly in North* Christian 10% *mainly in South* African 52% *mainly in South* Arab 39% *mainly in North*)

Age	13–17	18–22	23–32
Men	1,786,000	1,498,000	2,255,000
Women	1,706,000	1,431,000	2,170,000

Total Armed Forces

ACTIVE 79,700
(ε20,000 conscripts)
Terms of service: conscription (males 18–30), 3 years

Army 75,000

(ε20,000 conscripts)
1 armd div • 1 recce bde • 6 inf div (regional comd) • 10+ arty bde (incl AD) • 1 AB div (incl 1 SF bde) • 3 arty regt • 1 mech inf bde • 1 engr div • 1 border gd div • 24 inf bde
EQUIPMENT
  MBT 250 T-54/-55, 20 M-60A3, 10+ ORC Type-59
  LT TK 70 PRC Type-62
  RECCE 6 AML-90, 90 *Saladin*, 80 *Ferret*, 60 BRDM-1/-2
  AIFV 6 BMP-2
  APC 426: 90 BTR-50/-152, 80 OT-62/-64, 36 M-113, 100 V-100/-150, 120 *Walid*
  TOWED ARTY 600 incl: **85mm:** D-44; **105mm:** M-101 pack, Model 56 pack; **122mm:** D-74, M-1938, Type-54/D-30; **130mm:** M-46/PRC Type 59-1
  SP ARTY 155mm: 6 AMX Mk F-3
  MRL 107mm: 400 Type-63; **122mm:** 30 BM-21
  MOR 81mm: 120; **82mm; 120mm:** 12 M-43, 24 AM-49
  ATGW 4 *Swingfire*
  RCL 106mm: 40 M-40A1
  ATK GUNS 40 incl: **76mm:** M-1942; **100mm:** M-1944
  AD GUNS 425 incl: **14.5mm; 20mm:** M-167 towed, M-163 SP; **23mm:** ZU-23-2; **37mm:** M-1939/Type-63, Type-55; **57mm:** Type-59
  SAM SA-7
  SURV RASIT (veh, arty)

Navy ε1,700

BASES Port Sudan (HQ), Flamingo Bay (Red Sea), Khartoum (Nile)
PATROL AND COASTAL COMBATANTS 7
  PATROL, INSHORE 3 *Kadir* PCI< (1 non-op)
  PATROL, RIVERINE 4 PCI<, about 16 armed boats
AMPHIBIOUS craft only
  some 7 *Sobat* (FRY DTK-221) LCT (used for transporting stores)

Air Force 3,000

(incl Air Defence); 56† cbt ac, 9 armed hel

FGA 9 F-5 (7 -E, 2 -F), 9 PRC J-5 (MiG-17), 9 PRC J-6 (MiG-19), 11 F-7 (MiG-21)

FTR 6 MiG-23, PRC J-6 (MiG-19)

TPT 4 An-24, 4 C-130H, 4 C-212, 3 DHC-5D, 6 EMB-110P, 1 F-27, 2 *Falcon* 20/50

HEL 11 AB-412, 8 IAR/SA-330, 4 Mi-4, 8 Mi-8, 4 Mi-24 (armed), 5 Mi-35 (armed)

TRG incl 4* MiG-15UTI, 4* MiG-21U, 2* JJ-5, 2* JJ-6, 10 PT-6A

AD 5 bty SA-2 SAM (18 launchers)

AAM AA-2 *Atoll*

Paramilitary 15,000

POPULAR DEFENCE FORCE 15,000 active

85,000 reserve; mil wg of National Islamic Front; org in bn of 1,000

Opposition

NATIONAL DEMOCRATIC ALLIANCE

coalition of many groups, of which the main forces are:

SUDANESE PEOPLE'S LIBERATION ARMY (SPLA) 20–30,000

four factions, each org in bn, operating mainly in southern Sudan; some captured T-54/-55 tks, BM-21 MRL and arty pieces, but mainly small arms plus **60mm** and **120mm** mor, **14.5mm** AA, SA-7 SAM

SUDAN ALLIANCE FORCES ε500

based in Eritrea, operate in border area

BEJA CONGRESS FORCES ε500

operate on Eritrean border

NEW SUDAN BRIGADE ε2,000

operate on Ethiopian and Eritrean borders

Foreign Forces

IRAN some mil advisers

Tanzania

	1995	1996	1997	1998
GDP	εsh2.3tr	εsh2.8tr		
	($3.2bn)	($3.4bn)		
per capita	$500	$500		
Growth	3.8%	4.5%		
Inflation	27.6%	21.0%		
Debt	$7.3bn	$7.5bn		
Def exp	εsh50bn	εsh49bn		
	($87m)	($85m)		
Def bdgt			εsh54bn	
			($89m)	
FMA (US)	$0.1m	$0.1m	$0.2m	$0.2m

contd	1995	1996	1997	1998
$1 = shilling	575	580	609	
Population		30,220,000		
Age	13–17	18–22	23–32	
Men	1,728,000	1,397,000	2,093,000	
Women	1,801,000	1,466,000	2,257,000	

Total Armed Forces

ACTIVE ε34,600

Terms of service: incl civil duties, 2 years

RESERVES 80,000

Citizens' Militia

Army 30,000+

5 inf bde • 1 tk bde • 2 arty bn • 2 AD arty bn • 2 mor bn • 2 ATK bn • 1 engr regt (bn)

EQUIPMENT†

MBT 30 PRC Type-59 (15 op), 35 T-54 (all non-op)

LT TK 30 PRC Type-62, 40 *Scorpion*

RECCE 40 BRDM-2

APC 66 BTR-40/-152, 30 PRC Type-56

TOWED ARTY 76mm: 45 ZIS-3; **85mm**: 80 PRC Type-56; **122mm**: 20 D-30, 100 M-30; **130mm**: 40 M-46

MRL 122mm: 58 BM-21

MOR 82mm: 350 M-43; **120mm**: 135 M-43

RCL 75mm: 540 PRC Type-52

Navy† ε1,000

BASES Dar es Salaam, Zanzibar, Mwanza (Lake Victoria – 4 boats)

PATROL AND COASTAL COMBATANTS 16

TORPEDO CRAFT 4 PRC *Huchuan* PHT< with 2 533mm TT

PATROL, INSHORE 12

8 PRC *Shanghai* II PFI (6 non-op)

4 *Thornycroft* PC<

AMPHIBIOUS 2

2 *Yunnan* LCU

Air Force 3,600

(incl ε2,600 AD tps); 24 cbt ac†, no armed hel

FTR 3 sqn with 3 PRC J-5 (MiG-17), 10 J-6 (MiG-19), 11 J-7 (MiG-21)

TPT 1 sqn with 3 DHC-5D, 1 PRC Y-5, 2 CH Y-12, 3 HS-748, 2 F-28, 1 HS-125-700

HEL 4 AB-205

LIAISON ac 5 Cessna 310, 2 Cessna 404, 1 Cessna 206 **hel** 6 Bell 206B

TRG 2 MiG-15UTI, 5 PA-28

AD GUNS 14.5mm: 40 ZPU-2/-4; **23mm**: 40 ZU-23;

37mm: 120 PRC Type-55
SAM 20 SA-3, 20 SA-6, 120 SA-7

Forces Abroad

UN AND PEACEKEEPING
ANGOLA (UNOMA): 3 civ pol

Paramilitary 1,400 active

POLICE FIELD FORCE 1,400
18 sub-units incl Police Marine Unit
  MARINE UNIT (100)
    boats only
  AIR WING
    ac 1 Cessna U-206 **hel** 2 AB-206A, 2 Bell 206L, 2 Bell 47G
CITIZENS' MILITIA 80,000

Togo

	1995	1996	1997	1998
GDP	fr606bn	fr662bn		
	($1.1bn)	($1.1bn)		
per capita	$1,200	$1,300		
Growth	7.2%	5.9%		
Inflation	15.7%	4.6%		
Debt	$1.5bn	$1.5bn		
Def exp	εfr14bn	εfr14bn		
	($28m)	($28m)		
Def bdgt			εfr17bn	
			($30m)	
FMA (Fr)	$1.1m	$1.0m	$1.0m	
(US)			$0.03m	$0.03m
$1 = CFA fr	499	512	570	
Population		4,560,000		
Age	*13–17*	*18–22*	*23–32*	
Men	263,000	206,000	304,000	
Women	268,000	219,000	332,000	

Total Armed Forces

ACTIVE some 6,950
Terms of service: conscription, 2 years (selective)

Army 6,500

2 inf regt
  1 with 1 mech bn, 1 mot bn
  1 with 2 armd sqn, 3 inf coy; spt units (trg)
1 Presidential Guard regt: 2 bn (1 cdo), 2 coy
1 para cdo regt: 3 coy
1 spt regt: 1 fd arty, 2 AD arty bty; 1 log/tpt/engr bn

EQUIPMENT
MBT 2 T-54/-55
LT TK 9 *Scorpion*
RECCE 6 M-8, 3 M-20, 10 AML (3 -60, 7 -90), 36 EE-9 *Cascavel*, 2 VBL
APC 4 M-3A1 half-track, 30 UR-416
TOWED ARTY 105mm: 4 HM-2
MOR 82mm: 20 M-43
RCL 57mm: 5 ZIS-2; **75mm**: 12 PRC Type-52/-56; **82mm**: 10 PRC Type-65
AD GUNS 14.5mm: 38 ZPU-4; **37mm**: 5 M-39

Navy ε200

(incl Marine Infantry unit)
BASE Lomé
PATROL CRAFT, INSHORE 2
  2 *Kara* (Fr *Esterel*) PFI<

Air Force †250

15 cbt ac, no armed hel
FGA 4 *Alpha Jet*, 4 EMB-326G
TPT 2 *Baron*, 2 DHC-5D, 1 Do-27, 1 F-28-1000 (VIP), 1 Boeing 707 (VIP), 2 Reims-Cessna 337
HEL 1 AS-332, 2 SA-315, 1 SA-319, 1 SA-330
TRG 4* CM-170, 3* TB-30

Forces Abroad

UN AND PEACEKEEPING
CAR (MISAB). HAITI (UNTMIH): 7 civ pol. WESTERN SAHARA (MINURSO): 2 civ pol

Paramilitary 750

GENDARMERIE (Ministry of Interior) 750
1 trg school, 2 reg sections, 1 mob sqn

Uganda

	1995	1996	1997	1998
GDP	Ush5.9tr	Ush6.7tr		
	($5.9bn)	($6.4bn)		
per capita	$1,500	$1,600		
Growth	9.8%	7.0%		
Inflation	7.4%	5.0%		
Debt	$3.6bn	$3.8bn		
Def exp	Ush122bn	Ush140bn		
	($126m)	($134m)		
Def bdgt			Ush147bn	
			($137m)	
FMA (US)	$0.1m	$4.2m	$0.3m	$0.4m
$1 = shilling	969	1,046	1,057	

Population		20,398,000	
Age	13–17	18–22	23–32
Men	1,163,000	981,000	1,411,000
Women	1,162,000	995,000	1,567,000

Total Armed Forces

ACTIVE ε40–55,000

Ugandan Peoples' Defence Force ε40–55,000

4 div (1 with 5, 1 with 3, 2 with 2 bde)
EQUIPMENT†
  MBT 80 T-54/-55
  LT TK ε20 PT-76
  APC 20 BTR-60, 4 OT-64 SKOT, 10 *Mamba*
  TOWED ARTY 76mm: 60 M-1942; **122mm**: 20 M-1938
  MRL 122mm: BM-21
  MOR 81mm: L 16; **82mm**: M-43; **120mm**: Soltam
  ATGW 40 AT-3 *Sagger*
  AD GUNS 14.5mm: ZPU-1/-2/-4; **23mm**: 20 ZU-23; **37mm**: 20 M-1939
  SAM 10 SA-7
  AVN 1 cbt ac†
  TRG 3† L-39, 1 SF*-260
  TPT HEL 1 Bell 206, 1 Bell 412, 5 Mi-17
  TPT/LIAISON HEL 1 AS-202 *Bravo*, 1 *Gulfstream* II, 1 *Gulfstream* III

Paramilitary ε600 active

BORDER DEFENCE UNIT ε600
  small arms
POLICE AIR WING
  ac 1 DHC-2, 1 DHC-4, 1 DHC-6 **hel** 2 Bell 206, 4 Bell 212
MARINES (ε400)
  8 riverine patrol craft<, plus boats

Opposition

LORD'S RESISTANCE ARMY ε2,000
(ε1,000 in Uganda, remainder in Sudan)
ALLIED DEMOCRATIC FORCES ε500–1,000

Zambia

	1995	1996	1997	1998
GDP	K3.5tr	K4.7tr		
	($3.0bn)	($3.2bn)		
per capita	$800	$900		

contd	1995	1996	1997	1998
Growth	-1.5%	5.0%		
Inflation	23.1%	43.1%		
Debt	$6.9bn	$6.8bn		
Def exp	εK52bn	εK52bn		
	($61m)	($59m)		
Def bdgt			εK83bn	
			($64m)	
FMA (US)	$0.1m	$0.1m	$0.2m	$0.2m
(PRC)			$2.0m	
$1 = kwacha	857	1,204	1,294	
Population		9,574,000		
Age	13–17	18–22	23–32	
Men	574,000	468,000	688,000	
Women	565,000	469,000	723,000	

Total Armed Forces

ACTIVE 21,600

Army 20,000

(incl 3,000 reserves)
3 bde HQ • 1 arty regt • 9 inf bn (3 reserve) • 1 engr bn • 1 armd regt (incl 1 armd recce bn)
EQUIPMENT
  MBT 10 T-54/-55, 20 PRC Type-59
  LT TK 30 PT-76
  RECCE 88 BRDM-1/-2
  APC 13 BTR-60
  TOWED ARTY 76mm: 35 M-1942; **105mm**: 18 Model 56 pack; **122mm**: 25 D-30; **130mm**: 18 M-46
  MRL 122mm: 50 BM-21
  MOR 81mm: 55; **82mm**: 24; **120mm**: 14
  ATGW AT-3 *Sagger*
  RCL 57mm: 12 M-18; **75mm**: M-20; **84mm**: *Carl Gustav*
  AD GUNS 20mm: 50 M-55 triple; **37mm**: 40 M-1939; **57mm**: 55 S-60; **85mm**: 16 KS-12
  SAM SA-7

Air Force 1,600

63† cbt ac, some armed hel
FGA 1 sqn with 12 J-6 (MiG-19)†
FTR 1 sqn with 12 MiG-21 MF†
TPT 1 sqn with 4 An-26, 4 C-47, 3 DHC-4, 4 DHC-5D
VIP 1 fleet with 1 HS-748, 3 Yak-40
LIAISON 7 Do-28, 2 Y-12
TRG 2*-F5T, 2* MiG-21U†, 12* *Galeb* G-2, 15* MB-326GB, 8* SF-260MZ
HEL 1 sqn with 4 AB-205A, 5 AB-212, 12 Mi-8
LIAISON HEL 12 AB-47G
MISSILES
  ASM AT-3 *Sagger*
  SAM 1 bn; 3 bty: SA-3 *Goa*

Forces Abroad

UN AND PEACEKEEPING
ANGOLA (UNOMA): 499; 1 inf bn, 10 Obs plus 15 civ pol

Paramilitary 1,400

POLICE MOBILE UNIT (PMU) 700
1 bn of 4 coy
POLICE PARAMILITARY UNIT (PPMU) 700
1 bn of 3 coy

Zimbabwe

	1995	1996	1997	1998
GDP	εZ$48bn	εZ$60bn		
	($5.5bn)	($6.1bn)		
per capita	$2,000	$2,200		
Growth	-2.0%	8.1%		
Inflation	22.6%	21.4%		
Debt	$4.9bn	$4.9bn		
Def exp	Z$2.1bn	Z$2.3bn		
	($233m)	($237m)		
Def bdgt[a]			Z$5.4bn	
			($471m)	
FMA (US)	$0.2m	$0.2m	$0.3m	$0.4m
US$1 = Z$	8.66	9.92	11.29	

[a] 18-month funding to 31 Dec 1998

Population	11,577,000		
Age	*13–17*	*18–22*	*23–32*
Men	724,000	592,000	925,000
Women	720,000	591,000	927,000

Total Armed Forces

ACTIVE ε39,000

Army ε35,000

5 bde HQ • 1 Mech, 1 Presidential Guard bde • 1 armd sqn • 15 inf bn (incl 2 guard, 1 mech, 1 cdo, 1 para) • 2 fd arty regt • 1 AD regt • 1 engr regt
EQUIPMENT
MBT 32: 22 PRC Type-59, 10 PRC Type-69
RECCE 90 EE-9 *Cascavel* (**90mm** gun)
APC 30 PRC Type-63 (YW-531), UR-416, 75 *Crocodile*, 23 ACMAT
TOWED ARTY 16: **122mm**: 12 PRC Type-60, 4 PRC Type-54
MRL 107mm: 18 PRC Type-63; **122mm**: 52 RM-70
MOR 81mm/82mm 502; **120mm**: 14 M-43
AD GUNS 215 incl **14.5mm**: ZPU-1/-2/-4; **23mm**: ZU-23; **37mm**: M-1939
SAM 17 SA-7

Air Force 4,000

56 cbt ac, 24 armed hel
Flying hours 100
FGA 2 sqn
1 with 11 *Hunters* (9 FGA-90, 1 -F80, 1 T-81)
1 with 6 *Hawk* Mk 60 and 5 *Hawk* Mk 60A
FTR 1 sqn with 12 PRC F-7 (MiG-21)
RECCE 1 sqn with 15* Reims-Cessna 337 *Lynx*
TRG/RECCE/LIAISON 1 sqn with 16 SF-260 *Genet* (9 -C, 5* -W, 2* TP)
TPT 1 sqn with 6 BN-2, 11 C-212-200 (1 VIP)
HEL 1 sqn with 24 SA-319 (armed/liaison), 1 sqn with 10 AB-412, 4 AS-532UL (VIP)

Forces Abroad

UN AND PEACEKEEPING
ANGOLA (UNOMA): 664 incl 20 Obs plus 22 civ pol

Paramilitary 21,800

ZIMBABWE REPUBLIC POLICE FORCE 19,500 (incl Air Wg)
POLICE SUPPORT UNIT 2,300

The International Arms Trade

The international arms trade grew by some 8% in 1996 in real terms from $36.9 billion to $39.9bn, following a 13% increase in 1995, according to *The Military Balance* estimates. A combination of factors have contributed to the growth following seven years of continuous decline since 1987 – notably unpredictable tensions in North-east Asia and the Middle East, favourable oil prices for the Gulf states enabling them to finance large orders placed after the 1990–91 Gulf War, and sustained modernisation demand in East Asia and, more recently, South America.

The top three suppliers (the US, the UK and France) all recorded large increases in defence exports in 1996, the first two mostly as a result of higher combat aircraft deliveries. US military aerospace exports increased from $7.8bn in 1995 to $10.8bn in 1996, with new combat aircraft deliveries rising from $228m to $3.1bn. The UK's aerospace exports grew from $6.3bn in 1995 (over 40% higher than in 1994) to $8bn in 1996. Saudi Arabia's defence imports in 1996 were higher than those of any other country, nearly three times those of Egypt the next largest importer. Japan, the UK, China, Taiwan, South Korea and Kuwait imported defence equipment worth more than $1bn, while Turkey's and Israel's defence imports were each worth almost $1bn. Thailand ($700m), Singapore ($400m) and Malaysia ($350m) were again large weapons importers in 1996, while Indonesia's arms imports increased sharply from about $200m to some $700m.

A primary source for *The Military Balance* arms trade statistics is *World Military Expenditures and Arms Transfers 1996* (Washington DC: Arms Control and Disarmament Agency, 1997). A primary source for 1996 figures is *Conventional Arms Transfers to Developing Nations 1989–1996* (Washington DC: Congressional Research Service, 1997). Where IISS figures differ from those of ACDA and CRS, it is because *The Military Balance* uses figures released by national governments and, in some cases, IISS estimates.

Table 39 Country suppliers to the international arms trade, 1992–1996

$10m–$50m	$50m–$100m	$100m–$200m	$200m–$1bn	$1bn–$10bn	$10bn+
Chile	Australia	Argentina	Belarus	Canada	US
Denmark	Indonesia	Austria	Belgium	China	
Egypt	Norway	Bulgaria	Brazil	France	
Finland	Romania	Poland	Czech Rep	Germany	
Greece	Singapore	Portugal	FRY	Israel	
Hungary	South Korea		Iran	Russia	
India	Turkey		Italy	UK	
Japan			Netherlands		
Jordan			North Korea		
Kazakstan			South Africa		
Kyrgyzstan			Spain		
Malaysia			Sweden		
Mexico			Switzerland		
Pakistan			Ukraine		
Saudi Arabia					
Taiwan					
Uzbekistan					
Zimbabwe					
Market share (%)					
0–1%	1–2%	2–5%	5–10%	35–45%	40–50%

Note Ca defence exports were US$1.1bn ($800m to US) in 1995 and $1.6bn ($1.2bn to US) in 1996. Ca exports to the US are excluded from *The Military Balance* figures owing to the unavailability of data prior to 1995.

Sources National governments; Arms Control and Disarmament Agency (ACDA), Washington DC

Table 40 Value of arms deliveries and market share, 1987–1996

(constant 1995 US$m)

	Total	USSR/Russia	%	Warsaw Pact excl. USSR	%	US	%	UK	%	France	%	Germany	%	Total Western Europe	%	China	%	Israel	%	Others	%
1987	84,892	29,900	35.2	5,280	6.2	22,650	26.7	7,055	8.3	7,640	9.0	2,070	2.4	21,188	25.0	2,460	2.9	1,400	1.6	2,014	2.4
1988	77,121	27,470	35.6	4,400	5.7	17,480	22.7	5,980	7.8	8,017	10.4	2,250	2.9	20,515	26.6	3,750	4.9	1,530	2.0	1,976	2.6
1989	69,452	20,975	30.2	2,490	3.6	19,050	27.4	8,027	11.6	9,266	13.3	1,560	2.2	21,042	30.3	3,240	4.7	1,580	2.3	1,075	1.5
1990	59,799	17,153	28.7	950	1.6	16,320	27.3	8,448	14.1	7,867	13.2	1,950	3.3	20,414	34.1	2,300	3.8	1,630	2.7	1,032	1.7
1991	42,579	6,850	16.1	530	1.2	15,910	37.4	6,194	14.5	4,470	10.5	2,650	6.2	15,032	35.3	1,550	3.6	1,710	4.0	997	2.3
1992	35,909	2,690	7.5	n.a.	n.a.	14,200	39.5	5,304	14.8	4,420	12.3	1,800	5.0	14,332	39.9	1,180	3.3	1,580	4.4	1,927	5.4
1993	35,591	3,250	9.1	n.a.	n.a.	15,940	44.8	4,895	13.8	3,067	8.6	1,562	4.4	11,554	32.5	1,150	3.2	1,540	4.3	2,157	6.1
1994	32,699	2,786	8.5	n.a.	n.a.	13,800	42.2	4,756	14.5	3,432	10.5	1,440	4.4	11,778	36.0	740	2.3	1,420	4.3	2,175	6.7
1995	36,870	3,335	9.6	n.a.	n.a.	15,600	42.3	7,419	20.1	3,806	10.3	1,383	3.8	14,091	38.2	630	1.7	1,240	3.4	1,774	4.8
1996	39,863	3,435	8.6	n.a.	n.a.	17,000	42.6	8,800	22.1	5,629	14.1	657	1.6	16,391	41.1	584	1.5	1,300	3.3	1,153	2.9

Notes [1] Western Europe comprises EU countries plus Norway and Switzerland
[2] 1996 figures are provisional
Sources National governments; ACDA

Table 41 Regional distribution of international arms deliveries, 1987–1996

(constant 1995 US$m)

	NATO and W. Europe	%	Eastern Europe	%	USSR/CIS	%	Middle East & N. Africa	%	East Asia	%	South Asia	%	Latin America	%	Sub-Saharan Africa	%	Austra-lasia	%
1987	15,142	17.8	6,867	8.1	1,812	2.1	31,862	37.5	10,071	11.9	6,291	7.4	5,100	6.0	6,511	7.7	1,236	1.5
1988	15,946	20.7	4,994	6.5	1,498	1.9	25,277	32.8	9,793	12.7	7,802	10.1	4,857	6.3	5,331	6.9	1,623	2.1
1989	15,519	22.3	3,918	5.6	1,078	1.6	24,233	34.9	7,539	10.9	8,987	12.9	3,547	5.1	3,301	4.8	1,330	1.9
1990	13,613	22.8	3,091	5.2	115	0.2	23,142	38.7	6,825	11.4	7,337	12.3	2,712	4.5	1,931	3.2	1,034	1.7
1991	13,007	30.5	271	0.6	100	0.2	15,845	37.2	6,136	14.4	3,950	9.3	1,729	4.1	696	1.6	845	2.0
1992	10,600	29.5	250	0.7	100	0.3	15,672	43.6	6,007	16.7	1,392	3.9	904	2.5	575	1.6	409	1.1
1993	9,753	27.4	1,415	4.0	100	0.3	14,487	40.7	6,664	18.7	1,053	3.0	756	2.1	592	1.7	771	2.2
1994	9,311	28.5	1,300	4.0	92	0.3	11,883	36.3	6,993	21.4	875	2.7	775	2.4	1,040	3.2	431	1.3
1995	8,635	23.4	835	2.3	350	0.9	14,385	39.0	8,535	23.1	1,330	3.6	1,540	4.2	300	0.8	960	2.6
1996	8,500	22.0	1,200	3.1	300	0.8	15,276	39.5	8,900	23.0	1,390	3.6	1,600	4.1	750	1.9	732	1.9

Note 1996 figures are provisional
Sources National governments; ACDA; US Congressional Research Service (CRS), Washington DC

Analyses *and* Tables

Table 42 Deliveries by other major arms suppliers, 1987–1996

(constant 1995 US$m)

	Italy	Sweden and other W. Europe	Canada	Brazil	South Africa	Ukraine	Czech Republic
1987	938	3,484	938	841	200	n.a.	n.a.
1988	599	3,668	905	874	162	n.a.	n.a.
1989	324	1,865	629	144	240	n.a.	n.a.
1990	230	1,919	718	69	200	n.a.	n.a.
1991	332	1,386	635	88	180	n.a.	n.a.
1992	398	2,410	1,291	194	163	0	n.a.
1993	367	1,663	786	105	228	300	220
1994	350	1,800	750	195	236	200	308
1995	340	1,143	292	200	272	200	150
1996	200	1,105	447	50	150	200	100

Notes [1] 1996 figures are provisional
[2] Ca defence exports were US$1.1bn ($800m to US) in 1995 and $1.6bn ($1.2bn to US) in 1996. Ca exports to the US are excluded from *The Military Balance* figures owing to the unavailability of data prior to 1995.
Sources National governments; ACDA; CRS

Table 43 Arms deliveries to South Asia, 1987–1996

(constant 1995 US$m)

	Myanmar	India	Pakistan	Afghanistan	Bangladesh	Sri Lanka
1987	26	3,883	440	1,812	65	65
1988	25	3,870	574	3,246	62	25
1989	24	3,595	659	4,553	144	12
1990	126	2,069	1,063	4,022	46	11
1991	431	1,022	243	2,100	88	66
1992	161	699	484	0	43	5
1993	136	283	577	5	31	21
1994	103	320	297	21	31	103
1995	140	450	500	20	60	160
1996	150	500	410	60	70	200

Note 1996 figures are provisional
Sources National governments; ACDA; CRS; IISS

Table 44 NATO and West European arms trade, 1987–1996

(constant 1995 US$m)

	Intra-Europe	European exports to US	US exports to Europe	Canada imports	Turkey imports	Total	US trade surplus with Europe
1987	6,065	1,424	5,000	1,100	1,553	15,142	3,576
1988	6,525	1,748	5,000	1,300	1,373	15,946	3,252
1989	5,262	1,019	7,000	800	1,438	15,519	5,982
1990	5,199	1,035	5,000	1,000	1,379	13,613	3,966
1991	5,631	1,050	4,000	1,000	1,326	13,007	2,950
1992	5,163	861	2,800	700	1,076	10,600	1,940
1993	4,011	734	2,900	850	1,258	9,753	2,166
1994	3,969	564	2,900	750	1,128	9,311	2,336
1995	3,535	500	3,100	583	917	8,635	2,600

Note Ca defence exports were US$1.1bn ($800m to US) in 1995 and $1.6bn ($1.2bn to US) in 1996. Ca exports to the US are excluded from *The Military Balance* figures owing to the unavailability of data prior to 1995.
Sources National governments; ACDA; CRS; European Commission

Table 45 Arms deliveries to the Middle East and North Africa, 1987–1996

(constant 1995 US$m)

	Saudi Arabia	Iraq	Iran	Egypt	Israel	Syria	UAE	Kuwait	Libya	Algeria
1987	9,327	7,637	2,200	2,330	2,977	2,589	181	259	777	906
1988	7,869	5,214	3,246	1,124	1,498	1,623	162	162	1,186	1,061
1989	8,689	4,848	2,157	1,048	1,110	1,318	1,018	288	1,318	749
1990	9,573	4,340	2,184	919	690	1,092	1,724	368	425	356
1991	10,050	0	1,768	912	663	884	387	320	453	144
1992	10,369	0	914	1,183	861	409	366	1,049	86	150
1993	8,368	0	1,153	1,468	1,153	283	482	970	80	130
1994	7,449	0	400	1,230	615	141	410	828	80	144
1995	8,660	0	500	1,900	600	170	875	900	80	230
1996	9,050	0	400	2,300	900	90	650	1,036	80	250

Note 1996 figures are provisional
Sources National governments; ACDA; CRS; IISS

Table 46 Arms deliveries to East Asia, 1987–1996

(constant 1995 US$m)

	Japan	Taiwan	ROK	DPRK	Vietnam	China	Thailand	Malaysia	Singapore	Indonesia	Philippines
1987	1,553	1,891	906	544	2,459	841	557	91	401	337	91
1988	1,465	1,373	812	1,249	1,873	537	698	50	474	350	112
1989	2,037	697	697	719	1,558	599	360	84	216	252	120
1990	1,714	723	1,224	230	1,264	345	333	34	287	345	126
1991	1,524	1,179	1,216	99	221	332	635	122	420	33	155
1992	1,291	886	1,200	32	20	1,398	398	140	237	54	151
1993	2,738	1,048	1,327	5	20	603	147	283	136	94	63
1994	2,242	1,025	1,435	92	82	267	400	871	236	51	92
1995	2,300	1,200	1,500	100	200	725	1,100	750	200	170	90
1996	2,000	1,300	1,100	100	200	1,500	700	350	400	700	100

Note 1996 figures are provisional
Sources National governments; ACDA; CRS; IISS

With the Czech Republic, Hungary and Poland as NATO's next new members, the first stage of the NATO enlargement debate is over. The debate about its real cost, however, is only just beginning. Of the two, this second issue is likely to be much more contentious. This is not only because the proliferation of cost studies and the range of potential costs make it difficult to come to a settled conclusion. A number of assumptions about how the Alliance should be reconfigured not just to create new capabilities, but also to shift the burden of total NATO expenditure significantly towards the European allies, lie behind the different costings currently available.

COSTING NATO ENLARGEMENT

The actual cost of NATO enlargement is unknowable. It will cost as much or as little as the countries concerned want it to. It will depend on two key variables: first, on what the allies agree is required in terms of additional military capability; and second – and much more significantly – on what can be afforded in extra resources over and above existing defence-spending levels. While it makes some sense to attempt to estimate the cost according to projected requirements – additional reinforcement capacity for current allies, force projection and modernisation for new members – the severe restraints on defence budgets cannot be ignored. So far, no study has been undertaken of the allies' and new members' ability to pay. Nor has there been any sign that NATO's European members are ready to assume a heavier share of the burden.

The reassuring rhetoric about enlargement costs is that they are 'manageable' and 'affordable'. In a narrow sense this is true. NATO is essentially a coordinating body. There is no compulsion in its system. Its funding is therefore the result of its members' willingness to finance adequately the programmes they agree to. According to long-standing cost formulae, agreed by consensus, all current members pay into a series of common budgets which enable the Alliance to function as an organisation. The most important are the military budget, which covers the costs of running its internationally staffed headquarters and command structure, and the Security Investment Programme, which pays for the common infrastructure, such as communications, required for operational interoperability and cohesion between allies (see Table 47 for 1996 cost contributions).

However, by far the heaviest burden falls on national budgets. Each NATO member pays directly for the capabilities and military personnel it makes available to the Alliance. The common budgets only bear the costs of projects over and above those which could reasonably be expected to be covered from national resources. Otherwise, each member pays for what it commits to NATO. The total defence expenditure of member-states amounted to US$470.7 billion in 1996. The same year, contributions to NATO's common budgets amounted to $1.8bn – 0.38% of total Alliance defence expenditures.

Since the end of the Cold War, NATO has been driven by supply considerations, rather than by requirements. Defence budgets have fallen dramatically as individual allies have taken the initiative to reduce and restructure their forces in line with the diminishing threat. While acknowledging the need to restructure for new missions and force projection, there has been a slow shift towards investment for the required new capabilities. At their Defence Planning meeting in December 1996, NATO Defence Ministers noted that budgetary constraints were delaying the implementation of plans for modernising forces. Areas for improvement include: deployable command, control and communications systems; strategic mobility; sustainability; ground-based air defence; and strategic surveillance and intelligence systems.

Table 47 **NATO common-funded budgets, 1996**								
(US$m)	Civil budget	Military budget	Security & Investment	NATO AEW&C	Total	% Common Funding	1996 Defence Spending	% Defence Spending
Belgium	5.0	19.5	35.8	7.7	68.0	3.8	4,278	0.01
Canada	10.2	38.3	34.5	21.3	104.3	5.9	8,564	0.02
Denmark	2.9	11.5	28.7	4.5	47.6	2.7	3,041	0.01
France	30.1	29.3	37.1	n.a.	96.5	5.4	47,190	0.02
Germany	28.4	106.4	198.6	63.5	396.9	22.3	39,240	0.08
Greece	0.7	2.6	7.2	1.4	11.9	0.7	5,580	0.00
Iceland	0.1	0.3	0.0	n.a.	0.4	0.0	0.0	0.00
Italy	10.5	40.5	65.2	16.4	132.6	7.4	23,779	0.03
Luxembourg	0.2	0.6	1.7	0.2	2.7	0.2	135	0.00
Netherlands	5.0	19.5	39.8	8.5	72.8	4.1	8,082	0.02
Norway	2.0	7.9	24.4	3.3	37.6	2.1	3,766	0.01
Portugal	1.2	4.3	2.4	1.6	9.5	0.5	2,913	0.00
Spain	6.4	7.2	7.2	n.a.	20.8	1.2	8,617	0.00
Turkey	2.9	10.9	7.7	3.7	25.2	1.4	7,000	0.01
United Kingdom	34.3	120.4	90.4	0.2	245.3	13.8	33,453	0.05
United States	42.6	165.2	206.8	93.7	508.3	28.5	271,417	0.11
Total	**182.5**	**584.4**	**787.5**	**226.0**	**1,780.4**	**100.0**	**467,056**	**0.38**

There has been zero real growth for the past four years in NATO's common-funded budgets. In that period, these budgets have had to absorb significant short-term costs for operations in Bosnia, thus postponing other necessary long-term investments. The Security Investment Programme has almost halved from over $1.3bn in 1989 to $787 million in 1996. According to the Defence Ministers, 'common-funding levels now appear to have stabilised'. They did not point, however, to a prospective increase, even though over the next few years those budgets will have to cope with the common infrastructure demands of new projects such as the Combined Joint Task Force (CJTF) concept. The new NATO Command Structure, when it is agreed, may also call on additional common funding in the short term as international military headquarters are closed or relocated. In the longer term, NATO expects the new structure to reduce costs.

COST STUDIES SO FAR

The main studies in the public domain – most notably by researchers at RAND, the US Congressional Budget Office (CBO) and the US administration – take the requirement-driven approach.[1] While the 'headline' costs seem to have diminished with each successive study, this is not because the methodologies have become more refined and the figures more accurate over time. Each study demonstrates that costings are highly dependent on the assumptions made, or the outcome preferred.

RAND Researchers' Study

Asmus, Kugler and Larrabee assumed a limited initial enlargement to the four Visegrad countries – the Czech Republic, Hungary, Poland and Slovakia. They defined a spectrum of possible defence postures and calculated their associated budgetary costs. Over a 10–15-year period, the cost for the entire enlarged Alliance could be as low as $10bn or as high as $110bn, depending on the posture chosen. The authors preferred their 'joint-power projection' option, employing both ground and air capabilities to reinforce new NATO members, which would cost between $30 and $52bn over 10–15 years. The authors settle on a $42bn package – equivalent to 1–2% of NATO's current defence spending – to be spent largely on developing a force-projection capability of ten fighter wings and five divisions.

For current members, the cost is not seen as marginal or additional. Rather, apart from (undefined) modest spending increases, the costs can be accommodated through 'reprogramming'. The researchers point out that NATO, in its central and north-west regions, still has 25 mobilisable divisions and over 1,800 combat aircraft – more than sufficient, in their view, to meet future defence needs in the region. Also, in relation to what the Alliance spends on its entire European defence posture – current European member-states spend $160bn annually – the additional costs to current members are assessed to be 'small' and 'affordable'. NATO common infrastructure funds would pick up 20% of the cost and would thus have to be doubled. The burden on the new members would be heavier. With no scope to reprogramme or cut, these new members would have to find an additional $8bn over 10–15 years (19% of the $42bn package) to pay their share.

The RAND researchers' approach is based on NATO's simultaneous enlargement and internal reform. It assumes that the security situation in Europe is more than manageable within existing resources. Enlargement offers the opportunity to create the joint power-projection capabilities the authors consider necessary to manage crises beyond NATO and European borders.

Congressional Budget Office

The CBO study also assumed enlargement to the Visegrad four. It looked at a range of options for mounting a credible defence of new members, using Russian capabilities as a yardstick. The criticisms of the study for being threat driven, or unrealistically 'worst case', are misplaced. The CBO considered a range of options for fulfilling the Alliance's commitment: to defend new members against external attack. Table 48 sets out the incremental options and estimated cost from 1996–2010.

Table 48 **Costs of military options to expand NATO**

(1997 US$bn)	Costs to the US	Cost to NATO allies	Cost to new members	Total cost
1 Enhance Visegrad defence and facilitate NATO supplemental reinforcement	4.8	13.8	42.0	60.6
2 Project NATO air power eastward to defend the Visegrad states	4.6	10.3	3.6	18.6
3 Project power eastward with NATO ground forces based in Germany	3.6	20.3	6.2	30.1
4 Move stocks of prepositioned equipment to Visegrad states	0.3	0.9	0.1	1.3
5 Station limited number of forces forward	5.5	8.7	0.0	14.2
Total	**18.8**	**54.0**	**51.9**	**124.1**

Notes [1] The costs shown for options 2 and 3 are incremental increases above those of option 1

[2] Costs were estimated for 1996–2010

Source Congressional Budget Office, Washington DC

The CBO's middle option of projecting power eastward is costed at $109.3bn at 1997 prices. Although similar in concept to RAND's preferred joint-power-projection scenario, it would cost just over twice as much. This is mainly because of the high costs it attributes to enhancing new members' own defences to achieve NATO standards. The CBO does not speculate as to whether the costs can be met from reprogramming and savings from existing defence budgets. It assumes that existing expenditure goes to valid programmes. Thus the costs are presented as incremental or additional outlays.

US Administration Report to Congress

This report is an authoritative statement of US objectives in steering the enlargement process through the critical Senate ratification debate and beyond. It follows the RAND researchers' logic and methodology. It assumes a small group (implicitly three) of non-specified countries join the Alliance by 1999, no significant threat from Russia and reliance on reinforcement capabilities as the basis of Article 5 defence for new members. Like the RAND researchers' study, the US administration argues that many of the necessary enlargement costs are independent of expansion. Current members are already restructuring their forces to become more mobile and deployable as part of NATO's overall adaptation to new missions. New members would have to modernise in any case.

This report does not discuss options, but sets out a blueprint: an initial capability to defend new members by 2001; and a build-up to a mature capability for reinforcement and force projection by 2009. For costing existing shortfalls in Alliance reinforcement capability, the US has used a notional force-projection package of four divisions and six NATO fighter wings. This is smaller than Asmus, Kugler and Larrabee's preferred option, thus accounting for a large part of the lower price. The total package would cost $27–35bn for the period 1997–2009. The breakdown is as follows:

- **$9–12bn** 'Direct' enlargement costs funded by current and new members to ensure that their forces are interoperable – such as extending and adapting NATO headquarters, communications and air-defence systems. These steps are only being taken because NATO is enlarging.
- **$10–13bn** New member costs for military restructuring. Such modernisation would, according to the report, be necessary in any case, and should not be attributable to enlargement.
- **$8–10bn** Existing member costs for increasing reinforcement capabilities, to which they are in any case pledged by NATO's 1991 Strategic Concept.

Of these costs, the US expects to pay only about $1.5–2bn, or $150–200m a year from 1999–2000, of the direct costs. The US does not expect to pay for improving its regional reinforcement capabilities: as the report notes, 'the United States already has the capability, unmatched anywhere in the world, for such operations'. The implication is clear: Europe pays.

NATO Study

NATO undertook an internal study of the impact on its common budgets of accepting one large country and one small one. It assessed the cost of such expansion at $5bn over 10 years. Shared between 16 current members and two or three new ones, $500m additional a year does indeed appear 'manageable'. However, the US is reported to have rejected this figure, as it did not include the cost to each individual ally of restructuring their forces for reinforcement. To persuade the US Senate to ratify the accession of three new NATO members, the US administration evidently believes that its allies will have to agree to specific national commitments beyond the increases necessary to pay for common infrastructure.

AFFORDABILITY

There is, as yet, no agreed Alliance estimate of costs or statement of requirements. The US administration's report to Congress is, as it acknowledges, a US view alone.

The problem with such a goal-oriented approach is that, while it is clear about the required outcome, it is unlikely to be accurate about actual achievement. The real outcome, and thus the real cost, will be determined more by what the allies, new and old, are able to afford, than by what the US expects or regards as a military requirement. This creates a major problem. There is, as yet, no Alliance-wide agreement on the requirements of an enlarged NATO other than that it would rely on reinforcement rather than the forward stationing of troops to extend collective defence eastward. At the July 1997 Madrid summit, NATO's leaders called for a 'concrete analysis of the resource implications of the forthcoming enlargement'. They nevertheless declared themselves 'confident that, in line with the security environment of the Europe of today, Alliance costs associated with the integration of new members will be manageable and that the resources necessary to meet those costs will be provided'. There is probably less to the Allies' confidence on costs than meets the eye. Not yet committed to funding specific military requirements, European allies will assume that the costs can be accommodated within existing defence budgets. Both they and the new allies will spend as much on enlargement as they believe they can afford. In a benign security environment, some feel there is no urgency. And, in a Europe struggling towards economic convergence and monetary union, there is no scope to increase defence budgets without further painful reductions in social and welfare programmes.

The omens are not good for burden-sharing. Canada has already stated that it is ready to spend only $5–7.2m in total on enlargement over 12 years. It contests the estimate of $32.4–42.5m, which is calculated to be its share under the US administration study.[2] The UK is also reportedly questioning the US assessment. According to British officials, the UK already has a force optimised for operations outside the country. The implication is that its armed forces will not need radical restructuring to meet NATO's future defence needs, and enlargement costs would be containable within the existing budget, which in any case is under review and pressure from the new Labour government. France remains outside NATO's integrated command structure, so will not be participating in defence planning or contributing to the Alliance's common military budgets. Paris has also announced further reductions in defence spending to help meet the criteria of the 1992 Maastricht Treaty on European Union. French President Jacques Chirac has said that 'France will not pay any additional costs for NATO enlargement'. Germany, equally, is in no position to spend more and in no mood to reprogramme radically to create a major force-projection capability for the first time. Bonn prefers gradual adjustments over an extended time period.

As for new members, their ability to pay must be even more in doubt – despite the optimistic US assumption that 'they will acquire greater flexibility to fund ... as their economies successfully reform and grow'.[3] In a semi-official study, Polish economists estimate that Poland could accommodate an anticipated contribution of 2% to common budgets, or about $35–40m per annum.[4] However, the general modernisation of the country's defence system will involve costs 'far exceeding the current budget of the Ministry of Defence'.[5] Because of differing methodologies, it is not possible to compare Polish with US estimates. The US appears to assume higher contributions to an increased NATO common budget than the Polish study. In any case, there would have to be steady, real growth in the new members' defence budgets and increases in the defence burden if the scale of outlays envisaged by the US is to be met.

CONCLUSION

Funding NATO enlargement is more likely to be driven by what is affordable than by what is required. As various past initiatives have underlined – notably the Conventional Defence Improvement initiative of the mid-1980s – NATO members often agree to ambitious short-term projects, but allow their implementation to slip according to the resources available. Implementing NATO enlargement is likely to follow a similar pattern.

New NATO members will have to order their priorities to make the best use of the money likely to be available. First, they need to ensure interoperability with their new allies, which requires expenditure on command-and-control systems and communications – as well as training, including language training, and exercises. They also need to evolve their doctrines and long-term defence strategy to match NATO's new roles and the kinds of operations on which they are most likely to be deployed. This step leads to the acquisition of major new weapon systems, such as combat aircraft and armoured vehicles, which should be the second priority. Since the operational life of such systems is normally decades, there should be no rush to buy them. They can be afforded, in any case, only if the new members' economies continue their steady rate of growth. The new members have a greater opportunity to be more radical than existing NATO members in their new acquisition programmes to ensure that their armed forces are light and mobile enough to deal with the challenges they are most likely to face – rather then be equipped for yesterday's wars. Most of the present Alliance members still have a long way to go, and will have to spend more on restructuring and re-equipping themselves for likely future NATO operations.

Notes

[1] Ronald D. Asmus, Richard L. Kugler and F. Stephen Larrabee, 'What Will NATO Enlargement Cost?', *Survival*, vol. 38, no. 3, Autumn 1996, pp. 5–26; *The Costs of Expanding The NATO Alliance* (Washington DC: CBO, March 1996); 'Report to The Congress on The Enlargement of The North Atlantic Treaty Organisation: Rationale, Benefits, Costs, and Implications', released by the Bureau of European and Canadian Affairs, US Department of State, Washington DC, 24 February 1997.

[2] Prime Minister Jean Chrétien quoted by Agence France Presse, 7 July 1997.

[3] 'Report to Congress', p. 16.

[4] 'Estimated Cost of NATO Enlargement: A Contribution to the Debate', Polish Euro-Atlantic Association, February 1997 (foreword by Janusz Onyszkiewicz).

[5] *Ibid.*, p. 24.

Analyses *and* Tables

Peacekeeping Operations

UNITED NATIONS

On 1 August 1997, the United Nations was maintaining 16 peacekeeping operations around the world. These missions involve the deployment of 20,527 troops world-wide from 70 countries. After the final withdrawal of troops with the UN Observer Mission in Angola (UNOMA), due by the end of November 1997, this number will fall to just below 19,000. The leading troop suppliers to the UN's 1997 peacekeeping activities are shown below. The UN peacekeeping budget for the year to 30 June 1997 is $1.3 billion. For the year to 30 June 1998, the latest budgetary projection is $1.1bn. UN peacekeeping outlays in 1996 were $1.8bn, down from $3.3bn in 1995, $3.4bn in 1994 and $3.1bn in 1993. Arrears in payments of contributions to the UN peacekeeping budget amounted to $1.7bn at 30 June 1997, of which the US owed 58%, Russia 14% and Ukraine 12%.

Table 49 Leading troop contributors to UN operations (as at 1 August 1997)

Country	Strength	Country	Strength	Country	Strength
Pakistan	1,325	Finland	914	Zimbabwe	742
Poland	1,122	Austria	900	Ireland	740
Russia	1,057	US	848	Norway	723
Bangladesh	1,042	Belgium	829	Nepal	669
Canada	1,026	Ghana	761	India	649

Table 50 Leading financial contributors to UN operations, 1997

(US$m)	Assessment[1]	%	Arrears[2]		Assessment[1]	%	Arrears[2]
US	316	25.0	970	Brazil	20	1.6	10
Japan	195	15.4	41	Netherlands	20	1.6	—
Germany	114	9.0	17	Australia	19	1.5	—
France	99	7.8	5	Sweden	14	1.1	1
UK	82	6.5	—	Ukraine	14	1.1	203
Russia	68	5.4	234	Belgium	13	1.0	1
Italy	66	5.2	3	Sub-total	1,108	87.7	1,489
Canada	39	3.1	—	Other	155	12.3	185
Spain	30	2.4	3	Total	1,263	100.0	1,674

Note   [1] Figures for 1997 assessment are annualised figures based on IISS calculations from UN mission-cost projections
        [2] As at 30 June 1997

UNITED NATIONS STAND-BY ARRANGEMENTS

Under the UN Stand-by system, introduced in 1992, individual member-states agree to make resources available in their home country for specific tasks. The guidelines for response times are:

- seven days for individual personnel;
- 15 days for units involved in the reception phase of an operation; and
- 30 days for other units.

The resources involved are: **military units** (e.g., infantry, combat engineers, military police and air transport units); **specialised personnel** (such as medical doctors, bomb disposal and civil engineers); and **materiel and equipment**.

By 2 June 1997, 66 countries were willing to participate in the system, the latest being China. The list at that date was:

Argentina[1]	Australia[2]	Austria[3]	Bangladesh[2]	Belarus[1]
Belgium[2]	Bolivia[3]	Botswana	Brazil	Bulgaria[2]
Canada[2]	Chad[1]	China	Czech Republic[2]	Denmark[3]
Egypt	Estonia	Finland[1]	France[2]	Georgia
Germany[1]	Ghana[3]	Greece	Guatemala[2]	Hungary[1]
India[1]	Indonesia	Ireland[1]	Italy[3]	Jordan[3]
Kazakstan	Kenya	Kyrgyzstan	Malaysia[3]	Moldova
Myanmar[1]	Nepal[2]	Netherlands[2]	New Zealand[2]	Nigeria
Norway[1]	Pakistan[2]	Poland[2]	Portugal[2]	Republic of Korea[3]
Romania	Russian Federation[1]	Senegal[1]	Singapore[3]	Slovak Republic[1]
Slovenia	Spain[1]	Sri Lanka[1]	Sudan	Sweden[1]
Syria[2]	Tanzania	Tunisia	Turkey[1]	Ukraine[1]
UK[2]	Uruguay[2]	USA[1]	Uzbekistan	Zambia
Zimbabwe[1]				

Notes [1] Member-states which have provided lists of capabilities = 47

[2] Member-states which have provided data and technical information = 25

[3] Member-states which have signed a Memorandum of Understanding with the UN formalising their commitment = 8

From data and technical information provided, and from UN estimates, stand-by personnel resources available to the UN as at 2 June 1997 were:

Inf	HQ Spt	Comms	Engr	Log	Air	Health	Other
50,191	3,124	4,055	7,596	10,150	2,750	4,800	4,405
Estimated Total 87,071							

Data and information on the principal UN and other long-term (lasting at least a year) peacekeeping missions are given below.

United Nations Truce Supervision Organisation (UNTSO)

Mission UNTSO was established in 1948 to assist the Mediator and Truce Commission supervise the truce in Palestine. Since then, UNTSO has performed various tasks, including supervising the General Armistice Agreements of 1949 and the cease-fire in the Suez Canal area and the Golan Heights following the Arab–Israeli Six Day War of June 1967. UNTSO assists and cooperates with the UN Disengagement Observer Force (UNDOF) on the Golan Heights in the Israeli–Syrian sector, and with the UN Interim Force in Lebanon (UNIFIL) in the Israeli–Lebanese sector. UNTSO also has a presence in the Egyptian–Israeli sector in the Sinai, and maintains offices in Beirut and Gaza.
Headquarters Government House, Jerusalem.
Strength 154 military observers, supported by international and locally recruited civilian staff.

Contributors Arg, Aus, A, Be, Ca, Chl, PRC, Da, Ea, SF, Fr, Irl, It, Nl, NZ, No, RF, Swe, CH, US.
Cost *1995* $28m *1996* $27m *1997* $27. Total cost to date: $491m.

United Nations Disengagement Observer Force (UNDOF)

Mission UNDOF was established in 1974 after the 1973 Middle East war to maintain the cease-fire between Israel and Syria; supervise the disengagement of Israeli and Syrian forces; and supervise the areas of separation and limitation, as provided in the Agreement on Disengagement of 31 May 1974. The situation in the Israeli–Syrian sector has remained quiet and there have been no serious incidents.
Location Syrian Golan Heights.
Headquarters Damascus.
Strength 1,047 troops, supported by approximately 35 international and 80 locally recruited civilian staff.
Contributors A, Ca, J, Pl.
Cost *1995* $32m *1996* $32m *1997* $38m. Total cost to date: $681m.

United Nations Interim Force in Lebanon (UNIFIL)

Mission UNIFIL was established in March 1978 to confirm the withdrawal of Israeli forces from southern Lebanon; restore international peace and security; and help the Lebanese government maintain effective authority in the area. UNIFIL has, however, been prevented from fully implementing its mandate. Israeli forces continue to occupy parts of southern Lebanon, where they and their local auxiliary in turn remain targets for attack by groups resisting the occupation.
Location Southern Lebanon.
Headquarters Naqoura.
Current Strength 4,470 troops, plus approximately 140 international and 190 local civilian staff.
Contributors Fji, SF, Fr, Gha, Irl, It, N, No, Pl.
Cost *1995* $135m *1996* $135m *1997* $121m. Total cost to date: $2.7bn.

United Nations Iraq–Kuwait Observer Force (UNIKOM)

Mission UNIKOM was established in April 1991 as part of the cease-fire arrangement at the end of the Gulf War to monitor the Iraq–Kuwait border area in the Khor Abdullah and demilitarised zones. The demilitarised zone extends 10km into Iraq and 5km into Kuwait from the agreed boundary between the two countries. UNIKOM's function is to deter violations of the inter-state boundary by direct action, and observe and report hostile or potentially hostile actions.
Location Iraqi–Kuwaiti border area.
Headquarters Umm Qasr, Iraq.
Strength 1,093.
Contributors Units from Bng (infantry), Da (logistic support) and No (medical); Observers from Arg, A, Bng, Ca, PRC, Da, Fji, SF, Fr, Ge, Gha, Gr, Hu, Ind, Indo, Irl, It, Kya, Mal, Nga, Pak, Pl, R, RF, Sen, Sgp, Swe, Th, Tu, UK, Ury, US, Ve.
Cost *1995* $66m *1996* $62m *1997* $50m. Total cost to date: $353m.

United Nations Peacekeeping Force in Cyprus (UNFICYP)

Mission UNFICYP was established in March 1964 to prevent a recurrence of fighting between the

Greek Cypriot and Turkish Cypriot communities and to help restore and maintain law and order and peaceful conditions. Following a *de facto* cease-fire on 16 August 1974, UNFICYP's mandate was expanded to include supervising the cease-fire and maintaining a buffer zone between the lines of the Cyprus National Guard and the Turkish and Turkish Cypriot forces.

Location Cyprus.

Headquarters Nicosia.

Strength 1,235 troops and support personnel, 35 civilian police; there is also a provision for some 370 internationally and locally recruited civilian staff.

Contributors Arg, Aus, A, Ca, SF, Hu, Irl, UK.

Cost *1995* $43m *1996* $44m *1997* $46m (including voluntary contributions by Cyprus of one-third of the total cost and by Greece of $7m) Total cost to date: $862m.

United Nations Military Observer Group in India and Pakistan (UNMOGIP)

Mission UNMOGIP was established in January 1949 to supervise the cease-fire between India and Pakistan in the state of Jammu and Kashmir. Following the 1972 India–Pakistan agreement defining a Line of Control in Kashmir, India claimed that UNMOGIP's mandate had lapsed. Pakistan, however, did not agree. Consequently, the UN Secretary-General has declared that UNMOGIP's mission can only be terminated by the UN Security Council. In the absence of such a decision, UNMOGIP has been maintained with the same mandate and functions.

Location The cease-fire line between India and Pakistan in the state of Jammu and Kashmir.

Headquarters Rawalpindi (November–April); Srinagar (May–October).

Strength 44 military observers, supported by international and locally recruited civilian staff.

Contributors Be, Chl, Da, SF, It, ROK, Swe, Ury.

Cost *1995* $6m *1996* $7m *1997* $7m. Total cost to date: $107m.

United Nations Observer Mission in Angola (UNOMA)

Mission On 1 July 1997, UNOMA took over from the United Nations Angola Verification Mission (UNAVEM) III to continue the process of restoring peace on the basis of the accords signed on 31 May 1991, the Lusaka Protocol signed on 20 November 1994, and relevant Security Council resolutions. The main objectives of UNOMA are to:

- provide meditation for the Angolan parties in completing the peace process;
- monitor the normalisation of the state administration throughout the country;
- assist in resolving and managing any conflicts that may arise;
- monitor and verify the integration of the forces of the *União Nacional para a Independência Total de Angola* (UNITA) into the government structure;
- promote a climate of confidence by maintaining a presence in major population areas and areas of tension.

The formed military units left over from UNAVEM III after 30 June 1997 were being withdrawn in phases, with one infantry company remaining until the end of November 1997.

Location Angola.

Headquarters Luanda.

Strength 3,026 troops and other military personnel, 253 military observers, 289 police observers; there is also provision for approximately 33 international civilian staff; the mission is backed up by locally recruited support staff. A reduced military helicopter company and two small military medical stations will also support the mission

Contributors Bng, Br, Bg, RC, Da, Fr, GuB, Hu, HKJ, Ind, Kya, Mal, RMM, Nba, Nl, Nga, No, NZ, Pak, Pl, Po, R, RF, Sen, Slvk, Swe, Ukr, Ury Z, Zw; others provide military observers
Cost UNAVEM III *1995* $311m *1996* $344m; UNOMA *1997* $135m. Total cost to date: $734m.

United Nations Mission for the Referendum in Western Sahara (MINURSO)

Mission MINURSO was established in April 1991 in accordance with 'the settlement proposals', as accepted by Morocco and the *Frente Popular para la Liberación de Saguia el-Hamra y de Río de Oro* (POLISARIO) on 30 August 1988 to:
• monitor a cease-fire;
• verify the reduction of Moroccan troops in the territory;
• monitor the confinement of Moroccan and POLISARIO troops to designated locations, and ensure the release of all Western Saharan political prisoners or detainees;
• oversee the exchange of prisoners of war;
• implement the repatriation programme;
• identify and register qualified voters;
• organise and ensure a free referendum and proclaim the results.
In its limited deployment, MINURSO's primary function was restricted to complementing the identification process; verifying the cease-fire and cessation of hostilities; and monitoring local police and ensuring security and order at identification and registration sites. In May 1996, in the absence of any meaningful progress towards completing the settlement plan, the Security Council suspended the identification process, authorised the withdrawal of the civilian police component – except for a small number of officers to maintain contacts with the authorities on both sides – and decided to reduce the strength of MINURSO's military component by 20%. It also supported the UN Secretary-General's decision to maintain a political office in Laayoune, with a liaison office in Tindouf, to maintain a dialogue with the parties and the two neighbouring countries.
Location Western Sahara.
Headquarters Laayoune.
Strength 197 military observers, 27 military support personnel and nine police officers for liaison duties; there is also provision for approximately 320 international civilian personnel, 90 local civilian staff and 12 observers from the Organisation of African Unity.
Contributors Arg, A, Bng, PRC, Et, ElS, Fr, Gha, Gui, Hr, Irl, It, Kya, Mal, Nga, Pak, Pl, Por, ROK, RF, Ury, US, Ve.
Cost *1995* $41m *1996* $59m *1997* $29m. Total cost to date: $254m.

United Nations Observer Mission in Liberia (UNOMIL)

Mission UNOMIL was established in September 1993 to supervise and monitor, in cooperation with the Cease-Fire Monitoring Group (ECOMOG) of the Economic Community of West African States (ECOWAS), the Cotonou Peace Agreement signed on 25 July 1993. ECOMOG had primary responsibility for ensuring the Agreement's implementation, while UNOMIL's role was to monitor the implementation procedures and verify their impartial application. Delays in implementing the Peace Agreement and renewed fighting among Liberian factions made it impossible to hold elections in February–March 1994, as scheduled. In the following months, a number of supplementary peace agreements, amending and clarifying the Cotonou Agreement, were negotiated – the Akosombo Agreement of 12 September 1994, the Accra Agreement of 21 December 1994 and the Abuja Agreement of 19 August 1995. ECOWAS will continue to play the lead role in the peace process in Liberia, while ECOMOG retains the primary responsibility for helping to implement the military provisions of the peace agreements. For its part, UNOMIL will continue to observe and monitor the implementation of the peace agreements. Its main functions are to:

- support the efforts of ECOWAS and the Liberian transitional government to implement the peace agreements;
- investigate allegations of reported cease-fire violations;
- recommend measures to prevent their recurrence and report to the Secretary-General accordingly;
- monitor compliance with the other military provisions of the agreements and verify their impartial application, especially disarming and demobilising combatants;
- assist in maintaining assembly sites;
- assist in implementing a programme to demobilise combatants.

UNOMIL has also been requested to support humanitarian assistance and other activities including observing and verifying the legislative and presidential election process.

Location Liberia.

Headquarters Monrovia.

Strength 85 military observers, supported by seven military support personnel.

Contributors Bng, PRC, Cz, Et, Ind, Kya, Mal, N, Pak, Ury.

Cost *1995* $17m *1996* $34m *1997* $19m. Total cost to date: $97m.

United Nations Preventive Deployment Force (UNPREDEP)

Mission UNPREDEP was established on 31 March 1995 to replace UNPROFOR in the former Yugoslav Republic of Macedonia (FYROM). UNPREDEP's mandate is to monitor and report any developments in the border areas that could undermine confidence and stability in FYROM and threaten its territory. Effective on 1 February 1996, following the termination of the mandates of the UN Confidence-Restoration Operation in Croatia (UNCRO), the UN Protection Force (UNPROFOR) in Bosnia-Herzegovina and the UN Peace Forces Headquarters (UNPF-HQ), UNPREDEP became an independent mission, reporting directly to the UN Secretariat in New York. The operation retains the same mandate, strength and troop composition.

Location FYROM.

Headquarters Skopje.

Strength 1,043 troops, 36 military observers, 26 civilian police; there is also provision for 73 international civilian staff and 127 locally recruited staff.

Contributors Arg, Bng, Be, Br, Ca, Cz, Da, Et, SF, Gha, Indo, Irl, HKJ, Kya, N, NZ, Nga, No, Pak, Pl, Por, RF, Swe, CH, Tu, Ukr, US.

Cost *1995* $38m *1996* $50m *1997* $45m. Total cost to date: $133m.

United Nations Mission in Bosnia and Herzegovina (UNMIBH)

Mission On 21 December 1995, the Security Council established the UN International Police Task Force (IPTF) and a United Nations civilian office for one year in accordance with the General Framework Agreement for Peace in Bosnia and Herzegovina (the Dayton Agreement) signed by the leaders of Bosnia and Herzegovina, Croatia and the Federal Republic of Yugoslavia on 14 December 1995. The operation has come to be known as the United Nations Mission in Bosnia and Herzegovina (UNMIBH). IPTF tasks include:

- monitoring, observing and inspecting law-enforcement activities and facilities, including associated judicial organisations, structures and proceedings;
- advising law-enforcement personnel and forces;
- training law-enforcement personnel;
- facilitating, within the IPTF mission of assistance, the parties' law-enforcement activities;
- assessing threats to public order and advising on the capability of law-enforcement agencies to deal with such threats;
- advising government authorities in Bosnia-Herzegovina on organising effective civilian law-enforcement agencies;
- assisting the parties or law-enforcement agencies in Bosnia-Herzegovina, giving priority to ensuring conditions for free-and-fair elections.

Location Bosnia-Herzegovina.

Headquarters Sarajevo.

Strength 1,955 police monitors and five military liaison officers; there is also a provision for approximately 380 international staff and 900 locally recruited staff.

Contributors Arg, A, Bng, Bg, Ca, Chl, Da, Et, Ea, SF, Fr, Ge, Gha, Gr, Hu, Ind, Indo, Irl, It, HKJ, Mal, N, Nl, Nga, No, Pak, Pl, Por, RF, Sen, Sp, Swe, CH, Tn, Tu, Ukr, UK, US.

Cost *1996* $163m *1997* $170m. Total cost to date: $333m.

United Nations Transitional Administration for Eastern Slavonia, Baranja and Western Sirmium (UNTAES)

Mission The 12 November 1995 Basic Agreement on the Region of Eastern Slavonia, Baranja and Western Sirmium provides for the area's peaceful integration into Croatia. The Agreement requested the Security Council to establish an administration to govern the region for a 12-month transitional period, which may be extended by up to a further 12 months, and to authorise an international force to maintain peace and security during that period and to otherwise assist in implementing the Agreement. UNTAES was set up on 15 January 1996, with both military and civilian components. Its most recent mandate lasts until January 1998. The military component's task is to:

- supervise and facilitate the demilitarisation of the region;
- monitor the voluntary and safe return of refugees and displaced persons to their home of origin in cooperation with the UN High Commission for Refugees (UNHCR);
- contribute, by its presence, to maintaining peace and security in the region;
- otherwise assist in implementing the Basic Agreement.

The civilian component is to set up a temporary police force. UNTAES is also required to cooperate with the International Criminal Tribunal for the Former Yugoslavia in performing its mandate. UN member-states are authorised, acting nationally or through regional organisations, to take all necessary measures, including close air support, to defend or help withdraw UNTAES if threatened or attacked. Such actions would be based on UNTAES' request and procedures communicated to the United Nations.

Location Eastern Slavonia, Baranja and Western Sirmium (Croatia).

Headquarters Vukovar.

Authorised Strength 5,000 troops, 100 military observers and 600 civilian police; there is also provision for approximately 480 international civilian staff, 720 locally recruited staff and 100 UN volunteers.

Actual Strength 3,251 troops, 98 military observers and 438 civilian police.

Current Contributors Arg, A, Bng, Be, Br, Cz, Da, Et, Fji, SF, Gha, Indo, Irl, HKJ, Kya, L, N, Nl, NZ, Nga, No, Pak, Pl, RF, Slvk, Swe, CH, Tn, Ukr, UK, US.

Cost *1996* $292m *1997* $266m. Total cost to date: $558m.

United Nations Mission of Observers in Prevlaka (UNMOP)

Mission United Nations military observers have been deployed in the strategically important Prevlaka peninsula of Croatia since October 1992, when the Security Council authorised UNPROFOR to assume responsibility for monitoring the area's demilitarisation. Following UNPROFOR's restructuring in March 1995, those functions were carried out by UNCRO. With the termination of UNCRO's mandate in January 1996, the Security Council authorised UN military observers as UNMOP to continue monitoring the demilitarisation of the peninsula for three months, to be extended for a further three months following a report by the Secretary-General that this would continue to decrease tension there. UNMOP is under the command and direction of a Chief Military Observer, who reports directly to the UN Secretariat in New York.

Location Prevlaka peninsula, Croatia.

Headquarters Dubrovnik.

Strength 27 military observers.

Contributors Arg, Bng, Be, Br, Ca, Cz, Da, Et, SF, Gha, Indo, Irl, HKJ, Kya, N, NZ, Nga, No, Pak, Pl, Por, Swe, CH, Ukr.

Cost Included in UNMIBH cost.

United Nations Observer Mission in Georgia (UNOMIG)

Mission UNOMIG was originally established to verify compliance with the 27 July 1993 cease-fire agreement between the government of Georgia and the Abkhaz authorities with special attention to the situation in the city of Sukhumi; to investigate reports of cease-fire violations; and to attempt to resolve such incidents with the parties involved. After UNOMIG's original mandate was invalidated by renewed fighting in Abkhazia in September 1993, it was given an interim mandate to maintain contacts with both sides to the conflict and with Russian military contingents, and to monitor and report on the situation, with particular reference to developments relevant to UN efforts to promote a comprehensive political settlement. Following the signing in May 1994 of the Agreement on a Cease-fire and Separation of Forces by the Georgian and Abkhaz parties, UNOMIG's tasks are to:

- monitor and verify the implementation of the Agreement;
- observe the operation of the peacekeeping force of the Commonwealth of Independent States (CIS);
- verify that troops do not remain in or re-enter the security zone and that heavy military equipment does not remain and is not re-introduced into the security zone or the restricted weapons zone;
- monitor the storage areas for heavy military equipment withdrawn from the security zone and restricted weapons zone;
- monitor the withdrawal of Georgian troops from the Kodori valley to locations beyond the frontiers of Abkhazia;
- patrol the Kodori valley regularly;
- investigate reported or alleged violations of the Agreement and attempt to resolve such incidents.

Location Georgia.

Headquarters Sukhumi.

Strength 109 military observers; there is also provision for 64 international civilian staff and 75 locally recruited staff.

Contributors Alb, A, Bng, C, Cz, Da, Et, Fr, Ge, Gr, Hu, Indo, HKJ, ROK, Pak, Pl, RF, Swe, CH, Tu, UK, Ury, US.

Cost *1995* $18m *1996* $16m *1997* $18m. Total cost to date: $52m.

United Nations Mission of Observers in Tajikistan (UNMOT)

Mission UNMOT was established in December 1994 to assist a Joint Commission – composed of representatives of the Tajik government and the Tajik opposition – to monitor the implementation of the Agreement on a Temporary Cease-fire and the Cessation of Other Hostile Acts on the Tajik–Afghan Border and within Tajikistan. Since the June 1997 peace accord its tasks are to:

• monitor the implementation of the Agreement of National Reconciliation and Peace Establishment of 27 June 1997 and the cessation of other hostile acts on the Tajik–Afghan border and within the country;

• investigate alleged violations of the agreement and report them;

• provide its good offices in liaison with the mission of the Organisation for Security and Cooperation in Europe (OSCE), with the collective peacekeeping forces of the CIS in Tajikistan and with the border forces;

• provide support for the UN Secretary-General's Special Envoy;

• provide political liaison and coordination services to facilitate expeditious humanitarian assistance by the international community.

Location Tajikistan.

Headquarters Dushanbe.

Strength 41 military observers, supported by 18 international and 26 local civilian staff.

Contributors A, Bng, Bg, Da, HKJ, Pl, CH, Ukr, Ury.

Cost *1995* $9m *1996* $7m *1997* $8m. Total cost to date: $24m.

United Nations Transition Mission in Haiti (UNTMIH)

Mission Replacing the UN Support Mission in Haiti (UNSMIH) on 1 August 1997, UNTMIH's mission is to assist Haiti's government in training and re-organising the police and in maintaining a secure and stable environment in which to establish and train an effective national police force. In establishing UNTMIH, the Security Council also supported the role of the Special Representative of the Secretary-General in coordinating UN activities to promote institution-building, national reconciliation and economic rehabilitation in Haiti.

Location Haiti.

Headquarters Port-au-Prince.

Strength 222 civilian police; 1,287 troops for security duties paid for by voluntary contributions from Ca instead of the UN peacekeeping budget. Pak also supplies troops for security.

Contributors Ag, Bn, Ca, Fr, Ind, RMM, Pak, Tg, US.

Cost *1995* $258m *1996* $243m *1997* $10m. Total cost to date: $516m.

OTHER MISSIONS

A number of peacekeeping missions are currently under way which are not under UN control. The major operations are shown below. Not shown are those of very brief duration or those that are covered under the regional text and country section concerned (for example ECOMOG in Liberia and Sierra Leone, MISAB in CAR, and MOMEP in Ecuador and Peru). The OSCE conducts a number of observer missions in areas of conflict – for example, Chechnya and Nagorno-Karabakh – which fluctuate in size and contributors. The OSCE also undertakes a number of important security-related non-military missions, such as supervising elections and conflict mediation (as in Tajikistan). In addition to the two field missions in Chechnya and Nagorno-Karabakh, in August 1997 there were 10 long-term missions deployed in Bosnia-Herzegovina, Croatia, Estonia, Georgia, Latvia, Moldova, Sarajevo, Skopje, Tajikistan and Ukraine. A small number of military observers are participating in these missions, but no armed forces formations are involved. While the OSCE describes these missions as long term, their mandates vary from three to six months (renewable). In *Operation Alba* in Albania, a force of 7,214 troops was deployed from April to August 1997 to help protect the delivery of humanitarian aid and to help provide security during the July 1997 elections. Eight European countries contributed to the force, led by Italy which provided 3,777 troops. The other contingents were provided by Austria, Denmark, Spain, France, Greece, Romania and Turkey.

NATO Stabilisation Force (SFOR) for Bosnia and Herzegovina

Mission SFOR's mission is to support further implementation of the 1995 General Framework Agreement for Peace in Bosnia and Herzegovina and respond to the resolutions of the United Nation's Security Council. Its mandate expires on 30 June 1998. The North Atlantic Council (NAC) has authorised a NATO-led operation for 18 months to deter a resumption of hostilities and to stabilise the peace in Bosnia and Herzegovina. SFOR's principal tasks are:
- to maintain the Zone of Separation (ZOS) and keep it free from armed groups, ensuring heavy weapons remain in approved storage areas, and freedom of movement exists throughout the country for SFOR and civilian agencies. SFOR is to promote freedom of movement across the Inter Entity Boundary Line (IEBL) for all citizens of Bosnia and Herzegovina, but cannot be expected to guarantee the freedom of movement of individuals throughout Bosnia and Herzegovina or forcibly return refugees. By successfully accomplishing these principal military tasks, SFOR will contribute to a secure environment within which civilian agencies can continue to undertake economic development, reconstruction, establish political institutions, and create an overall climate of reconciliation for the people of Bosnia and Herzegovina;
- to maintain control of the airspace over Bosnia and Herzegovina and of the movement of military traffic over key ground routes;
- to continue to use Joint Military Commissions;
- to give selective support to international organisations in their humanitarian missions;
- to assist in observing and preventing interference with the movement of civilian populations, refugees and displaced persons, and respond appropriately to deliberate violence;
- to assist in monitoring the clearance of minefields and obstacles.

SFOR will also remain ready to support the UN Transitional Administration for Eastern Slavonia when needed.

Location Bosnia-Herzegovina with supporting elements in Croatia and bases in Italy and Hungary. A maritime component is at sea in the Adriatic.

Headquarters
- The Commander of SFOR (COMSFOR) has a headquarters in Sarajevo and commands three divisions with their headquarters based in Mostar, Tuzla and Banja Luka.
- The Commander of the SFOR Air Component is the NATO Commander Allied Air Forces Southern Europe who exercises his operational control through his Combined Air Operations Centre (CAOC) at Vincenza, Italy.
- The SFOR Naval Component is commanded by NATO's Commander Allied Naval Forces Southern Europe. This component comprises ships from several nations which are formed into task forces and are available or can be called upon for support.
- NATO's Commander Allied Striking Forces Southern Europe commands carrier-based aviation and amphibious forces in the region, which are not an integral part of SFOR, but are earmarked to support it if needed.

Strength 36,179 (29,580 NATO forces and 6,599 from non-NATO countries).

Contributors

NATO Be, Ca, Da, Fr, Ge, Gr, It, Lu, Nl, No, Po, Sp, Tu, UK, US.

Iceland, which has no armed forces, is contributing civilian medical personnel.

Non-NATO A, Alb, Bg, Cz, Et, Ea, SF, Hu, HKJ, Lat, L, Mal, Mor, Pl, R, RF, Slvk (civilian personnel only), Swe, Ukr.

Cost *1996ε* $5bn (IFOR) *1997ε* $4bn.

Multinational Force and Observers (MFO)

Mission The MFO was established in August 1981, under the peace treaty between Israel and Egypt (the Camp David accords), to verify the withdrawal of Israeli forces from the Sinai peninsula and to monitor the force levels permitted in the zone covered by the treaty. The force is also required to help ensure freedom of navigation through the Strait of Tiran.

Location Sinai peninsula.

Headquarters Main headquarters in Rome with a forward headquarters in the Sinai.

Strength 1,896.

Contributors Aus, Ca, Co, Fji, Fr, Hu, It, NZ, No, Ury, US. The force includes a number of civilians on private contracts to fly air-observation missions and for logistic-support duties.

Cost *1995* $51m *1996* $50m *1997* $51m.

The most influential event affecting arms control in 1997 was the US–Russia summit meeting in Helsinki in March. This outlined a programme of action for the two countries over the next decade in nuclear, chemical and conventional arms-control matters. On 29 April 1997, the Chemical Weapons Convention (CWC) entered into force, without Russia as a member. Although the Preparatory Commission setting up the organisation for the Comprehensive Test Ban Treaty (CTBT) began work, the prospects for the Treaty's early entry into force are not good.

NUCLEAR WEAPONS

Strategic Arms Reduction Treaty

In their March 1997 summit declarations, US President Bill Clinton and Russian President Boris Yeltsin set out their understandings on the Strategic Arms Reduction Treaty (START) II. The essential elements are:

- Once Russia ratifies START II, negotiations for START III should begin. START III aims to reach lower aggregate levels of 2,000–2,500 strategic warheads each for the US and Russia.
- START II reductions to below 3,500 warheads on each side – due to be completed by 2003 – are to be phased over a longer period to 2007. This will coincide with the proposed target date for START III reductions.

Dovetailing the dates for START II and III reductions will allow Russia to retain parity with the US once both are left with only the single-warhead inter-continental ballistic missile systems required by START II. Once its multiple-warhead systems are dismantled, Russia would have to build up its single-warhead systems (SS-27) to reach the 3,000–3,500 START II level. It is doubtful whether the Russians could afford to do this, even if they so wished. The new understanding avoids this strategic imbalance. The US hoped that it would help to ease the ratification of START II in the Russian Duma. Among other important elements relating to transparency and promoting the irreversibility of the reductions, the Presidents agreed that all warheads on strategic delivery vehicles due to be eliminated by the new date set for START II should nevertheless be 'either removed or by other means (jointly agreed) placed in a deactivated status by 31 December 2003'. The US is to provide funds through the Nunn–Lugar programme to assist early deactivation.

The implementation of START I continues. The numbers of strategic delivery vehicles formally declared by Russia and the US under their Memorandum of Understanding as at 1 January 1997 are shown below.

Table 51	**Aggregate numbers of strategic offensive delivery vehicles**		
(as at 1 January 1997)	**ICBMs**	**SLBMs**	**Bombers**
US	755	480	329
Russia	762	664	79
Belarus	0	0	0
Kazakstan	0	0	0
Ukraine	115[1]	0	44
Totals	1,632	1,144	452

Note [1] There are no warheads with these missiles

OTHER NUCLEAR DEVELOPMENTS

Comprehensive Test Ban Treaty

In March 1997, the Preparatory Commission of the Comprehensive Test Ban Treaty Organisation (CTBTO) agreed the structure of the Provisional Technical Secretariat (PTS) and made key appointments. The PTS has five divisions:

As at 10 July 1997, 144 states had signed the Treaty and four had ratified it. According to Article XIV, the Treaty will enter into force after the following 44 states (listed in Annex 2 to the Treaty) have ratified it:

Algeria	Brazil	DPRK[1]	Hungary	Japan	Poland	Spain	US
Argentina	Bulgaria	DRC	India[1]	Mexico	Romania	Sweden	Vietnam
Australia	Canada	Egypt	Indonesia	Netherlands	ROK	Switzerland	
Austria	Chile	Finland	Iran	Norway	Russia	Turkey	
Bangladesh	China	France	Israel	Pakistan[1]	Slovakia	Ukraine	
Belgium	Colombia	Germany	Italy	Peru	South Africa	UK	

Note [1] These countries have not signed the Treaty

In present circumstances, there is little chance of India joining the Treaty – and thus neither will Pakistan. There is a provision in the Treaty that, four years after it opened for signature (on 24 September 1996), the signatories can call a conference to decide what measures to take to bring about entry into force. Despite delays, and barring a dramatic change in the general security situation, the five nuclear weapon states (NWS) are likely to maintain their moratorium on testing.

The CTBTO cannot activate its verification system until 180 days after the Treaty enters into force. However, time is needed to set up the system, recruit and train staff, and carry out research and development (R&D) on the technical aspects of the global monitoring system. Seismic monitoring is well established, but the other three methods – hydroacoustic, radionuclide atmospheric monitoring and infrasound – require more work if they are to form part of a global system within the next three or four years. The US Department of Energy (DoE) Sandia National Laboratory at Albuquerque, New Mexico, has a major R&D programme to support the CTBTO. This programme is expected to cost at least US$19 million in 1998.

International Atomic Energy Agency Safeguards

In June 1997, Brazil joined the Treaty on the Non-Proliferation of Nuclear Weapons (NPT), bringing the total membership of the Treaty to 186. Since 1993, the International Atomic Energy

Agency (IAEA) has been engaged in a programme to strengthen the 'safeguards' (or verification) system: by June 1995, Part I of the plan was approved by the Board of Governors and put into effect. Its main components are:

- taking environmental samples at locations to which the IAEA already has access for design information verification or inspections;
- using no-notice inspections at key places in all nuclear facilities; such inspections are intended to improve the verification of movement of declared materials and provide another means of detecting undeclared material;
- confirmation of the Agency's right of access to records of activities carried out before entry into force of a safeguards agreement to help ensure that all material has been properly declared; and
- use of monitoring systems that can operate unattended to transmit information direct to IAEA headquarters.

On 15 May 1997, Part II of the package was agreed by the Board of Governors. This contains a model protocol for NPT members to agree individually with the IAEA. The main elements of the protocol include:

- an 'expanded declaration' to provide information on nuclear-fuel-cycle-related activities not involving nuclear material, including R&D and non-nuclear activities that support the nuclear fuel cycle, to give the IAEA a better understanding of a state's nuclear programme, its future direction, and the kinds of nuclear activities the programme's infrastructure could support;
- access to any place on the site of a nuclear facility, to any decommissioned facility, and to any other location where nuclear material is present, and to nuclear-related manufacturing and other locations identified by the IAEA; and
- the use of environmental sampling as well as other measures at these locations.

Judging by the experience of implementing earlier bilateral agreements with the IAEA, it will take some years before this protocol is widely used. While these additional measures strengthen the Agency's safeguards system, as with any other global verification system, they will not provide a guarantee against covert nuclear-weapons programmes. Other national technical measures will still be needed to monitor the relatively small number of states likely to try to conduct clandestine weapons programmes. Certain non-declared nuclear states – India, Israel and Pakistan – still remain outside the NPT.

ANTI-BALLISTIC MISSILE TREATY

The March 1997 Joint Statement from the US–Russia Helsinki summit included an understanding on the Anti-Ballistic Missile (ABM) Treaty which aimed to provide the basis for concluding negotiations to distinguish strategic from theatre missile defences (TMD). The Joint Statement re-affirmed the two Presidents' commitment to the Treaty and included the following under-standings, intended to appear in the final agreement:

- the velocity of target missiles used in TMD tests should be limited to 5km/sec and the range to 3,500km;
- a provision should be included not to develop, test or deploy space-based TMD interceptors or components based on alternative technologies that could substitute for such interceptors (these interceptors would conflict with the ABM Treaty's ban on space-based ABM systems);
- transparency provisions to provide mutual confidence. The Presidents stated that neither country has plans for TMD interceptors with velocities greater than 5.5km/sec for land-based and air-based TMD systems, and of 4.5km/sec for sea-based TMD systems; nor are there plans

for tests against a target missile with multiple independently targetable re-entry vehicles or strategic ballistic-missile re-entry vehicles. The two sides also stated that neither has plans before April 1999 to flight test a higher-velocity TMD system against a ballistic target missile.

The Joint Statement also covered potential new technologies by calling for consultations in the event that new technologies arise for TMD systems. Such consultations would be undertaken to preclude violation or circumvention of the ABM Treaty, but they would not give either side a veto over the other's programmes.

CHEMICAL AND BIOLOGICAL WEAPONS

The CWC entered into force fully on 29 April 1997. The US ratified the Convention on 25 April, just in time to retain the right to appoint US nationals to the implementation body, the Organisation for the Prohibition of Chemical Weapons (OPCW). Russia, a declared possessor of one of the largest arsenals of chemical weapons (CW), had not ratified as at 1 August 1997. By 25 July 1997, 97 of the 165 signatories had ratified the Convention. Inspections by the OPCW under the global verification regime have already begun.

Progress by the Group of Governmental Experts attempting to draft a verification protocol for the Biological and Toxin Weapons Convention (BTWC) is limited. At the last BTWC Review Conference (on 25 November–7 December 1996), the Group was given more time to complete its work. It is required to report as soon as possible, but no later than the next Review Conference in 2001. The matters on which the group has most difficulty in finding consensus are:

- Definitions of terms, in particular whether or not a list of bacteriological (biological) agents and toxins, should be agreed. Some countries believe that this would aid verification by focusing on agents considered most dangerous. Others believe that such a list would *de facto* limit the scope of the Convention and would not take account of rapid advances in biotechnology.
- Which equipment and activities should be subject to verification measures that might be agreed. As with listing agents, too narrow a focus on certain activities could allow for circumvention. It is difficult to define the limits of the relevant biotechnological activities – they could range from producing therapeutic drugs and veterinary vaccines to the food industry (for example, yoghurt production and brewing) and agriculture (such as biopesticide production).

THE UN WEAPONRY CONVENTION

The UN Weaponry Convention (the 'Convention on Prohibitions or Restrictions on the Use of Certain Conventional Weapons which may be deemed to be Excessively Injurious or to have Indiscriminate Effects'), opened for signature in April 1981 and came into force on 2 October 1983. By 30 June 1997, 66 states had ratified the Convention and one or more of its protocols.

The Convention contains four protocols. Protocol I prohibits the use of any weapon intended to injure by fragments which escape x-ray detection. Protocol II restricts the use of mines, booby traps and 'other devices', and aims to prevent or at least reduce civilian casualties caused by these weapons during and after hostilities. Protocol III restricts the use of incendiary weapons. Protocol IV bans anti-personnel blinding laser weapons.

The Convention was amended in May 1996 to:

- apply Protocol II to internal as well as international conflicts;
- ban undetectable (plastic) mines and mines which explode on electro-magnetic detection;
- introduce a set of criteria for self-destructing or self-deactivating remotely delivered mines;

- introduce new standards for marking minefields.

Countries have nine years in which to replace existing stocks with land-mines built to the new specification. The Convention bans the transfer of land-mines to non-member-states and to non-state armed groups. Annual meetings are to take place to review the implementation of the amended Protocol II.

The next UN Weaponry Convention Review Conference will not take place until 2001. Some countries felt that more urgent action was needed; on 3–5 October 1996, a conference 'Towards a Global Ban on Anti-Personnel Mines' organised by the Canadian government was held in Ottawa. The 50 countries participating adopted the Declaration of the Ottawa Conference, urging the earliest possible conclusion of a legally binding international agreement to prohibit all anti-personnel mines (APLs). The Canadian initiative aimed to draft a treaty which could be opened for signature before the end of December 1997.

Some countries, in particular the US, preferred to work towards a ban through the Geneva-based Conference on Disarmament (CD) to achieve a broader consensus for a global treaty. However, in August 1997 the US changed its policy and joined the Ottawa process which by then was supported by more than 100 countries. There is strong opposition to a ban from some CD members, notably China, Israel, Pakistan, Russia, South Korea, Syria and Turkey. This route to a legally binding ban would be slower, and would probably become blocked in the present security and political circumstances.

In addition to attempts to achieve international agreement on prohibiting APLs, many governments have adopted unilateral APL prohibitions: some have banned production; others have stopped all exports; a limited number of states have embarked on programmes to destroy their APL stockpiles. These efforts have been bolstered by conferences and declarations in Europe and Africa (sponsored by the Organisation for African Unity (OAU) with the International Committee of the Red Cross (ICRC)).

UN REGISTER OF CONVENTIONAL ARMS

During 1997, a group of 25 governmental experts met to review the performance of the UN Register of Conventional Arms and to examine ways of developing it further. Participation in the Register is growing; nearly 100 countries report annually on the seven categories of major conventional weapons it covers.[1] An increasing number of these countries detail the weapons (designations and types) being transferred rather than simply stating quantities. In addition to reporting transfers, some countries voluntarily report their military holdings and procurement from national production. These include NATO and other European countries, Australia, Japan and the larger Latin American countries – Argentina, Brazil and Mexico. Attempts by these countries to require the same level of commitment for reporting procurement through national production and military holdings as for transfers has yet to succeed.

Many Arab states do not participate because they believe weapons of mass destruction (WMD) should be covered by the Register. Their main concern is Israel, which regularly reports to the Register. Nevertheless, as Arab states are importers of the seven categories of major weapons systems, most of these states' acquisitions are reported by the exporting countries.

---

[1] The categories are main battle tanks, armoured combat vehicles, large calibre artillery (100mm and above), combat aircraft, armed helicopters (only with integrated fire-control systems), warships (750 tonnes and above) and missiles and their launchers (25km range and above).

Analyses *and* Tables

THE WASSENAAR ARRANGEMENT

Member Countries (as at 1 August 1997)

Argentina	Denmark	Italy	Portugal	Switzerland
Australia	Finland	Japan	Romania	Turkey
Austria	France	Luxembourg	Russia	Ukraine
Belgium	Germany	Netherlands	Slovakia	UK
Bulgaria	Greece	New Zealand	South Korea	US
Canada	Hungary	Norway	Spain	
Czech Republic	Ireland	Poland	Sweden	

The Regime

Established in July 1996, the Wassenaar Arrangement is a voluntary system to coordinate national controls on exporting conventional arms and dual-use technologies by promoting information exchange through a consultative forum. The regime has two sets of guidelines, one relating to conventional weapons, the other to dual-use goods. The guidelines on conventional arms transfers call for regular information exchanges, consultations and reviews of arms exports. Members have agreed in principle to exchange information every six months on deliveries of weapons covered by the UN Register of Conventional Arms (including details of model and type, together with quantity and recipient). The guidelines on exports of dual-use goods are based on an agreed list of controlled goods comprising: a 'Basic List' (Tier 1, for example, telecommunications equipment); and two annexes made up of a 'Sensitive List' (Tier 2, such as super computers) and a 'Very Sensitive List' (a sub-set of Tier 2, for instance, stealth technology). All exports of dual-use goods are at the discretion of national governments, but members have agreed: to exchange information twice a year on all denials of export licences for Tier 1 items; to notify denials of licences for the export of Tier 2 items within 60 days; and twice a year to provide information on licences to export any Tier 2 items to non-members. Members have also agreed to inform all other members, within 60 days, of approval of a licence which has been denied by another member during the previous three years.

Table 52 **Summary of the Wassenaar Arrangement notification requirements**

	Notification Required After:		
	Licence Approval	Licence Denial	Counter-Approval
UN Register Categories (Conventional Weapons)	Bi-annually	No	No
Dual-Use: Tier 1	No	Bi-annually	No
Dual-Use: Tier 2	Bi-annually	Within 60 days	Within 60 days

MISSILE TECHNOLOGY CONTROL REGIME

The Missile Technology Control Regime (MTCR) was formed in April 1987 to control the transfer of equipment and technology that might help to build missile-delivery systems capable of carrying nuclear weapons. The warhead performance threshold was defined in terms of the ability to deliver at least 500kg over a distance of at least 300km. In 1992, the guidelines were extended to include missile-delivery systems capable of carrying biological and chemical warheads. The MTCR is politically binding only and not part of a legal treaty regime. The members unilaterally implement the agreed export control standards.

Membership

In 1995 Brazil, Russia and South Africa joined the MTCR, raising membership to 28 states.

Members and adherents (as at 1 August 1997)						
Argentina	Canada[1]	Germany[1]	Israel[2]	New Zealand	Spain	US[1]
Australia	China[2]	Greece	Italy[1]	Norway	Sweden	
Austria	Denmark	Hungary	Japan[1]	Portugal	Switzerland	
Belgium	Finland	Iceland	Luxembourg	Russia	Ukraine[2]	
Brazil	France[1]	Ireland	Netherlands	South Africa	UK[1]	

Notes [1] Founding member

[2] Adherent to the guidelines, but not member

In 1993, additional requirements for membership were introduced. To prevent countries joining the Regime to gain access to missile technology that would otherwise be denied, new criteria established that potential members dispense with the development, or deployment, of their own Category 1 missile systems. Exceptions were conceded to Russia, and to China, if it were to move to full membership. The controversy these exceptions generated also stemmed from the fact that the MTCR's express purpose was to coordinate export-control efforts rather than impose arms-control limits. The response to this new precondition was mixed. Argentina, Brazil, Hungary and South Africa accepted it; Ukraine rejected membership on the grounds that such missile systems were an integral part of its national-defence requirements, although it subsequently committed itself to adhere to the guidelines.

The Regime

The original MTCR guidelines listed controlled items in two categories. Category 1 covers the most sensitive items; particular restraint is to be exercised with a 'strong presumption to deny such transfers'. Category 2 covers dual-use equipment and technology that might be incorporated in Category 1 items. Export-licensing decisions are to be made on a case-by-case basis and approval should be denied if there is a significant risk of the goods and technology being used for missile development. The extension of the guidelines in 1992 to cover missiles capable of carrying any WMD included an enlarged reference list of controlled items agreed in December 1993 that member-states should have embodied in their national export-control regulations by July 1994. The structure of the revised control list was changed to accommodate two sub-categories (termed Item 1 and Item 2) under Category 1. Category 2 was also altered to include complete systems and sub-systems for missiles with ranges greater than 300km, regardless of their payload capacity.

MTCR Issues

- The inclusion of biological and chemical warheads has brought new classes of missiles into the Regime, but modifications to missiles which can significantly alter their performance must also be taken into account. Systems that perform beneath the MTCR thresholds can be upgraded, or modified, in such a way that their warhead or range is above the thresholds. Such modifications can be covert and are difficult to verify.
- Although ballistic-missile technology has been the focus of the MTCR, there is increasing need for specific criteria to ensure cruise-missile technology is fully covered. The MTCR includes

the key missile and dual-technology goods needed for such cruise-missile programmes, but the exemptions in Category 2 controls for aircraft components leave loopholes that could be exploited for cruise-missile production purposes. The current weight and range thresholds need to be reviewed to take account, for example, of air-launched cruise missiles (ALCMs).

- There have been a number of suspected breaches of the Regime by both members and adherents. China, Russia and Ukraine have reportedly exchanged technology and hardware. In the last two years, a number of reports have suggested that these states attempted to transfer prohibited technology to other countries, including Egypt, Iran, Libya and Pakistan.

There is a case for expanding membership of the MTCR. The commitment at the 1996 Edinburgh plenary to approach missile-technology proliferation on a regional basis is significant. Hungary is the only MTCR member among the East European former Warsaw Pact countries. Several countries which have ballistic- and cruise-missile programmes are outside the Regime. They include North and South Korea, India and Pakistan, and, although Israel is an adherent, Egypt, Iran, Iraq and Turkey are not. Finally, an increasing number of countries may acquire the necessary indigenous capability, although they do not necessarily possess missile programmes, such as Indonesia, Malaysia, Mexico, Singapore, South Korea and Taiwan. Applying MTCR guidelines to space-launch programmes for civilian purposes remains the area in which the Regime's controls are most challenged. Although the guidelines state that the Regime is not designed to impede national space programmes, there is now a strong presumption within the MTCR to deny exports of Category 1 goods even for civilian space-launcher programmes. There is also increasing pressure to restrain Category 2 exports destined for civil programmes. However, there is a perception that membership of the MTCR facilitates access to controlled dual-use technology. Technological cooperation between member-states does take place, for example, through the European Space Agency. Some members are rigorous in their demands for end-use guarantees; others assume that membership of the MTCR means that export controls for Regime members can be eased with no added risk.

Table 53 International comparisons of defence expenditure and military manpower in 1985, 1995 and 1996

(1995 constant prices)

	Defence Expenditure US$m			US$ per capita			% of GDP			Numbers in Armed Forces (000)		Estimated Reservists (000)	Para-military (000)
	1985	1995	1996	1985	1995	1996	1985	1995	1996	1985	1996	1996	1996
Canada	10,688	9,126	8,387	421	324	295	2.2	1.6	1.5	83.0	70.5	27.7	9.3
US	352,551	277,834	265,823	1,473	1,056	1,001	6.5	3.8	3.6	2,151.6	1,483.8	1,880.6	88.3
NATO Europe													
Belgium	5,621	4,449	4,190	570	442	416	3.0	1.8	1.6	91.6	46.3	60.0	n.a.
Denmark	2,855	3,118	2,978	558	598	570	2.2	1.8	1.7	29.6	32.9	70.4	n.a.
France	44,604	47,768	46,217	808	822	792	4.0	3.1	3.1	464.3	398.9	337.0	92.4
Germany	48,149	41,157	38,432	634	507	474	3.2	1.9	1.7	478.0	358.4	304.9	25.1
Greece	3,180	5,056	5,465	320	484	520	7.0	4.4	4.8	201.5	168.3	291.0	30.5
Iceland	n.a.	n.a.	n.a.	n.a.	n.a.	n.a.	n.a.	n.a.	n.a.	n.a.	n.a.	n.a.	0.1
Italy	23,462	19,376	23,289	411	335	402	2.3	1.8	2.2	385.1	325.2	584.0	255.7
Luxembourg	87	142	133	238	350	324	0.9	0.7	0.7	0.7	0.8	n.a	0.6
Netherlands	8,121	8,011	7,915	561	519	510	3.1	2.3	2.1	105.5	63.1	81.0	3.6
Norway	2,826	3,508	3,689	681	806	844	3.1	2.7	2.4	37.0	30.0	255.0	0.7
Portugal	1,674	2,670	2,853	164	271	289	3.1	3.1	2.8	73.0	54.2	210.0	49.8
Spain	10,289	8,652	8,439	267	221	215	2.4	1.5	1.5	320.0	206.8	420.0	75.5
Turkey	3,134	6,606	6,856	62	108	110	4.5	3.8	3.9	630.0	525.0	378.7	182.2
United Kingdom	43,536	33,406	32,764	770	573	561	5.2	3.1	3.0	327.1	226.0	327.4	n.a.
Sub-total NATO Europe	197,539	183,920	183,219	432	431	431	3.1	2.3	2.2	3,143.4	2,435.9	3,319.4	716.2
Total NATO	560,777	470,880	457,430	496	463	458	3.3	2.3	2.3	5,378.0	3,990.2	5,227.7	813.8
Non-NATO Europe													
Albania	258	89	98	87	25	27	5.3	6.3	6.7	40.4	54.0	155.0	13.5
Armenia	n.a.	79	87	n.a.	21	23	n.a.	5.9	6.2	n.a.	57.4	300.0	1.0
Austria	1,763	2,129	2,011	233	267	251	1.2	1.0	0.9	54.7	55.8	91.8	n.a.
Azerbaijan	n.a.	107	131	n.a.	14	17	n.a.	5.0	5.8	n.a.	70.7	560.0	40.0
Belarus	n.a.	496	480	n.a.	48	46	n.a.	4.8	4.2	n.a.	85.5	289.5	8.0
Bosnia-Herzegovina	n.a.	600	245	n.a.	137	56	n.a.	20.0	6.3	n.a.	92.0	100.0	n.a.
Bulgaria	2,235	417	335	250	50	40	6.6	3.2	3.3	148.5	103.5	303.0	34.0
Croatia	n.a.	1,773	1,254	n.a.	375	266	n.a.	9.8	6.8	n.a.	64.7	220.0	40.0
Cyprus	119	368	420	179	443	500	3.6	4.7	5.2	10.0	10.0	88.0	4.0
Czech Republic	n.a.	1,120	988	n.a.	108	96	n.a.	2.7	2.4	n.a.	70.0	240.0	5.6
Czechoslovakia	3,200	n.a.	n.a.	205	n.a.	n.a.	8.2	n.a.	n.a.	203.3	n.a.	n.a.	n.a.
Estonia	n.a.	101	106	n.a.	67	72	n.a.	2.8	2.4	n.a.	3.5	6.0	2.0
Finland	2,051	2,385	2,162	418	467	422	2.8	2.3	2.0	36.5	32.5	500.0	3.5
FYROM	n.a.	116	117	n.a.	20	20	n.a.	9.0	9.2	n.a.	10.4	100.0	7.5
Georgia	n.a.	106	110	n.a.	20	20	n.a.	3.5	3.4	n.a.	10.0	250.0	5.0
Hungary	3,241	613	757	304	60	75	7.2	1.4	1.7	106.0	64.3	173.0	13.8
Ireland	437	688	725	123	191	200	1.8	1.1	1.1	13.7	12.7	15.6	n.a.
Latvia	n.a.	121	130	n.a.	46	50	n.a.	3.3	3.5	n.a.	8.0	16.5	4.3
Lithuania	n.a.	115	122	n.a.	31	33	n.a.	4.2	4.3	n.a.	5.1	11.0	4.8

(1995 constant prices)

	Defence Expenditure US$m			US$ per capita			% of GDP			Numbers in Armed Forces (000)		Estimated Reservists (000)	Para-military (000)
	1985	1995	1996	1985	1995	1996	1985	1995	1996	1985	1996	1996	1996
Malta	22	32	32	61	88	87	1.4	1.1	1.1	0.8	2.0	n.a.	n.a.
Moldova	n.a.	45	46	n.a.	10	11	n.a.	3.8	4.2	n.a.	11.9	66.0	3.4
Poland	7,864	2,753	3,020	211	72	78	8.1	2.7	2.8	319.0	248.5	466.0	24.4
Romania	1,905	872	730	84	38	32	4.5	2.9	2.3	189.5	228.4	427.0	79.1
Slovakia	n.a.	455	438	n.a.	84	81	n.a.	2.9	2.6	n.a.	42.6	20.0	4.0
Slovenia	n.a.	277	275	n.a.	138	137	n.a.	1.9	1.8	n.a.	9.6	53.0	4.5
Sweden	4,359	6,035	5,941	522	687	674	3.3	2.9	2.9	65.7	62.6	729.0	35.6
Switzerland	2,636	4,952	4,479	408	702	633	2.1	1.6	1.6	20.0	27.3	396.0	n.a.
Ukraine	n.a.	1,005	1,306	n.a.	20	25	n.a.	2.2	3.0	n.a.	400.8	1,000.0	66.0
FRY (Serbia-Montenegro)	4,562	3,111	1,440	196	288	127	3.8	19.6	8.7	241.0	113.9	400.0	n.a.
Total	**34,652**	**30,960**	**27,986**	**234**	**162**	**148**	**4.8**	**4.7**	**3.8**	**1,449.1**	**1,957.1**	**6,976.4**	**404.0**
Russia	n.a.	82,000	69,537	n.a.	554	470	n.a.	7.4	6.5	n.a.	1,270.0	2,400.0	352.0
Soviet Union	329,449	n.a.	n.a.	1,181	n.a.	n.a.	16.1	n.a.	n.a.	5,300.0	n.a.	n.a.	n.a.
Middle East and North Africa													
Algeria	1,301	1,427	1,764	59	51	62	1.7	3.3	4.0	170.0	123.7	150.0	41.2
Bahrain	206	273	279	494	477	476	3.5	5.4	5.5	2.8	11.0	n.a.	9.3
Egypt	3,527	2,506	2,629	73	43	43	7.2	4.5	4.5	445.0	440.0	254.0	232.0
Gaza and Jericho	n.a.	n.a.	n.a.	n.a.	n.a.	n.a.	n.a.	n.a.	n.a.	n.a.	n.a.	n.a.	16.5
Iran	19,423	3,000	3,301	435	46	49	36.0	4.8	5.0	305.0	513.0	350.0	350.0
Iraq	17,573	1,250	1,224	1,105	59	56	25.9	8.3	8.3	520.0	382.5	650.0	50.0
Israel	6,899	9,298	9,359	1,630	1,655	1,624	21.2	12.2	12.1	142.0	175.0	430.0	6.1
Jordan	822	448	390	235	102	85	15.9	6.8	5.6	70.3	98.7	35.0	30.0
Kuwait	2,453	3,489	3,505	1,434	2,318	2,218	9.1	13.1	12.9	12.0	15.3	23.7	5.5
Lebanon	273	490	474	102	122	116	9.0	4.9	4.4	17.4	48.9	n.a.	18.5
Libya	1,844	1,401	1,272	490	259	227	6.2	5.6	5.1	73.0	65.0	40.0	0.5
Mauritania	71	29	31	42	13	13	6.5	2.7	2.9	8.5	15.7	n.a.	5.0
Morocco	875	1,464	1,539	40	53	54	5.4	4.5	4.3	149.0	194.0	150.0	42.0
Oman	2,946	2,018	1,876	1,841	1,073	955	20.8	17.1	15.6	2.5	43.5	n.a.	4.4
Qatar	410	700	740	1,301	1,286	1,334	6.0	9.8	10.2	6.0	11.8	n.a.	n.a.
Saudi Arabia	24,530	17,196	16,999	2,125	1,082	1,030	19.6	13.8	12.8	62.5	162.5	n.a.	16.0
Syria	4,756	1,738	1,553	453	122	105	16.4	5.6	4.8	402.5	421.0	500.0	8.0
Tunisia	569	369	390	80	41	42	5.0	2.1	2.0	35.1	35.0	n.a.	23.0
UAE	2,790	1,950	2,028	1,993	820	830	7.6	5.1	5.2	43.0	64.5	n.a.	1.0
Yemen	668	345	354	66	24	24	9.9	3.7	3.7	64.1	42.0	40.0	70.0
Total	**91,937**	**49,391**	**49,705**	**737**	**508**	**492**	**12.3**	**7.0**	**6.8**	**2,530.7**	**2,863.1**	**2,622.7**	**929.0**
Central and Southern Asia													
Afghanistan	392	200	200	22	9	9	8.7	15.4	15.4	47.0	429.0	n.a.	n.a.
Bangladesh	341	500	517	3	4	4	1.4	1.7	1.7	91.3	117.5	n.a.	49.7

(1995 constant prices)

| | Defence Expenditure | | | | | | | | | Numbers in Armed Forces (000) | | Estimated Reservists (000) | Para-military (000) |
| | US$m | | | US$ per capita | | | % of GDP | | | | | | |
	1985	1995	1996	1985	1995	1996	1985	1995	1996	1985	1996	1996	1996
India	8,553	9,992	10,158	11	11	11	3.0	2.9	2.8	1,260.0	1,145.0	535.0	1,944.0
Kazakstan	n.a.	427	460	n.a.	25	28	n.a.	2.4	2.6	n.a.	40.0	n.a.	34.5
Kyrgyzstan	n.a.	56	47	n.a.	12	10	n.a.	3.5	2.6	n.a.	7.0	n.a.	5.0
Myanmar	1,200	1,880	1,929	32	40	40	5.1	7.5	7.6	186.0	321.0	n.a.	85.3
Nepal	49	37	39	3	2	2	1.5	1.0	0.9	25.0	43.0	n.a.	28.0
Pakistan	2,835	3,642	3,579	29	28	27	6.9	6.2	5.7	482.8	587.0	513.0	248.0
Sri Lanka	311	663	867	20	37	47	3.8	5.1	6.5	21.6	115.0	4.2	110.2
Tajikistan	n.a.	111	113	n.a.	19	19	n.a.	10.1	11.0	n.a.	7.0	n.a.	16.5
Turkmenistan	n.a.	135	135	n.a.	30	30	n.a.	2.8	2.8	n.a.	18.0	n.a.	n.a.
Uzbekistan	n.a.	385	412	n.a.	17	17	n.a.	3.8	3.8	n.a.	30.0	n.a.	16.0
Total	13,682	18,029	18,456	17	19	20	4.3	5.2	5.3	2,113.7	2,859.5	1,052.2	2,537.2
East Asia and Australasia													
Australia	7,436	8,399	8,394	472	460	455	3.4	2.4	2.2	70.4	57.8	49.5	1.0
Brunei	280	268	330	1,250	909	1,091	6.0	6.0	6.5	4.1	5.0	0.7	4.1
Cambodia	n.a.	174	177	n.a.	18	18	n.a.	5.9	5.7	35.0	87.7	n.a.	220.0
China	27,107	32,929	34,684	26	27	29	7.9	5.9	5.7	3,900.0	2,935.0	1,275.0	1,200.0
Fiji	19	48	47	27	61	60	1.2	2.7	2.6	2.7	3.6	6.0	n.a.
Indonesia	3,197	4,403	4,599	20	23	23	2.8	2.2	2.1	278.1	299.2	400.0	186.0
Japan	29,350	50,219	43,626	243	401	348	1.0	1.0	1.0	243.0	235.5	47.9	12.0
Korea, North	5,675	5,232	5,330	278	240	243	23.0	25.6	27.2	838.0	1,054.0	4,700.0	115.0
Korea, South	8,592	14,179	15,168	209	316	336	5.1	3.4	3.3	598.0	660.0	4,500.0	8.0
Laos	75	73	76	21	15	15	7.8	4.2	4.1	53.7	37.0	n.a.	100.0
Malaysia	2,409	3,514	3,542	155	153	148	5.6	4.5	4.2	110.0	114.5	35.8	25.8
Mongolia	47	19	14	24	8	6	9.0	2.4	1.7	33.0	21.0	140.0	12.5
New Zealand	882	1,024	729	271	290	205	2.9	1.9	1.3	12.4	9.9	6.7	n.a.
Papua New Guinea	49	66	77	14	15	17	1.5	1.3	1.5	3.2	3.7	n.a.	n.a.
Philippines	647	1,361	1,457	12	20	21	1.4	2.0	2.0	114.8	107.5	131.0	42.5
Singapore	1,622	3,970	3,959	634	1,349	1,325	6.7	5.9	5.5	55.0	53.9	221.0	11.6
Taiwan	8,793	13,143	13,297	453	622	624	7.0	5.0	4.9	444.0	376.0	1,657.5	26.7
Thailand	2,559	4,006	4,212	49	66	69	5.0	2.4	2.5	235.3	254.0	200.0	139.5
Vietnam	3,277	910	930	53	12	12	19.4	4.3	4.0	1,027.0	572.0	3,000.0	50.0
Total	102,018	143,937	140,650	234	264	266	6.5	4.7	4.6	8,057.7	6,887.3	16,371.0	2,154.7

Caribbean, Central and Latin America

Caribbean

	1985	1995	1996	1985	1995	1996	1985	1995	1996	1985	1996	1996	1996
Antigua and Barbuda	3	3	3	39	47	46	0.5	0.7	0.8	0.1	0.2	0.1	n.a.
Bahamas	13	19	21	56	74	80	0.5	0.6	0.6	0.5	0.9	n.a.	2.3
Barbados	16	14	14	71	50	50	0.9	0.7	0.7	1.0	0.6	0.4	n.a.
Cuba	2,181	700	686	216	64	62	9.6	5.8	5.4	161.5	100.0	135.0	19.0

(1995 constant prices)	Defence Expenditure US$m			US$ per capita			% of GDP			Numbers in Armed Forces (000)		Estimated Reservists (000)	Para-military (000)
	1985	1995	1996	1985	1995	1996	1985	1995	1996	1985	1996	1996	1996
Dominican Republic	70	109	101	11	14	13	1.1	1.3	1.1	22.2	24.5	n.a.	15.0
Haiti	42	59	62	7	8	9	1.5	3.4	3.5	6.9	n.a.	n.a.	7.0
Jamaica	27	28	28	12	11	11	0.9	0.6	0.6	2.1	3.3	0.9	0.2
Trinidad and Tobago	100	72	71	84	55	54	1.4	1.2	1.1	2.1	2.1	n.a.	4.8
Central America													
Belize	5	13	14	33	62	64	1.4	2.4	2.5	0.6	1.1	0.7	n.a.
Costa Rica	40	48	50	15	14	14	0.7	0.6	0.6	n.a.	n.a.	n.a.	7.0
El Salvador	344	145	122	72	26	21	4.4	1.8	1.5	41.7	28.4	n.a.	12.0
Guatemala	160	150	154	20	14	14	1.8	1.4	1.4	31.7	44.2	35.0	12.3
Honduras	98	54	57	22	9	9	2.1	1.3	1.3	16.6	18.8	60.0	5.5
Mexico	1,695	2,366	2,582	22	26	28	0.7	0.8	0.8	129.1	175.0	300.0	15.0
Nicaragua	301	39	36	92	9	8	17.4	1.8	1.5	62.9	17.0	12.0	n.a.
Panama	123	107	109	56	40	40	2.0	1.3	1.4	12.0	n.a.	n.a.	11.8
South America													
Argentina	4,945	3,879	3,732	162	113	108	3.8	1.7	1.5	108.0	72.5	375.0	31.2
Bolivia	173	146	152	27	18	18	2.0	2.1	2.1	27.6	33.5	n.a.	30.6
Brazil	3,209	9,824	10,341	24	61	63	0.8	2.0	2.1	276.0	295.0	1115.0	385.6
Chile	1,696	1,947	1,990	140	137	138	7.8	3.7	3.5	101.0	89.7	50.0	31.2
Colombia	579	1,791	1,846	20	51	52	1.6	2.6	2.6	66.2	146.3	60.7	87.0
Ecuador	388	530	528	41	45	44	1.8	3.4	3.4	42.5	57.1	100.0	0.3
Guyana	43	7	7	54	9	9	6.8	1.1	1.0	6.6	1.6	1.5	1.5
Paraguay	82	112	110	22	23	22	1.3	1.4	1.3	14.4	20.2	164.5	14.8
Peru	875	874	1,061	47	37	44	4.5	1.6	1.9	128.0	125.0	188.0	68.6
Suriname	11	14	14	29	34	33	2.4	3.9	3.5	2.0	1.8	n.a.	n.a.
Uruguay	326	331	270	108	104	85	3.5	2.9	2.3	31.9	25.6	n.a.	2.5
Venezuela	1,125	882	903	65	40	40	2.1	1.1	1.2	49.0	46.0	8.0	23.0
Total	18,671	24,264	25,063	56	43	42	3.0	1.9	1.8	1,344.2	1,330.4	2,606.8	788.2
Sub-Saharan Africa													
Horn Of Africa													
Djibouti	44	22	20	102	35	31	7.9	5.5	5.2	3.0	8.4	n.a.	4.2
Eritrea	n.a.	40	59	n.a.	11	16	n.a.	5.7	7.5	n.a.	55.0	n.a.	n.a.
Ethiopia	610	119	122	14	2	2	17.9	2.2	2.0	217.0	120.0	n.a.	n.a.
Somali Republic	63	43	43	12	7	7	6.2	4.9	4.8	62.7	225.0	n.a.	n.a.
Sudan	146	389	397	7	14	13	3.2	4.3	4.3	56.6	89.0	n.a.	75.0
Central Africa													
Burundi	48	46	49	10	7	7	3.0	5.3	4.1	5.2	18.5	n.a.	3.5
Cameroon	217	202	218	21	15	16	1.4	2.4	2.4	7.3	13.1	n.a.	9.0
Cape Verde	5	4	4	15	10	9	0.9	2.0	1.7	7.7	1.1	n.a.	0.1

(1995 constant prices)

	Defence Expenditure US$m			US$ per capita			% of GDP			Numbers in Armed Forces (000)		Estimated Reservists (000)	Para-military (000)
	1985	1995	1996	1985	1995	1996	1985	1995	1996	1985	1996	1996	1996
Central African Republic	24	24	29	9	7	8	1.4	2.0	2.4	2.3	2.7	n.a.	2.3
Chad	51	34	38	10	5	6	2.9	2.5	2.7	12.2	25.4	n.a.	9.5
Congo	76	49	54	41	18	19	1.9	1.9	1.9	8.7	10.0	n.a.	5.0
Equatorial Guinea	4	2	2	11	5	5	2.0	1.5	1.0	2.2	1.3	n.a.	0.3
Gabon	108	102	109	108	78	81	1.8	1.9	2.0	2.4	4.7	n.a.	4.8
Rwanda	45	90	93	7	12	12	1.9	6.9	6.3	5.2	33.0	n.a.	n.a.
Zaire	111	185	166	4	4	4	1.5	3.2	2.8	48.0	28.1	n.a.	37.0
East Africa													
Kenya	350	206	207	17	7	7	3.1	2.3	2.2	13.7	24.2	n.a.	5.0
Madagascar	74	33	36	7	2	3	2.0	0.8	0.8	21.1	21.0	n.a.	7.5
Mauritius	3	14	60	3	12	52	0.3	0.6	2.3	1.0	1.3	n.a.	0.5
Seychelles	11	12	10	168	163	144	2.1	3.6	3.1	1.2	0.3	n.a.	1.0
Tanzania	191	87	83	9	3	3	4.4	2.7	2.5	40.4	34.6	80.0	1.4
Uganda	72	126	150	5	7	8	1.8	2.1	2.4	20.0	50.0	n.a.	1.5
West Africa													
Benin	29	24	26	7	4	5	1.1	1.4	1.4	4.5	4.8	n.a.	2.5
Burkina Faso	46	68	65	6	6	6	1.1	2.6	2.4	4.0	5.8	n.a.	4.5
Côte d'Ivoire	104	98	92	10	7	6	0.8	1.0	0.9	13.2	8.4	12.0	7.8
Gambia, The	3	15	14	4	14	13	1.5	4.1	3.9	0.5	0.8	n.a.	n.a.
Ghana	86	121	118	7	7	7	1.0	1.5	1.4	15.1	7.0	n.a.	7.5
Guinea	71	51	55	12	8	8	1.8	1.8	1.9	9.9	9.7	n.a.	9.6
Guinea Bissau	15	8	8	17	8	7	5.7	3.1	2.9	8.6	7.3	n.a.	2.0
Liberia	38	45	44	17	15	14	2.4	3.5	3.3	6.8	22.0	n.a.	n.a.
Mali	41	50	40	5	5	4	1.4	2.3	1.8	4.9	7.4	n.a.	7.8
Niger	16	21	21	3	2	2	0.5	0.9	0.9	2.2	5.3	n.a.	5.4
Nigeria	1,475	1,507	1,521	16	15	15	1.7	3.5	3.5	94.0	77.1	n.a.	12.0
Senegal	86	74	73	13	9	8	1.1	1.9	1.7	10.1	13.4	n.a.	4.0
Sierra Leone	7	41	45	2	9	9	1.0	5.7	5.9	3.1	14.2	n.a.	0.8
Togo	26	28	27	9	7	6	1.3	2.7	2.5	3.6	7.0	n.a.	0.8
Southern Africa													
Angola	883	400	441	101	38	40	15.1	6.3	6.4	49.5	97.0	n.a.	40.0
Botswana	51	225	224	47	152	147	1.1	7.0	6.7	4.0	7.5	n.a.	1.0
Lesotho	63	33	31	41	17	15	4.6	6.0	5.0	2.0	2.0	n.a.	n.a.
Malawi	29	21	23	4	2	2	1.0	1.3	1.2	5.3	9.8	1.0	1.0
Mozambique	326	58	61	24	3	3	8.5	3.7	3.7	15.8	11.0	n.a.	n.a.
Namibia	n.a.	65	71	n.a.	39	42	n.a.	2.7	3.0		8.1	n.a.	0.1
South Africa	3,922	3,177	2,506	117	75	58	2.7	2.4	1.8	106.4	137.9	550.7	140.0
Zambia	55	61	58	8	7	6	1.1	2.0	1.8	16.2	21.6	n.a.	1.4
Zimbabwe	232	233	232	28	21	20	3.1	4.2	3.9	41.0	43.0	n.a.	21.8
Total	9,856	8,252	7,745	26	20	20	3.0	3.1	3.0	958.5	1,069.8	643.7	407.5

(1995 constant prices)

	Defence Expenditure US$m			US$ per capita			% of GDP			Numbers in Armed Forces (000)		Estimated Reservists (000)	Para-military (000)
	1985	1995	1996	1985	1995	1996	1985	1995	1996	1985	1996	1996	1996
Global Totals													
NATO	560,777	470,880	457,430	496 / 907	463 / 670	458 / 647	3.3 / 4.7	2.3 / 3.0	2.3 / 2.9	5,378.0	3,990.2	5,227.7	813.8
Non-NATO Europe	34,652	30,960	27,986	234 / n.a.	162 / 125	148 / 113	4.8 / n.a.	4.7 / 2.4	3.8 / 2.2	1,449.1	1,957.7	6,976.4	404.0
Russia	n.a.	82,000	69,537	n.a.	554	470	n.a.	7.4	6.5	n.a.	1,270.0	2,400.0	352.0
Soviet Union	329,449	n.a.	n.a.	1,181	n.a.	n.a.	16.1	n.a.	n.a.	5,300.0	n.a.	n.a.	n.a.
Middle East and North Africa	91,937	49,391	49,705	737 / 431	508 / 174	492 / 169	12.3 / 15.1	7.0 / 8.2	6.8 / 7.9	2,530.7	2,863.1	2,622.7	929.0
Central and South Asia	13,682	18,029	18,456	17 / n.a.	19 / 13	20 / 13	4.3 / n.a.	5.2 / 3.6	5.3 / 3.4	2,113.7	2,859.5	1,052.2	2,537.2
East Asia and Australasia	102,018	143,937	140,650	234 / 63	264 / 77	266 / 74	6.5 / 2.3	4.7 / 1.9	4.6 / 2.0	8,057.7	6,887.3	16,371.0	2,154.7
Caribbean, Central and Latin America	18,671	24,264	25,063	56 / 47	43 / 51	42 / 52	3.0 / 1.9	1.9 / 1.7	1.8 / 1.7	1,344.2	1,330.4	2,606.8	788.2
Sub-Saharan Africa	9,856	8,252	7,745	26 / 22	20 / 15	20 / 13	3.0 / 3.3	3.1 / 2.7	3.0 / 2.4	958.5	1,069.8	643.7	407.5
Global totals	1,161,042	827,714	796,572	373 / 275	254 / 146	240 / 139	6.7 / 5.2	4.5 / 2.9	4.3 / 2.8	27,131.9	22,227.9	37,900.6	8,386.4

Notes

1   For an explanation of the IISS defence-expenditure calculation, see 'Explanatory Notes'
2   Under *Defence expenditure per capita* and *Defence expenditure as a proportion of GDP*, the top figure is the average of individual country values and the lower figure is the average of aggregated regional and global values

Table 54 **Warships** *Submarines*

Class name	Displacement[1] (Tons – dived)	No. in service	Countries operating	Missile launchers	Torpedo tubes	Remarks
Abato	1,400	2	Pe	0	4 533mm (bow), 2 533mm (stern)	1 127mm gun aft
Agosta	1,760	4	Fr	0	4 533mm (bow)	20 torpedoes or 36 mines
Akula	9,100	13	RF	see remarks	4 533mm, 4 650mm	SS-N-21 SLCM
Albacora	1,043	3	Por	0	12 533mm	Fr *Daphné*
Benjamin Franklin	8,250	2	US	0	4 533mm (bow)	Special Forces ops; nuclear-powered
Canakkale/Burakreis	2,440	6	Tu	0	6 533mm (bow), 4 533mm (stern)	Ex-US *Guppy* II; 40 mines in lieu of torpedoes
Charlie II	5,550	2	RF	8 SS-N-7 or SS-N-9 USGW SS-N-15 ASW	6 533mm	SS-N-15 ASW fired from 533mm TT; 2 tubes may be 650mm for SS-N-16; nuclear-powered
Collins	3,353	1	Aus	see remarks	6 533mm	Sub-*Harpoon* SSM fired from 533mm TT
Daphné	1,038	2	Fr	0	12 550mm	Fr *Daphné*
Delphin	1,043	4	Sp	0	12 550mm	
Delta I (SSBN)	10,200	5	RF	12 SS-N-8 SLBM	4 533mm (bow), 2 406mm (bow)	Nuclear-powered
Delta II (SSBN)	11,750	3	RF	16 SS-N-8 SLBM	4 533mm (bow), 2 406mm (bow)	Nuclear-powered
Delta III (SSBN)	11,450	10	RF	16 SS-N-18 SLBM	4 533mm (bow), 2 406mm (bow)	Nuclear-powered
Delta IV (SSBN)	12,600	7	RF	16 SS-N-23 SLBM	4 533mm (bow), 2 650mm (bow)	Nuclear-powered
Dolgorae	175	1	ROK	0	2 406mm	Special Forces ops; can carry 8 swimmers
Dolphin	1,900	1	Il	Sub-harpoon USGW	2 650mm, 4 533mm	Ge new design, 2 more building
Echo II	5,800	1	RF	8 SS-N-12 USGW	5 533mm	Nuclear-powered
Foxtrot	2,475	2	C	0	6 533mm (bow), 4 533mm (stern)	44 mines in lieu of torpedoes (non-op)
		4	RF			
		5	Ind			
		2	LAR			
		2	Pl			
Gal	600	3	Il	Sub-*Harpoon* USGW	8 533mm	UK Vickers 540
Galerna	1,740	4	Sp	0	4 533mm	Fr *Agosta*; 19 mines with reduced torpedo load
Gotland	1,490	2	Swe	0	4 533mm, 2 400mm	AIP; can carry up to 48 mines
Hai Lung	2,660	2	ROC	0	6 533mm (bow)	Ex-Nl *Zwaardvis*-class
Hai Shih	2,420	2	ROC	0	6 533mm (bow), 4 533mm (stern)	Ex-US *Guppy* II
Han	5,500	5	PRC	0	6 533mm	36 mines in lieu of torpedoes; nuclear-powered
Hangor	1,043	4	Pak	Sub-*Harpoon* USGW	12 550mm	Fr *Daphné*
Harushio	3,000	7	J	see remarks	6 533mm	Sub-*Harpoon* SSM can be fired from TT
Hashmat	1,740	2	Pak	Sub-*Harpoon* USGW	4 533mm	Fr *Agosta*; mining capability; TT launcher
Heroj	705	2	FRY	0	4 533mm	12 mines in lieu of torpedoes
Kilo	3,076	17	RF	0	6 533mm	24 mines in lieu of torpedoes
		3	PRC	0	6 533mm	24 mines in lieu of torpedoes
		8	Ind	0	6 533mm	24 mines in lieu of torpedoes
		2	Ag	0	6 533mm	24 mines in lieu of torpedoes

Class name	Displacement (Tons – dived)	No. in service	Countries operating	Missile launchers	Torpedo tubes	Remarks
Kilo continued		3	Ir	0	6 533mm	24 mines in lieu of torpedoes
		1	R	0	6 533mm	24 mines in lieu of torpedoes
Kobben	524	6	No	0	8 533mm	Ge Type 207
Le Redoutable (SSBN)	8,920	4	Fr	16 M4 SLBM	4 533mm	Nuclear-powered
Le Triomphant (SSBN)	14,335	1	Fr	16 M45 SLBM	4 533mm	
Los Angeles	6,927	55	US	12 *Tomahawk* SLCM *Harpoon* USGW	4 533mm	Nuclear-powered; basic, modified and improved variants in service
Maria Van Riebeek	1,043	3	RSA	0	8 550mm (bow), 4 550mm (stern)	Ex-Fr *Daphné*; no torpedo reloads
Ming	2,113	13	PRC	0	8 533mm	32 mines in lieu of torpedoes
Näcken	1,085	1	Swe	0	6 533mm, 2 400mm	48 mines externally
Narhvalen	450	3	Da	0	8 533mm	Ge Type 205 design
Narwhal	5,830	1	US	8 *Tomahawk* USGW	4 533mm	Nuclear-powered
Oberon	2,410	2	Aus	Sub-*Harpoon* USGW	6 533mm	Combined total of 20 *Harpoon* and torpedoes
		3	Br			
		3	Ca			
		2	Chl			
Ohio (SSBN)	18,750	18	US	8 with 24 *Trident* C-4 SLBM, 8 with 24 *Trident*	4 533mm	Nuclear-powered
Oscar	12,500	12	RF	24 SS-N-19 USGW SS-N-15 and SSN-16	4 533mm, 2 or 4 650mm	Nuclear-powered
Romeo	1,830	2	Bg	TT launch	6 533mm (bow), 2 533mm (stern)	28 mines in lieu of torpedoes
		36	PRC			
		8	Et			4 units only USGW
		22	DPRK			Non-op
		3	Syr			
Rubis	2,670	6	Fr	*Exocet* USGW from TT	4 533mm	32 mines in lieu of torpedoes
Santa Cruz	2,264	3	Arg	0	6 533mm	Ge TR-1700; mining capability
Sauro	1,631	8	It	0	6 533mm	20 mines in lieu of torpedoes
Sava	960	2	FRY	0	6 533mm	
Seawolf	9,150	1	US	*Tomahawk* USGW Sub-*Harpoon* USGW	8 660mm	100 mines in lieu of torpedoes
Sierra	7,900	4	RF	SS-N-21 SLCM Sub-*Harpoon* USGW	8 650mm	Nuclear-powered
Song	2,250	1	PRC	YJ-82 USGW	6 533mm	Mines in lieu of torpedoes; msl op late 1998
Sturgeon	4,960	18	US	*Tomahawk* USGW Sub-*Harpoon*	4 533mm	Mining capability; 4 of class DDS for 1 pl SEAL; 4 of class can support DSRV
Swiftsure	4,900	5	UK	Sub-*Harpoon* USGW	5 533mm	Mines can be carried in lieu of torpedoes
Type 205	450	2	Ge	0	8 533mm	
Type 206/206A	498	14	Ge	0	8 533mm	Mining capability

Class name	Displacement[1] (Tons – dived)	No. in service	Countries operating	Missile launchers	Torpedo tubes	Remarks
(Type 209) *Salta*	1,440	1	Arg	0	8 533mm	Ge design; mining capability
Local class names						
Atilay	"	6	Tu	0	"	
Cakra	"	2	Indo	0	"	
Casma	"	6	Pe	0	"	
Chang Bogo	"	6	ROK	0	"	
Glavkos	"	8	Gr	see remarks	"	1 with sub-*Harpoon* USGW
Pijao	"	2	Co	0	"	
Preveze	"	2	Tu	Sub-*Harpoon* USGW	"	
Sabalo	"	2	Ve	0	"	
Shishumar	"	4	Ind	0	"	
Shyri	"	2	Ec	0	"	
Thompson	"	2	Chl	0	"	
Tupi	"	3	Br	0	"	
Tang	2,700	2	Tu	0	8 533mm	Mining capability
Tango	3,800	5	RF	0	6 533mm	24 mines in lieu of torpedoes
Trafalgar	5,900	7	UK	see remarks	5 533mm	Nuclear-powered; sub-*Harpoon* USGW
Tumleren	524	3	Da	0	8 533mm	Mod Ge *Kobben*
Typhoon (SSBN)	26,500	6	RF	20 SS-N-20 SLBM	2 533mm, 4 650mm	Nuclear-powered; mines in lieu of torpedoes can fire SS-N-15 ASW from 533mm TT
Ula	1,150	6	No	0	8 533mm	
Vanguard (SSBN)	15,900	3	UK	16 *Trident* D-5 SLBM	4 533mm	Nuclear-powered
Västergötland	1,143	4	Swe	0	6 533mm, 3 400mm	Can carry 48 mines in external girdle
Victor 3	6,300	26	RF	see remarks	2 533mm, 4 650mm	Nuclear-powered; SS-N-21 SLCM, SS-N-15 ASW, SS-N-16 ASW
Walrus	2,800	4	Nl	see remarks	4 533mm	Provision for sub-*Harpoon* USGW
Whiskey	1,350	1	Alb	0	6 533mm	Mining capability
		4	DPRK			
Xia (SSBN)	8,000	1	PRC	12 CSS-N-3 SLBM	6 533mm	Nuclear-powered
Yankee	10,000	1	RF	12 SS-NX-24 SLCM	n.k.	Trials boat nuclear-powered
Yankee Notch	10,300	3	RF	40 SS-N-21 SLCM	6 533mm	Nuclear-powered
Yuushio	2,450	9	J	Sub-*Harpoon* USGW	6 533mm	

Note

[1] For an explanation of the displacement and tonnage used, see 'Structure and Methodology'

Table 55 **Conventional Armed Forces in Europe** (CFE) **Treaty**

Manpower and Treaty Limited Equipment: current holdings and CFE limits on the forces of the Treaty members

Current holdings are derived from data declared as at 1 January 1997 and so may differ from *The Military Balance* listings

	Manpower Holding	Manpower Limit	Tanks¹ Holding	Tanks¹ Limit	ACV¹ Holding	ACV¹ Limit	Artillery¹ Holding	Artillery¹ Limit	Attack Helicopters Holding	Attack Helicopters Limit	Combat Aircraft² Holding	Combat Aircraft² Limit
Budapest/Tashkent Group												
Armenia	54,658	60,000	102	220	218	220	225	285	7	50	6	100
Azerbaijan	69,254	70,000	270	220	557	220	301	285	15	50	48	100
Belarus	83,817	100,000	1,778	1,800	2,518	2,600	1,533	1,615	71	80	286	294
Bulgaria	93,731	104,000	1,475	1,475	1,985	2,000	1,750	1,750	43	67	235	235
Czech Republic	61,647	93,333	952	957	1,367	1,367	767	767	36	50	144	230
Georgia	30,000	40,000	79	220	102	220	92	285	3	50	6	100
Hungary	49,958	100,000	797	835	1,300	1,700	840	840	59	108	142	180
Moldova	11,075	20,000	0	210	209	210	155	250	0	50	27	50
Poland	227,860	234,000	1,729	1,730	1,442	2,150	1,581	1,610	94	130	384	460
Romania	228,195	230,000	1,375	1,375	2,091	2,100	1,466	1,475	16	120	372	430
Russia*a*	817,139	1,450,000	5,541	6,400	10,198	11,480	6,011	6,415	812	890	2,891	3,416
Slovakia	45,483	46,667	478	478	683	683	383	383	19	25	113	115
Ukraine	370,847	450,000	4,063	4,080	4,847	5,050	3,764	4,040	294	330	940	1,090
North Atlantic Treaty Group												
Belgium	44,057	70,000	334	334	678	1,099	312	320	46	46	166	232
Canada*b*	0	10,660	0	77	0	277	0	38	0	0	0	90
Denmark	29,629	39,000	343	353	286	316	503	553	12	12	74	106
France	281,647	325,000	1,156	1,306	3,574	3,820	1,192	1,292	326	396	650	800
Germany	285,326	345,000	3,248	4,166	2,537	3,446	2,058	2,705	205	306	560	900
Greece	158,621	158,621	1,735	1,735	2,325	2,534	1,878	1,878	20	30	486	650
Italy	245,575	315,000	1,283	1,348	3,031	3,339	1,932	1,955	132	139	516	650
Netherlands	43,856	80,000	722	743	610	1,080	448	607	12	50	181	230
Norway	24,421	32,000	170	170	199	225	246	527	0	0	74	100
Portugal	45,731	75,000	186	300	346	430	320	450	0	26	105	160
Spain	180,063	300,000	725	794	1,194	1,588	1,230	1,310	28	90	200	310
Turkey*a*	527,670	530,000	2,563	2,795	2,424	3,120	2,843	3,523	25	103	362	750
UK	224,351	260,000	521	1,015	2,411	3,176	436	636	289	371	624	900
US	107,481	250,000	1,115	4,006	1,849	5,372	612	2,492	126	431	220	784

Notes

¹ Includes TLE with land-based maritime forces (Marines, Naval Infantry etc.)
² Does not include land-based maritime aircraft for which a separate limit has been set

a Manpower and TLE is for that in the Atlantic to the Urals (ATTU) zone only
b Canada has now withdrawn all its TLE from the ATTU

Table 56 **Military Satellites**

This table includes only satellites dedicated to military use. It does not include other military satellites such as those used for scientific research, nor civilian communications, photographic and remote-sensing satellites which could also have a military use.

	Designation/Name Launch Date	Purpose/ Operator	Capabilities	Orbit/ Lifetime	Remarks
United States	*Leasat 5* Jan 1990	Comms Navy	UHF band 240–400 MHz; SHF band 7,250–7,500 MHz and 7,975–8,025 MHz	GEO 7 years	Last satellite in *Leasat* series, also known as *Syncom* IV; to replace and supplement *Fleetsatcom*
	Fleetsatcom (FSC) 4 Oct 1980	Comms Navy	23 channels in UHF band 244–263 MHz: 10 Navy, 12 Air Force, 1 US National Command		Likely to provide command and control of Navy nuclear forces into late 1990s; to be replaced by UFO system (see below)
	Fleetsatcom 7 Dec 1986 *Fleetsatcom* 8 Sep 1989	Air Force	FSC 7 and 8 carry additional EHF equipment	GEO 10 years	
	Ultra-high Frequency Follow-On (UFO) Communications Satellite UFO 2 Sep 1993		39 channels: 21 narrow band, 17 relay, 1 fleet broadcast		To replace US Navy's Fleet Satellite Communications System (FLTSAT)
	UFO 3 Jun 1994 UFO 4 Jan 1995 UFO 5 May 1995 UFO 6 Oct 1995 UFO 7 Jul 1996	Comms Navy	Enhanced anti-jamming and hardening against electro-magnetic pulse UHF uplink and downlink, SHF anti-jamming command link, and S-band	GEO 14 years	Full system to consist of nine satellites; UFO 8, 9 and 10 scheduled for launch to 1999
	Defense Space Communications Satellite System (DSCS) II-16 Sep 1989	Comms Army Navy Air Force	Some tactical voice and data communications 7/8 GHz X-band, up/down; 1,300 duplex voice channels or 100Mbit/s of data	GEO 7.5 years	DCSC II-16 is probably the only remaining operational DSCS II, but will be replaced by DSCSIII
	DSCS III-2 Oct 1985 DSCS III-3 Oct 1985 DSCS III-4 Sep 1989 DSCS III-5 Feb 1982 DSCS III-6 Jul 1992 DSCS III-7 Jul 1993 DSCS III-8 Nov 1993		1,300 duplex voice channels, hardening against EMPs, X-rays, and gamma rays; can detect jamming attempts and determine location of jammer; six SHF up/down channels	GEO 10 years	DSCS III constellation will eventually consist of 14 satellites

United States *continued*

Designation/Name Launch Date	Purpose/ Operator	Capabilities	Orbit/ Lifetime	Remarks
DSCS III-9 Jul 1995				Launch of DSCS-III 10 expected late 1997 or 1998
NAVSTAR (Block 2) GPS 13, 14, 15, 16, 17, 18, 19, 20, 21 Feb 1989–Oct 1990	Nav Air Force	System can fix military users to 16m, but is downgraded for civil users	MEO 7.5 years	The more advanced Block 2R system with an accuracy of 1m will replace expired satellites; they will have improved stability and survivability, and 180 days' service without ground control; will also have improved atomic clocks. First Block 2R launched Jul 1997
NAVSTAR (Block 2A) GPS 22, 23, 24, 25, 26, 27, 28, 29, 31, 33, 34, 35, 36, 37, 38, 39, 40 Nov 1990–Sep 1996	Nav			Sensors to detect and evaluate nuclear detonations deployed in NAVSTAR system
Defense Support Program (DSP) 1 DSP-F14 (DSP 3-2) Jun 1989 **DSP-F15 (DSP 3-3)** Nov 1990 **DSP-F16 (DSP 3-4)** Nov 1991 **DSP-F17 (DSP 3-5)** Dec 1994 **DSP-F18 (DSP 3-6)** Feb 1997	EW/Intel Air Force	Wide-field IR sensor senses at two wavelengths; detects missile launches, nuclear detonations, aircraft in after-burner, spacecraft and terrest-rial infra-red events	GEO 5–9 years	Ten DSP-1 satellites planned; 4 more to be launched before programme termination. To be succeeded by Space-Based Infra-red System in GEOSY, highly elliptical and low-earth orbits
Orion (fomerly *Magnum*) Nov 1989	SIGINT NRO, CIA	Intercepts and relays commu-nications and missile tele-metric signals	GEOSY 7–9 years	Programmes at or near end of life; only 2 built, first launched 1985
Name unknown Aug 1994, May 1995 Apr 1996	SIGINT NRO, NSA, CIA	Intercepts and relays commu-nications and missile tele-metric signals	GEOSY	Indicates that the three launches correspond to 2 GEOSY programmes
Jumpseat May 1994, Jul 1995, Apr 1996	SIGINT NSA	Capabilities not known		
Trumpet May 1994, July 1995	SIGINT NSA	Intercepts coomunications and perhaps electronic signals	Highly ellip-tical (*Molniya*) orbit	Successor to *Jumpseat*. Programme reportedly termin-ated after initial order of 3; third launch due in 1997
Defense Meteoro-logical Satellite Program (DMSP) DMSP B5D2 7 (S11) Nov 1991 **DMSP B5D2 8 (S12)** Apr 1995 **DMSP B5D2 9 (S13)** Mar 1995	Met	Operational Linescan Imaging System, Microwave Imager, Microwave temperature sounder, IR temperature/ moisture sounder; 0.5km reso--lution, 2,960km scan width	LEO, Sun-Synch 4–5 years	Next generation, DMSP 5D3, planned to launch summer 1997 To be followed by DMSP 6 in 2004–5

	Designation/Name Launch Date	Purpose/ Operator	Capabilities	Orbit/ Lifetime	Remarks
US *continued*	*Lacrosse* (formerly *Indigo*) Dec 1988, Nov 1991	**Radar Imaging** NRO	All-weather, 24-hour imaging capability; resolution 1–2m	LEO	Originally developed to give US capability to monitor events in cloud-covered eastern Europe and Soviet Union; most recent codename may be *Vega*
	Improved Crystal advanced KH-11 Nov 1992, Dec 1995 Dec 1996	**Photo Recce** NRO, CIA	Visible light and infra-red imagery	LEO 8 years	Real-time return; 6-inch resolution; replaced KH-11
NATO	**NATO 3D** Nov 1984	Comms	Secure communications within Europe and US; three X-band channels	GEO 7 years	NATO 3D remains as back-up system
	NATO 4A Jan 1991		Four channels of 60–135 MHz two UHF transponders with 25 KHz channel Anti-jamming features	GEO 7 years	NATO 4A and B are almost identical to UK's *Skynet* 4
	NATO 4B Dec 1993				
CIS/Russia	*Molniya-1* periodic (2–4 annually)	Comms	X-band transponder at 1.0/0.8 GHz up/down	GEO 2 years	Eight-satellite constellation for secure government/military communications
	Strela-2 Dec 1994			LEO 1.5 years	For long-range military communications using small, low-power, perhaps clandestine transmitters; stores data and sends to CIS receiving station during pass
	Strela-3 Feb 1996, Feb 1997			LEO 2 years	Tactical communications, six-satellite constellation also known as *Locsyst*; provides communication between military units, ships, bases, etc.
	Glonass 41, 46, 47, 48, 49, 52, 53, 54, 55, 56, 57, 58, 59, 60, 61, 62, 63, 64, 65, 66, 67, 68, 69, 70, 71 Dec 1990–Dec 1995	Nav	Horizontal position accuracy of 60m, vertical position accuracy of 75m for civil users; transmits spread spectrum signals at 1.2 and 1.6 GHz; Channel High Accuracy (CHA) available to authorised users	MEO 3 years	Full constellation consists of 24 satellites in three orbital planes; full complement of satellites began operation in January 1996; similar to US GPS NAVSTAR system
	Parus Feb 1993, Apr 1993, Mar 1995, Jan 1996, Apr 1997	Nav	80–100m positioning for naval vessels; VHF and UHF broadcast at approximately 150 and 400 MHz	LEO 2 years	Six-satellite constellation on planes spaced by 30 degrees; *Tsikada/Nadezhda* is civilian counterpart
	Prognoz Dec 1992	EW	S-band capacity	GEO	
	Oko Oct 1992–May 1997	EW		GEO/Ellip	Nine-satellite missile and nuclear-test monitoring Early Warning constellation
	Electronic Ocean Reconnaissance Satellite Surveillance (EORSAT) Jun 1995, Dec 1995, Dec 1996	Ocean		LEO 1.5 years	Passive electronic detection of radio/radar transmission frequencies from foreign ships

	Designation/Name Launch Date	Purpose/ Operator	Capabilities	Orbit/ Lifetime	Remarks
CIS/Russia continued	**Generation 3 Zenit** **Resurs-F** Periodic		Remote Sensing	LEO ± 30 days	
	Generation 4 Yantar **Kometa** Periodic	EW/Recce Photo Recce	Cameras, film-return capsule; topographic capability with 10m resolution	LEO 44 days 2 months	
	Generation 5 Periodic	Remote Sensing	Panchromatic, 3m resolution	LEO ± 300 days	
	Generation 6/7 Periodic	Remote Sensing		LEO 6–8 weeks	
	Tselina-2 Mar 1993–May 1997	Elint/ Sigint		LEO 3 years	
	Tselina-D Nov–Dec 1992	Elint/ Sigint		LEO	
France	**Hélios I** Jul 1995	Remote Sensing	1m multispectral resolution; revisit time 48hrs for 1 sat	LEO 5 years	With Ge, It and Sp
	Cerise Jul 1995	EW/ Recce		LEO 2.5 years	Military research satellite
China	**Fanhui Shi Weixing (FSW) I, 2** Periodic: short mission durations	Remote Sensing		LEO FSW 1: 7–10 days FSW 2: 15–18 days	—
UK	**Skynet 4A** Jan 1990	Comms	As Skynet 4B	GEO 7 years	
	Skynet 4B Dec 1988		3 X-band 7.25–8.40 GHz; 4 SHF channels; 2 UHF 305–315/250–260 MHz up/down transponders; hardened against EMP; has anti-jamming devices		
	Skynet 4C Aug 1990		As Skynet 4B		
Israel	**Offeq 3** Apr 1995	EW/Recce	Resolution 2m	LEO 2 years	

Abbreviations

CIA	Central Intelligence Agency (US)	NAV	Navigation
Comms	Communications	NAVSTAR	Navigation Satellite Timing and Ranging
DSCS	Defence Space Communications Satellite	NRO	National Reconnaissance Office (US)
EHF	Extra High Frequency		
Ellip	Elliptical	NSA	National Security Agency (US)
EW	Early Warning		
GEO	Geostationary orbit	SAT	Satellite
GEOSY	Geosynchronous	SHF	Super-High Frequency
GPS	Global Positioning System	UFO	UHF Follow-On
LEO	Low-earth orbit	UHF	Ultra-High Frequency

Definitions

Armoured Infantry Fighting Vehicle (AIFV) An armoured combat vehicle designed and equipped to transport an infantry squad, armed with integral/organic cannons of at least 20mm

Armoured Personnel Carrier (APC) A lightly armoured combat vehicle designed and equipped to transport an infantry squad, armed with integral/organic weapons of less than 20mm calibre

Table 57 **AIFV and APC** *key characteristics*

Armoured Infantry Fighting Vehicles (AIFV)

Designation	Country of origin	In-service date	Variants	Crew	W/T	Max road speed (km/h)	Max range (km)	Armament (mm)	Ammo	In service with
AIFV	US	1977–		3+7	T	61.2	490	25	324	Be, Et, Nl, Pi, Tu
AMX-10P	Fr	1973–94		3+8	T	65	500	20	760	Fr, Indo, Q, Sau, Sgp, UAE
AMX-VCI	Fr	1957–89		3+10	T	64	500–550	20	n.a.	Arg, Cy, Ec, Indo, RL, Mex, Q, Ve
ASCOD/*Pizarro*	A, Sp	1996		3+8	T	70	600	30	200	Sp
BMD-1	RF	1969–88?		3+4	T	70	320	73	40	Az, Bel, Mol, RF, Ukr, Uz
BMD-2	RF	1989–90?		2+5	T	60	500	30	300	RF
BMD-3	RF	1990–		2+5	T	71	500	30	860	RF
BMP-1	RF	1967–79		3+8	T	65	550–600	73	40	Afg, Ag, Ang, Arm, Az, Bel, C, Gr, Hu, Ind, Ir, Irq, Kaz, Kgz, LAR, Mgl, Moz, Pl, R, RF, Slvk, Ska, Swe, Syr, Tjk, Tkm, Ukr, Vn, Ye
BMP-2	RF	1979–?	D	3+7	T	65	550–600	30	500	Afg, Ag, Ang, Arm, Az, Bel, Cz, SF, Ind, Ir, Irq, HK, Kaz, Kwt, RF, Slvk, Syr, Ukr, Uz, Ye
BMP-23	Bg	1990	A	3+7	T	61.5	550–600	23	600	Bg
BMP-3	RF	1990–		3+7	T	70	600	100	40	Az, Cy, Kwt, RF, Ukr, UAE
BMP-30	Bg	1995–		3+7	T	61.5	600	30	1,000	Bg
CV 9030	Swe	1997		3+8	T	70	600	30	400	No
CV 9040	Swe	1995		3+8	T	70	600	40	238	Swe
M-80	FRY	1975–91	A	3+7	T	60	500	20	400	Cr, Slvn, FRY
M2/M3	US	1981–95	A1, A2	3+6	T	66	483	25	900	Sau, US
Marder 1	Ge	1968–75	A1/-A1A/-A2/-A3	9	T	75	520	20	1,250	Ge

Designation	Country of origin	In-service date	Variants	Crew	W/T	Max road speed (km/h)	Max range (km)	Armament (mm)	Ammo	In service with
MLI-84	R	1990–95		2+9	T	65	550–600	73	40	R
Pbv 302	Swe	1966–71		2+10	T	66	300	20	505	Swe
Ratel	RSA	1976–87	Mk 2, Mk 3	11	W	105	860	20	1,200	Mor, RSA
TAMSE VCTP	Arg	1981–		2+10	T	80	590	20	1,400	Arg
Type-89	J	1992–		3+7	T	70	400	35	n.a.	J
Warrior	UK	1987–		3+7	T	75	660	30	250	Kwt, UK
WZ-501	PRC	1991?		3+8	T	65	460–510	73	40	PRC
WZ-551	PRC	1995–?		3+9	W	85	600	25	400	PRC

Armoured Personnel Carriers (APC)

Designation	Country of origin	In-service date	Variants	Crew	W/T	Max road speed (km/h)	Max range (km)	Armament (mm)	Ammo	In service with
AAV7	US	1971–	A1	3+25	T	64	482	12.7	1,000	Arg, Br, It, ROK, Sp, Th, US, Ve
ACMAT	Fr	1980–		2+10	W	95	1,600	7.62	n.a.	CAR
Armadillo	Gua	1983–		3+13	W	100	1,200	12.7	n.a.	Gua
BDX/Timoney	Be	1978–82		2+10	W	100	500–900	7.62	n.a.	Be, Irl, Mex
BLR	Sp	1980?		1+12	W	93	570	7.62	n.a.	Sp
BMR-600	Sp	1979–89		2+10	W	103	1,000	12.7	2,500	Et, Sau, Pe, Sp
BOV	FRY	1980–?		2+8	W	95	500–800	7.62	n.a.	FRY
Bravia Commando Mk III	Por	1977–		3+5	W	90	800	7.62	n.a.	Por
Bravia Mk 1 (V-200 Chaimite)	Por	1963–		11	W	110	1,050	7.62	9,500	RL, Pe, Pi, Por
BTR-152	RF	1950–62	V/V1/V2/V3/K	2+17	W	75	600	7.62	1,250	Afg, Ang, Cam, RC, C, Eth, Gui, Gub, Irq, DPRK, RMM, Mgl, Moz, Nic, RF, Ska, Sdn, Syr, Tz, Vn
BTR-40		1950–?	B	2+8	W	80	285	7.62	1,250	Afg, Bu, C, Gui, GuB, Indo, DPRK, Lao, RF, Syr, Tz, Vn, Ye
BTR-60P	RF	1960–76	PA/PB/PU	2+16	W	80	500	7.62	2,000	Afg, Ag, Ang, Arm, Az, Bel, Bwa, Bg, Cam, RC, C, Dj, Ea, Eth, SF, Gui, GuB, Ir, Irq, DPRK, Lao, LAR, L, RMM, Mgl, Moz, Nic, Pe, R, RF, Syr, Tjk, Tu, Uga, Vn, Ye, Z
BTR-70	RF	1972–82		2+9	W	80	600	14.5	500	Arm, Az, Bel, Ea, Ga, Hu, Kaz, Mol, R, RF, Tjk, Tkm, Ukr, Uz
BTR-80	RF	1984–		3+7	W	90	600	14.5	500	Arm, Az, Bng, Bel, Ea, Ga, Hu, Kaz, RF, Tu, Ukr, Uz
BTR-80A	RF	1994–		2+8	W	90	600–800	30	300	RF
Buffel	RSA	1978–?		1+10	W	96	1000			RSA, Ska
Casspir	RSA	1979–	MkII, MkIII	2+10	W	90	850	7.62		Nba, Pe, RSA

Designation	Country of origin	In-service date	Variants	Crew	W/T	Max road speed (km/h)	Max range (km)	Armament (mm)	Ammo	In service with
Condor	Ge	1981–		2+12	W	100	900	20	220	Mal, Por, Tu, Ury
Dragoon	US	1983–		12	W	116	885	7.62	2,600	Ve
EE-11 Urutu	Br	1974–?		1+12	W	105	850	12.7	n.a.	Bol, Br, Chl, Co, Ec, Gbn, Irq, HKJ, LAR, Py, Sme, Tn, UAE, Ve
Fahd	Et	1986–		10	W	85	750	7.62	n.a.	Ag, Et, Kwt
Fiat 6614	It	1977–?		1+10	W	100	700	12.7	n.a.	It, ROK, Pe, Tn, Ve
FV 432	UK	1963–71		2+10	T	52.2	480	7.62	1,600	UK
Hotspur Hussar	UK	1987–		1+13	W	120	300	7.62	n.a.	Et, Ska
HWK-11	Ge	1964		2+10	T	65	320	12.7	n.a.	Mex
KIFV	ROK	1985–		3+9	T	74	480	7.62	n.a.	ROK, Mal
LAV-150	US	1964	-100, -200, S, ST	3+7	W	112	800	7.62	2,400	Bol, Btwa, Cm, Cha, DR, Gbn, Gua, Indo, Ja, Mal, Mex, Pi, Por, Sau, Sgp, Sdn, ROC, Th, Ve
LAV-300	US	1982–		3+9	W	105	925	7.62	n.a.	Pi
LOV-OP	Cr	1995–?		2+8	W	65	500–700		n.a.	Cr
M-113	US	1960–	A1/-A2/-A3	2+11	T	60–65	480	12.7	2,000	Arg, Aus, Be, Bol, Br, Cam, Ca, Chl, Da, Ec, Et, Ge, Gr, Gua, Il, HK, ROK, KWT, RL, Mor, NZ, No, Pak, Pe, Pi, Por, Sau, Sgp, Sp, CH, ROC, Th, Tu, US, Ye
M-60	FRY	1965–?		3+10	T	45	400	12.7	n.a.	Cr, FRY
MLVM	R	1990–95		2+7	T	48	370–400	14.5	600	R
MOWAG Roland	CH	1964–80		3+3	W	110	550	7.62	n.a.	Arg, Bol, Chl, Gr, Mex, Pe
MT-LB	RF	1971–?		2+11	T	61.5	500	7.62	2,500	Az, Bel, Bg, SF, Hu, Irq, Kaz, Mol, RF, Swe, Ukr
OT-62	Cz, Pl	1964–96	A/-B/-C	2+18	T	58	460	7.62	1,250	Et, Ind, Irq, LAR, Mor, Sdn
OT-64A (SKOT)	Cz, Pl	1964–	SKOT-2/-2A/-2AP	2+18	W	94.4	710	7.62	1,250	Cam, Cz, Ind, Irq, LAR, Mor, Pl, Slvk, Sdn, Uga, Ury
OT-90	Cz	1991?		3+8	T	65	550–600	14.5	n.a.	Cz, Slvk
Pandur	A	1995–		2+8	W	100	700	12.7	n.a.	A
Panhard M-3	Fr	1971–87?		2+10	W	90	600	7.62	n.a.	Ag, Brn, BF, Bu, Gbn, Irq, Irl, CI, Kya, RL, Mal, Ngr, Sau, Sen, UAE, Zr
Piranha/LAV (8x8)	CH	1976–	Category II	15	W	100	780	12.7	n.a.	Aus, Ca, Chl, Gha, Nga, O, Sau, CH, US
PSZH-IV	Hu	1970–?		3+6	W	80	500	14.5	500	Cz, Hu
Saracen	UK	1952–63		2+10	W	72	400	7.62	3,000	Indo, HKJ, RL, Nga, Ska

Designation	Country of origin	In-service date	Variants	Crew	W/T	Max road speed (km/h)	Max range (km)	Armament (mm)	Ammo	In service with
Saurer 4K 4FA	A	1961–69		2+8	T	65	370	12.7	n.a.	A
Saxon	UK	1976–93		2+10	W	96	480	12.7	n.a.	Brn, Mal, Nga, O, UK
Simba	UK	1994–		2+10	W	100	660	12.7	n.a.	Pi
SKPF m/42	Swe	1943–46		2+13	W	70	n.a.	7.62	n.a.	Lat, L, Swe
Steyr 4K 7FA G 127	A	1977		2+8	T	70	520	12.7	n.a.	Nga
Stormer	UK	1982–		3+8	T	80	650	7.62	n.a.	Indo, Mal, O, UK
TABC-79	R	1988–?		3+4	W	85	700	14.5	600	R
Tpz-1 (Fuchs)	Ge	1979–		2+10	W	105	800	7.62	n.a.	Ge, UK, US, Ve
Type-60	J	1960–72		4+6	T	45	300	12.7	n.a.	J
Type-73	J	1973		3+9	T	45	300	12.7	n.a.	J
Type-90	PRC	1995		2+13	T	65	500	12.7	1,000	PRC
UR-416	Ge	1969–78?		2+8	W	81	600–700	7.62	n.a.	Arg, EIS, Gr, Kya, Nga, Pak, Pe, Sau, Tg, Tu, Ve
VAB	Fr	1976–93		2+10	W	92	1000	12.7	n.a.	Bru, CAR, Cy, Fr, CI, RL, Ms, Mor, O, Q
VCC-1	It	1976–82?	–2	2+7	T	64.4	550	12.7	1,050	It,
VCR	Fr	1978–		3+9	W	90	700	7.62	n.a.	Mex, UAE
VXB-170	Fr	1971–78?		1+11	W	85	750	7.62	n.a.	Fr, Gbn, Sen
Walid	Et	1960–86?	–2	2+8–10	W	86	800	7.62	n.a.	Bu, Et, Sdn,
WZ-523	PRC	1995–?		2+10	W	80	600	12.7	600	PRC
XA-180/XA-185	SF	1984–		2+10	W	95	800–900	12.7	n.a.	SF, No
YW-531 (Type-63)	PRC	1969?		2+13	T	65	500	12.7	1,120	Alb, PRC, Irq, DPRK, Zr, Zw
YW-531 H (Type-85)	PRC	1986?		2+13	T	65	500	12.7	1,120	PRC, Th
YW-534	PRC	1986?		2+13	T	65	500	12.7	1,100	PRC

Notes

[1] The table shows only the original producer of each equipment. Other licensed producer countries are not listed.

[2] In service date indicates the period during which an equipment was brought into service. Where dates cannot be firmly established, '?' is used. Where equipment remains in production, an open date is given, i.e. 1979–

[3] W/T = Wheeled/Tracked

[4] Only the basic vehicle is listed. '/' is used to separate variants of each equipment. Variants with larger calibre cannons and those converted for other purposes (such as weapons platforms, command posts, communication terminals, etc) are not included.

[5] Maximum speed and range assumes travel by road.

[6] Maximum range does not include the fitting of long-range, additional, external or supplementary fuel tanks.

[8] Ammo = Ammunition. Where available, figures are given for the maximum number of main armament rounds.

[9] n.a. = not available.

[10] In service with – an index of country abbreviations can be found at pp. 317–18

Table 58 **Designations of aircraft and helicopters**

Notes

[1] [Square brackets] indicate the type from which a variant was derived: 'Q-5 ... [MiG-19]' indicates that the design of the Q-5 was based on that of the MiG-19.

[2] (Parentheses) indicate an alternative name by which an aircraft is known, sometimes in another version: 'L-188 ... *Electra* (P-3 *Orion*)' shows that in another version the Lockheed Type 188 *Electra* is known as the P-3 *Orion*.

[3] Names given in 'quotation marks' are NATO reporting names, e.g., 'Su-27... *"Flanker"'*.

[4] When no information is listed under 'Country of origin' or 'Maker', the primary reference given under 'Name/ designation' should be looked up under 'Type'.

[5] For country abbreviations, see 'Index of Countries and Territories' (pp. 317–18).

Type	Name/ designation	Country of origin•Maker

Aircraft

Type	Name/ designation	Country of origin•Maker
A-1	AMX	Br/It•AMX
A-1B	AMX	Br/It•AMX
A-3	*Skywarrior*	US•Douglas
A-4	*Skyhawk*	US•MD
A-5	*Fantan*	PRC•Nanchang
A-6	*Intruder*	US•Grumman
A-7	*Corsair* II	US•LTV
A-10	*Thunderbolt*	US•Fairchild
A-36	*Halcón* (C-101)	
A-37	*Dragonfly*	US•Cessna
AC-47	(C-47)	
AC-130	(C-130)	
Air Beetle		Nga•AIEP
Airtourer		NZ•Victa
AJ-37	(J-37)	
Alizé		Fr•Breguet
Alpha Jet		Fr/Ge•Dassault–Breguet/Dornier
AM-3	*Bosbok* (C-4M)	It•Aermacchi
An-2	*'Colt'*	Ukr•Antonov
An-12	*'Cub'*	Ukr•Antonov
An-14	*'Clod'*	Ukr•Antonov
An-22	*'Cock'*	Ukr•Antonov
An-24	*'Coke'*	Ukr•Antonov
An-26	*'Curl'*	Ukr•Antonov
An-30	*'Clank'*	Ukr•Antonov
An-32	*'Cline'*	Ukr•Antonov
An-124	*'Condor'*	Ukr•Antonov
Andover	[HS-748]	
AS-202	*Bravo*	CH•FFA
AT-3		ROC•AIDC
AT-6	(T-6)	
AT-11		US•Beech
AT-26	EMB-326	
AT-33	(T-33)	
Atlantic	(*Atlantique*)	Fr•Dassault–Breguet
AU-23	*Peacemaker* [PC-6B]	US•Fairchild
AV-8	*Harrier* II	US/UK•MD/BAe
Aztec	PA-23	US•Piper
B-1	*Lancer*	US•Rockwell
B-2	*Spirit*	US•Northrop Grumman
B-52	*Stratofortress*	US•Boeing
B-65	*Queen Air*	US•Beech
BAC-167	*Strikemaster*	UK•BAe
BAe-146		UK•BAe
BAe-748	(HS-748)	UK•BAe
Baron	(T-42)	
Be-6	*'Madge'*	RF•Beriev
Be-12	*'Mail'* (*Tchaika*)	RF•Beriev
Beech 50	*Twin Bonanza*	US•Beech
Beech 95	*Travel Air*	US•Beech
BN-2	*Islander, Defender, Trislander*	UK•Britten-Norman
Boeing 707		US•Boeing
Boeing 727		US•Boeing
Boeing 737		US•Boeing
Boeing 747		US•Boeing
Bonanza		US•Beech
Bronco	(OV-10)	
Bulldog		UK•BAe
C-1		J•Kawasaki
C-2	*Greyhound*	US•Grumman
C-4M	*Kudu* (AM-3)	RSA•Atlas
C-5	*Galaxy*	US•Lockheed
C-7	DHC-7	
C-9	*Nightingale* (DC-9)	
C-12	*Super King Air* (*Huron*)	US•Beech
C-17	*Globemaster* III	US•McDonnell Douglas
C-18	[Boeing 707]	
C-20	(*Gulfstream* III)	
C-21	(*Learjet*)	
C-22	(Boeing 727)	
C-23	(*Sherpa*)	UK•Short
C-42	(Neiva *Regente*)	Br•Embraer
C-45	*Expeditor*	US•Beech
C-46	*Commando*	US•Curtis
C-47	DC-3 (*Dakota*) (C-117 *Skytrain*)	US•Douglas
C-54	*Skymaster* (DC-4)	US•Douglas
C-91	HS-748	
C-93	HS-125	
C-95	EMB-110	
C-97	EMB-121	
C-101	*Aviojet*	Sp•CASA
C-115	DHC-5	Ca•De Havilland
C-117	(C-47)	
C-118	*Liftmaster* (DC-6)	
C-119	*Packet*	US•Fairchild
C-123	*Provider*	US•Fairchild
C-127	(Do-27)	Sp•CASA
C-130	*Hercules* (L-100)	US•Lockheed
C-131	Convair 440	US•Convair
C-135	[Boeing 707]	
C-137	[Boeing 707]	
C-140	(*Jetstar*)	US•Lockheed
C-141	*Starlifter*	US•Lockheed
C-160		Fr/Ge•Transall
C-212	*Aviocar*	Sp•CASA
C-235		Sp•CASA
CA-25	*Winjeel*	Aus•Commonwealth
Canberra		UK•BAe

Type	Name/designation	Country of origin • Maker
CAP-10		Fr•Mudry
CAP-20		Fr•Mudry
CAP-230		Fr•Mudry
Caravelle	SE-210	Fr•Aérospatiale
CC-109	(Convair 440)	US•Convair
CC-115	DHC-5	
CC-117	(Falcon 20)	
CC-132	(DHC-7)	
CC-137	(Boeing 707)	
CC-138	(DHC-6)	
CC-144	CL-600/-601	Ca•Canadair
CF-18	F/A-18	
CF-116	F-5	
Cheetah	[Mirage III]	RSA•Atlas
Cherokee	PA-28	US•Piper
Cheyenne	PA-31T [Navajo]	US•Piper
Chieftain	PA-31-350 [Navajo]	US•Piper
Ching-Kuo		ROC•AIDC
Citabria		US•Champion
Citation	(T-47)	US•Cessna
CJ-6	[Yak-18]	PRC•Nanchang
CL-44		Ca•Canadair
CL-215		Ca•Canadair
CL-601	*Challenger*	Ca•Canadair
CM-170	*Magister [Tzukit]*	Fr•Aérospatiale
CM-175	*Zéphyr*	Fr•Aérospatiale
CN-235		Sp/Indo•CASA/IPTN
Cochise	T-42	
Comanche	PA-24	US•Piper
Commander	Aero-/TurboCommander	US•Rockwell
Commodore	MS-893	Fr•Aérospatiale
CP-3	P-3 Orion	
CP-121	S-2	
CP-140	*Aurora (P-3 Orion)*	US•Lockheed
	Acturas	
CT-4	*Airtrainer*	NZ•Victa
CT-39	*Sabreliner*	US•Rockwell
CT-114	CL-41 *Tutor*	Ca•Canadair
CT-133	*Silver Star [T-33]*	Ca•Canadair
CT-134	*Musketeer*	
Dagger	(Nesher)	
Dakota		US•Piper
Dakota	(C-47)	
DC-3	(C-47)	US•Douglas
DC-4	(C-54)	US•Douglas
DC-6	(C-118)	US•Douglas
DC-7		US•Douglas
DC-8		US•Douglas
DC-9		US•MD
Deepak	(HPT-32)	
Defender	BN-2	
DHC-3	*Otter*	Ca•DHC
DHC-4	*Caribou*	Ca•DHC
DHC-5	*Buffalo*	Ca•DHC
DHC-6	*Twin Otter, CC-138*	Ca•DHC
DHC-7	*Dash-7 (Ranger, CC-132)*	Ca•DHC
DHC-8		Ca•DHC
Dimona	H-36	Ge•Hoffman
Do-27	(C-127)	Ge•Dornier
Do-28	*Skyservant*	Ge•Dornier
Do-128		Ge•Dornier
Do-228		Ge•Dornier
E-2	*Hawkeye*	US•Grumman
E-3	*Sentry*	US•Boeing
E-4	[Boeing 747]	US•Boeing
E-6	[Boeing 707]	
E-26	T-35A (Tamiz)	Chl•Enear
EA-3	[A-3]	
EA-6	*Prowler [A-6]*	
EC-130	[C-130]	
EC-135	[Boeing 707]	
EF-11	*Raven*	US•General Dynamic
Electra	(L-188)	
EMB-110	*Bandeirante*	
EMB-111	*Maritime Bandeirante*	Br•Embraer
EMB-120	*Brasilia*	Br•Embraer
EMB-121	*Xingu*	Br•Embraer
EMB-312	*Tucano*	Br•Embraer
EMB-326	*Xavante (MB-326)*	Br•Embraer
EMB-810	[Seneca]	Br•Embraer
EP-3	(P-3 Orion)	
Etendard		Fr•Dassault
EV-1	(OV-1)	
F-1	[T-2]	J•Mitsubishi
F-4	*Phantom*	US•MD
F-5	-A/-B *Freedom Fighter*	
	-E/-F *Tiger* II	US•Northrop
F-5T	JJ-5	PRC•Shenyang
F-6	J-6	
F-7	J-7	
F-8	J-8	
F-8	*Crusader*	US•Republic
F-14	*Tomcat*	US•Grumman
F-15	*Eagle*	US•MD
F-16	*Fighting Falcon*	US•GD
F-18	[F/A-18], *Hornet*	
F-21	*Kfir*	Il•IAI
F-27	*Friendship*	Nl•Fokker
F-28	*Fellowship*	Nl•Fokker
F-35	*Draken*	Swe•SAAB
F-104	*Starfighter*	US•Lockheed
F-111	EF-111	US•GD
F-117	*Nighthawk*	US•Lockheed
F-172	(Cessna 172)	Fr/US•Reims-Cessna
F/A-18	*Hornet*	US•MD
Falcon	*Mystère-Falcon*	
FB-111	(F-111)	
FH-227	(F-27)	US•Fairchild-Hiller
Firefly	(T-67M)	UK•Slingsby
Flamingo	MBB-233	Ge•MBB
FT-5	JJ-5	PRC•CAC
FT-6	JJ-6	
FTB-337	[Cessna 337]	
G-91		It•Aeritalia
G-222		It•Aeritalia
Galaxy	C-5	
Galeb		FRY•SOKO
Genet	SF-260W	
GU-25	(Falcon 20)	
Guerrier	R-235	
Gulfstream		US•Gulfstream Aviation
Gumhuria	(Bücker 181)	Et•Heliopolis
H-5	[Il-28]	PRC•Harbin
H-6	[Tu-16]	PRC•Xian
H-36	*Dimona*	
Halcón	[C-101]	
Harrier	(AV-8)	UK•BAe
Hawk		UK•BAe

Type	Name/ designation	Country of origin	Maker
HC-130	(C-130)		
HF-24	*Marut*	Ind•HAL	
HFB-320	*Hansajet*	Ge•Hamburger FB	
HJ-5	(H-5)		
HJT-16	*Kiran*	Ind•HAL	
HPT-32	*Deepak*	Ind•HAL	
HS-125	(*Dominie*)	UK•BAe	
HS-748	[*Andover*]	UK•BAe	
HT-2		Ind•HAL	
HU-16	*Albatross*	US•Grumman	
HU-25	(*Falcon 20*)		
Hunter		UK•BAe	
HZ-5	(H-5)		
IA-35	*Huanquero*	Arg•FMA	
IA-50	*Guaraní*	Arg•FMA	
IA-58	*Pucará*	Arg•FMA	
IA-63	*Pampa*	Arg•FMA	
IAI-201/-202	*Arava*	Il•IAI	
IAI-1124	*Westwind, Seascan*	Il•IAI	
IAR-28		R•IAR	
IAR-93	*Orao*	FRY/R•SOKO/IAR	
Il-14	'Crate'	RF•Ilyushin	
Il-18	'Coot'	RF•Ilyushin	
Il-20	(Il-18)		
Il-28	'Beagle'	RF•Ilyushin	
Il-38	'May'	RF•Ilyushin	
Il-62	'Classic'	RF•Ilyushin	
Il-76	'Candid' (tpt), 'Mainstay' (AEW), 'Midas' (tkr)	RF•Ilyushin	
Impala	[MB-326]	RSA•Atlas	
Islander	BN-2		
J-2	[MiG-15]	PRC•	
J-5	[MiG-17F]	PRC•Shenyang	
J-6	[MiG-19]	PRC•Shenyang	
J-7	[MiG-21]	PRC•Xian	
J-8	[Sov Ye-142]	PRC•Shenyang	
J-32	*Lansen*	Swe•SAAB	
J-35	*Draken*	Swe•SAAB	
J-37	*Viggen*	Swe•SAAB	
JA-37	(J-37)		
Jaguar		Fr/UK•SEPECAT	
JAS-39	*Gripen*	Swe•SAAB	
Jastreb		FRY•SOKO	
Jet Provost		UK•BAe	
Jetstream		UK•BAe	
JJ-6	(J-6)		
JZ-6	(J-6)		
K-8		PRC/Pak•NAMC/PAC	
KA-3	[A-3]		
KA-6	[A-6]		
KC-10	*Extender* [DC-10]	US•MD	
KC-130	[C-130]		
KC-135	[Boeing 707]		
KE-3A	[Boeing 707]		
Kfir		Il•IAI	
King Air		US•Beech	
Kiran	HJT-16		
Kraguj		FRY•SOKO	
Kudu	C-4M		
L-4	*Cub*		
L-18	*Super Cub*	US•Piper	
L-19	O-1		
L-21	*Super Cub*	US•Piper	
L-29	*Delfin*	Cz•Aero	

Type	Name/ designation	Country of origin	Maker
L-39	*Albatros*	Cz•Aero	
L-70	*Vinka*	SF•Valmet	
L-90TP	*Redigo*	SF•Valmet	
L-100	C-130 (civil version)		
L-188	*Electra* (P-3 *Orion*)	US•Lockheed	
L-410	*Turbolet*	Cz•LET	
L-1011	*Tristar*	US•Lockheed	
LAC52	YAK52	RF•Aerostar	
Learjet	(C-21)	US•Gates	
LR-1	(MU-2)	J•Mitsubishi	
M-28	*Skytruck*	Pl•MIELEC	
Magister	CM-170		
Marut	HF-24		
Mashshaq	MFI-17	Pak/Swe•PAC/SAAB	
Matador	(AV-8)		
MB-326		It•Aermacchi	
MB-339	(*Veltro*)	It•Aermacchi	
MBB-233	*Flamingo*		
MC-130	(C-130)		
Mercurius	(HS-125)		
Merlin		US•Fairchild	
Mescalero	T-41		
Metro		US•Fairchild	
MFI-15	*Safari*	Swe•SAAB	
MFI-17	*Supporter* (T-17)	Swe•SAAB	
MH-1521	*Broussard*	Fr•Max Holste	
MiG-15	'Midget' trg	RF•MiG	
MiG-17	'Fresco'	RF•MiG	
MiG-19	'Farmer'	RF•MiG	
MiG-21	'Fishbed'	RF•MiG	
MiG-23	'Flogger'	RF•MiG	
MiG-25	'Foxbat'	RF•MiG	
MiG-27	'Flogger D'	RF•MiG	
MiG-29	'Fulcrum'	RF•MiG	
MiG-31	'Foxhound'	RF•MiG	
Mirage		Fr•Dassault	
Missionmaster	N-22		
Mohawk	OV-1		
MS-760	*Paris*	Fr•Aérospatiale	
MS-893	*Commodore*		
MU-2	LR-1	J•Mitsubishi	
Musketeer	Beech 24	US•Beech	
Mya-4	'Bison'	RF•Myasishchev	
Mystère-Falcon		Fr•Dassault	
N-22	*Floatmaster, Missionmaster*	Aus•GAF	
N-24	*Searchmaster* B/L	Aus•GAF	
N-262	*Frégate*	Fr•Aérospatiale	
N-2501	*Noratlas*	Fr•Aérospatiale	
Navajo	PA-31	US•Piper	
NC-212	C-212	Sp/Indo•CASA/Nurtanio	
NC-235	C-235	Sp/Indo•CASA/Nurtanio	
Nesher	[*Mirage* III]	Il•IAI	
NF-5	(F-5)		
Nightingale	(DC-9)		
Nimrod		UK•BAe	
Nomad		Aus•GAF	
O-1	*Bird Dog*	US•Cessna	
O-2	(Cessna 337 *Skymaster*)	US•Cessna	
OA-4	(A-4)		
OA-37	*Dragonfly*		
Orao	IAR-93		
Ouragan		Fr•Dassault	

Type	Name/designation	Country of origin Maker
OV-1	*Mohawk*	US•Rockwell
OV-10	*Bronco*	US•Rockwell
P-2J	[SP-2]	J•Kawasaki
P-3		CH•Pilatus
P-3	*Orion*	US•Lockheed
P-92		It•Teenam
P-95	EMB-110	
P-149		It•Piaggio
P-166		It•Piaggio
P-180	*Avanti*	It•Piaggio
PA-18	*Super Cub*	US•Piper
PA-23	*Aztec*	US•Piper
PA-24	*Comanche*	US•Piper
PA-28	*Cherokee*	US•Piper
PA-31	*Navajo*	US•Piper
PA-34	*Seneca*	US•Piper
PA-44	*Seminole*	US•Piper
PBY-5	*Catalina*	US•Consolidated
PC-6	*Porter*	CH•Pilatus
PC-6A/B	*Turbo Porter*	CH•Pilatus
PC-7	*Turbo Trainer*	CH•Pilatus
PC-9		CH•Pilatus
PC-12		CH•Pilatus
PD-808		It•Piaggio
Pembroke		UK•BAe
Pillán	T-35	
PL-1	*Chien Shou*	ROC•AIDC
Porter	PC-6	
PS-5	[SH-5]	PRC•HAMC
PT-6	[CJ-6]	PRC•Nanchang
PZL-104	*Wilga*	Pl•PZL
PZL-130	*Orlik*	Pl•PZL
Q-5	'Fantan' [MiG-19]	PRC•Nanchang
Queen Air	(U-8)	
R-160		Fr•Socata
R-235	*Guerrier*	Fr•Socata
RC-21	(C-21, *Learjet*)	
RC-47	(C-47)	
RC-95	(EMB-110)	
RC-135	[Boeing 707]	
RF-4	(F-4)	
RF-5	(F-5)	
RF-35	(F-35)	
RF-104	(F-104)	
RG-8A		US•Schweizer
RT-26	(EMB-326)	
RT-33	(T-33)	
RU-21	(*King Air*)	
RV-1	(OV-1)	
S-2	*Tracker*	US•Grumman
S-3	*Viking*	US•Lockheed
S-208		It•SIAI
S-211		It•SIAI
SA 2-37A		US•Schweizer
Sabreliner	(CT-39)	US•Rockwell
Safari	MFI-15	
Safir	SAAB-91 (SK-50)	Swe•SAAB
SC-7	*Skyvan*	UK•Short
SE-210	*Caravelle*	
Sea Harrier	(*Harrier*)	
Seascan	IAI-1124	
Searchmaster	N-24 B/L	
Seneca	PA-34 (EMB-810)	US•Piper

Type	Name/designation	Country of origin Maker
Sentry	(O-2)	US•Summit
SF-37	(J-37)	
SF-260	(SF-260W *Warrior*)	It•SIAI
SH-37	(J-37)	
Sherpa	Short 330, C-23	UK•Short
Short 330	(*Sherpa*)	UK•Short
Sierra 200	(*Musketeer*)	
SK-35	(J-35)	Swe•SAAB
SK-37	(J-37)	
SK-50	(*Safir*)	
SK-60	(SAAB-105)	Swe•SAAB
SK-61	(*Bulldog*)	
Skyvan		UK•Short
SM-90		RF•Technoavia
SM-1019		It•SIAI
SP-2H	*Neptune*	US•Lockheed
SR-71	*Blackbird*	US•Lockheed
Su-7	'Fitter A'	RF•Sukhoi
Su-15	'Flagon'	RF•Sukhoi
Su-17/-20/-22	'Fitter'	RF•Sukhoi
Su-24	'Fencer'	RF•Sukhoi
Su-25	'Frogfoot'	RF•Sukhoi
Su-27	'Flanker'	RF•Sukhoi
Su-29		RF•Sukhoi
Super		Fr•Dassault
Shrike Aerocommander		US•Rockwell
Super Galeb		FRY•SOKO
T-1		J•Fuji
T-1A	*Jayhawk*	US•Beech
T-2	*Buckeye*	US•Rockwell
T-2		J•Mitsubishi
T-3		J•Fuji
T-17	(*Supporter*, MFI-17)	Swe•SAAB
T-23	*Uirapurú*	Br•Aerotec
T-25	Neiva *Universal*	Br•Embraer
T-26	EMB-326	
T-27	*Tucano*	Br•Embraer
T-28	*Trojan*	US•N. American
T-33	*Shooting Star*	US•Lockheed
T-34	*Mentor*	US•Beech
T-35	*Pillán* [PA-28]	Chl•Enaer
T-36	(C-101)	
T-37	(A-37)	
T-38	*Talon*	US•Northrop
T-39	(*Sabreliner*)	US•Rockwell
T-41	*Mescalero* (Cessna 172)	US•Cessna
T-42	*Cochise* (*Baron*)	US•Beech
T-43	(Boeing 737)	
T-44	(*King Air*)	
T-47	(*Citation*)	
T-67M	(*Firefly*)	UK • Slingsby
T-400	(T-1A)	US•Beech
TB-20	*Trinidad*	Fr•Aérospatiale
TB-21	*Trinidad*	Fr•Socata
TB-30	*Epsilon*	Fr•Aérospatiale
TB-200	*Tobago*	Fr•Socata
TBM-700		Fr•Socata
TC-45	(C-45, trg)	
TCH-1		ROC•AIDC
Texan	T-6	
TL-1	(KM-2)	J•Fuji
Tornado		UK/Ge/It•Panavia
TR-1	[U-2]	US•Lockheed
Travel Air	Beech 95	

Type	Name/ designation	Country of origin	Maker
Trident		UK•BAe	
Trislander	BN-2		
Tristar	L-1011		
TS-8	*Bies*	Pl•PZL	
TS-11	*Iskra*	Pl•PZL	
Tu-16	*'Badger'*	RF•Tupolev	
Tu-22	*'Blinder'*	RF•Tupolev	
Tu-26	*'Backfire'*, (Tu-22M)	RF•Tupolev	
Tu-28	*'Fiddler'*	RF•Tupolev	
Tu-95	*'Bear'*	RF•Tupolev	
Tu-126	*'Moss'*	RF•Tupolev	
Tu-134	*'Crusty'*	RF•Tupolev	
Tu-142	*'Bear F'*	RF•Tupolev	
Tu-154	*'Careless'*	RF•Tupolev	
Tu-160	*'Blackjack'*	RF•Tupolev	
Turbo Porter	PC-6A/B		
Twin Bonanza	Beech 50		
Twin Otter	DHC-6		
Tzukit	[CM-170]	Il•IAI	
U-2		US•Lockheed	
U-3	(Cessna 310)	US•Cessna	
U-7	(L-18)		
U-8	(Twin Bonanza/Queen Air)	US•Beech	
U-9	(EMB-121)		
U-10	*Super Courier*	US•Helio	
U-17	(Cessna 180, 185)	US•Cessna	
U-21	(King Air)		
U-36	(Learjet)		
U-42	(C-42)		
U-93	(HS-125)		
U-125	BAe 125-800	UK•BAe	
UC-12	(King Air)		
UP-2J	(P-2J)		
US-1		J•Shin Meiwa	
US-2A	(S-2A, tpt)		
US-3	(S-3, tpt)		
UTVA-66		FRY•UTVA	
UTVA-75		FRY•UTVA	
UV-18	(DHC-6)		
V-400	*Fantrainer 400*	Ge•VFW	
V-600	*Fantrainer 600*	Ge•VFW	
Vampire	DH-100		
VC-4	*Gulfstream I*		
VC-10		UK•BAe	
VC-11	*Gulfstream II*		
VC-91	(HS-748)		
VC-93	(HS-125)		
VC-97	(EMB-120)		
VC-130	(C-130)		
VFW-614		Ge•VFW	
Vinka	L-70		
VU-9	(EMB-121)		
VU-93	(HS-125)		
WC-130	[C-130]		
WC-135	[Boeing 707]	US•Boeing	
Westwind	IAI-1124		
Winjeel	CA-25		
Xavante	EMB-326		
Xingu	EMB-121		
Y-5	[An-2]	PRC•Hua Bei	
Y-7	[An-24]	PRC•Xian	
Y-8	[An-12]	PRC•Shaanxi	
Y-12		PRC•Harbin	
Yak-11	*'Moose'*	RF•Yakovlev	

Type	Name/ designation	Country of origin	Maker
Yak-18	*'Max'*	RF•Yakovlev	
Yak-28	*'Firebar'* ('Brewer')	RF•Yakovlev	
Yak-38	*'Forger'*	RF•Yakovlev	
Yak-40	*'Codling'*	RF•Yakovlev	
YS-11		J•Nihon	
Z-43		Cz•Zlin	
Z-226		Cz•Zlin	
Z-326		Cz•Zlin	
Z-526		Cz•Zlin	
Zéphyr	CM-175		

Helicopters

A-109	*Hirundo*	It•Agusta	
A-129	*Mangusta*	It•Agusta	
AB-...	(Bell 204/205/206/ 212/214, etc.)	It/US•Agusta/Bell	
AH-1	*Cobra/Sea Cobra*	US•Bell	
AH-6	(Hughes 500/530)	US•MD	
AH-64	*Apache*	US•Hughes	
Alouette II	SA-318, SE-3130	Fr•Aérospatiale	
Alouette III	SA-316, SA-319	Fr•Aérospatiale	
AS-61	(SH-3)	US/It•Sikorsky/Agusta	
AS-332	*Super Puma*	Fr•Aérospatiale	
AS-350	*Ecureuil*	Fr•Aérospatiale	
AS-355	*Ecureuil II*	Fr•Aérospatiale	
AS-365	*Dauphin*	Fr•Aérospatiale	
AS-532	*Super Puma*	Fr•Aérospatiale	
AS532 UL	*Cougar*	Fr•Eurocopter	
AS-550	*Fennec*	Fr•Aérospatiale	
AS-565	*Panthar*	Fr•Eurocopter	
ASH-3	(Sea King)	It/US•Agusta/Sikorsky	
AUH-76	(S-76)		
Bell 47		US•Bell	
Bell 204		US•Bell	
Bell 205		US•Bell	
Bell 206		US•Bell	
Bell 212		US•Bell	
Bell 214		US•Bell	
Bell 406		US•Bell	
Bell 412		US•Bell	
Bo-105	(NBo-105)	Ge•MBB	
CH-3	(SH-3)		
CH-34	*Choctaw*	US•Sikorsky	
CH-46	*Sea Knight*	US•Boeing-Vertol	
CH-47	*Chinook*	US•Boeing-Vertol	
CH-53	*Stallion (Sea Stallion)*	US•Sikorsky	
CH-54	*Tarhe*	US•Sikorsky	
CH-113	(CH-46)		
CH-124	SH-3		
CH-139	Bell 206		
CH-146	Bell 412	Ca•Bell	
CH-147	CH-47		
Cheetah	[SA-315]	Ind•HAL	
Chetak	[SA-319]	Ind•HAL	
Commando	(SH-3)	UK/US•Westland/Sikorsky	
EH-60	(UH-60)		
EH-101		UK/It•Westland/Agusta	
F-28F		US•Enstrom	
FH-1100	(OH-5)	US•Fairchild-Hiller	
Gazela	(SA-342)	Fr/FRY•Aérospatiale/SOKO	
Gazelle	SA-341/-342		
H-34	(S-58)		

Analyses and Tables

Type	Name/ designation	Country of origin	Maker
H-76	S-76		
HA-15	Bo-105		
HB-315	*Gavião* (SA-315)	Br/Fr•Helibras Aérospatiale	
HB-350	*Esquilo* (AS-350)	Br/Fr•Helibras Aérospatiale	
HD-16	SA-319		
HH-3	(SH-3)		
HH-34	(CH-34)		
HH-53	(CH-53)		
HH-65	(AS-365)	Fr•Eurocopter	
Hkp-2	*Alouette* II/SE-3130		
Hkp-3	AB-204		
Hkp-4	KV-107		
Hkp-5	Hughes 300		
Hkp-6	AB-206		
Hkp-9	Bo-105		
Hkp-10	AS-332		
HR-12	OH-58		
HSS-1	(S-58)		
HSS-2	(SH-3)		
HT-17	CH-47		
HT-21	AS-332		
HU-1	(UH-1)	J/US•Fuji/Bell	
HU-8	UH-1B		
HU-10	UH-1H		
HU-18	AB-212		
Hughes 269		US•MD	
Hughes 300		US•MD	
Hughes 369		US•MD	
Hughes 500/520	*Defender*	US•MD	
IAR-316/-330	(SA-316/-330)	R/Fr•IAR/Aérospatiale	
Ka-25	*'Hormone'*	RF•Kamov	
Ka-27	*'Helix'*	RF•Kamov	
Ka-50	*Hokum*	RF•Kamov	
KH-4	(Bell 47)	J/US•Kawasaki/Bell	
KH-300	(Hughes 269)	J/US•Kawasaki/MD	
KH-500	(Hughes 369)	J/US•Kawasaki/MD	
Kiowa	OH-58		
KV-107	[CH-46]	J/US•Kawasaki/Vertol	
Lynx		UK•Westland	
MD-500/530	*Defender*	US•McDonnell Douglas	
MH-6	(AH-6)		
MH-53	(CH-53)		
Mi-1	*'Hare'*	RF•Mil	
Mi-2	*'Hoplite'*	RF•Mil	
Mi-4	*'Hound'*	RF•Mil	
Mi-6	*'Hook'*	RF•Mil	
Mi-8	*'Hip'*	RF•Mil	
Mi-14	*'Haze'*	RF•Mil	
Mi-17	*'Hip'*	RF•Mil	
Mi-24	*'Hind'*	RF•Mil	
Mi-25	*'Hind'*	RF•Mil	
Mi-26	*'Halo'*	RF•Mil	
Mi-28	*'Havoc'*	RF•Mil	
Mi-35	(Mi-25)		
NAS-332	AS-332	Indo/Fr•Nurtanio/Aérospatiale	
NB-412	Bell 412	Indo/US•Nurtanio/Bell	
NBo-105	Bo-105	Indo/Ge•Nurtanio/MBB	
NH-300	(Hughes 300)	It/US•Nardi/MD	
NSA-330	(SA-330)	Indo/Fr•Nurtanio/Aérospatiale	
OH-6	*Cayuse* (Hughes 369)	US•MD	
OH-13	(Bell 47G)		
OH-23	*Raven*	US•Hiller	
OH-58	*Kiowa* (Bell 206)		
OH-58D	(Bell 406)		
PAH-1	(Bo-105)		
Partizan	(*Gazela*, armed)		
PZL-W3	*Sokol*	Pl•Swidnik	
RH-53	(CH-53)		
S-55	(*Whirlwind*)	US•Sikorsky	
S-58	(*Wessex*)	US•Sikorsky	
S-61	SH-3		
S-65	CH-53		
S-70	UH-60	US•Sikorsky	
S-76		US•Sikorsky	
S-80	CH-53		
SA-315	*Lama* [*Alouette* II]	Fr•Aérospatiale	
SA-316	*Alouette* III (SA-319)	Fr•Aérospatiale	
SA-318	*Alouette* II (SE-3130)	Fr•Aérospatiale	
SA-319	*Alouette* III (SA-316)	Fr•Aérospatiale	
SA-321	*Super Frelon*	Fr•Aérospatiale	
SA-330	*Puma*	Fr•Aérospatiale	
SA-341/-342	*Gazelle*	Fr•Aérospatiale	
SA-360	*Dauphin*	Fr•Aérospatiale	
SA-365	*Dauphin* II (SA-360)		
Scout	(*Wasp*)	UK•Westland	
SE-316	(SA-316)		
SE-3130	(SA-318)		
Sea King	[SH-3]	UK•Westland	
SH-2	*Sea Sprite*	US•Kaman	
SH-3	(*Sea King*)	US•Sikorsky	
SH-34	(S-58)		
SH-57	Bell 206		
SH-60	*Sea Hawk* (UH-60)		
Sioux	(Bell 47)	UK•Westland	
TH-50	*Esquilo* (AS-550)		
TH-55	Hughes 269		
TH-57	*Sea Ranger* (Bell 206)		
TH-67	*Creek* (Bell 206B-3)	Ca•Bell	
UH-1	*Iroquois* (Bell 204/205/212)		
UH-12	(OH-23)	US•Hiller	
UH-13	(Bell 47J)		
UH-19	(S-55)		
UH-34T	(S-58T)		
UH-46	(CH-46)		
UH-60	*Black Hawk* (SH-60)	US•Sikorsky	
VH-4	(Bell 206)		
VH-60	(S-70)		
Wasp	(*Scout*)	UK•Westland	
Wessex	(S-58)	US/UK•Sikorsky/Westland	
Whirlwind	(S-55)	US/UK•Sikorsky/Westland	
Z-5	[Mi-4]	PRC•Harbin	
Z-6	[Z-5]	PRC•Harbin	
Z-8	[SA-321]	PRC•Changhe	
Z-9	[SA-365]	PRC•Harbin	

Index of Countries and Territories

References

Index of **Country Abbreviations**

A	Austria	Ga	Georgia	Pan	Panama
AB	Antigua and Barbuda	Gam	Gambia, The	Pe	Peru
Afg	Afghanistan	Gbn	Gabon	Pi	Philippines
Ag	Algeria	Ge	Germany	Pl	Poland
Alb	Albania	Gha	Ghana	PNG	Papua New Guinea
Ang	Angola	Gr	Greece	Por	Portugal
Arg	Argentina	Gua	Guatemala	PRC	China
Arm	Armenia	GuB	Guinea-Bissau	Py	Paraguay
Aus	Australia	Gui	Guinea		
Az	Azerbaijan	Guy	Guyana	Q	Qatar
		GzJ	Palestinian Autonomous		
Bds	Barbados		Areas of Gaza and Jericho	R	Romania
Be	Belgium			RC	Congo
Bel	Belarus	HKJ	Jordan	RF	Russia
BF	Burkina Faso	Hr	Honduras	RH	Haiti
Bg	Bulgaria	Hu	Hungary	RIM	Mauritania
BiH	Bosnia-Herzegovina			RL	Lebanon
Bn	Benin	Icl	Iceland	RMM	Mali
Bng	Bangladesh	Il	Israel	ROC	Taiwan
Bol	Bolivia	Ind	India	ROK	Korea: Republic of
Br	Brazil	Indo	Indonesia		(South)
Brn	Bahrain	Ir	Iran	RSA	South Africa
Bru	Brunei	Irl	Ireland	Rwa	Rwanda
Btwa	Botswana	Irq	Iraq		
Bu	Burundi	It	Italy	Sau	Saudi Arabia
Bze	Belize			Sdn	Sudan
		J	Japan	Sen	Senegal
C	Cuba	Ja	Jamaica	Sey	Seychelles
Ca	Canada			SF	Finland
Cam	Cambodia	Kaz	Kazakstan	Sgp	Singapore
CAR	Central African Republic	Kgz	Kyrgyzstan	Ska	Sri Lanka
CH	Switzerland	Kwt	Kuwait	SL	Sierra Leone
Cha	Chad	Kya	Kenya	Slvk	Slovakia
Chl	Chile			Slvn	Slovenia
CI	Côte d'Ivoire	L	Lithuania	Sme	Suriname
Co	Colombia	Lao	Laos	Sp	Spain
Cr	Croatia	LAR	Libya	SR	Somali Republic
CR	Costa Rica	Lat	Latvia	Swe	Sweden
Crn	Cameroon	Lb	Liberia	Syr	Syria
CV	Cape Verde	Ls	Lesotho		
Cy	Cyprus	Lu	Luxembourg	Tg	Togo
Cz	Czech Republic			Th	Thailand
		M	Malta	Tjk	Tajikistan
Da	Denmark	Mal	Malaysia	Tkm	Turkmenistan
Dj	Djibouti	Mdg	Madagascar	Tn	Tunisia
DROC	Democratic Republic of	Mex	Mexico	TT	Trinidad and Tobago
	Congo	Mgl	Mongolia	Tu	Turkey
DPRK	Korea: Democratic People's	Mlw	Malawi	Tz	Tanzania
	Republic (North)	Mol	Moldova		
DR	Dominican Republic	Mor	Morocco	UAE	United Arab Emirates
		Moz	Mozambique	Uga	Uganda
Ea	Estonia	Ms	Mauritius	UK	United Kingdom
Ec	Ecuador	My	Myanmar (Burma)	Ukr	Ukraine
EG	Equatorial Guinea			Ury	Uruguay
ElS	El Salvador	N	Nepal	US	United States
Er	Eritrea	Nba	Namibia	Uz	Uzbekistan
Et	Egypt	Nga	Nigeria		
Eth	Ethiopia	Ngr	Niger	Ve	Venezuela
		Nic	Nicaragua	Vn	Vietnam
Fji	Fiji	Nl	Netherlands		
Fr	France	No	Norway	Ye	Yemen, Republic of
FRY	Federal Republic of	NZ	New Zealand		
	Yugoslavia			Z	Zambia
	(Serbia-Montenegro)	O	Oman	Zw	Zimbabwe
FYROM	Former Yugoslav				
	Republic of Macedonia	Pak	Pakistan		

See 'Index of Countries and Territories' (pp. 317–18) for country abbreviations

<	under 100 tonnes
–	part of unit is detached/less than
+	unit reinforced/more than
*	training aircraft considered combat-capable
†	serviceability in doubt
ε	estimated
' '	unit with overstated title/ship class nickname
AAA	anti-aircraft artillery
AAM/R	air-to-air missile/refuelling
AAV	amphibious armoured vehicle
AAW	anti-air warfare
AB(D)	airborne (division)
ABM	anti-ballistic missile
about	the total could be higher
ac	aircraft
ACM	advanced cruise missile
ACV	air cushion vehicle/vessel/ armoured combat vehicle
AD	air defence
adj	adjusted
AE	auxiliary, ammunition carrier
AEW	airborne early warning
AF	stores ship with RAS
AFB/S	Air Force Base/Station
AG	misc auxiliary
AGHS	hydrographic survey vessel
AGI	intelligence collection vessel
AGM	air-to-ground missile
AGOR	oceanographic research vessel
AGOS	ocean surveillance vessel
AH	hospital ship
AIFV	armoured infantry fighting vehicle
AIP	air-independent propulsion
AK	cargo ship
AKR	fast sealift ship
ALCM	air-launched cruise missile
amph	amphibious/amphibian
AMRAAM	advanced medium-range air-to-air missile
AO/T	tanker(s) with/without RAS capability
AOE	auxiliary, fuel and ammu-nition, RAS capability
AP	passenger ship
APC	armoured personnel carrier
APL	anti-personnel land-mine
AR	repair ship
ARG	amphibious ready group
ARM	anti-radiation (radar) missile
armd	armoured
ARS	salvage ship
arty	artillery
AR(R)V	armoured recovery (and repair) vehicle
AS	submarine depot ship
aslt	assault
ASM	air-to-surface missile
ASR	submarine rescue craft
ASROC	anti-submarine rocket
ASTT/W	anti-submarine TT/warfare
ASUW	anti-surface-unit warfare
AT	tug

ATACMS	army tactical missile system
ATBM	anti-tactical ballistic missile
ATGW	anti-tank guided weapon
ATK	anti-tank
avn	aviation
AWACS	airborne warning and control system
BB	battleship
bbr	bomber
bde	brigade
bdgt	budget
BG	battle group
BMD	ballistic missile defence
bn	battalion/billion
BOFI	Bofors Optronic Fire control Instrument
bty	battery
cal	calibration
CALCM	conventional air-launched cruise missile
CAS	close air support
casevac	casualty evacuation
CASM	conventionally armed stand-off missiles
Cat	category
cav	cavalry
cbt	combat
CBU	cluster bomb unit
CC	cruiser
CCT	combat-capable trainer
cdo	commando
CET	combat engineer tractor
CFE	Conventional Armed Forces in Europe
CG/H/N	SAM cruiser/with helicopters/nuclear-fuelled
cgo	freight aircraft
civ pol	civilian police
CMDS	command ship
comb	combined/combination
comd	command
comms	communications
CONUS	continental United States
coy	company
CV/N/V	aircraft carrier/nuclear-fuelled/V/STOL and hel
CVBG	carrier battle group
CW	chemical warfare/weapons
DD/G/H	destroyer/with area SAM/ with hel
DDS	dry dock shelter
def	defence
defn	definition
det	detachment
div	division
DMS	defence mobilisation ship
ECM	electronic countermeasures
Econ aid	economic aid with a military use
ECR	electronic combat and reconnaissance
EDA	Excess Defense Articles (US)
EEZ	exclusive economic zone
ELINT	electronic intelligence
elm	element
EmDA	Emergency Drawdown Authority (US)
engr	engineer
EOD	explosive ordnance disposal
eqpt	equipment

ESM	electronic support measures
est	estimate(d)
EW	electronic warfare
excl	excludes/excluding
exp	expenditure
FAC	forward air control
fd	field
FF/G/H	frigate/with area SAM/with helicopter
FGA	fighter, ground-attack
flo-flo	float-on, float-off
flt	flight
FMA/F/S	Foreign Military Assistance/ Financing/Sales
FPS	fleet patrol ship
FROG	Free Rocket Over Ground
ftr	fighter (aircraft)
FW	fixed-wing
FY	fiscal year
gd	guard
GDP	gross domestic product
GNP	gross national product
gp	group
GS	General Service (UK)
GW	guided weapon
HACV	heavy armoured combat vehicle
HARM	high-speed anti-radiation missile
hel	helicopter
HMMWV	high-mobility multipurpose wheeled vehicle
HOT	High-subsonic Optically Teleguided
how	howitzer
HS	Home Service (UK)
HWT	heavy-weight torpedo
hy	heavy
ICBM	intercontinental ballistic missile
IMET	International Military Education and Training
imp	improved
incl	includes/including
indep	independent
inf	infantry
IRBM	intermediate-range ballistic missile
JSTARS	joint strategic airborne reconnaissance system
KT	kiloton
LACV	light armoured combat vehicle
LAMPS	light airborne multi-purpose system
LANTIRN	low-altitude navigation and targeting infra-red system night
LASH	cargo ship barge
LAW	light anti-tank weapon
LCA	landing craft, assault
LCAC	landing craft, air cushion
LCC	amphibious command ship
LCH/M/T/ U/VP	landing craft, heavy/ mechanised/tank/utility/ vehicles and personnel
LGB	laser-guided bomb
LHA	landing ship, assault
LKA	assault cargo ship
log	logistic

Index of **Abbreviations**

LPD/H	landing platform, dock/helicopter
LSD/H/M/T	landing ship, dock/heavy/medium/tank
lt	light
LWT	light-weight torpedo
maint	maintenance
MBT	main battle tank
MCC/I/O	mine countermeasures vessel, coastal/inshore/offshore
MCDV	maritime coastal defence vessel
MCM/CS	mine countermeasures/command and support ship
MD	Military District
mech	mechanised
med	medium
MEF/B/U	Marine Expeditionary Force/Brigade/Unit (US)
MG	machine gun
MHC/I/O	minehunter, coastal/inshore/offshore
mil	military
MIRV	multiple independently targetable re-entry vehicle
misc	miscellaneous
MIUW	mobile inshore undersea warfare
Mk	mark (model number)
ML	minelayer
MLRS	multiple launch rocket system
mob	mobilisation/mobile
mod	modified/modification
mor	mortar
mot	motorised/motor
MP	Military Police
MPA	maritime patrol aircraft
MPS	marine prepositioning squadron
MR	maritime reconnaissance/motor rifle
MRAAM	medium-range air-to-air missile
MRBM	medium-range ballistic missile
MRD	motor rifle division
MRL	multiple rocket launcher
MRR	motor rifle regiment
MRV	multiple re-entry vehicle
MSA	minesweeper, auxiliary
MSC	military sealift command
MSC/I/O/R	minesweeper, coastal/inshore/offshore/riverine
msl	missile
MT	megaton
mtn	mountain
n.a.	not applicable
Narcs	narcotics (funding for anti-drug operations)
NASAMS	Norwegian Advanced SAM System
NBC	nuclear, biological and chemical
NCO	non-commissioned officer
n.k.	not known
nm	nautical mile
NMP	net material product
nuc	nuclear
obs	observation
OCU	operational conversion unit(s)
off	official
O&M	operations and maintenance
OOA	out of area
OOV	objects of verification
op/ops	operational/operations
OPV	offshore patrol vessel
org	organised/organisation
OTH/-B	over-the-horizon/backscatter (radar)
OTHR/T	over-the-horizon radar/targeting
PAAMS	principal anti-air missile system
para	paratroop/parachute
pax	passenger/passenger transport aircraft
PCC/I/O/R/H	patrol craft, coastal/inshore/offshore/riverine/harbour
PDMS	point defence missile system
pdr	pounder
PFC/I/O	fast patrol craft, coastal/inshore/offshore
PFM/T	fast patrol craft, SSM/torpedo
PGG	patrol craft with SSM
PHM/T	hydrofoil, SSM/torpedo
PKO	peacekeeping operation
pl	platoon
POMCUS	prepositioning of materiel configured to unit sets
PPP	purchasing-power parity
PSC	principal surface combatant
publ	public
RAPID	Reorganised Army Plains Infantry Division
RAM	Rolling Airframe Missile
RAS	replenishment at sea
RCL	recoilless launcher
R&D	research and development
recce	reconnaissance
regt	regiment
RL	rocket launcher
ro-ro	roll-on, roll-off
RPV	remotely piloted vehicle
RRC	rapid-reaction corps
RV	re-entry vehicle
SAM	surface-to-air missile
SAR	search and rescue
SDV	swimmer delivery vehicles
SEAL	sea–air–land
SES	surface-effect ship
SEWS	satellite early-warning system
SF	Special Forces
SIGINT	signals intelligence
sigs	signals
SLAM	stand-off land attack missile
SLBM	submarine-launched ballistic missile
SLCM	sea-launched cruise missile
SLEP	service life extension programme
SMAW	shoulder-launched multi-purpose assault weapon
SOC	special operations capable
some	up to
Sov	Soviet
SP	self-propelled
spt	support
sqn	squadron
SRAM	short-range attack missile
SRBM	short-range ballistic missile
SS(C/I)	submarine (coastal/inshore)
SSB/N	ballistic-missile submarine/nuclear-fuelled
SSGN	SSN with dedicated non-ballistic missile launchers
SSM	surface-to-surface missile
SSN	nuclear-fuelled submarine
START	Strategic Arms Reduction Talks/Treaty
STO(V)L	short take-off and (vertical) landing
str	strength
SUGW	surface-to-underwater GW
SURV	surveillance
SWATH	small waterplane area twin hulled (vessel)
sy	security
t	tonnes
TA	Territorial Army (UK)
tac	tactical
TACS	auxiliary crane ship
T-AFS	combat stores ship
TAGOS	towed array AGOS
T-AH	hospital ship
T-AOT	transport oiler
T-AVB	maintenance aviation support ship
TASM	tactical air-to-surface missile
TD	tank division
tempy	temporary
tk	tank
tkr	tanker
TLE	treaty-limited equipment (CFE)
TMD	theater missile defense (US)
TOW	Tube-launched Optically-tracked Wire-guided missile
tp	troop
tpt	transport
tr	trillion
trg	training
TT	torpedo tube
UAV	unmanned aerial vehicle
UN	United Nations
URG	under way replenishment group
USGW	underwater-to-surface GW
utl	utility
UUGW	underwater-to-underwater GW
veh	vehicle
VIP	very important person
VLS	vertical launch system
V(/S)TOL	vertical(/short) take-off and landing
wg	wing
WMD	weapon(s) of mass destruction
wpn	weapon
XFPB	extra-fast patrol boat